BERND MANTZ

THE
NORTH &
CENTRAL AMERICAN
FOOTBALL YEARBOOK

2021-2022

British Library Cataloguing in Publication Data
A catalogue record for this book is available from the British Library

ISBN: 978-1-86223-465-9

Copyright © 2021, SOCCER BOOKS LIMITED (01472 696226)
72 St. Peter's Avenue, Cleethorpes, N.E. Lincolnshire, DN35 8HU, England
Web site www.soccer-books.co.uk
e-mail info@soccer-books.co.uk

All rights are reserved. No part of this publication may be reproduced, stored in a retrieval system or transmitted, in any form or by any means, electronic, mechanical, photocopying, recording, or otherwise, without the prior written permission of Soccer Books Limited.

Printed in the UK by 4edge Ltd

Dear Readers,

As expected, the 2020/2021 football season was badly affected by the ongoing COVID-19 pandemic. Many of the CONCACAF members were forced to postpone play in the national leagues to be continued at a later date, or even to cancel their national championship altogether. As a result, no national champions were declared in several countries.

Some changes were also necessary at international level. The qualifying matches for the 2022 World Cup were postponed several times, so games scheduled to be played during October and November 2020 were moved to March 2021. This meant that the games originally to be played in March 2021 were postponed until June 2021 and it was decided that it would not be possible to play the groups with both home and away matches. Instead, just a single game was played between the teams in each group with the match played on a neutral ground. This prevented unnecessary travel, but the "smaller nations" also had to play their games on neutral grounds belonging to "stronger nations", which made upsets much less likely without home advantage. Nevertheless, Curaçao managed to advance in Group C, so Guatemala were eliminated despite not suffering a defeat or even conceding a single goal! Saint Kitts and Nevis also surprised by winning Group F, mainly because group favourites, Trinidad and Tobago weren't able to beat Puerto Rico.

The second round, which was also played on neutral ground in mid-June for scheduling reasons, brought no more surprises, with the favourites prevailing so Curaçao and Saint Kitts and Nevis were eliminated by Panama and El Salvador respectively. The third (and final) qualification round is scheduled to be played between September 2021 and March 2022, when eight teams are due to fight for three direct qualification places, with a fourth team entering Intercontinental play-offs for a place in Qatar 2022. That is the plan today, but it remains to be seen if these scheduled dates are influenced by the pandemic again in the future.

At the international club level, scheduled matches were also moved due to the pandemic. The CONCACAF Champions League, originally planned for spring 2020, was also postponed and eventually ended in December 2020. As expected, a Mexican club won yet again, this time CF Tigres de la Universidad Autonoma de Nuevo León. Los Angeles FC made it to the Final, where they led 1-0 for 11 second half minutes, but the Mexican team proved too strong and scored twice to win their first Champions League title. It should also be mentioned that the semi-finals and final were all played in Orlando (United States) and these matches were decided by a single game instead of the usual two-legged format.

The second competition, the CONCACAF League 2020, was also affected by the pandemic so, instead of being played from July to November 2020, the matches were instead played from October 2020 to February 2021. Again, all the ties were decided in just a single game and this was played at the venue of the club team drawn first. Liga Deportiva Alajuelense from Costa Rica won this fourth edition, so three of the four winners have been from Costa Rica.

This new edition of the North and Central Football Yearbook presents the 2020-2021 football season in North, Central America and the Caribbean Zone in the usual manner, both at club and at representative team level, nationally and internationally. An improvement this year is that the player statistics for clubs in the larger CONCACAF countries now also includes the number of substitute appearances, in addition to the number of games started and goals scored. All international matches are listed with complete statistics, including those played during early July 2021 as qualifiers for the CONCACAF Gold Cup which is scheduled to be held in the second half of July 2021!

I hope you enjoy the read!

The Author

ABBREVIATIONS

GK	Goalkeeper		**Ape**	Apertura
DF	Defender		**Cla**	Clausura
MF	Midfielder		**M**	Matches played
FW	Forward		**(s)**	Matches played as a substitute
DOB	Date of birth		**G**	Goals scored
			FT	Final Tournament

(F) International friendly matches
(CNL) CONCACAF Nations League Finals
(GCQ) 2021 Golf Cup Qualifiers
(WCQ) 2022 FIFA World Cup Qualifiers

FIFA COUNTRY CODES – NORTH & CENTRAL AMERICA

AIA	Anguilla		**GUI**	Guyana
ATG	Antigua and Barbuda		**HAI**	Haiti
ARU	Aruba		**HON**	Honduras
BAH	Bahamas		**JAM**	Jamaica
BRB	Barbados		**MTQ**	Martinique
BLZ	Belize		**MEX**	Mexico
BER	Bermuda		**MSR**	Montserrat
BOE	Bonaire		**NIC**	Nicaragua
VGB	British Virgin Islands		**PAN**	Panama
CAN	Canada		**PUR**	Puerto Rico
CAY	Cayman Islands		**LCA**	Saint Lucia
CRC	Costa Rica		**SKN**	Saint Kitts and Nevis
CUB	Cuba		**SMN**	Saint-Martin
CUW	Curaçao		**VIN**	St. Vincent and the Grenadines
DMA	Dominica		**SMA**	Sint Maarten
DOM	Dominican Republic		**SUR**	Suriname
SLV	El Salvador		**TRI**	Trinidad and Tobago
GYF	French Guiana		**TCA**	Turks and Caicos Islands
GRN	Grenada		**USA**	United States of America
GLP	Guadeloupe		**VIR**	US Virgin Islands
GUA	Guatemala		**BOE**	Bonaire (non-FIFA member)

FIFA COUNTRY CODES – AFRICA

ALG	Algeria		**LBY**	Libya
ANG	Angola		**MAD**	Madagascar
CMR	Cameroon		**MLI**	Mali
CPV	Cape Verde Islands		**MAR**	Morocco
COD	D.R. Congo		**NGA**	Nigeria
EGY	Egypt		**STP**	São Tomé e Príncipe
EQG	Equatorial Guinea		**SEN**	Senegal
GAM	Gambia		**SLE**	Sierra Leone
GHA	Ghana		**RSA**	South Africa
GNB	Guinea-Bissau		**TUN**	Tunisia
KEN	Kenya		**UGA**	Uganda
LBR	Liberia			

FIFA COUNTRY CODES – ASIA

AUS	Australia		MAS	Malaysia
BAN	Bangladesh		MDV	Maldives
IND	India		QAT	Qatar
IRQ	Iraq		KSA	Saudi Arabia
JPN	Japan		THA	Thailand
KOR	Korea Republic		UAE	United Arab Emirates

FIFA COUNTRY CODES – EUROPE

ALB	Albania		LVA	Latvia
AUT	Austria		LUX	Luxembourg
AZB	Azerbaijan		MAL	Malta
BLR	Belarus		MDV	Moldova
BEL	Belgium		NED	Netherlands
BIH	Bosnia and Herzegovina		NIR	Northern Ireland
BUL	Bulgaria		NOR	Norway
CRO	Croatia		POL	Poland
CYP	Cyprus		POR	Portugal
CZE	Czech Republic		IRL	Republic of Ireland
DEN	Denmark		ROU	Romania
ENG	England		SMR	San Marino
EST	Estonia		SCO	Scotland
FIN	Finland		SRB	Serbia
FRA	France		SVK	Slovakia
GEO	Georgia		SVN	Slovenia
GER	Germany		ESP	Spain
GRE	Greece		SWE	Sweden
HUN	Hungary		SUI	Switzerland
ISL	Iceland		TUR	Turkey
ISR	Israel		WAL	Wales
ITA	Italy			

FIFA COUNTRY CODES – OCEANIA

NZL	New Zealand

FIFA COUNTRY CODES – SOUTH AMERICA

ARG	Argentina		ECU	Ecuador
BOL	Bolivia		PAR	Paraguay
BRA	Brazil		PER	Peru
CHI	Chile		URU	Uruguay
COL	Colombia		VEN	Venezuela

SUMMARY

Editorial   *3*
Abbreviations, FIFA Country Codes   *4*
Summary   *6*

COMPETITIONS FOR NATIONAL TEAMS
    CONCACAF Nations League 2019-2020   *7*
    2022 FIFA World Cup – CONCACAF Qualifiers   *8*
    2021 CONCACAF Gold Cup   *12*

CONCACAF CONTINENTAL COMPETITIONS FOR CLUB TEAMS
    CONCACAF League 2020   *14*
    CONCACAF Champions League 2020   *24*
    CFU Club Championship 2021   *36*
    CONCACAF Caribbean Club Shield 2021   *40*

NATIONAL ASSOCIATIONS
    Anguilla   *42*
    Antigua and Barbuda   *47*
    Aruba   *52*
    Bahamas   *58*
    Barbados   *64*
    Belize   *70*
    Bermuda   *75*
    Bonaire   *83*
    British Virgin Islands   *87*
    Canada   *93*
    Cayman Islands   *102*
    Costa Rica   *108*
    Cuba   *138*
    Curaçao   *145*
    Dominica   *153*
    Dominican Republic   *160*
    El Salvador   *168*
    French Guiana   *196*
    Grenada   *203*
    Guadeloupe   *210*
    Guatemala   *218*
    Guyana   *251*
    Haiti   *256*
    Honduras   *267*
    Jamaica   *292*
    Martinique   *298*
    Mexico   *305*
    Montserrat   *346*
    Nicaragua   *351*
    Panama   *374*
    Puerto Rico   *395*
    Saint Kitts and Nevis   *401*
    Saint Lucia   *408*
    Saint-Martin   *411*
    Saint Vincent and the Grenadines   *415*
    Sint Maarten   *420*
    Suriname   *423*
    Trinidad and Tobago   *429*
    Turks and Caicos Islands   *437*
    United States of America   *441*
    U.S. Virgin Islands   *490*

CONCACAF NATIONS LEAGUE 2019-2020

The 2019–2020 CONCACAF Nations League was the inaugural season of the CONCACAF Nations League, involving national teams of the all member associations of CONCACAF.

The final tournament, originally scheduled to be played in June 2020, was postponed to June 2021 due to the COVID-19 pandemic. United States defeated Mexico in the final match and became first winner of the competition.

FINAL TOURNAMENT

All matches were played in Denver (United States).

SEMI-FINALS

| 03.06.2021 | Denver | Honduras - United States | 0-1 (0-0) |
| 03.06.2021 | Denver | Mexico - Costa Rica | 0-0; 5-4 pen |

THIRD PLACE PLAY_OFF

| 06.06.2021 | Denver | Honduras - Costa Rica | 2-2 (0-1, 2-2, 2-2); 5-4 pen |

FINAL

06.06.2021, 1st CONCACAF Nations League, Final
Empower Field at Mile High Stadium, Denver; Attendance: 34,451
Referee: Bryan López Castellanos (Guatemala)

UNITED STATES - MEXICO 3-2 (1-1, 2-2)

USA: Zackary Thomas Steffen (69.Ethan Shea Horvath), Timothy Michael Ream (82.Tyler Shaan Adams), John Anthony Brooks, DeAndre Roselle Yedlin (105+1.Reginald Jacob Cannon), Mark Alexander McKenzie, Sergiño Gianni Dest (60.Timothy Tarpeh Weah), Kellyn Kai Perry-Acosta, Christian Mate Pulisic, Weston James Earl McKennie, Giovanni Alejandro Reyna (82.Sebastian Francisco Lletget), Joshua Thomas Sargent (68.Theoson-Jordan Siebatcheu Pefok). Trainer: Gregg Berhalter.

MEX: Francisco Guillermo Ochoa Magaña, Héctor Alfredo Moreno Herrera (100.Carlos Joel Salcedo Hernández), Luis Alfonso Rodríguez Alanís, Néstor Alejandro Araujo Razo, Jesús Daniel Gallardo Vasconcelos, Héctor Miguel Herrera López (100.José Andrés Guardado Hernández), Carlos Alberto Rodríguez Gómez (66.Luis Francisco Romo Barrón), Edson Omar Álvarez Velázquez (117.Orbelín Pineda Alvarado), Carlos Uriel Antuna Romero (78.Diego Lainez Leyva), Jesús Manuel Corona Ruíz (66.Henry Josué Martín Mex), Hirving Rodrigo Lozano Bahena. Trainer: Gerardo Daniel Martino (Argentina).

Goals: 0-1 Jesús Manuel Corona Ruíz (2), 1-1 Giovanni Alejandro Reyna (27), 1-2 Diego Lainez Leyva (79), 2-2 Weston James Earl McKennie (82), 3-2 Christian Mate Pulisic (114 penalty).

FIFA WORLD CUP 2022

FIFA WORLD CUP Qatar 2022

The qualification for the FIFA World Cup 2022 started with the CONCACAF First Round – originally scheduled for October 2020 - in March 2021. Due to COVID-19 pandemic and related quarantine and travel restrictions, teams played against each other in a single round-robin format (a total of four matches per team, two "home" and two "away"), also a lot of matches took place at a neutral venue. Group winners advanced to the CONCACAF Second Round.

FIRST ROUND
(24.03.2021-08.06.2021)

GROUP A

Date	Venue	Match	Result
24.03.2021	Willemstad	Antigua and Barbuda - Montserrat	2-2(2-2)
25.03.2021	San Salvador	El Salvador - Grenada	2-0(1-0)
27.03.2021	Upper Bethlehem	U.S. Virgin Islands - Antigua and Barbuda	0-3(0-3)
28.03.2021	Willemstad	Montserrat - El Salvador	1-1(0-1)
30.03.2021	St. George's	Grenada - U.S. Virgin Islands	1-0(1-0)
02.06.2021	San Cristóbal	Montserrat - U.S. Virgin Islands	4-0(1-0)
04.06.2021	North Sound	Antigua and Barbuda - Grenada	1-0(1-0)
05.06.2021	Upper Bethlehem	U.S. Virgin Islands - El Salvador	0-7(0-2)
08.06.2021	St. George's	Grenada - Montserrat	1-2(0-0)
08.06.2021	San Salvador	El Salvador - Antigua and Barbuda	3-0(1-0)

FINAL STANDINGS

1.	**El Salvador**	4	3	1	0	13	-	1	10
2.	Montserrat	4	2	2	0	9	-	4	8
3.	Antigua and Barbuda	4	2	1	1	6	-	5	7
4.	Grenada	4	1	0	3	2	-	5	3
5.	U.S. Virgin Islands	4	0	0	4	0	-	15	0

GROUP B

Date	Venue	Match	Result
24.03.2021	Paramaribo	Suriname - Cayman Islands	3-0(2-0)
25.03.2021	Orlando	Canada - Bermuda	5-1(2-0)
27.03.2021	Bradenton	Aruba - Suriname	0-6(0-3)
29.03.2021	Bradenton	Cayman Islands - Canada	0-11(0-6)
30.03.2021	Bradenton	Bermuda - Aruba	5-0(2-0)
02.06.2021	Bradenton	Cayman Islands - Aruba	1-3(1-2)
04.06.2021	Paramaribo	Suriname - Bermuda	6-0(4-0)
05.06.2021	Bradenton	Aruba - Canada	0-7(0-3)
08.06.2021	Bradenton	Bermuda - Cayman Islands	1-1(0-1)
08.06.2021	Bridgeview	Canada - Suriname	4-0(1-0)

FINAL STANDINGS

1.	**Canada**	4	4	0	0	27	-	1	12
2.	Suriname	4	3	0	1	15	-	4	9
3.	Bermuda	4	1	1	2	7	-	12	4
4.	Aruba	4	1	0	3	3	-	19	3
5.	Cayman Islands	4	0	1	3	2	-	18	1

GROUP C

Date	Venue	Match	Result
24.03.2021	Ciudad de Guatemala	Guatemala - Cuba	1-0(0-0)
25.03.2021	Willemstad	Curaçao - Saint Vincent and the Grenadines	5-0(4-0)
27.03.2021	Willemstad	British Virgin Islands - Guatemala	0-3(0-2)
28.03.2021	Ciudad de Guatemala	Cuba - Curaçao	1-2(1-2)
30.03.2021	Willemstad	Saint Vincent and the Grenadines – British Virgin Islands	3-0(2-0)
02.06.2021	Ciudad de Guatemala	Cuba - British Virgin Islands	5-0(1-0)
04.06.2021	Ciudad de Guatemala	Guatemala - Saint Vincent and the Grenadines	10-0(5-0)
05.06.2021	Ciudad de Guatemala	British Virgin Islands - Curaçao	0-8(0-6)
08.06.2021	St. George's	Saint Vincent and the Grenadines - Cuba	0-1(0-0)
08.06.2021	Willemstad	Curaçao - Guatemala	0-0

FINAL STANDINGS

1.	**Curaçao**	4	3	1	0	15	-	1	10
2.	Guatemala	4	3	1	0	14	-	0	10
3.	Cuba	4	2	0	2	7	-	3	6
4.	Saint Vincent and the Grenadines	4	1	0	3	3	-	16	3
5.	British Virgin Islands	4	0	0	4	0	-	19	0

GROUP D

Date	Venue	Match	Result
24.03.2021	Santo Domingo	Dominican Republic - Dominica	1-0(0-0)
25.03.2021	Santo Domingo	Panama - Barbados	1-0(0-0)
27.03.2021	Fort Lauderdale	Anguilla - Dominican Republic	0-6(0-3)
28.03.2021	Santo Domingo	Dominica - Panama	1-2(0-1)
30.03.2021	Santo Domingo	Barbados - Anguilla	1-0(0-0)
02.06.2021	Santo Domingo	Dominica - Anguilla	3-0(3-0)
04.06.2021	Santo Domingo	Dominican Republic - Barbados	1-1(0-1)
05.06.2021	Ciudad de Panamá	Anguilla - Panama	0-13(0-4)
08.06.2021	Santo Domingo	Barbados - Dominica	1-1(0-0)
08.06.2021	Ciudad de Panamá	Panama - Dominican Republic	3-0(1-0)

FINAL STANDINGS

#	Team	P	W	D	L	GF	-	GA	Pts
1.	**Panama**	4	4	0	0	19	-	1	12
2.	Dominican Republic	4	2	1	1	8	-	4	7
3.	Barbados	4	1	2	1	3	-	3	5
4.	Dominica	4	1	1	2	5	-	4	4
5.	Anguilla	4	0	0	4	0	-	23	0

GROUP E

Please note: Saint Lucia withdrew before playing.

Date	Venue	Match	Result
25.03.2021	Port-au-Prince	Haiti - Belize	2-0(0-0)
27.03.2021	San Cristóbal	Turks and Caicos Islands - Nicaragua	0-7(0-3)
30.03.2021	San Cristóbal	Belize - Turks and Caicos Islands	5-0(1-0)
04.06.2021	Managua	Nicaragua - Belize	3-0(1-0)
05.06.2021	Providenciales	Turks and Caicos Islands - Haiti	0-10(0-5)
08.06.2021	Port-au-Prince	Haiti - Nicaragua	1-0(0-0)

FINAL STANDINGS

#	Team	P	W	D	L	GF	-	GA	Pts
1.	**Haiti**	3	3	0	0	13	-	0	9
2.	Nicaragua	3	2	0	1	10	-	1	6
3.	Belize	3	1	0	2	5	-	5	3
4.	Turks and Caicos Islands	3	0	0	3	0	-	22	0
5.	Saint Lucia (*withdrew*)								

GROUP F

24.03.2021	San Cristóbal	Saint Kitts and Nevis - Puerto Rico	1-0(1-0)
25.03.2021	San Cristóbal	Trinidad and Tobago - Guyana	3-0(3-0)
27.03.2021	Nassau	Bahamas - Saint Kitts and Nevis	0-4(0-1)
28.03.2021	Mayagüez	Puerto Rico - Trinidad and Tobago	1-1(0-0)
30.03.2021	Santo Domingo	Guyana - Bahamas	4-0(1-0)
02.06.2021	Mayagüez	Puerto Rico - Bahamas	7-0(4-0)
04.06.2021	Basseterre	Saint Kitts and Nevis - Guyana	3-0(2-0)
05.06.2021	Nassau	Bahamas - Trinidad and Tobago	0-0
08.06.2021	Basseterre	Guyana - Puerto Rico	0-2(0-2)
08.06.2021	Santo Domingo	Trinidad and Tobago - Saint Kitts and Nevis	2-0(1-0)

FINAL STANDINGS

1.	**Saint Kitts and Nevis**	4	3	0	1	8	-	2	9
2.	Trinidad and Tobago	4	2	2	0	6	-	1	8
3.	Puerto Rico	4	2	1	1	10	-	2	7
4.	Guyana	4	1	0	3	4	-	8	3
5.	Bahamas	4	0	1	3	0	-	15	1

SECOND ROUND
(12.06.2021-15.06.2021)

12.06.2021	Basseterre	Saint Kitts and Nevis - El Salvador	0-4(0-3)
15.06.2021	San Salvador	El Salvador - Saint Kitts and Nevis	2-0(1-0)

[El Salvador won 6-0 on aggregate and were qualified for the Third Round].

12.06.2021	Port-au-Prince	Haiti - Canada	0-1(0-1)
15.06.2021	Bridgeview	Canada - Haiti	3-0(0-0)

[Canada won 4-0 on aggregate and were qualified for the Third Round].

12.06.2021	Ciudad de Panamá	Panama - Curaçao	2-1(0-0)
15.06.2021	Willemstad	Curaçao - Panama	0-0

[Panama won 2-1 on aggregate and were qualified for the Third Round].

THID ROUND
(02.09.2021-30.03.2022)

The third round will be disputed by eight teams. The top-5 CONCACAF teams of the FIFA Rankings from July 2020 (Mexico, United States, Costa Rica, Jamaica and Honduras) were joined by the three winners of the second round (El Salvador, Canada and Panama).

The top-3 teams will qualify directly for the 2022 FIFA World Cup Final Tournament, while the fourth ranked team will play in the Inter-Confederation play-offs for a possible fouth place.

GOLD CUP 2021

The 2021 CONCACAF Gold Cup will be the 16th edition of the CONCACAF Gold Cup competition and 26th CONCACAF regional championship overall in CONCACAF's existence. The final tournament will be hosted – as usually – by the United States, between 10 July - 1 August, 2021. The tournament was originnaly scheduled between 2-25 July 2021, but was postponed due to COVID-19 pandemic.

The 2019-2020 CONCACAF Nations League determined 12 teams for the Final Tournament:
8 from League A (top-2 of each group from Nations League A):
United States, Canada, Mexico, Panama, Honduras, Martinique, Costa Rica, Curaçao.

and 4 from League B (winners of each group from nations League B):
Grenada, El Salvador, Jamaica, Suriname.

Another twelve teams competed in the qualifiers for the last 3 places:

CONCACAF GOLD CUP QUALIFIERS

Please note: all matches were played in Fort Lauderdale (United States).

First Round
(between League C group winners, League B group runners-up third placed teams from League A)

02.07.2021	Fort Lauderdale	Haiti - Saint Vincent and the Grenadines	6-1(3-1)
02.07.2021	Fort Lauderdale	Trinidad and Tobago - Montserrat	6-1(3-0)
02.07.2021	Fort Lauderdale	Bermuda - Barbados	8-1(4-1)
03.07.2021	Fort Lauderdale	Guatemala - Guyana	4-0(1-0)
03.07.2021	Fort Lauderdale	Cuba - French Guiana	0-3(awarded)
03.07.2021	Fort Lauderdale	Guadeloupe - Bahamas	2-0(0-0)

Second Round *(between First Round winners)*

06.07.2021	Fort Lauderdale	Haiti - Bermuda	4-1(3-0)
06.07.2021	Fort Lauderdale	Guatemala - Guadeloupe	1-1; 9-10 pen
06.07.2021	Fort Lauderdale	Trinidad and Tobago - French Guiana	1-1; 8-7 pen

Haiti, Guadeloupe and Trinidad and Tobago were qualified for the Final Tournament.

Qatar will participate for the first time as invited guest.
Curaçao eventually withdrew just before the start of the competition due to an outbreak of COVID-19 in the team. Guatemala, as best ranked team of the qualifiers, will replace Curaçao in the final tournament.

List of venues:

City	Stadium	Capacity
Arlington	AT&T Stadium	80,000
Austin	Q2 Stadium	20,500
Dallas	Cotton Bowl	92,100
Frisco	Toyota Stadium	20,500
Houston	BBVA Compass Stadium	22,039
Houston	NRG Stadium	71,795
Glendale	State Farm Stadium	63,400
Paradise	Allegiant Stadium	61,000
Orlando	Exploria Stadium	25,500
Kansas City	Children's Mercy Park	18,467

The draw for the Final Tournament was held on 28.09.2020, in Miami. The 16 teams were drawn in four groups as follows:

Group A	Venues and matches	
	10.07.2021 Arlington	Mexico - Trinidad and Tobago
Mexico	11.07.2021 Frisco	El Salvador - Guatemala
El Salvador	14.07.2021 Frisco	Trinidad and Tobago - El Salvador
Curaçao*	14.07.2021 Dallas	Guatemala - Mexico
Trinidad and Tobago	18.07.2021 Dallas	Mexico - El Salvador
	18.07.2021 Frisco	Guatemala - Trinidad and Tobago

*replaced by Guatemala

Group B	Venues and matches	
	11.07.2021 Kansas City	Canada - Martinique
United States	11.07.2021 Kansas City	United States - Haiti
Canada	15.07.2021 Kansas City	Haiti - Canada
Martinique	15.07.2021 Kansas City	Martinique - United States
Haiti	18.07.2021 Frisco	Martinique - Haiti
	18.07.2021 Kansas City	United States - Canada

Group C	Venues and matches	
	12.07.2021 Orlando	Jamaica - Suriname
Costa Rica	12.07.2021 Orlando	Costa Rica - Guadeloupe
Jamaica	16.07.2021 Orlando	Guadeloupe - Jamaica
Suriname	16.07.2021 Orlando	Suriname - Costa Rica
Guadeloupe	20.07.2021 Orlando	Costa Rica - Jamaica
	20.07.2021 Houston	Suriname - Guadeloupe

Group D	Venues and matches	
	13.07.2021 Houston	Qatar - Panama
Honduras	13.07.2021 Houston	Honduras - Grenada
Panama	17.07.2021 Houston	Grenada - Qatar
Grenada	17.07.2021 Houston	Panama - Honduras
Qatar	20.07.2021 Orlando	Panama - Grenada
	20.07.2021 Houston	Honduras - Qatar

Group winners and runners-up will advance to the quarter finals.
Quarter-Finals: 24/25.07.2021 – Glendale & Arlington
Semi-Finals: 29.07.2021 – Austin or Houston
Final: 01.08.2021 – Paradise

NORTH & CENTRAL AMERICAN CLUB COMPETITIONS 2020/2021

CONCACAF LEAGUE 2020

22 clubs from 11 CONCACAF member associations entered the 2020 edition of the CONCACAF League.

List of participating clubs:

North America	
Canada (1 team)	Forge FC Hamilton*

Central America	
Belize (1 team)	Verdes FC San Ignacio*
Costa Rica (3 teams)	Deportivo Saprissa San José CS Herediano Heredia Liga Deportiva Alajuelense*
El Salvador (3 teams)	Alianza FC San Salvador CD FAS Santa Ana* CD Municipal Limeño Santa Rosa de Lima*
Guatemala (3 teams)	CSD Municipal Ciudad de Guatemala Comunicaciones FC Ciudad de Guatemala* Antigua Guatemala FC*
Honduras (3 teams)	CD Olimpia Tegucigalpa CD Marathón San Pedro Sula CD Motagua Tegucigalpa*
Nicaragua (2 teams)	Real Estelí FC Managua FC*
Panama (3 teams)	Tauro FC Ciudad de Panamá San Francisco FC La Chorrera CA Independiente La Chorrera*

Caribbean	
Dominican Republic (1 team)	Cibao FC Santiago de Caballeros*
Haiti (1 team)	Arcahaie FC*
Jamaica (1 team)	Waterhouse FC Kingston

(*teams entered the Preliminary Round)

Please note: due to the COVID-19 pandemic, the start of the tournament (originally scheduled to begin on 28.07.2020 and end in November 2020), had been postponed. To ease the schedule, CONCACAF announced that the Preliminary Round and Round of 16 would be played as single-leg matches, but on 29.10.2020, this format had been extended to all rounds, with ties hosted by the higher-seeded teams based on the CONCACAF Club Ranking. Finally, the competition was played from 20.10.2020 to 03.02.2021.

PRELIMINARY ROUND

20.10.2020, Estadio Cuscatlán, San Salvador
Referee: Oliver Amet Vergara Rodríguez (Panama)
CD FAS Santa Ana - Managua FC   **1-1(1-0,1-1,1-1); 4-5 on penalties**
FAS Santa Ana: Kévin Edenilson Carabantes Rivera, Moisés Xavier García Orellana, Diego José Chávez Rivas, Edwin Mauricio Cuellar Linares, Alberto Siliazar Henríquez, Julio César Amaya Sibrián (75.Walter Ernesto Ayala Chiguila), Guillermo Nicolás Stradella (73.Luis Fernando Rodríguez Barrios), Wilma Enrique Torres Peña, Erivan Stiven Flores Morales, Raúl Eduardo Peñaranda Contreras, Diego Daniel Areco Sayas. Trainer: Jorge Humberto Rodríguez Álvarez.
Managua: Lester José Acevedo García, Kevin José Serapio Oviedo, Rigoberto Fuentes, Ulises Pozo, Wesner De Trinidad, Nahúm Elieth Peralta Arce, Danilo Zuñiga Araúz, Pablo Gállego Lardiés, Agenor Báez Cano (68.Diego Peláez Silva), Leandro Figueroa, Ricardo Mendieta Dolmos (77.Brayan Josué Castillo Arzú). Trainer: Emilio Aburto.
Goals: Diego Daniel Areco Sayas (13 penalty) / Ricardo Mendieta Dolmos (58).
Penalties: Diego Peláez Silva (missed); Moisés Xavier García Orellana 1-0; Pablo Gállego Lardiés 1-1; Diego Daniel Areco Sayas (missed); Danilo Zuñiga Araúz 1-2; Raúl Eduardo Peñaranda Contreras 2-2; Brayan Josué Castillo Arzú 2-3; Wilma Enrique Torres Peña 3-3; Kevin José Serapio Oviedo 3-4; Luis Fernando Rodríguez Barrios 4-4; Leandro Figueroa 4-5; Walter Ernesto Ayala Chiguila (saved).

20.10.2020, Estadio Olímpico „Félix Sánchez", Santo Domingo (Dominican Republic)
Referee: Reon Radix (Grenada)
Arcahaie FC - Verdes FC San Ignacio   **3-0 (awarded)**
The match was originally scheduled on 20.10.2020, but postponed as players and staff members of Verdes FC San Ignacio were tested positive for COVID-19. Verdes FC San Ignacio later withdrew from the competition.

21.10.2020, Estadio Olímpico „Rommel Fernández Gutiérrez", Ciudad de Panamá
Referee: Diego Montaño Robles (Mexico)
CA Independiente La Chorrera - Antigua Guatemala FC   **0-0; 2-4 on penalties**
Independiente: José Carlos Guerra, Azmahar Anibal Ariano Navarro, Francisco Javier Vence Gómez, Omar Federico Córdoba Quintero, Jiovany Javier Ramos Díaz, Joseph Yeramid Rosales Erazo (85.Martín Moran), Rafael Águila (70.Juan Alberto González Pineda), Omar Ezequiel Browne Zuñiga, Alfredo Horacio Stephens Francis (70.Guido Adalberto Rouse Luzcando), Alexis Venancio Palacios Curley (56.Andrés Alejandro Peñalba Martínez), José Fajardo Nelson. Trainer: Francisco Perlo (Venezuela).
Antigua: Víctor Manuel Ayala González, José Antonio Mena Alfaro, Moises Edwardo Hernandez Moralez, Jairo Randolfo Arreola Silva (82.Allan Ricardo Miranda Albertazzi), Emmanuel Giovani Hernández Neri (82.Pablo Andrés Aguilar Palacios), Marco Leonel Domínguez-Ramírez, Kener Hairon Lemus Méndez, Kervin René García Sandoval, Josué Isaac Martínez Areas (70.Christian Omar Ojeda Ramírez), Robin Osvaldo Betancourth Cue, Nicolás Iván Martínez Vargas (74.Kevin Eduardo Arriola García). Trainer: Antonio Torres Servín (Mexico).
Penalties: Kevin Eduardo Arriola García 0-1; José Fajardo Nelson (saved); Marco Leonel Domínguez-Ramírez 0-2; Guido Adalberto Rouse Luzcando 1-2; Moises Edwardo Hernandez Moralez 1-3; Omar Ezequiel Browne Zuñiga 2-3; Christian Omar Ojeda Ramírez 2-4; Juan Alberto González Pineda (missed).

22.10.2020, Estadio Cuscatlán, San Salvador
Referee: Selvin Brown Chavarria (Honduras)
CD Municipal Limeño Santa Rosa de Lima - Forge FC Hamilton   1-2(1-1)
Municipal Limeño: William Ernesto Torres Peña, Mario Ernesto Machado Salamanca, Walter Eliseo Guevara Canales (88.Ever Leonel Rodríguez Moreno), Ever Alexander González Acosta (73.Arnulfo Beitar Córdoba), Luis Fernando Méndez Hernández, Edwin Ernesto Sánchez Vigil (74.Hugo Alexis Oviedo Jara), Samuel Esteban Giménez Cáceres, Kevin Arquímides Oviedo, Ramón Antonio Viera López (87.Jeison Arley Quiñónez Angulo), Harold Rafael Alas Rodríguez, William Alfredo Canales Belloso (57.Ramón Adalberto Rodríguez Moreno). Trainer: Álvaro Misael Alfaro Sánchez.
Forge FC: Triston Henry, David Edward Edgar, Dominic Samuel, Jonathan Grant [*sent off 64*], Daniel Krutzen, Kyle Edward Bekker, Alexander Achinioti-Jönsson, Paolo Sabak (70.Jordan Dunstan), Molham Babouli (85.Maxim Tissot), David Choinière (61.Elimane Oumar Cissé), Kadell Thomas (62.Anthony Joseph Novak). Trainer: Bobby Smyrniotis.
Goals: Kevin Arquímides Oviedo (38) / David Choinière (21), Anthony Joseph Novak (83).

22.10.2020, Estadio „Tiburcio Carías Andino", Tegucigalpa
Referee: Keylor Antonio Herrera Villalobos (Costa Rica)
CD Motagua Tegucigalpa - Comunicaciones FC Ciudad de Guatemala   2-2(0-1,2-2,2-2);
15-14 on penalties
Motagua: Jonathan Felipe Rougier, Juan Pablo Montes Montes, Marcelo Antonio Pereira Rodríguez, Omar Josué Elvir Casco (76.Emilio Arturo Izaguirre Giron), Matías Alejandro Galvaliz, Raúl Marcelo Santos Colindres (74.Wilmer Crisanto Casildo), Héctor Enrique Castellanos Villatoro, Kevin Josué López Maldonado, Gonzalo Martín Klusener (46.Román Rubilio Castillo Álvarez), Roberto Moreira Aldana, Walter Joel Martínez Betanco (77.Bayron Edimar Dionicio Méndez). Trainer: Diego Martín Vásquez Castro (Argentina).
Comunicaciones: José de Jesús Calderón Frías, Michael Umaña Corrales (86.José Manuel Murillo Morán), Gerardo Arturo Gordillo Olivero, José Carlos Pinto Samayoa [*sent off 62*], Manfred Russell Russell (65.Carlos Anselmo Mejía del Cid), Rafael Andrés Lezcano Montero, Jorge Eduardo Aparicio Grijalva (75.Alejandro Miguel Galindo), Stheven Adán Robles Ruiz (66.Carlos Mauricio Castrillo Alonzo), Rodrigo Saravia Samayoa (87.José Manuel Contreras y Contreras, Agustín Enrique Herrera Osuna, Kevin Josué Grijalva González. Trainer: Mauricio Antonio Tapia (Argentina).
Goals: Matías Alejandro Galvaliz (55), Kevin Josué López Maldonado (60) / Rafael Andrés Lezcano Montero (38), Agustín Enrique Herrera Osuna (49).
Penalties: Roberto Moreira Aldana 1-0; José Manuel Contreras y Contreras 1-1; Wilmer Crisanto Casildo 2-1; Alejandro Miguel Galindo (missed); Matías Alejandro Galvaliz 3-1; José Manuel Murillo Morán 3-2; Kevin Josué López Maldonado (saved); Rafael Andrés Lezcano Montero 3-3; Román Rubilio Castillo Álvarez 4-3; Agustín Enrique Herrera Osuna 4-4; Bayron Edimar Dionicio Méndez 5-4; Carlos Anselmo Mejía del Cid 5-5; Juan Pablo Montes Montes (missed); Gerardo Arturo Gordillo Olivero (saved); Emilio Arturo Izaguirre Giron 6-5; Kevin Josué Grijalva González 6-6; Héctor Enrique Castellanos Villatoro 7-6; Carlos Mauricio Castrillo Alonzo 7-7; Jonathan Felipe Rougier 8-7; José de Jesús Calderón Frías 8-8; Roberto Moreira Aldana 9-8; José Manuel Contreras y Contreras 9-9; Wilmer Crisanto Casildo 10-9; Alejandro Miguel Galindo 10-10; Matías Alejandro Galvaliz 11-10; José Manuel Murillo Morán 11-11; Román Rubilio Castillo Álvarez 12-11; Rafael Andrés Lezcano Montero 12-12; Kevin Josué López Maldonado 13-12; Agustín Enrique Herrera Osuna 13-13; Bayron Edimar Dionicio Méndez 14-13; Carlos Anselmo Mejía del Cid 14-14; Emilio Arturo Izaguirre Giron (saved); Gerardo Arturo Gordillo Olivero (missed); Juan Pablo Montes Montes 15-14; Kevin Josué Grijalva González (missed).

04.11.2020, Estadio „Alejandro Morera Soto", Alajuela
Referee: Selvin Brown Chavarria (Honduras)
Liga Deportiva Alajuelense - Cibao FC Santiago de Caballeros   3-0(1-0)
LD Alajuelense: Mauricio José Vargas Campos, Adolfo Abdiel Machado, Ian Rey Smith Quiros, Bernald Alfaro Alfaro, Yurguin Alberto Román Alfaro, Fernán José Faerrón Tristán, Carlos Andrei Mora Montoya (86.Juan Pablo Ledezma Porras), Alexander Agustín López Rodríguez (85.Facundo Zabala), Barlon Andrés Sequeira Sibaja (62.Brandon Aguilera Zamora), Geancarlo Castro González (69.Dylan Armando Flores Knowles), Álvaro Alberto Saborío Chacón. Trainer: Andrés José Carevic Ghelfi (Argentina).
Cibao FC: Alan Emanuel Aciar, Javier Francisco Graieb, Luis Ismael Díaz Ramírez, Hérold Charles Jr., Eduardo Matías Rotondi (72.Frantzety Herard), Jorge Ivan Pérez, Jean Carlos López Moscoso (81.Roberto Peraza Santos), Leandro Rodríguez (81.Pavel Estefan Bergaglio Cruz), Pablo Daniel Cofe (55.Mateo Zazo Ortíz), Enzo Rafael Guzmán Espinal, Germán Adolfo Sosa (72.Yohan Eduardo Parra Francisco). Trainer: Jorge Rolando Alfonso Avalos (Argentina).
Goals: Álvaro Alberto Saborío Chacón (23 penalty), Carlos Andrei Mora Montoya (36), Álvaro Alberto Saborío Chacón (82).

ROUND OF 16

03.11.2020, Estadio Olímpico Metropolitano, San Pedro Sula
Referee: Ismael Alexander Cornejo Meléndez (El Salvador)
CD Marathón San Pedro Sula - Antigua Guatemala FC   1-1(1-1,1-1,1-1); 4-3 on penalties
Marathón: Denovan Galileo Torres Pérez, Bryan Arturo Johnson Sacasa, Mathías Sebastián Techera Pizarro, Luis Fernando Garrido Garrido (90.Cristian Neptali Calix Alvarado), John Paul Suazo Caballero, Allan Alexander Banegas Murillo, Edwin Solani Solano Martínez (79.José Enrique Vigil Lobo), Luis Fernando Vega Cillacorta, Yaudel Lahera García (52.Marlon Roberto Ramírez Arauz), Ryduan Palermo Bruno Volpi. Trainer: Héctor Vargas Baldús (Argentina).
Antigua: Víctor Manuel Ayala González, José Antonio Mena Alfaro, Moises Edwardo Hernandez Moralez, Jairo Randolfo Arreola Silva, Emmanuel Giovani Hernández Neri (89.Cristian Alexander Jiménez Martínez), Marco Leonel Domínguez-Ramírez, Kener Hairon Lemus Méndez [*sent off 39*], Kervin René García Sandoval, Josué Isaac Martínez Areas (72.Kevin Eduardo Arriola García), Robin Osvaldo Betancourth Cue (88.Christian Omar Ojeda Ramírez), Nicolás Iván Martínez Vargas (65.Allan Ricardo Miranda Albertazzi). Trainer: Antonio Torres Servín (Mexico).
Goals: Allan Alexander Banegas Murillo (41 penalty) / Nicolás Iván Martínez Vargas (5).
Penalties: Bruno Volpi 1-0; Kevin Eduardo Arriola García (saved); Allan Alexander Banegas Murillo (saved); Marco Leonel Domínguez-Ramírez 1-1; Ryduan Palermo 2-1; Moises Edwardo Hernandez Moralez 2-2; Cristian Neptali Calix Alvarado 3-2; Christian Omar Ojeda Ramírez 3-3; Bryan Arturo Johnson Sacasa 4-3; Jairo Randolfo Arreola Silva (saved).

03.11.2020, Estadio Olímpico „Rommel Fernández Gutiérrez", Ciudad de Panamá
Referee: Nima Saghafi (United States)
Tauro FC Ciudad de Panamá - Forge FC Hamilton   1-2(1-1)
Tauro FC: Luis Alfonso Hurtado Osorio (45+3.Jorginho Antonio Frías Bethancourt), Richard Amed Peralta Robledo, Gerardo Omar Negrete Caballero, Luis Yohan Asprilla (46.Ismael Díaz de León), Rolando Vicente Botello Garibaldo, Rigoberto Niño Cabrera, Justin Alberto Simmons Samaniego (68.Cristian Josué Quintero Carvajal), Diego Ezequiel Valanta Del Busto (46.Ernesto Emanuel Walker Willis; 69.Jorge Samuel Clement Gutiérrez), Edilson Denilson Carrasquilla Alcazar, Iván Alejandro Anderson Hernández, Edwin Enrique Aguilar Samaniego. Trainer: Rafael Loreto Mea Vital (Venezuela).
Forge FC: Triston Henry, David Edward Edgar, Dominic Samuel, Daniel Krutzen, Kyle Edward Bekker, Alexander Achinioti-Jönsson, Kwame Awuah, Elimane Oumar Cissé (74.Paolo Sabak), Molham Babouli (88.Maxim Tissot), David Choinière (73.Anthony Joseph Novak), Kadell Thomas (46.Christopher Lenroy Nanco; 90+3.Jordan Dunstan). Trainer: Bobby Smyrniotis.
Goals: Edwin Enrique Aguilar Samaniego (18) / Molham Babouli (11), Daniel Krutzen (90+1 penalty).

04.11.2020, Estadio Cuscatlán, San Salvador
Referee: John Francis Pitti Hernández (Panama)
Alianza FC San Salvador - CD Motagua Tegucigalpa   1-1(0-0,1-1,1-1); 3-4 on penalties
Alianza: Mario Antonio González Martínez, Iván Roberto Mancia Ramirez, Bryan Alexander Tamacas López, Rudy Geovanny Clavel Mendoza, Marvin Wilfredo Monterrosa Delzas, Juan Carlos Portillo Leal (76.Wilfredo Ulises Cienfuegos), Jonathan David Jiménez Guzmán, César Noé Flores Linares (72.Rodolfo Antonio Zelaya García), Narciso Oswaldo Orellana Guzmán, Oswaldo Enrique Blanco Mancilla, Michell Mercado Martínez. Trainer: Juan Cortés Diéguez.
Motagua: Jonathan Felipe Rougier, Emilio Arturo Izaguirre Giron (84.Omar Josué Elvir Casco), Juan Pablo Montes Montes, Marcelo Antonio Pereira Rodríguez, Reinieri Joel Mayorquín Gámez (24.Sergio Salvador Peña Zelaya; 83.Marco Tulio Vega Ordoñez), Raúl Marcelo Santos Colindres, Héctor Enrique Castellanos Villatoro, Kevin Josué López Maldonado, Gonzalo Martín Klusener (62.Roberto Moreira Aldana), Román Rubilio Castillo Álvarez, Walter Joel Martínez Betanco (61.Matías Alejandro Galvaliz). Trainer: Diego Martín Vásquez Castro (Argentina).
Goals: Rodolfo Antonio Zelaya García (80 penalty) / Héctor Enrique Castellanos Villatoro (90+1).
Penalties: Wilfredo Ulises Cienfuegos (saved); Roberto Moreira Aldana 0-1; Michell Mercado Martínez 1-1; Matías Alejandro Galvaliz 1-2; Oswaldo Enrique Blanco Mancilla (saved); Omar Josué Elvir Casco 1-3; Rodolfo Antonio Zelaya García 2-3; Kevin Josué López Maldonado (missed); Bryan Alexander Tamacas López 3-3; Román Rubilio Castillo Álvarez 3-4.

05.11.2020, Estadio „Ricardo Saprissa Aymá", San José
Referee: Luis Santander Aguirre (Mexico)
Deportivo Saprissa San José - CSD Municipal Ciudad de Guatemala   4-1(2-1)
Deportivo Saprissa: Aarón Moises Cruz Esquivel, Aubrey Robert David, Esteban Ezequiel Espíndola López, Luis José Hernández Paniagua, Michael Francisco Barrantes Rojas (84.Johnny Gerardo Acosta Zamora), Mariano Néstor Torres (74.Esteban Eduardo Rodríguez Ballestero), Marvin Angulo Borbón (74.Warren Steven Madrigal Molina), David Alberto Guzmán Pérez, Johan Alberto Venegas Ulloa (84.Yostín Tellería Alfaro), Ricardo José Blanco Mora, Jimmy Marín Vílchez (74.Daniel Colindres Solera). Trainer: Walter Centeno Corea.
Municipal: Víctor Rafael García Muníz, Carlos Eduardo Gallardo Nájera, José Alfredo Morales Concua (56.Rudy Ronaldo Barrientos Reyes), Carlos Fernando Alvarado López, Jaime Enrique Alas Morales, Brandon Andrés de León Ramos (56.Janderson Kione Pereira Rodrigues), Luis Enrique de León Valenzuela, Manuel Estuardo López Rodas, José Mario Rosales Marroquín (84.José Carlos Martínez Navas), Ramiro Iván Rocca, Alejandro Matías Díaz. Trainer: Sebastián Alejandro Bini (Argentina).
Goals: Johan Alberto Venegas Ulloa (33, 38, 50, 54) / Ramiro Iván Rocca (20).

05.11.2020, Stadium East, Kingston
Referee: Ricangel de Leça (Aruba)
Waterhouse FC Kingston - Arcahaie FC **1-3(0-2)**
Waterhouse: Akeem Chambers, Ryan Ricardo Wellington (84.André Omare Leslie), Shawn Lawes, Damion Richard Binns, Ricardo Thomas (84.Rafeik Thomas), Fabion McCarthy, Stephen David Williams (74.Rohan Beadle), Andre Fletcher (53.Roshane Nicholas Sharpe), Kenroy Howell, Colorado Murray, Shaquille Bradford (53.Denaro Thomas). Trainer: Marcel Gayle.
Arcahaie: Guerry Romondt, Richard Calixte, Alland Pierre, Marc Sully, Sylvenson Colin, Clifford Thomas (86.Esdras Philippe), Wendy Louis-Jean, Richardson Thomas (76.Ose Charles), Eguynor Cineus, Kervens Jolicoeur (75.Mylove Dorvilien), Johnny Pierre Paul (86.Wilmane Exume). Trainer: Gabriel Michel.
Goals: Kenroy Howell (81) / Richard Calixte (12), Wendy Louis-Jean (31), Johnny Pierre Paul (60).

05.11.2020, Estadio „Tiburcio Carías Andino", Tegucigalpa
Referee: Óscar Donaldo Moncada Godoy (Honduras)
CD Olimpia Tegucigalpa - Managua FC **6-0(2-0)**
Olimpia: Edrick Eduardo Menjívar Jonhnson, Johnny Harold Leverón Uclés, Maylor Alberto Nuñez Flores, Elvin Oliva Casildo (70.Samuel Arturo Córdova Howe), Javier Arnaldo Portillo Martínez, Deybi Aldair Flores Flores, Carlos Enrique Pineda López (66.Jorge Daniel Álvarez Rodas), Edwin Alexander Rodríguez Castillo (72.Luis Fernando Garrido Garrido), Jerry Ricardo Bengtson Bodden (72.Eddie Gabriel Hernández Padilla), Justin Arboleda Buenaños, Michael Anthony Chirinos López (67.Marvin Javier Bernárdez García). Trainer: Pedro Antonio Troglio (Argentina).
Managua: Lester José Acevedo García (69.Erly Rolando Méndez Ocampo), Kevin José Serapio Oviedo, Rigoberto Fuentes, Ulises Pozo, Wesner De Trinidad, Nahúm Elieth Peralta Arce (63.Jeremy Cuarezma), Danilo Zuñiga Araúz, Pablo Gállego Lardiés, Diego Peláez Silva (63.Camphers Santiago Pérez Bermudez), Leandro Figueroa (55.Agenor Báez Cano), Ricardo Mendieta Dolmos (70.Brayan Josué Castillo Arzú). Trainer: Emilio Aburto.
Goals: Elvin Oliva Casildo (8), Michaell Anthony Chirinos López (17), Justin Arboleda Buenaños (51), Edwin Alexander Rodríguez Castillo (62), Jerry Ricardo Bengtson Bodden (64), Marvin Javier Bernárdez García (82).

24.11.2020, Estadio „Alejandro Morera Soto", Alajuela
Referee: Daneon Parchment (Jamaica)
Liga Deportiva Alajuelense - San Francisco FC La Chorrera **1-0(0-0)**
LD Alajuelense: Leonel Gerardo Moreira Ledezma, Júnior Enrique Díaz Campbell, Adolfo Abdiel Machado, Ian Rey Smith Quiros (89.José Andrés Salvatierra López), Facundo Zabala, Carlos Andrei Mora Montoya (58.Adrián Alonso Martínez Batista), Alexander Agustín López Rodríguez (79.Bernald Alfaro Alfaro), Barlon Andrés Sequeira Sibaja (89.Geancarlo Castro González), Bryan Jafet Ruiz González, Jonathan Alonso Moya Aguilar, Jurguens Josafat Montenegro Vallejo (79.Álvaro Alberto Saborío Chacón). Trainer: Andrés José Carevic Ghelfi (Argentina).
San Francisco: Eric Hughes Guevara, Martín Antonio Gómez Rodríguez (74.Sergio Cunningham Torres), Fernando Vidal Mena González (88.Jean Carlos Sánchez Rose), Roderick Alonso Miller Molina, Roberto Leandro Chen Rodríguez, Francisco Antonio Palacios Alleyne, Mauricio José Vargas Campos, Jhamal Adonis Rodríguez Thomas, Luis Aurelio Pereira Lewis (79.Wesley Alberto Cabrera Duarte), Jorge Luis Serrano Francis, Jair Ibrahim Catuy Arosemena. Trainer: Gonzálo Soto Cortázar (Colombia).
Goal: Jurguens Josafat Montenegro Vallejo (61).

24.11.2020, Estadio Nacional de Costa Rica, San José
Referee: Bryan López Castellanos (Guatemala)
CS Herediano Heredia - Real Estelí FC **0-1(0-1)**
Herediano: Bryan Andrés Segura Cruz, Keyner Yamal Brown Blackwood, Keysher Fuller Spence (51.Yael Andrés López Fuentes), Orlando Moisés Galo Calderón, Rándall Azofeifa Corrales (51.Berny Thomas Burke Montiel), Yeltsin Ignacio Tejeda Valverde, Aarón Salazar Arias, Leandro Barrios Rita dos Martires "Leandrinho" (65.Zuhander Manuel Zúñiga Cordero), Yendrick Alberto Ruiz González, Jonathan Andrés McDonald Porras (46.Jordy Francisco Hernández Molina), John Jairo Ruiz Barrantes. Trainer: Jafet Soto Molina.
Real Estelí: Rodrigo Pérez Romo, Rodrigo José Bronzatti, Josué Abraham Quijano Potosme, Manuel Rosas Arreola (69.Óscar Acevedo), Oscar Renan López, Juan Ramón Barrera Pérez (84.Brandon Ayerdis), Yohn Géiler Mosquera Martínez (85.Marlon Andrés López Moreno), Richard Andrés Rodríguez Álvez, Carlos Alberto Chavarria Rodríguez (75.Fernando Mercado Villar), Henry García (85.Luis Alberto Acuña), Jorge Andrés Betancur Bustamante. Trainer: Holver Flores.
Goal: Jorge Andrés Betancur Bustamante (19).

QUARTER-FINALS

01.12.2020, Estadio „Tiburcio Carías Andino", Tegucigalpa
Referee: Oscar Macías Romo (Mexico)
CD Marathón San Pedro Sula - Deportivo Saprissa San José **0-2(0-1)**
Marathón: Luis Enrique Ortíz Hernández, Bryan Arturo Johnson Sacasa, Mathías Sebastián Techera Pizarro, Luis Fernando Garrido Garrido, John Paul Suazo Caballero (67.Yaudel Lahera García), Allan Alexander Banegas Murillo (76.Selvin Rolando Guevara Casco), Edwin Solani Solano Martínez, Luis Fernando Vega Cillacorta, Marlon Roberto Ramírez Arauz (57.Cristian Neptali Calix Alvarado), Ryduan Palermo (76.Frelys Edilson López Saravia), Bruno Volpi. Trainer: Héctor Vargas Baldús (Argentina).
Deportivo Saprissa: Aarón Moises Cruz Esquivel, Alexander Robinson Delgado, Aubrey Robert David, Luis José Hernández Paniagua (82.Jordy Jafeth Evans Solano), Michael Francisco Barrantes Rojas (77.Jaylon Jahi Hadden Scarlett), Mariano Néstor Torres (82.Jonathan Josué Martínez Solano), Marvin Angulo Borbón, David Alberto Guzmán Pérez (77.Esteban Ezequiel Espíndola López), Johan Alberto Venegas Ulloa, Ricardo José Blanco Mora, Jimmy Marín Vílchez (77.Daniel Colindres Solera). Trainer: Walter Centeno Corea.
Goals: Johan Alberto Venegas Ulloa (13, 55).

01.12.2020, Estadio Olímpico „Félix Sánchez", Santo Domingo (Dominican Republic)
Referee: Oshane Nation (Jamaica)
Arcahaie FC - Forge FC Hamilton **1-1(0-1,1-1,1-1); 4-2 on penalties**
Arcahaie: Guerry Romondt, Alland Pierre, Marc Sully, Hantz Billy Anacius, Sylvenson Colin, Olnick Alesy, Clifford Thomas, Wendy Louis-Jean (90+4.Esdras Philippe), Richardson Thomas (90+2.Wilmane Exume), Kervens Jolicoeur, Johnny Pierre Paul (76.Ose Charles). Trainer: Gabriel Michel.
Forge FC: Triston Henry, David Edward Edgar, Dominic Samuel, Jonathan Grant (70.Anthony Joseph Novak), Daniel Krutzen, Kyle Edward Bekker, Alexander Achinioti-Jönsson, Kwame Awuah, Paolo Sabak (79.Montther Mohsen), Molham Babouli, David Choinière (79.Kadell Thomas). Trainer: Bobby Smyrniotis.
Goals: Kervens Jolicoeur (59) / Daniel Krutzen (45+1 penalty).
Penalties: Daniel Krutzen (saved); Clifford Thomas 1-0; Alexander Achinioti-Jönsson (saved); Olnick Alesy 2-0; David Edward Edgar 2-1; Hantz Billy Anacius 3-1; Molham Babouli 3-2; Ose Charles 4-2.

02.12.2020, Estadio „Tiburcio Carías Andino", Tegucigalpa
Referee: Adonai Escobedo González (Mexico)
CD Olimpia Tegucigalpa - CD Motagua Tegucigalpa   2-0(1-0)
Olimpia: Edrick Eduardo Menjívar Jonhnson, Jonathan Josué Paz Hernández, Maylor Alberto Nuñez Flores, Elvin Oliva Casildo, Javier Arnaldo Portillo Martínez, Deybi Aldair Flores Flores, Carlos Enrique Pineda López, Edwin Alexander Rodríguez Castillo (90.Jorge Daniel Álvarez Rodas), Jerry Ricardo Bengtson Bodden, Justin Arboleda Buenaños (78.Eddie Gabriel Hernández Padilla), Marvin Javier Bernárdez García (71.José Mario Pinto Paz). Trainer: Pedro Antonio Troglio (Argentina).
Motagua: Jonathan Felipe Rougier, Emilio Arturo Izaguirre Giron (69.Omar Josué Elvir Casco), Wesly Roberto Decas, Christopher Aaron Meléndez Suazo, Reinieri Joel Mayorquín Gámez (46.Gonzalo Martín Klusener [*sent off 81*]), Matías Alejandro Galvaliz (76.Félix Joan Crisanto Velásquez), Raúl Marcelo Santos Colindres, Héctor Enrique Castellanos Villatoro, Kevin Josué López Maldonado (70.Bayron Edimar Dionicio Méndez), Roberto Moreira Aldana (23.Walter Joel Martínez Betanco), Román Rubilio Castillo Álvarez. Trainer: Diego Martín Vásquez Castro (Argentina).
Goals: Maylor Alberto Nuñez Flores (32), Deybi Aldair Flores Flores (54).

02.12.2020, Estadio „Alejandro Morera Soto", Alajuela
Referee: Rubiel Vazquez (United States)
Liga Deportiva Alajuelense - Real Estelí FC   2-1(1-1)
LD Alajuelense: Leonel Gerardo Moreira Ledezma, Adolfo Abdiel Machado, José Andrés Salvatierra López, Fernán José Faerrón Tristán, Facundo Zabala, Alexander Agustín López Rodríguez, Barlon Andrés Sequeira Sibaja (65.Carlos Andrei Mora Montoya), Bryan Jafet Ruiz González, Álvaro Alberto Saborío Chacón (60.Jonathan Alonso Moya Aguilar), Jurguens Josafat Montenegro Vallejo (82.Dylan Armando Flores Knowles), Adrián Alonso Martínez Batista (81.Ian Rey Smith Quiros). Trainer: Andrés José Carevic Ghelfi (Argentina).
Real Estelí: Rodrigo Pérez Romo, Rodrigo José Bronzatti, Josué Abraham Quijano Potosme, Manuel Rosas Arreola, Oscar Renan López, Juan Ramón Barrera Pérez, Yohn Géiler Mosquera Martínez (46.Marlon Andrés López Moreno), Richard Andrés Rodríguez Álvez, Henry García (75.Fernando Mercado Villar), Jorge Andrés Betancur Bustamante (62.Luis Alberto Acuña), Brandon Ayerdis (74.Luis Alfredo López Pineda). Trainer: Holver Flores.
Goals: Bryan Jafet Ruiz González (24), Adrián Alonso Martínez Batista (56) / Juan Ramón Barrera Pérez (44).

PLAY-IN ROUND

The winners were qualified for the 2021 CONCACAF Champions League.

08.12.2020, Estadio „Tiburcio Carías Andino", Tegucigalpa
Referee: Bryan López Castellanos (Guatemala)
CD Marathón San Pedro Sula - Forge FC Hamilton   1-0(1-0)
Marathón: Luis Enrique Ortíz Hernández, Bryan Arturo Johnson Sacasa, José Carlos López Perdomo, Mathías Sebastián Techera Pizarro, Luis Fernando Garrido Garrido, Allan Alexander Banegas Murillo, Kervin Fabián Arriaga Villanueva, Selvin Rolando Guevara Casco (63.Ryduan Palermo), Edwin Solani Solano Martínez, Luis Fernando Vega Cillacorta, Bruno Volpi. Trainer: Héctor Vargas Baldús (Argentina).
Forge FC: Triston Henry, David Edward Edgar, Maxim Tissot, Jonathan Grant, Daniel Krutzen, Kyle Edward Bekker [*sent off 86*], Alexander Achinioti-Jönsson (78.Paolo Sabak), Kwame Awuah (78.Jordan Dunstan), Molham Babouli, David Choinière (88.Dominic Samuel), Kadell Thomas (46.Christopher Lenroy Nanco; 76.Anthony Joseph Novak). Trainer: Bobby Smyrniotis.
Goal: Edwin Solani Solano Martínez (18).

09.12.2020, Estadio „Tiburcio Carías Andino", Tegucigalpa
Referee: Keylor Antonio Herrera Villalobos (Costa Rica)
CD Motagua Tegucigalpa - Real Estelí FC　　　　**2-2(1-0,2-2,2-2); 2-4 on penalties**
Motagua: Marlon Javier Licona López, Emilio Arturo Izaguirre Giron (85.Reinieri Joel Mayorquín Gámez), Marcelo Antonio Pereira Rodríguez, Wesly Roberto Decas, Christopher Aaron Meléndez Suazo, Omar Josué Elvir Casco, Matías Alejandro Galvaliz (80.Bayron Edimar Dionicio Méndez), Raúl Marcelo Santos Colindres (85.Félix Joan Crisanto Velásquez), Héctor Enrique Castellanos Villatoro (90+1.Sergio Salvador Peña Zelaya), Kevin Josué López Maldonado, Marco Tulio Vega Ordoñez (90+1.Wilmer Crisanto Casildo). Trainer: Diego Martín Vásquez Castro (Argentina).
Real Estelí: Denver Fox, Rodrigo José Bronzatti, Josué Abraham Quijano Potosme, Manuel Rosas Arreola, Oscar Renan López, Juan Ramón Barrera Pérez (84.Luis Alfredo López Pineda), Yohn Géiler Mosquera Martínez (58.Marlon Andrés López Moreno), Richard Andrés Rodríguez Álvez, Carlos Alberto Chavarria Rodríguez (80.Brandon Ayerdis), Henry García (84.Fernando Mercado Villar), Jorge Andrés Betancur Bustamante (58.Luis Alberto Acuña). Trainer: Holver Flores.
Goals: Kevin Josué López Maldonado (37), Matías Alejandro Galvaliz (52 penalty) / Juan Ramón Barrera Pérez (66), Fernando Mercado Villar (90).
Penalties: Wilmer Crisanto Casildo 1-0; Manuel Rosas Arreola 1-1; Bayron Edimar Dionicio Méndez 2-1; Richard Andrés Rodríguez Álvez 2-2; Omar Josué Elvir Casco (missed); Luis Alberto Acuña 2-3; Sergio Salvador Peña Zelaya (missed); Luis Alfredo López Pineda 2-4.

SEMI-FINALS

20.01.2021, Estadio „Alejandro Morera Soto", Alajuela
Referee: Mario Alberto Escobar Toca (Guatemala)
Liga Deportiva Alajuelense - CD Olimpia Tegucigalpa　　　　**0-0; 5-4 on penalties**
LD Alajuelense: Leonel Gerardo Moreira Ledezma, Daniel Arreola Argüello, José Andrés Salvatierra López, Yurguin Alberto Román Alfaro, Fernán José Faerrón Tristán, Alexander Agustín López Rodríguez, Marcel Hernández Campanioni, Brandon Aguilera Zamora (62.José Miguel Cubero Loría), Bryan Jafet Ruiz González, Jurguens Josafat Montenegro Vallejo, Adrián Alonso Martínez Batista (81.Carlos Andrei Mora Montoya). Trainer: Andrés José Carevic Ghelfi (Argentina).
Olimpia: Harold Geovanny Fonseca Baca, Johnny Harold Leverón Uclés, Jonathan Josué Paz Hernández, Maylor Alberto Nuñez Flores, Elvin Oliva Casildo, Deybi Aldair Flores Flores, German Noe Mejía Briceño, Edwin Alexander Rodríguez Castillo (81.Michael Anthony Chirinos López), Eddie Gabriel Hernández Padilla, Jerry Ricardo Bengtson Bodden (69.Justin Arboleda Buenaños), José Mario Pinto Paz (68.Marvin Javier Bernárdez García). Trainer: Pedro Antonio Troglio (Argentina).
Penalties: Justin Arboleda Buenaños 0-1; Bryan Jafet Ruiz González 1-1; Michaell Anthony Chirinos López 1-2; Yurguin Alberto Román Alfaro 2-2; Eddie Gabriel Hernández Padilla 2-3; José Miguel Cubero Loría 3-3; Harold Geovanny Fonseca Baca (missed); Fernán José Faerrón Tristán 4-3; Johnny Harold Leverón Uclés 4-4; Daniel Arreola Argüello 5-4.

22.01.2021, Estadio „Ricardo Saprissa Aymá", San José
Referee: Reon Radix (Grenada)
Deportivo Saprissa San José - Arcahaie FC   **5-0(2-0)**
Deportivo Saprissa: Aarón Moises Cruz Esquivel, Aubrey Robert David, Esteban Ezequiel Espíndola López (58.Kendall Jamaal Waston Manley), Luis José Hernández Paniagua (67.Matthew Bolaños García), Jordy Jafeth Evans Solano, Michael Francisco Barrantes Rojas (67.Marvin Angulo Borbón), Mariano Néstor Torres, Christian Bolaños Navarro (58.Daniel Colindres Solera), David Alberto Guzmán Pérez, Jimmy Marín Vílchez, Ariel Francisco Rodríguez Araya (58.Orlando Alexis Sinclair Hernández). Trainer: Walter Centeno Corea.
Arcahaie: Guerry Romondt, Richard Calixte (69.Hantz Billy Anacius), Alland Pierre (51.Esdras Philippe), Reginald Cadet, Marc Sully (10.Eguynor Cineus), Olnick Alesy, Clifford Thomas (69.Richardson Thomas), Wendy Louis-Jean, Kervens Jolicoeur, Mylove Dorvilien, Johnny Pierre Paul (51.Ose Charles). Trainer: Gabriel Michel.
Goals: Esteban Ezequiel Espíndola López (16), Ariel Francisco Rodríguez Araya (31), Jimmy Marín Vílchez (48), Christian Bolaños Navarro (56), Mariano Néstor Torres (66).

FINAL

03.02.2021, Estadio „Alejandro Morera Soto", Alajuela
Referee: Iván Arcides Barton Cisneros (El Salvador)
Liga Deportiva Alajuelense - Deportivo Saprissa San José   **3-2(1-1)**
LD Alajuelense: Leonel Gerardo Moreira Ledezma, Daniel Arreola Argüello, José Andrés Salvatierra López, Yurguin Alberto Román Alfaro, Fernán José Faerrón Tristán, Alexander Agustín López Rodríguez (83.José Miguel Cubero Loría), Marcel Hernández Campanioni, Barlon Andrés Sequeira Sibaja (83.Geancarlo Castro González), Bryan Jafet Ruiz González, Jurguens Josafat Montenegro Vallejo (90+3.Bernald Alfaro Alfaro), Adrián Alonso Martínez Batista (76.Carlos Andrei Mora Montoya). Trainer: Andrés José Carevic Ghelfi (Argentina).
Deportivo Saprissa: Aarón Moises Cruz Esquivel, Kendall Jamaal Waston Manley, Aubrey Robert David, Esteban Ezequiel Espíndola López, Jordy Jafeth Evans Solano, Michael Francisco Barrantes Rojas (64.Esteban Eduardo Rodríguez Ballestero), Mariano Néstor Torres (76.Marvin Angulo Borbón), Christian Bolaños Navarro, David Alberto Guzmán Pérez (76.Ricardo José Blanco Mora), Daniel Colindres Solera (76.Jimmy Marín Vílchez), Ariel Francisco Rodríguez Araya (67.Orlando Alexis Sinclair Hernández). Trainer: Walter Centeno Corea.
Goals: 0-1 Christian Bolaños Navarro (18), 1-1 Barlon Andrés Sequeira Sibaja (33), 2-1 Yurguin Alberto Román Alfaro (63), 3-1 Alexander Agustín López Rodríguez (66), 3-2 Marvin Angulo Borbón (87).

2020 CONCACAF League Winner: **Liga Deportiva Alajuelense** (Costa Rica)

Best Goalscorer: Johan Alberto Venegas Ulloa (Deportivo Saprissa San José) - 6 goals

CONCACAF LEAGUE (since 2017) TABLE OF HONOURS		
2017	CD Olimpia Tegucigalpa	(HON)
2018	CS Herediano Heredia	(CRC)
2019	Deportivo Saprissa San José	(CRC)
2020	Liga Deportiva Alajuelense	(CRC)

CONCACAF CHAMPIONS LEAGUE 2020

16 clubs from 8 CONCACAF member associations entered the 2020 edition of the CONCACAF Champions League.

List of participating clubs:

North America	
Canada (1 team)	Montreal Impact
Mexico (4 teams)	CF América Ciudad de México
	CF Tigres de la Universidad Autónoma de Nuevo León
	Cruz Azul FC Ciudad de México
	Club León
United States (4 teams)	Seattle Sounders FC
	Los Angeles FC
	New York City FC
	Atlanta United FC

Central America	
Costa Rica (2 teams)	Deportivo Saprissa San José (*2019 CONCACAF League winner*)
	AD San Carlos
El Salvador (1 team)	Alianza FC San Salvador
Guatemala (1 team)	Comunicaciones FC Ciudad de Guatemala
Honduras (2 teams)	FC Motagua Tegucigalpa
	CD Olimpia Tegucigalpa

Caribbean	
Jamaica (1 team)	Portmore United FC

The competition was originally scheduled to be organized from 25.02. to 07.05.2020. The Round of 16 was played as expected (18-27.02.2020).

On 12.03.2020, CONCACAF announced the decision to suspend the tournament with immediate effect due to the COVID-19 pandemic. On 02.11.2020 it was announced that the tournament would resume at a centralized location in the United States from 15 to 22.12.2020, with all remaining rounds played as single-leg matches. The Exploria Stadium in Orlando (Florida, United States) was designated as the host for the remainder of the tournament.

ROUND OF 16

18.02.2020, Estadio Olímpico Metropolitano, San Pedro Sula
Referee: Adonai Escobedo González (Mexico)
FC Motagua Tegucigalpa - Atlanta United FC 1-1(1-1)
Motagua: Jonathan Felipe Rougier, Félix Joan Crisanto Velásquez, Marcelo Antonio Pereira Rodríguez, Reinieri Joel Mayorquín Gámez (70.Walter Joel Martínez Betanco), Omar Josué Elvir Casco, Matías Alejandro Galvaliz (82.Emilio Arturo Izaguirre Giron), Raúl Marcelo Santos Colindres, Héctor Enrique Castellanos Villatoro, Kevin Josué López Maldonado, Roberto Moreira Aldana, Román Rubilio Castillo Álvarez (66.Gonzalo Martín Klusener). Trainer: Diego Martín Vásquez Castro (Argentina).
Atlanta United: Bradley Edwin Guzan, Fernando Nicolás Meza, Franco Nicolás Escobar, Anton Charles Walkes, Jeffrey Adam Larentowicz, Emerson Schellas Hyndman, Eric Daian Remedi, Mohammed Adams (65.Brooks Howard Lennon), Ezequiel Omar Barco, Gonzalo Nicolás Martínez (81.Adam Jahn), Josef Alexander Martínez Mencia. Trainer: Franciscus de Boer (Netherlands).
Goals: Roberto Moreira Aldana (33) / Josef Alexander Martínez Mencia (35).

25.02.2020, Fifth Third Bank Stadium, Kennesaw; Attendance: 8,474
Referee: Keylor Antonio Herrera Villalobos (Costa Rica)
Atlanta United FC - FC Motagua Tegucigalpa 3-0(1-0)
Atlanta United: Bradley Edwin Guzan, Fernando Nicolás Meza, Brooks Howard Lennon, Franco Nicolás Escobar, Anton Charles Walkes, Jake David Mulraney (81.Luiz Fernando Nascimento), Emerson Schellas Hyndman (88.Mohammed Adams), Eric Daian Remedi, Ezequiel Omar Barco, Gonzalo Nicolás Martínez (88.Jeffrey Adam Larentowicz), Josef Alexander Martínez Mencia. Trainer: Franciscus de Boer (Netherlands).
Motagua: Jonathan Felipe Rougier, Juan Pablo Montes Montes, Félix Joan Crisanto Velásquez (64.Walter Joel Martínez Betanco), Marcelo Antonio Pereira Rodríguez, Reinieri Joel Mayorquín Gámez (69.Román Rubilio Castillo Álvarez), Omar Josué Elvir Casco, Matías Alejandro Galvaliz (58.Gonzalo Martín Klusener), Raúl Marcelo Santos Colindres, Héctor Enrique Castellanos Villatoro, Kevin Josué López Maldonado, Roberto Moreira Aldana. Trainer: Diego Martín Vásquez Castro (Argentina).
Goals: Gonzalo Nicolás Martínez (40), Josef Alexander Martínez Mencia (61), Gonzalo Nicolás Martínez (83).
[Atlanta United FC won 4-1 on aggregate]

18.02.2020, Independence Park, Kingston
Referee: Reon Radix (Grenada)
Portmore United FC - Cruz Azul FC Ciudad de México 1-2(0-0)
Portmore United: Kemar Foster, Ryan Wellington, Roberto Johnson, Osani Ricketts, Damano Rio Solomon, Ricardo Wayne Morris, Seigel Knight, Shande James, Chavany Willis (90+6.Rosario Harriott), Shai Smith (72.Cleon Pryce), Rondee Smith (82.Kevon Farquharson). Trainer: Ricardo Wayne Gardner.
Cruz Azul: Sebastián Jurado Roca, Pablo César Aguilar Benítez, Julio César Domínguez Juárez, Juan Marcelo Escobar Chena, Jaiber Jiménez Ramírez, Pablo Daniel Ceppelini Gatto (78.Santiago Tomás Giménez), Rafael Baca Miranda, Orbelín Pineda Alvarado (62.Roberto Carlos Alvarado Hernández), Alex Stik Castro Giraldo, Jonathan Darwin Borja Colorado (62.Jonathan Javier Rodríguez Portillo), Lucas Giuliano Passerini. Trainer: Robert Dante Siboldi Badiola (Uruguay).
Goals: Rondee Smith (74) / Lucas Giuliano Passerini (90+5), Jonathan Javier Rodríguez Portillo (90+9).

25.02.2020, Estadio Azteca, Ciudad de México
Referee: Drew Fischer (Canada)
Cruz Azul FC Ciudad de México - Portmore United FC **4-0(1-0)**
Cruz Azul: Guillermo Allison Revuelta, Jaiber Jiménez Ramírez, Luis Francisco Romo Barrón (82.Diego Barraza González), Jorge Luis García Rivas, Josué Emmanuel Reyes Santacruz, Pablo Daniel Ceppelini Gatto, Rafael Baca Miranda (66.Victor Yoshimar Yotún Flores), Orbelín Pineda Alvarado (71.Josué Misael Domínguez González), Alex Stik Castro Giraldo, Jonathan Darwin Borja Colorado, Lucas Giuliano Passerini. Trainer: Robert Dante Siboldi Badiola (Uruguay).
Portmore United: Kemar Foster, Rosario Harriott, Ryan Wellington (58.Damano Rio Solomon), Roberto Johnson, Osani Ricketts, Emelio Rousseau, Ricardo Wayne Morris, Seigel Knight (46.Chavany Willis), Tevin Shaw, Shande James, Rondee Smith (67.Revaldo Mitchell). Trainer: Ricardo Wayne Gardner.
Goals: Orbelín Pineda Alvarado (22), Lucas Giuliano Passerini (59), Pablo Daniel Ceppelini Gatto (76 penalty), Jonathan Darwin Borja Colorado (90).
[Cruz Azul FC Ciudad de México won 6-1 on aggregate]

18.02.2020, Estadio León, León; Attendance: 32,000
Referee: Ismael Alexander Cornejo Meléndez (El Salvador)
Club León - Los Angeles FC **2-0(1-0)**
León: Rodolfo Cota Robles, Fernando Navarro Morán, William José Tesillo Gutiérrez, Ramiro González Hernández, Luis Arturo Montes Jiménez (90+3.Saúl Zamora Romero), Jaine Stiven Barreiro Solis, Pedro Jesús Aquino Sánchez (63.Leonardo Javier Ramos), José Iván Rodríguez Rebollar, Víctor Ismael Sosa (87.Jown Anderson Cardona Agudelo), Ángel Israel Mena Delgado, Jean David Meneses Villarroel. Trainer: Marcos Ignacio Ambriz Espinoza.
Los Angeles: Kenneth Vermeer, Dejan Jaković, Eddie Livington Segura Martínez, Diego José Palacios Espinoza (68.Mohamed El-Mounir Abdussalam), Tristan Michael Blackmon, Mark-Anthony Kaye (62.Bryce Duke), Paul Brian Rodríguez Bravo, Francisco Ginella Dabezies, Carlos Alberto Vela Garrido, Diego Martín Rossi Marachlian (76.Adrien Alfredo Perez), Latif Atta Blessing. Trainer: Robert Frank Bradley.
Goals: Jean David Meneses Villarroel (21), Ángel Israel Mena Delgado (89).

27.02.2020, Banc of California Stadium, Los Angeles; Attendance: 22,300
Referee: Mario Alberto Escobar Toca (Guatemala)
Los Angeles FC - Club León **3-0(1-0)**
Los Angeles: Kenneth Vermeer, Dejan Jaković, Eddie Livington Segura Martínez, Diego José Palacios Espinoza, Tristan Michael Blackmon, Mark-Anthony Kaye, Eduard Andrés Atuesta Velasco (83.Francisco Ginella Dabezies), Paul Brian Rodríguez Bravo (75.Adrien Alfredo Perez), Carlos Alberto Vela Garrido, Diego Martín Rossi Marachlian, Latif Atta Blessing. Trainer: Robert Frank Bradley.
León: Rodolfo Cota Robles, Fernando Navarro Morán, William José Tesillo Gutiérrez, Ramiro González Hernández, Luis Arturo Montes Jiménez, Jaine Stiven Barreiro Solis, Pedro Jesús Aquino Sánchez (82.Leonardo Javier Ramos), José Iván Rodríguez Rebollar, Víctor Ismael Sosa, Jean David Meneses Villarroel *[sent off 90+4]*, José de Jesús Godínez Navarro (84.Jown Anderson Cardona Agudelo). Trainer: Marcos Ignacio Ambriz Espinoza.
Goals: Carlos Alberto Vela Garrido (27, 77), Diego Martín Rossi Marachlian (79).
[Los Angeles FC won 3-2 on aggregate]

19.02.2020, Estadio „Doroteo Guamuch Flores", Ciudad de Guatemala
Referee: Jair Marrufo (United States)
Comunicaciones FC Cd. de Guatemala - CF América Ciudad de México   1-1(0-0)
Comunicaciones: José de Jesús Calderón Frías, Michael Umaña Corrales, Gerardo Arturo Gordillo Olivero, Allan Ricardo Miranda Albertazzi, Allen José Yanes Pinto, Rafael Andrés Lezcano Montero (79.Bladimir Yovany Díaz Saavedra), Alejandro Miguel Galindo (62.Maximiliano Lombardi Rodríguez), Jorge Eduardo Aparicio Grijalva, Rodrigo Saravia Samayoa, Jostin Akeem Daly Cordero (74.Carlos Anselmo Mejía del Cid), Agustín Enrique Herrera Osuna. Trainer: Mauricio Antonio Tapia (Argentina).
América: Óscar Francisco Jiménez Fabela, Luis Fernando Fuentes Vargas, Víctor Emanuel Aguilera, Bruno Amílcar Valdez, Jorge Eduardo Sánchez Ramos, Leonardo Gabriel Suárez (61.Jesús Alonso Escoboza Lugo), Richard Rafael Sánchez Guerrero (90+1.Román Arturo Martínez Canales), Francisco Sebastián Córdova Reyes, Santiago Cáseres, Andrés Felipe Ibargüen García (73.Antonio de Jesús López Amenábar), Federico Sebastián Viñas Barboza. Trainer: Miguel Ernesto Herrera Aguirre.
Goals: Gerardo Arturo Gordillo Olivero (81) / Francisco Sebastián Córdova Reyes (90).

26.02.2020, Estadio Azteca, Ciudad de México
Referee: Henry Alberto Bejarano Matarrita (Costa Rica)
CF América Ciudad de México - Comunicaciones FC Cd. de Guatemala   1-1(0-0,1-1,1-1);
5-3 on penalties
América: Óscar Francisco Jiménez Fabela, Paul Nicolás Aguilar Rojas, Víctor Emanuel Aguilera, Bruno Amílcar Valdez, Jorge Eduardo Sánchez Ramos (71.Andrés Felipe Ibargüen García), Leonardo Gabriel Suárez (82.Jesús Alonso Escoboza Lugo), Richard Rafael Sánchez Guerrero, Francisco Sebastián Córdova Reyes, Santiago Cáseres, Giovani Álex dos Santos Ramírez, Federico Sebastián Viñas Barboza (46.Román Arturo Martínez Canales). Trainer: Miguel Ernesto Herrera Aguirre.
Comunicaciones: José de Jesús Calderón Frías, Michael Umaña Corrales, Gerardo Arturo Gordillo Olivero, Allan Ricardo Miranda Albertazzi, Allen José Yanes Pinto [*sent off 68*], Rafael Andrés Lezcano Montero, Alejandro Miguel Galindo (76.Maximiliano Lombardi Rodríguez), Jorge Eduardo Aparicio Grijalva (86.Fredy William Thompson León), Rodrigo Saravia Samayoa, Jostin Akeem Daly Cordero (70.Carlos Mauricio Castrillo Alonzo), Agustín Enrique Herrera Osuna. Trainer: Mauricio Antonio Tapia (Argentina).
Goals: Víctor Emanuel Aguilera (80 penalty) / Agustín Enrique Herrera Osuna (62 penalty).
Penalties: Víctor Emanuel Aguilera 1-0; Fredy William Thompson León 1-1; Jesús Alonso Escoboza Lugo 2-1; Maximiliano Lombardi Rodríguez 2-2; Bruno Amílcar Valdez 3-2; Rafael Andrés Lezcano Montero 3-3; Andrés Felipe Ibargüen García 4-3; Agustín Enrique Herrera Osuna (saved); Francisco Sebastián Córdova Reyes 5-3.
[CF América Ciudad de México won 5-3 on penalties (after 2-2 on aggregate)]

19.02.2020, Estadio Cuscatlán, San Salvador
Referee: Daneon Parchment (Jamaica)
Alianza FC San Salvador - CF Tigres de la UA de Nuevo León   2-1(0-1)
Alianza: Víctor Rafael García Muníz, Mario Alberto Jacobo Segovia, Rudy Geovanny Clavel Mendoza, Alexander Vidal Larín Hernández, Jonathan David Jiménez Guzmán, Óscar Elías Cerén Delgado, Marvin Wilfredo Monterrosa Delzas, Juan Carlos Portillo Leal (87.José Pablo Varela Rebollo), Felipe Ponce Ramírez (70.Oscar Oswaldo Rodríguez Maldonado), Narciso Oswaldo Orellana, Oswaldo Enrique Blanco Mancilla (78.Gerardo Maximiliano Freitas Talpamiz). Trainer: Wilson Jaime Gutiérrez Cardona (Colombia).
Tigres: Nahuel Ignacio Guzmán, Luis Alfonso Rodríguez Alanís, Carlos Joel Salcedo Hernández, Juan José Sánchez Purata (67.Jordan Steeven Sierra Flores), Rafael de Souza Pereira "Rafael Carioca", Jesús Alberto Dueñas Manzo, Javier Ignacio Aquino Carmona, Guido Hernán Pizarro Demestri, André-Pierre Christian Gignac, Enner Remberto Valencia Lastra, Nicolás Federico López Alonso (62.Julián Andrés Quiñones Quiñones). Trainer: Ricardo Ferretti de Oliveira (Brazil).
Goals: Felipe Ponce Ramírez (47 penalty), Oswaldo Enrique Blanco Mancilla (55) / Jorge Eduardo Sánchez Ramos (34).

26.02.2020, Estadio Universitario, San Nicolás de los Garza; Attendance: 38,894
Referee: Héctor Saíd Martínez Sorto (Honduras)
CF Tigres de la UA de Nuevo León - Alianza FC San Salvador   **4-2(3-2)**
Tigres: Nahuel Ignacio Guzmán, Luis Alfonso Rodríguez Alanís, Francisco Javier Meza Palma, Carlos Joel Salcedo Hernández (70.Eduardo Jesús Vargas Rojas), Jordan Steeven Sierra Flores (85.Julián Andrés Quiñones Quiñones), Rafael de Souza Pereira "Rafael Carioca", Jesús Alberto Dueñas Manzo, Javier Ignacio Aquino Carmona, Guido Hernán Pizarro Demestri, André-Pierre Christian Gignac, Enner Remberto Valencia Lastra. Trainer: Ricardo Ferretti de Oliveira (Brazil).
Alianza: Víctor Rafael García Muníz, Iván Roberto Mancia Ramirez, Mario Alberto Jacobo Segovia, Rudy Geovanny Clavel Mendoza (39.José Pablo Varela Rebollo), Alexander Vidal Larín Hernández, Óscar Elías Cerén Delgado, Marvin Wilfredo Monterrosa Delzas, Juan Carlos Portillo Leal (77.Rubén Eduardo Marroquín Meléndez), Felipe Ponce Ramírez (81.José Isaac Portillo Molina), Narciso Oswaldo Orellana, Oswaldo Enrique Blanco Mancilla. Trainer: Wilson Jaime Gutiérrez Cardona (Colombia).
Goals: Enner Remberto Valencia Lastra (10), André-Pierre Christian Gignac (18, 23 penalty), Nahuel Ignacio Guzmán (90+4) / Juan Carlos Portillo Leal (34, 42).
[CF Tigres de la Universidad Autónoma de Nuevo León won 5-4 on aggregate]

19.02.2020, Estadio „Ricardo Saprissa Aymá", San José
Referee: Kimbell Ward (Saint Kitts and Nevis)
Deportivo Saprissa San José - Montreal Impact   **2-2(0-2)**
Saprissa: Aarón Moises Cruz Esquivel, Roy Miller Hernández, Aubrey Robert David, Yostin Jafet Salinas Phillips (46.Michael Francisco Barrantes Rojas), Mariano Néstor Torres, Marvin Angulo Borbón, David Alberto Guzmán Pérez (66.Ariel Francisco Rodríguez Araya), Ricardo José Blanco Mora, Christian Bolaños Navarro, Johan Alberto Venegas Ulloa, Manfred Alonso Ugalde Arce (77.Jonathan Josué Martínez Solano). Trainer: Walter Centeno Corea.
Impact: Clément Diop Degoud, Rod Dodji Fanni, Jukka Raitala, Rudy Camacho (17.Joel Robert Waterman), Jorge Luis Corrales Cordero, Zachary Bichotte Paul Brault-Guillard, Samuel Piette, Amar Sejdič, Bojan Krkić Pérez, Romell Samir Quioto Robinson (71.Ballou Jean-Yves Tabla), Orji Okwonkwo (28.Maximiliano Nicolás Urruti Mussa). Trainer: Thierry Daniel Henry (France).
Goals: Johan Alberto Venegas Ulloa (80), Ariel Francisco Rodríguez Araya (90) / Orji Okwonkwo (12), Romell Samir Quioto Robinson (22).

26.02.2020, Olympic Stadium, Montreal; Attendance: 21,505
Referee: Fernando Guerrero Ramírez (Mexico)
Montreal Impact - Deportivo Saprissa San José   **0-0**
Impact: Clément Diop Degoud, Rod Dodji Fanni, Jukka Raitala (46.Joel Robert Waterman), Jorge Luis Corrales Cordero, Zachary Bichotte Paul Brault-Guillard, Luis Thomas Binks, Samuel Piette, Shamit Shome, Amar Sejdič (67.Saphir Sliti Taïder), Bojan Krkić Pérez (78.Anthony Jackson-Hamel), Romell Samir Quioto Robinson. Trainer: Thierry Daniel Henry (France).
Saprissa: Aarón Moises Cruz Esquivel, Aubrey Robert David, Jean Carlo Agüero Duarte, Walter Eduardo Cortés Pérez (71.Yael Andrés López Fuentes), Mariano Néstor Torres, Marvin Angulo Borbón (64.Ariel Francisco Rodríguez Araya), David Alberto Guzmán Pérez (74.Jonathan Josué Martínez Solano), Ricardo José Blanco Mora, Christian Bolaños Navarro, Johan Alberto Venegas Ulloa, Manfred Alonso Ugalde Arce. Trainer: Walter Centeno Corea.
[Montreal Impact won on away goals rule (2-2 on aggregate)]

20.02.2020, Estadio „Alejandro Morera Soto", Alajuela
Referee: César Arturo Ramos (Mexico)
AD San Carlos - New York City FC **3-5(1-2)**
San Carlos: Patrick Alberto Pemberton Bernard, Jordan Hakeem Smith Wint, José David Sánchez Cruz, Lucas Maximiliano Meza, Esteban Ramírez Segnini, Carlos Acosta Evans (54.Cristian Alonso Martínez Mena), Fernando Brenes Arrieta, Randy Yormein Chirino Serrano (70.Juan Vicente Solís Brenes), Marco Julián Mena Rojas, Jorman Isreal Aguilar Bustamante, Julio César Cruz González (53.Omar Ezequiel Browne Zuñiga). Trainer: Luis Antonio Marín Murillo.
New York City: Sean Everet Johnson, Anton Lars Tinnerholm (62.Joseph Scally), Alexander Martín Marquinho Callens Asín, Maxime Chanot, Rónald Alberto Matarrita Ulate, Alexander Michael Ring, Jesús Manuel Medina Maldonado, Keaton Alexander Parks (64.Maximiliano Nicolás Moralez), James Hoban Sands, Héber Araujo dos Santos (64.Valentín Mariano José Castellanos Giménez), Alexandru Ionuț Mitriță. Trainer: Ronny Deila (Norway).
Goals: Jorman Isreal Aguilar Bustamante (45), Marco Julián Mena Rojas (63), Omar Ezequiel Browne Zuñiga (79) / Héber Araujo dos Santos (13, 35, 52 penalty), Alexander Martín Marquinho Callens Asín (61), Alexandru Ionuț Mitriță (90+3).

26.02.2020, Red Bull Arena, Harrison; Attendance: 4,396
Referee: John Francis Pitti Hernández (Panama)
New York City FC - AD San Carlos **1-0(1-0)**
New York City: Sean Everet Johnson, Anton Lars Tinnerholm, Alexander Martín Marquinho Callens Asín, Maxime Chanot, Rónald Alberto Matarrita Ulate (63.Sebastien Uchechukwu Ibeagha), Maximiliano Nicolás Moralez (63.Ismael Tajouri), Alexander Michael Ring, Jesús Manuel Medina Maldonado, James Hoban Sands, Alexandru Ionuț Mitriță (76.Gary Sean Mackay-Steven), Valentín Mariano José Castellanos Giménez. Trainer: Ronny Deila (Norway).
San Carlos: Patrick Alberto Pemberton Bernard, José David Sánchez Cruz, Lucas Maximiliano Meza, Pablo César Arboine Carmona, Fernando Brenes Arrieta, Randy Yormein Chirino Serrano, Cristian Alonso Martínez Mena, Greivin Méndez Venegas (54.Esteban Ramírez Segnini), Roberto José Córdoba Durán (60.Rashid Enrique Chirino Serrano), Omar Ezequiel Browne Zuñiga, Jorman Isreal Aguilar Bustamante (69.Julio César Cruz González). Trainer: Luis Antonio Marín Murillo.
Goal: Alexander Martín Marquinho Callens Asín (41).
[New York City FC won 6-3 on aggregate]

20.02.2020, Estadio Olímpico Metropolitano, San Pedro Sula
Referee: Juan Gabriel Calderón Pérez (Costa Rica)
CD Olimpia Tegucigalpa - Seattle Sounders FC **2-2(0-1)**
Olimpia: Edrick Eduardo Menjívar Jonhnson, Johnny Harold Leverón Uclés, Ever Gonzalo Alvarado Sandoval, Jonathan Josué Paz Hernández, Deybi Aldair Flores Flores, German Noe Mejía Briceño, Carlos Enrique Pineda López (73.Leonardo Matías Garrido), Edwin Alexander Rodríguez Castillo, Jerry Ricardo Bengtson Bodden (69.Jorge Renán Benguche Ramírez), Justin Arboleda Buenaños, José Mario Pinto Paz (58.Cristian Omar Maidana). Trainer: Pedro Antonio Troglio (Argentina).
Seattle Sounders: Stefan Frei, Kelvin Leerdam, Yeimar Pastor Gómez Andrade, Xavier Ricardo Arreaga Bermello, Nouhou Tolo, Joevin Martin Jones (69.Shane Edward O'Neill), João Paulo Mior (79. Daniel Ulises Leyva), Jordy José Delem, Cristian Roldan, Raúl Mario Ruidíaz Misitich, Jordan Perry Morris (84.Alexander Roldán). Trainer: Brian Schmetzer.
Goals: Justin Arboleda Buenaños (63, 81) / João Paulo Mior (6), Jordan Perry Morris (54).

27.02.2020, CenturyLink Field, Seattle; Attendance: 34,016
Referee: Iván Arcides Barton Cisneros (El Salvador)
Seattle Sounders FC - CD Olimpia Tegucigalpa   2-2(1-1,2-2,2-2); 2-4 on penalties
Seattle Sounders: Stefan Frei, Kelvin Leerdam, Shane Edward O'Neill, Xavier Ricardo Arreaga Bermello, Nouhou Tolo, Joevin Martin Jones (70.Miguel Ángel Ibarra Andrade), João Paulo Mior, Jordy José Delem, Cristian Roldan, Raúl Mario Ruidíaz Misitich, Jordan Perry Morris (84.Justin Shane Dhillon). Trainer: Brian Schmetzer.
Olimpia: Edrick Eduardo Menjívar Jonhnson, Johnny Harold Leverón Uclés, Maylor Alberto Nuñez Flores, Elvin Oliva Casildo, Leonardo Matías Garrido (72.Jorge Renán Benguche Ramírez), Deybi Aldair Flores Flores, German Noe Mejía Briceño, Carlos Enrique Pineda López, Jerry Ricardo Bengtson Bodden (81.Edwin Alexander Rodríguez Castillo), Justin Arboleda Buenaños, José Mario Pinto Paz (58.Cristian Omar Maidana). Trainer: Pedro Antonio Troglio (Argentina).
Goals: Cristian Roldan (21), João Paulo Mior (64) / Elvin Oliva Casildo (4), Carlos Enrique Pineda López (86).
Penalties: Raúl Mario Ruidíaz Misitich 1-0; Justin Arboleda Buenaños 1-1; João Paulo Mior 2-1; Jorge Renán Benguche Ramírez 2-2; Cristian Roldan (missed); Edwin Alexander Rodríguez Castillo 2-3; Kelvin Leerdam (saved); Johnny Harold Leverón Uclés 2-4.
[CD Olimpia Tegucigalpa won 4-2 on penalties (after 4-4 on aggregate)]

QUARTER-FINALS

10.12.2020, Olympic Stadium, Montreal; Attendance: 22,704
Referee: Adonai Escobedo González (Mexico)
Montreal Impact - CD Olimpia Tegucigalpa 1-2(0-2)
Impact: Clément Diop Degoud, Rod Dodji Fanni, Jorge Luis Corrales Cordero, Zachary Bichotte Paul Brault-Guillard (46.Orji Okwonkwo), Joel Robert Waterman, Luis Thomas Binks, Victor Mugubi Wanyama, Saphir Sliti Taïder, Samuel Piette, Romell Samir Quioto Robinson (72.Ballou Jean-Yves Tabla), Maximiliano Nicolás Urruti Mussa (58.Anthony Jackson-Hamel). Trainer: Thierry Daniel Henry (France).
Olimpia: Edrick Eduardo Menjívar Jonhnson (14.Alex Naíd Guity Barrios), Johnny Harold Leverón Uclés, Maylor Alberto Nuñez Flores, Elvin Oliva Casildo, Leonardo Matías Garrido (85.José Mario Pinto Paz), Deybi Aldair Flores Flores, German Noe Mejía Briceño (90.José Arnaldo Cañete Prieto), Carlos Enrique Pineda López, Edwin Alexander Rodríguez Castillo, Jerry Ricardo Bengtson Bodden, Jorge Renán Benguche Ramírez. Trainer: Pedro Antonio Troglio (Argentina).
Goals: Saphir Sliti Taïder (47) / Jerry Ricardo Bengtson Bodden (15), Jorge Renán Benguche Ramírez (41).

15.12.2020, Exploria Stadium, Orlando
Referee: Ricardo Montero Araya (Costa Rica)
CD Olimpia Tegucigalpa - Montreal Impact 0-1(0-0)
Olimpia: Edrick Eduardo Menjívar Jonhnson, Johnny Harold Leverón Uclés, Maylor Alberto Nuñez Flores, Elvin Oliva Casildo, Javier Arnaldo Portillo Martínez, Deybi Aldair Flores Flores, Carlos Enrique Pineda López, Edwin Alexander Rodríguez Castillo (84.Diego Antonio Reyes Sandoval), Jerry Ricardo Bengtson Bodden (76.Eddie Gabriel Hernández Padilla), Justin Arboleda Buenaños (83.Samuel Arturo Córdova Howe), Marvin Javier Bernárdez García (58.Josmán Alexander Figueroa Arzú). Trainer: Pedro Antonio Troglio (Argentina).
Impact: Clément Diop Degoud, Rudy Camacho, Zachary Bichotte Paul Brault-Guillard, Luis Thomas Binks, Mustafa Kizza, Victor Mugubi Wanyama, Samuel Piette (83.Jean-Aniel Assi), Amar Sejdič, Romell Samir Quioto Robinson, Orji Okwonkwo, Mason Vincent Toye (56.Anthony Jackson-Hamel). Trainer: Thierry Daniel Henry (France).
Goal: Amar Sejdič (57).
[CD Olimpia Tegucigalpa won on away goals rule (2-2 on aggregate)]

11.12.2020, Red Bull Arena, Harrison; Attendance: 10,212
Referee: Juan Gabriel Calderón Pérez (Costa Rica)
New York City FC - CF Tigres de la Universidad Autónoma de Nuevo León 0-1(0-0)
New York City: Sean Everet Johnson, Anton Lars Tinnerholm, Alexander Martín Marquinho Callens Asín, Maxime Chanot, Rónald Alberto Matarrita Ulate, Alexander Michael Ring, Keaton Alexander Parks (75.Maximiliano Nicolás Moralez), James Hoban Sands, Héber Araujo dos Santos (65.Valentín Mariano José Castellanos Giménez), Alexandru Ionuț Mitriță, Ismael Tajouri (73.Jesús Manuel Medina Maldonado). Trainer: Ronny Deila (Norway).
Tigres: Nahuel Ignacio Guzmán, Hugo Ayala Castro, Luis Alfonso Rodríguez Alanís, Francisco Javier Meza Palma, Jordan Steeven Sierra Flores (46.Luis Enrique Quiñones García), Rafael de Souza Pereira "Rafael Carioca", Jesús Alberto Dueñas Manzo, Javier Ignacio Aquino Carmona, Guido Hernán Pizarro Demestri, André-Pierre Christian Gignac, Eduardo Jesús Vargas Rojas. Trainer: Ricardo Ferretti de Oliveira (Brazil).
Goal: Eduardo Jesús Vargas Rojas (90+3).

15.12.2020, Exploria Stadium, Orlando
Referee: Daneon Parchment (Jamaica)
CF Tigres de la Universidad Autónoma de Nuevo León - New York City FC   4-0(1-0)
Tigres: Nahuel Ignacio Guzmán, Hugo Ayala Castro, Luis Alfonso Rodríguez Alanís, Carlos Joel Salcedo Hernández (72.Francisco Javier Meza Palma), Rafael de Souza Pereira "Rafael Carioca", Jesús Alberto Dueñas Manzo, Javier Ignacio Aquino Carmona, Guido Hernán Pizarro Demestri, Leonardo Cecilio Fernández López (72.Raymundo de Jesús Fulgencio Román), André-Pierre Christian Gignac, Luis Enrique Quiñones García (86.Nicolás Federico López Alonso). Trainer: Ricardo Ferretti de Oliveira (Brazil).
New York City: Luis Barraza, Anton Lars Tinnerholm, Alexander Martín Marquinho Callens Asín, Maxime Chanot (89.Sebastien Uchechukwu Ibeagha), Rónald Alberto Matarrita Ulate (70.Guðmundur Þórarinsson), Maximiliano Nicolás Moralez, Gary Sean Mackay-Steven, Jesús Manuel Medina Maldonado (69.Keaton Alexander Parks), Nicolás Brian Acevedo Tabarez (89.Antonio Rocha), Ismael Tajouri (70.Andres Jasson), Valentín Mariano José Castellanos Giménez. Trainer: Ronny Deila (Norway).
Goals: André-Pierre Christian Gignac (30), Leonardo Cecilio Fernández López (49), Rafael de Souza Pereira "Rafael Carioca" (64), Javier Ignacio Aquino Carmona (85).
[CF Tigres de la Universidad Autónoma de Nuevo León won 5-0 on aggregate]

11.12.2020, Estadio Azteca, Ciudad de México; Attendance: 20,731
Referee: John Francis Pitti Hernández (Panama)
CF América Ciudad de México - Atlanta United FC   3-0(3-0)
América: Óscar Francisco Jiménez Fabela, Luis Fernando Fuentes Vargas, Víctor Emanuel Aguilera, Bruno Amílcar Valdez, Jorge Eduardo Sánchez Ramos, Leonardo Gabriel Suárez, Richard Rafael Sánchez Guerrero, Santiago Cáseres (89.Fernando Rubén González Pineda), Giovani Álex dos Santos Ramírez (72.Federico Sebastián Viñas Barboza), Andrés Felipe Ibargüen García (57.Francisco Sebastián Córdova Reyes), Henry Josué Martín Mex. Trainer: Miguel Ernesto Herrera Aguirre.
Atlanta United: Bradley Edwin Guzan, Fernando Nicolás Meza, Brooks Howard Lennon, Anton Charles Walkes, Jeffrey Adam Larentowicz, Jake David Mulraney (66.Adam Jahn), Emerson Schellas Hyndman, Eric Daian Remedi (46.Matheus Rossetto; 58.Luis Manuel Castro Cáceres), Mohammed Adams, Ezequiel Omar Barco, Gonzalo Nicolás Martínez. Trainer: Franciscus de Boer (Netherlands).
Goals: Leonardo Gabriel Suárez (11), Henry Josué Martín Mex (13), Bruno Amílcar Valdez (36).

16.12.2020, Exploria Stadium, Orlando
Referee: Ismael Alexander Cornejo Meléndez (El Salvador)
Atlanta United FC - CF América Ciudad de México   1-0(0-0)
Atlanta United: Bradley Edwin Guzan, Fernando Nicolás Meza, Franco Nicolás Escobar, Miles Gordon Robinson, George Bello, Jake David Mulraney (80.Jackson Conway), Emerson Schellas Hyndman, Eric Daian Remedi (80.Matheus Rossetto), Ezequiel Omar Barco (62.Erick Estéfano Torres Padilla), Adam Jahn (62.Damián Marcelino Moreno [*sent off 90*]), Erik Nicolás López Samaniego (76.Jack William Gurr). Trainer: Stephen Glass (Scotland).
América: Francisco Guillermo Ochoa Magaña, Jorge Eduardo Sánchez Ramos, Sebastián Enzo Cáceres Ramos, Ramón Juárez del Castillo, Jesús Alonso Escoboza Lugo (86.Luis Ricardo Reyes Moreno), Leonardo Gabriel Suárez (74.Antonio de Jesús López Amenábar), Richard Rafael Sánchez Guerrero, Francisco Sebastián Córdova Reyes, Santiago Cáseres, Roger Beyker Martínez Tobinson (74.Santiago Naveda Lara), Federico Sebastián Viñas Barboza (82.Esteban Lozano Solana). Trainer: Miguel Ernesto Herrera Aguirre.
Goal: Jackson Conway (82).
[CF América Ciudad de México won 3-1 on aggregate]

16.12.2020, Exploria Stadium, Orlando
Referee: Héctor Saíd Martínez Sorto (Honduras)
Los Angeles FC - Cruz Azul FC Ciudad de México**2-1(1-1)**
Los Angeles: Kenneth Vermeer, Eddie Livington Segura Martínez, Diego José Palacios Espinoza, Tristan Michael Blackmon (88.Mohamed El-Mounir Abdussalam), Jesús David Murillo Largacha, José Andoni Cifuentes Charcopa (80.Paul Brian Rodríguez Bravo), Mark-Anthony Kaye, Eduard Andrés Atuesta Velasco, Diego Martín Rossi Marachlian (80.Latif Atta Blessing), Carlos Alberto Vela Garrido, Danny Musovski (58.Kwadwo Opoku). Trainer: Robert Frank Bradley.
Cruz Azul: Sebastián Jurado Roca, Julio César Domínguez Juárez, Luis Francisco Romo Barrón, Pablo César Aguilar Benítez, Juan Marcelo Escobar Chena, Elías Hernán Hernández Jacuinde (51.Adrián Alexei Aldrete Rodríguez), Victor Yoshimar Yotún Flores, Rafael Baca Miranda, Roberto Carlos Alvarado Hernández (84.José Ignacio Rivero Segade), Orbelín Pineda Alvarado (83.Josué Misael Domínguez González), Santiago Tomás Giménez (51.Milton Joel Caraglio Lugo). Trainer: Robert Dante Siboldi Badiola (Uruguay).
Goals: Carlos Alberto Vela Garrido (38 penalty), Kwadwo Opoku (71) / Victor Yoshimar Yotún Flores (15 penalty).

SEMI-FINALS

19.12.2020, Exploria Stadium, Orlando
Referee: Iván Arcides Barton Cisneros (El Salvador)
CF Tigres de la UA de Nuevo León - CD Olimpia Tegucigalpa**3-0(1-0)**
Tigres: Nahuel Ignacio Guzmán, Hugo Ayala Castro, Luis Alfonso Rodríguez Alanís (81.Diego Antonio Reyes Rosales), Carlos Joel Salcedo Hernández, Rafael de Souza Pereira "Rafael Carioca", Jesús Alberto Dueñas Manzo, Javier Ignacio Aquino Carmona (42.Raymundo de Jesús Fulgencio Román), Guido Hernán Pizarro Demestri, Leonardo Cecilio Fernández López (58.Nicolás Federico López Alonso), André-Pierre Christian Gignac, Luis Enrique Quiñones García. Trainer: Ricardo Ferretti de Oliveira (Brazil).
Olimpia: Edrick Eduardo Menjívar Jonhnson, Johnny Harold Leverón Uclés, Maylor Alberto Nuñez Flores, Elvin Oliva Casildo, Javier Arnaldo Portillo Martínez (64.Samuel Arturo Córdova Howe), Deybi Aldair Flores Flores [*sent off 45+3*], Carlos Enrique Pineda López, Edwin Alexander Rodríguez Castillo (77.José Mario Pinto Paz), Jerry Ricardo Bengtson Bodden (79.Eddie Gabriel Hernández Padilla), Justin Arboleda Buenaños (46.Jorge Daniel Álvarez Rodas), Marvin Javier Bernárdez García (65.Michaell Anthony Chirinos López). Trainer: Pedro Antonio Troglio (Argentina).
Goals: André-Pierre Christian Gignac (45+4 penalty, 57 penalty), Elvin Oliva Casildo (78 own goal).

19.12.2020, Exploria Stadium, Orlando
Referee: Juan Gabriel Calderón Pérez (Costa Rica)
Los Angeles FC - CF América Ciudad de México**3-1(0-1)**
Los Angeles: Kenneth Vermeer, Jesús David Murillo Largacha, Eddie Livington Segura Martínez, Diego José Palacios Espinoza, Tristan Michael Blackmon, Mark-Anthony Kaye, Eduard Andrés Atuesta Velasco [*sent off 45+5*], José Andoni Cifuentes Charcopa (69.Francisco Ginella Dabezies), Carlos Alberto Vela Garrido, Diego Martín Rossi Marachlian, Danny Musovski (46.Latif Atta Blessing). Trainer: Robert Frank Bradley.
América: Francisco Guillermo Ochoa Magaña, Luis Fernando Fuentes Vargas, Luis Ricardo Reyes Moreno [*sent off 79*], Jorge Eduardo Sánchez Ramos, Sebastián Enzo Cáceres Ramos, Ramón Juárez del Castillo (76.Roger Beyker Martínez Tobinson), Leonardo Gabriel Suárez (83.Sergio Ismael Díaz Velázquez), Richard Rafael Sánchez Guerrero (68.Andrés Felipe Ibargüen García), Francisco Sebastián Córdova Reyes (83.Jesús Alonso Escoboza Lugo), Santiago Cáseres (83.Santiago Naveda Lara), Federico Sebastián Viñas Barboza. Trainer: Miguel Ernesto Herrera Aguirre.
Goals: Carlos Alberto Vela Garrido (46, 47), Latif Atta Blessing (90+5) / Sebastián Enzo Cáceres Ramos (12).

FINAL

22.12.2020, Exploria Stadium, Orlando
Referee: Mario Alberto Escobar Toca (Guatemala)
CF Tigres de la Universidad Autónoma de Nuevo León - Los Angeles FC   2-1(0-0)
Tigres: Nahuel Ignacio Guzmán, Hugo Ayala Castro (74.Francisco Javier Meza Palma), Luis Alfonso Rodríguez Alanís, Carlos Joel Salcedo Hernández, Rafael de Souza Pereira "Rafael Carioca", Jesús Alberto Dueñas Manzo (71.Raymundo de Jesús Fulgencio Román), Javier Ignacio Aquino Carmona (87.Eduardo Santiago Tercero Méndez), Guido Hernán Pizarro Demestri, Leonardo Cecilio Fernández López (71.Nicolás Federico López Alonso), André-Pierre Christian Gignac, Luis Enrique Quiñones García (87.Francisco Eduardo Venegas Moreno). Trainer: Ricardo Ferretti de Oliveira (Brazil).
Los Angeles: Kenneth Vermeer, Jesús David Murillo Largacha (88.Paul Brian Rodríguez Bravo), Eddie Livington Segura Martínez, Diego José Palacios Espinoza, Tristan Michael Blackmon, Mark-Anthony Kaye, José Andoni Cifuentes Charcopa (67.Francisco Ginella Dabezies), Carlos Alberto Vela Garrido, Diego Martín Rossi Marachlian, Latif Atta Blessing, Danny Musovski (46.Kwadwo Opoku). Trainer: Robert Frank Bradley.
Goals: 0-1 Diego Martín Rossi Marachlian (61), 1-1 Hugo Ayala Castro (72), 2-1 André-Pierre Christian Gignac (84).

2020 CONCACAF Champions League Winner:
CF Tigres de la Universidad Autónoma de Nuevo León (Mexico)

Best Goalscorer:
André-Pierre Christian Gignac (FRA, CF Tigres de la Universidad Autónoma de Nuevo León) – 8 goals

CONCACAF CUP OF CHAMPIONS CLUBS (1962-2008)
CONCACAF CHAMPIONS LEAGUE (since 2008/2009)
TABLE OF HONOURS

1962	Club Deportivo Guadalajara	(MEX)
1963	Racing Club Haïtien	(HAI)
1967	Alianza FC San Salvador	(SLV)
1968	Deportivo Toluca Fútbol Club	(MEX)
1969	CDSC Cruz Azul	(MEX)
1970	CDSC Cruz Azul	(MEX)
1971	CDSC Cruz Azul	(MEX)
1972	Club Deportivo Olimpia Tegucigalpa	(HON)
1973	Sport Vereniging Transvaal	(SUR)
1974	CSD Municipal Ciudad de Guatemala	(GUA)
1975	Atlético Español FC Ciudad de México	(MEX)
1976	Club Deportivo Águila San Miguel	(SLV)
1977	Club América Ciudad de México	(MEX)
1978	Club Universidad de Guadalajara*	(MEX)
1978	CSD Comunicaciones Ciudad de Guatemala	(GUA)
1978	Defence Force FC Chaguaramas	(TRI)
1979	CD FAS Santa Ana	(SLV)
1980	Club UNAM Ciudad de México	(MEX)
1981	Sport Vereniging Transvaal	(SUR)
1982	Club UNAM Ciudad de México	(MEX)
1983	Atlante FC Ciudad de México	(MEX)
1984	Violette Athletic Club Port-au-Prince	(HAI)

Year	Club	Country
1985	Defence Force FC Chaguaramas	(TRI)
1986	LD Alajuelense	(CRC)
1987	Club América Ciudad de México	(MEX)
1988	Club Deportivo Olimpia Tegucigalpa	(HON)
1989	Club UNAM Ciudad de México	(MEX)
1990	Club América Ciudad de México	(MEX)
1991	Puebla FC	(MEX)
1992	Club América Ciudad de México	(MEX)
1993	CD Saprissa San José	(CRC)
1994	CS Cartaginés Deportiva	(CRC)
1995	CD Saprissa San José	(CRC)
1996	CDSC Cruz Azul	(MEX)
1997	CDSC Cruz Azul	(MEX)
1998	Washington DC United	(USA)
1999	Necaxa CF	(MEX)
2000	Los Angeles Galaxy	(USA)
2002	CF Pachuca	(MEX)
2003	Deportivo Toluca Fútbol Club	(MEX)
2004	LD Alajuelense	(CRC)
2005	CD Saprissa San José	(CRC)
2006	Club América Ciudad de México	(MEX)
2007	CF Pachuca	(MEX)
2008	CF Pachuca	(MEX)
2008/2009	Atlante FC	(MEX)
2009/2010	CF Pachuca	(MEX)
2010/2011	CF Monterrey	(MEX)
2011/2012	CF Monterrey	(MEX)
2012/2013	CF Monterrey	(MEX)
2013/2014	Cruz Azul FC Ciudad de México	(MEX)
2014/2015	CF América Ciudad de México	(MEX)
2015/2016	CF América Ciudad de México	(MEX)
2016/2017	CF Pachuca	(MEX)
2018	Club Deportivo Guadalajara	(MEX)
2019	CF Monterrey	(MEX)
2020	CF Tigres de la Universidad Autónoma de Nuevo León	(MEX)

*all declared joint winners after the final tournament was cancelled due to administrative problems and disagreement on the dates

CONCACAF CARIBBEAN CLUB CHAMPIONSHIP 2021

13 clubs from 11 member associations entered the 2021 edition of the CONCACAF Caribbean Club Championship hosted in San Cristóbal & Santo Domingo (Dominican Republic).

List of participating clubs:

Dominican Republic (2 teams)	Universidad Organización y Métodos FC Santo Domingo
	Delfines del Este FC La Romana
Haiti (2 teams)	AS Cavaly Léogâne
	Don Bosco FC Pétion-Ville
Bonaire (1 team)	SV Real Rincón
Curaçao (1 team)	RKSV Scherpenheuvel
French Guiana (1 team)	Olympique de Cayenne
Guadeloupe (1 team)	AS Le Gosier
Martinique (1 team)	AS Samaritaine Sainte-Marie
Puerto Rico (1 team)	Metropolitan Football Academy San Juan
Saint Vincent and the Grenadines (1 team)	Hope International FC Kingstown
Sint Maarten (1 team)	Flames United SC Philipsburg
Suriname (1 team)	Inter Moengotapoe

Withdrawn teams: SV Racing Club Aruba Oranjestad (Aruba), Sagicor South East United La Plaine (Dominica), Portmore United FC & Waterhouse FC Kingston (Jamaica), Platinum FC Vieux Fort (Saint Lucia).
Teams from Trinidad and Tobago did not enter the competition.

GROUP STAGE
Winners were qualified for the Semi-Finals.

Group A

15.05.2021, Estádio Olímpico „Félix Sánchez", Santo Domingo
Referee: Tori Penso (United States)
Universidad Organización y Métodos FC Santo Domingo - Flames United SC   11-1(6-1)
Goals: Harold Sanon (3, 6), Hilario Mena (28), Arichel Hernández Mora (35), Daniel Jamesley (41), Shane Weekes (45+1 own goal), Daniel Jamesley (50), Hilario Mena (58), Jackson Tineo (75), Daniel Jamesley (79), Wilman Modesta (90) / Jayan Gordon (15).

17.05.2021, Estadio Panamericano, San Cristóbal
Referee: Edgar Alonso Ramírez (El Salvador)
Flames United SC Philipsburg - Inter Moengotapoe   0-12(0-5)
Goals: Rievaldo Doorson (9), Romeo Kastiel (21, 31), Miquel Danny Darson (35 penalty), Sergino Rahi Eduard (37), Miquel Danny Darson (48), Damian Brunswijk (64), Rievaldo Doorson (70), Anduelo Amoeferie (83 penalty), Basil Germaine Wong (86 own goal), Chamille Eduard (89), Jerrel Wijks (90+2).

19.05.2021, Estádio Olímpico „Félix Sánchez", Santo Domingo
Referee: Tori Penso (United States)
Universidad Organización y Métodos FC Santo Domingo - Inter Moengotapoe   1-1(1-0)
Goals: Hilario Mena (11) / Donnegy Seraino Fer (57).

	FINAL STANDINGS							
1.	**Inter Moengotapoe**	2	1	1	0	13	- 1	4
2.	Universidad Organización y Métodos FC Santo Domingo	2	1	1	0	12	- 2	4
3.	Flames United SC Philipsburg	2	0	0	2	1	- 23	0

Group B

15.05.2021, Estádio Olímpico „Félix Sánchez", Santo Domingo
Referee: Ricangel de Leça (Aruba)
**Delfines del Este FC La Romana –
Metropolitan Football Academy San Juan**　　　　　**1-1(0-0); 0-3 awarded**
Goals: Yessy Mena (90+5) / Jorge Luis Rivera (83).
Please note: the match was awarded as a 3-0 win for Metropolitan Football Academy San Juan due to the fact that Delfines del Este FC La Romana have fielded six ineligible players.

17.05.2021, Estadio Panamericano, San Cristóbal
Referee: Odette Hamilton (Jamaica)
Metropolitan Football Academy San Juan - SV Real Rincón　　**4-0(2-0)**
Goals: Héctor Omar Ramos Lebrón (6), Rilove Janga (39 own goal), Jorge Luis Rivera (75, 90+4).

19.05.2021, Estádio Olímpico „Félix Sánchez", Santo Domingo
Referee: Jamar Springer (Barbados)
Delfines del Este FC La Romana - SV Real Rincón　　**10-0(6-0)**
Goals: Roberto Victoria (3), Yessy Mena (16), Roberto Victoria (17, 19, 20), Carlos Heredia Fontana (37 penalty), Randy Valdez (38), Roberto Victoria (48), Dayron Michel (54), Carlos Heredia Fontana (84).

	FINAL STANDINGS							
1.	**Metropolitan Football Academy San Juan**	2	2	0	0	7	- 0	6
2.	Delfines del Este FC La Romana	2	1	0	1	10	- 3	3
3.	SV Real Rincón	2	0	0	2	0	- 14	0

Group C

Please note: Sagicor South East United La Plaine withdrew after being unable to travel to the Dominican Republic in time for the tournament due to travel challenges resulting from the COVID-19 pandemic.

16.05.2021, Estádio Olímpico „Félix Sánchez", Santo Domingo
Referee: Rubiel Vázquez (United States)
Don Bosco FC Pétion-Ville - AS Samaritaine Sainte-Marie　　**2-2(1-1)**
Goals: Elyvens Dejan (14), Jean Innocent (79) / Patrick Percin (27), Dylan Florent (70).

18.05.2021, Estadio Panamericano, San Cristóbal
Referee: Oliver Amet Vergara Rodríguez (Panama)
AS Samaritaine Sainte-Marie - AS Le Gosier　　**3-1(2-1)**
Goals: Patrick Percin (26), Jordan Lise (44), Dylan Florent (90+5) / Hilaire Orilus (19).

20.05.2021, Estádio Olímpico „Félix Sánchez", Santo Domingo
Referee: Trevester Richards (Saint Kitts and Nevis)
Don Bosco FC Pétion-Ville - AS Le Gosier 1-0(0-0)
Goal: Andreville Zavarov (55).

FINAL STANDINGS

1.	**AS Samaritaine Sainte-Marie**	2	1	1	0	5	-	3	4
2.	Don Bosco FC Pétion-Ville	2	1	1	0	3	-	2	4
3.	AS Le Gosier	2	0	0	2	1	-	4	0

Group D

16.05.2021, Estadio Panamericano, San Cristóbal
Referee: William Anderson (Puerto Rico)
Olympique de Cayenne - Hope International FC Kingstown 1-4(1-2)
Goals: Delano Batiste (45+3) / Kevin Samuel (13), Enrique Millington (45+1), Nazir Obain McBurnette (72), Joseph Douglas (90+3).

16.05.2021, Estádio Olímpico „Félix Sánchez", Santo Domingo
Referee: Francia María González Martínez (Mexico)
AS Cavaly Léogâne - RKSV Scherpenheuvel 3-0(2-0)
Goals: Roody Joseph (3 penalty), Dorvil Gamaël (12), Joseph Fenelson (86).

18.05.2021, Estádio Olímpico „Félix Sánchez", Santo Domingo
Referee: Randy Encarnación Solano (Dominican Republic)
AS Cavaly Léogâne - Olympique de Cayenne 5-0(2-0)
Goals: Elistin Eddyson (26), Dorvil Gamaël (40), Dorley Jean (53), Dorvil Gamaël (62), Joseph Fenelson (87).

18.05.2021, Estadio Panamericano, San Cristóbal
Referee: Trevester Richards (Saint Kitts and Nevis)
RKSV Scherpenheuvel - Hope International FC Kingstown 3-1(1-0)
Goals: Nicolás Rocha (34), Maximiliano Ciarnello (61), Benjamin Gill (86) / Joseph Douglas (70).

20.05.2021, Estádio Olímpico „Félix Sánchez", Santo Domingo
Referee: Oliver Amet Vergara Rodríguez (Panama)
AS Cavaly Léogâne - Hope International FC Kingstown 2-1(1-1)
Goals: Roody Joseph (31, 79) / Nazir Obain McBurnette (34).

20.05.2021, Estadio Panamericano, San Cristóbal
Referee: Odette Hamilton (Jamaica)
RKSV Scherpenheuvel - Olympique de Cayenne 3-1(3-1)
Goals: Maximiliano Ciarnello (10), Nicolás Rocha (16, 27) / Delano Batiste (5).

FINAL STANDINGS

1.	**AS Cavaly Léogâne**	3	3	0	0	10	-	1	9
2.	RKSV Scherpenheuvel	3	2	0	1	6	-	5	6
3.	Hope International FC Kingstown	3	1	0	2	6	-	6	3
4.	Olympique de Cayenne	3	0	0	3	2	-	12	0

SEMI-FINALS

23.05.2021, Estádio Olímpico „Félix Sánchez“, Santo Domingo
Referee: Rubiel Vázquez (United States)
Inter Moengotapoe - Metropolitan Football Academy San Juan **3-1(0-0)**
Goals: Romeo Kastiel (53), Miquel Danny Darson (69), Rievaldo Doorson (86) / Marc Nieves (90+5).

23.05.2021, Estádio Olímpico „Félix Sánchez“, Santo Domingo
Referee: Oliver Amet Vergara Rodríguez (Panama)
AS Samaritaine Sainte-Marie - AS Cavaly Léogâne **0-2(0-1)**
Goals: Dorley Jean (30), Karl Vitulin (77 own goal).

FINAL

25.05.2021, Estádio Olímpico „Félix Sánchez“, Santo Domingo
Referee: Francia María González Martínez (Mexico)
Inter Moengotapoe - AS Cavaly Léogâne **0-3(0-1)**
Goals: Constant Monuma (29), Dorvil Gamaël (47, 77).

CARIBBEAN FOOTBALL UNION CLUB CHAMPIONSHIP (1997-2021) TABLE OF HONOURS		
1997	United Petrotrin Palo Seco	(TRI)
1998	Joe Public FC Tunapuna	(TRI)
1999	*Not held*	(TRI)
2000	Joe Public FC Tunapuna	(TRI)
2001	Defence Force FC Chaguaramas	(TRI)
2002	Williams Connection FC Marabella	(TRI)
2003	San Juan Jabloteh FC Port of Spain	(TRI)
2004	Harbour View FC Kingston	(JAM)
2005	Portmore United FC	(JAM)
2006	Williams Connection FC Marabella	(TRI)
2007	Harbour View FC Kingston	(JAM)
2008	*Not held*	(JAM)
2009	Williams Connection FC Marabella	(TRI)
2010	Puerto Rico Islanders FC	(PUR)
2011	Puerto Rico Islanders FC	(PUR)
2012	Caledonia AIA Malabar	(TRI)
2013	*No winner*[1]	
2014	*No winner*[1]	
2015	Central FC California	(TRI)
2016	Central FC California	(TRI)
2017	Cibao FC Santiago de Caballeros	(DOM)
2018	Club Atlético Pantoja Santo Domingo	(DOM)
2019	Portmore United FC	(JAM)
2020	*Competition cancelled*	
2021	AS Cavaly Léogâne	(HAI)

[1] - *No final matches were held.*

CONCACAF CARIBBEAN CLUB SHIELD
2021

14 clubs from 14 member associations entered the 2021 edition of the CONCACAF Caribbean Club Shield.

List of participating clubs:

Aruba (1 team)	SV Racing Club Aruba Oranjestad
Bonaire (1 team)	SV Real Rincón
Curaçao (1 team)	RKSV Scherpenheuvel
Dominica (1 team)	South East United La Plaine
French Guiana (1 team)	Olympique de Cayenne
Guadeloupe (1 team)	AS Le Gosier
Guyana (1 team)	Fruta Conquerors FC Georgetown
Martinique (1 team)	AS Samaritaine Sainte-Marie
Puerto Rico (1 team)	Metropolitan Football Academy San Juan
Saint Kitts and Nevis (1 team)	St. Paul United FC
Saint Lucia (1 team)	Platinum FC Vieux-Fort
Saint Vincent and the Grenadines (1 team)	Hope International FC Kingstown
Sint Maarten (1 team)	Flames United SC Philipsburg
Suriname (1 team)	Inter Moengotapoe

Associations which did not enter a team: Anguilla, Antigua and Barbuda, Bahamas, Barbados, Bermuda, British Virgin Islands, Cayman islands, Cuba, Grenada, Montserrat, Saint Martin, Turks and Caicos Islands and U.S. Virgin Islands.

The tournament was originally scheduled to be played between 23.04.2021 and 02.05.2021 in Curaçao. In early April, CONCACAF postponed the competition due to COVID-19 pandemic. Eventually CONCACAF cancelled the tournament, and a numner of teams participated in the 2021 CONCACAF Caribbean Club Championship.

	**CONCACAF CARIBBEAN CLUB SHIELD (since 2018)** **TABLE OF HONOURS**
2018	Club Franciscain Le François	(MTQ)
2019	SV Robinhood Paramaribo	(SUR)
2020	*Competition cancelled*	
2021	*Competition cancelled*	

NATIONAL ASSOCIATIONS

The CONCACAF (**Confederation of North and Central American and Caribbean Association Football**) is the continental governing body for football in North America, Central America and the Caribbean. Three South American countries, Guyana, Suriname and the French department of French Guiana are also members of CONCACAF.

MEMBER NATIONS

North American Zone
(NAFU = North American Football Union)

Canada
Mexico
United States

Central American Zone
(UNCAF = Unión Centroamericana de Fútbol)

Belize
Costa Rica
El Salvador
Guatemala
Honduras
Nicaragua
Panama

Caribbean Zone
(CFU = Caribbean Football Union)

Anguilla	Guyana
Antigua and Barbuda	Haiti
Aruba	Jamaica
Bahamas	Martinique*
Barbados	Montserrat
Bermuda	Puerto Rico
British Virgin Islands	Saint Kitts and Nevis
Cayman Islands	Saint Lucia
Cuba	Saint Vincent and the Grenadines
Curaçao	Saint-Martin*
Dominica	Sint Maarten*
Dominican Republic	Suriname
French Guiana*	Trinidad and Tobago
Grenada	Turks and Caicos Islands
Guadeloupe*	U.S. Virgin Islands

*CONCACAF members, but not FIFA-affiliated countries.

ANGUILLA

The Country:	The FA:
Anguilla	Anguilla Football Association
Capital: The Valley	2 Queen Elizabeth Avenue, P.O. Box 1318
Surface: 91 km²	The Valley, AI-2640
Population: 14,731 [2018]	Year of Formation: 1990
Time: UTC-4	Member of FIFA since: 1996
	Member of CONCACAF since: 1994

Anguilla is an internally self-governing overseas territory of the United Kingdom.

NATIONAL TEAM RECORDS	
First international match:	14.05.1991, Saint Lucia: Anguilla - Montserrat 1-1
Most international caps:	Kelvin Ryan Liddie – 31 caps (since 2000)
Most international goals:	Richard O'Connor – 5 goals / 6 caps (2000-2006)
	Terrence Rogers – 5 goals / 16 caps (2000-2012)
	Girdon Connor – 5 goals / 29 caps (2000-2018)

CONCACAF GOLD CUP	
1991	Qualifiers
1993	Qualifiers
1996	Qualifiers
1998	Qualifiers
2000	Qualifiers
2002	Qualifiers
2003	Did not enter
2005	*Withdrew*
2007	Qualifiers
2009	Qualifiers
2011	Qualifiers
2013	Qualifiers
2015	Qualifiers
2017	Qualifiers
2019	Qualifiers
2021	Qualifiers

FIFA WORLD CUP	
1930	-
1934	-
1938	-
1950	-
1954	-
1958	-
1962	-
1966	-
1970	-
1974	-
1978	-
1982	-
1986	-
1990	-
1994	-
1998	Did not enter
2002	Qualifiers
2006	Qualifiers
2010	Qualifiers
2014	Qualifiers
2018	Qualifiers

F.I.F.A. CONFEDERATIONS CUP 1992-2017
None

OLYMPIC FOOTBALL TOURNAMENTS 1900-2016
None

CCCF (Confederación Centroamericana y del Caribe de Fútbol) CHAMPIONSHIPS 1941-1961
None

CONCACAF CHAMPIONSHIPS 1963-1989
None

CONCACAF NATIONS LEAGUE	
2019-2020	League C

CARIBBEAN CHAMPIONSHIPS 1989-2017			
1989	Did not enter	1999	Did not enter
1991	Qualifiers	2001	Qualifiers
1992	Qualifiers	2005	Did not enter
1993	Qualifiers	2007	Qualifiers
1994	Qualifiers	2008	Qualifiers
1995	Qualifiers	2010	Qualifiers
1996	Qualifiers	2012	Qualifiers
1997	Qualifiers	2014	Qualifiers
1998	Qualifiers	2017	Qualifiers

ANGUILLAN CLUB HONOURS IN CONCACAF CLUB COMPETITIONS:

CONCACAF Champions Cup / CONCACAF Champions League 1962-2020
None

CONCACAF League 2017-2020
None

Caribbean Club Championship 1997-2021
None

CONCACAF Cup Winners Cup 1991-1995*
None

Copa Interamericana 1968-1998*
None

*defunct competitions

NATIONAL COMPETITIONS
TABLE OF HONOURS

	CHAMPIONS
1997/1998	Spartans International FC The Valley
1998/1999	Attackers FC The Valley-North
1999/2000	*No competition*
2000/2001	Roaring Lions FC Stoney Ground
2001/2002	Roaring Lions FC Stoney Ground
2002/2003	Roaring Lions FC Stoney Ground
2004	Spartans International FC The Valley
2005/2006	Roaring Lions FC Stoney Ground
2006/2007	Kicks United FC The Valley
2007/2008	Attackers FC The Valley-North
2008/2009	Attackers FC The Valley-North
2009/2010	Roaring Lions FC Stoney Ground
2010/2011	Kicks United FC The Valley
2011/2012	Kicks United FC The Valley
2012/2013	Attackers FC The Valley-North
2013/2014	Roaring Lions FC Stoney Ground
2014/2015	Kicks United FC The Valley
2015/2016	Salsa Ballers FC George Hill
2016/2017	Roaring Lions FC Stoney Ground
2017/2018	Kicks United FC The Valley
2018/2019	*Championship abandoned*
2020	Roaring Lions FC Stoney Ground
2021	*Championship not yet finished*

NATIONAL CHAMPIONSHIP
AFA Football League 2021

The 2021 championship started on 05.03.2021, but was interrupted several times due to CIVID-19 pandemic. A lot of matches have to be rescheduled, it is not clear whether the game will continue and when it will end.

NATIONAL TEAM
INTERNATIONAL MATCHES 2020/2021

21.03.2021	Fort Lauderdale	U.S. Virgin Islands - Anguilla	0-0	(F)
27.03.2021	Fort Lauderdale	Anguilla - Dominican Republic	0-6(0-3)	(WCQ)
30.03.2021	Santo Domingo	Barbados - Anguilla	1-0(0-0)	(WCQ)
02.06.2021	Santo Domingo	Dominica - Anguilla	3-0(3-0)	(WCQ)
05.06.2021	Ciudad de Panamá	Anguilla - Panama	0-13(0-4)	(WCQ)

21.03.2021, Friendly International
Training Ground at Inter Miami CF Stadium, Fort Lauderdale (USA); Attendance: 0
Referee: Juan Pablo Casas (United States)
U.S. VIRGIN ISLANDS - ANGUILLA   0-0
AIA: Kareem Burris, Luke Paris, Tafari Smith (88.Jauron Gayle), Kion Lee, Javille Brooks, Germain Hughes, Kian Duncan (66.Sedu Bradshaw), Cyrus Williams Sylvan-Vanterpool (23.Kayini Brooks-Belle), Jonathan Guishard, Aedan Scipio, Calvin Morgan. Trainer: Stern Christopher James John (Trinidad and Tobago).

27.03.2021, 22nd FIFA World Cup Qualifiers, CONCACAF First Round
DRV PNK Stadium, Fort Lauderdale
Referee: Rubiel Vásquez (United States)
ANGUILLA - DOMINICAN REPUBLIC   0-6(0-3)
AIA: Kareem Burris, Tafari Smith, Tyrique Lake (40.Cyrus Williams Sylvan-Vanterpool; 89.Jauron Gayle), Javille Brooks, Luke Paris, Germain Hughes, Kian Duncan, Kapil Assent Battice (46.Noah Bradshaw), Jonathan Guishard, Calvin Morgan, Aedan Scipio (73.Stewart Murray). Trainer: Stern Christopher James John (Trinidad and Tobago).

30.03.2021, 22nd FIFA World Cup Qualifiers, CONCACAF First Round
Estadio Olímpico "Félix Sánchez", Santo Domingo (Dominican Republic)
Referee: Diego Montaño Robles (Mexico)
BARBADOS - ANGUILLA   1-0(0-0)
AIA: Darius Lantan, Kion Lee, Tafari Smith, Javille Brooks, Tyrique Lake, Luke Paris, Germain Hughes, Kian Duncan, Kapil Assent Battice (53.Cyrus Williams Sylvan-Vanterpool), Calvin Morgan, Jonathan Guishard (79.Steven Austin). Trainer: Stern Christopher James John (Trinidad and Tobago).

02.06.2021, 22nd FIFA World Cup Qualifiers, CONCACAF First Round
Estadio Olímpico "Félix Sánchez", Santo Domingo (Dominican Republic)
Referee: Kimbell Ward (Saint Kitts and Nevis)
DOMINICA - ANGUILLA   3-0(3-0)
AIA: Darius Lantan, Kion Lee, Tafari Smith, Javille Brooks, Tyrique Lake, Germain Hughes, Steven Austin, Kian Duncan (88.Stewart Murray), Lamar Carpenter, Jonathan Guishard, Kyle Lake-Bryan (71.Kayini Brooks-Belle). Trainer: Stern Christopher James John (Trinidad and Tobago).

05.06.2021, 22nd FIFA World Cup Qualifiers, CONCACAF First Round
Estadio Nacional Rod Carew, Ciudad de Panamá
Referee: Sergio Armando Reyna Moller (Guatemala)
ANGUILLA - PANAMA   0-13(0-4)
AIA: Darius Lantan, Kion Lee, Javille Brooks, Tafari Smith, Tyrique Lake, Steven Austin, Simon Anthony, Kayini Brooks-Belle (88.Shemari Bryan), Jonathan Guishard, Kyle Lake-Bryan (81.Rodondo Alphonse Roach), Stewart Murray (62.Jermal Richardson). Trainer: Stern Christopher James John (Trinidad and Tobago).

NATIONAL TEAM PLAYERS 2020/2021

Name	DOB	Club
Goalkeepers		
Kareem BURRIS	13.09.1991	*Roaring Lions FC Stoney Ground*
Darius LANTAN	15.02.1979	*Dock's United FC*
Defenders		
Noah BRADSHAW	18.04.2004	*Lymers FC*
Sedu BRADSHAW	13.11.2002	*Lymers FC*
Javille BROOKS	21.09.1984	*Attackers FC The Valley-North*
Shemari BRYAN	09.02.2002	*Roaring Lions FC Stoney Ground*
Germain HUGHES	15.11.1996	*Roaring Lions FC Stoney Ground*
Tyrique LAKE	04.01.1999	*Crowder Colle Roughriders (USA)*
Kion LEE	02.09.1993	*Roaring Lions FC Stoney Ground*
Luke PARIS	11.11.1994	*Windsor FC (ENG)*
Rodondo Alphonse ROACH		*Diamond FC*
Tafari SMITH	26.03.2000	*Roaring Lions FC Stoney Ground*
Midfielders		
Simon ANTHONY	02.11.1977	*Unattached*
Steven AUSTIN	27.12.1990	*Dock's United FC*
Kian DUNCAN	26.05.2000	*Burnham FC (ENG)*
Stewart MURRAY	19.01.1988	*Dock's United FC*
Jermal RICHARDSON	10.05.1994	*Roaring Lions FC Stoney Ground*
Cyrus Williams SYLVAN-VANTERPOOL	30.12.1990	*Frimley Green FC (ENG)*
Forwards		
Kapil Assent BATTICE	26.10.1982	*Roaring Lions FC Stoney Ground*
Kayini BROOKS-BELLE	23.07.1994	*Roaring Lions FC Stoney Ground*
Lamar CARPENTER	23.01.2004	
Jauron GAYLE	04.03.2004	*Diamond FC*
Jonathan GUISHARD	02.07.1996	*Dock's United FC*
Kyle LAKE-BRYAN	23.10.2001	*Wingate & Finchlay FC (ENG)*
Calvin MORGAN	18.05.1995	*Chalvey Sports FC (ENG)*
Aedan SCIPIO	03.09.1990	*Roaring Lions FC Stoney Ground*

National coaches		
Stern Christopher James JOHN (Trinidad and Tobago) [from 31.10.2020]		30.10.1976

ANTIGUA AND BARBUDA

The Country:		The FA:
Antigua and Barbuda Capital: Saint John's Surface: 442 km² Population: 96,286 [2018] Time: UTC-4 Independent since: 1981		Antigua and Barbuda Football Association Ground Floor, Sydney Walling Stand, Antigua Recreation Grounds, St. John's Year of Formation: 1928 Member of FIFA since: 1970 Member of CONCACAF since: 1972

NATIONAL TEAM RECORDS

First international match: 10.11.1972, Port of Spain:
Trinidad and Tobago - Antigua and Barbuda 11-1
Most international caps: Peter Junior Byers – 90 caps (2004-2018)
Most international goals: Derrick Edwards – 59 goals / 63 caps (1988-2003)

CONCACAF GOLD CUP	
1991	Did not enter
1993	Qualifiers
1996	Qualifiers
1998	Qualifiers
2000	Qualifiers
2002	Qualifiers
2003	Qualifiers
2005	Qualifiers
2007	Qualifiers
2009	Qualifiers
2011	Qualifiers
2013	Qualifiers
2015	Qualifiers
2017	Qualifiers
2019	Qualifiers
2021	Qualifiers

FIFA WORLD CUP	
1930	-
1934	-
1938	-
1950	-
1954	-
1958	-
1962	-
1966	-
1970	Did not enter
1974	Qualifiers
1978	Did not enter
1982	Did not enter
1986	Qualifiers
1990	Qualifiers
1994	Qualifiers
1998	Qualifiers
2002	Qualifiers
2006	Qualifiers
2010	Qualifiers
2014	Qualifiers
2018	Qualifiers

F.I.F.A. CONFEDERATIONS CUP 1992-2017

None

OLYMPIC FOOTBALL TOURNAMENTS 1908-2016							
1908	-	1948	-	1972	-	1996	Qualifiers
1912	-	1952	-	1976	-	2000	-
1920	-	1956	-	1980	-	2004	*Suspended*
1924	-	1960	-	1984	Qualifiers	2008	Qualifiers
1928	-	1964	-	1988	Qualifiers	2012	Qualifiers
1936	-	1968	-	1992	Qualifiers	2016	Qualifiers

CCCF (Confederación Centroamericana y del Caribe de Fútbol) CHAMPIONSHIPS 1941-1961
None

CONCACAF CHAMPIONSHIPS 1963-1989
None

CONCACAF NATIONS LEAGUE	
2019-2020	League B

CARIBBEAN CHAMPIONSHIPS 1989-2017			
1989	Qualifiers	1999	Qualifiers
1991	Did not enter	2001	Qualifiers
1992	Final Tournament - Group Stage	2005	Qualifiers
1993	Qualifiers	2007	Qualifiers
1994	Qualifiers	2008	Final Tournament - Group Stage
1995	Final Tournament - Group Stage	2010	Final Tournament - Group Stage
1996	*Withdrew*	2012	Final Tournament - Group Stage
1997	Final Tournament - Group Stage	2014	Final Tournament - Group Stage
1998	Final Tournament - 4th Place	2017	Qualifiers

ANTIGUA AND BARBUDA CLUB HONOURS IN CONCACAF CLUB COMPETITIONS:

CONCACAF Champions Cup / CONCACAF Champions League 1962-2020
None

CONCACAF League 2017-2020
None

Caribbean Club Championship 1997-2021
None

CONCACAF Cup Winners Cup 1991-1995*
None

Copa Interamericana 1968-1998*
None

**defunct competitions*

NATIONAL COMPETITIONS
TABLE OF HONOURS

	CHAMPIONS	CUP WINNERS
1968/1969	Empire FC Gray's Farm	-
1969/1970	Empire FC Gray's Farm	-
1970/1971	Empire FC Gray's Farm	-
1971/1972	Empire FC Gray's Farm	-
1972/1973	Empire FC Gray's Farm	-
1973/1974	Empire FC Gray's Farm	-

1974/1975	*Not known*	-
1975/1976	*Not known*	-
1976/1977	*Not known*	-
1977/1978	*Not known*	-
1978/1979	Empire FC Gray's Farm	-
1979/1980	*Not known*	-
1980/1981	*Not known*	-
1981/1982	*Not known*	-
1982/1983	*Not known*	-
1983/1984	Villa Lions FC Saint John's	-
1984/1985	Liberta FC	-
1985/1986	Villa Lions FC Saint John's	-
1986/1987	Liberta FC	-
1987/1988	Empire FC Gray's Farm	-
1988/1989	*Not known*	-
1989/1990	J & J Construction FC Parham	-
1990/1991	*Not known*	-
1991/1992	Empire FC Gray's Farm	-
1992/1993	*Not known*	-
1993/1994	Lion Hill Spliff FC Saint John's	-
1994/1995	English Harbour FC	-
1995/1996	English Harbour FC	-
1996/1997	English Harbour FC	-
1997/1998	Empire FC Gray's Farm	-
1998/1999	Empire FC Gray's Farm	-
1999/2000	Empire FC Gray's Farm	-
2000/2001	Empire FC Gray's Farm	-
2001/2002	Parham FC	-
2002/2003	Parham FC	-
2003/2004	Bassa FC All Saint's	-
2004/2005	Bassa FC All Saint's	SAP FC Bolans
2005/2006	SAP FC Bolans	Freemansville FC
2006/2007	Bassa FC All Saint's	*Tournament cancelled*
2007/2008	Bassa FC All Saint's	Bassa FC All Saint's
2008/2009	SAP FC Bolans	SAP FC Bolans
2009/2010	Bassa FC All Saint's	Bassa FC All Saint's
2010/2011	Parham FC	*No competition*
2011/2012	Old Road FC St. Marys	Parham FC
2012/2013	Old Road FC St. Marys	*No competition*
2013/2014	SAP FC Bolans	*No competition*
2014/2015	Parham FC	*No competition*
2015/2016	Hoppers FC Green Bay	*No competition*
2016/2017	Parham FC	*No competition*
2017/2018	Hoppers FC Green Bay	*No competition*
2018/2019	Liberta Blackhawks FC	*No competition*
2019/2020	*Competition abandoned*	*No competition*
2020/2021	*No competition*	*No competition*

NATIONAL CHAMPIONSHIP
Digicel/Red Stripe Premier Division 2020/2021

No championship was played due to COVID-19 pandemic.

NATIONAL TEAM
INTERNATIONAL MATCHES 2020/2021

24.03.2021	*Willemstad*	*Antigua and Barbuda - Montserrat*	*2-2(2-2)*	*(WCQ)*
27.03.2021	*Upper Bethlehem*	*US Virgin Islands - Antigua and Barbuda*	*0-3(0-3)*	*(WCQ)*
04.06.2021	*North Sound*	*Antigua and Barbuda - Grenada*	*1-0(1-0)*	*(WCQ)*
08.06.2021	*San Salvador*	*El Salvador - Antigua and Barbuda*	*3-0(1-0)*	*(WCQ)*

24.03.2021, 22nd FIFA World Cup Qualifiers, CONCACAF First Round
Stadion „Ergilio Hato", Willemstad (Curaçao)
Referee: Melvin Orlando Matamoros (Honduras)
ANTIGUA AND BARBUDA - MONTSERRAT **2-2(2-2)**
ATG: Molvin Alfanso James, Karanja Khari Afeba Mack, Jervez Lee (46.Juwan Roberts), Zaine Sebastian Francis-Angol, Kendukar Challenger, Quinton Travis Peterson Griffith, Eugene Kirwan (83.Calaum Jahraldo-Martin), Joshua Kevin Stanley Parker, Denie Henry, Junior Benjamin, D'Andre Bishop (89.Peter Junior Byers). Trainer: Thomas David Curtis (England).
Goals: Eugene Kirwan (23), D'Andre Bishop (45).

27.03.2021, 22nd FIFA World Cup Qualifiers, CONCACAF First Round
Bethlehem Soccer Stadium, Upper Bethlehem
Referee: Trevester Richards (Saint Kitts and Nevis)
U.S. VIRGIN ISLANDS - ANTIGUA AND BARBUDA **0-3(0-3)**
ATG: Molvin Alfanso James, Karanja Khari Afeba Mack, Kendukar Challenger, Denie Henry, Juwan Roberts, Quinton Travis Peterson Griffith, Leroy Graham, Peter Junior Byers (87.Jajuan Williams), Javorn Stevens, Junior Benjamin, D'Andre Bishop (87.Tyrique Tonge). Trainer: Thomas David Curtis (England).
Goals: Peter Junior Byers (26), Quinton Travis Peterson Griffith (34 penalty, 42).

04.06.2021, 22nd FIFA World Cup Qualifiers, CONCACAF First Round
"Sir Vivian Richards" Stadium, North Sound
Referee: Francia María González Martínez (Mexico)
ANTIGUA AND BARBUDA - GRENADA **1-0(1-0)**
ATG: Molvin Alfanso James, Aaron Taylor-Sinclair, Karanja Khari Afeba Mack, Kendukar Challenger, Daniel Robert Bowry, Quinton Travis Peterson Griffith, Eugene Kirwan, Joshua Kevin Stanley Parker, Stephen Rhys Browne (76.Denie Henry), Peter Junior Byers (76.Javorn Stevens), D'Andre Bishop (64.Thomas James Everton Bramble). Trainer: Thomas David Curtis (England).
Goal: Stephen Rhys Browne (20).

08.06.2021, 22nd FIFA World Cup Qualifiers, CONCACAF First Round
Estadio Cuscatlán, San Salvador
Referee: Keylor Antonio Herrera Villalobos (Costa Rica)
EL SALVADOR - ANTIGUA AND BARBUDA **3-0(1-0)**
ATG: Molvin Alfanso James, Aaron Taylor-Sinclair, Karanja Khari Afeba Mack (79.Ranaldo Flowers), Shevorn Philip (79.Keon Kevin Greene), Kendukar Challenger, Quinton Travis Peterson Griffith, Daniel Robert Bowry, Joshua Kevin Stanley Parker, Stephen Rhys Browne, Junior Benjamin (66.Peter Junior Byers), D'Andre Bishop (63.Tamarley Kaharie Thomas). Trainer: Thomas David Curtis (England) & Mikele Benjamin Leigertwood.

NATIONAL TEAM PLAYERS 2020/2021

Name	DOB	Club

Goalkeepers

Molvin Alfanso JAMES	08.05.1989	*Tryum FC*

Defenders

Daniel Robert BOWRY	29.04.1998	*Wealdstone FC (ENG)*
Kendukar CHALLENGER	24.01.1998	*All Saint's United FC*
Zaine Sebastian FRANCIS-ANGOL	30.06.1993	*Hartlepool United FC (ENG)*
Jervez LEE	10.09.1992	*Ottos Rangers FC*
Karanja Khari Afeba MACK	24.08.1987	*Parham FC*
Shevorn PHILLIP	09.09.1996	*Liberta Blackhawks FC*
Aaron TAYLOR-SINCLAIR	08.04.1991	*Livingston FC (SCO)*
Jajuan WILLIAMS	24.01.2001	*Old Road FC St. Marys*

Midfielders

Thomas James Everton BRAMBLE	09.05.2001	*Dover Athletic FC (ENG)*
Ranaldo FLOWERS	09.03.2003	*Aston Villa FC Saint John's*
Quinton Travis Peterson GRIFFITH	27.02.1992	*Five Islands FC*
Leroy GRAHAM	07.12.1999	*Five Islands FC*
Denie HENRY	07.05.1998	*Parham FC*
Eugene KIRWAN	01.01.1993	*Five Islands FC*
Joshua Kevin Stanley PARKER	01.12.1990	*Burton Albion FC (ENG)*
Juwan ROBERTS	05.04.1996	*Swetes FC*
Tamarley Kaharie THOMAS	28.07.1983	*Hoppers FC Green Bay*

Forwards

Junior BENJAMIN	13.08.1992	*Ottos Rangers FC*
D'Andre BISHOP	02.10.2002	*Ottos Rangers FC*
Stephen Rhys BROWNE	16.11.1995	*Sutton United FC (ENG)*
Peter Junior BYERS	20.10.1984	*SAP FC Bolans*
Keon Kevin GREENE	27.07.2000	
Calaum JAHRALDO-MARTIN	27.04.1993	*Unattached*
Javorn STEVENS	09.05.1998	*Hoppers FC Green Bay*
Tyrique TONGE	14.03.2001	*SAP FC Bolans*

National coaches

Thomas David CURTIS (England) [from 01.01.2021]	01.03.1973
Mikele Benjamin LEIGERTWOOD	12.11.1982

ARUBA

ARUBAANSE VOETBAL BOND

The Country:	The FA:
Aruba	Arubaanse Voetbal Bond
Capital: Oranjestad	Technical Centre „Angel Botta"
Surface: 193 km²	Shaba 24, P.O. Box 368, Noord
Population: 116,576 [2019]	Year of Formation: 1932
Time: UTC-4	Member of FIFA since: 1988
Independent since: 1986	Member of CONCACAF since: 1986

NATIONAL TEAM RECORDS

First international match: 06.04.1924, Aruba: Aruba - Curaçao 0-4
Most international caps: Theric Ruiz – 28 caps (2004-2016)
Most international goals: Frederick Ronald Gómez – 6 goals / 20 caps (from 2002)

CONCACAF GOLD CUP	
1991	Did not enter
1993	*Withdrew*
1996	Qualifiers
1998	Qualifiers
2000	Qualifiers
2002	Qualifiers
2003	Qualifiers
2005	*Withdrew*
2007	Did not enter
2009	Qualifiers
2011	Did not enter
2013	Did not enter
2015	Qualifiers
2017	Qualifiers
2019	Qualifiers
2021	Qualifiers

FIFA WORLD CUP	
1930	-
1934	-
1938	-
1950	-
1954	-
1958	-
1962	-
1966	-
1970	-
1974	-
1978	-
1982	-
1986	-
1990	Did not enter
1994	Did not enter
1998	Qualifiers
2002	Qualifiers
2006	Qualifiers
2010	Qualifiers
2014	Qualifiers
2018	Qualifiers

F.I.F.A. CONFEDERATIONS CUP 1992-2017
None

OLYMPIC FOOTBALL TOURNAMENTS 1908-2016

1908	-	1948	-	1972	-	1996	-
1912	-	1952	-	1976	-	2000	Qualifiers
1920	-	1956	-	1980	-	2004	-
1924	-	1960	-	1984	-	2008	Qualifiers
1928	-	1964	-	1988	-	2012	Qualifiers
1936	-	1968	-	1992	Qualifiers	2016	Qualifiers

CCCF (Confederación Centroamericana y del Caribe de Fútbol) CHAMPIONSHIPS 1941-1961

1955	

CONCACAF CHAMPIONSHIPS 1963-1989

None

CONCACAF NATIONS LEAGUE

2019-2020	League B *(relegated to League C)*

CARIBBEAN CHAMPIONSHIPS 1989-2017

1989	Qualifiers	1999	*Withdrew*
1991	Did not enter	2001	Qualifiers
1992	Qualifiers	2005	Did not enter
1993	*Withdrew*	2007	Did not enter
1994	Did not enter	2008	Qualifiers
1995	Qualifiers	2010	Did not enter
1996	Did not enter	2012	Qualifiers
1997	Qualifiers	2014	Qualifiers
1998	Qualifiers	2017	Qualifiers

ARUBAN CLUB HONOURS IN CONCACAF CLUB COMPETITIONS:

CONCACAF Champions Cup / CONCACAF Champions League 1962-2020

None

CONCACAF League 2017-2020

None

Caribbean Club Championship 1997-2021

None

CONCACAF Cup Winners Cup 1991-1995*

None

Copa Interamericana 1968-1998*

None

*defunct competitions

NATIONAL COMPETITIONS
TABLE OF HONOURS

	CHAMPIONS	CUP WINNERS
1960	SV Racing Club Aruba Oranjestad	-
1961	SV Dakota Oranjestad	-
1962	SV Dakota Oranjestad	-
1963	SV Dakota Oranjestad	-
1964	SV Racing Club Aruba Oranjestad	-
1965	SV Dakota Oranjestad	-
1966	SV Dakota Oranjestad	-
1967	SV Racing Club Aruba Oranjestad	-
1968	SV Estrella Papilon	-
1969	SV Dakota Oranjestad	-
1970	SV Dakota Oranjestad	-
1971	SV Dakota Oranjestad	-
1972	*No competition*	-
1973	SV Estrella Papilon	-
1974	SV Dakota Oranjestad	-
1975	SV Bubali	-
1976	SV Dakota Oranjestad	-
1977	SV Estrella Papilon	-
1978	SV Racing Club Aruba Oranjestad	-
1979	SV Racing Club Aruba Oranjestad	-
1980	SV Dakota Oranjestad	-
1981	SV Dakota Oranjestad	-
1982	SV Dakota Oranjestad	-
1983	SV Dakota Oranjestad	-
1984	SV San Luis Deportivo	-
1985	SV Estrella Papilon	-
1986	SV Racing Club Aruba Oranjestad	-
1987	SV Racing Club Aruba Oranjestad	-
1988	SV Estrella Papilon	-
1989	SV Estrella Papilon	-
1990	SV Estrella Papilon	-
1991	SV Racing Club Aruba Oranjestad	-
1992	SV Estrella Papilon	-
1993	SV Riverplate Oranjestad	
1994	SV Racing Club Aruba Oranjestad	-
1995	SV Dakota Oranjestad	-
1996	SV Estrella Papilon	-
1997	SV Riverplate Oranjestad	-
1998	SV Estrella Papilon	-
1999	SV Estrella Papilon	-
2000	SV Deportivo Nacional Palm Beach	-
2001	SV Deportivo Nacional Palm Beach	-
2002	SV Racing Club Aruba Oranjestad	-
2003	SV Deportivo Nacional Palm Beach	-
2004	*No competition*	-
2004/2005	SV Britannia Piedra Plat	SV Sportboys Angochi
2005/2006	SV Estrella Papilon	SV Estudiantes Oranjestad

2006/2007	SV Deportivo Nacional Palm Beach	SV Dakota Oranjestad
2007/2008	SV Racing Club Aruba Oranjestad	SV Britannia Piedra Plat
2008/2009	SV Britannia Piedra Plat	SV Britannia Piedra Plat
2009/2010	SV Britannia Piedra Plat	SV Britannia Piedra Plat
2010/2011	SV Racing Club Aruba Oranjestad	SV Britannia Piedra Plat
2011/2012	SV Racing Club Aruba Oranjestad	SV Racing Club Aruba Oranjestad
2012/2013	SV La Fama Savaneta	SV Britannia Piedra Plat
2013/2014	SV Britannia Piedra Plat	SV Estrella Papilon Santa Cruz
2014/2015	SV Racing Club Aruba Oranjestad	SV Britannia Piedra Plat
2015/2016	SV Racing Club Aruba Oranjestad	SV Racing Club Aruba Oranjestad
2016/2017	SV Deportivo Nacional Noord	SV Britannia Piedra Plat
2017/2018	SV Dakota Oranjestad	SV Estrella Papilon Santa Cruz
2018/2019	SV Racing Club Aruba Oranjestad	SV Dakota Oranjestad
2019/2020	*Competition cancelled*	SV Racing Club Aruba Oranjestad
2021	*Competition not yet finished*	SV Racing Club Aruba Oranjestad

NATIONAL CHAMPIONSHIP
Division di Honor 2021

The championship mode was changed to a spring-autumn rhythm, the first matchday was played on May 8, 2021.

NATIONAL CUP
Copa Libertador "Betico Croes" Final 2021

14.04.2021
SV Racing Club Aruba Oranjestad - SV La Fama Savaneta   7-0(1-0)
Goals: Jean-Luc Bergen (26 penalty), Walter Bennet (50), Jhon Silva (52), Walter Bennet (63), Juan Pérez (66), Jhon Silva (69), Juan Pérez (70).

		NATIONAL TEAM INTERNATIONAL MATCHES 2020/2021		
27.03.2021	Bradenton	Aruba - Suriname	0-6(0-3)	(WCQ)
30.03.2021	Bradenton	Bermuda - Aruba	5-0(2-0)	(WCQ)
02.06.2021	Bradenton	Cayman Islands - Aruba	1-3(1-2)	(WCQ)
05.06.2021	Bradenton	Aruba - Canada	0-7(0-3)	(WCQ)

27.03.2021, 22nd FIFA World Cup Qualifiers, CONCACAF First Round
IMG Academy, Bradenton (United States)
Referee: Ismail Elfath (United States)
ARUBA - SURINAME   **0-6(0-3)**
ARU: Eric Abdul, Nickenson Stephan Paul, Jean-Pierre Eugene Heyden (75.François Croes), Mark Carvin Jacobs, Javier Alejandro Jiménez Paris (89.Jeamirr Howell-Brokken), Erik Santos de Gouveia, Walter Bennett (89.Shermar Miguel Monticeuex), Edward Jamir Clarissa (72.Daniel Linscheer), Ericson Eustin Croes, Kenderick Junel Roderick Poulina, Shakame Isiah Stamper. Trainer: Stanley Purl Menzo (Netherlands).

30.03.2021, 22nd FIFA World Cup Qualifiers, CONCACAF First Round
IMG Academy, Bradenton (United States)
Referee: Jaime Alfredo Herrera Bonilla (El Salvador)
BERMUDA - ARUBA   **5-0(2-0)**
ARU: Eric Abdul (69.José Gregorio Cruz Ayora), François Croes (85.Jean-Pierre Eugene Heyden), Nickenson Stephan Paul, Mark Carvin Jacobs, Javier Alejandro Jiménez Paris, Erik Santos de Gouveia, Walter Bennett, Edward Jamir Clarissa (88.Shakame Isiah Stamper), Ericson Eustin Croes (28.Daniel Linscheer; 85.Shermar Miguel Monticeuex), Kenderick Junel Roderick Poulina, Frederick Ronald Gómez. Trainer: Stanley Purl Menzo (Netherlands).

02.06.2021, 22nd FIFA World Cup Qualifiers, CONCACAF First Round
IMG Academy, Bradenton (United States)
Referee: Luis Enrique Santander Aguirre (Mexico)
CAYMAN ISLANDS - ARUBA   **1-3(1-2)**
ARU: Eric Abdul, Fernando Lewis, Diederick Luigi Luydens, Darryl Bäly, Javier Alejandro Jiménez Paris (79.Glenbert Denilson Croes), Noah Lucho Harms (66.Ericson Eustin Croes), Marlon Pereira Freire (66.Erik Santos de Gouveia), Jonathan Jordan Richard (90+2.François Croes), Walter Bennett, Joshua Arnold John, Terence Clyde Leon Groothusen (79.Frederick Ronald Gómez). Trainer: Stanley Purl Menzo (Netherlands).
Goals: Joshua Arnold John (40), Terence Clyde Leon Groothusen (45+2), Joshua Arnold John (75).

08.06.2021, 22nd FIFA World Cup Qualifiers, CONCACAF First Round
IMG Academy, Bradenton (United States)
Referee: Marco Antonio Ortíz Nava (Mexico)
ARUBA - CANADA   **0-7(0-3)**
ARU: Eric Abdul, Fernando Lewis, Diederick Luigi Luydens, Darryl Bäly, Javier Alejandro Jiménez Paris (71.Frederick Ronald Gómez), Noah Lucho Harms (71.Nickenson Stephan Paul), Marlon Pereira Freire (90.Kenderick Junel Roderick Poulina), Jonathan Jordan Richard, Walter Bennett (90.Erik Santos de Gouveia), Joshua Arnold John, Terence Clyde Leon Groothusen (83.Glenbert Denilson Croes). Trainer: Stanley Purl Menzo (Netherlands).

NATIONAL TEAM PLAYERS 2020/2021

Name	DOB	Club
Goalkeepers		
Eric ABDUL	26.02.1986	SV Dakota Oranjestad
José Gregorio CRUZ Ayora	24.11.1993	SV Deportivo Nacional Noord
Defenders		
Darryl BÄLY	19.01.1998	FC Volendam (NED)
François CROES	28.10.1999	SV Estrella Papilon Santa Cruz
Noah Lucho HARMS	05.05.1997	VV Spijkenisse (NED)
Jean-Pierre Eugene HEYDEN	25.02.2000	SV Dakota Oranjestad
Mark Carvin JACOBS	28.10.1999	SV Bubali Noord
Fernando LEWIS	31.01.1993	Quick Boys Katwijk aan Zee (NED)
Diederick Luigi LUYDENS	18.02.1999	KSF Prespa Birlik Malmö (SWE)
Nickenson Stephan PAUL	24.08.1997	SV Dakota Oranjestad
Midfielders		
Walter BENNETT	18.03.1997	SV Racing Club Aruba Oranjestad
Edward Jamir CLARISSA	26.03.2000	SV Deportivo Nacional Noord
Ericson Eustin CROES	28.11.1999	SV Caiquetio Paradera
Glenbert Denilson CROES	17.06.2001	SV Racing Club Aruba Oranjestad
Jeamirr HOWELL-BROKKEN	16.11.1992	SV Racing Club Aruba Oranjestad
Javier Alejandro JIMÉNEZ Paris	27.05.2000	FCBrandenburg 03 Berlin (GER)
Shermar Miguel MONTICEUEX	07.08.2000	SV Dakota Oranjestad
Marlon PEREIRA Freire	26.03.1987	SteDoCo Hoornaar (NED)
Kenderick Junel Roderick POULINA	10.06.1999	SV Riverplate Oranjestad
Jonathan Jordan RICHARD	21.06.1991	HBOK Zunderdorp (NED)
Erik SANTOS de Gouveia	30.08.1990	SV Racing Club Aruba Oranjestad
Forwards		
Frederick Ronald GÓMEZ	25.10.1984	SV Racing Club Aruba Oranjestad
Terence Clyde Leon GROOTHUSEN	16.09.1996	Alemannia Aachen 1900 (GER)
Joshua Arnold JOHN	01.10.1988	VVV-Venlo (NED)
Daniel LINSCHEER	21.01.1994	SV Britannia Piedra Plat
Shakame Isiah STAMPER	26.12.2000	SV Riverplate Oranjestad
National coaches		
Stanley Purl MENZO (Netherlands) [from 12.03.2021]		15.10.1963

BAHAMAS

The Country:	The FA:
The Commonwealth of The Bahamas Capital: Nassau Surface: 13,878 km² Population: 385,637 [2018] Time: UTC-5 Independent since: 1973	Bahamas Football Association Rosetta Street, PO-Box N-8434, Nassau Year of Formation: 1967 Member of FIFA since: 1968 Member of CONCACAF since: 1981

NATIONAL TEAM RECORDS

First international match: 03.03.1970: Netherlands Antilles - Bahamas 8-1
Most international caps: Lesly St. Fleur – 22 caps (since 2006)
Most international goals: Lesly St. Fleur – 10 goals / 22 caps (since 2006)

CONCACAF GOLD CUP		FIFA WORLD CUP	
1991	Did not enter	1930	-
1993	Did not enter	1934	-
1996	Did not enter	1938	-
1998	Did not enter	1950	-
2000	Qualifiers	1954	-
2002	*Withdrew*	1958	-
2003	Did not enter	1962	-
2005	*Withdrew*	1966	-
2007	Qualifiers	1970	Did not enter
2009	Did not enter	1974	Did not enter
2011	Did not enter	1978	Did not enter
2013	Did not enter	1982	Did not enter
2015	Did not enter	1986	Did not enter
2017	Did not enter	1990	Did not enter
2019	Qualifiers	1994	Did not enter
2021	Qualifiers	1998	*Withdrew*
		2002	Qualifiers
		2006	Qualifiers
		2010	Qualifiers
		2014	*Withdrew*
		2018	Qualifiers

F.I.F.A. CONFEDERATIONS CUP 1992-2017

None

OLYMPIC FOOTBALL TOURNAMENTS 1908-2016							
1908	-	1948	-	1972	-	1996	-
1912	-	1952	-	1976	-	2000	*Withdrew*
1920	-	1956	-	1980	-	2004	Qualifiers
1924	-	1960	-	1984	Qualifiers	2008	Qualifiers
1928	-	1964	-	1988	Qualifiers	2012	Did not enter
1936	-	1968	-	1992	-	2016	Did not enter

CCCF (Confederación Centroamericana y del Caribe de Fútbol) CHAMPIONSHIPS 1941-1961
None

CONCACAF CHAMPIONSHIPS 1963-1989
None

CONCACAF NATIONS LEAGUE	
2019-2020	League C (*promoted to League B*)

CARIBBEAN CHAMPIONSHIPS 1989-2017			
1989	Did not enter	1999	Qualifiers
1991	Did not enter	2001	*Withdrew*
1992	Did not enter	2005	*Withdrew*
1993	Did not enter	2007	Qualifiers
1994	Did not enter	2008	Did not enter
1995	Did not enter	2010	Did not enter
1996	Did not enter	2012	Did not enter
1997	Did not enter	2014	Did not enter
1998	Did not enter	2017	Did not enter

BAHAMIAN CLUB HONOURS IN CONCACAF CLUB COMPETITIONS:

CONCACAF Champions Cup / CONCACAF Champions League 1962-2020
None
CONCACAF League 2017-2020
None
Caribbean Club Championship 1997-2021
None
CONCACAF Cup Winners Cup 1991-1995*
None
Copa Interamericana 1968-1998*
None

**defunct competitions*

NATIONAL COMPETITIONS
TABLE OF HONOURS

	CHAMPIONS	CUP WINNERS	
		New Providence	Grand Bahamas
1991/1992	Britam United FC	-	-
1992/1993	Britam United FC	-	-
1993/1994	Britam United FC	-	-
1994/1995	Britam United FC	-	-
1995/1996	Freeport FC	*Not known*	Pub on the Mall Red Dogs**
1996/1997	Cavalier FC Nassau	*Not known*	*Not known*
1997/1998	Cavalier FC Nassau	*Not known*	*Not known*
1998/1999	Cavalier FC Nassau	*Not known*	*Not known*
1999/2000	Abacom United FC Marsh Town	Cavalier FC Nassau	*Not known*
2000/2001	Cavalier FC Nassau	Cavalier FC Nassau	Abacom United FC Marsh Town
2001/2002	*Championship final not played*	J.J. Johnson United	*Not known*
2002/2003	Bears FC Nassau	Bears FC Nassau	Playtime Sports Tigers
2003/2004	*Championship final not played**	Bears FC Nassau	Freeport FC
2005	*Championship final not played**	*Not known*	*Not known*
2005/2006	*Championship final not played**	Bears FC Nassau	*Not known*
2007	*Championship final not played**	Bears FC Nassau	*Not known*
2008	*Championship final not played**	FC Nassau	*Not known*
	Bahamas FA Senior League		
2008/2009	Bears FC Nassau	IM Bears FC	*Not known*
2009/2010	Insurance Management Bears FC Nassau	J.J. Johnson United	*Not known*
2010/2011	Insurance Management Bears FC Nassau	Cavalier FC Nassau	*Not known*
2011/2012	Insurance Management Bears FC Nassau	IM Bears FC	*Not known*
2012/2013	Insurance Management Bears FC Nassau	*Not known*	*Not known*
2013/2014	Lyford Cay Dragons FC	*Not known*	*Not known*
2014/2015	Western Warriors SC Nassau	Western Warriors SC	*Not known*
2015/2016	Insurance Management Bears FC Nassau	Western Warriors SC	*Not known*
2016/2017	Western Warriors SC Nassau	*Not known*	*Not known*
2017/2018	University of the Bahamas FC	*Not known*	*Not known*
2018/2019	Dynamos FC Nassau	*Not known*	*Not known*
2019/2020	*Competition suspended*	*Not known*	*Not known*
2020/2021	*No competition*	*Not known*	*Not known*

*the final between the winner of the New Providence Football League and the Grand Bahamas Football League was not played.
**became later Freeport FC

President's Cup winners:
1999: Cavalier FC Nassau; 2000: Cavalier FC Nassau; 2001: Khaki Superstars Air; 2009: Insurance Management Bears FC Nassau; 2010: Insurance Management Bears FC Nassau; 2011: Cavalier FC Nassau.

	New Providence Football League winners	Grand Bahamas Football League winners
1996	J.S. Johnson UNited	Pub on the Mall Red Dogs
1997	Cavalier FC Nassau	*Not known*
1998	Cavalier FC Nassau	*Not known*
1999	Cavalier FC Nassau	*Not known*
2000	Cavalier FC Nassau	Abacom United FC Marsh Town
2001	Cavalier FC Nassau	Abacom United FC Marsh Town
2002	Bears FC Nassau	Abacom United FC Marsh Town
2003	Bears FC Nassau	Abacom United FC Marsh Town
2004	Bears FC Nassau	Haitian Superstars
2005	Caledonia Celtic FC	*Not known*
2006	Caledonia Celtic FC	Brita Red Bulls
2007	Bears FC Nassau	*Not known*
2008	*No competition*	*No competition*

NATIONAL CHAMPIONSHIP
Bahamas FA Senior League 2020/2021

No championship was played due to COVID-19 pandemic.

NATIONAL TEAM
INTERNATIONAL MATCHES 2020/2021

27.03.2021	Nassau	Bahamas - Saint Kitts and Nevis	0-4(0-1)	(WCQ)
30.03.2021	Santo Domingo	Guyana - Bahamas	4-0(1-0)	(WCQ)
02.06.2021	Mayagüez	Puerto Rico - Bahamas	7-0(4-0)	(WCQ)
05.06.2021	Nassau	Bahamas - Trinidad and Tobago	0-0	(WCQ)
02.07.2021	Fort Lauderdale	Guadeloupe - Bahamas	2-0(0-0)	(GCQ)

27.03.2021, 22nd FIFA World Cup Qualifiers, CONCACAF First Round
"Thomas Robinson" Stadium, Nassau
Referee: Óscar Macías Romo (Mexico)
BAHAMAS - SAINT KITTS AND NEVIS   0-4(0-1)
BAH: Michael Benaiah Peter Butler, Ambry Moss, Dylan Pritchard, Logan Russell (65.Happy McNair Hall), Isiah Claudius Collie, Cameron Robert Hepple, Terrence Decarlo Delancy Jr., Marcel Maximi Joseph (82.Elijah Mitchell), Jean Rivenson Francois (50.Troy Milton Pinder), Lesly St. Fleur, Peter Julmis. Trainer: Nesley Jean.

30.03.2021, 22nd FIFA World Cup Qualifiers, CONCACAF First Round
Estadio Olímpico "Félix Sánchez", Santo Domingo (Dominican Republic)
Referee: Sergio Armando Reyna Moller (Guatemala)
GUYANA - BAHAMAS   4-0(1-0)
BAH: Ian Lowe, Ambry Moss, Dylan Pritchard (50.Troy Milton Pinder), Logan Russell (61.Happy McNair Hall), Cameron Robert Hepple, Isiah Claudius Collie, Terrence Decarlo Delancy Jr., Marcel Maximi Joseph, Jean Rivenson Francois (77.Elijah Mitchell), Lesly St. Fleur, Peter Julmis. Trainer: Nesley Jean.

02.06.2021, 22nd FIFA World Cup Qualifiers, CONCACAF First Round
Mayagüez Athletics Stadium, Mayagüez
Referee: Tori Penso (United States)
PUERTO RICO - BAHAMAS   7-0(4-0)
BAH: Ian Lowe, Cameron Kemp (46.Roen Davis), Dylan Pritchard, Troy Milton Pinder, Jaelin Williams (75.Swain Kenaz), Logan Russell, Terrence Decarlo Delancy Jr., Marcel Maximi Joseph (81.Alexander Thompson), Nicolas Lopez (81.Nathan Wells), Ethan Wesley Willie, Quinton Carey. Trainer: Nesley Jean.

05.06.2021, 22nd FIFA World Cup Qualifiers, CONCACAF First Round
"Thomas Robinson" Stadium, Nassau; Attendance: n/a
Referee: Oliver Amet Vergara Rodríguez (Panama)
BAHAMAS - TRINIDAD AND TOBAGO   0-0
BAH: Ian Lowe, Dylan Pritchard, Troy Milton Pinder, Logan Russell (90+2.Peter Julmis), Evelt Julmis, Terrence Decarlo Delancy Jr., Marcel Maximi Joseph, Nicolas Lopez, Roen Davis (68.Ethan Wesley Willie), Lesly St. Fleur, Quinton Carey. Trainer: Nesley Jean.

03.07.2021, 16th CONCACAF Gold Cup Qualifiers, First Round
DRV PNK Stadium, Fort Lauderdale (United States); Attendance: 0
Referee: Reon Radix (Grenada)
GUADELOUPE - BAHAMAS   2-0(0-0)
BAH: Ian Lowe, Ambry Moss (89.Troy Milton Pinder), Logan Russell (63.Roen Davis), Evelt Julmis, Cameron Robert Hepple, Isiah Claudius Collie (56.Christopher Godet), Terrence Decarlo Delancy Jr., Marcel Maximi Joseph, Lesly St. Fleur, Quinton Carey (56.Ethan Wesley Willie), Peter Julmis (89.Nicolas Lopez). Trainer: Nesley Jean.

NATIONAL TEAM PLAYERS 2020/2021

Name	DOB	Club
Goalkeepers		
Michael Benaiah Peter BUTLER	02.03.1999	*University of the Bahamas FC*
Swain KENAZ*	16.04.2005	*Western Warriors SC Nassau*
Ian LOWE	29.08.2002	*Dynamos FC Nassau*

* was used as field player.

Name	DOB	Club
Defenders		
Christopher GODET	30.03.1998	*Cubs FC*
Happy McNair HALL	15.10.1987	*Westside SC-Renegades FC*
Evelt JULMIS	10.09.1999	
Cameron KEMP		
Ambry MOSS	02.11.1990	
Troy Milton PINDER	30.10.1997	*Western Warriors SC Nassau*
Dylan PRITCHARD	01.11.1993	
Logan RUSSELL	26.10.1999	
Jaelin WILLIAMS	29.11.1997	*Lassen Cougars (USA)*
Midfielders		
Isiah Claudius COLLIE	22.04.1997	*Cavalier FC Nassau*
Roen DAVIS	21.04.2004	*Western Warriors SC Nassau*
Terrence Decarlo DELANCY Jr.	28.02.1994	*Cavalier FC Nassau*
Jean Rivenson FRANCOIS	13.12.1991	*Western Warriors SC Nassau*
Cameron Robert HEPPLE	19.05.1988	*Westside SC-Renegades FC*
Marcel Maximi JOSEPH	30.03.1997	*Side FC 92 Tulsa (USA)*
Nicolas LOPEZ	08.03.2003	
Elijah MITCHELL	23.02.2003	
Alexander THOMPSON	21.02.1990	*Westside SC-Renegades FC*
Nathan WELLS	07.10.2000	*Western Warriors SC Nassau*
Forwards		
Quinton CAREY	26.11.1996	
Peter JULMIS	28.05.2001	*Dynamos FC Nassau*
Lesly ST. FLEUR	31.02.1989	*Bears FC Nassau*
Ethan Wesley WILLIE	21.02.1999	*Western Warriors SC Nassau*

National coaches		
Nesley JEAN [from 01.01.2019]		27.08.1975

BARBADOS

The Country:	The FA:
Barbados	Barbados Football Association
Capital: Bridgetown	Sir Garfield Sobers Sports Complex, Wildey
Surface: 431 km²	St. Michael BB11000, Bridgetown
Population: 287,025 [2019]	Year of Formation: 1910
Time: UTC-4	Member of FIFA since: 1968
Independent since: 1966	Member of CONCACAF since: 1967

NATIONAL TEAM RECORDS

First international match: 09.02.1931: Barbados - Martinique 1-2
Most international caps: Norman Forde – 74 caps (1998-2011)
Most international goals: Llewellyin Riley – 23 goals / 43 caps (1995-2005)

CONCACAF GOLD CUP	
1991	Did not enter
1993	Qualifiers
1996	Qualifiers
1998	Qualifiers
2000	Qualifiers
2002	Qualifiers
2003	Qualifiers
2005	Qualifiers
2007	Qualifiers
2009	Qualifiers
2011	Qualifiers
2013	Qualifiers
2015	Qualifiers
2017	Qualifiers
2019	Qualifiers
2021	Qualifiers

FIFA WORLD CUP	
1930	-
1934	-
1938	-
1950	-
1954	-
1958	-
1962	-
1966	-
1970	Did not enter
1974	Did not enter
1978	Qualifiers
1982	Did not enter
1986	*Withdrew*
1990	Did not enter
1994	Qualifiers
1998	Qualifiers
2002	Qualifiers
2006	Qualifiers
2010	Qualifiers
2014	Qualifiers
2018	*Disqualified*

F.I.F.A. CONFEDERATIONS CUP 1992-2017

None

OLYMPIC FOOTBALL TOURNAMENTS 1908-2016

1908	-	1948	-	1972	Qualifiers	1996	Did not enter
1912	-	1952	-	1976	Qualifiers	2000	Qualifiers
1920	-	1956	-	1980	Qualifiers	2004	Qualifiers
1924	-	1960	-	1984	Qualifiers	2008	Qualifiers
1928	-	1964	-	1988	Qualifiers	2012	Did not enter
1936	-	1968	-	1992	Qualifiers	2016	Qualifiers

CCCF (Confederación Centroamericana y del Caribe de Fútbol) CHAMPIONSHIPS 1941-1961
None

CONCACAF CHAMPIONSHIPS 1963-1989
None

CONCACAF NATIONS LEAGUE

2019-2020	League C (*promoted to League B*)

CARIBBEAN CHAMPIONSHIPS 1989-2017

1989	Final Tournament - Group Stage	1999	Qualifiers
1991	Did not enter	2001	Final Tournament - Group Stage
1992	Qualifiers	2005	Final Tournament - 4th Place
1993	Qualifiers	2007	Final Tournament - Group Stage
1994	Final Tournament - Group Stage	2008	Final Tournament - Group Stage
1995	Qualifiers	2010	Qualifiers
1996	Qualifiers	2012	Qualifiers
1997	Qualifiers	2014	Qualifiers
1998	Qualifiers	2017	Qualifiers

BARBADIAN CLUB HONOURS IN CONCACAF CLUB COMPETITIONS:

CONCACAF Champions Cup / CONCACAF Champions League 1962-2020
None

CONCACAF League 2017-2020
None

Caribbean Club Championship 1997-2021
None

CONCACAF Cup Winners Cup 1991-1995*
None

Copa Interamericana 1968-1998*
None

*defunct competitions

NATIONAL COMPETITIONS
TABLE OF HONOURS

Barbados FA Cup winners before 1947/1948:
1910: Kensington Rovers; 1911: Kensington Rovers; 1912: Kensington Rovers & Harrison College (shared); 1913: Harrison College; 1914: Kensington Rovers; 1915: Kensington Rovers; 1916: Kensington Rovers; 1917: Kensington Rovers; 1918: Kensington Rovers; 1919: Kensington Rovers; 1920: Harrison College; 1921: Kensington Rovers; 1922: Kensington Rovers; 1923: Harrison College Bridgetown; 1924: Empire; 1925: Empire; 1926: Empire; 1927: Spartan Bridgetown; 1928: Empire.

	CHAMPIONS	CUP WINNERS
1947/1948	Spartan Bridgetown	Everton Bridgetown
1960	Everton Bridgetown	Everton Bridgetown
1962	Everton Bridgetown	Everton Bridgetown
1966	Everton Bridgetown	-
1967	New South Wales Bridgetown[1]	New South Wales Bridgetown
1969	New South Wales Bridgetown	New South Wales Bridgetown
1970	New South Wales Bridgetown	New South Wales Bridgetown
1972	-	New South Wales Bridgetown
1975	-	New South Wales Bridgetown
1984	Weymouth Wales Bridgetown	Weymouth Wales Bridgetown
1986	Weymouth Wales Bridgetown	Everton Bridgetown
1987	Everton Bridgetown	Weymouth Wales Bridgetown
1988	Pride of Gall Hill FC	-
1989	Paradise SC Dover	Pinelands
1990	Brittons Hill FC Valery	Everton Bridgetown
1992	Pinelands	-
1993	Pride of Gall Hill FC	Pride of Gall Hill FC
1994	-	Barbados Defence Force SC Paragon
1995	Barbados Defence Force SC Paragon	Pride of Gall Hill FC
1996	Paradise SC Dover	Paradise SC Dover
1997	Notre Dame SC Bayville	Notre Dame SC Bayville
1998	Notre Dame SC Bayville	Pride of Gall Hill FC
1999	Notre Dame SC Bayville	Paradise SC Dover
2000	Notre Dame SC Bayville	Paradise SC Dover
2001	Paradise SC Dover	Notre Dame SC Bayville
2002	Notre Dame SC Bayville	Youth Milan FC Checker Hall
2003	Paradise SC Dover	Paradise SC Dover
2004	Notre Dame SC Bayville	Notre Dame SC Bayville
2005	Notre Dame SC Bayville	Paradise SC Dover
2006	Youth Milan FC Checker Hall	Pride of Gall Hill FC
2007	Barbados Defence Force SC Paragon	Brittons Hill FC Valery
2008	Notre Dame SC Bayville	Notre Dame SC Bayville
2009	Brittons Hill FC Valery	Youth Milan FC Checker Hall
2010	Notre Dame SC Bayville	Notre Dame SC Bayville
2011	Youth Milan FC Checker Hall	Weymouth Wales FC Carrington Village
2012	Weymouth Wales FC Carrington Village	Barbados Defence Force SC Paragon
2013	Barbados Defence Force SC Paragon	Rendezvous FC
2014	Barbados Defence Force SC Paragon	Weymouth Wales FC Carrington Village
2015	Barbados Defence Force SC Paragon	Barbados Defence Force SC Paragon

2016	University of West Indies Blackbirds FC Cave Hill	Weymouth Wales FC Carrington Village
2017	Weymouth Wales FC Carrington Village	Weymouth Wales FC Carrington Village
2018	Weymouth Wales FC Carrington Village	Paradise SC Dover
2018/2019	Barbados Defence Force SC Paragon	Weymouth Wales FC Carrington Village
2020	*Championship suspended*	*Competition cancelled*

[1]caled later Weymouth Wales Bridgetown, then Weymouth Wales FC Carrington Village.

NATIONAL CHAMPIONSHIP
Premier Division – Digicel Premier League 2020

Please note: the league was suspended on 17.03.2020 due to COVID-19 pandemic.

League table at time of suspension:

1.	Weymouth Wales FC Carrington Village	7	5	1	1	16 - 4	16
2.	Barbados Defence Force SC Paragon	7	4	3	0	19 - 8	15
3.	Paradise SC Dover	7	3	2	2	13 - 8	11
4.	Notre Dame SC Bayville	7	3	2	2	12 - 13	11
5.	Empire Club FC	7	3	1	3	13 - 10	10
6.	Deacons FC	7	3	1	3	10 - 11	10
7.	Wotton FC	7	3	0	4	9 - 12	9
8.	University of West Indies Blackbirds FC Cave Hill	7	1	4	2	12 - 13	7
9.	Ellerton FC (*Relegated*)	7	1	4	2	10 - 12	7
10.	Saint Andrew Lions FC (*Relegated*)	7	1	4	2	10 - 13	7
11.	Silver Sands FC (*Relegated*)	7	2	0	5	7 - 19	6
12.	Brittons Hill United FC Valery (*Relegated*)	7	1	2	4	3 - 11	5

NATIONAL TEAM
INTERNATIONAL MATCHES 2020/2021

25.03.2021	Santo Domingo	*Panama - Barbados*	*1-0(0-0)*	*(WCQ)*
30.03.2021	Santo Domingo	*Barbados - Anguilla*	*1-0(0-0)*	*(WCQ)*
04.06.2021	Santo Domingo	*Dominican Republic - Barbados*	*1-1(0-1)*	*(WCQ)*
08.06.2021	Santo Domingo	*Barbados - Dominica*	*1-1(0-0)*	*(WCQ)*
02.07.2021	Fort Lauderdale	*Bermuda - Barbados*	*8-1(4-1)*	*(GCQ)*

25.03.2021, 22nd FIFA World Cup Qualifiers, CONCACAF First Round
Estadio Olímpico "Félix Sánchez", Santo Domingo (Dominican Republic)
Referee: Nima Saghafi (United States)
PANAMA - BARBADOS   **1-0(0-0)**
BRB: Kishmar Primus, Krystian Mitchell Victor Pearce, Carl Hinkson, Rashad Smith, Jomo Harris, Hadan Holligan, Rashad Jules (80.Ackeel Applewhaite), Mario Williams, Niall Reid-Stephen (59.Keon Atkins), Emile Saimovici (68.Ryan Lara Trotman), Omani Leacock (83.Jamol Williams). Trainer: Russell Nigel Latapy (Trinidad and Tobago).

30.03.2021, 22nd FIFA World Cup Qualifiers, CONCACAF First Round
Estadio Olímpico "Félix Sánchez", Santo Domingo (Dominican Republic)
Referee: Diego Montaño Robles (Mexico)
BARBADOS - ANGUILLA   **1-0(0-0)**
BRB: Kishmar Primus, Krystian Mitchell Victor Pearce, Carl Hinkson (81.Keon Atkins), Rashad Smith (46.Ackeel Applewhaite), Jomo Harris, Hadan Holligan, Rashad Jules, Mario Williams, Emile Saimovici, Omani Leacock (46.Niall Reid-Stephen), Ryan Lara Trotman. Trainer: Russell Nigel Latapy (Trinidad and Tobago).
Goal: Emile Saimovici (81).

04.06.2021, 22nd FIFA World Cup Qualifiers, CONCACAF First Round
Estadio Olímpico "Félix Sánchez", Santo Domingo
Referee: Germán Stanley Martínez Miranda (El Salvador)
DOMINICAN REPUBLIC - BARBADOS   **1-1(0-1)**
BRB: Kishmar Primus (32.Liam Brathwaite), Krystian Mitchell Victor Pearce, Rashad Smith, Andreas Applewhaite, Hadan Holligan, Mario Williams, Ackeel Applewhaite, Niall Reid-Stephen (65.Romario Drakes), Emile Saimovici (65.Thierry Gale), Hallam Robert Hope, Omani Leacock. Trainer: Russell Nigel Latapy (Trinidad and Tobago).
Goal: Niall Reid-Stephen (42).

08.06.2021, 22nd FIFA World Cup Qualifiers, CONCACAF First Round
Estadio Olímpico "Félix Sánchez", Santo Domingo (Dominican Republic)
Referee: Jaime Herrera Bonilla (El Salvador)
BARBADOS - DOMINICA   **1-1(0-0)**
BRB: Liam Brathwaite, Carl Hinkson, Rashad Smith, Andreas Applewhaite, Jomo Harris, Hadan Holligan, Devonte Richards (46.Niall Reid-Stephen), Hallam Robert Hope (90.Keon Atkins), Akeem Hill, Omani Leacock (71.Romario Drakes), Antone Greaves (46.Emile Saimovici). Trainer: Russell Nigel Latapy (Trinidad and Tobago).
Goal: Emile Saimovici (48).

02.07.2021, 16th CONCACAF Gold Cup Qualifiers, First Round
DRV PNK Stadium, Fort Lauderdale (United States); Attendance: 0
Referee: Drew Fischer (Canada)

BERMUDA - BARBADOS   **8-1(4-1)**

BRB: Liam Brathwaite, Krystian Mitchell Victor Pearce (73.Akeem Hill), Rashad Smith (42.Ackeel Applewhaite), Andre Applewhaite (46.Dwayne Pascal Green), Jomo Harris (63.Antone Greaves), Hadan Holligan, Mario Williams, Emile Saimovici, Nicholas Alexander Blackman, Hallam Robert Hope, Omani Leacock (42.Ryan Lara Trotman). Trainer: Russell Nigel Latapy (Trinidad and Tobago).
Goal: Hadan Holligan (45+1).

NATIONAL TEAM PLAYERS 2020/2021

Name	DOB	Club
Goalkeepers		
Liam BRATHWAITE	06.11.2000	*UWI Blackbirds FC Cave Hill*
Kishmar PRIMUS	09.04.1998	*Barbados Defence Force SC Paragon*
Defenders		
Ackeel APPLEWHAITE	17.07.1990	*Paradise SC Dover*
Andre APPLEWHAITE	03.06.2002	*Weymouth Wales FC Carrington Village*
Dwayne Pascal GREEN	03.09.1996	*FC Den Bosch (NED)*
Carl HINKSON	14.04.1997	
Krystian Mitchell Victor PEARCE	05.01.1990	*Boreham Wood FC (ENG)*
Rashad SMITH	31.07.1996	*Barbados Defence Force SC Paragon*
Midfielders		
Jomo HARRIS	15.02.1995	*Paradise SC Dover*
Akeem HILL	01.11.1996	*Barbados Defence Force SC Paragon*
Hadan HOLLIGAN	11.09.1996	*Weymouth Wales FC Carrington Village*
Rashad JULES	24.06.1992	*Barbados Defence Force SC Paragon*
Niall REID-STEPHEN	08.09.2001	*UWI Blackbirds FC Cave Hill*
Devonte RICHARDS	27.09.2002	
Emile SAIMOVICI	10.04.1993	
Jamol WILLIAMS	20.04.2003	*Saint Andrew Lions FC*
Mario WILLIAMS	19.08.1992	*Weymouth Wales FC Carrington Village*
Forwards		
Keon ATKINS	19.05.1995	*Deacons FC*
Nicholas Alexander BLACKMAN	11.11.1989	*Maccabi Tel Aviv (ISR)*
Romario DRAKES	31.12.2000	*Youth Milan FC*
Thierry GALE	01.05.2002	*Budapest Honvéd FC (HUN)*
Antone GREAVES	04.12.1999	*Weymouth Wales FC Carrington Village*
Hallam Robert HOPE	17.03.1994	*Swindon Town FC (ENG)*
Omani LEACOCK	01.05.1998	*Barbados Defence Force SC Paragon*
Ryan Lara TROTMAN	27.06.1999	*FC Den Bosch (NED)*
National coaches		
Russell Nigel LATAPY (Trinidad and Tobago) [from 01.04.2019]		02.08.1968

BELIZE

The Country:	The FA:
Belize	Football Federation of Belize
Capital: Belmopán	26 Hummingbird Highway, Belmopán,
Surface: 22,966 km²	P.O. Box 1742, Belize City
Population: 419,199 [2020]	Year of Formation: 1980
Time: UTC-6	Member of FIFA since: 1986
Independent since: 1981	Member of CONCACAF since: 1986

NATIONAL TEAM RECORDS

First international match: 29.11.1995, San Salvador: El Salvador - Belize 3-0
Most international caps: Elroy Alexander Smith – 61 caps (2004-2019)
Most international goals: Deon McCaulay – 27 goals / 55 caps (since 2007)

CONCACAF GOLD CUP	
1991	Did not enter
1993	Did not enter
1996	Qualifiers
1998	Qualifiers
2000	Qualifiers
2002	Qualifiers
2003	Did not enter
2005	Qualifiers
2007	Qualifiers
2009	Qualifiers
2011	Qualifiers
2013	Final Tournament (Group Stage)
2015	Qualifiers
2017	Qualifiers
2019	Qualifiers
2021	Qualifiers

FIFA WORLD CUP	
1930	-
1934	-
1938	-
1950	-
1954	-
1958	-
1962	-
1966	-
1970	-
1974	-
1978	-
1982	-
1986	-
1990	Did not enter
1994	Did not enter
1998	Qualifiers
2002	Qualifiers
2006	Qualifiers
2010	Qualifiers
2014	Qualifiers
2018	Qualifiers

F.I.F.A. CONFEDERATIONS CUP 1992-2017

None

OLYMPIC FOOTBALL TOURNAMENTS 1908-2016

1908	-	1948	-	1972	-	1996	Qualifiers
1912	-	1952	-	1976	-	2000	Qualifiers
1920	-	1956	-	1980	-	2004	Qualifiers
1924	-	1960	-	1984	-	2008	Did not enter
1928	-	1964	-	1988	-	2012	Qualifiers
1936	-	1968	-	1992	Qualifiers	2016	Qualifiers

CCCF (Confederación Centroamericana y del Caribe de Fútbol) CHAMPIONSHIPS 1941-1961
None

CONCACAF CHAMPIONSHIPS 1963-1989
None

CONCACAF NATIONS LEAGUE

2019-2020	League B

COPA CENTROAMERICANA (UNCAF NATIONS CHAMPIONSHIPS) 1991-2017

1991	Did not enter	2005	Final Round – Group Stage
1993	Did not enter	2007	Final Round – Group Stage
1995	Final Round – Group Stage	2009	Final Round – Group Stage
1997	Preliminary Round	2011	Final Round – Group Stage
1999	Final Round – Group Stage	2013	Final Round - 4th Place
2001	Final Round – Group Stage	2014	Final Round – Group Stage
2003	Did not enter	2017	Final Round - 6th Place

BELIZEAN CLUB HONOURS IN CONCACAF CLUB COMPETITIONS:

CONCACAF Champions Cup / CONCACAF Champions League 1962-2020
None

CONCACAF League 2017-2020
None

Caribbean Club Championship 1997-2021
None

CONCACAF Cup Winners Cup 1991-1995*
None

Copa Interamericana 1968-1998*
None

*defunct competitions

NATIONAL COMPETITIONS
TABLE OF HONOURS

	CHAMPIONS
	Interdistrict Championship
1969/1970	FC San Joaquín
1976/1977	Queens Park Rangers Stann Creek Town
1978/1979	Queens Park Rangers Stann Creek Town
	National Division
1991/1992	La Victoria FC Corozal*
1992/1993	Acros Caribe Belize City

1993/1994	La Victoria FC Corozal
1994/1995	Acros Crystal Belize City
1995/1996	Juventus FC Orange Walk
1996/1997	Juventus FC Orange Walk
1997/1998	Juventus FC Orange Walk
1998/1999	Juventus FC Orange Walk
1999/2000	Sagitún Independence
2000/2001	Kulture Yabra FC Belize City
2001/2002	Kulture Yabra FC Belize City
	BPFL Regent Challenge Champions Cup
2002/2003	Sagitún Independence
2003	Kulture Yabra FC Belize City
2004	Sagitún Independence
	National League
2005	Juventus FC Orange Walk
2005/2006	New Site Erei Dangriga
2006	New Site Erei Dangriga
	RFG Insurance League
2006	FC Belize Belize City
2007	FC Belize Belize City
2007/2008	Hankook Real Verdes FC San Ignacio
2008	Ilagulei FC Dangriga
2009 Spring	Nizhee Corozal FC
2009 Fall	Belize Defence Force FC San Ignacio
2010 Spring	Belize Defence Force FC San Ignacio
2010/2011 Fall	Belize Defence Force FC San Ignacio
	Premier League
2012	Placencia Assassins FC
2012/2013 Opening	Belmopán Bandits FSC
2012/2013 Closing	Police United FC Belmopán
2013/2014 Opening	Belmopán Bandits FSC
2013/2014 Closing	Belmopán Bandits FSC
2014/2015 Fall	Belmopán Bandits FSC
2014/2015 Spring	Verdes FC San Ignacio
2015 Opening	Police United FC Belmopán
2016 Closing	Belmopán Bandits FSC
2016 Opening	Belmopán Bandits FSC
2017 Closing	Belmopán Bandits FSC
2017 Opening	Verdes FC San Ignacio
2018 Closing	Belmopán Bandits FSC
2018 Opening	Belmopán Bandits FSC
2019 Closing	San Pedro Pirates FC
2019 Opening	Verdes FC San Ignacio
2020 Closing	*Championship cancelled*
2020 Opening	*Championship cancelled*
2021 Closing	*Championship cancelled*

*called later FC Corozal (1997-1998), La Vicria Dolphins FC Corozal Town (1998-1999), Corozal FC (2001-2002), Corozal Victory FC (2002), Nizhee Corozal FC (since 2008).

NATIONAL CHAMPIONSHIP
Premier League of Belize 2020/2021

The season was cancelled due to COVID-19 pandemic.

NATIONAL TEAM
INTERNATIONAL MATCHES 2020/2021

25.03.2021	Port-au-Prince	Haiti - Belize	2-0(0-0)	(WCQ)
30.03.2021	San Cristóbal	Belize - Turks and Caicos Islands	5-0(1-0)	(WCQ)
04.06.2021	Managua	Nicaragua - Belize	3-0(1-0)	(WCQ)

25.03.2021, 22nd FIFA World Cup Qualifiers, CONCACAF First Round
Stade "Sylvio Cator", Port-au-Prince
Referee: Walter Alexander López Castellanos (Guatemala)

HAITI - BELIZE   **2-0(0-0)**

BLZ: Woodrow West, Asrel Kimmani Sutherland, Everal Trapp, Ian Gaynair (70.Norman Anderson), Deshawon Nembhard, Michael Thomas Atkinson (56.Nana-Yaw Gyedu Amankwah-Mensah), Collin Westby, Jordi Leonel Polanco (57.Andrés Makin), Deon Lincoln McCaulay, Carlos Roberto Bernárdez García (61.Ean Lewis), Angelo Capello (69.Jesse August). Trainer: Dale Daniel Pelayo Sr.

30.03.2021, 22nd FIFA World Cup Qualifiers, CONCACAF First Round
Estadio Panamericano, San Cristóbal (Dominican Republic)
Referee: Nima Saghafi (United States)

BELIZE - TURKS AND CAICOS ISLANDS   **5-0(1-0)**

BLZ: Woodrow West, Asrel Kimmani Sutherland, Everal Trapp, Deshawon Nembhard, Nana-Yaw Gyedu Amankwah-Mensah (61.José Reuben Urbina), Collin Westby, Jordi Leonel Polanco (70.Ean Lewis), Deon Lincoln McCaulay, Carlos Roberto Bernárdez García (70.Desmond Wade), Krisean Kyle López (46.Jesse August), Angelo Capello (56.Nahjib Kazim Guerra). Trainer: Dale Daniel Pelayo Sr.
Goals: Carlos Roberto Bernárdez García (45+3), Jesse August (47), Carlos Roberto Bernárdez García (48), Deshawon Nembhard (81), Deon Lincoln McCaulay (90+1).

04.06.2021, 22nd FIFA World Cup Qualifiers, CONCACAF First Round
Estadio Nacional, Managua
Referee: Nelson Alcides Salgado Trujillo (Honduras)

NICARAGUA - BELIZE   **3-0(1-0)**

BLZ: Charles Tillett, Ian Gaynair, Norman Anderson, Deshawon Nembhard, Nana-Yaw Gyedu Amankwah-Mensah (79.Jordan Casanova), Donell Eric Arzú (61.Darrel Myvett), Denmark Raymond Casey Jr., Jordi Leonel Polanco (78.Jahlin Pelayo), Deon Lincoln McCaulay, Gilroy Ronald Thurton (78.Izon Ainsley Gill), Krisean Kyle López (54.Ean Lewis). Trainer: Dale Daniel Pelayo Sr.

NATIONAL TEAM PLAYERS 2020/2021

Name	DOB	Club

Goalkeepers

Charles TILLETT	29.07.2001	*Verdes FC San Ignacio*
Woodrow WEST	19.09.1985	*Juticalpa FC (HON)*

Defenders

Donell Eric ARZÚ	27.09.1999	*Wagiya FC Dangriga*
Jordan CASANOVA	30.04.2004	*San Pedro Pirates FC*
Ian GAYNAIR	26.02.1986	*Belmopán Bandits FSC*
Deshawon NEMBHARD	08.10.1994	*Unattached*
Asrel Kimmani SUTHERLAND	08.03.1993	*San Pedro Pirates FC*
Everal TRAPP	22.01.1987	*Verdes FC San Ignacio*
José Reuben URBINA	13.02.1995	*Altitude FC Independence*

Midfielders

Nana-Yaw Gyedu AMANKWAH-MENSAH	19.01.1989	*New York Greek American AA (USA)*
Norman ANDERSON	25.01.1997	*Belmopán Bandits FSC*
Michael Thomas ATKINSON	02.12.1994	*Hungerford Town FC (ENG)*
Jesse AUGUST	22.01.1994	*Altitude FC Independence*
Denmark Raymond CASEY Jr.	14.01.1994	*Belmopán Bandits FSC*
Izon Ainsley GILL	27.12.1999	*Verdes FC San Ignacio*
Nahjib Kazim GUERRA	18.08.1994	*Verdes FC San Ignacio*
Ean LEWIS	25.02.1991	*Belize Defence Force FC San Ignacio*
Andrés MAKIN	11.04.1992	*Police United FC Belmopán*
Darrel MYVETT	15.12.1993	*Verdes FC San Ignacio*
Jahlin PELAYO	29.08.2001	*Belmopán Bandits FSC*
Jordi Leonel POLANCO	08.06.1996	*Belmopán Bandits FSC*
Gilroy Ronald THURTON	07.09.1993	*San Pedro Pirates FC*
Collin WESTBY	19.02.1995	*Altitude FC Independence*

Forwards

Carlos Roberto BERNÁRDEZ García	28.12.1992	*Platense FC Puerto Cortés (HON)*
Angelo CAPELLO	27.01.2002	*Sheffield United FC (ENG)*
Krisean Kyle LÓPEZ	02.11.1998	*Verdes FC San Ignacio*
Deon Lincoln McCAULAY	20.09.1987	*Ginga Atlanta (USA)*
Desmond WADE	31.08.1997	*Belize Defence Force FC San Ignacio*

National coaches

Dale Daniel PELAYO Sr. [from 31.07.2020]	02.03.1977

BERMUDA

Bermuda Football Association

The Country:	The FA:
Bermuda	Bermuda Football Association
Capital: Hamilton	1 BFA Way, DV02, Devonshire
Surface: 53,2 km²	Year of Formation: 1928
Population: 71,176 [2018]	Member of FIFA since: 1967
Time: UTC-4	Member of CONCACAF since: 1962

NATIONAL TEAM RECORDS

First international match: 10.08.1964, Reykjavík: Iceland - Bermuda 4-3
Most international caps: Damon Jason Ming – 42 caps (2003-2013)
Most international goals: Leonard Shaun Goater – 20 goals / 22 caps (1987-2004)

CONCACAF GOLD CUP		FIFA WORLD CUP	
1991	Did not enter	1930	-
1993	Did not enter	1934	-
1996	Did not enter	1938	-
1998	Qualifiers	1950	-
2000	Qualifiers	1954	-
2002	*Withdrew*	1958	-
2003	Did not enter	1962	-
2005	Qualifiers	1966	-
2007	Qualifiers	1970	Qualifiers
2009	Qualifiers	1974	Did not enter
2011	Did not enter	1978	Did not enter
2013	Qualifiers	1982	Did not enter
2015	Did not enter	1986	Did not enter
2017	Qualifiers	1990	Did not enter
2019	Final Tournament (Group Stage)	1994	Qualifiers
2021	Qualifiers	1998	*Withdrew*
		2002	Qualifiers
		2006	Qualifiers
		2010	Qualifiers
		2014	Qualifiers
		2018	Qualifiers

F.I.F.A. CONFEDERATIONS CUP 1992-2017

None

OLYMPIC FOOTBALL TOURNAMENTS 1908-2016							
1908	-	1948	-	1972	Qualifiers	1996	Qualifiers
1912	-	1952	-	1976	Qualifiers	2000	Qualifiers
1920	-	1956	-	1980	Qualifiers	2004	Did not enter
1924	-	1960	-	1984	Qualifiers	2008	Qualifiers
1928	-	1964	-	1988	Qualifiers	2012	Did not enter
1936	-	1968	Qualifiers	1992	Did not enter	2016	Did not enter

CCCF (Confederación Centroamericana y del Caribe de Fútbol) CHAMPIONSHIPS 1941-1961
None

CONCACAF CHAMPIONSHIPS 1963-1989
1969, 1971

CONCACAF NATIONS LEAGUE	
2019-2020	League A (*relegated to League B*)

CARIBBEAN CHAMPIONSHIPS 1989-2017			
1989	Did not enter	1999	Qualifiers
1991	Did not enter	2001	Qualifiers
1992	Did not enter	2005	Qualifiers
1993	Did not enter	2007	Qualifiers
1994	Did not enter	2008	Qualifiers
1995	Did not enter	2010	Did not enter
1996	Did not enter	2012	Qualifiers
1997	Qualifiers	2014	Did not enter
1998	Qualifiers	2017	Qualifiers

BERMUDIAN CLUB HONOURS IN CONCACAF CLUB COMPETITIONS:

CONCACAF Champions Cup / CONCACAF Champions League 1962-2020
None
CONCACAF League 2017-2020
None
Caribbean Club Championship 1997-2021
None
CONCACAF Cup Winners Cup 1991-1995*
None
Copa Interamericana 1968-1998*
None

*defunct competitions

NATIONAL COMPETITIONS
TABLE OF HONOURS

The first League championship started 1929 only with white players. Clubs having black players formed 1944 their own league called the „Bermuda Football League", they entered in 1954 the Bermuda FA Cup too. The first „black-and-white" league started in 1963.

	CHAMPIONS	CUP WINNERS
1955/1956	Pembroke Juniors	Bermuda AA Wanderers
1956/1957	*Not known*	Pembroke Hamilton Club Zebras
1957/1958	*Not known*	Wellington Rovers
1958/1959	*Not known*	Dock Hill Rangers
1959/1960	*Not known*	Pembroke Hamilton Club Zebras
1960/1961	*Not known*	Pembroke Hamilton Club Zebras
1961/1962	*Not known*	Pembroke Hamilton Club Zebras
1962/1963	*Not known*	Young Men's Social Club
1963/1964	Young Men's Social Club	Young Men's Social Club
1964/1965	Young Men's Social Club	Young Men's Social Club
1965/1966	Young Men's Social Club	Casuals
1966/1967	Somerset Cricket Club	Pembroke Hamilton Club Zebras
1967/1968	Somerset Cricket Club	Somerset Trojans
1968/1969	Somerset Cricket Club	Somerset Trojans
1969/1970	Somerset Cricket Club	Somerset Trojans
1970/1971	Pembroke Hamilton Club Zebras	Pembroke Hamilton Club Zebras
1971/1972	Devonshire Colts FC	Somerset Trojans
1972/1973	Devonshire Colts FC	Devonshire Colts FC
1973/1974	North Village Community Club	Devonshire Colts FC
1974/1975	Hotels International FC	Pembroke Hamilton Club Zebras
1975/1976	North Village Community Club	Somerset Trojans
1976/1977	Pembroke Hamilton Club Zebras	Somerset Trojans
1977/1978	North Village Community Club	North Village Community Club
1978/1979	North Village Community Club	Somerset Trojans
1979/1980	Hotels International FC	Pembroke Hamilton Club Zebras
1980/1981	Southampton Rangers SC	Vasco da Gama FC
1981/1982	Somerset Cricket Club	Vasco da Gama FC
1982/1983	Somerset Cricket Club	North Village Community Club
1983/1984	Somerset Cricket Club	Southampton Rangers SC
1984/1985	Pembroke Hamilton Club Zebras	Hotels International FC
1985/1986	Pembroke Hamilton Club Zebras	North Village Community Club
1986/1987	Somerset Cricket Club	Dandy Town SC
1987/1988	Dandy Town SC	Somerset Trojans
1988/1989	Pembroke Hamilton Club Zebras	North Village Community Club
1989/1990	Pembroke Hamilton Club Zebras	Somerset Trojans
1990/1991	Boulevard Community Club	Boulevard Blazers FC
1991/1992	Pembroke Hamilton Club Zebras	Pembroke Hamilton Club Zebras
1992/1993	Somerset Cricket Club	Boulevard Blazers FC
1993/1994	Dandy Town SC	Vasco da Gama FC
1994/1995	Boulevard Community Club	Vasco da Gama FC
1995/1996	Vasco da Gama FC	Boulevard Blazers FC
1996/1997	Devonshire Colts FC	Boulevard Blazers FC
1997/1998	Vasco da Gama FC	Vasco da Gama FC

1998/1999	Vasco da Gama FC	Devonshire Colts FC
1999/2000	Pembroke Hamilton Club Zebras	North Village Community Club
2000/2001	Dandy Town Hornets SC	Devonshire Colts FC
2001/2002	North Village Community Club	North Village Community Club
2002/2003	North Village Community Club	North Village Community Club
2003/2004	Dandy Town Hornets SC	North Village Community Club
2004/2005	Devonshire Recreation Club Cougars	North Village Community Club
2005/2006	North Village Community Club	North Village Community Club
2006/2007	Devonshire Recreation Club Cougars	Devonshire Colts FC
2007/2008	Pembroke Hamilton Club Zebras	Pembroke Hamilton Club Zebras
2008/2009	Devonshire Recreation Club Cougars	Boulevard Blazers FC
2009/2010	Dandy Town Hornets SC	Devonshire Recreation Club Cougars
2010/2011	North Village Community Club Rams	Devonshire Recreation Club Cougars
2011/2012	Dandy Town Hornets SC	Dandy Town Hornets SC
2012/2013	Devonshire Recreation Club Cougars	Devonshire Recreation Club Cougars
2013/2014	Dandy Town Hornets SC	Dandy Town Hornets SC
2014/2015	Somerset Cricket Club Trojans	Dandy Town Hornets SC
2015/2016	Dandy Town Hornets SC	Robin Hood FC Pembroke
2016/2017	Robin Hood FC Pembroke	Pembroke Hamilton Club Zebras
2017/2018	Pembroke Hamilton Club Zebras	Robin Hood FC Pembroke
2018/2019	Pembroke Hamilton Club Zebras	Robin Hood FC Pembroke
2019/2020	North Village Community Club Rams	*Competition cancelled*
2020/2021	*Championship cancelled*	*Competition cancelled*

NATIONAL CHAMPIONSHIP
Cingular Wireless Premier Division 2020/2021

Please note: the league was suspended after 10 Rounds on 05.12.2020 due to COVID-19 pandemic. The season was declared void on 15.03.2021. No title was awarded.

League table at time of suspension:

1.	Robin Hood FC Pembroke	8	7	1	0	26	-	5	22
2.	Devonshire Recreation Club Cougars	9	5	2	2	17	-	7	17
3.	Pembroke Hamilton Club Zebras	9	5	2	2	17	-	14	17
4.	Dandy Town Hornets SC	7	4	2	1	15	-	9	14
5.	Somerset Cricket Club Trojans	8	4	2	2	8	-	8	14
6.	North Village Community Club Rams	8	3	2	3	10	-	12	11
7.	Devonshire Colts FC	8	2	2	4	15	-	13	8
8.	Southampton Rangers SC	8	2	2	4	8	-	12	8
9.	X'roads Warriors FC St. George's	8	1	2	5	7	-	17	5
10.	Saint George's Cricket Club	8	1	1	6	5	-	13	4
11.	Somerset Eagles Recreation Club Sandys	7	1	0	6	6	-	24	3

NATIONAL CUP
BFA Challenge Cup Final 2020/2021

The competition was cancelled due to COVID-19 pandemic.

THE CLUBS

DANDY TOWN HORNETS SPORTS CLUB PEMBROKE PARISH
Year of Formation: 1973
Stadium: St. John's Field, Pembroke Parish (1,000)

DEVONSHIRE COLTS FOOTBALL CLUB
Year of Formation: 1958
Stadium: Police Recreation Field (7,000)

DEVONSHIRE RECREATION CLUB COUGARS
Year of Formation: n/a
Stadium: Devonshire Recreation Club (10,000)

NORTH VILLAGE COMMUNITY CLUB RAMS
Year of Formation: 1957
Stadium: Bernard Park Field, Hamilton (1,000)

PEMBROKE HAMILTON CLUB ZEBRAS
Year of Formation: 1950
Stadium: Southampton Rangers Field (1,000)

ROBIN HOOD FOOTBALL CLUB PEMBROKE
Year of Formation: 1977
Stadium: Goose Gosling Field, Pembroke Parish (n/a)

SOMERSET EAGLES RECREATION CLUB SANDYS
Year of Formation: n/a
Stadium: White Hill Field 1, Sandys (1,000

SOMERSET CRICKET CLUB TROJANS
Year of Formation: 1964
Stadium: Somerset Cricket Club Field, Somerset (1,000)

ST. GEORGE'S CRICKET CLUB
Year of Formation: 1965
Stadium: Southampton Oval, Southampton (1,000)

SOUTHAMPTON RANGERS SPORTS CLUB
Year of Formation: 1892
Stadium: Wellington Oval, St. George's (1,000)

X-ROADS WARRIORS FOOTBALL CLUB ST. GEORGE'S
Year of Formation: n/a
Stadium: Garrison Field, St. George's (1,000)

NATIONAL TEAM
INTERNATIONAL MATCHES 2020/2021

25.03.2021	Orlando	Canada - Bermuda	5-1(2-0)	(WCQ)
30.03.2021	Bradenton	Bermuda - Aruba	5-0(2-0)	(WCQ)
04.06.2021	Paramaribo	Suriname - Bermuda	6-0(4-0)	(WCQ)
08.06.2021	Bradenton	Bermuda - Cayman Islands	1-1(0-1)	(WCQ)
02.07.2021	Fort Lauderdale	Bermuda - Barbados	8-1(4-1)	(GCQ)
06.07.2021	Fort Lauderdale	Haiti - Bermuda	4-1(3-0)	(GCQ)

25.03.2021, 22nd FIFA World Cup Qualifiers, CONCACAF First Round
Exploria Stadium, Orlando (United States)
Referee: Armando Villareal (United States)
CANADA - BERMUDA   **5-1(2-0)**
BER: Dale Donald Eve, Dante Roger David Leverock (83.Jomei Bean-Lindo), Roger Colville Lee, Jaylon Wayne Bather, Eusebio Blankendal, Calon Minors, Kane Sinclair Crichlow, Lejuan Simmons (64.Knory Scott), Cecoy Robinson (73.London Steede-Jackson), Jordan Outerbridge (73.Jahkari Furbert), Chae Brangman. Trainer: Kyle Lavince Lightbourne.
Goal: Kane Sinclair Crichlow (63).

30.03.2021, 22nd FIFA World Cup Qualifiers, CONCACAF First Round
IMG Academy, Bradenton (United States)
Referee: Jaime Alfredo Herrera Bonilla (El Salvador)
BERMUDA - ARUBA   **5-0(2-0)**
BER: Dale Donald Eve, Dante Roger David Leverock, Roger Colville Lee, Jaylon Wayne Bather, Eusebio Blankendal, Jahkari Furbert (62.Zeiko Troy Jahmiko Lewis), Keishon Bean (82.London Steede-Jackson), Calon Minors (90.Jomei Bean-Lindo), Kane Sinclair Crichlow, Lejuan Simmons (62.Knory Scott), Tokia Enrique Zidane Russell Jr. (62.Chae Brangman). Trainer: Kyle Lavince Lightbourne.
Goals: Kane Sinclair Crichlow (36), Jaylon Wayne Bather (40), Dante Roger David Leverock (57), Knory Scott (64), Kane Sinclair Crichlow (80).

04.06.2021, 22nd FIFA World Cup Qualifiers, CONCACAF First Round
Stadion "Dr. Ir. Franklin Essed", Paramaribo
Referee: Mario Alberto Escobar Toca (Guatemala)
SURINAME - BERMUDA   **6-0(4-0)**
BER: Dale Donald Eve, Roger Colville Lee, Tahzeiko Soloman Harris, Eusebio Blankendal, Trey Tucker, Willie Minkah Ajani Clemons, Rashad Smith-Jones, Jomei Bean-Lindo (81.Azende Furbert), Luke Robinson (72.Jordan Outerbridge), Lejuan Simmons (19.Keishon Bean), Kole Hall (72.Tokia Enrique Zidane Russell Jr.). Trainer: Kyle Lavince Lightbourne.

08.06.2021, 22nd FIFA World Cup Qualifiers, CONCACAF First Round
IMG Academy, Bradenton (United States)
Referee: Rubiel Vazquez (United States)
BERMUDA - CAYMAN ISLANDS   **1-1(0-1)**
BER: Detre Bell, Tahzeiko Soloman Harris, Eusebio Blankendal (71.Daren Usher), Richard Jones Jr. (46.Jordan Outerbridge), Willie Minkah Ajani Clemons, London Steede-Jackson, Rashad Smith-Jones (61.Cecoy Robinson), Justin Bell (71.Keishon Bean), Luke Robinson, Azende Furbert, Kole Hall (71.Tokia Enrique Zidane Russell Jr.). Trainer: Kyle Lavince Lightbourne.
Goal: Kole Hall (65).

02.07.2021, 16th CONCACAF Gold Cup Qualifiers, First Round
DRV PNK Stadium, Fort Lauderdale (United States); Attendance: 0
Referee: Drew Fischer (Canada)
BERMUDA - BARBADOS **8-1(4-1)**
BER: Dale Donald Eve, Dante Roger David Leverock (73.Richard Jones Jr.), Jaylon Wayne Bather, Eusebio Blankendal (64.Jonté Jahki Smith), Calon Minors, Reginald Everard Vibart Thompson Lambe (59.Kane Sinclair Crichlow), Kacy Milan Butterfield, Willie Minkah Ajani Clemons (59.Roger Colville Lee), Zeiko Troy Jahmiko Lewis (73.Luke Robinson), Nakhi Wells, Justin Donawa. Trainer: Kyle Lavince Lightbourne.
Goals: Nakhi Wells (1, 14), Reginald Everard Vibart Thompson Lambe (29), Dante Roger David Leverock (39), Krystian Mitchell Victor Pearce (60 own goal), Kane Sinclair Crichlow (66), Zeiko Troy Jahmiko Lewis (67), Nakhi Wells (87 penalty).

06.07.2021, 16th CONCACAF Gold Cup Qualifiers, Second Round
DRV PNK Stadium, Fort Lauderdale (United States); Attendance: 0
Referee: Iván Arcides Barton Cisneros (El Salvador)
HAITI - BERMUDA **4-1(3-0)**
BER: Dale Donald Eve, Dante Roger David Leverock, Jaylon Wayne Bather, Eusebio Blankendal (46.Kole Hall), Calon Minors (69.Richard Jones Jr.), Reginald Everard Vibart Thompson Lambe (46.Kane Sinclair Crichlow), Kacy Milan Butterfield (80.Jonté Jahki Smith), Willie Minkah Ajani Clemons, Zeiko Troy Jahmiko Lewis (69.Lejuan Simmons), Nakhi Wells, Justin Donawa. Trainer: Kyle Lavince Lightbourne.
Goals: Nakhi Wells (80).

NATIONAL TEAM PLAYERS
2020/2021

Name	DOB	Club

Goalkeepers

Detre BELL	08.03.1997	*CSU Bakersfield Roadrunners (USA)*
Dale Donald EVE	09.02.1995	*Spennymoor Town FC (ENG)*

Defenders

Jaylon Wayne BATHER	31.12.1992	*Robin Hood FC Pembroke*
Jomei BEAN-LINDO	09.05.1998	*Dandy Town Hornets SC*
Eusebio BLANKENDAL	03.11.1998	*Dandy Town Hornets SC*
Azende FURBERT	18.03.1998	*Dandy Town Hornets SC*
Tahzeiko Soloman HARRIS	07.05.1999	*Louisville Cardinals (USA)*
Richard JONES Jr.		*Devonshire Colts FC*
Dante Roger David LEVEROCK	04.11.1992	*Robin Hood FC Pembroke*
Calon MINORS	11.07.1996	*BAA Wanderers Hamilton*
Daren USHER	07.12.1995	*Pembroke Hamilton Club Zebras*

Midfielders

Kacy Milan BUTTERFIELD	24.01.1998	*Guiseley AFC (ENG)*
Willie Minkah Ajani CLEMONS	24.09.1994	*Dalkurd FF (SWE)*
Kane Sinclair CRICHLOW	21.08.2000	*Watford FC (ENG)*
Jahkari FURBERT	06.03.1999	*BAA Wanderers Hamilton*
Reginald Everard Vibart Thompson LAMBE	04.02.1991	*Stowmarket Town FC (ENG)*
Roger Colville LEE	01.07.1991	*JK Tallinna Kalev (EST)*
Jordan OUTERBRIDGE	26.02.1996	*Hamilton Parish Workman's Club*
Knory SCOTT	06.06.1999	*Hastings United FC (ENG)*
Lejuan SIMMONS	07.04.1993	*Robin Hood FC Pembroke*
London STEEDE-JACKSON	30.12.1994	*BAA Wanderers Hamilton*
Trey TUCKER	20.01.1996	*Devonshire Recreation Club Cougars*

Forwards

Keishon BEAN	19.02.2000	*North Village Community Club Rams*
Justin BELL	20.03.1998	*Robin Hood FC Pembroke*
Chae BRANGMAN	12.02.1995	*Robin Hood FC Pembroke*
Justin DONAWA	27.06.1996	*Solihull Moors FC (ENG)*
Kole HALL	22.08.1998	*Radcliffe FC (ENG)*
Zeiko Troy Jahmiko LEWIS	06.04.1995	*Charleston Battery (USA)*
Cecoy ROBINSON	10.10.1987	*Pembroke Hamilton Club Zebras*
Luke ROBINSON	20.10.1998	*Staines Town FC (ENG)*
Tokia Enrique Zidane RUSSELL Jr.	05.02.2000	*Unattached*
Jonté Jahki SMITH	10.07.1994	*Woking FC (ENG)*
Nakhi WELLS	01.06.1990	*Bristol City FC (ENG)*

National coaches

Kyle Lavince LIGHTBOURNE		29.09.1968

BONAIRE

The Country:	The FA:
Bonaire	Federashon Futbòl Boneriano
Capital: Kralendijk	P/A Kaya Akuamarin 4, Kralendijk
Surface: 294 km²	Year of Formation: 1960
Population: 20,104 [2019]	Member of FIFA since: *not affiliated*
Time: UTC-4	Member of CONCACAF since: 2013

Bonaire is a special municipality within the country of the Netherlands.

NATIONAL TEAM RECORDS

First international match: 15.11.2013: Suriname – Bonaire 2-0
Most international caps: Not known
Most international goals: Not known

CONCACAF GOLD CUP		FIFA WORLD CUP	
1991	-	1930	-
1993	-	1934	-
1996	-	1938	-
1998	-	1950	-
2000	-	1954	-
2002	-	1958	-
2003	-	1962	-
2005	-	1966	-
2007	-	1970	-
2009	-	1974	-
2011	-	1978	-
2013	-	1982	-
2015	Qualifiers	1986	-
2017	Did not enter	1990	-
2019	Qualifiers	1994	-
2021	Qualifiers	1998	-
		2002	-
		2006	-
		2010	-
		2014	-
		2018	-

F.I.F.A. CONFEDERATIONS CUP 1992-2017

None

OLYMPIC FOOTBALL TOURNAMENTS 1900-2016	
None	

CCCF (Confederación Centroamericana y del Caribe de Fútbol) CHAMPIONSHIPS 1941-1961	
None	
CONCACAF CHAMPIONSHIPS 1963-1989	
None	
NAFC (North American Football Confederation) CHAMPIONSHIPS 1947-1991	
None	

CONCACAF NATIONS LEAGUE	
2019-2020	League C

CARIBBEAN CHAMPIONSHIPS 1989-2017			
1989	-	1999	-
1991	-	2001	-
1992	-	2005	-
1993	-	2007	-
1994	-	2008	-
1995	-	2010	-
1996	-	2012	-
1997	-	2014	
1998	-	2017	Did not enter

BONAIRE CLUB HONOURS IN CONCACAF CLUB COMPETITIONS:

CONCACAF Champions Cup / CONCACAF Champions League 1962-2020	
None	
CONCACAF Cup Winners Cup 1991-1995	
None	
Copa Interamericana 1968-1998	
None	

NATIONAL COMPETITIONS
TABLE OF HONOURS

	CHAMPIONS
1960/1961	SV Deportivo
1961/1962	SV Estrellas Nort Saliña Kunuku Bieu
1962/1963	SV Estrellas Nort Saliña Kunuku Bieu
1963/1964	SV Estrellas Nort Saliña Kunuku Bieu
1964/1965	*No competition*
1965/1966	SV Estrellas Nort Saliña Kunuku Bieu
1966/1967	*No competition*
1967/1968	SV Vitesse Antriòl
1968/1969	SV Vitesse Antriòl
1969/1970	SV Vitesse Antriòl
1970/1971	SV Vitesse Antriòl
1971/1972	SV Real Rincon
1973	SV Real Rincon
1973/1974	*No competition*
1974/1975	SV Estrellas Nort Saliña Kunuku Bieu
1976	SV Juventus Antriòl
1977	SV Juventus Antriòl
1978	SV Estrellas Nort Saliña Kunuku Bieu
1979	SV Real Rincon
1980/1981	SV Vitesse Antriòl
1982	*No competition*
1983	SV Uruguay Antriòl
1984	SV Juventus Antriòl
1984/1985	SV Juventus Antriòl
1986	SV Real Rincon
1987	SV Juventus Antriòl
1988	SV Estrellas Nort Saliña Kunuku Bieu
1989	SV Juventus Antriòl
1990/1991	SV Vitesse Antriòl
1992	SV Juventus Antriòl
1993	SV Vitesse Antriòl
1994	SV Juventus Antriòl
1995	SV Vespo Rincon
1996	SV Real Rincon
1997	SV Real Rincon
1998/1999	SV Estrellas Nort Saliña Kunuku Bieu
1999/2000	SV Estrellas Nort Saliña Kunuku Bieu
2000/2001	SV Estrellas Nort Saliña Kunuku Bieu
2001/2002	SV Estrellas Nort Saliña Kunuku Bieu
2002/2003	SV Real Rincon
2003/2004	SV Real Rincon
2004/2005	SV Juventus Antriòl
2005/2006	SV Real Rincon
2006/2007	SV Vespo Rincon
2007/2008	SV Juventus Antriòl
2009	SV Juventus Antriòl
2010	SV Juventus Antriòl

2011	*No competition*
2012	SV Juventus Antriòl
2013	SV Juventus Antriòl
2014	SV Real Rincon
2015/2016	SV Atlétiko Flamingo Nikiboko
2016/2017	SV Real Rincon
2017/2018	SV Real Rincon
2018/2019	SV Real Rincon
2019/2020	*Championship abandoned*
2021	*Championship suspended*

NATIONAL CHAMPIONSHIP
Bonaire League / Kampionato 2021

The 2021 championship started on 17.02.2021, being interrupted later due to COVID-19 pandemic. It is not clear when the competition will end.

NATIONAL TEAM
INTERNATIONAL MATCHES 2020/2021

No international activities for the Bonaire national team during the 2020/2021 season.

BRITISH VIRGIN ISLANDS

The Country:	
British Virgin Islands	
Capital: Road Town	
Surface: 153 km²	
Population: 30,030 [2019]	
Time: UTC-4	

The FA:
British Virgin Islands Football Association
East End/Long Look Stadium, Tortola
Year of Formation: 1974
Member of FIFA since: 1996
Member of CONCACAF since: 1994

NATIONAL TEAM RECORDS

First international match: 10.05.1991, Basseterrre (SKN): Cayman Islands - British Virgin Isl. 2-1
Most international caps: Carlos Septus – 21 caps (since 2011)
Most international goals: Avondale Williams – 5 goals / 15 caps (2000-2012)

CONCACAF GOLD CUP	
1991	Qualifiers
1993	Qualifiers
1996	*Withdrew*
1998	Qualifiers
2000	Qualifiers
2002	Qualifiers
2003	Qualifiers
2005	Qualifiers
2007	Withdrew
2009	Qualifiers
2011	Qualifiers
2013	Qualifiers
2015	Qualifiers
2017	Qualifiers
2019	Qualifiers
2021	Qualifiers

FIFA WORLD CUP	
1930	-
1934	-
1938	-
1950	-
1954	-
1958	-
1962	-
1966	-
1970	-
1974	-
1978	-
1982	-
1986	-
1990	-
1994	-
1998	Did not enter
2002	Qualifiers
2006	Qualifiers
2010	Qualifiers
2014	Qualifiers
2018	Qualifiers

F.I.F.A. CONFEDERATIONS CUP 1992-2017
None

OLYMPIC FOOTBALL TOURNAMENTS 1900-2016	
None	

CCCF (Confederación Centroamericana y del Caribe de Fútbol) CHAMPIONSHIPS 1941-1961	
None	

CONCACAF CHAMPIONSHIPS 1963-1989	
None	

CONCACAF NATIONS LEAGUE	
2019-2020	League C

CARIBBEAN CHAMPIONSHIPS 1989-2017			
1989	Qualifiers	1999	Qualifiers
1991	Qualifiers	2001	Qualifiers
1992	Qualifiers	2005	Qualifiers
1993	Qualifiers	2007	*Withdrew*
1994	Qualifiers	2008	Qualifiers
1995	Did not enter	2010	Qualifiers
1996	Did not enter	2012	Qualifiers
1997	Qualifiers	2014	Qualifiers
1998	Qualifiers	2017	Qualifiers

BRITISH VIRGIN ISLANDS CLUB HONOURS IN CONCACAF CLUB COMPETITIONS:

CONCACAF Champions Cup / CONCACAF Champions League 1962-2020
None
CONCACAF League 2017-2020
None
Caribbean Club Championship 1997-2021
None
CONCACAF Cup Winners Cup 1991-1995*
None
Copa Interamericana 1968-1998*
None

defunct competitions

NATIONAL COMPETITIONS
TABLE OF HONOURS

	TORTOLA CHAMPIONS	VIRGIN GORDA CHAMPIONS
1970	The Bronze	-
1971	*Not known*	-
1972	*Not known*	-
1973	*Not known*	-
1974	*Not known*	-
1975	*Not known*	-
1976	*Not known*	-
1977	*Not known*	-
1978	*Not known*	-
1979	SKB Budweiser	-
1980	Queen City Strikers	-
1981	SKB Budweiser	-
1982	International Motors	-
1983	International Motors	-
1984	SKB Budweiser	-
1985	SKB Budweiser	-
1986	SKB Budweiser	-
1987	SKB Budweiser	-
1988	*Championship abandoned*	-
1989	Popeye Bombers	-
1990	Jolly Rogers Strikers	-
1991	Hiaroun	-
1992	Hiaroun	-
1993	Interfada	-
1994	Interfada	-
1995	Interfada	-
1996	Black Lions Road Town	Spice United
1997	Interfada	Beverly Hills
1997/1998	BDO Binder Stingers Road Town	United Kickers
1998/1999	Veterans Road Town	*Not known*
1999/2000	HBA Panthers	Rangers
2000/2001	HBA Panthers	-
2001	Future Stars United Road Town	Rangers
2002	HBA Panthers	-
2003	Old Madrid FC	Rangers (2002/2003)
2004	Valencia I FC	Rangers
2005	*Championship abandoned*	Rangers (2004/2005); Hairoun Stars (2005)
2006	*No competition*	Rangers
2007	*No competition*	Rangers
2008	*No competition*	Hairoun Stars
2009	*No competition*	*No competition*
	BVI Football Associations Football League	
2009/2010	Islanders FC Tortola	
2010/2011	Islanders FC Tortola	
2011/2012	Islanders FC Tortola	
2012/2013	Islanders FC Tortola	
2013/2014	Islanders FC Tortola	

2014/2015	Islanders FC Tortola
2015/2016	Sugar Boys FC Virgin Gorda
2016/2017	Islanders FC Tortola
2018	One Love United FC Road Town
2018/2019	*No competition*
2019/2020	Islanders FC Tortola
2020/2021	*Competition not yet finished*

NATIONAL CHAMPIONSHIP
BVIFA National League 2020/2021

The league was suspended between 16.03.2020 and 25.07.2020 due to Covid-19 pandemic. The rest of competition was rescheduled, but FC Sea Argo (who already forfeited four games and lost other six) withdrew from competition. Here the final table to make complete missing data from last year's yearbook.

1.	**Islanders FC Tortola**	19	15	2	2	45 - 16	47
2.	Wolues FC Road Town	19	13	3	3	53 - 21	42
3.	Sugar Boys FC Virgin Gorda	19	11	2	6	45 - 21	35
4.	Panthers FC Road Town	19	9	2	8	43 - 37	29
5.	One Caribbean FC Spanish Town	19	9	2	8	44 - 42	29
6.	Lion Heart FC Parham Town	19	6	7	6	32 - 31	25
7.	One Love United FC Road Town	19	6	3	10	31 - 39	21
8.	Virgin Gorda United	19	5	5	9	25 - 31	20
9.	Rebels FC Road Town	19	6	1	12	32 - 53	19
10.	Old Madrid FC	19	5	3	11	43 - 48	18
11.	FC Sea Argo (*withdrew*)	10	0	0	10	1 - 55	0

NATIONAL CHAMPIONSHIP
BVIFA National League / Super Six League 2021/2022

Regular Stage

1.	Sugar Boys FC Virgin Gorda	9	7	1	1	17 - 7	22
2.	Islanders FC Tortola	9	7	0	2	18 - 7	21
3.	Wolues FC Road Town	9	6	1	2	23 - 11	19
4.	Lion Heart FC Parham Town	9	5	2	2	19 - 14	17
5.	Virgin Gorda United	9	3	2	4	11 - 15	11
6.	Panthers FC Road Town	9	3	1	5	15 - 17	10
7.	One Caribbean FC Spanish Town	9	2	4	3	10 - 12	10
8.	Old Madrid FC	9	2	1	6	13 - 23	7
9.	Rebels FC Road Town	9	1	2	6	11 - 20	5
10.	One Love United FC Road Town	9	1	2	6	10 - 21	5

Top-6 teams were qualified for the Second Stage (Super Six).

Super Six

1.	Sugar Boys FC Virgin Gorda	5	4	0/0	1	13 - 4	12
2.	Lion Heart FC Parham Town	5	4	0/0	1	11 - 8	12
3.	Virgin Gorda United	4	1	1/0	2	4 - 6	6
4.	Panthers FC Road Town	4	0	2/0	2	5 - 10	6
5.	Wolues FC Road Town	5	1	0/1	3	6 - 8	3
6.	Islanders FC Tortola	5	1	0/2	2	6 - 9	3

Matches that ended in a draw were decided by penalty shoot-outs (3 points for the winner).
Top-2 were qualified for the Championship Final.

Championship Final [27.06.2021	
Sugar Boys FC Virgin Gorda - Lion Heart FC Parham Town	3-3; 5-4 pen
Lion Heart FC Parham Town - Sugar Boys FC Virgin Gorda	*postponed*

Please note: the second leg were postponed indefinitely due to COVID-19 pandemic.

Super Six League 2020/2021 Champions: *to be determined*

NATIONAL TEAM
INTERNATIONAL MATCHES 2020/2021

27.03.2021	Willemstad	*British Virgin Islands - Guatemala*	*0-3(0-2)*	*(WCQ)*
30.03.2021	Willemstad	*Saint Vincent and the Grenadines - British Virgin Islands*	*3-0(2-0)*	*(WCQ)*
02.06.2021	Ciudad de Guatemala	*Cuba - British Virgin Islands*	*5-0(1-0)*	*(WCQ)*
05.06.2021	Ciudad de Guatemala	*British Virgin Islands - Curaçao*	*0-8(0-6)*	*(WCQ)*

27.03.2021, 22nd FIFA World Cup Qualifiers, CONCACAF First Round
Stadion „Ergilio Hato", Willemstad (Curaçao)
Referee: Óscar Donaldo Moncada (Honduras)
BRITISH VIRGIN ISLANDS - GUATEMALA   0-3(0-2)
VGB: Phillip Jules Graham, Joshua Bertie, Jerry Junior Wiltshire, Charles Robert Medway [*sent off 88*], Jamie Wilson, T'Sharne Gallimore, Kristian Javier Samuel (69.Giovanni Grant), Carlos Septus, William Robert Green (75.Miguel Ryan Marshall), Kevin Fisher-Daniel (61.Luka Chalwell), Tyler Cecil Hornby-Forbes. Trainer: Daniel Neville (England).

30.03.2021, 22nd FIFA World Cup Qualifiers, CONCACAF First Round
Stadion „Ergilio Hato", Willemstad (Curaçao)
Referee: Henry Alberto Bejarano Matarrita (Costa Rica)
SAINT VINCENT AND THE GRENADINES - BRITISH VIRGIN ISLANDS   3-0(2-0)
VGB: Phillip Jules Graham, Joshua Bertie, Jerry Junior Wiltshire, Giovanni Grant (46.Luka Chalwell), Jamie Wilson, T'Sharne Gallimore, Kristian Javier Samuel (90.Justin Smith), Carlos Septus (90.Ikyjah Williams), William Robert Green (67.Miguel Ryan Marshall), Kevin Fisher-Daniel (46.Luca Reich), Tyler Cecil Hornby-Forbes. Trainer: Daniel Neville (England).

02.06.2021, 22nd FIFA World Cup Qualifiers, CONCACAF First Round
Estadio "Doroteo Guamuch Flores", Ciudad de Guatemala (Guatemala)
Referee: Jose Raul Torres Rivera (Puerto Rico)
CUBA - BRITISH VIRGIN ISLANDS   5-0(1-0)
VGB: Phillip Jules Graham, Joshua Bertie, Giovanni Grant, Jamie Wilson, T'Sharne Gallimore, Kristian Javier Samuel (41.Luca Reich), Miguel Ryan Marshall, Luka Chalwell (80.Charley McMillan-López), Carlos Septus (80.Denvin Jones), Kevin Fisher-Daniel (75.Justin Smith), Tyler Cecil Hornby-Forbes. Trainer: Daniel Neville (England).

05.06.2021, 22nd FIFA World Cup Qualifiers, CONCACAF First Round
Estadio El Trébol, Ciudad de Guatemala (Guatemala)
Referee: William Anderson (Puerto Rico)
BRITISH VIRGIN ISLANDS - CURAÇAO 0-8(0-6)
VGB: Phillip Jules Graham (77.William Butler), Joshua Bertie, Giovanni Grant (65.Kevin Fisher-Daniel), Jamie Wilson (17.Justin Smith; 77.Denvin Jones), T'Sharne Gallimore, Kristian Javier Samuel, Miguel Ryan Marshall, Luka Chalwell, Luca Reich (77.Charley McMillan-López), Carlos Septus, Tyler Cecil Hornby-Forbes. Trainer: Daniel Neville (England).

NATIONAL TEAM PLAYERS 2020/2021

Name	DOB	Club
Goalkeepers		
William BUTLER	04.06.2004	*Poole Town FC (ENG)*
Phillip Jules GRAHAM	11.09.2000	*Panthers FC Road Town*
Defenders		
Joshua BERTIE	09.10.1996	*Andover Town FC (ENG)*
Giovanni GRANT	28.12.2002	*Old Madrid FC*
Charles Robert MEDWAY	02.06.2002	*Poole Town FC (ENG)*
Ikyjah WILLIAMS	14.04.2003	*Rebels FC Road Town*
Jerry Junior WILTSHIRE	04.02.1996	*Maidenhead United FC (ENG)*
Midfielders		
Luka CHALWELL	11.04.2004	*Poole Town FC (ENG)*
T'Sharne GALLIMORE	20.08.2000	*Chesham United FC (ENG)*
Kristian JAVIER Samuel	07.06.1996	*Lionsbridge FC (USA)*
Miguel Ryan MARSHALL	11.04.2002	*Poole Town FC (ENG)*
Luca REICH	29.07.2003	*Wolues FC Road Town*
Carlos SEPTUS	16.06.1991	*One Caribbean FC Spanish Town*
Jamie WILSON	31.01.1996	*Bridgwater United FC (ENG)*
Forwards		
Kevin FISHER-DANIEL	27.03.1995	*Islanders FC Tortola*
William Robert GREEN	05.09.1997	*Wolues FC Road Town*
Tyler Cecil HORNBY-FORBES	18.04.2002	*Poole Town FC (ENG)*
Denvin JONES		*Rebels FC Road Town*
Charley MCMILLAN-LÓPEZ	27.03.1996	*Ashford United FC (ENG)*
Justin SMITH	12.08.2003	*One Love United FC Road Town*
National coaches		
Daniel NEVILLE (England) [from 20.03.2021]		18.11.1978

CANADA

The Country:	The FA:
Canada Capital: Ottawa Surface: 9,984,670 km² Population: 38,048,738 [2021] Time: UTC -3.5 to -8	Canadian Soccer Association Place Soccer Canada, 237 Metcalfe Street, Ottawa, Ontario K2P 1R2 Year of Formation: 1912 Member of FIFA since: 1913 Member of CONCACAF since: 1961

NATIONAL TEAM RECORDS

First international match: 28.11.1885, East Newark: United States - Canada 0-1
Most international caps: Julien Bobby de Guzman – 89 caps (since 2002)
Most international goals: Dwayne Anthony De Rosario – 22 goals / 81 caps (1997-2015)

CONCACAF GOLD CUP		FIFA WORLD CUP	
1991	Final Tournament (Group Stage)	1930	Did not enter
1993	Final Tournament (Group Stage)	1934	Did not enter
1996	Final Tournament (Group Stage)	1938	Did not enter
1998	*Withdrew*	1950	Did not enter
2000	**Final Tournament (Winners)**	1954	Did not enter
2002	Final Tournament (3rd Place)	1958	Qualifiers
2003	Final Tournament (Group Stage)	1962	*Withdrew*
2005	Final Tournament (Group Stage)	1966	Did not enter
2007	Final Tournament (Semi-Finals)	1970	Qualifiers
2009	Final Tournament (Quarter-Finals)	1974	Qualifiers
2011	Final Tournament (Group Stage)	1978	Qualifiers
2013	Final Tournament (Group Stage)	1982	Qualifiers
2015	Final Tournament (Group Stage)	1986	Final Tournament (Group Stage)
2017	Final Tournament (Quarter-Finals)	1990	Qualifiers
2019	Final Tournament (Quarter-Finals)	1994	Qualifiers
2021	Final Tournament (*to be played*)	1998	Qualifiers
		2002	Qualifiers
		2006	Qualifiers
		2010	Qualifiers
		2014	Qualifiers
		2018	Qualifiers

F.I.F.A. CONFEDERATIONS CUP 1992-2017

2001 (Group Stage)

OLYMPIC FOOTBALL TOURNAMENTS 1908-2016							
1908	-	1948	-	1972	Qualifiers	1996	Qualifiers
1912	-	1952	-	1976	FT/Group Stage	2000	Qualifiers
1920	-	1956	-	1980	Qualifiers	2004	Qualifiers
1924	-	1960	-	1984	Quarter-Finals	2008	Qualifiers
1928	-	1964	-	1988	Qualifiers	2012	Qualifiers
1936	-	1968	Qualifiers	1992	Qualifiers	2016	Qualifiers

CCCF (Confederación Centroamericana y del Caribe de Fútbol) CHAMPIONSHIPS 1941-1961
None

NAFC (North American Football Confederation) CHAMPIONSHIPS 1947-1991
1990 (Winners), 1991

CONCACAF CHAMPIONSHIPS 1963-1989
1977, 1981, **1985 (Winners)**

CONCACAF NATIONS LEAGUE	
2019-2020	League A

CANADIAN CLUB HONOURS IN CONCACAF CLUB COMPETITIONS:

CONCACAF Champions Cup / CONCACAF Champions League 1962-2020
None

CONCACAF League 2017-2020
None

Caribbean Club Championship 1997-2021
None

CONCACAF Cup Winners Cup 1991-1995*
None

Copa Interamericana 1968-1998*
None

*defunct competitions

NATIONAL COMPETITIONS
TABLE OF HONOURS

Canadian National Soccer League

1922	Toronto Ulster United
1923	Toronto Ulster United
1924	Toronto Ulster United
1925	*No competition*
1926	Toronto Ulster United
1927	*No competition*
1928	Montral NCR
1929	Montreal CNR
1930	Toronto Scottish
1931	Toronto Scottish
1932	Toronto Ulster United
1933	Toronto Ulster United
1934	Toronto Ulster United
1935	Frood Mines Tigers
1936	Montreal Carsteel
1937	Toronto British Consols
1938	Montreal Victorias
1939	Toronto British Consols
1940	Montreal Carsteel
1941	Toronto Ulster United
1942	*No competition*
1943	*No competition*
1944	*No competition*
1945	*No competition*
1946	*No competition*
1947	Montréal Stelco
1948	Montreal Carsteel
1949	Toronto Canadians
1950	Hamilton Westinghouse
1951	Toronto Saint Andrews
1952	Toronto East End Canadians
1953	Toronto Ukrainians
1954	Toronto Ukrainians
1955	Toronto Ukrainians
1956	Toronto Polish White Eagles
1957	Toronto Italia
1958	Montreal Hungaria
1959	Montreal Cantalia
1960	Toronto Italia
1961	Toronto Roma
1962	Toronto Olympia
1963	Toronto Ukrainians
1964	Toronto Ukrainians
1965	Toronto Ukrainians
1966	Windsor Teutonia
1967	Hamilton Primos
1968	Sudbury Italian Flyers
1969	Toronto First Portuguese
1970	CNSC Toronto Croatia
1971	CNSC Toronto Croatia
1972	CNSC Toronto Croatia
1973	CNSC Toronto Croatia
1974	Serbia White Eagles
1975	Toronto Italia
1976	Toronto Italia
1977	Montréal Castors
1978	Montréal Castors
1979	Toronto First Portuguese
1980	Toronto Falcons
1981	Hamilton Steelers
1982	Toronto Italia
1983	*No competition*
1984	Toronto Italia
1985	London Marconi
1986	Toronto Blizzard
1987	Windsor Wheels
1988	Toronto Italia
1989	Toronto Italia
1990	Toronto First Portuguese
1991	Scarbourough International
1992	Woodbridge Azurri
1993	St. Catharines Roma
1994	Toronto Italia
1995	St. Catharines Wolves
1996	Toronto Italia
1997	St. Catharines Wolves

Canadian Professional Soccer League

1998	Toronto Olympians

Canadian Premier Soccer League

1999	Toronto Olympians
2000	CNSC Toronto Croatia
2001	St. Catharines Roma Wolves
2002	Ottawa Wizards
2003	Brampton Hitmen
2004	CNSC Toronto Croatia
2005	Oakville Blue Devils

Canadian Soccer League

2006	Italia Shooters SC
2007	CNSC Toronto Croatia
2008	Serbian White Eagles FC
2009	Trois-Rivières Attak FC
2010	Brantford Galaxy SC
2011	CNSC Toronto Croatia
2012	CNSC Toronto Croatia
2013	Soccer Club Waterloo Region
2014	York Region Shooters
2015	CNSC Toronto Croatia
2016	Serbian White Eagles FC
2017	York Region Shooters
2018	FC Vorkuta Toronto
2019	Scarborough SC
2020	FC Vorkuta Vaughan

Canadian Soccer Championship

2008	Montreal Impact
2009	Toronto FC
2010	Toronto FC
2011	Toronto FC
2012	Toronto FC
2013	Montreal Impact
2014	Montreal Impact
2015	Vancouver Whitecaps FC
2016	Toronto FC
2017	Toronto FC
2018	Toronto FC
2019	Montreal Impact
2020	*Not yet finished*

Canadian Premier League

2019	Forge FC Hamilton
2020	Forge FC Hamilton

CANADIAN SOCCER CHAMPIONSHIP 2020

On 13.08.2020, the Canadian Soccer Association announced that the tournament will consist solely of a single final match to be held between the winner of the head-to-head series between a Canadian team from Major League Soccer and the champion of the Canadian Premier League.

First Stage

1. **Toronto FC**	6	4	0	2	9	-	5	12
2. Montreal Impact	6	3	0	3	9	-	8	9
3. Vancouver Whitecaps FC	6	2	0	4	8	-	13	6

Until 11.03.2021, the final match was multiple times postponed.

On March 11, 2021, it was announced that the final would be postponed beyond March and that Toronto FC would automatically qualify for the CONCACAF Champions League.

Championship Final

Forge FC Hamilton - Toronto FC   *To be played*

NATIONAL CHAMPIONSHIP
Canadian Premier League 2020

First Stage

1. Cavalry FC Calgary	7	4	1	2	10	-	7	13
2. HFX Wanderers FC Halifax	7	3	3	1	12	-	7	12
3. Forge FC Hamilton	7	3	3	1	13	-	9	12
4. Pacific FC Greater Victoria	7	3	2	2	10	-	8	11
5. York9 FC Toronto	7	2	4	1	8	-	7	10
6. Valour FC Winnipeg	7	2	2	3	8	-	9	8
7. Atlético Ottawa	7	2	2	3	7	-	12	8
8. FC Edmonton	7	0	1	6	5	-	14	1

Top-4 teams were qualified for the Group Stage.

Group Stage

1. Forge FC Hamilton	3	2	1	0	4	-	1	7
2. HFX Wanderers FC Halifax	3	1	1	1	3	-	7	4
3. Cavalry FC Calgary	3	1	0	2	4	-	4	3
4. Pacific FC Greater Victoria	3	1	0	2	6	-	5	3

Top-2 teams were qualified for the Championship Final.

Championship Final [19.09.2020]

19.09.2020, Alumni Field, Charlottetown; Referee: Juam Márquez
Forge FC Hamilton - HFX Wanderers FC Halifax   2-0 (0-0)

2020 Canadian Premier League Champions: **Forge FC Hamilton**

Best goalscorer 2020: Akeem Garcia (TRI, HFX Wanderers FC Halifax) – 6 goals

THE CLUBS

ATLÉTICO OTTAWA
Year of Formation: 2020
Stadium: TD Place, Ottawa (24,000)

CAVALRY FOOTBALL CLUB CALGARY
Year of Formation: 2018
Stadium: ATCO Field, Calgary (5,288)

FOOTBALL CLUB EDMONTON
Year of Formation: 2010
Stadium: Clarke Stadium, Edmonton (5,100)

FORGE FOOTBALL CLUB HAMILTON
Year of Formation: 2017
Stadium: "Tim Hortons" Field, Hamilton (10,016)

HFX WANDERERS FOOTBALL CLUB HALIFAX
Year of Formation: 2018
Stadium: Wanderers Grounds, Halifax (6,200)

PACIFIC FOOTBALL CLUB GREATER VICTORIA
Year of Formation: 2018
Stadium: Westhills Stadium, Langford (6,200)

VALOUR FOOTBALL CLUB WINNIPEG
Year of Formation: 2017
Stadium: IG Field Stadium, Winnipeg (10,000)

YORK9 FOOTBALL CLUB TORONTO
Year of Formation: 2018
Stadium: York Lions Stadium, Toronto (8,000)

NATIONAL TEAM
INTERNATIONAL MATCHES 2020/2021

25.03.2021	Orlando	Canada - Bermuda	5-1(2-0)	(WCQ)
29.03.2021	Bradenton	Cayman Islands - Canada	0-11(0-6)	(WCQ)
05.06.2021	Bradenton	Aruba - Canada	0-7(0-3)	(WCQ)
08.06.2021	Bridgeview	Canada - Suriname	4-0(1-0)	(WCQ)
12.06.2021	Port-au-Prince	Haiti - Canada	0-1(0-1)	(WCQ)
15.06.2021	Bridgeview	Canada - Haiti	3-0(0-0)	(WCQ)

25.03.2021, 22nd FIFA World Cup Qualifiers, CONCACAF First Round
Exploria Stadium, Orlando (United States)
Referee: Armando Villareal (United States)
CANADA - BERMUDA   **5-1(2-0)**
CAN: Milan Borjan, Steven de Sousa Vitória, Samuel Ayomide Adekugbe (77.David Wotherspoon), Alphonso Boyle Davies, Kamal Anthony Miller, Atiba Hutchinson, Stephen Antunes Eustáquio (77.Samuel Piette), Richmond Laryea (69.Alistair Johnston), David Wayne Hoilett (77.Theodor Alexander Corbeanu), Lucas Daniel Cavallini (70.Liam Alan Millar), Cyle Christopher Larin. Trainer: John Herdman (England).
Goals: Cyle Christopher Larin (19, 27), Richmond Laryea (53), Cyle Christopher Larin (69), Theodor Alexander Corbeanu (81).

29.03.2021, 22nd FIFA World Cup Qualifiers, CONCACAF First Round
IMG Academy, Bradenton (United States)
Referee: Ted Unkel (United States)
CAYMAN ISLANDS - CANADA   **0-11(0-6)**
CAN: Maxime Crépeau, Ricardo José Araújo Ferreira, Frank Sturing, Alphonso Boyle Davies, David Wotherspoon, Samuel Piette (68.Stephen Antunes Eustáquio), Mark-Anthony Kaye, Alistair Johnston (68.Richmond Laryea), Cyle Christopher Larin (60.Lucas Daniel Cavallini), Liam Alan Millar (70.Samuel Ayomide Adekugbe), Theodor Alexander Corbeanu (61.David Wayne Hoilett). Trainer: John Herdman (England).
Goals: Frank Sturing (6), Cyle Christopher Larin (14), David Wotherspoon (25), Alphonso Boyle Davies (28 penalty), Mark-Anthony Kaye (33), Alistair Johnston (43), Mark-Anthony Kaye (63), Lucas Daniel Cavallini (68), Alphonso Boyle Davies (73), Lucas Daniel Cavallini (74, 76).

05.06.2021, 22nd FIFA World Cup Qualifiers, CONCACAF First Round
IMG Academy, Bradenton (United States)
Referee: Marco Antonio Ortíz Nava (Mexico)
ARUBA - CANADA   **0-7(0-3)**
CAN: Dayne St. Clair, Steven de Sousa Vitória, Samuel Ayomide Adekugbe (66.Alphonso Boyle Davies), Frank Sturing, David Wotherspoon (66.Jonathan Christian David), Mark-Anthony Kaye, Liam Fraser, Tajon Buchanan, David Wayne Hoilett (34.Zachary Bichotte Paul Brault-Guillard), Lucas Daniel Cavallini (73.Cyle Christopher Larin), Liam Alan Millar (46.Theodor Alexander Corbeanu). Trainer: John Herdman (England).
Goals: Lucas Daniel Cavallini (18), David Wayne Hoilett (20 penalty), Lucas Daniel Cavallini (45+3), Zachary Bichotte Paul Brault-Guillard (49), Alphonso Boyle Davies (78), Cyle Christopher Larin (88), Jonathan Christian David (90).

08.06.2021, 22nd FIFA World Cup Qualifiers, CONCACAF First Round
SeatGeek Stadium, Bridgeview (United States)
Referee: Nima Saghafi (United States)
CANADA - SURINAME **4-0(1-0)**
CAN: Milan Borjan, Denie Henry, Richmond Laryea (81.Tajon Buchanan), Scott Fitzgerald Kennedy, Alistair Johnston, Samuel Piette, Jonathan Osorio (66.Mark-Anthony Kaye), Stephen Antunes Eustáquio, Cyle Christopher Larin (66.Lucas Daniel Cavallini), Alphonso Boyle Davies (81.Samuel Ayomide Adekugbe), Jonathan Christian David (81.David Wotherspoon). Trainer: John Herdman (England).
Goals: Alphonso Boyle Davies (37), Jonathan Christian David (59, 72, 77 penalty).

12.06.2021, 22nd FIFA World Cup Qualifiers, CONCACAF Second Round
Stade "Sylvio Cator", Port-au-Prince
Referee: John Francis Pitti Hernández (Panama)
HAITI - CANADA **0-1(0-1)**
CAN: Milan Borjan, Steven de Sousa Vitória, Richmond Laryea (78.Tajon Buchanan), Alphonso Boyle Davies, Scott Fitzgerald Kennedy, Alistair Johnston, Jonathan Osorio (82.Samuel Piette), Mark-Anthony Kaye (62.Samuel Ayomide Adekugbe), Stephen Antunes Eustáquio, Cyle Christopher Larin (78.Doneil Jor-Dee Ashley Henry), Jonathan Christian David (81.Lucas Daniel Cavallini). Trainer: John Herdman (England).
Goal: Cyle Christopher Larin (14).

15.06.2021, 22nd FIFA World Cup Qualifiers, CONCACAF Second Round
SeatGeek Stadium, Bridgeview (United States)
Referee: Rubiel Vasquez (United States)
CANADA - HAITI **3-0(0-0)**
CAN: Milan Borjan, Steven de Sousa Vitória, Doneil Jor-Dee Ashley Henry, Alphonso Boyle Davies (82.David Wayne Hoilett), Scott Fitzgerald Kennedy, Alistair Johnston, Jonathan Osorio (65.David Wotherspoon), Mark-Anthony Kaye, Stephen Antunes Eustáquio, Cyle Christopher Larin (75.Samuel Ayomide Adekugbe), Jonathan Christian David (82.Tajon Buchanan). Trainer: John Herdman (England).
Goals: Josué Duverger (46 own goal), Cyle Christopher Larin (74), David Wayne Hoilett (89).

NATIONAL TEAM PLAYERS 2020/2021

Name	DOB	Club
Goalkeepers		
Milan BORJAN	23.10.1987	FK Crvena zvezda Beograd (SRB)
Maxime CRÉPEAU	11.05.1994	Vancouver Whitecaps FC
Dayne ST. CLAIR	09.05.1997	Minnesota United FC (USA)
Defenders		
Samuel Ayomide ADEKUGBE	16.01.1995	Vålerenga Fotball Oslo (NOR)
Zachary Bichotte Paul BRAULT-GUILLARD	30.12.1998	CF Montréal
Ricardo José Araújo FERREIRA	25.11.1992	SC Farense (POR)
Doneil Jor-Dee Ashley HENRY	20.04.1993	Suwon Samsung Bluewings (KOR)
Alistair JOHNSTON	08.10.1998	Nashville SC (USA)
Scott Fitzgerald KENNEDY	31.03.1997	SSV Jahn Regensburg (GER)
Richmond LARYEA	07.01.1995	Toronto FC
Kamal Anthony MILLER	16.05.1997	CF Montréal
Frank STURING	29.05.1997	FC Den Bosch (NED)
Steven de Sousa VITÓRIA	11.01.1987	Moreirense FC (POR)
Midfielders		
Alphonso Boyle DAVIES	02.11.2000	FC Bayern München (GER)
Stephen Antunes EUSTÁQUIO	21.12.1996	FC Paços de Ferreira (POR)
Liam FRASER	13.02.1998	Columbus Crew SC (USA)
Atiba HUTCHINSON	08.02.1983	Beşiktaş JK İstanbul (TUR)
Mark-Anthony KAYE	02.12.1994	Los Angeles FC (USA)
Jonathan OSORIO	12.06.1992	Toronto FC
Samuel PIETTE	12.11.1994	CF Montréal
David WOTHERSPOON	16.01.1990	St. Johnstone FC (SCO)
Forwards		
Tajon BUCHANAN	08.02.1999	New England Revolution (USA)
Lucas Daniel CAVALLINI	28.12.1992	Vancouver Whitecaps FC
Theodor Alexander CORBEANU	17.05.2002	Wolverhampton Wanderers FC (ENG)
Jonathan Christian DAVID	14.01.2000	Lille OSC (FRA)
David Wayne "Junior" HOILETT	05.06.1990	Cardiff City FC (WAL)
Cyle Christopher LARIN	17.04.1995	Beşiktaş JK İstanbul (TUR)
Liam Alan MILLAR	27.09.1999	Charlton Athletic FC (ENG); 31.05.21-> Liverpool FC U23 (ENG)
National coaches		
John HERDMAN (England) [from 08.01.2018]		19.07.1975

CAYMAN ISLANDS

The Country:	The FA:
Cayman Islands Capital: George Town Surface: 264 km² Population: 65,813 [2019] Time: UTC-5	Cayman Islands Football Association Cayman Centre of Excellence, Poindexter Road P.O. Box 178, George Town, KYI-1104 Year of Formation: 1966 Member of FIFA since: 1992 Member of CONCACAF since: 1990

NATIONAL TEAM RECORDS

First international match: 10.05.1991, Basseterre (SKN): Cayman Islands - British Virgin Isl. 9-1
Most international caps: Ian Albert Lindo – 23 caps (2001-2011)
Most international goals: Not known

CONCACAF GOLD CUP	
1991	Qualifiers
1993	Qualifiers
1996	Qualifiers
1998	*Withdrew*
2000	Qualifiers
2002	Qualifiers
2003	Qualifiers
2005	Qualifiers
2007	Qualifiers
2009	Qualifiers
2011	Qualifiers
2013	Did not enter
2015	Did not enter
2017	Did not enter
2019	Qualifiers
2021	Qualifiers

FIFA WORLD CUP	
1930	-
1934	-
1938	-
1950	-
1954	-
1958	-
1962	-
1966	-
1970	-
1974	-
1978	-
1982	-
1986	-
1990	-
1994	Did not enter
1998	Qualifiers
2002	Qualifiers
2006	Qualifiers
2010	Qualifiers
2014	Qualifiers
2018	Qualifiers

F.I.F.A. CONFEDERATIONS CUP 1992-2017
None

OLYMPIC FOOTBALL TOURNAMENTS 1908-2016

1908	-	1948	-	1972	-	1996	Qualifiers
1912	-	1952	-	1976	-	2000	Did not enter
1920	-	1956	-	1980	-	2004	Qualifiers
1924	-	1960	-	1984	-	2008	Qualifiers
1928	-	1964	-	1988	-	2012	Qualifiers
1936	-	1968	-	1992	-	2016	Qualifiers

CCCF (Confederación Centroamericana y del Caribe de Fútbol) CHAMPIONSHIPS 1941-1961
None

CONCACAF CHAMPIONSHIPS 1963-1989
None

CONCACAF NATIONS LEAGUE

2019-2020	League C

CARIBBEAN CHAMPIONSHIPS 1989-2017

1989	Did not enter	1999	Qualifiers
1991	Final Tournament - Group Stage	2001	Qualifiers
1992	Qualifiers	2005	Qualifiers
1993	Qualifiers	2007	Qualifiers
1994	Final Tournament - Group Stage	2008	Qualifiers
1995	Final Tournament - 4th Place	2010	Qualifiers
1996	Qualifiers	2012	Did not enter
1997	*Withdrew*	2014	Did not enter
1998	Final Tournament - Group Stage	2017	Did not enter

CAYMAN ISLANDS CLUB HONOURS IN CONCACAF CLUB COMPETITIONS:

CONCACAF Champions Cup / CONCACAF Champions League 1962-2020
None

CONCACAF League 2017-2020
None

Caribbean Club Championship 1997-2021
None

CONCACAF Cup Winners Cup 1991-1995*
None

Copa Interamericana 1968-1998*
None

*defunct competitions

NATIONAL COMPETITIONS
TABLE OF HONOURS

	CHAMPIONS	CUP WINNERS
1980	Yama Sun Oil	-
1981	*Not known*	-
1982	*Not known*	-
1983	St. George's	-
1984	Mont Joly	-
1985	*Not known*	-
1986	*Not known*	-
1987	*Not known*	-
1988	*Not known*	-
1989	*Not known*	-
1990	*Not known*	-
1991	*Not known*	-
1992	*Not known*	-
1993	*Not known*	-
1994	*Not known*	-
1995	*Not known*	-
1995/1996	*Not known*	East End United
1996/1997	George Town SC	*Not known*
1997/1998	Scholars International FC West Bay	George Town SC
1998/1999	George Town SC	*Not known*
1999/2000	Western Union FC George Town	*Not known*
2000/2001	Scholars International FC West Bay	Bodden Town SC
2001/2002	George Town SC	George Town SC
2002/2003	Scholars International FC West Bay	Scholars International FC West Bay
2003/2004	Latinos FC George Town	Latinos FC George Town
2004/2005	Western Union FC George Town	Western Union FC George Town
2005/2006	Scholars International FC West Bay	Scholars International FC West Bay
2006/2007	Scholars International FC West Bay	Latinos FC George Town
2007/2008	Scholars International FC West Bay	Scholars International FC West Bay
2008/2009	Elite SC George Town	Bodden Town SC
2009/2010	Scholars International FC West Bay	George Town SC
2010/2011	Elite SC George Town	George Town SC
2011/2012	Scholars International FC West Bay	Scholars International FC West Bay
2012/2013	Bodden Town SC	Bodden Town SC
2013/2014	Bodden Town SC	Elite SC George Town
2014/2015	Scholars International FC West Bay	Cayman Athletic SC George Town
2015/2016	Scholars International FC West Bay	Elite SC George Town
2016/2017	Bodden Town SC	Bodden Town SC
2017/2018	Scholars International FC West Bay	Academy SC George Town
2018/2019	Scholars International FC West Bay	Elite SC George Town
2019/2020	*Championship suspended*	*Competition abandoned*
2020/2021	Scholars International FC West Bay	Bodden Town SC

NATIONAL CHAMPIONSHIP
Cayman Islands FA Premier League 2020/2021

1.	**Scholars International FC West Bay**	18	14	3	1	51 - 7	45
2.	Bodden Town SC	18	10	5	3	25 - 17	35
3.	Future SC West Bay	18	9	5	4	32 - 26	32
4.	Academy SC George Town	18	9	3	6	33 - 23	30
5.	Latinos FC George Town	18	9	2	7	26 - 24	29
6.	Elite SC George Town	18	8	5	5	22 - 23	29
7.	East End United FC	18	6	3	9	23 - 32	21
8.	George Town SC	18	5	3	10	14 - 25	18
9.	Sunset FC George Town (*Relegation Play-off*)	18	3	1	14	18 - 37	10
10.	Roma United SC (*Relegated*)	18	2	0	16	17 - 47	6

Promoted for the 2020/2021 season: Alliance FC.
Relegation Play-off: Sunset FC George Town – Cayman Athletic FC 2-0.

NATIONAL CUP
CIFA Cup Final 2020/2021

16.05.2021
Bodden Town SC - Academy SC George Town   1-1 aet; 5-4 pen

THE CLUBS

ACADEMY SPORTS CLUB GEORGE TOWN
Year of Formation: n/a
Stadium: Academy Sports Field, George Town (250)

BODDEN TOWN SPORTS CLUB
Year of Formation: 1970
Stadium: Bodden Town Stadium, Bodden Town (1,500)

EAST END UNITED FOOTBALL CLUB
Year of Formation: n/a
Stadium: "Donovan Rankine" Stadium, East End (1,500)

ELITE SPORTS CLUB GEORGE TOWN
Year of Formation: 1982
Stadium: T.E. McField Sports Centre, George Town (2,500)

FUTURE SPORTS CLUB WEST BAY
Year of Formation: 1998

GEORGE TOWN SPORTS CLUB
Year of Formation: 1996
Stadium: The Annex Stadium, George Town (2,500)

LATINOS FOOTBALL CLUB GEORGE TOWN
Year of Formation: 2006
Stadium: Bodden Town Stadium, Bodden Town (1,500)

ROMA UNITED SPORTS CLUB GEORGE TOWN
Year of Formation: 2002

SCHOLARS INTERNATIONAL FOOTBALL CLUB WEST BAY
Year of Formation: 1986
Stadium: „Ed Bush" Stadium, West Bay (2,500)

SUNSET FOOTBALL CLUB GEORGE TOWN
Year of Formation: 1982
Stadium: T.E. McField Sports Centre, George Town (2,500)

NATIONAL TEAM
INTERNATIONAL MATCHES 2020/2021

24.03.2021	Paramaribo	Suriname - Cayman Islands	3-0(2-0)	(WCQ)
29.03.2021	Bradenton	Cayman Islands - Canada	0-11(0-6)	(WCQ)
02.06.2021	Bradenton	Cayman Islands - Aruba	1-3(1-2)	(WCQ)
08.06.2021	Bradenton	Bermuda - Cayman Islands	1-1(0-1)	(WCQ)

24.03.2021, 22nd FIFA World Cup Qualifiers, CONCACAF First Round
Stadion "Dr. Ir. Franklin Essed", Paramaribo
Referee: Jorge Antonio Pérez Durán (Mexico)
SURINAME - CAYMAN ISLANDS 3-0(2-0)
CAY: David Lee, Tyler Lee, Mason Duval, Ackeem Hyde, Cameron Gray, Wesley Robinson, Jermaine Wilson (25.Justin Byles; 83.Jason Kirkconnell), Joshewa Leandro Frederick-Charley (58.Jonah Ebanks), Trey Ebanks (59.Jabari Campbell), D'Andre Rowe, Gunnar Studenthofft (83.Kion Parchmont). Trainer: Benjamin Robert Pugh (England).

29.03.2021, 22nd FIFA World Cup Qualifiers, CONCACAF First Round
IMG Academy, Bradenton (United States)
Referee: Ted Unkel (United States)
CAYMAN ISLANDS - CANADA 0-11(0-6)
CAY: Albertini Holness, Tyler Lee, Jonah Ebanks (70.Justin Byles), Mason Duval (65.Jabari Campbell), Ackeem Hyde, Cameron Gray, Wesley Robinson, Joshewa Leandro Frederick-Charley (85.Romario Dixon), Christopher Reeves (65.Kion Parchmont), D'Andre Rowe, Mark Samuel Ebanks (84.Trey Ebanks). Trainer: Benjamin Robert Pugh (England).

02.06.2021, 22nd FIFA World Cup Qualifiers, CONCACAF First Round
IMG Academy, Bradenton (United States)
Referee: Luis Enrique Santander Aguirre (Mexico)
CAYMAN ISLANDS - ARUBA 1-3(1-2)
CAY: Albertini Holness, André McFarlane, Romario Dixon (67.Mason Duval), Jonah Ebanks (67.Trey Ebanks), Jabari Campbell, Cameron Gray (81.Joshewa Leandro Frederick-Charley), Wesley Robinson, D'Andre Rowe, Kareem Foster (79.Jamaal Seymour), Theron Magnus Wood (81.Barry Dre Tibbetts), Mark Samuel Ebanks. Trainer: Benjamin Robert Pugh (England).
Goal: Jonah Ebanks (30 penalty).

08.06.2021, 22nd FIFA World Cup Qualifiers, CONCACAF First Round
IMG Academy, Bradenton (United States)
Referee: Rubiel Vazquez (United States)
BERMUDA - CAYMAN ISLANDS 1-1(0-1)
CAY: Albertini Holness, André McFarlane, Jonah Ebanks (90+2.Andrew Browning), Mason Duval, Cameron Gray, Wesley Robinson, Joshewa Leandro Frederick-Charley, D'Andre Rowe (85.Barry Dre Tibbetts), Kareem Foster, Theron Magnus Wood (57.Kion Parchmont), Mark Samuel Ebanks. Trainer: Benjamin Robert Pugh (England).
Goal: Mark Samuel Ebanks (23).

NATIONAL TEAM PLAYERS 2020/2021

Name	DOB	Club
Goalkeepers		
Albertini HOLNESS	06.03.2000	*Cayman Athletic SC George Town*
David LEE	15.05.1998	*Academy SC George Town*
Defenders		
Jabari CAMPBELL	23.06.2000	*Academy SC George Town*
Joshewa Leandro FREDERICK-CHARLERY	24.01.1997	*Bodden Town SC*
Cameron GRAY	22.10.1998	
Ackeem HYDE	03.11.1999	
Tyler LEE	05.09.1994	*Future SC West Bay*
André McFARLANE	01.11.1989	*Future SC West Bay*
Wesley ROBINSON	07.09.1993	*Elite SC George Town*
D'Andre ROWE	05.01.2001	*Cayman Athletic SC George Town*
Midfielders		
Justin BYLES	22.01.2005	
Romario DIXON	19.09.1996	*Academy SC George Town*
Mason DUVAL	24.08.2001	*Academy SC George Town*
Jonah EBANKS	07.05.1996	*Scholars International FC West Bay*
Trey EBANKS	05.06.2000	*Academy SC George Town*
Kareem FOSTER	06.09.2000	*Westfield FC (ENG)*
Jason KIRKCONNELL	30.08.2003	*Bhrooke House College FC (ENG)*
Kion PARCHMONT	28.01.2000	
Barry Dre TIBBETTS	15.06.2002	*Future SC West Bay*
Jermaine WILSON	05.02.1995	*Academy SC George Town*
Forwards		
Andrew BROWNING		*East End United FC*
Mark Samuel EBANKS	26.12.1990	*Future SC West Bay*
Christopher REEVES	27.02.1997	*Elite SC George Town*
Jamaal SEYMOUR	21.06.1996	*Academy SC George Town*
Gunnar STUDENTHOFFT	05.04.2002	
Theron Magnus WOOD	07.02.1990	*Bodden Town SC*
National coaches		
Benjamin Robert PUGH (England) [from 01.07.2019]		23.11.1989

COSTA RICA

The Country:	The FA:
República de Costa Rica (Republic of Costa Rica) Capital: San José Surface: 51,100 km² Population: 5,094,118 [2020] Time: UTC-7 Independent since: 1821	Federación Costarricense de Fútbol Radial Santa Ana Belén, Costado Norte Estatua Leon Cortes, 600 mts sur del Cruce de la Panasonic, San José 670-1000 Year of Formation: 1921 Member of FIFA since: 1927 Member of CONCACAF since: 1962

NATIONAL TEAM RECORDS

First international match: 14.09.1921, Ciudad de Guatemala: Costa Rica - El Salvador 7-0
Most international caps: Wálter Centeno Corea – 137 caps (1995-2009)
Most international goals: Rolando Fonseca Jiménez – 47 goals / 113 caps (1992-2011)

CONCACAF GOLD CUP		FIFA WORLD CUP	
1991	Final Tournament (4th Place)	1930	Did not enter
1993	Final Tournament (3rd Place)	1934	Did not enter
1996	Qualifiers	1938	*Withdrew*
1998	Final Tournament (Group Stage)	1950	Did not enter
2000	Final Tournament (Quarter-Finals)	1954	Entry not accepted by FIFA
2002	Final Tournament (Runners-up)	1958	Qualifiers
2003	Final Tournament (4th Place)	1962	Qualifiers
2005	Final Tournament (Quarter-Finals)	1966	Qualifiers
2007	Final Tournament (Quarter-Finals)	1970	Qualifiers
2009	Final Tournament (Semi-Finals)	1974	Qualifiers
2011	Final Tournament (Quarter-Finals)	1978	Qualifiers
2013	Final Tournament (Quarter-Finals)	1982	Qualifiers
2015	Final Tournament (Quarter-Finals)	1986	Qualifiers
2017	Final Tournament (Semi-Finals)	1990	Final Tournament (2nd Round)
2019	Final Tournament (Quarter-Finals)	1994	Qualifiers
2021	Final Tournament (*to be played*)	1998	Qualifiers
		2002	Final Tournament (Group Stage)
		2006	Final Tournament (Group Stage)
		2010	Qualifiers
		2014	Final Tournament (Quarter-Finals)
		2018	Final Tournament (Group Stage)

F.I.F.A. CONFEDERATIONS CUP 1992-2017

None

OLYMPIC FOOTBALL TOURNAMENTS 1908-2016

1908	-	1948	-	1972	Did not enter	1996	Qualifiers
1912	-	1952	-	1976	Qualifiers	2000	Qualifiers
1920	-	1956	-	1980	FT/Group Stage	2004	Quarter-Finals
1924	-	1960	-	1984	FT/Group Stage	2008	Qualifiers
1928	-	1964	-	1988	Did not enter	2012	Qualifiers
1936	-	1968	Qualifiers	1992	*Suspended*	2016	Qualifiers

CCCF (Confederación Centroamericana y del Caribe de Fútbol) CHAMPIONSHIPS 1941-1961

1941 (Winners), 1943, **1946-1948 (Winners)**, 1951, **1953-1955-1960-1961 (Winners)**

CONCACAF CHAMPIONSHIPS 1963-1989

1963 (Winners), 1965, **1969 (Winners)**, 1971, 1985 (3rd Place), **1989 (Winners)**

COPA AMÉRICA (invited as guests)

1997, 2001, 2004, 2011, 2016

CONCACAF NATIONS LEAGUE

2019-2020

COPA CENTROAMERICANA (UNCAF NATIONS CHAMPIONSHIPS) 1991-2017

1991	**Final Round - Winners**	2005	**Final Round - Winners**
1993	Final Round - Runners-up	2007	**Final Round - Winners**
1995	Final Round - 4th Place	2009	Final Round - Runners-up
1997	**Final Round - Winners**	2011	Final Round - Runners-up
1999	**Final Round - Winners**	2013	**Final Round - Winners**
2001	Final Round - Runners-up	2014	**Final Round - Winners**
2003	**Final Round - Winners**	2017	Final Round - 4th

COSTA RICAN CLUB HONOURS IN CONCACAF CLUB COMPETITIONS:

CONCACAF Champions Cup / CONCACAF Champions League 1962-2020

Club Deportivo Saprissa San José	3	1993, 1995, 2005
Liga Deportiva Alajuelense	2	1986, 2004

CONCACAF League 2017-2020

CS Herediano Heredia	1	2018
Club Deportivo Saprissa San José	1	2019
Liga Deportiva Alajuelense	1	2020

Caribbean Club Championship 1997-2021

None

*CONCACAF Cup Winners Cup 1991-1995**

None

*Copa Interamericana 1968-1998**

None

*defunct competitions

NATIONAL COMPETITIONS
TABLE OF HONOURS

	CHAMPIONS
1921	CS Herediano Heredia
1922	CS Herediano Heredia
1923	CS Cartaginés Deportiva SA
1924	CS Herediano Heredia
1925	CS La Libertad San José
1926	CS La Libertad San José
1927	CS Herediano Heredia
1928	Liga Deportiva Alajuelense
1929	CS La Libertad San José
1930	CS Herediano Heredia
1931	CS Herediano Heredia
1932	CS Herediano Heredia
1933	CS Herediano Heredia
1934	CS La Libertad San José
1935	CS Herediano Heredia
1936	CS Cartaginés Deportiva SA
1937	CS Herediano Heredia
1938	Orión FC Curridabat
1939	Liga Deportiva Alajuelense
1940	CS Cartaginés Deportiva SA
1941	Liga Deportiva Alajuelense
1942	CS La Libertad San José
1943	ADFC Universidad de Costa Rica San José
1944	Orión FC Curridabat
1945	Liga Deportiva Alajuelense
1946	CS La Libertad San José
1947	CS Herediano Heredia
1948	CS Herediano Heredia
1949	Liga Deportiva Alajuelense
1950	Liga Deportiva Alajuelense
1951	CS Herediano Heredia
1952	Deportivo Saprissa San José
1953	Deportivo Saprissa San José
1954	*No competition*
1955	CS Herediano Heredia
1956	*No competition*
1957	Deportivo Saprissa San José
1958	Liga Deportiva Alajuelense
1959	Liga Deportiva Alajuelense
1960	Liga Deportiva Alajuelense
1961	CS Herediano Heredia (ASOFUTBOL) / Carmen FC (FEDEFUTBOL)
1962	Deportivo Saprissa San José
1963	CS Uruguay de Coronado
1964	Deportivo Saprissa San José
1965	Deportivo Saprissa San José
1966	Liga Deportiva Alajuelense
1967	Deportivo Saprissa San José

Year		Champion
1968		Deportivo Saprissa San José
1969		Deportivo Saprissa San José
1970		Liga Deportiva Alajuelense
1971		Liga Deportiva Alajuelense
1972		Deportivo Saprissa San José
1973		Deportivo Saprissa San José
1974		Deportivo Saprissa San José
1975		Deportivo Saprissa San José
1976		Deportivo Saprissa San José
1977		Deportivo Saprissa San José
1978		CS Herediano Heredia
1979		CS Herediano Heredia
1980		Liga Deportiva Alajuelense
1981		CS Herediano Heredia
1982		Deportivo Saprissa San José
1983		Liga Deportiva Alajuelense
1984		Liga Deportiva Alajuelense
1985		CS Herediano Heredia
1986		AD Municipal Puntarenas
1987		CS Herediano Heredia
1988		Deportivo Saprissa San José
1989		Deportivo Saprissa San José
1990		*No competition*
1990/1991		Liga Deportiva Alajuelense
1991/1992		Liga Deportiva Alajuelense
1992/1993		CS Herediano Heredia
1993/1994		Deportivo Saprissa San José
1994/1995		Deportivo Saprissa San José
1995/1996		Liga Deportiva Alajuelense
1996/1997		Liga Deportiva Alajuelense
1997/1998		Deportivo Saprissa San José
1998/1999		Deportivo Saprissa San José
1999/2000		Liga Deportiva Alajuelense
2000/2001		Liga Deportiva Alajuelense
2001/2002		Liga Deportiva Alajuelense
2002/2003		Liga Deportiva Alajuelense
2003/2004		Deportivo Saprissa San José
2004/2005		Liga Deportiva Alajuelense
2005/2006		Deportivo Saprissa San José
2006/2007		Deportivo Saprissa San José
2007/2008	Ape:	Deportivo Saprissa San José
	Cla:	Deportivo Saprissa San José
2008/2009	Ape:	Deportivo Saprissa San José
	Cla:	Liberia Mía CF
2009/2010	Ape:	Brujas FC Escazú
	Cla:	Deportivo Saprissa San José
2010/2011	Ape:	Liga Deportiva Alajuelense
	Cla:	Liga Deportiva Alajuelense
2011/2012	Ape:	Liga Deportiva Alajuelense
	Cla:	CS Herediano Heredia
2012/2013	Inv:	Liga Deportiva Alajuelense
	Ver:	CS Herediano Heredia

2013/2014	Inv:	Liga Deportiva Alajuelense
	Ver:	Deportivo Saprissa San José
2014/2015	Inv:	Deportivo Saprissa San José
	Ver:	CS Herediano Heredia
2015/2016	Inv:	Deportivo Saprissa San José
	Ver:	CS Herediano Heredia
2016/2017	Inv:	Deportivo Saprissa San José
	Ver:	CS Herediano Heredia
2017/2018	Inv:	AD Municipal Pérez Zeledón
	Ver:	Deportivo Saprissa San José
2018/2019	Inv:	CS Herediano Heredia
	Ver:	AD San Carlos Ciudad Quesada
2019/2020	Inv:	CS Herediano Heredia
	Ver:	Deportivo Saprissa San José
2020/2021	Inv:	Liga Deportiva Alajuelense
	Cla:	Deportivo Saprissa San José

NATIONAL CHAMPIONSHIP
Primera División - Liga Promérica 2020/2021

Torneo Apertura 2020

Results

Round 1 [15-16.08.2020]
Guadalupe FC - Santos de Guápiles 2-2(2-2)
Pérez Zeledón - LD Alajuelense 0-2(0-1)
Deportivo Saprissa - Limón FC 4-0(0-0)
ADR Jicaral - AD San Carlos 0-1(0-0)
CS Herediano - Municipal Grecia 3-0(1-0)
Sporting FC - CS Cartaginés 2-3(1-2) [09.09.]

Round 2 [21-23.08.2020]
Limón FC - Sporting FC 1-1(0-1)
Santos de Guápiles - CS Herediano 1-1(0-0)
LD Alajuelense - Guadalupe FC 0-1(0-0)
Municipal Grecia - Pérez Zeledón 3-1(2-0)
CS Cartaginés - ADR Jicaral 2-2(2-1) [16.09.]
AD San Carlos - Dep.Saprissa 1-1(0-0) [16.09.]

Round 3 [29-30.08.2020]
Pérez Zeledón - Guadalupe FC 3-2(2-1)
Santos de Guápiles - Municipal Grecia 1-1(0-1)
CS Herediano - LD Alajuelense 1-2(0-0)
Sporting FC - ADR Jicaral 1-0(0-0)
AD San Carlos - Limón FC 2-2(1-1)
Dep. Saprissa - CS Cartaginés 0-4(0-3) [23.09.]

Round 4 [01-03.09.2020]
LD Alajuelense - Santos de Guápiles 2-1(0-1)
Guadalupe FC - Municipal Grecia 1-0(0-0)
CS Herediano - Pérez Zeledón 2-1(1-0)
Limón FC - CS Cartaginés 1-1(0-0)
Sporting FC - AD San Carlos 1-0(0-0)
ADR Jicaral – Dep. Saprissa 0-1(0-0) [30.09.]

Round 5 [05-06.09.2020]
Municipal Grecia - LD Alajuelense 2-3(1-0)
Guadalupe FC - CS Herediano 2-3(2-1)
Pérez Zeledón - Santos de Guápiles 0-2(0-1)
CS Cartaginés - AD San Carlos 4-0(1-0)
ADR Jicaral - Limón FC 0-2(0-0)
Dep. Saprissa - Sporting FC 2-1(1-0) [07.10.]

Round 6 [12-13.09.2020]
Pérez Zeledón - CS Herediano 1-0(1-0)
AD San Carlos - Sporting FC 0-1(0-0)
Deportivo Saprissa - ADR Jicaral 1-0(1-0)
CS Cartaginés - Limón FC 4-0(3-0)
Municipal Grecia - Guadalupe FC 0-1(0-1)
Santos de Guápiles - LD Alajuelense 0-4(0-1)

Round 7 [18-20.09.2020]
LD Alajuelense - Municipal Grecia 3-1(1-1)
Sporting FC - Deportivo Saprissa 1-2(0-0)
Santos de Guápiles - Pérez Zeledón 1-4(1-2)
CS Herediano - Guadalupe FC 3-1(2-0)
Limón FC - ADR Jicaral 1-0(1-0)
AD San Carlos - CS Cartaginés 1-0(1-0)

Round 8 [26-27.09.2020]
Municipal Grecia - Santos de Guápiles 0-1(0-1)
Guadalupe FC - Pérez Zeledón 4-1(3-1)
LD Alajuelense - CS Herediano 2-0(1-0)
CS Cartaginés - Deportivo Saprissa 2-1(1-1)
ADR Jicaral - Sporting FC 3-1(2-0)
Limón FC - AD San Carlos 0-2(0-1) [14.10.]

Round 9 [02-05.10.2020]
Pérez Zeledón - Municipal Grecia 3-3(1-1)
Sporting FC - Limón FC 0-1(0-1)
Guadalupe FC - LD Alajuelense 1-2(0-2)
CS Herediano - Santos de Guápiles 0-0
ADR Jicaral - CS Cartaginés 1-0(1-0)
Dep. Saprissa - AD San Carlos 0-0 [18.10.]

Round 10 [11.10.2020]
CS Cartaginés - Sporting FC 2-0(0-0)
Limón FC - Deportivo Saprissa 1-0(0-0)
AD San Carlos - ADR Jicaral 0-0
Municipal Grecia - Herediano 2-2(2-0) [24.10.]
Alajuelense - Pérez Zeledón 0-2(0-0) [25.10.]
Santos de G. - Guadalupe FC 1-1(0-0) [05.11.]

Round 11 [27-29.10.2020]
Limón FC - Municipal Grecia 1-0(1-0)
CS Herediano - AD San Carlos 1-1(0-0)
Sporting FC - Pérez Zeledón 2-0(1-0)
LD Alajuelense - ADR Jicaral 2-2(1-1)
Guadalupe FC - CS Cartaginés 1-0(1-0)
Santos de Guápiles - Dep. Saprissa 0-0 [18.11.]

Round 12 [31.10.-02.11.2020]
CS Herediano - Sporting FC 4-2(3-0)
Deportivo Saprissa - LD Alajuelense 2-3(0-0)
CS Cartaginés - Municipal Grecia 2-1(0-0)
ADR Jicaral - Guadalupe FC 3-1(1-1)
Pérez Zeledón - Limón FC 1-1(1-1)
AD San Carlos - Santos de Guápiles 2-0(0-0)

Round 13 [07-08.11.2020]
Municipal Grecia - AD San Carlos 1-0(0-0)
LD Alajuelense - CS Cartaginés 4-1(2-1)
Deportivo Saprissa - Pérez Zeledón 4-0(2-0)
Guadalupe FC - Sporting FC 2-2(0-1)
Santos de Guápiles - ADR Jicaral 1-1(0-0)
Limón FC - CS Herediano 1-4(0-2) [02.12.]

Round 14 [11-12.11.2020]
CS Cartaginés - Santos de Guápiles 3-0(2-0)
Limón FC - Guadalupe FC 2-1(1-0)
Sporting FC - LD Alajuelense 2-3(0-0)
AD San Carlos - Pérez Zeledón 3-1(0-1)
ADR Jicaral - Municipal Grecia 1-0(0-0)
CS Herediano - Dep. Saprissa 2-3(1-1) [22.11.]

Round 15 [14-17.11.2020]
Santos de Guápiles - Limón FC 0-0
Municipal Grecia - Sporting FC 0-0
Deportivo Saprissa - Guadalupe FC 5-1(2-1)
AD San Carlos - LD Alajuelense 1-0(0-0)
Pérez Zeledón - ADR Jicaral 1-1(0-1)
CS Cartaginés - CS Herediano 0-1(0-1)

Round 16 [05-06.12.2020]
ADR Jicaral - CS Herediano 0-0
Sporting FC - Santos de Guápiles 3-1(1-0)
LD Alajuelense - Limón FC 4-1(2-0)
Municipal Grecia - Deportivo Saprissa 0-3(0-2)
Guadalupe FC - AD San Carlos 3-0(1-0)
Pérez Zeledón - CS Cartaginés 1-4(1-2)

Grupo A - Final Standings

1	Liga Deportiva Alajuelense	16	12	1	3	36 - 18	37
2	CS Herediano Heredia	16	7	5	4	27 - 19	26
3	Guadalupe FC	16	6	3	7	24 - 27	21
4	AD Municipal Pérez Zeledón	16	4	3	9	20 - 34	15
5	Santos de Guápiles FC	16	2	8	6	12 - 24	14
6	AD Municipal Grecia FC	16	2	4	10	14 - 26	10

Grupo B - Final Standings

1	Deportivo Saprissa San José	16	9	3	4	29	-	16	30
2	CS Cartaginés Deportiva SA	16	9	2	5	32	-	16	29
3	AD San Carlos Ciudad Quesada	16	6	5	5	14	-	14	23
4	Limón FC	16	6	5	5	15	-	24	23
5	ADR Jicaral Sercoba	16	4	6	6	14	-	15	18
6	Sporting FC San José	16	5	3	8	20	-	24	18

Both group winners and runners-up were qualified for the Torneo Apertura Play-offs, while teams ranked last were qualified for the Relegation Play-offs.

Relegation Play-offs (Liguilla por la Permanencia) [09-13.12.2020]

AD Municipal Grecia FC - Sporting FC San José   1-1(1-1)   1-0(1-0)

Apertura Play-offs

Play-offs Semi-Finals [09-13.12.2020]

CS Cartaginés Deportiva SA - Liga Deportiva Alajuelense   2-3(2-1)   1-1(0-1)
CS Herediano Heredia - Deportivo Saprissa San José   3-0(1-0)   1-1(0-1)

Torneo Apertura Finals

16.12.2020, Estadio Nacional, San José; Attendance: 0
Referee: Pedro Navarro
CS Herediano Heredia - Liga Deportiva Alajuelense   0-1(0-1)
Herediano: Bryan Andrés Segura Cruz, Aarón Salazar Arias, Orlando Moisés Galo Calderón, Yael Andrés López Fuentes [*sent off 90*], Christian Antonio Reyes Alemán, Yeltsin Ignacio Tejeda Valverde, Suhander Manuel Zúñiga Cordero, Jefferson Brenes Rojas (67.Berny Thomas Burke Montiel), Gerson Torres Barrantes, Nextali Rodríguez Medina (56.Yendrick Alberto Ruiz González), Leandro Barrios Rita dos Martires "Leandrinho" (81.Fabrizio Antonio Ramírez Montero). Trainer: Jafet Soto Molina.
LD Alajuelense: Leonel Gerardo Moreira Ledezma, Fernán José Faerrón Tristán (83.Bernald Alfaro Alfaro), José Andrés Salvatierra López, Adolfo Abdiel Machado, Facundo Gabriel Zabala, Alexander Agustín López Rodríguez (83.José Miguel Cubero Loría), Barlon Andrés Sequeira Sibaja (71.Carlos Andrei Mora Montoya), Jurguens Josafat Montenegro Vallejo (83.Álvaro Alberto Saborío Chacón), Jonathan Alonso Moya Aguilar, Bryan Jafet Ruiz González, Adrián Alonso Martínez Batista (75.Dylan Armando Flores Knowles). Trainer: Andrés José Carevic Ghelfi (Argentina).
Goal: 0-1 Adrián Alonso Martínez Batista (37).

20.12.2020, Estadio „Alejandro Morera Soto", Alajuela; Attendance: 0
Referee: Hugo Armando Cruz Alvarado
Liga Deportiva Alajuelense - CS Herediano Heredia   1-0(1-0)
LD Alajuelense: Leonel Gerardo Moreira Ledezma, Fernán José Faerrón Tristán, José Andrés Salvatierra López, Adolfo Abdiel Machado, Facundo Gabriel Zabala (85.Júnior Enrique Díaz Campbell), Alexander Agustín López Rodríguez (85.Bernald Alfaro Alfaro), Barlon Andrés Sequeira Sibaja (63.Carlos Andrei Mora Montoya), Jurguens Josafat Montenegro Vallejo (72.Dylan Armando Flores Knowles), Jonathan Alonso Moya Aguilar, Bryan Jafet Ruiz González, Adrián Alonso Martínez Batista (72.José Miguel Cubero Loría). Trainer: Andrés José Carevic Ghelfi (Argentina).
Herediano: Bryan Andrés Segura Cruz, Aarón Salazar Arias, Orlando Moisés Galo Calderón (52.Keysher Fuller Spence), Christian Antonio Reyes Alemán (46.Yendrick Alberto Ruiz González [*sent off 77*]), Keyner Yamal Brown Blackwood, Yeltsin Ignacio Tejeda Valverde, Suhander Manuel Zúñiga Cordero, Berny Thomas Burke Montiel (52.Fabrizio Antonio Ramírez Montero), Jefferson Brenes Rojas (46.Leandro Barrios Rita dos Martires "Leandrinho"), Gerson Torres Barrantes, Nextali Rodríguez Medina (79.Óscar Esteban Granados Maroto). Trainer: Jafet Soto Molina.
Goal: 1-0 Jonathan Alonso Moya Aguilar (30).

2020 Torneo Apertura Champions: **Liga Deportiva Alajuelense**

Best goalscorer Torneo Apertura 2020:
Marcel Hernández Campanioni (CUB, CS Cartaginés Deportiva SA) – 13 goals

Torneo Clausura 2021

Results

Round 1 [12-14.01.2021]
Guadalupe FC - Limón FC 3-0 *awarded*
ADR Jicaral - AD San Carlos 1-1(1-1)
Municipal Grecia - Deportivo Saprissa 0-0
LD Alajuelense - Pérez Zeledón 2-0(2-0)
Sporting FC - CS Herediano 3-2(3-0)
CS Cartaginés - Santos de Guápiles 1-0(1-0)

Round 2 [16-17.01.2021]
Limón FC - LD Alajuelense 0-2(0-2)
Deportivo Saprissa - ADR Jicaral 2-2(1-1)
CS Cartaginés - Guadalupe FC 2-1(0-1)
Municipal Grecia - Sporting FC 1-1(0-0)
Santos de Guápiles - Pérez Zeledón 2-0(2-0)
AD San Carlos - CS Herediano 2-1(0-0)

Round 3 [20-21.01.2021]
AD San Carlos - Guadalupe FC 1-0(0-0)
CS Herediano - Municipal Grecia 1-1(1-1)
ADR Jicaral - Limón FC 2-0(0-0)
Pérez Zeledón - CS Cartaginés 2-1(0-1)
Santos de Guáp. - Alajuelense 0-3(0-2) [27.01.]
Dep. Saprissa - Sporting FC 4-0(2-0) [27.01.]

Round 4 [23-25.01.2021]
Sporting FC - Santos de Guápiles 0-1(0-0)
LD Alajuelense - AD San Carlos 1-1(0-1)
Municipal Grecia - Pérez Zeledón 0-0
ADR Jicaral - CS Herediano 2-0(0-0)
CS Cartaginés - Limón FC 1-1(1-1)
Guadalupe FC - Deportivo Saprissa 2-2(0-0)

Round 5 [30-31.01.2021]
Limón FC - Municipal Grecia 0-0
AD San Carlos - Sporting FC 0-0
CS Herediano - LD Alajuelense 1-1(0-0)
Deportivo Saprissa - CS Cartaginés 4-1(1-0)
Santos de Guápiles - Guadalupe FC 2-2(1-2)
Pérez Zeledón - ADR Jicaral 1-2(0-2)

Round 6 [02-03.02.2021]
Sporting FC - Limón FC 0-1(0-0)
ADR Jicaral - Santos de Guápiles 0-1(0-0)
CS Herediano - Guadalupe FC 2-2(0-1)
AD San Carlos - CS Cartaginés 1-1(1-1)
Alajuelense - Munic. Grecia 3-0(2-0) [10.02.]
Pérez Zeledón - Dep. Saprissa 1-1(1-0) [11.02.]

Round 7 [06-08.02.2021]
Municipal Grecia - ADR Jicaral 2-0(2-0)
Guadalupe FC - Sporting FC 0-0
CS Cartaginés - CS Herediano 1-2(0-0)
LD Alajuelense - Deportivo Saprissa 3-1(0-1)
Santos de Guápiles - AD San Carlos 3-1(0-0)
Limón FC - Pérez Zeledón 1-1(1-1)

Round 8 [13-15.02.2021]
Sporting FC - CS Cartaginés 3-1(1-0)
CS Herediano - Santos de Guápiles 2-1(2-1)
ADR Jicaral - LD Alajuelense 1-1(1-0)
Deportivo Saprissa - Limón FC 4-2(4-0)
AD San Carlos - Municipal Grecia 1-4(0-2)
Pérez Zeledón - Guadalupe FC 1-3(0-0)

Round 9 [20-21.02.2021]
Limón FC - Santos de Guápiles 3-2(3-1)
Sporting FC - ADR Jicaral 0-0
Pérez Zeledón - AD San Carlos 1-1(1-1)
CS Cartaginés - LD Alajuelense 1-1(0-1)
Guadalupe FC - Municipal Grecia 1-1(0-0)
Deportivo Saprissa - CS Herediano 1-0(1-0)

Round 10 [27-28.02.2021]
ADR Jicaral - Guadalupe FC 3-2(2-0)
Municipal Grecia - CS Cartaginés 1-2(0-1)
Santos de Guápiles - Dep. Saprissa 1-1(1-0)
CS Herediano - Pérez Zeledón 1-1(0-1)
LD Alajuelense - Sporting FC 3-0(2-0)
AD San Carlos - Limón FC 0-3(0-0)

Round 11 [02-04.03.2021]
CS Cartaginés - ADR Jicaral 1-1(0-0)
Limón FC - CS Herediano 0-2(0-1)
Sporting FC - Pérez Zeledón 0-1(0-0)
Guadalupe FC - LD Alajuelense 1-3(1-1)
Deportivo Saprissa - AD San Carlos 1-1(0-0)
Municipal Grecia - Santos de Guápiles 1-2(1-0)

Round 12 [06-08.03.2021]
Limón FC - Guadalupe FC 1-7(1-2)
Pérez Zeledón - LD Alajuelense 1-5(1-2)
CS Herediano - Sporting FC 2-1(0-0)
Deportivo Saprissa - Municipal Grecia 1-2(1-1)
AD San Carlos - ADR Jicaral 0-0
Santos de Guápiles - CS Cartaginés 1-0(0-0)

Round 13 [12-14.03.2021]
CS Herediano - AD San Carlos 0-1(0-1)
Sporting FC - Municipal Grecia 0-0
Guadalupe FC - CS Cartaginés 0-3(0-2)
LD Alajuelense - Limón FC 0-0
ADR Jicaral - Deportivo Saprissa 0-0
Pérez Zeledón - Santos de Guápiles 1-1(1-1)

Round 14 [19-20.03.2021]
Limón FC - ADR Jicaral 2-1(0-1)
CS Cartaginés - Pérez Zeledón 0-0
Municipal Grecia - CS Herediano 1-4(1-1)
Guadalupe FC - AD San Carlos 1-2(0-1)
LD Alajuelense - Santos de Guápiles 1-1(0-0)
Sporting FC - Deportivo Saprissa 1-0(1-0)

Round 15 [30-31.03.2021]
Limón FC - CS Cartaginés 1-0(0-1)
AD San Carlos - LD Alajuelense 0-1(0-0)
CS Herediano - ADR Jicaral 2-2(1-1)
Santos de Guápiles - Sporting FC 3-1(0-1)
Deportivo Saprissa - Guadalupe FC 1-1(1-0)
Pérez Zeledón - Mun. Grecia 1-1(1-0) [14.04.]

Round 16 [02-05.04.2021]
LD Alajuelense - CS Herediano 1-1(1-0)
Municipal Grecia - Limón FC 2-2(1-0)
Guadalupe FC - Santos de Guápiles 2-4(0-1)
CS Cartaginés - Deportivo Saprissa 0-0
Sporting FC - AD San Carlos 2-0(2-0)
ADR Jicaral - Pérez Zeledón 1-1(0-1)

Round 17 [09-11.04.2021]
Municipal Grecia - LD Alajuelense 1-4(1-2)
CS Cartaginés - AD San Carlos 1-1(1-0)
Limón FC - Sporting FC 3-1(1-0)
Guadalupe FC - CS Herediano 2-2(0-1)
Deportivo Saprissa - Pérez Zeledón 1-1(0-0)
Santos de Guápiles - ADR Jicaral 3-0(1-0)

Round 18 [17-18.04.2021]
Pérez Zeledón - Limón FC 3-2(1-1)
Sporting FC - Guadalupe FC 0-3(0-1)
CS Herediano - CS Cartaginés 1-2(0-1)
ADR Jicaral - Municipal Grecia 1-0(0-0)
Deportivo Saprissa - LD Alajuelense 0-5(0-2)
AD San Carlos - Santos de Guápiles 1-0(0-0)

Round 19 [20-22.04.2021]
CS Cartaginés - Sporting FC 0-1(0-0)
Limón FC - Deportivo Saprissa 1-2(1-2)
Guadalupe FC - Pérez Zeledón 0-1(0-1)
LD Alajuelense - ADR Jicaral 3-0(1-0)
Municipal Grecia - AD San Carlos 2-1(0-1)
Santos de Guápiles - CS Herediano 2-2(1-1)

Round 20 [24-26.04.2021]
LD Alajuelense - CS Cartaginés 4-1(1-0)
Municipal Grecia - Guadalupe FC 0-0
ADR Jicaral - Sporting FC 1-2(1-0)
CS Herediano - Deportivo Saprissa 2-2(1-0)
Santos de Guápiles - Limón FC 3-2(2-2)
AD San Carlos - Pérez Zeledón 0-1(0-0)

Round 21 [30.04.-02.05.2021]
CS Cartaginés - Municipal Grecia 2-0(0-0)
Limón FC - AD San Carlos 0-3(0-3)
Guadalupe FC - ADR Jicaral 0-0
Pérez Zeledón - CS Herediano 0-3(0-0)
Deport. Saprissa - Santos de Guápiles 3-1(3-0)
Sporting FC - LD Alajuelense 1-2(1-0) [10.05.]

Round 22 [13.05.2021]
ADR Jicaral - CS Cartaginés 1-0(0-0)
LD Alajuelense - Guadalupe FC 0-0
CS Herediano - Limón FC 2-0(0-0)
AD San Carlos - Deportivo Saprissa 2-0(1-0)
Santos de Guápiles - Municipal Grecia 2-2(1-0)
Pérez Zeledón - Sporting FC 3-1(2-0)

<u>Please note</u>: Due to outstanding payments at the Caja Costarricense de Seguro Social (CCSS), Limón FC was not allowed to play in the game against Guadalupe FC (Round 1).

Final Standings

1	Liga Deportiva Alajuelense	22	14	8	0	49	-	12	50
2	Santos de Guápiles FC	22	10	6	6	36	-	29	36
3	CS Herediano Heredia	22	7	9	6	35	-	29	30
4	Deportivo Saprissa San José	22	6	11	5	31	-	29	29
5	AD San Carlos Ciudad Quesada	22	7	8	7	21	-	24	29
6	ADR Jicaral Sercoba	22	6	10	6	21	-	24	28
7	AD Municipal Pérez Zeledón	22	6	10	6	22	-	29	28
8	CS Cartaginés Deportiva SA	22	6	8	8	23	-	27	26
9	AD Municipal Grecia FC	22	4	11	7	22	-	29	23
10	Sporting FC San José	21	6	5	11	18	-	31	23
11	Guadalupe FC	21	4	10	8	33	-	31	22
12	Limón FC	22	5	6	11	25	-	42	21

Top-4 advanced to the Clausura Play-offs.

Relegation Play-offs (Liguilla del no descenso) [18-25.05.2021]
Limón FC - Sporting FC San José   0-1(0-0)   2-2(1-1)

Clausura Play-offs

Play-offs Semi-Finals [16-20.05.2020]
Deportivo Saprissa San José - Liga Deportiva Alajuelense   4-3(3-1)   2-2(1-0)
CS Herediano Heredia - Santos de Guápiles FC   2-1(1-0)   0-0

Torneo Clausura Finals

23.05.2021, Estadio „Ricardo Saprissa Aymá", San José; Attendance: 0
Referee: Juan Gabriel Calderón Pérez
Deportivo Saprissa San José - CS Herediano Heredia   3-2(1-1)
Deportivo Saprissa: Aarón Moises Cruz Esquivel, Ricardo José Blanco Mora, Aubrey Robert David, Jordy Jafeth Evans Solano, Michael Francisco Barrantes Rojas, David Alberto Guzmán Pérez, Mariano Néstor Torres (Cap), Christián Bolaños Navarro (90.Orlando Alexis Sinclair Hernández), Ariel Francisco Rodríguez Araya (75.Esteban Eduardo Rodríguez Ballestero), Daniel Colindres Solera (84.Luis José Hernández Paniagua). Trainer: Wilber Mauricio Wright Reynolds.
Herediano: Minor Jesús Álvarez Cordero, Aarón Salazar Arias, Ariel Román Soto González, Orlando Moisés Galo Calderón (70.Keysher Fuller Spence), Suhander Manuel Zúñiga Cordero (65.Óscar Esteban Granados Maroto), Fabrizio Antonio Ramírez Montero (65.Berny Thomas Burke Montiel), Jefferson Brenes Rojas, Gerson Torres Barrantes, Yendrick Alberto Ruiz González (Cap) (83.Anthony Daniel Contreras Enríquez), Francisco Javier Rodríguez Hernández (70.Brayan Andrés Rojas Jiménez). Trainer: Luis Antonio Marín Murillo.
Goals: 1-0 Daniel Colindres Solera (21), 1-1 Yendrick Alberto Ruiz González (45+1), 2-1 Michael Francisco Barrantes Rojas (57), 3-1 Aubrey Robert David (64), 3-2 Anthony Daniel Contreras Enríquez (85).

26.05.2021, Estadio "Abel Rodríguez Sequeira", Guadalupe; Attendance: 0
Referee: Adrián Chinchilla
CS Herediano Heredia - Deportivo Saprissa San José   0-1(0-1)
Herediano: Minor Jesús Álvarez Cordero, Aarón Salazar Arias, Yael Andrés López Fuentes (80.Keyner Yamal Brown Blackwood), Keysher Fuller Spence (58.Anthony Daniel Contreras Enríquez), Ariel Román Soto González, Suhander Manuel Zúñiga Cordero, Óscar Esteban Granados Maroto (65.Rándall Azofeifa Corrales), Jefferson Brenes Rojas (46.Berny Thomas Burke Montiel), Gerson Torres Barrantes, Yendrick Alberto Ruiz González (Cap) (65.Brayan Andrés Rojas Jiménez), Francisco Javier Rodríguez Hernández. Trainer: Luis Antonio Marín Murillo.
Deportivo Saprissa: Aarón Moises Cruz Esquivel, Ricardo José Blanco Mora, Aubrey Robert David, Walter Eduardo Cortés Pérez, Michael Francisco Barrantes Rojas (78.Esteban Ezequiel Espíndola López), David Alberto Guzmán Pérez, Mariano Néstor Torres (Cap) (90.Jordy Jafeth Evans Solano), Christián Bolaños Navarro (90.Marvin Angulo Borbón), Ariel Francisco Rodríguez Araya (65.Orlando Alexis Sinclair Hernández), Jimmy Marín Vílchez, Daniel Colindres Solera (84.Luis José Hernández Paniagua). Trainer: Wilber Mauricio Wright Reynolds.
Goal: 0-1 Ariel Francisco Rodríguez Araya (13).

2021 Torneo Clausura Champions: **Deportivo Saprissa San José**

Best goalscorer Torneo Clausura 2021:
Javon Romario East (JAM, Santos de Guápiles FC) &
Johan Alberto Venegas Ulloa (Liga Deportiva Alajuelense) – both 13 goals

Aggregate Table 2020/2021

1.	Liga Deportiva Alajuelense	38	26	9	3	85	-	30	87
2.	Deportivo Saprissa San José	38	15	14	9	60	-	45	59
3.	CS Herediano Heredia	38	14	14	10	62	-	48	56
4.	CS Cartaginés Deportiva SA	38	15	10	13	55	-	43	55
5.	Santos de Guápiles FC	38	12	14	12	48	-	53	50
6.	AD San Carlos Ciudad Quesada	38	13	13	12	35	-	38	52
7.	ADR Jicaral Sercoba	38	10	16	12	35	-	39	46
8.	Limón FC (*Relegated*)	38	11	11	16	40	-	66	44
9.	AD Municipal Pérez Zeledón	38	10	13	15	42	-	63	43
10.	Guadalupe FC	38	10	13	15	57	-	58	43
11.	Sporting FC San José	38	11	8	19	38	-	55	41
12.	AD Municipal Grecia FC	38	6	15	17	36	-	55	33

THE CLUBS 2020/2021

Please note: number of matches, subtitutes and goals are including Regular Seasons and all Play-offs!

LIGA DEPORTIVA ALAJUELENSE

Foundation date: June 18, 1919
Address: Avenida 3, Calles 13 y 15, Alajuela
Stadium: Estadio „Alejandro Morera Soto", Alajuela (17,895)

THE SQUAD

	DOB	Ape M	(s)	G	Cla M	(s)	G
Goalkeepers:							
Leonel Gerardo Moreira Ledezma	02.04.1990	18			22		
Mauricio José Vargas Campos (USA)	10.08.1992	2			2	(1)	
Defenders:							
Daniel Arreola Argüello (MEX)	08.10.1985				18		2
Júnior Enrique Díaz Campbell	12.09.1983	4	(1)	1	5	(9)	
Fernán José Faerrón Tristán	22.08.2000	15	(1)	3	12	(5)	
Alexis Yohaslin Gamboa Rojas	20.03.1999				7	(3)	1
Ian Elijah Lawrence Escoe	28.05.2002				6	(1)	
Adolfo Abdiel Machado (PAN)	14.02.1985	19	(1)				
Marcos Josué Meneses Salazar	12.07.1995	1	(3)	1			
Carlos Andrei Mora Montoya	18.03.2001	7	(12)	1			
Yurguin Alberto Román Alfaro	19.01.1997	3	(4)		15		
José Andrés Salvatierra López	10.10.1989	13	(2)		15	(2)	
Ian Rey Smith Quiros	06.03.1998	7	(7)		8	(4)	
Facundo Gabriel Zabala (ARG)	02.01.1999	17		2			
Midfielders:							
Brandon Aguilera Zamora	28.06.2003	4	(5)		2	(15)	1
Bernald Alfaro Alfaro	26.01.1997	4	(8)		11	(7)	
Geancarlo Castro González	12.02.2002		(4)		1	(10)	
José Miguel Cubero Loría	14.02.1987	2	(3)		10	(3)	
Dylan Armando Flores Knowles	30.05.1993	5	(12)				
Alexander Agustín López Rodríguez (HON)	05.06.1992	17	(1)	1	18		3
Rashir Shakir Parkins Harris	23.02.2001		(3)				
Barlon Andrés Sequeira Sibaja	25.05.1998	20		2	14	(1)	1
Forwards:							
Marcel Hernández Campanioni (CUB)	11.07.1989				19	(2)	11
Adrián Alonso Martínez Batista	15.10.1998	13	(3)	4	18	(1)	7
Jurguens Josafat Montenegro Vallejo	13.12.2000	13	(5)	5	13	(9)	8
Carlos Mora Montoya	18.03.2001				8	(12)	1
Jonathan Alonso Moya Aguilar	06.01.1992	15	(2)	12			
Bryan Jafet Ruiz González	18.08.1985	15	(2)	4	17	(6)	3
Álvaro Alberto Saborío Chacón	25.03.1982	6	(12)	6			
Aaron Suárez Zuñiga	27.06.2002				5	(6)	2
Johan Alberto Venegas Ulloa	27.11.1988				18	(5)	13
Trainer:							
Andrés José Carevic Ghelfi (ARG)	13.12.1978	20			24		

CLUB SPORT CARTAGINÉS DEPORTIVO S.A. CARTAGO

Foundation date: July 1, 1906
Address: Calle 8, Avenida 11 y 13, Barrio Asís, Cartago
Stadium: Estadio "José Rafael Fello Meza Ivankovich", Cartago (8,831)

THE SQUAD

Name	DOB	Ape M	Ape (s)	Ape G	Cla M	Cla (s)	Cla G
Goalkeepers:							
Marco Antonio Madrigal Villalobos	03.08.1985	1			11		
Darryl Jared Parker Cortes	07.03.1993	17			11		
Defenders:							
Bismar Gilberto Acosta Evans	19.12.1986				7	(2)	
Antonio Aguilar Jiménez	22.11.1996		(2)				
Carlos Luis Barahona Jiménez	21.08.2002		(1)		16		
Ryan Bolaños Davis	19.12.1998	8	(1)		10	(1)	
Kenner Gutiérrez Cerdas	09.06.1989	13			12	(1)	1
Carlos Adriel Montenegro Rodríguez (NCA)	07.01.1991	2	(5)		3	(1)	
William Quirós Espinoza	19.10.1994	14		2	13	(2)	
Diego Andrés Sánchez Corrales	07.08.1998	6	(4)	1	10	(6)	
Heyreel Antonio Saravia Vargas	06.10.1992	10			10	(1)	
José Eduardo Sosa Centeno	04.10.1994	10	(1)	2	9	(6)	1
Román Aureliano Torres Morcillo (PAN)	20.03.1986				13	(2)	1
Midfielders:							
Luis Ronaldo Araya Hernández	03.08.1999	3	(8)	1	4	(10)	
Kevin Arrieta Maroto	13.02.1991	4	(7)	2			
Daniel Chacón Salas	11.04.2001	18		1	3	(1)	1
Esthuar Raúl Dávila Garita	11.08.2000	2	(4)	1		(2)	
Diego Alonso Estrada Valverde	25.05.1989		(2)		2	(3)	
Allen Esteban Guevara Zúñiga	16.04.1989	10	(5)	1	5	(16)	
Carlos Alonso Hernández Espinoza	29.08.1989	2	(9)		4	(2)	
Isaí Orlando Molina Víquez	03.01.2001					(1)	
Ronald Mauricio Montero Lobo	28.03.1987	15		2	20		1
Cristopher Antonio Núñez González	08.12.1997	17		4	18	(1)	2
Jacke Fabián Rojas Ramírez	04.09.1998		(1)			(1)	
Jeikel Francisco Venegas McCarthy	06.04.1988	10	(2)	2	11	(5)	1
Forwards:							
Byron Bonilla Martínez (NCA)	30.08.1993	13	(5)	1	16	(3)	4
Jonathan Alberto Hansen (ARG)	10.09.1988		(10)				
Marcel Hernández Campanioni (CUB)	11.07.1989	18		13			
David Gerardo Ramírez Ruiz	28.05.1993				7	(7)	2
Andy Josué Reyes Vado	06.04.1999	5	(6)	1	11	(11)	3
Roger Fabricio Rojas Lazo (HON)	09.06.1990				16	(1)	6
David Alonso Vargas Masís	31.08.1993		(1)				
Steve Taylor Fallas	18.06.1999		(3)				
Trainer:							
Hernán Evaristo Medford Bryan	23.05.1968	18			17		
[12.04.2021] Danny Alberto Fonseca Bravo	07.11.1979				2		
[20.04.2021] Geiner Isidro Segura Mora	14.10.1974				3		

ASOCIACIÓN DEPORTIVA MUNICIPAL GRECIA FÚTBOL CLUB
Foundation date: August 16, 1998
Address: Avenida Colón, Grecia
Stadium: Estadio „Allen Riggioni Suárez", Grecia (3,354)

THE SQUAD

	DOB	M	Ape (s)	G	M	Cla (s)	G
Goalkeepers:							
Víctor Bolívar Ordóñez	03.09.1983	3					
Bryan Alejandro Morales Carrillo	04.07.1993				2		
Brayan Adiak Rodríguez Torres	23.09.1996		(1)				
Kevin Ruiz Rojas	10.06.1988	15			20		
Defenders:							
Jean Carlo Agüero Duarte	06.07.1993	10	(4)	2	18	(1)	
Shain Joshua Brown	25.01.1996	6	(1)				
Adrián Alberto Chévez Alanis	27.02.1998	2	(1)				
José Esteban Espinoza Sibaja	22.11.1997	3					
José Guillermo Garro González	07.06.1986				4	(1)	
Pablo Herrera Barrantes	14.02.1987				9	(6)	1
Marvin Andrés Obando Mata	18.05.1982				2	(3)	
Leonel Héctor Peralta (ARG)	09.07.1992	8	(2)		1		
Jefferson Ronaldo Rivera Stuart	02.11.1996				13	(3)	
Alejandro José Rodríguez Hernández	11.01.1997		(2)			(1)	
Jean Carlos Sánchez Gutiérrez	19.04.1992	10	(3)		9	(4)	1
Luis José Sequeira Guerrero	11.05.1994	8	(5)				
Richard Steven Gutiérrez	24.12.1996	14	(1)		8	(2)	
José Gabriel Vargas Barrantes	07.11.1989	17		1	21		6
Midfielders:							
José Rodolfo Alfaro Vargas	18.03.2000		(7)	1	1	(2)	
Juan Pablo Arguedas Chacón	21.04.1997	3	(6)				
Osvaldo Alonso Barrantes Segura	10.09.2003				1		
Roger Daniel Cortés Guevara	23.10.2000		(1)				
Luis Carlos Fallas Treminio	12.04.1998	4	(8)		17	(1)	
Yecxy Jarquín Ramos	22.05.2000		(3)		8	(6)	
José Martín Leitón Rodríguez	06.08.1993				5	(5)	
Anthony Josué López Muñoz	19.01.1996	9		1	4	(11)	1
Axell Quirós Cruz	03.06.1998	9			7	(2)	
Jason Reyes Mora	22.12.1997	3	(3)	1			
Youstin Delfin Salas Gómez	17.06.1996	15		1	17	(2)	
Álvaro de Jesús Sánchez Alfaro	02.08.1984	16	(2)	2	18	(2)	
Rubén Andrés Silva Castillo	11.05.2002					(2)	
Kenneth Gerardo Vargas Vargas	17.04.2002				8	(3)	2
Forwards:							
Abraham Darío Carreño Rohan (MEX)	13.01.1988				1		
Jorge Alejandro Castro Salazar	11.09.1990				13	(4)	2
Naël Wellofky Élysée (HAI)	28.05.2001	4	(12)		4	(7)	
Aldo Xavier Magaña Padilla (MEX)	08.04.1996	9	(3)	1			
Luis Alfredo Rodríguez Arroyo	06.02.1993	8	(7)	2	1	(9)	1
Harry José Rojas Cabeza	20.12.1996	15	(2)	2	15	(4)	3
Carlos Daniel Small Cardenas (PAN)	13.03.1995				6	(9)	3
Alberth Mauricio Villalobos Solís	25.01.1995	7	(3)	2	9	(5)	1
Trainer:							
Fernando Palomeque Díaz (MEX)	20.03.1968	8					

[28.09.2020] Luis Diego Arnáez Villegas	05.11.1967	9	
[10.12.2020] José Enrique Rodríguez Carranza	01.12.1982	1	
[01.01.2021] Gilberto Martínez Vidal	01.10.1979		14
[25.03.2021] Johnny Gerardo Chaves Arias	26.09.1960		8

GUADALUPE FÚTBOL CLUB

Foundation date: April 24, 2017
Address: n/a
Stadium: Estadio „José Joaquín Fonseca", Guadalupe (4,200)

THE SQUAD

	DOB	Ape M	(s)	G	Cla M	(s)	G
Goalkeepers:							
Luis Alejandro Barrientos Arguedas	11.02.1998	5					
Jorge Eduardo Jara Lemaire	05.01.1996	1			5		
Luis Fernando Torres Brenes	16.03.1985	10			16		
Defenders:							
Lautaro Jesús Ayala (ARG)	23.06.1997	8		2	14	(1)	1
Brandón Bonilla Zárate	10.08.1996	14	(2)	1	18	(3)	1
Darío Alejandro Delgado Mora	14.12.1985	12			15	(2)	2
Kevin José Espinoza Campos	11.02.1997	13	(1)	2	4	(3)	
John Ángel Flores Barquero	02.12.0000	1			1	(1)	
Sebastián González Muñoz	11.03.1997	4	(5)	1	9	(8)	
Marcos Josué Meneses Salazar	12.07.1995				20	(1)	1
René Miranda Yubank	04.05.1996	4	(4)		19		2
Andrey Gerardo Mora Matarrita	18.09.1996	14	(2)		9	(1)	
Jason Andrés Prendas Cruz	15.02.1989	8	(1)				
Josué David Rodríguez Ramírez	10.03.1992	2	(5)		4	(2)	
Midfielders:							
Keven Steven Alemán-Bustos (CAN)	25.03.1994				2	(8)	1
Freyman Stivi Arce Ramírez	22.01.2002					(1)	
Din John Arias Álvarez	25.10.1992	1	(6)	2		(7)	
José Luis Cordero Manzanares	31.01.1987	12	(3)	1	4	(4)	1
Malcom Nackey Frago Mayers	19.07.1995		(1)				
Eduardo Luis Juárez Viales	22.09.1998	5	(3)		20		2
José Martín Leitón Rodríguez	06.08.1993	1	(2)				
Aaron Gerardo Murillo Fonseca	20.03.1998	2	(6)	1	5	(13)	
Victor Josué Murillo Villegas	18.06.1995	3	(5)		1	(4)	1
Sergio Antonio Nuñez Gutierrez	14.02.1998	13		1	8	(7)	
Jossimar Jesús Pemberton Segura	21.04.1993	16		4	19		5
Reiby Ling Smith Dixon	31.10.1992				4	(4)	
Forwards:							
Nicolás Azofeifa Valverde	10.08.2000				3	(6)	1
Anthony Daniel Contreras Enríquez	29.01.2000	9	(1)	5			
Diego Huacuja Martínez (MEX)	01.10.2001				4	(2)	
Andrés Gómez Rodríguez	07.05.2000	12	(1)	2			
Darryn Eduardo Rojas Jiménez	05.02.1999		(7)				
Royner Andrey Rojas Dinarte	11.06.2002	1	(4)	1	16	(1)	5
Arley Sandí Martínez	31.03.2001					(4)	
Frank Andrés Zamora García	16.08.1991	5		2	11	(5)	6
Trainer:							
Alexander José Vargas Villalobos	27.11.1978	16			21		

CLUB SPORT HEREDIANO HEREDIA

Foundation date: June 12, 1921
Address: Avenida 2, Calles 14 y 16, 325-300 Heredia
Stadium: Estadio „Eladio Rosabal Cordero", Heredia (8,068)

THE SQUAD

	DOB	Ape M	(s)	G	Cla M	(s)	G
Goalkeepers:							
Esteban Alvarado Brown	28.04.1989	8					
Minor Jesús Álvarez Cordero	14.11.1989				10		
Luis Alejandro Barrientos Arguedas	11.02.1998	1					
Bryan Andrés Segura Cruz	14.01.1997	11	(1)		16		
Defenders:							
Keyner Yamal Brown Blackwood	30.12.1991	10			15	(1)	
Keysher Fuller Spence	12.07.1994	7	(4)		4	(15)	
Orlando Moisés Galo Calderón	11.08.2000	16		1	19	(2)	1
Yael Andrés López Fuentes	17.12.1998	5	(2)		12	(4)	1
Mauricio de Jesús Núñez Morales	28.10.1993	9	(1)		1		
Christian Antonio Reyes Alemán	02.11.1995	6			3	(4)	
Aarón Salazar Arias	15.05.1999	17	(1)	2	17	(2)	3
Ariel Román Soto González	14.05.1992	10			22		2
Midfielders:							
Rándall Azofeifa Corrales	30.12.1984	5	(3)			(5)	
Jefferson Brenes Rojas	13.04.1997	15	(2)	3	8	(8)	1
Berny Thomas Burke Montiel	16.03.1996	2	(10)	1	7	(6)	
Óscar Esteban Granados Maroto	25.10.1985	7	(8)	1	9	(12)	
Jordy Francisco Hernández Molina	26.03.2002	1	(9)	1			
Dilan Andrés Moraga Corrales	21.04.2003		(1)				
Fabrizio Antonio Ramírez Montero	01.04.1997	3	(11)		16	(4)	2
Nextali Rodríguez Medina	03.03.1998	10	(2)	1	3	(10)	
Yeltsin Ignacio Tejeda Valverde	17.03.1992	15	(2)		19	(1)	
Gerson Torres Barrantes	28.08.1997	18		2	23		4
Suhander Manuel Zúñiga Cordero	15.01.1997	8	(5)	2	22	(2)	2
Forwards:							
Geovanni Arturo Campos Villalobos	14.12.1995	3	(7)	2			
Anthony Daniel Contreras Enríquez	29.01.2000				17	(9)	3
Leandro Barrios Rita dos Martires "Leandrinho" (BRA)	06.06.1986	7	(4)	2		(3)	
Jonathan Andrés McDonald Porras	28.10.1987	9		5	4	(4)	
Francisco Javier Rodríguez Hernández	08.02.1993				13	(7)	5
Brayan Andrés Rojas Jiménez	30.11.1997				4	(9)	3
John Jairo Ruiz Barrantes	10.01.1994	9	(1)	3	10	(7)	3
Yendrick Alberto Ruiz González	12.04.1987	8	(10)	3	12	(7)	7
Trainer:							
Jafet Soto Molina	01.04.1976	20					
[01.01.2021] Fernando Palomeque Díaz (MEX)	20.03.1968				6		
[05.02.2021] Pablo Andrés Salazar Sánchez	21.11.1982				1		
[09.02.2021] Luis Antonio Marín Murillo	10.08.1974				19		

ASOCIACIÓN DEPORTIVA Y RECREATIVA JICARAL SERCOBA

Foundation date: May 12, 2007
Address: *Not known*
Stadium: Estadio Asociación Cívica Jicaraleña, Jicaral (1,500)

THE SQUAD

	DOB	Ape M	(s)	G	Cla M	(s)	G
Goalkeepers:							
Kevin Andrés Briceño Toruño	21.10.1991	14			22		
Bryan Stid Cordero Varela	13.11.1994	1					
Jussef Nelson Delgado López	27.1.1994	1	(1)				
Defenders:							
Horacio Joaquín Aguirre Santellán (URU)	23.03.1991	15		1			
Kevin Arrieta Maroto	13.02.1991				6	(3)	
Esteban Cano Arias	08.05.1995	11	(1)	1	15	(6)	2
Kevin José Fajardo Martínez	05.09.1989	7			22		2
William Alban Fernández González	15.05.1994	13			18	(1)	
Francisco Roberto Flores Zapata	02.04.1988	16		1	6	(11)	
Rafael Ángel Núñez Jimenez	09.04.1984	11			4	(4)	
Marvin Andrés Obando Mata	18.05.1982	4	(3)				
Jason Andrés Prendas Cruz	15.02.1989				21		2
Kevin Enrique Vega Garro	05.04.1992				17	(1)	
Midfielders:							
Alejandro Jesús Bran Flores	05.03.2001				8	(6)	
Sebastián Gerardo Castro Rodríguez	16.08.2000		(1)				
Wálter de Jesús Chévez Ruiz	06.05.1986	13	(3)			(1)	
Kendall Alejandro Gallardo Sequeira	03.03.2000	4	(6)		12	(7)	
Rodrigo Alonso Garita Valverde	23.12.1993				1	(4)	
Ismael Alberto Gómez (ARG)	26.01.1984	4	(6)	1			
Luis José Gutiérrez García	21.02.1999	1	(2)		7		
Omar Alberto López Guzmán (MEX)	27.06.1989				13	(8)	1
Gustavo Adolfo Méndez Chaves	23.08.2000	1	(5)				
Néstor Monge Guevara	07.01.1990				7	(11)	
Yonaiker Samir Mora González	12.07.1998	3	(5)				
Kevin Javier Patiño Guerra	23.12.1999	7	(7)			(2)	
José Carlos Pérez González	04.07.1987	3	(1)		15	(4)	2
Bryan Gerardo Solórzano Chacón	05.01.1988		(1)				
Edder Gerardo Solórzano Leal	21.09.1995	4	(7)	2			
José Andrés Torres Jiménez	26.01.1997				1	(6)	
Joaquín Azzem Vergés Collazo (URU)	01.06.1992				11	(5)	1
Forwards:							
Nicolás Azofeifa Valverde	10.08.2000	4	(2)				
Javier Alexander Camareno Álvarez	05.01.1998	8	(3)		1	(1)	
Giovanni Pierre Clunie Asenjo	20.12.1994	14	(1)	4	1	(3)	
Habraham Javier González Henry	07.02.2001				1	(1)	
Kennedy Rocha Pereira (BRA)	30.10.1996	9	(2)	3	15	(2)	6
Cristhiam Lagos Navarro	17.08.1984		(2)				
Joshua Parra Mesén	27.04.2001				10	(7)	3
Arley Sandí Martínez	31.03.2001	1					
Juan Vicente Solís Brenes	26.10.1987	7	(6)	1	8	(10)	
Trainer:							
Erick Alberto Rodríguez Santamaría	04.12.1973	3					
[07.09.2020] José Antonio Giacone Garita (ARG)	05.01.1971	13					
[01.01.2021] Martín Marcelo Arriola Sobrino (URU)	03.10.1973				22		

LIMÓN FÚTBOL CLUB

Foundation date: 1964
Address: *Not known*
Stadium: Estadio „Juan Gobán", Limón (2,349)

THE SQUAD	DOB	Ape M	(s)	G	Cla M	(s)	G
Goalkeepers:							
Esteban Alvarado	28.04.1989				20		
Minor Jesús Álvarez Cordero	14.11.1989	11					
Dexter Alberto Lewis Bonilla	02.02.1981	5			3		
Defenders:							
Jorkaeff Mauricio Azofeifa Rivas	09.02.2001	12	(1)		12	(1)	1
Jefferson Barnett Vargas	01.04.2000	2	(3)		2		
Rasheed Rahem García Clarke	06.06.1999	1	(3)		1	(5)	
Jemark Gersinio Hernández Hall	14.12.1994				10	(4)	
Kareem Jabbar McLean Powell	14.07.1983	12			18	(2)	
Greivin Méndez Venegas	24.02.1992	6	(4)		18	(4)	
Luis Alejandro Pérez Castillo	08.01.1991	11	(1)		22		2
Jeikol James Peterkin Maxwell	12.08.1991	3					
Roy Alexander Smith Lewis	19.04.1990	14		1	18	(1)	
Midfielders:							
Darryl Yorel Araya Samuels	08.11.2000	10	(6)	2	2	(18)	
Ryan Germaine Cane Box	05.07.2003					(2)	
Kadeem Alexandre Coles Martínez	12.05.1999	4	(5)		9	(4)	
Kevin Mauricio Cunningham Brown	07.06.1985				8	(5)	
Alexánder Alberto Espinoza Barrantes	04.02.1985	10	(3)	1	18	(2)	5
Jurguen Esquivel					1	(1)	
Marvin Lorenzo Esquivel Paz	24.06.1993	10	(4)	2	12	(4)	
Johnny Delroy Gordon Benwell	12.01.1991	13	(2)		20	(1)	
Sheldon Ricard Harris Gregory	26.12.1999	1	(2)			(1)	
Derrickson Quirós Sánchez	21.12.2001	5	(5)				
Jefferson Ronaldo Rivera Stuart	03.11.1996	14	(1)	2			
Mauricio Salas Vargas	09.02.1997	5	(1)				
Jonathan Esteban Tejada Matute (HON)	13.09.1994					(6)	
Carlos Arturo Villegas Retana	03.03.1999				19		5
Roan Roberto Wilson Gordon	01.05.2002	2	(5)		15	(5)	1
Forwards:							
Keyder Bernard Cordero	26.09.1996	5	(1)	1	1	(2)	
Mynor Javier Escoe Miller	06.04.1991				1	(11)	1
Andrey Anthony Francis Carmona	15.12.1990	4	(2)	2	2	(10)	1
Kishurn Gouldbourne Brown	11.03.2004		(1)				
Carlos Andrés Soza Quezada (CHI)	19.09.1989	1	(6)	1			
John Dario Vizcaíno Piedra	02.09.1994				12	(2)	6
Steven Andrey Williams Barnett	20.01.1987	3	(7)				
Yuaycell Shamir Wright Parks	22.06.1992	12	(2)	3	9	(1)	3
Trainer:							
Luis Fernando Fallas Arias	24.07.1974	16					
[16.01.2021] Ricardo Augusto Allen Thomas	26.12.1979				3		
[27.01.2021] Daniel Alberto Casas Lago (URU)	29.04.1959				17		
[03.05.2021] Ricardo Augusto Allen Thomas	26.12.1979				3		

ASOCIACIÓN DEPORTIVA MUNICIPAL DE PÉREZ ZELEDÓN

Foundation date: 1962
Address: Parque de San Isidro de El General, San Isidro de El General
Stadium: Estadio Municipal, Pérez Zeledón (3,259)

THE SQUAD

	DOB	Ape M	(s)	G	Cla M	(s)	G
Goalkeepers:							
Jussef Nelson Delgado López	27.01.1994				13		
Guido Jiménez López	11.06.1997	6					
Brayan Alejandro Morales Carrillo	04.07.1993	10					
Luis Diego Rivas Méndez	24.08.1997				8		
Justin Vargas Hernández	02.10.2001				1		
Defenders:							
Johnny Gerardo Acosta Zamora	21.07.1983				8		
Guillermo Daniel Alán Villalobos	09.05.1999				8	(5)	
Dennis Esteban Castillo Romero	30.04.1993	10		1			
Johán Enrique Cortés Alfaro	05.12.1999	3	(1)				
José Esteban Espinoza Sibaja	22.11.1997				7	(1)	
Asdrúbal Enrique Gibbons Hidalgo	10.06.1987	6		1			
Henrique Moura Perillo (BRA)	08.02.1991	3			21		
Jaikel Medina Scarlett	28.01.1992	8		1			
Diego Armando Mesen Calvo	28.03.1999	7	(2)		11	(3)	
Sebastían Monge Quesada	28.08.2000	5					
Jhamir Kareem Ordain Alexander	29.07.1993	5			11	(1)	
Keral Yanfer Ríos Castillo	05.03.2003				2	(1)	
Midfielders:							
Axel Mauriel Amador Rojas	06.11.2000	1	(2)		1	(2)	
Anderson Barboza Ureña	05.04.2002		(2)			(1)	
Luis Carlos Barrantes Campos	28.09.1991	9	(4)		11	(4)	
Geiner Leonardo Castillo Rojas	02.03.2001	2	(5)		1	(4)	
Kenneth Josué Cerdas Barrantes	29.12.1995	5	(5)	2	9	(8)	1
Junior Antonio Delgado Solís	24.09.1993	5			15	(1)	
Juan Gabriel Guzmán Otárola	17.06.1987	6	(9)		7	(1)	
Gabriel Fernando Leiva Rojas	27.08.1994	12	(2)	4	18	(2)	6
Anthony Emanuel Mata Flores	28.07.1995	1	(6)		1	(2)	
Néstor Monge Guevara	07.01.1990	13					
Joshua Navarro Sandí	11.03.1999	14		3	9	(5)	
Luis Stewart Pérez Alguera	17.03.1987	4	(3)	2	16	(5)	6
Francisco Ramírez Mora	12.08.1999				1		
José Paulo Rodríguez Santamaria	24.05.2001				7	(4)	
Reimond Ademar Salas Gómez	11.03.1994	13	(1)	3	5	(8)	
Edder Gerardo Solórzano Leal	21.09.1995				15	(4)	
Daniel Villegas Mora	06.01.1998	11	(3)	1	14	(3)	1
Álvaro José Zamora Mata	09.03.2002					(4)	
Forwards:							
César Gerardo Elizondo Quesada	10.02.1988	4	(2)				
Hernán Gustavo Fener (ARG)	21.06.1990	6	(4)	2			
Craig Jeffrey Foster (JAM)	07.09.1991	1	(2)				
Deybis Augusto Jiménez	01.07.1995					(3)	
Starling Matarrita González	20.06.1990				16	(4)	6
Josué Mitchell Omier	11.11.1989	5	(9)		1	(7)	
Justin Monge Calderón	30.06.2002	1	(1)		1	(1)	

| Oscar Javier Móvil Castillo (COL) | 01.05.1987 | | 4 | (2) | |

Trainer:				
Johnny Gerardo Chaves Arias	26.09.1960	16		5
[02.02.2021] Paul César Wanchope Watson	31.07.1976			17

ASOCIACIÓN DEPORTIVA SAN CARLOS

Foundation date: May 9, 1965
Address: Estadio "Carlos Ugalde Álvarez", San Martín, Ciudad Quesada
Stadium: Estadio "Carlos Ugalde Álvarez", Ciudad Quesada (4,000)

THE SQUAD

	DOB	Ape M	(s)	G	Cla M	(s)	G
Goalkeepers:							
Luis Gabriel Alpízar Sibaja	23.05.1995	6			4		
Kevin José Chamorro Rodríguez	08.04.2000	10			17		
Jason Alonso Vega Carmona	06.11.1995				1		
Defenders:							
Sebastián Acuña Murillo	25.06.2002				1	(3)	
Álvaro Gerardo Aguilar Sánchez	24.01.1992	11			12		1
Randall Alberto Alvarado Brenes	17.12.1988				3	(4)	
Pablo César Arboine Carmona	03.04.1998	5	(4)				
Erick Anthony Cabalceta Giacchero	09.01.1993	12		2			
Jorge Andrés Gutiérrez Solano	24.04.1994	4	(4)		5	(2)	
Adolfo Abdiel Machado (PAN)	14.02.1985				21		
Carlos Manuel Martínez Castro	30.03.1999	14	(1)		1		
Juan Luis Pérez Rodríguez	29.06.1999				10	(3)	2
José David Sánchez Cruz	12.12.1994	12	(3)		18	(2)	1
Keylor Ubaldo Soto Vega	26.07.1984	13	(1)	3	19	(2)	1
Midfielders:							
Carlos Acosta Evans	31.08.1983	1					
Wilmer Jesús Azofeifa Valverde	04.06.1994	8	(6)	1	19	(2)	1
Raheem Cole Martínez	12.05.1999	4	(4)		9	(9)	
Roberto José Córdoba Durán	16.07.1998	7	(7)		5	(5)	1
Cristian Alonso Martínez Mena	19.04.1994	13	(1)		15	(4)	
Gustavo Adolfo Méndez Chaves	23.08.2000					(6)	
José Guillermo Mora Campos	02.06.1992	9	(2)		12	(6)	1
Bayron David Múrcia Barberena	19.07.2003		(1)			(1)	
Joseth Gael Peraza Serrano	09.12.2004		(1)				
Esteban Ramírez Segnini	02.02.1987	2	(6)				
Andrey Josué Soto Ruíz	08.04.2003	2	(2)		1	(7)	
Jefry Antonio Valverde Rojas	10.06.1995	11	(2)	1	21	(1)	
Luis Alfredo Zúñiga González (NCA)	05.04.2001		(1)				
Forwards:							
Jormán Isreal Aguilar Bustamante (PAN)	11.01.1994	10	(1)	3			
Jean Carlo Alvarado Solis	23.02.2002		(3)			(1)	
Pedro Federico Báez Benítez (PAR)	15.01.1997				5	(12)	
Rashid Enrique Chirino Serrano	21.10.2000	4	(6)	1	11	(7)	2
Julio César Cruz González (MEX)	23.11.1995	4	(3)				
Javon Romario East (JAM)	22.03.1995	7	(5)				
Aldo Xavier Magaña Padilla (MEX)	08.04.1996				1	(7)	
Marco Julián Mena Rojas	03.11.1989	3	(5)	1	9	(9)	2
Álvaro Alberto Saborío Chacón	25.03.1982				21	(1)	9
Alberth Mauricio Villalobos Solís	25.01.1995	4	(1)	1			

Luis Alfredo Zuñiga González (PAN)	27.01.1997		1	
Trainer:				
Carlos Alberto Restrepo Isaza (COL)	05.03.1961	4		
[08.09.2020] Jeaustin Campos Madriz	30.06.1971	12	10	
[01.03.2021] Gustavo Adrián Martínez Rocha (ARG)	12.11.1972		12	

ASOCIACIÓN DEPORTIVA SANTOS DE GUÁPILES

Foundation date: 1961
Address: *Not known*
Stadium: Estadio „Ebal Rodríguez", Guápiles (3,300)

THE SQUAD

	DOB	Ape M	(s)	G	Cla M	(s)	G
Goalkeepers:							
Daniel Arturo Cambronero Solano	08.01.1986	10					
Emer Jesús Espinoza Matarrita	02.04.1995				1		
Douglas Forvis Espinoza (NCA)	17.05.1992	6			23		
Defenders:							
Randall Alberto Alvarado Brenes	17.12.1988	8	(4)				
Pablo César Arboine Carmona	03.04.1998				13	(2)	
Yeremy Gerardo Araya Molina	07.10.1988		(7)				
Michael Vinicio Barquero Abarca	10.02.1991		(2)		2	(10)	
Alvin Jamier Bennett Freckleton	12.11.1994	13			12	(4)	
Pablo Esteban Fonseca Brenes	13.08.1998				4	(3)	
José Guillermo Garro González	07.06.1986	7	(2)	1			
Byron Jhosué Gutiérrez Piña	10.04.1998		(3)				
Jemark Gersinio Hernández Hall	14.12.1994		(2)				
Jason Telemaco Ingram Oporta (NCA)	20.08.1997	16			9	(5)	
Alexander Freiber Jiménez Fuentes	06.07.2001	16		1	5	(3)	
Douglas Andrey López Araya	21.09.1998	5	(4)		13	(6)	2
Juan Diego Madrigal Espinoza	21.05.1987	15	(1)	2	23	(1)	
Cristopher Josué Meneses Barrantes	02.05.1990				22		1
Roy Miller Hernández	24.11.1984				18	(1)	
Midfielders:							
Keyshwen Kermey Arboine Peterkin	02.11.2001				2		
Adán Alberto Clímaco Calderón	05.01.2001					(1)	
Geremy Gómez Stuart	31.08.2001				1	(7)	
Víctor Alfredo Griffith Mullins (PAN)	12.12.2000	8	(4)				
Brayan Steven López Ramírez	03.06.1990	15		1	15	(5)	2
Denilson Mason Gutiérrez	09.09.1998	8	(3)		20	(2)	1
Denilson Jhonn Mora Marín	08.10.1999	1	(4)		3	(6)	
Anderson Jesús Núñez Ruiz	27.02.1998		(2)				
Osvaldo Roberto Rodríguez Flores	17.12.1990	15		1	17	(2)	4
Jourgen Isacc Salas Ortega	19.07.2001				1	(3)	
Mauricio Salas Vargas	09.02.1997				1	(8)	
Ariel Antonio Zapata Pizarro	03.01.1997		(1)				
Forwards:							
Kenny Martin Cunningham Brown	07.06.1985	7			15	(4)	7
Javon Romario East (JAM)	22.03.1995				23		13
Starling Doney Matarrita González	20.06.1990	14		5			
Erson Jossimar Méndez James	19.09.2001	11	(5)	1	10	(10)	3
Luis Paradela (CUB)	21.01.1997				11	(5)	3
José Alejandro Ruiz Suárez	22.03.1999	1	(7)				
Trainer:							
Luis Antonio Marín Murillo	10.08.1974	16			7		
[08.02.2021] Erick Alberto Rodríguez Santamaría	04.12.1973				17		

DEPORTIVO SAPRISSA SAN JUAN S.A.D.

Foundation date: July 16, 1935
Address: Frente clinica Rodrigo Fournier 2834-1000, San Juan de Tíbás, San José
Stadium: Estadio „Ricardo Saprissa Aymá", San José (20,558)

THE SQUAD

Name	DOB	Ape M	(s)	G	Cla M	(s)	G
Goalkeepers:							
Aarón Moises Cruz Esquivel	25.05.1991	18			20		
Francisco Alejandro Gómez Bermúdez	08.04.1989				6		
Defenders:							
Johnny Gerardo Acosta Zamora	21.07.1983	8	(5)	1			
Ricardo José Blanco Mora	12.05.1989	12			17	(4)	
Matthew Bolaños García	05.07.2002		(4)		3		
Walter Eduardo Cortés Pérez	05.02.2000				5	(3)	
Aubrey Robert David (TRI)	11.10.1990	14		1	21	(2)	2
Esteban Ezequiel Espíndola López (ARG)	22.03.1992	8	(3)		17	(3)	3
Jordy Jafeth Evans Solano	17.04.2002	4	(2)		19	(6)	
Luis José Hernández Paniagua	07.02.1998	16			10	(8)	
Alexander Robinson Delgado	21.11.1988	7	(5)				
Atim Rooper García	25.05.2001	1	(1)			(1)	
Kendall Jamaal Waston Manley	01.01.1988				13	(2)	4
Midfielders:							
Marvin Angulo Borbón	30.09.1986	16		3	13	(3)	
Michael Francisco Barrantes Rojas	04.10.1983	13	(4)	3	16	(5)	1
Daniel Colindres Solera	10.01.1985	13	(5)	3	19	(1)	6
David Alberto Guzmán Pérez	18.02.1990	12	(3)	1	19	(3)	2
Jaylon Jahi Hadden Scarlett	09.04.1998	1	(4)				
Jedwin Hohao Lester Arroyo	21.08.2002		(2)		2	(2)	
Warren Steven Madrigal Molina	24.07.2004		(3)			(4)	
Jimmy Marín Vílchez	08.10.1997	15	(1)	3	20	(4)	5
Samuel Dimark Maroto Monge	16.07.2003				1	(1)	
Jonathan Josué Martínez Solano	19.03.1998	1	(10)		3	(7)	
Esteban Eduardo Rodríguez Ballestero	25.01.1988	9	(6)		4	(15)	
Douglas Esteban Sequeira Borbón	16.09.2003		(1)		1		
Yostín Tellería Alfaro	09.04.2003		(5)	1		(3)	
Mariano Néstor Torres (ARG)	19.05.1987	15	(2)	3	19	(3)	1
Forwards:							
Johel Fabricio Alemán Gaitán	26.07.2003		(3)		3	(1)	
Jeiner Steven Ballestero Chinchilla	19.01.2001				1	(5)	1
Christián Bolaños Navarro	17.05.1984				17	(2)	8
Keimark Yamark Davis Kelly	08.11.2002					(4)	
Ariel Francisco Rodríguez Araya	27.09.1989				11	(4)	6
Orlando Alexis Sinclair Hernández	19.04.1998				6	(7)	2
Johan Alberto Venegas Ulloa	27.11.1988	13		9			
Frank Andrés Zamora García	16.08.1991	2	(10)	2		(2)	
Trainer:							
Wálter Centeno Corea	06.10.1974	18			6		
[08.02.2021] Roy Anthony Myers Francis	13.04.1969				12		
[20.04.2021] Marco Antonio Herrera Marín	27.01.1969				1		
[21.04.2021] Wilber Mauricio Wright Reynolds	20.12.1970				7		

SPORTING FOOTBALL CLUB SAN JOSÉ

Foundation date: June 24, 2016
Address: Pavas, 10109 San José
Stadium: Estadio "Ernesto Rohrmoser Lahmann", San José (3,000)

THE SQUAD

	DOB	Ape M	(s)	G	Cla M	(s)	G
Goalkeepers:							
Carlos Andrés Méndez Segura	21.12.1982	5	(1)		21		
Érick Adonis Pineda Castrillo	02.04.1997	13			3		
Defenders:							
Horacio Joaquín Aguirre Santellán (URU)	23.03.1991				18	(1)	2
Darío José Alfaro González	25.02.1997	3	(4)				
Irving Esteban Calderón Reid	15.04.1994	14	(3)				
Dennis Castillo Romero	30.04.1993				20	(1)	1
Rudy Anthony Dawson Forbes	08.05.1988				7	(1)	
Luis Alejandro Flores Cordero	23.01.1994	18			24		
Rigoberto Alonso Jiménez Chavarría	21.02.1989	15	(1)		21		
Jaikel Medina Scarlett	28.01.1992				14	(3)	
Edder Jersinio Munguio Villegas	22.07.1985	14			16	(1)	1
José Luis Quirós Espinoza	05.08.1999				1	(4)	
Yostin Jafet Salinas Phillips	14.09.1998	16			6	(1)	1
Kevin Enrique Vega Garro	05.04.1992	1	(2)				
Midfielders:							
Michael Josué Arias Ugalde	31.01.1996	7	(9)	1		(7)	
Juan Gabriel Bustos Golobio	09.07.1992	7	(3)	3			
Rodrigo Alonso Garita Valverde	23.12.1993	10	(2)				
Jaylon Jahi Hadden Scarlett	09.04.1998				13	(2)	1
Diego Josué Madrigal Ulloa	19.03.1989				14	(3)	2
José Miguel Marín Calderón	29.09.1984	2	(9)				
Elian Andrés Morales Traña	29.05.2000	5	(5)	1	9	(8)	1
Josimar Ademir Olivero Rodríguez	20.02.1992	12	(3)		1	(6)	
Rashir Shakir Parkins Harris	23.02.2001				14	(4)	
Esteban Ramírez Segnini	02.02.1987				13	(10)	2
Jorman Esteban Sánchez Tencio	16.02.1998	2	(6)				
Jaime Valderramos Montero	16.03.1990		(5)	1			
Bryan Isaias Vega Chavez	27.05.1991	15	(3)	3	18	(1)	2
Forwards:							
Jorge Alejandro Castro Salazar	11.09.1990	9	(5)	1			
Jostin Akeem Daly Cordero	23.04.1998	14	(2)	8	10	(11)	2
Hernán Gustavo Fener (ARG)	21.06.1990					(2)	
Jonathan Alberto Hansen (ARG)	19.09.1988				13	(4)	2
Cristhiam Lagos Navarro	17.08.1984				7	(9)	4
Jeffry Montenegro Zúñiga	22.04.1995	1	(10)	1	1	(1)	
Jean Andrés Scott Hernández	14.03.1994	4	(8)	2			
Derrickson Quirós Sánchez	21.12.2001					(5)	
Randall Jhoan Row Solano	08.10.1998	11	(3)				
Trainer:							
Randall Enrique Alberto Row Arias	21.04.1971	18					
José Antonio Giacone Garita (ARG) [01.01.2021]	05.01.1971				24		

SECOND LEVEL
Segunda División de Costa Rica – Liga de Ascenso 2020/2021

Torneo Apertura 2020

First Stage

Grupo A

1.	AD Municipal Liberia	10	5	2	3	14	-	11	17
2.	AD Guanacasteca Nicoya	10	3	6	1	12	-	9	15
3.	Puntarenas FC	10	3	5	2	11	-	11	14
4.	Marineros FC de Puntarenas	10	2	6	2	12	-	13	12
5.	Municipal Garabito Jacó	10	2	5	3	11	-	13	11
6.	AD Santa Rosa	10	1	4	5	11	-	14	7

Grupo B

1.	AD COFUTPA Palmares	10	5	2	3	15	-	10	17
2.	AD Cariari de Pococí	10	5	2	3	14	-	12	17
3.	*AD Juventud Escazuceña*	10	4	3	3	12	-	11	15
4.	AD Carmelita Alajuela	10	3	3	4	9	-	10	12
5.	AD Municipal San Ramón	10	3	2	5	10	-	13	11
6.	AD Municipal Santa Ana	10	2	4	4	10	-	14	10

Grupo C

1.	ADC Barrio México San José	10	6	2	2	13	-	7	20
2.	Fútbol Consultants Desamparados	10	5	3	2	18	-	10	18
3.	*Puerto Golfito FC*	10	3	5	2	13	-	9	14
4.	Aserrí FC	10	3	4	3	11	-	13	13
5.	CS Uruguay de Coronado	10	3	2	5	12	-	14	11
6.	AD Municipal Turrialba	10	1	2	7	7	-	21	5

Top-2 of each group and the best two teams ranked third were qualified for the Play-offs Quarter-Finals.

Play-offs

Quarter-Finals [21-25.11.2020]

AD Cariari de Pococí - AD Municipal Liberia	2-1(2-0)	2-2(0-0)
AD Guanacasteca Nicoya - AD COFUTPA Palmares	0-0	2-1(0-1)
AD Juventud Escazuceña - ADC Barrio México San José	1-0(0-0)	0-0
Puerto Golfito FC - ADC Barrio México San José	1-0(1-0)	1-1(0-1)

Semi-Finals [28.11.-06.12.2020]

AD Juventud Escazuceña - AD Guanacasteca Nicoya	0-1(0-1)	0-1(0-0)
Puerto Golfito FC - AD Cariari de Pococí	2-0(2-0)	2-2(0-1)

Final [13-20.12.2020]

Puerto Golfito FC - AD Guanacasteca Nicoya	0-1(0-1)	1-2(0-1)

2020 Torneo Apertura Champions: **AD Guanacasteca Nicoya**

Torneo Clausura 2021

Grupo A

1.	Puntarenas FC	10	6	1	3	11	-	8	19
2.	AD Guanacasteca Nicoya	10	4	5	1	11	-	5	17
3.	*AD Municipal Liberia*	10	4	4	2	14	-	10	16
4.	Municipal Garabito Jacó	10	4	3	3	17	-	15	15
5.	Marineros FC de Puntarenas	10	3	2	5	9	-	14	11
6.	AD Santa Rosa	10	0	3	7	7	-	17	3

Grupo B

1.	AD Carmelita Alajuela	10	7	0	3	22	-	16	21
2.	AD Municipal San Ramón	10	5	2	3	12	-	10	17
3.	*AD COFUTPA Palmares*	10	5	1	4	17	-	16	16
4.	AD Juventud Escazuceña	10	4	2	4	21	-	16	14
5.	AD Municipal Santa Ana	9	2	2	5	7	-	15	8
6.	AD Cariari de Pococí	9	2	1	6	13	-	19	7

Grupo C

1.	ADC Barrio México San José	10	8	2	0	29	-	14	26
2.	Fútbol Consultants Desamparados	10	5	3	2	18	-	10	18
3.	AD Municipal Turrialba	10	4	3	3	16	-	14	15
4.	Puerto Golfito FC	10	3	2	5	20	-	21	11
5.	Aserrí FC	10	2	2	6	9	-	20	8
6.	CS Uruguay de Coronado	10	2	0	8	7	-	20	6

Top-2 of each group and the best two teams ranked third were qualified for the Play-offs Quarter-Finals.

Play-offs

Quarter-Finals [10-18.04.2021]

AD COFUTPA Palmares - ADC Barrio México San José	0-4(0-1)	1-6(0-3)
AD Guanacasteca Nicoya - Fútbol Consultants Desamparados	6-2(2-1)	4-1(3-0)
AD Municipal Liberia - AD Carmelita Alajuela	1-2(0-1)	2-2(1-2)
AD Municipal San Ramón - Puntarenas FC	0-0	1-2(0-1)

Semi-Finals [24.04.-02.05.2021]

AD Guanacasteca Nicoya - ADC Barrio México San José	1-2(0-2)	1-0 aet 4-2 pen
Puntarenas FC - AD Carmelita Alajuela	2-3(2-3)	5-0(3-0)

Final [09-15.05.2021]

AD Guanacasteca Nicoya - Puntarenas FC	2-2(2-1)	3-2(3-1)

2021 Torneo Clausura Champions: **AD Guanacasteca Nicoya**

AD Guanacasteca Nicoya (as winner of both Apertura and Clausura) promoted for the Primera División 2021/2022.

NATIONAL TEAM
INTERNATIONAL MATCHES 2020/2021

10.10.2020	San José	Costa Rica - Panama	0-1(0-0)	(F)
13.10.2020	San José	Costa Rica - Panama	0-1(0-1)	(F)
13.11.2020	Maria Enzersdorf	Costa Rica - Qatar	1-1(0-1)	(F)
27.03.2021	Zenica	Bosnia and Herzegovina - Costa Rica	0-0	(F)
30.03.2021	Wiener Neustadt	Costa Rica - Mexico	0-1(0-0)	(F)
03.06.2021	Denver	Mexico - Costa Rica	0-0; 5-4p	(CNL)
06.06.2021	Denver	Honduras - Costa Rica	2-2; 5-4p	(CNL)
09.06.2021	Sandy	United States - Costa Rica	4-0(2-0)	(F)

10.10.2020, Friendly International
Estadio Nacional, San José; Attendance: 0
Referee: Keylor Antonio Herrera Villalobos (Costa Rica)
COSTA RICA - PANAMA 0-1(0-0)
CRC: Minor Jesús Álvarez Cordero, Óscar Esau Duarte Gaitán, Keyner Yamal Brown Blackwood, Mauricio de Jesús Núñez Morales, Marvin Angulo Borbón (75.Cristopher Antonio Núñez González), Jeikel Francisco Venegas Mc Carthy, Yeltsin Ignacio Tejeda Valverde (75.Jefferson Brenes Rojas), Ricardo José Blanco Mora, Johan Alberto Venegas Ulloa (73.Brayan Steven López Ramírez), Jostin Akeem Daly Cordero (61.Yuaycell Shamir Wright Parks), John Jairo Ruiz Barrantes (61.Osvaldo Roberto Rodríguez Flores). Trainer: Rónald Alfonso González Brenes.

13.10.2020, Friendly International
Estadio Nacional, San José; Attendance: 0
Referee: Juan Gabriel Calderón Pérez (Costa Rica)
COSTA RICA - PANAMA 0-1(0-1)
CRC: Minor Jesús Álvarez Cordero, Óscar Esau Duarte Gaitán, Ariel Román Soto González, Mauricio de Jesús Núñez Morales (46.Brayan Steven López Ramírez), Yostin Jafet Salinas Phillips, Marvin Angulo Borbón (64.Starling Doney Matarrita González), Johan Alberto Venegas Ulloa, Yeltsin Ignacio Tejeda Valverde, Osvaldo Roberto Rodríguez Flores (46.Jeikel Francisco Venegas Mc Carthy), Ricardo José Blanco Mora (83.John Jairo Ruiz Barrantes), Jostin Akeem Daly Cordero (57.Yuaycell Shamir Wright Parks). Trainer: Rónald Alfonso González Brenes.

13.11.2020, Friendly International
BSFZ-Arena, Maria Enzersdorf (Austria); Attendance: 0
Referee: Sebastian Gishamer (Austria)
COSTA RICA - QATAR 1-1(0-1)
CRC: Keylor Antonio Navas Gamboa, Óscar Esau Duarte Gaitán, Cristian Esteban Gamboa Luna, Kendall Jamaal Waston Manley, Francisco Javier Calvo Quesada, Celso Borges Mora, David Alberto Guzmán Pérez (64.Bernald Alfaro Alfaro), Johan Alberto Venegas Ulloa (81.Luis Mario Díaz Espinoza), Joël Nathaniel Campbell Samuels (80.Deyver Antonio Vega Álvarez), Felicio Anando Brown Forbes (57.Jonathan Alonso Moya Aguilar), Ariel Daniel Lassiter Acuña (46.Randall Enrique Leal Arley). Trainer: Rónald Alfonso González Brenes.
Goal: Joël Nathaniel Campbell Samuels (67).

27.03.2021, Friendly International
Stadion Bilino Polje, Zenica; Attendance: 0
Referee: Nejc Kajtazovič (Slovenia)
BOSNIA AND HERZEGOVINA - COSTA RICA   **0-0**
CRC: Leonel Gerardo Moreira Ledezma, Bryan Josué Oviedo Jiménez, Kendall Jamaal Waston Manley, Francisco Javier Calvo Quesada, Keysher Fuller Spence, Johan Alberto Venegas Ulloa, Yeltsin Ignacio Tejeda Valverde (73.Cristian Alonso Martínez Mena), Barlon Andrés Sequeira Sibaja (63.Allan Enzo Cruz Leal), Bryan Jafet Ruiz González (63.Ariel Daniel Lassiter Acuña), Joël Nathaniel Campbell Samuels (89.Suhander Manuel Zúñiga Cordero), Felicio Anando Brown Forbes. Trainer: Rónald Alfonso González Brenes.

30.03.2021, Friendly International
Wiener Neustadt Stadion, Wiener Neustadt (Austria); Attendance: 0
Referee: Christian-Petru Ciochirca (Austria)
COSTA RICA - MEXICO   **0-1(0-0)**
CRC: Keylor Antonio Navas Gamboa, Bryan Josué Oviedo Jiménez (46.Ariel Daniel Lassiter Acuña), Kendall Jamaal Waston Manley, Francisco Javier Calvo Quesada, Keysher Fuller Spence, Johan Alberto Venegas Ulloa, Allan Enzo Cruz Leal, Barlon Andrés Sequeira Sibaja (46.Rónald Alberto Matarrita Ulate), Bryan Jafet Ruiz González (81.Cristian Alonso Martínez Mena), Joël Nathaniel Campbell Samuels (90+1.Suhander Manuel Zúñiga Cordero), Felicio Anando Brown Forbes (74.Cristopher Antonio Núñez González). Trainer: Rónald Alfonso González Brenes.

03.06.2021, 1st CONCACAF Nations League, Semi-Finals
Empower Field at Mile High Stadium, Denver (United States); Attendance: 34,451
Referee: Bryan López Castellanos (Guatemala)
MEXICO - COSTA RICA   **0-0; 5-4 on penalties**
CRC: Leonel Gerardo Moreira Ledezma, Bryan Josué Oviedo Jiménez, Óscar Esau Duarte Gaitán, Francisco Javier Calvo Quesada, Keysher Fuller Spence, Celso Borges Mora (82.Bernald Alfaro Alfaro), Yeltsin Ignacio Tejeda Valverde, Randall Enrique Leal Arley (85.Jurguens Josafat Montenegro Vallejo), Bryan Jafet Ruiz González (62.Allan Enzo Cruz Leal), Joël Nathaniel Campbell Samuels (85.Johan Alberto Venegas Ulloa), Adrián Alonso Martínez Batista (62.Ariel Daniel Lassiter Acuña). Trainer: Rónald Alfonso González Brenes.
Penalties: Johan Alberto Venegas Ulloa, Óscar Esau Duarte Gaitán (missed), Bernald Alfaro Alfaro, Ariel Daniel Lassiter Acuña, Francisco Javier Calvo Quesada, Allan Enzo Cruz Leal (saved).

06.06.2021, 1st CONCACAF Nations League, Third Place Play-off
Empower Field at Mile High Stadium, Denver (United States); Attendance: 37,648
Referee: Reon Radix (Grenada)
HONDURAS - COSTA RICA   **2-2(0-1,2-2,2-2); 5-4 on penalties**
CRC: Leonel Gerardo Moreira Ledezma, Bryan Josué Oviedo Jiménez (48.Joseph Martín Mora Cortéz), Óscar Esau Duarte Gaitán, Francisco Javier Calvo Quesada, Keysher Fuller Spence, Celso Borges Mora (57.Allan Enzo Cruz Leal), Yeltsin Ignacio Tejeda Valverde, Randall Enrique Leal Arley (57.Ariel Daniel Lassiter Acuña), Bryan Jafet Ruiz González (57.Johan Alberto Venegas Ulloa), Joël Nathaniel Campbell Samuels (72.Gerson Torres Barrantes), Adrián Alonso Martínez Batista. Trainer: Rónald Alfonso González Brenes.
Goals: Joël Nathaniel Campbell Samuels (8), Francisco Javier Calvo Quesada (85).
Penalties: Johan Alberto Venegas Ulloa, Francisco Javier Calvo Quesada (saved), Ariel Daniel Lassiter Acuña, Gerson Torres Barrantes, Joseph Martín Mora Cortéz, Yeltsin Ignacio Tejeda Valverde (saved).

09.06.2021, Friendly International
Rio Tinto Stadium. Sandy; Attendance: 19,007
Referee: Tristley Bassue (Saint Kitts and Nevis)
UNITED STATES - COSTA RICA   **4-0(2-0)**
CRC: Leonel Gerardo Moreira Ledezma, Giancarlo González Castro, Aarón Salazar Arias (46.Randall Enrique Leal Arley), Joseph Martín Mora Cortéz, Francisco Javier Calvo Quesada, Bernald Alfaro Alfaro (46.Celso Borges Mora), Keysher Fuller Spence, Johan Alberto Venegas Ulloa (64.Jurguens Josafat Montenegro Vallejo), Yeltsin Ignacio Tejeda Valverde (75.Bryan Josué Oviedo Jiménez), Gerson Torres Barrantes (46.Ariel Daniel Lassiter Acuña), Joël Nathaniel Campbell Samuels (64.Allan Enzo Cruz Leal). Trainer: Rónald Alfonso González Brenes.

NATIONAL TEAM PLAYERS 2020/2021

Name	DOB	Club
Goalkeepers		
Minor Jesús ÁLVAREZ Cordero	14.11.1989	CS Herediano Heredia
Leonel Gerardo MOREIRA Ledezma	02.04.1990	Liga Deportiva Alajuelense
Keylor Antonio NAVAS Gamboa	15.12.1986	Paris Saint-Germain FC (FRA)
Defenders		
Keyner Yamal BROWN Blackwood	30.12.1991	CS Herediano Heredia
Francisco Javier CALVO Quesada	08.07.1992	Chicago Fire (USA)
Óscar Esau DUARTE Gaitán	03.06.1989	Levante UD Valencia (ESP)
Keysher FULLER Spence	12.07.1994	CS Herediano Heredia
Cristian Esteban GAMBOA Luna	24.10.1989	VfL Bochum (GER)
Giancarlo GONZÁLEZ Castro	08.02.1988	Los Angeles Galaxy (USA)
Rónald Alberto MATARRITA Ulate	09.07.1994	FC Cincinnati (USA)
Joseph Martín MORA Cortéz	15.01.1993	Washington DC United (USA)
Mauricio de Jesús NUÑEZ Morales	28.10.1993	CS Herediano Heredia
Bryan Josué OVIEDO Jiménez	18.02.1990	FC København (DEN)
Aarón SALAZAR Arias	15.05.1999	CS Herediano Heredia
Yostin Jafet SALINAS Phillips	14.09.1998	Sporting FC San José
Ariel Román SOTO González	14.05.1992	CS Herediano Heredia
Kendall Jamaal WASTON Manley	01.01.1988	Deportivo Saprissa San José
Midfielders		
Bernald ALFARO Alfaro	26.01.1997	Liga Deportiva Alajuelense
Marvin ANGULO Borbón	30.09.1986	Deportivo Saprissa San José
Ricardo José BLANCO Mora	12.05.1989	Deportivo Saprissa San José
Celso BORGES Mora	27.08.1988	RC Deportivo La Coruña (ESP)
Jefferson BRENES Rojas	13.04.1997	CS Herediano Heredia
Allan Enzo CRUZ Leal	24.02.1996	FC Cincinnati (USA)
Luis Mario DÍAZ Espinoza	06.12.1998	Columbus Crew (USA)
David Alberto GUZMÁN Pérez	18.02.1990	Deportivo Saprissa San José
Ariel Daniel LASSITER Acuña	27.09.1994	Houston Dynamo FC (USA)
Randall Enrique LEAL Arley	14.01.1997	Nashville SC (USA)
Cristian Alonso MARTÍNEZ Mena	19.04.1994	AD San Carlos
Cristopher Antonio NUÑEZ González	08.12.1997	CS Cartaginés Deportiva SA

Osvaldo Roberto RODRÍGUEZ Flores	17.12.1990	*Santos de Guápiles FC*
Bryan Jafet RUIZ González	18.08.1985	*Liga Deportiva Alajuelense*
John Jairo RUIZ Barrantes	10.01.1994	*CS Herediano Heredia*
Barlon Andrés SEQUEIRA Sibaja	25.05.1998	*Liga Deportiva Alajuelense*
Yeltsin Ignacio TEJEDA Valverde	17.03.1992	*CS Herediano Heredia*
Gerson TORRES Barrantes	28.08.1997	*CS Herediano Heredia*
Jeikel Francisco VENEGAS Mc Carthy	06.04.1988	*CS Cartaginés Deportiva SA*
Suhander Manuel ZUÑIGA Cordero	15.01.1997	*CS Herediano Heredia*

Forwards

Felicio Anando BROWN Forbes	28.08.1991	*Wisła Kraków (POL)*
Joël Nathaniel CAMPBELL Samuels	10.02.1992	*Club León (MEX)*
Jostin Akeem DALY Cordero	23.04.1998	*Sporting FC San José*
Brayan Steven LÓPEZ Ramírez	03.06.1990	*Santos de Guápiles FC*
Adrián Alonso MARTÍNEZ Batista	15.10.1998	*Liga Deportiva Alajuelense*
Starling Doney MATARRITA González	20.06.1990	*AD Municipal Pérez Zeledón*
Jurguens Josafat MONTENEGRO Vallejo	13.12.2000	*Liga Deportiva Alajuelense*
Jonathan Alonso MOYA Aguilar	06.01.1992	*FC Anyang (KOR)*
Deyver Antonio VEGA Álvarez	19.09.1992	*FC Politehnica Iaşi (ROU)*
Johan Alberto VENEGAS Ulloa	27.11.1988	*Liga Deportiva Alajuelense*
Yuaycell Shamir WRIGHT Parks	22.06.1992	*Limón FC*

National coaches

Rónald Alfonso GONZÁLEZ Brenes [30.09.2019 – 10.06.2021]	08.08.1970

CUBA

The Country:	The FA:
República de Cuba (Republic of Cuba)	Asociación de Fútbol de Cuba
Capital: Havana	Estadio "Pedro Marrero", Escuela Nacional de
Surface: 110,861 km²	Futbol - Mario López Ave 41, 44 y 46
Population: 11,193,470 [2019]	Municipio Playa, La Habana
Time: UTC-4	Year of Formation: 1924
Independent since: 1868	Member of FIFA since: 1932
	Member of CONCACAF since: 1961

NATIONAL TEAM RECORDS

First international match:	16.03.1930: Cuba - Jamaica 3-1
Most international caps:	Yénier Márquez Molina – 126 caps (2000-2015)
Most international goals:	Léster Oriel Moré Hennynghom – 30 goals / 62 caps (1995-2007)

CONCACAF GOLD CUP

1991	*Withdrew*
1993	Did not enter
1996	Qualifiers
1998	Final Tournament (Group Stage)
2000	Qualifiers
2002	Final Tournament (Group Stage)
2003	Final Tournament (Quarter-Finals)
2005	Final Tournament (Group Stage)
2007	Final Tournament (Group Stage)
2009	*Withdrew after qualifying*
2011	Final Tournament (Group Stage)
2013	Final Tournament (Quarter-Finals)
2015	Final Tournament (Quarter-Finals)
2017	Qualifiers
2019	Final Tournament (Group Stage)
2021	Qualifiers

FIFA WORLD CUP

1930	Did not enter
1934	Qualifiers
1938	Final Tournament (Quarter-Finals)
1950	Qualifiers
1954	Entry not accepted by FIFA
1958	Did not enter
1962	Did not enter
1966	Qualifiers
1970	Entry not accepted by FIFA
1974	Did not enter
1978	Qualifiers
1982	Qualifiers
1986	Did not enter
1990	Qualifiers
1994	*Withdrew*
1998	Qualifiers
2002	Qualifiers
2006	Qualifiers
2010	Qualifiers
2014	Qualifiers
2018	Qualifiers

F.I.F.A. CONFEDERATIONS CUP 1992-2017

None

OLYMPIC FOOTBALL TOURNAMENTS 1908-2016

1908	-	1948	-	1972	Qualifiers	1996	Did not enter
1912	-	1952	-	1976	FT/Group Stage	2000	Qualifiers
1920	-	1956	-	1980	Quarter-Finals	2004	Qualifiers
1924	-	1960	-	1984	Qualifiers	2008	Qualifiers
1928	-	1964	-	1988	Did not enter	2012	Qualifiers
1936	-	1968	-	1992	Qualifiers	2016	Qualifiers

CCCF (Confederación Centroamericana y del Caribe de Fútbol) CHAMPIONSHIPS 1941-1961
1955, 1957, 1960, 1961

CONCACAF CHAMPIONSHIPS 1963-1989
1967, 1971, 1981

NAFC (North American Football Confederation) CHAMPIONSHIPS 1947-1991
1947, 1949

CONCACAF NATIONS LEAGUE
2019-2020

CARIBBEAN CHAMPIONSHIPS 1989-2017

1989	Did not enter	1999	Final Tournament - Runners-up
1991	Final Tournament - *Withdrew*	2001	Final Tournament - 4th Place
1992	Final Tournament - 4th Place	2005	Final Tournament - Runners-up
1993	Did not enter	2007	Final Tournament - 3rd Place
1994	Did not enter	2008	Final Tournament - 4th Place
1995	Final Tournament - 3rd Place	2010	Final Tournament - 3rd Place
1996	Final Tournament - Runners-up	2012	**Final Tournament - Winners**
1997	Did not enter	2014	Final Tournament - 4th Place
1998	Qualifiers	2017	Qualifiers

CUBAN CLUB HONOURS IN CONCACAF CLUB COMPETITIONS:

CONCACAF Champions Cup / CONCACAF Champions League 1962-2020
None

CONCACAF Cup Winners Cup 1991-1995
None

Copa Interamericana 1968-1998
None

NATIONAL COMPETITIONS
TABLE OF HONOURS

	CHAMPIONS
1912	Rovers AC La Habana
1913	CD Hatuey La Habana
1914	Rovers AC La Habana
1915	Hispano América La Habana
1916	La Habana FC
1917	Iberia La Habana[1]
1918	Iberia La Habana
1919	Hispano América La Habana
1920	Hispano América La Habana
1921	Hispano América La Habana

1922	Iberia La Habana
1923	Iberia La Habana
1924	Olimpia
1925	Fortuna
1926	Real Iberia La Habana
1927	Juventud Asturiana La Habana
1928	Real Iberia La Habana
1929	Real Iberia La Habana
1930	Deportivo Español Santiago de Cuba
1931	DC Gallego La Habana
1932	DC Gallego La Habana
1933	Juventud Asturiana La Habana
1934	Real Iberia La Habana
1935	Juventud Asturiana La Habana
1936	Juventud Asturiana La Habana
1937	DC Gallego La Habana
1938	DC Gallego La Habana
1939	DC Gallego La Habana
1940	DC Gallego La Habana
1941	Juventud Asturiana La Habana
1942	Deportivo Puentes Grandes
1943	Deportivo Puentes Grandes
1944	Juventud Asturiana La Habana
1945	DC Gallego La Habana
1946	*No competition*
1947	DC Gallego La Habana
1948	Juventud Asturiana La Habana
1949	Diablos Rojos Santiago de Cuba
1950	Hispano América La Habana
1951	Deportivo San Francisco
1952	Deportivo San Francisco
1953	Deportivo San Francisco
1954	Deportivo San Francisco
1955	Deportivo San Francisco
1956	Casino Español
1957	Deportivo San Francisco
1958	Deportivo Mordazo
1959	Deportivo Mordazo
1960	Cerro La Habana
1961	Deportivo Mordazo
1962	*No competition*
1963	Industriales La Habana
1964	Industriales La Habana
1965	La Habana FC
1966	La Habana FC
1967	La Habana FC
1968	Granjeros
1969	Granjeros
1970	Granjeros
1971	*No competition*
1972	Industriales La Habana
1973	Industriales La Habana

1974	Azucareros
1975	Granjeros
1976	Azucareros
1977	Granjeros
1978/1979	Ciudad de La Habana
1979	Ciudad de La Habana
1980	FC Villa Clara Zulueta
1981	FC Villa Clara Zulueta
1982	FC Villa Clara Zulueta
1983	FC Villa Clara Zulueta
1984	Ciudad de La Habana
1985	FC Cienfuegos
1986	FC Villa Clara Zulueta
1987	FC Pinar del Río
1988/1989	FC Pinar del Río
1989/1990	FC Pinar del Río
1990/1991	FC Cienfuegos
1991/1992	FC Pinar del Río
1992	FC Villa Clara Zulueta
1993	FC Ciego de Ávila
1994	Ciudad de La Habana
1995	FC Pinar del Río
1996	FC Villa Clara Zulueta
1997	FC Villa Clara Zulueta
1998	Ciudad de La Habana
1999/2000	FC Pinar del Río
2000/2001	Ciudad de La Habana
2001/2002	FC Ciego de Ávila
2002/2003	FC Villa Clara Zulueta
2003	FC Ciego de Ávila
2004/2005	FC Villa Clara Zulueta
2005/2006	FC Holguín
2006	FC Pinar del Río
2007/2008	FC Cienfuegos
2008/2009	FC Cienfuegos
2009/2010	FC Ciego de Ávila
2010/2011	FC Villa Clara Zulueta
2011/2012	FC Villa Clara Zulueta
2013	FC Villa Clara Zulueta
2014	FC Ciego de Ávila Morón
2015	CF de Camagüey
2016	FC Villa Clara Zulueta
2017	FC Santiago de Cuba
2018	FC Santiago de Cuba
2019	FC Santiago de Cuba
2019/2020	*Championship cancelled*
2020/2021	*No competition*

[1]became later Real Iberia La Habana.

NATIONAL CHAMPIONSHIP
Campeonato Nacional de Fútbol de Cuba 2020/2021

The championship was cancelled due to COVID-19 pandemic.

NATIONAL TEAM
INTERNATIONAL MATCHES 2020/2021

24.03.2021	*Ciudad de Guatemala*	*Guatemala - Cuba*	*1-0(0-0)*	*(WCQ)*
28.03.2021	*Ciudad de Guatemala*	*Cuba - Curaçao*	*1-2(1-2)*	*(WCQ)*
02.06.2021	*Ciudad de Guatemala*	*Cuba - British Virgin Islands*	*5-0(1-0)*	*(WCQ)*
08.06.2021	*St. George's*	*Saint Vincent and the Grenadines - Cuba*	*0-1(0-0)*	*(WCQ)*
02.07.2021	*Fot Lauderdale*	*Cuba - French Guiana*	*0-3 awarded*	*(GCQ)*

24.03.2021, 22nd FIFA World Cup Qualifiers, CONCACAF First Round
Estadio "Doroteo Guamuch Flores", Ciudad de Guatemala
Referee: Benjamin Pineda Ávila (Costa Rica)
GUATEMALA - CUBA   **1-0(0-0)**
CUB: Sandy Sánchez Mustellier, Jorge Luis Corrales Cordero, Yosel Piedra Guillén, Dariel Alejandro Morejón Rodríguez (75.Sánder Fernández Cervantes), Karel Aldair Espino Contreras [*sent off 61*], Carlos Alberto Vázquez Fernández, Arichel Hernández Mora, Jean Carlos Rodríguez Quiñones (46.Onel Lázaro Hernández Mayea), Joel Apezteguía Hijuelos (68.Sandro Cutiño Castellano), Maykel Alejandro Reyes Azcuy (81.Asmel Núñez Artires), Luis Javier Paradela Díaz (81.Yasniel Matos Rodríguez). Trainer: Pablo Elier Sánchez Salgado.

28.03.2021, 22nd FIFA World Cup Qualifiers, CONCACAF First Round
Estadio "Doroteo Guamuch Flores", Ciudad de Guatemala (Guatemala)
Referee: Germán Stanley Martínez Miranda (El Salvador)
CUBA - CURAÇAO   **1-2(1-2)**
CUB: Sandy Sánchez Mustellier, Jorge Luis Corrales Cordero, Yosel Piedra Guillén (79.Yunior Yuri Pérez Pérez), Dariel Alejandro Morejón Rodríguez, Carlos Alberto Vázquez Fernández, Onel Lázaro Hernández Mayea, Arichel Hernández Mora, Sandro Cutiño Castellano (56.Jean Carlos Rodríguez Quiñones), Joel Apezteguía Hijuelos (12.Sánder Fernández Cervantes), Maykel Alejandro Reyes Azcuy (56.José Alberto Pérez Oquendo), Luis Javier Paradela Díaz (79.Yasniel Matos Rodríguez). Trainer: Pablo Elier Sánchez Salgado.
Goal: Onel Lázaro Hernández Mayea (28).

02.06.2021, 22nd FIFA World Cup Qualifiers, CONCACAF First Round
Estadio "Doroteo Guamuch Flores", Ciudad de Guatemala (Guatemala)
Referee: José Raúl Torres Rivera (Puerto Rico)
CUBA - BRITISH VIRGIN ISLANDS   **5-0(1-0)**
CUB: Nelson Johnston Barrientos, Jorge Luis Corrales Cordero, Yosel Piedra Guillén, Karel Aldair Espino Contreras (64.Yunior Yuri Pérez Pérez), Carlos Alberto Vázquez Fernández, Onel Lázaro Hernández Mayea, Arichel Hernández Mora, Asmel Núñez Artires (64.Dairon Reyes Ruedas), Davide Fabrizio Incerti (76.Rolando Domingo Abreu Canela), Willian Pozo-Venta Angell (64.Maykel Alejandro Reyes Azcuy), Luis Javier Paradela Díaz (76.Yasniel Matos Rodríguez). Trainer: Pablo Elier Sánchez Salgado.
Goals: Luis Javier Paradela Díaz (35), Onel Lázaro Hernández Mayea (68), Maykel Alejandro Reyes Azcuy (76), Carlos Alberto Vázquez Fernández (80), Dairon Reyes Ruedas (90+1).

08.06.2021, 22nd FIFA World Cup Qualifiers, CONCACAF First Round
Kirani James Athletic Stadium, St. George's (Grenada); Attendance: 50
Referee: Fernando Guerrero Ramírez (Mexico)
SAINT VINCENT AND THE GRENADINES - CUBA   **0-1(0-0)**
CUB: Nelson Johnston Barrientos, Jorge Luis Corrales Cordero, Yosel Piedra Guillén, Karel Aldair Espino Contreras, Carlos Alberto Vázquez Fernández (72.Yunior Yuri Pérez Pérez), Modesto Méndez Amador, Onel Lázaro Hernández Mayea, Arichel Hernández Mora, Davide Fabrizio Incerti (59.Dairon Reyes Ruedas), Willian Pozo-Venta Angell (59.Asmel Núñez Artires), Luis Javier Paradela Díaz (82.Yasniel Matos Rodríguez). Trainer: Pablo Elier Sánchez Salgado.
Goal: Maykel Alejandro Reyes Azcuy (64).

03.07.2021, 16th CONCACAF Gold Cup Qualifiers, First Round
DRV PNK Stadium, Fort Lauderdale (United States); Attendance: 0
CUBA - FRENCH GUIANA   **0-3 (awarded)**
Please note: due to COVID-19 pandemic related travel and visa challenges, Cuba forfeited the match, a 3-0 win was awarded for French Guiana.

NATIONAL TEAM PLAYERS 2020/2021

Name	DOB	Club
Goalkeepers		
Nelson JOHNSTON Barrientos	25.02.1990	*FC Santiago de Cuba*
Sandy SÁNCHEZ Mustellier	24.05.1994	*Porto Velho EC (BRA)*
Defenders		
Jorge Luis CORRALES Cordero	20.05.1991	*FC Tulsa (USA)*
Sandro CUTIÑO Castellano	03.03.1995	*Porto Velho EC (BRA)*
Modesto MÉNDEZ Amador	06.01.1998	*Fort Lauderdale CF (USA)*
Dariel Alejandro MOREJÓN Rodríguez	21.12.1998	*Navegantes EC (BRA)*
Yunior Yuri PÉREZ Pérez		*FC Guantánamo*
Yosel PIEDRA Guillén	27.03.1994	*CSD Sanarate (GUA)*
Carlos Alberto VÁZQUEZ Fernández	25.04.1999	*CDA Navalcarnero (ESP)*
Midfielders		
Rolando Domingo ABREU Canela	15.05.1992	*FC Santiago de Cuba*
Karel Aldair ESPINO Contreras	27.10.2001	*FC Artemisa Guanajay*
Arichel HERNÁNDEZ Mora	20.09.1993	*Universidad O&M Santo Domingo (DOM)*
Davide Fabrizio INCERTI	22.06.2002	*Ternana Calcio (ITA)*
Asmel NÚÑEZ Artires	03.05.1992	*FC Ciego de Ávila*
José Alberto PÉREZ Oquendo	15.09.1999	*FC La Habana*
Dairon REYES Ruedas	18.09.2003	*Fort Lauderdale CF (USA)*
Jean Carlos RODRÍGUEZ Quiñones	27.05.1999	*FC Pinar del Río*
Forwards		
Joel APEZTEGUÍA Hijuelos	17.12.1983	*SP Tre Fiori (SMR)*
Sánder FERNÁNDEZ Cervantes	19.07.1987	*FC Ciego de Ávila*
Onel Lázaro HERNÁNDEZ Mayea	01.02.1993	*Norwich City FC (ENG)*
Yasniel MATOS Rodríguez		*FC Holguín Banes*
Luis Javier PARADELA Díaz	21.01.1997	*Santos de Guápiles FC (CRC)*
Willian POZO-VENTA Angell	27.08.1997	*Strømmen IF (NOR)*
Maykel Alejandro REYES Azcuy	04.03.1993	*CD Real Sociedad Tocoa (HON)*
National coaches		
Pablo Elier SÁNCHEZ Salgado [from 16.07.2019]		

CURAÇAO

The Country:	The FA:
Land Curaçao (Country of Curaçao)	Curaçao Football Federation
Capital: Willemstad	Kaya Andrew Jones 49, Willemstad
Surface: 800 km²	Year of Formation: 1921
Population: 163,424 [2019]	Member of FIFA since: 1932
Time: UTC-4	Member of CONCACAF since: 1961

Netherlands overseas territory, called earlier Netherlands Antilles.

NATIONAL TEAM RECORDS

First international match:	06.04.1924: Aruba - Curaçao 0-4
Most international caps:	Rhu-endly Aurelio Jean-Carlo "Cuco" Martina – 51 caps (since 2011)
Most international goals:	Leandro Jones Johan Bacuna – 13 goals / 36 caps (since 2016)

CONCACAF GOLD CUP		FIFA WORLD CUP	
1991	Did not enter	1930	-
1993	*Withdrew*	1934	Did not enter
1996	Qualifiers	1938	Did not enter
1998	Qualifiers	1950	Did not enter
2000	Qualifiers	1954	Did not enter
2002	Did not enter	1958	Qualifiers
2003	Qualifiers	1962	Qualifiers
2005	*Withdrew*	1966	Qualifiers
2007	Qualifiers	1970	Qualifiers
2009	Qualifiers	1974	Qualifiers
2011	Qualifiers	1978	Qualifiers
2013	Qualifiers	1982	Qualifiers
2015	Qualifiers	1986	Qualifiers
2017	Final Tournament (Group Stage)	1990	Qualifiers
2019	Final Tournament (Quarter-Finals)	1994	Qualifiers
2021	Final Tournament (*withdrew*)	1998	Qualifiers
		2002	Qualifiers
		2006	Qualifiers
		2010	Qualifiers
		2014	Qualifiers
		2018	Qualifiers

F.I.F.A. CONFEDERATIONS CUP 1992-2017

None

OLYMPIC FOOTBALL TOURNAMENTS 1908-2016

Year	Result	Year	Result	Year	Result	Year	Result
1908	-	1948	-	1972	Qualifiers*	1996	Did not enter
1912	-	1952	FT - 1/8 Finals	1976	Did not enter	2000	Qualifiers*
1920	-	1956	Did not enter	1980	Qualifiers*	2004	Did not enter
1924	-	1960	Qualifiers*	1984	Qualifiers*	2008	Qualifiers*
1928	-	1964	Qualifiers*	1988	Did not enter	2012	Qualifiers
1936		1968	Qualifiers*	1992	Qualifiers*	2016	*Withdrew*

*as Netherlands Antilles

CCCF (Confederación Centroamericana y del Caribe de Fútbol) CHAMPIONSHIPS 1941-1961
1948, 1953, 1955 (Runners-up), 1957 (Runners-up, as Curaçao), 1960 (Runners-up), 1961

CONCACAF CHAMPIONSHIPS 1963-1989
1963 (3rd Place), 1965, 1967, 1969 (3rd Place), 1973

CONCACAF NATIONS LEAGUE
2019-2020	League A

CARIBBEAN CHAMPIONSHIPS 1989-2017

Year	Result	Year	Result
1989	Final Tournament - Group Stage	1999	Qualifiers*
1991	Qualifiers*	2001	Did not enter
1992	Qualifiers*	2005	*Withdrew*
1993	Did not enter	2007	Qualifiers*
1994	Did not enter	2008	Qualifiers*
1995	Qualifiers*	2010	Qualifiers*
1996	Qualifiers*	2012	Qualifiers
1997	Qualifiers*	2014	Final Tournament - Group Stage
1998	Final Tournament - Group Stage*	2017	**Final Tournament (Winners)**

*as Netherlands Antilles.

CURAÇAO CLUB HONOURS IN CONCACAF CLUB COMPETITIONS:

CONCACAF Champions Cup / CONCACAF Champions League 1962-2020
None

CONCACAF League 2017-2020
None

Caribbean Club Championship 1997-2021
None

CONCACAF Cup Winners Cup 1991-1995*
None

Copa Interamericana 1968-1998*
None

*defunct competitions

NATIONAL COMPETITIONS
TABLE OF HONOURS

		CHAMPIONS
1921	CVV Sparta	
1921/22	MVC Juliana	
1922/23	CVV Sparta	
1924/25	CVV Sparta	
1925/26	CRKSV Jong Holland Willemstad	
1926/27	Dutch Football Club	
1928	CRKSV Jong Holland Willemstad	
1929	Sportclub Asiento	
1930	Sportclub Asiento	
1931	CVV Volharding	
1932	CRKSV Jong Holland Willemstad	
1933	VV Transvaal	
1934	Sportclub Asiento	
1935	CRKSV Jong Holland Willemstad	
1936	SV Racing Club Curaçao	
1937	CRKSV Jong Holland Willemstad	
1938	SV Sport Unie Brion Trappers Willemstad	
1940	CRKSV Jong Holland Willemstad	
1941	SV Sport Unie Brion Trappers Willemstad	
1942	Sportclub Independiente	
1943	CRKSV Jong Holland Willemstad	
1944	*No competition*	
1945	SV Sport Unie Brion Trappers Willemstad	
1946	*No competition*	
1947	SV Sport Unie Brion Trappers Willemstad	
1948	CRKSV Jong Holland Willemstad	
1949	SV Sport Unie Brion Trappers Willemstad	
1950	SV Sport Unie Brion Trappers Willemstad	
1951	SV Sport Unie Brion Trappers Willemstad	
1952	CRKSV Jong Holland Willemstad	
1953	SV Sport Unie Brion Trappers Willemstad	
1954	SV Sport Unie Brion Trappers Willemstad	
1955	SV Sport Unie Brion Trappers Willemstad	
1956	SV Sport Unie Brion Trappers Willemstad	
1957	*No competition*	
1958	SV Sport Unie Brion Trappers Willemstad	
1959	CRKSV Jong Holland Willemstad	
1960	RKV FC Sithoc Mahuma	
1961	RKV FC Sithoc Mahuma	
1962	Veendam	
1963	CRKSV Jong Colombia Willemstad	
1964	RKSV Scherpenheuvel	
1965	CRKSV Jong Colombia Willemstad	
1966	CRKSV Jong Colombia Willemstad	
1967	CRKSV Jong Colombia Willemstad	
1968	RKSV Scherpenheuvel	
1969	CRKSV Jong Colombia Willemstad	

1970	*No competition*
1971	SV Sport Unie Brion Trappers Willemstad
1972	CRKSV Jong Colombia Willemstad
1973	CRKSV Jong Colombia Willemstad
1974	*No competition*
1974/1975	CRKSV Jong Colombia Willemstad
1976	SV Sport Unie Brion Trappers Willemstad
1976/1977	CRKSV Jong Holland Willemstad
1978	SV Sport Unie Brion Trappers Willemstad
1979	CRKSV Jong Colombia Willemstad
1980	SV Sport Unie Brion Trappers Willemstad
1981	CRKSV Jong Holland Willemstad
1982	SV Sport Unie Brion Trappers Willemstad
1983	SV Sport Unie Brion Trappers Willemstad
1984	SV Sport Unie Brion Trappers Willemstad
1985	SV Sport Unie Brion Trappers Willemstad
1986	RKSV Sithoc Mahuma
1987	RKSV Centro Dominguito
1988	CRKSV Jong Colombia Willemstad
1989	RKSV FC Sithoc Mahuma
1990/1991	RKSV FC Sithoc Mahuma
1991	RKSV FC Sithoc Mahuma
1992	RKSV FC Sithoc Mahuma
1993	RKSV FC Sithoc Mahuma
1994	CRKSV Jong Colombia Willemstad
1995/1996	RKSV FC Sithoc Mahuma
1996	Union Deportivo Banda Abou
1997	Union Deportivo Banda Abou
1998	*No competition*
1998/1999	CRKSV Jong Holland Willemstad
2000	CRKSV Jong Colombia Willemstad
2000/2001	*No competition*
2001/2002	SV Centro Social Deportivo Barber
2002/2003	SV Centro Social Deportivo Barber
2003/2004	SV Centro Social Deportivo Barber
2004/2005	SV Centro Social Deportivo Barber
2005/2006	Union Deportivo Banda Abou
2006/2007	SV Centro Social Deportivo Barber
2007/2008	Union Deportivo Banda Abou
2008/2009	SV Hubentut Fortuna Seru Fortuna
2009/2010	SV Hubentut Fortuna Seru Fortuna
2010/2011	SV Hubentut Fortuna Seru Fortuna
2012	RKSV Centro Dominguito
2013	RKSV Centro Dominguito
2014	SV Centro Social Deportivo Barber
2015	RKSV Centro Dominguito
2016	RKSV Centro Dominguito
2017/2018	RKSV Centro Dominguito
2018/2019	SV VESTA Willemstad
2019/2020	RKSV Scherpenheuvel

List of Netherlands Antilles Champions:
1959: CRKSV Jong Holland Willemstad; 1960: RKV FC Sithoc Mahuma; 1961: RKV FC Sithoc Mahuma; 1962: RKV FC Sithoc Mahuma; 1963: *No competition*; 1964: SV Racing Club Oranjestad [Aruba]; 1965: SV Racing Club Oranjestad [Aruba]; 1966: CRKSV Jong Colombia Willemstad; 1967: RKSV Scherpenheuvel; 1968: CRKSV Jong Colombia Willemstad; 1969: SV Sport Unie Brion Trappers Willemstad; 1970: SV Estrella Santa Cruz [Aruba]; 1971: CRKSV Jong Colombia Willemstad; 1972: CRKSV Jong Colombia Willemstad; 1973: CRKSV Jong Colombia Willemstad; 1974: CRKSV Jong Colombia Willemstad; 1975: CRKSV Jong Colombia Willemstad; 1976: CRKSV Jong Holland Willemstad; 1977: CRKSV Jong Holland Willemstad; 1978: CRKSV Jong Colombia Willemstad; 1979: SV Sport Unie Brion Trappers Willemstad; 1980: SV Sport Unie Brion Trappers Willemstad; 1981: CRKSV Jong Holland Willemstad; 1982: SV Sport Unie Brion Trappers Willemstad; 1983: SV Sport Unie Brion Trappers Willemstad; 1984: SV Sport Unie Brion Trappers Willemstad; 1985: Union Deportivo Banda Abou; 1986: SV Victory Boys Noord Zapateer; 1987: Union Deportivo Banda Abou; 1988: CRKSV Jong Colombia Willemstad; 1989: Union Deportivo Banda Abou; 1990: RKV FC Sithoc Mahuma; 1991: RKV FC Sithoc Mahuma; 1992: RKV FC Sithoc Mahuma; 1993: RKV FC Sithoc Mahuma; 1994: CRKSV Jong Colombia Willemstad; 1995: RKV FC Sithoc Mahuma; 1996/1997: Union Deportivo Banda Abou; 1997: CRKSV Jong Colombia Willemstad; 1998: *No competition;* 1998/1999: RKV FC Sithoc Mahuma; 2000: *No competition;* 2000/2001: CRKSV Jong Colombia Willemstad; 2001/2002: SV Centro Social Deportivo Barber; 2002/2003: SV Centro Social Deportivo Barber; 2003/2004: SV Centro Social Deportivo Barber; 2004/2005: SV Centro Social Deportivo Barber; 2005/2006: SV Centro Social Deportivo Barber; 2006/2007: SV Centro Social Deportivo Barber; 2007/2008: SV Centro Social Deportivo Barber; 2008/2009: SV Hubentut Fortuna Seru Fortuna; 2009/2010: SV Centro Social Deportivo Barber.
Note: Aruban club participated up to 1985.

NATIONAL CHAMPIONSHIP
Kampionato Liga MCB - Promé Divishon 2021

The championship mode was changed to a spring-autumn rhythm, the first matchday was played on March 7-14, 2021.

NATIONAL TEAM
INTERNATIONAL MATCHES 2020/2021

25.03.2021	Willemstad	Curaçao - Saint Vincent and the Grenadines	5-0(4-0)	(WCQ)
28.03.2021	Ciudad de Guatemala	Cuba - Curaçao	1-2(1-2)	(WCQ)
05.06.2021	Ciudad de Guatemala	British Virgin Islands - Curaçao	0-8(0-6)	(WCQ)
08.06.2021	Willemstad	Curaçao - Guatemala	0-0	(WCQ)
12.06.2021	Ciudad de Panamá	Panama - Curaçao	2-1(0-0)	(WCQ)
15.06.2021	Willemstad	Curaçao - Panama	0-0	(WCQ)

25.03.2021, 22nd FIFA World Cup Qualifiers, CONCACAF First Round
Stadion „Ergilio Hato", Willemstad
Referee: Benjamin Pineda Ávila (Costa Rica)
CURAÇAO - SAINT VINCENT AND THE GRENADINES   5-0(4-0)
CUW: Eloy Victor Room, Rhuendly Aurelio Jean-Carlo Martina, Suently Alberto (70.Roshon van Eijma), Juriën Godfried Juan Gaari, Vurnon San Benito Anita, Leandro Jones Johan Bacuna (61.Elson Quincy Hooi), Jeremy de Nooijer, Juninho Bacuna, Jarchinio Angelo Roberto Antonia (61.Jeremy Antonisse), Gevaro Giomar Magno Nepomuceno (40.Michaël Madionis Mateo Maria), Anthony Edsel Johannes van den Hurk (61.Rangelo Maria Janga). Trainer: Guus Hiddink (Netherlands).
Goals: Juninho Bacuna (1), Anthony Edsel Johannes van den Hurk (17), Juninho Bacuna (36), Jarchinio Angelo Roberto Antonia (44), Elson Quincy Hooi (87).

28.03.2021, 22nd FIFA World Cup Qualifiers, CONCACAF First Round
Estadio "Doroteo Guamuch Flores", Ciudad de Guatemala (Guatemala)
Referee: Germán Stanley Martínez Miranda (El Salvador)
CUBA - CURAÇAO   1-2(1-2)
CUW: Eloy Victor Room, Rhuendly Aurelio Jean-Carlo Martina, Michaël Madionis Mateo Maria, Suently Alberto, Juriën Godfried Juan Gaari, Vurnon San Benito Anita, Leandro Jones Johan Bacuna, Rolieny Nonato Luis Bonevacia (46.Jeremy Antonisse), Juninho Bacuna, Rolieny Nonato Luis Bonevacia (62.Elson Quincy Hooi), Jarchinio Angelo Roberto Antonia (62.Anthony Edsel Johannes van den Hurk). Trainer: Guus Hiddink (Netherlands).
Goals: Leandro Jones Johan Bacuna 810), Rolieny Nonato Luis Bonevacia (44).

05.06.2021, 22nd FIFA World Cup Qualifiers, CONCACAF First Round
Estadio El Trébol, Ciudad de Guatemala (Guatemala)
Referee: William Anderson (Puerto Rico)
BRITISH VIRGIN ISLANDS - CURAÇAO   0-8(0-6)
CUW: Eloy Victor Room, Rhuendly Aurelio Jean-Carlo Martina, Michaël Madionis Mateo Maria, Suently Alberto, Juriën Godfried Juan Gaari, Vurnon San Benito Anita (46.Gervane Zjandric Adonnis Kastaneer), Leandro Jones Johan Bacuna, Juninho Bacuna (46.Rolieny Nonato Luis Bonevacia), Rolieny Nonato Luis Bonevacia (71.Anthony Edsel Johannes van den Hurk), Jarchinio Angelo Roberto Antonia (46.Kenji Joel Gorré), Brandley Mack-olien Kuwas (46.Elson Quincy Hooi). Trainer: Guus Hiddink (Netherlands).
Goals: Brandley Mack-olien Kuwas (7), Michaël Madionis Mateo Maria (9), Leandro Jones Johan Bacuna (11), Rolieny Nonato Luis Bonevacia (18 penalty, 22), Michaël Madionis Mateo Maria (27), Kenji Joel Gorré (57), Kenji Joel Gorré (90+1).

08.06.2021, 22nd FIFA World Cup Qualifiers, CONCACAF First Round
Stadion „Ergilio Hato", Willemstad; Attendance: 3,000
Referee: Armando Villareal (United States)

CURAÇAO - GUATEMALA   0-0

CUW: Eloy Victor Room, Rhuendly Aurelio Jean-Carlo Martina, Michaël Madionis Mateo Maria (89.Ayrton Daryl Statie), Suently Alberto, Juriën Godfried Juan Gaari, Vurnon San Benito Anita, Leandro Jones Johan Bacuna, Juninho Bacuna, Jarchinio Angelo Roberto Antonia, Anthony Edsel Johannes van den Hurk (72.Rangelo Maria Janga), Brandley Mack-olien Kuwas (77.Kevin Felida). Trainer: Guus Hiddink (Netherlands).

12.06.2021, 22nd FIFA World Cup Qualifiers, CONCACAF Second Round
Estadio Nacional, Ciudad de Panamá; Attendance: 7,000
Referee: Jaime Herrera Bonilla (El Salvador)

PANAMA - CURAÇAO   2-1(0-0)

CUW: Eloy Victor Room, Rhuendly Aurelio Jean-Carlo Martina, Michaël Madionis Mateo Maria, Suently Alberto, Juriën Godfried Juan Gaari (46.Darryl Brian Ricky Lachman), Vurnon San Benito Anita, Leandro Jones Johan Bacuna, Juninho Bacuna (64.Gervane Zjandric Adonnis Kastaneer), Kevin Felida (46.Brandley Mack-olien Kuwas), Rangelo Maria Janga, Jarchinio Angelo Roberto Antonia (89.Rolieny Nonato Luis Bonevacia). Trainer: Guus Hiddink (Netherlands).
Goal: Rangelo Maria Janga (87).

15.06.2021, 22nd FIFA World Cup Qualifiers, CONCACAF Second Round
Stadion „Ergilio Hato", Willemstad
Referee: Marco Antonio Ortíz Nava (Mexico)

CURAÇAO - PANAMA   0-0

CUW: Eloy Victor Room, Darryl Brian Ricky Lachman, Michaël Madionis Mateo Maria (79.Ayrton Daryl Statie), Juriën Godfried Juan Gaari, Shermar Martina, Vurnon San Benito Anita, Leandro Jones Johan Bacuna, Juninho Bacuna, Rangelo Maria Janga (63.Jarchinio Angelo Roberto Antonia), Elson Quincy Hooi (18.Kenji Joel Gorré; 79.Rolieny Nonato Luis Bonevacia), Brandley Mack-olien Kuwas. Trainer: Guus Hiddink (Netherlands).

NATIONAL TEAM PLAYERS 2020/2021

Name	DOB	Club
Goalkeepers		
Eloy Victor ROOM	06.02.1989	*Columbus Crew (USA)*
Defenders		
Suently ALBERTO	09.06.1996	*Unattached*
Juriën Godfried Juan GAARI	23.12.1993	*RKC Waalwijk (NED)*
Darryl Brian Ricky LACHMAN	11.11.1989	*Perth Glory FC (AUS)*
Michaël Madionis Mateo MARIA	31.01.1995	*NAC Breda (NED)*
Rhuendly Aurelio Jean-Carlo "Cuco" MARTINA	25.09.1989	*Unattached*
Roshon VAN EIJMA	06.06.1998	*SC Preußen Münster (GER)*
Midfielders		
Vurnon San Benito ANITA	04.04.1989	*RKC Waalwijk (NED)*
Juninho BACUNA	07.08.1997	*Huddersfield Town AFC (ENG)*
Leandro Jones Johan BACUNA	21.08.1991	*Cardiff City FC (WAL)*
Rolieny Nonato Luis BONEVACIA	08.10.1991	*Al Fujairah FC (UAE)*
Jeremy DE NOOIJER	15.03.1992	*Al-Shamal SC (QAT)*
Kevin FELIDA	11.11.1999	*FC Den Bosch (NED)*
Brandley Mack-olien KUWAS	19.09.1992	*Al Jazira SCC Abu Dhabi (UAE)*
Ayrton Daryl STATIE	22.07.1994	*Unattached*
Forwards		
Jarchinio Angelo Roberto ANTONIA	27.12.1990	*SC Cambuur-Leewarden (NED)*
Jeremy ANTONISSE	29.03.2002	*PSV Eindhoven (NED)*
Charlison Girigorio BENSCHOP	21.08.1989	*Apollon FC Limassol (CYP)*
Kenji Joel GORRÉ	29.09.1994	*CD Nacional Funchal (POR)*
Elson Quincy HOOI	01.10.1991	*Muaither SC (QAT)*
Rangelo Maria JANGA	16.04.1992	*NEC Nijmegen (NED)*
Gervane Zjandric Adonnis KASTANEER	09.06.1996	*Heart of Midlothian FC (SCO)*
Gevaro Giomar Magno NEPOMUCENO	10.11.1992	*FC Dinamo București (ROU)*
Anthony Edsel Johannes VAN DEN HURK	19.01.1993	*Helsingborgs IF (SWE)*
National coaches		
Guus HIDDINK (Netherlands) [from 01.09.2020]		08.11.1946

DOMINICA

The Country:	The FA:
Commonwealth of Dominica	Dominica Football Association
Capital: Roseau	Patrick John Football House, Bath Estate
Surface: 754 km²	P.O. Box 1080, Roseau
Population: 71,625 [2018]	Year of Formation: 1970
Time: UTC-4	Member of FIFA since: 1994
Independent since: 1978	Member of CONCACAF since: 1994

NATIONAL TEAM RECORDS

First international match: 1932: Dominica - Martinique 1-0
Most international caps: Glenson Price – 64 caps (since 2005)
Most international goals: Julian Wade – 17 goals / 39 caps (since 2010)

CONCACAF GOLD CUP	
1991	Did not enter
1993	Qualifiers
1996	Qualifiers
1998	Qualifiers
2000	Qualifiers
2002	Qualifiers
2003	*Withdrew*
2005	Qualifiers
2007	Qualifiers
2009	Qualifiers
2011	Qualifiers
2013	Qualifiers
2015	Qualifiers
2017	Qualifiers
2019	Qualifiers
2021	Qualifiers

FIFA WORLD CUP	
1930	-
1934	-
1938	-
1950	-
1954	-
1958	-
1962	-
1966	-
1970	-
1974	-
1978	-
1982	-
1986	-
1990	-
1994	-
1998	Qualifiers
2002	Qualifiers
2006	Qualifiers
2010	Qualifiers
2014	Qualifiers
2018	Qualifiers

F.I.F.A. CONFEDERATIONS CUP 1992-2017

None

OLYMPIC FOOTBALL TOURNAMENTS 1908-2016							
1908	-	1948	-	1972	-	1996	-
1912	-	1952	-	1976	-	2000	Qualifiers
1920	-	1956	-	1980	-	2004	Qualifiers
1924	-	1960	-	1984	-	2008	Qualifiers
1928	-	1964	-	1988	-	2012	Qualifiers
1936	-	1968	-	1992	-	2016	Qualifiers

CCCF (Confederación Centroamericana y del Caribe de Fútbol) CHAMPIONSHIPS 1941-1961
None

CONCACAF CHAMPIONSHIPS 1963-1989
None

CONCACAF NATIONS LEAGUE	
2019-2020	League B (*relegated to League C*)

CARIBBEAN CHAMPIONSHIPS 1989-2017			
1989	Qualifiers	1999	Qualifiers
1991	Did not enter	2001	Qualifiers
1992	Qualifiers	2005	Qualifiers
1993	Qualifiers	2007	Qualifiers
1994	Final Tournament - Group Stage	2008	Qualifiers
1995	Qualifiers	2010	Qualifiers
1996	Qualifiers	2012	Qualifiers
1997	Qualifiers	2014	Qualifiers
1998	Final Tournament - Group Stage	2017	Qualifiers

DOMINICA CLUB HONOURS IN CONCACAF CLUB COMPETITIONS:

CONCACAF Champions Cup / CONCACAF Champions League 1962-2020
None
CONCACAF League 2017-2020
None
Caribbean Club Championship 1997-2021
None
CONCACAF Cup Winners Cup 1991-1995*
None
Copa Interamericana 1968-1998*
None

*defunct competitions

NATIONAL COMPETITIONS
TABLE OF HONOURS

	CHAMPIONS	CUP WINNERS
1970	Harlem United FC Newtown	Harlem United FC Newtown
1971	*Not known*	Harlem United FC Newtown
1972	Harlem United FC Newtown	*Not known*
1973	Harlem United FC Newtown	Harlem United FC Newtown
1974	Harlem United FC Newtown	Harlem United FC Newtown
1975	*No competition*	*No competition*
1976	*Not known*	Harlem United FC Newtown
1977	*Not known*	*Not known*
1978	*Not known*	Harlem United FC Newtown
1979	*Not known*	*Not known*
1980	*Not known*	Harlem United FC Newtown
1981	Harlem United FC Newtown	*Not known*
1982	*Not known*	*Not known*
1983	Harlem United FC Newtown	*Not known*
1984	*Not known*	Harlem United FC Newtown
1985	Antilles Kensboro Roseau & Harlem United FC Newtown (shared)	*Not known*
1986	*Not known*	*Not known*
1987	*Not known*	*Not known*
1988	*Not known*	*Not known*
1989	Harlem United FC Newtown	*Not known*
1990	*Not known*	*Not known*
1991	*Not known*	*Not known*
1992	Harlem United FC Newtown	Harlem United FC Newtown
1993	Harlem United FC Newtown	*Not known*
1994	Harlem United FC Newtown	Harlem United FC Newtown
1995	Harlem United FC Newtown	*Not known*
1996	Black Rocks Roseau	*Not known*
1997	Harlem United FC Newtown	Harlem United FC Newtown
1998	ACS Zebbians Goodwill	Pointe Michel FC
1999	Harlem United FC Newtown	*No competition*
2000	Harlem United FC Newtown	*No competition*
2001	Harlem United FC Newtown	*No competition*
2001/2002	Kubuli All Stars FC Saint Joseph	Sagicor South East United La Plaine
2002/2003	Harlem United FC Newtown	Harlem United FC Newtown
2003/2004	Harlem United FC Newtown	Harlem United FC Newtown
2004/2005	Dublanc Strikers SC	Sagicor South East United La Plaine
2005/2006	Harlem United FC Newtown	-
2006/2007	Sagicor South East United La Plaine	-
2007/2008	Centre Bath Estate FC Roseau	-
2008/2009	Centre Bath Estate FC Roseau	-
2009/2010	Centre Bath Estate FC Roseau	-
2010/2011	*No competition*	-
2011/2012	Harlem United FC Newtown	-
2012/2013	Centre Bath Estate FC Roseau	-
2013/2014	Northern Concrete & Steel Bombers	-
2014/2015	Exodus FC St. Joseph	-

2015/2016	Dublanc FC	-
2016/2017	Dublanc FC	-
2017/2018	*Championship abandoned*	-
2018/2019	Sagicor South East United La Plaine	-
2020	Sagicor South East United La Plaine	-

NATIONAL CHAMPIONSHIP
Premier League 2020

1.	**Sagicor South East United La Plaine**	18	10	5	3	33 - 18	35
2.	Happi Bath Estate FC Roseau	18	10	4	4	25 - 14	34
3.	LA Enterprises Bombers FC Portsmouth	18	10	3	5	39 - 23	33
4.	Promex Harlem United FC Newtown	18	9	2	7	44 - 30	29
5.	CCCUL Dublanc FC	18	8	5	5	31 - 20	29
6.	WE United FC Castle Bruce	18	8	3	7	26 - 20	27
7.	Petro Caribe Pointe Michel FC	18	7	3	8	29 - 33	24
8.	East Central FC Castle Bruce	18	5	7	6	24 - 21	22
9.	Belfast Estate Mahaut Soca Strikers FC (*Relegation Play-offs*)	18	5	3	10	30 - 41	18
10.	Exodus FC Saint Joseph (*Relegated*)	18	0	1	17	9 - 70	1

Relegation Play-off: Belfast Estate Mahaut Soca Strikers FC – LA Stars FC 2-3

SECOND LEVEL
First Division 2020

Regular Stage

Group 1

1.	Promex Harlem United FC Newtown "B"	10	7	1	2	33	-	15	22
2.	Police SC	10	5	4	1	19	-	13	19
3.	Middleham United FC Cockrane	10	5	3	2	29	-	12	18
4.	Belfast Estate Mahaut Soca Strikers FC "B"	10	5	2	3	24	-	18	17
5.	ACS Pottersville Tarish Unted	10	5	2	3	21	-	17	17
6.	Busta Warner	10	5	1	4	22	-	30	16
7.	Denise Charles Pointe Michel FC	10	4	3	3	23	-	14	15
8.	Exodus FC "B" Saint Joseph	10	3	3	4	20	-	19	12
9.	All Saints FC	10	2	3	5	15	-	21	9
10.	Kensborough United FC	10	2	1	7	12	-	31	7
11.	Do It Centre Might Avengers FC	10	0	1	9	11	-	39	1

Group 2

1.	East Central FC "B" Castle Bruce	9	7	1	1	25	-	7	22
2.	LA Enterprises Bombers "B" Portsmouth	9	7	0	2	41	-	7	21
3.	LA Stars FC	9	6	2	1	22	-	10	20
4.	CCCUL Dublanc FC "B" Dublanc	9	5	2	2	18	-	15	17
5.	RC Doctors FC	9	3	1	5	8	-	16	10
6.	BAA Sharks Bense	9	2	3	4	17	-	19	9
7.	WE United FC "B" Castle Bruce	9	2	3	4	13	-	29	9
8.	Sagicor South East FC "B" La Plaine	9	2	2	5	17	-	25	8
9.	Itassi United FC	9	2	0	7	9	-	32	6
10.	Diaspora Calibishie FC	9	1	2	6	11	-	21	5

Top-4 of each group were qualified for the Play-off Stage.

Play-off Stage

Quarter-Finals [09-11.12.2020]

Promex Harlem United FC Newtown "B" - CCCUL Dublanc FC "B" Dublanc	1-0
Police SC - LA Stars FC	1-2
Middleham United FC Cockrane - LA Enterprises Bombers "B" Portsmouth	3-0
Belfast Estate Mahaut Soca Strikers FC "B" - East Central FC "B" Castle Bruce	2-3

Semi-Finals [12-16.12.2020]

Promex Harlem United FC Newtown "B" - LA Stars FC	5-1
East Central FC "B" Castle Bruce - Middleham United FC Cockrane	3-0

Please note: as both finalists already have their first team at First Level, the two losing semi-finalists played for promotion in the Third Place Play-off.

Third Place Play-off [19.12.2020]

Middleham United FC Cockrane - LA Stars FC	2-1

Middleham United FC Cockrane promoted for the 2021 Premier League, while LA Stars FC played in the Relegation Play-off.

Final [20.12.2020]

Promex Harlem United FC Newtown "B" - East Central FC "B" Castle Bruce	3-0

NATIONAL TEAM
INTERNATIONAL MATCHES 2020/2021

24.03.2021	Santo Domingo	*Dominican Republic - Dominica*	*1-0(0-0)*	*(WCQ)*
28.03.2021	Santo Domingo	*Dominica - Panama*	*1-2(0-1)*	*(WCQ)*
02.06.2021	Santo Domingo	*Dominica - Anguilla*	*3-0(3-0)*	*(WCQ)*
08.06.2021	Santo Domingo	*Barbados - Dominica*	*1-1(0-0)*	*(WCQ)*

24.03.2021, 22nd FIFA World Cup Qualifiers, CONCACAF First Round
Estadio Olímpico "Félix Sánchez", Santo Domingo
Referee: William Anderson (Puerto Rico)
DOMINICAN REPUBLIC - DOMINICA **1-0(0-0)**
DMA: Glenson Prince, Sidney Martin Lockhart, Erskim Williams, Briel Thomas, Malcolm Anthony Joseph, Kelrick Walter, Chad Bertrand, Travist Joseph (84.Audel Josiah O'Neal Laville), Fitz Jolly, Julian Michael Wade (86.Darryl Longdon), Javid George. Trainer: Rajesh Joseph Latchoo (Trinidad and Tobago).

28.03.2021, 22nd FIFA World Cup Qualifiers, CONCACAF First Round
Estadio Olímpico "Félix Sánchez", Santo Domingo
Referee: Marco Antonio Ortíz Nava (Mexico)
DOMINICA - PANAMA **1-2(0-1)**
DMA: Glenson Prince, Sidney Martin Lockhart, Erskim Williams, Briel Thomas, Malcolm Anthony Joseph, Kelrick Walter, Chad Bertrand, Travist Joseph, Fitz Jolly (68.Audel Josiah O'Neal Laville), Triston Sandy (38.Darryl Longdon), Julian Michael Wade (87.Reon Cuffy). Trainer: Rajesh Joseph Latchoo (Trinidad and Tobago).
Goal: Audel Josiah O'Neal Laville (82).

02.06.2021, 22nd FIFA World Cup Qualifiers, CONCACAF First Round
Estadio Olímpico "Félix Sánchez", Santo Domingo (Dominican Republic)
Referee: Kimbell Ward (Saint Kitts and Nevis)
DOMINICA - ANGUILLA **3-0(3-0)**
DMA: Glenson Prince, Erskim Williams, Travist Joseph (62.Marcelus Shane Bonney), Fitz Jolly, Malcolm Anthony Joseph, Kelrick Walter (67.Sidney Martin Lockhart), Chad Bertrand (75.Kassim Peltier), Briel Thomas, Anfernee Frederick (67.Audel Josiah O'Neal Laville), Julian Michael Wade (75.Triston Sandy), Javid George. Trainer: Rajesh Joseph Latchoo (Trinidad and Tobago).
Goals: Briel Thomas (3), Chad Bertrand (34), Julian Michael Wade (42).

08.06.2021, 22nd FIFA World Cup Qualifiers, CONCACAF First Round
Estadio Olímpico "Félix Sánchez", Santo Domingo (Dominican Republic)
Referee: Jaime Herrera Bonilla (El Salvador)
BARBADOS - DOMINICA **1-1(0-0)**
DMA: Glenson Prince, Erskim Williams, Travist Joseph, Sidney Martin Lockhart, Anfernee Frederick (78.Marcelus Shane Bonney), Malcolm Anthony Joseph, Chad Bertrand (28.Donan Jervier), Briel Thomas (46.Triston Sandy), Julian Michael Wade, Javid George, Audel Josiah O'Neal Laville (81.Euclid Bertrand). Trainer: Rajesh Joseph Latchoo (Trinidad and Tobago).
Goal: Julian Michael Wade (57).

NATIONAL TEAM PLAYERS
2020/2021

Name	DOB	Club
Goalkeepers		
Glenson PRINCE	17.09.1987	*Phare du Petit-Canal (GLP)*
Defenders		
Euclid BERTRAND	23.07.1974	*Dublanc FC*
Malcolm Anthony JOSEPH	10.10.1993	*LA Enterprise Bombers Portsmouth*
Sidney Martin LOCKHART	08.03.1996	*Morvant Caledonia United (TRI)*
Kassim PELTIER	07.09.1998	*Promex Harlem United FC Newtown*
Erskim WILLIAMS	21.10.1994	*LA Enterprise Bombers Portsmouth*
Midfielders		
Chad BERTRAND	19.12.1986	*Solidarité Scolaire Baie-Mahault (GLP)*
Marcelus Shane BONNEY	16.02.2000	*Bath Estate FC Roseau*
Anfernee FREDERICK	23.01.1996	*Bath Estate FC Roseau*
Javid GEORGE	14.06.1998	*Sagicor South East United La Plaine*
Donan JERVIER	04.11.1989	*Promex Harlem United FC Newtown*
Fitz JOLLY	16.03.1999	*Bath Estate FC Roseau*
Triston SANDY		*LA Enterprise Bombers Portsmouth*
Briel THOMAS	25.11.1994	*Williams Connection FC (TRI)*
Kelrick WALTER	06.11.1989	*Bath Estate FC Roseau*
Forwards		
Reon CUFFY	17.01.1999	*East Central FC*
Travist JOSEPH	23.05.1994	*Dublanc FC*
Audel Josiah O'Neal LAVILLE	14.09.2002	*Promex Harlem United FC Newtown*
Darryl LONGDON	08.11.2000	*FC Tucson (USA)*
Julian Michael WADE	12.07.1990	*Solidarité Scolaire Baie-Mahault (GLP)*
National coaches		
Rajesh Joseph LATCHOO (Trinidad and Tobago) [from 05.03.2017]		08.06.1984

DOMINICAN REPUBLIC

Federación Dominicana de Fútbol

The Country:
República Dominicana (Dominican Republic)
Capital: Santo Domingo
Surface: 48,442 km²
Population: 10,878,246 [2018]
Time: UTC-4
Independent since: 1865

The FA:
Federación Dominicana de Fútbol
Centro Olímpico „Juan Pablo Duarte",
Ensanche Miraflores, Apartado Postal 1953,
Santo Domingo
Year of Formation: 1953
Member of FIFA since: 1958
Member of CONCACAF since: 1964

NATIONAL TEAM RECORDS

First international match: 21.05.1967: Dominican Republic - Haiti 0-8
Most international caps: Miguel Starling Lloyd Troncoso – 48 caps (since 2004)
Most international goals: Jonathan Rafael Faña Frías – 24 goals / 45 caps (2006-2016)

CONCACAF GOLD CUP	
1991	Qualifiers
1993	Qualifiers
1996	Qualifiers
1998	*Withdrew*
2000	Qualifiers
2002	Qualifiers
2003	Qualifiers
2005	*Withdrew*
2007	*Withdrew during qualifiers*
2009	Did not enter
2011	Qualifiers
2013	Qualifiers
2015	Qualifiers
2017	Qualifiers
2019	Qualifiers
2021	Qualifiers

FIFA WORLD CUP	
1930	-
1934	-
1938	-
1950	-
1954	-
1958	-
1962	Did not enter
1966	Did not enter
1970	Did not enter
1974	Did not enter
1978	Qualifiers
1982	Did not enter
1986	Did not enter
1990	Did not enter
1994	Qualifiers
1998	Qualifiers
2002	Qualifiers
2006	Qualifiers
2010	Qualifiers
2014	Qualifiers
2018	Qualifiers

F.I.F.A. CONFEDERATIONS CUP 1992-2017
None

OLYMPIC FOOTBALL TOURNAMENTS 1908-2016

1908	-	1948	-	1972	Did not enter	1996	Did not enter
1912	-	1952	-	1976	Qualifiers	2000	Qualifiers
1920	-	1956	-	1980	Qualifiers	2004	Qualifiers
1924	-	1960	-	1984	Did not enter	2008	Qualifiers
1928	-	1964	-	1988	Qualifiers	2012	Did not enter
1936	-	1968	Qualifiers	1992	Did not enter	2016	Qualifiers

CCCF (Confederación Centroamericana y del Caribe de Fútbol) CHAMPIONSHIPS 1941-1961
None

CONCACAF CHAMPIONSHIPS 1963-1989
None

CONCACAF NATIONS LEAGUE

2019-2020	League B

CARIBBEAN CHAMPIONSHIPS 1989-2017

1989	Did not enter	1999	Qualifiers
1991	Final Tournament - Group Stage	2001	Qualifiers
1992	Did not enter	2005	*Withdrew*
1993	Qualifiers	2007	Qualifiers
1994	Qualifiers	2008	Did not enter
1995	Qualifiers	2010	Qualifiers
1996	Qualifiers	2012	Final Tournament - Group Stage
1997	Qualifiers	2014	Qualifiers
1998	Qualifiers	2017	Qualifiers

DOMINICAN REPUBLIC CLUB HONOURS IN CONCACAF CLUB COMPETITIONS:

CONCACAF Champions Cup / CONCACAF Champions League 1962-2020
None

CONCACAF League 2017-2020
None

Caribbean Club Championship 1997-2021

Cibao FC Santiago de Caballeros	1	2017
Club Atlético Pantoja Santo Domingo	1	2018

CONCACAF Cup Winners Cup 1991-1995*
None

Copa Interamericana 1968-1998*
None

*defunct competitions

NATIONAL COMPETITIONS
TABLE OF HONOURS

	CAMPEONATO NACIONAL - CHAMPIONS
1970	España FC
1971	España FC
1972	UCMM Santiago de los Caballeros
1973	UCMM Santiago de los Caballeros
1974	UCMM Santiago de los Caballeros
1975	*Not known*
1976	Moca FC Don Bosco
1977	Moca FC Don Bosco
1978	Moca FC Don Bosco
1979	*Not known*
1980	*Not known*
1981	Universidad Autónoma Santo Domingo
1982	*Not known*
1983	*Not known*
1984	*Not known*
1985	Moca FC Don Bosco
1986	Moca FC Don Bosco
1987	Moca FC Don Bosco
1988/1898	Universidad Autónoma Santo Domingo
1989/1990	Universidad Autónoma Santo Domingo
1991	Bancredicard Santo Domino
1992	Bancredicard Santo Domino
1993	San Cristóbal FC
1994	Bancredicard Santo Domino
1995	Moca FC Don Bosco
1996	*Not known*
1997	FC Santos San Cristóbal
1998	Domingo Savio La Vega
1999	Moca FC Don Bosco
2000/2001	Club Atlético Pantoja Santo Domingo
2001/2002	*Not known*
2002/2003	Club Atlético Pantoja Santo Domingo
2003/2004	Casa de España
2005	Baninter Jarabacoa
2006	La Vega

	LIGA MAYOR - CHAMPIONS
2001/2002	Baninter Jarabacoa
2002/2003	Baninter Jarabacoa
2003/2004	*No competition*
2004/2005	Club Atlético Pantoja Santo Domingo
2005/2006	*No competition*
2007	Barcelona FC Santo Domingo
2007/2008	*No competition*
2009	Club Atlético Pantoja Santo Domingo
2010	Moca FC Don Bosco
2011/2012	Club Atlético Pantoja Santo Domingo

2012/2013	Moca FC Don Bosco
2014	Moca FC Don Bosco
2015	Club Atlético Pantoja Santo Domingo
2016	Club Barcelona Atlético Santo Domingo
2017	Club Atlético Pantoja Santo Domingo
2018	Cibao FC Santiago de Caballeros
2019	Club Atlético Pantoja Santo Domingo
2020	Universidad Organización y Métodos FC Santo Domingo

NATIONAL CHAMPIONSHIP
Liga Dominicana de Fútbol "Banco Popular" – Liga Mayor 2020

Group Stage

Zona Norte

1. Cibao FC Santiago de Caballeros	6	3	2	1	11	-	5	11
2. Atlántico FC Puerto Plata	6	2	4	0	8	-	4	10
3. Atlético Vega Real La Vega	6	1	4	1	10	-	8	7
4. Jarabacoa FC	6	0	2	4	3	-	15	2

Zona Sur

1. Universidad Organización y Métodos FC Santo Domingo	6	4	1	1	8	-	2	13
2. Delfines del Este FC La Romana	6	3	2	1	8	-	8	11
3. Club Atlético San Cristóbal	6	2	0	4	8	-	12	6
4. Club Atlético Pantoja Santo Domingo	6	1	1	4	7	-	9	4

Group winners were qualified for the Play-off Semi-Finals, while teams ranked second and third were qualified for the Play-off Quarter-Finals.

Play-off Stage

Quarter-Finals [14-15.11.2020]

Atlántico FC Puerto Plata - Club Atlético San Cristóbal	1-3
Delfines del Este FC La Romana - Atlético Vega Real La Vega	2-1

Semi-Finals [21-29.11.2020]

- Universidad Organización y Métodos FC Santo Domingo	0-3	1-2
Delfines del Este FC La Romana - Cibao FC Santiago de Caballeros	2-1	1-0

Final [06-13-.12.2020]

Delfines del Este FC La Romana - Universidad Organización y Métodos FC Santo Domingo	0-2
Universidad Organización y Métodos FC Santo Domingo - Delfines del Este FC La Romana	2-1

Liga Mayor 2020 Champions: **Universidad Organización y Métodos FC Santo Domingo**

THE CLUBS

ATLÁNTICO FÚTBOL CLUB PUERTO PLATA
Year of Formation: 2014
Stadium: Estadio "Leonel Plácido", Puerto Plata (2,000)

CLUB ATLÉTICO SAN CRISTÓBAL
Year of Formation: 2015
Stadium: Estadio Panamericano, San Cristóbal (2,800)

ATLÉTICO VEGA REAL LA VEGA
Year of Formation: 2014
Stadium: Estadio Olímpico, La Vega (7,000)

CIBAO FÚTBOL CLUB SANTIAGO DE CABALLEROS
Year of Formation: 2015
Stadium: Estadio Cibao FC, Santiago de Caballeros (5,000)

CLUB ATLÉTICO PANTOJA SANTO DOMINGO
Year of Formation: 2000
Stadium: Estadio Olímpico „Félix Sánchez", Santo Domingo (27,000)

DELFINES DEL ESTE FÚTBOL CLUB LA ROMANA
Year of Formation: 2015
Stadium: Estadio Municipal, La Romana (2,000)

JARABACOA FÚTBOL CLUB
Year of Formation: n/a
Stadium: Estadio Olímpico, La Vega (10,000

UNIVERSIDAD ORGANIZACIÓN Y MÉTODOS FÚTBOL CLUB SANTO DOMINGO
Year of Formation: 2010
Stadium: Estadio Olímpico „Félix Sánchez", Santo Domingo (27,000)

NATIONAL TEAM
INTERNATIONAL MATCHES 2020/2021

19.01.2021	Santo Domingo	Dominican Republic - Puerto Rico	0-1(0-1)	(F)
25.01.2021	Santo Domingo	Dominican Republic - Serbia	0-0	(F)
24.03.2021	Santo Domingo	Dominican Republic - Dominica	1-0(0-0)	(WCQ)
27.03.2021	Fort Lauderdale	Anguilla - Dominican Republic	0-6(0-3)	(WCQ)
04.06.2021	Santo Domingo	Dominican Republic - Barbados	1-1(0-1)	(WCQ)
08.06.2021	Ciudad de Panamá	Panama - Dominican Republic	3-0(1-0)	(WCQ)

19.01.2021, Friendly International
Estadio Olímpico "Félix Sánchez", Santo Domingo; Attendance: 0
Referee: Randy Encarnación (Dominican Republic)
DOMINICAN REPUBLIC - PUERTO RICO   **0-1(0-1)**
DOM: Johan Snick Guzmán de los Santos, Brian López Nina, Benjamín Rafael Núñez Rodríguez (80.Ernesto Chet Trinidad Reyes), Alejandro Jiménez García, Edarlyn Reyes Ureña (80.Alexander Joseph Francois), Kelvin Durán (67.Kelvin Martínez Rodríguez), Wilman Modesta (81.Alexis Weidenbach), Carlos Heredia Fontana (68.Domingo Antonio Peralta Florencio), Edison Alexander Azcona Vélez, Dorny Alexander Romero Chalas, Nowend Yenrique Lorenzo Cabrera (58.Erick Odali Paniagua Japa [*sent off 90+3*]). Trainer: Jacques Antonio Passy Kahn (Mexico).

25.01.2021, Friendly International
Estadio Olímpico "Félix Sánchez", Santo Domingo; Attendance: 0
Referee: William Anderson (Puerto Rico)
DOMINICAN REPUBLIC - SERBIA   **0-0**
DOM: Rafael Alejandro Díaz Jr., Andrea Bosco, Luiyi Ramón de Lucas Pérez, Edarlyn Reyes Ureña, José Luis de la Cruz Melo (78.Alexis Weidenbach), Wilman Modesta, Carlos Heredia Fontana (50.Antonio Natalucci Berroa), Gerard Paul Lavergne Matos (68.Gabriel Ernesto Núñez D´Alessandro), Edison Alexander Azcona Vélez (78.Ronaldo Junior Vásquez Herasme), Dorny Alexander Romero Chalas (68.Nowend Yenrique Lorenzo Cabrera), Juan Carlos Pineda Torres (50.Rudolf Karl González Vass). Trainer: Jacques Antonio Passy Kahn (Mexico).

24.03.2021, 22nd FIFA World Cup Qualifiers, CONCACAF First Round
Estadio Olímpico "Félix Sánchez", Santo Domingo
Referee: William Anderson (Puerto Rico)
DOMINICAN REPUBLIC - DOMINICA   **1-0(0-0)**
DOM: Rafael Alejandro Díaz Jr., Cayetano Bonnín Vásquez, Andrea Bosco, Luiyi Ramón de Lucas Pérez, Rudolf Karl González Vass (72.Manny Alexander Rodríguez Baldera, Francisco José Núñez Rodríguez (64.Domingo Antonio Peralta Florencio), Enmy Manuel Peña Beltré, Luis Ángel Núñez Coordes (84.Benjamín Rafael Núñez Rodríguez), Wilman Modesta, Carlos Heredia Fontana (72.Jean Carlos López Moscoso), Ronaldo Junior Vásquez Herasme (84.Gianluigi Sueva). Trainer: Jacques Antonio Passy Kahn (Mexico).
Goal: Francisco José Núñez Rodríguez (52).

27.03.2021, 22nd FIFA World Cup Qualifiers, CONCACAF First Round
DRV PNK Stadium, Fort Lauderdale
Referee: Rubiel Vásquez (United States)

ANGUILLA - DOMINICAN REPUBLIC   **0-6(0-3)**

DOM: Rafael Alejandro Díaz Jr., Hansley Alexander Martínez García, Luis Ismael Díaz Ramírez, Rafael Leonardo Flores (71.Carlos Eduardo Ventura Soriano), Gabriel Ernesto Núñez D´Alessandro, Carlos Heredia Fontana, Ronaldo Junior Vásquez Herasme, Domingo Antonio Peralta Florencio (67.Luis José Espinal Florencio), Ernesto Chet Trinidad Reyes, Dorny Alexander Romero Chalas (71.Richard Joel Dabas Pérez), Nowend Yenrique Lorenzo Cabrera. Trainer: Jacques Antonio Passy Kahn (Mexico).

Goals: Dorny Alexander Romero Chalas (22 penalty), Nowend Yenrique Lorenzo Cabrera (25), Dorny Alexander Romero Chalas (27), Nowend Yenrique Lorenzo Cabrera (46), Domingo Antonio Peralta Florencio (66), Luis José Espinal Florencio (76).

04.06.2021, 22nd FIFA World Cup Qualifiers, CONCACAF First Round
Estadio Olímpico "Félix Sánchez", Santo Domingo
Referee: Germán Stanley Martínez Miranda (El Salvador)

DOMINICAN REPUBLIC - BARBADOS   **1-1(0-1)**

DOM: Rafael Alejandro Díaz Jr., Cayetano Bonnín Vásquez, Andrea Bosco, Luiyi Ramón de Lucas Pérez, Edarlyn Reyes Ureña, Enmy Manuel Peña Beltré (64.Antonio Natalucci Berroa), Manny Alexander Rodríguez Baldera, Wilman Modesta (46.Jean Carlos López Moscoso), Ronaldo Junior Vásquez Herasme (70.Carlos Heredia Fontana), Domingo Antonio Peralta Florencio (46.Francisco José Núñez Rodríguez), Dorny Alexander Romero Chalas (82.Nowend Yenrique Lorenzo Cabrera). Trainer: Jacques Antonio Passy Kahn (Mexico).

Goal: Manny Alexander Rodríguez Baldera (90+2).

08.06.2021, 22nd FIFA World Cup Qualifiers, CONCACAF First Round
Estadio Nacional "Rod Carew", Ciudad de Panamá
Referee: Walter Alexander López Castellanos (Guatemala))

PANAMA - DOMINICAN REPUBLIC   **3-0(1-0)**

DOM: Rafael Alejandro Díaz Jr., Cayetano Bonnín Vásquez (70.Brian López Nina), Luis Ismael Díaz Ramírez, Andrea Bosco (46.Enmy Manuel Peña Beltré), Luiyi Ramón de Lucas Pérez, Edarlyn Reyes Ureña, Jean Carlos López Moscoso (65.Rafael Leonardo Flores), Manny Alexander Rodríguez Baldera, Wilman Modesta (54.Ronaldo Junior Vásquez Herasme), Dorny Alexander Romero Chalas (46.Antonio Natalucci Berroa), Nowend Yenrique Lorenzo Cabrera. Trainer: Jacques Antonio Passy Kahn (Mexico).

Goals:

NATIONAL TEAM PLAYERS 2020/2021		
Name	DOB	Club
Goalkeepers		
Rafael Alejandro DÍAZ Jr.	08.10.1991	*Sacramento Republic (USA)*
Johan Snick GUZMÁN de los Santos	03.07.1987	*Real Ávila CF (ESP)*
Defenders		
Cayetano BONNÍN Vásquez	30.06.1990	*Hercules de Alicante CF (ESP)*
Andrea BOSCO	06.10.1995	*Pro Sesto 1913 (ITA)*
José Luis DE LA CRUZ Melo	05.07.2000	*RCD Carabanchel (ESP)*

Luiyi Ramón DE LUCAS Pérez	31.08.1994	*FC Haka Valkeakoski (FIN)*
Luis Ismael DÍAZ Ramírez	21.08.1990	*Cibao FC Santiago de los Caballeros*
Kelvin DURÁN	05.08.1994	*Universidad O&M FC Santo Domingo*
Alexander Joseph FRANCOIS	29.04.2003	*Lonestar SC (USA)*
Alejandro JIMÉNEZ García	13.01.2002	*UE Cornellà (ESP)*
Brian LÓPEZ Nina	20.11.1999	*Atlético Porcuna CF (ESP)*
Hansley Alexander MARTÍNEZ García	03.03.1991	*Universidad O&M FC Santo Domingo*
Antonio NATALUCCI Berroa	01.08.2000	*Cavese 1919 (ITA)*
Benjamín Rafael NÚÑEZ Rodríguez	15.05.1995	*AD Ceuta FC (ESP)*
Edarlyn REYES Ureña	30.09.1997	*Club Real Santa Cruz de la Sierra (BOL)*
Ernesto Chet TRINIDAD Reyes	02.01.1996	*Club Atlético Pantoja Santo Domingo*

Midfielders

Edison Alexander AZCONA Vélez	21.11.2003	*Inter Miami CF (USA)*
Richard Joel DABAS Pérez	04.08.1994	*Cibao FC Santiago de los Caballeros*
Rafael Leonardo FLORES	24.04.1992	*Cibao FC Santiago de los Caballeros*
Rudolf Karl GONZÁLEZ Vass	02.07.1998	*Bonner SC (GER)*
Gerard Paul LAVERGNE Matos	25.01.1999	*FC Tucson (USA)*
Jean Carlos LÓPEZ Moscoso	09.11.1993	*Cibao FC Santiago de los Caballeros*
Kelvin MARTÍNEZ Rodríguez	11.09.1997	*Jarabacoa FC*
Wilman MODESTA	24.12.1995	*Universidad O&M FC Santo Domingo*
Gabriel Ernesto NÚÑEZ D´Alessandro	24.01.1994	*CD Luis Ángel Firpo Usulután (SLV)*
Enmy Manuel PEÑA Beltré	07.09.1992	*Valletta FC (MLT)*
Manny Alexander RODRÍGUEZ Baldera	23.05.1998	*CF Rajo Majahadonda (ESP)*
Ronaldo Junior VÁSQUEZ Herasme	30.06.1999	*Club Atlético Pantoja Santo Domingo*
Alexis WEIDENBACH	24.09.1996	*TuS Rot-Weiß Koblenz (GER)*

Forwards

Luis Ángel Núñez COORDES	02.01.1999	*FC St. Pauli Hamburg (GER)*
Luis José ESPINAL Florencio	20.02.1994	*Club Atlético Pantoja Santo Domingo*
Carlos HEREDIA Fontana	28.09.1998	*Delfines del Este FC La Romana*
Nowend Yenrique LORENZO Cabrera	02.11.2002	*CA Osasuna Pamplona Juvenil A (ESP)*
Francisco José NÚÑEZ Rodríguez	15.05.1995	*SCR Peña Deportiva Santa Eulària des Riu (ESP)*
Erick Odali PANIAGUA Japa	06.04.1999	*Club Atlético Pantoja Santo Domingo*
Domingo Antonio PERALTA Florencio	28.07.1986	*Atlético Vega Real La Vega*
Juan Carlos PINEDA Torres	12.01.2000	*CD Mirandés "B" (ESP)*
Dorny Alexander ROMERO Chalas	24.01.1998	*Venados FC Mérida (MEX)*
Gianluigi SUEVA	01.01.2001	*Cosenza Calcio (ITA)*
Carlos Eduardo VENTURA Soriano	1997	*Cibao FC Santiago de los Caballeros*

National coaches

Jacques Antonio PASSY Kahn (Mexico) [from 03.08.2020]	30.09.1975

EL SALVADOR

The Country:	The FA:
República de El Salvador	Federación Salvadoreña de Fútbol
(Republic of El Salvador)	Avenida José Matias Delgado, Frente al Centro
Capital: San Salvador	Espanol Colonia Escalón, Zona 10,
Surface: 21,040 km²	San Salvador 1029
Population: 6,420,746 [2018]	Year of Formation: 1935
Time: UTC-6	Member of FIFA since: 1938
Independent since: 1821	Member of CONCACAF since: 1962

NATIONAL TEAM RECORDS

First international match: 14.09.1921, Ciudad de Guatemala: Guatemala - El Salvador 1-2
Most international caps: Alfredo Alberto Pacheco – 85 caps (2002-2013)
Most international goals: Raúl Ignacio Díaz Arce – 39 goals / 72 caps (1991-2000)

CONCACAF GOLD CUP	
1991	Qualifiers
1993	Qualifiers
1996	Final Tournament (Group Stage)
1998	Final Tournament (Group Stage)
2000	Qualifiers
2002	Final Tournament (Quarter-Finals)
2003	Final Tournament (Quarter-Finals)
2005	Qualifiers
2007	Final Tournament (Group Stage)
2009	Final Tournament (Group Stage)
2011	Final Tournament (2nd Round)
2013	Final Tournament (Quarter-Finals)
2015	Final Tournament (Group Stage)
2017	Final Tournament (Quarter-Finals)
2019	Final Tournament (Group Stage)
2021	Final Tournament (*to be played*)

FIFA WORLD CUP	
1930	Did not enter
1934	Did not enter
1938	*Withdrew*
1950	Did not enter
1954	Did not enter
1958	Did not enter
1962	Did not enter
1966	Did not enter
1970	Final Tournament (Group Stage)
1974	Qualifiers
1978	Qualifiers
1982	Final Tournament (Group Stage)
1986	Qualifiers
1990	Qualifiers
1994	Qualifiers
1998	Qualifiers
2002	Qualifiers
2006	Qualifiers
2010	Qualifiers
2014	Qualifiers
2018	Qualifiers

F.I.F.A. CONFEDERATIONS CUP 1992-2017

None

OLYMPIC FOOTBALL TOURNAMENTS 1908-2016

1908	-	1948	-	1972	Qualifiers	1996	Qualifiers
1912	-	1952	-	1976	Qualifiers	2000	Qualifiers
1920	-	1956	-	1980	Qualifiers	2004	Qualifiers
1924	-	1960	-	1984	Qualifiers	2008	Qualifiers
1928	-	1964	-	1988	Qualifiers	2012	Qualifiers
1936	-	1968	FT/Group Stage	1992	Qualifiers	2016	Qualifiers

CCCF (Confederación Centroamericana y del Caribe de Fútbol) CHAMPIONSHIPS 1941-1961
1941 (Runners-up), **1943 (Winners)**, 1946 (3rd Place), 1948, 1953, 1955, 1961 (Runners-up)

CONCACAF CHAMPIONSHIPS 1963-1989
1963 (Runners-up), 1965, 1971, 1977 (3rd Place), 1981 (Runners-up), 1985, 1989

CONCACAF NATIONS LEAGUE

2019-2020	League B (*promoted to League A*)

COPA CENTROAMERICANA (UNCAF NATIONS CHAMPIONSHIPS) 1991-2017

1991	Final Round - 4th Place	2005	Final Round - Group Stage
1993	Final Round - 4th Place	2007	Final Round - 4th Place
1995	Final Round - 3rd Place	2009	Final Round - 4th Place
1997	Final Round - 3rd Place	2011	Final Round - 4th Place
1999	Final Round - 4th Place	2013	Final Round - 3rd Place
2001	Final Round - 3rd Place	2014	Final Round - 4th Place
2003	Final Round - 3rd Place	2017	Final Round - 3rd Place

SALVADORAN CLUB HONOURS IN CONCACAF CLUB COMPETITIONS:

CONCACAF Champions Cup / CONCACAF Champions League 1962-2020		
Alianza Fútbol Club San Salvador	1	1967
Club Deportivo Águila San Miguel	1	1976
Club Deportivo Futbolistas Asociados Santanecos (FAS) Santa Ana	1	1979

CONCACAF League 2017-2020
None

Caribbean Club Championship 1997-2021
None

CONCACAF Cup Winners Cup 1991-1995*		
Club Deportivo Atlético Marte San Salvador	1	1991

Copa Interamericana 1968-1998*
None

*defunct competitions

NATIONAL COMPETITIONS
TABLE OF HONOURS

CHAMPIONS	
1926/1927	Chinameca SC
1927/1928	Hércules
1928/1929	Hércules
1929/1930	Hércules
1930/1931	Hércules

1931/1932	Hércules
1932/1933	Hércules
1933/1934	Hércules
1934/1935	CD Maya
1935/1936	CD Maya
1936/1937	CD 33
1937/1938	CD 33
1938/1939	CD 33
1939/1940	España FC
1940/1941	Quequeisque
1941/1942	Quequeisque
1942/1943	Quequeisque
1943/1944	Quequeisque
1944/1945	Quequeisque
1945/1946	Quequeisque
1946	Libertad FC
NATIONAL LEAGUE	
1947	Libertad FC
1947/1948	*No competition*
1948/1949	CD Once Municipal Ahuachapán
1949/1950	*No competition*
1950/1951	CD Dragón
1951/1952	CD FAS Santa Ana
1952/1953	CD Dragón
1953/1954	CD FAS Santa Ana
1955	CD Atlético Marte San Salvador
1955/1956	CD Atlético Marte San Salvador
1956/1957	CD Atlético Marte San Salvador
1957/1958	CD FAS Santa Ana
1959	CD Águila San Miguel
1960/1961	CD Águila San Miguel
1961/1962	CD FAS Santa Ana
1962	CD FAS Santa Ana
1963/1964	CD Águila San Miguel
1964	CD Águila San Miguel
1965/1966	Alianza FC San Salvador
1966/1967	Alianza FC San Salvador
1967/1968	CD Águila San Miguel
1968/1969	CD Atlético Marte San Salvador
1970	CD Atlético Marte San Salvador
1971	Juventud Olímpica
1972	CD Águila San Miguel
1973	Juventud Olímpica
1974/1975	CD Platense
1975/1976	CD Águila San Miguel
1976/1977	CD Águila San Miguel
1977/1978	CD FAS Santa Ana
1978/1979	CD FAS Santa Ana
1979/1980	CD Santiagueño
1980/1981	CD Atlético Marte San Salvador
1981	CD FAS Santa Ana
1982	CD Atlético Marte San Salvador

Año		Campeón
1983		CD Águila San Miguel
1984		CD FAS Santa Ana
1985		CD Atlético Marte San Salvador
1986/1987		Alianza FC San Salvador
1987/1988		CD Águila San Miguel
1988/1989		CD Luis Ángel Firpo Usulután
1989/1990		Alianza FC San Salvador
1990/1991		CD Luis Ángel Firpo Usulután
1991/1992		CD Luis Ángel Firpo Usulután
1992/1993		CD Luis Ángel Firpo Usulután
1993/1994		Alianza FC San Salvador
1994/1995		CD FAS Santa Ana
1995/1996		CD FAS Santa Ana
1996/1997		Alianza FC San Salvador
1997/1998		CD Luis Ángel Firpo Usulután
1998/1999	Ape:	Alianza FC San Salvador
	Cla:	CD Luis Ángel Firpo Usulután
1999/2000	Ape:	CD Águila San Miguel
	Cla:	CD Luis Ángel Firpo Usulután
2000/2001	Ape:	CD Águila San Miguel
	Cla:	CD Águila San Miguel
2001/2002	Ape:	Alianza FC San Salvador
	Cla:	CD FAS Santa Ana
2002/2003	Ape:	CD FAS Santa Ana
	Cla:	San Salvador FC
2003/2004	Ape:	CD FAS Santa Ana
	Cla:	Alianza FC San Salvador
2004/2005	Ape:	CD FAS Santa Ana
	Cla:	CD FAS Santa Ana
2005/2006	Ape:	CD Vista Hermosa San Francisco Gotera
	Cla:	CD Águila San Miguel
2006/2007	Ape:	CD Once Municipal Ahuachapán
	Cla:	AD Isidro Metapán Santa Ana
2007/2008	Ape:	CD Luis Ángel Firpo Usulután
	Cla:	CD Luis Ángel Firpo Usulután
2008/2009	Ape:	AD Isidro Metapán Santa Ana
	Cla:	AD Isidro Metapán Santa Ana
2009/2010	Ape:	CD FAS Santa Ana
	Cla:	AD Isidro Metapán Santa Ana
2010/2011	Ape:	AD Isidro Metapán Santa Ana
	Cla:	Alianza FC San Salvador
2011/2012	Ape:	AD Isidro Metapán Santa Ana
	Cla:	CD Águila San Miguel
2012/2013	Ape:	AD Isidro Metapán Santa Ana
	Cla:	CD Luis Ángel Firpo Usulután
2013/2014	Ape:	AD Isidro Metapán Santa Ana
	Cla:	AD Isidro Metapán Santa Ana
2014/2015	Ape:	AD Isidro Metapán Santa Ana
	Cla:	Santa Tecla FC
2015/2016	Ape:	Alianza FC San Salvador
	Cla:	CD Dragón San Miguel
2016/2017	Ape:	Santa Tecla FC

2017/2018	Cla:	Santa Tecla FC
	Ape:	Alianza FC San Salvador
2018/2019	Cla:	Alianza FC San Salvador
	Ape:	Santa Tecla FC
2019/2020	Cla:	CD Águila San Miguel
	Ape:	Alianza FC San Salvador
2020/2021	Cla:	Once Deportivo FC Ahuachapán
	Ape:	Alianza FC San Salvador
	Cla:	CD FAS Santa Ana

NATIONAL CHAMPIONSHIP
Primera División de Fútbol Profesional – La Liga Mayor 2020/2021

Torneo Apertura 2020

Primera Fase / Group Stage - Results

Grupo occidental [11.10.-15.11.2020]
Isidro Metapán - FAS Santa Ana 3-1(1-1)
Once Deportivo - Sonsonate FC 4-1(2-0)
FAS Santa Ana - Sonsonate FC 0-2(0-2)
Isidro Metapán - Once Deportivo 6-0(2-0)
Sonsonate FC - Isidro Metapán 1-1(0-1)
Once Deportivo - FAS Santa Ana 0-0
Sonsonate FC - Once Deportivo 0-1(0-1)
FAS Santa Ana - Isidro Metapán 4-0(2-0)
Sonsonate FC - FAS Santa Ana 0-3(0-1)
Once Deportivo - Isidro Metapán 3-1(0-1)
Isidro Metapán - Sonsonate FC 2-0(1-0)
FAS Santa Ana - Once Deportivo 1-0(1-0)

Grupo central [11.10.-15.11.2020]
AD Chalatenango - Atlético Marte 3-1(1-1)
Alianza FC - Santa Tecla FC 3-0(1-0)
AD Chalatenango - Alianza FC 0-3(0-3)
Atlético Marte - Santa Tecla FC 1-1(1-0)
Santa Tecla FC - AD Chalatenango 1-1(0-0)
Alianza FC - Atlético Marte 1-0(0-0)
Santa Tecla FC - Alianza FC 1-3(0-1)
Atlético Marte - AD Chalatenango 3-2(0-1)
Santa Tecla FC - Atlético Marte 2-1(2-0)
Alianza FC - AD Chalatenango 1-1(1-1)
AD Chalatenango - Santa Tecla FC 1-1(0-0)
Atlético Marte - Alianza FC 1-3(0-1)

Grupo oriental [10.10.-15.11.2020]
Jocoro FC - Luis Ángel Firpo 1-0(0-0)
CD Águila - Municipal Limeño 2-1(1-1)
Municipal Limeño - Luis Ángel Firpo 0-0
CD Águila - Jocoro FC 2-0(0-0)
Jocoro FC - Municipal Limeño 5-1(2-1)
Municipal Limeño - CD Águila 1-0(1-0)
Luis Ángel Firpo - Jocoro FC 0-1(0-1)
Luis Ángel Firpo - CD Águila 2-1(1-0)
Jocoro FC - CD Águila 2-1(1-1)
Luis Ángel Firpo - Municipal Limeño 1-0(0-0)
CD Águila - Luis Ángel Firpo 1-2(1-1)
Municipal Limeño - Jocoro FC 4-0(2-0)

Final Standings – occidental

1. AD Isidro Metapán Santa Ana	6	3	1	2	13 - 9	10
2. CD FAS Santa Ana	6	3	1	2	9 - 5	10
3. Once Deportivo FC Ahuachapán	6	3	1	2	8 - 9	10
4. Sonsonate FC	6	1	1	4	4 - 11	4

Final Standings – central							
1. Alianza FC San Salvador	6	5	1	0	14 - 3	16
2. AD Chalatenango	6	1	3	2	8 - 10	6
3. Santa Tecla FC	6	1	3	2	6 - 11	6
4. CD Atlético Marte San Salvador	6	1	1	4	7 - 12	4

Final Standings – oriental							
1. Jocoro FC	6	4	0	2	9 - 8	12
2. CD Luis Ángel Firpo Usulután	6	3	1	2	5 - 4	10
3. CD Municipal Limeño Santa Rosa de Lima	6	2	1	3	7 - 8	7
4. CD Águila San Miguel	6	2	0	4	7 - 8	6

Segunda Fase / Second Stage - Results

Grupo A [21.11.2020-09.01.2021]
Jocoro FC - CD Águila 0-0
Sonsonate FC - Isidro Metapán 1-1(0-0)
Atlético Marte - Alianza FC 3-5(1-2)
Sonsonate FC - Atlético Marte 2-2(1-0)
Alianza FC - Jocoro FC 4-1(2-0)
Isidro Metapán - CD Águila 0-1(0-0)
CD Águila - Alianza FC 1-0(0-0)
Jocoro FC - Sonsonate FC 0-0
Atlético Marte - Isidro Metapán 1-1(1-0)
Sonsonate FC - CD Águila 0-0
Isidro Metapán - Alianza FC 1-1(0-1)
Atlético Marte - Jocoro FC 2-1(0-1)
CD Águila - Atlético Marte 2-2(0-2)
Jocoro FC - Isidro Metapán 3-1(2-1)
Alianza FC - Sonsonate FC 2-1(1-0)
CD Águila - Jocoro FC 2-1(2-0)
Alianza FC - Atlético Marte 1-0(0-0)
Isidro Metapán - Sonsonate FC 2-3(0-0)
CD Águila - Isidro Metapán 3-1(0-0)
Jocoro FC - Alianza FC 1-0(1-0)
Atlético Marte - Sonsonate FC 1-1(1-0)
Alianza FC - CD Águila 1-2(0-1)
Sonsonate FC - Jocoro FC 1-1(1-0)
Isidro Metapán - Atlético Marte 3-2(2-1)
CD Águila - Sonsonate FC 1-1
Alianza FC - Isidro Metapán 1-0
Jocoro FC - Atlético Marte 2-2
Atlético Marte - CD Águila 0-3(0-2)
Sonsonate FC - Alianza FC 2-3
Isidro Metapán - Jocoro FC 0-0

Grupo B [21.11.2020-09.01.2021]
FAS Santa Ana - AD Chalatenango 0-0
Luis Ángel Firpo - Municipal Limeño 0-0
Once Deportivo - Santa Tecla FC 2-0(1-0)
FAS Santa Ana - Luis Ángel Firpo 2-0(1-0)
Municipal Limeño - Once Deportivo 1-0(0-0)
AD Chalatenango - Santa Tecla FC 0-0
Santa Tecla FC - Municipal Limeño 1-2(1-2)
Luis Ángel Firpo - AD Chalatenango 0-0
Once Deportivo - FAS Santa Ana 4-2(1-2)
AD Chalatenango - Municipal Limeño 3-3(3-1)
FAS Santa Ana - Santa Tecla FC 1-1(0-1)
Luis Ángel Firpo - Once Deportivo 0-1(0-0)
Santa Tecla FC - Luis Ángel Firpo 0-2(0-1)
Once Deportivo - AD Chalatenango 1-0(0-0)
Municipal Limeño - FAS Santa Ana 2-3(1-0)
Municipal Limeño - Luis Ángel Firpo 1-2(1-1)
Santa Tecla FC - Once Deportivo 1-1(1-1)
AD Chalatenango - FAS Santa Ana 1-2(0-0)
Luis Ángel Firpo - FAS Santa Ana 1-2(0-2)
Once Deportivo - Municipal Limeño 0-1(0-1)
Santa Tecla FC - AD Chalatenango 3-1(2-0)
AD Chalatenango - Luis Ángel Firpo 1-2(1-1)
Municipal Limeño - Santa Tecla FC 3-0(1-0)
FAS Santa Ana - Once Deportivo 0-1(0-0)
Municipal Limeño - AD Chalatenango 2-1
Santa Tecla FC - FAS Santa Ana 0-2
Once Deportivo - Luis Ángel Firpo 1-1
AD Chalatenango - Once Deportivo 2-1
FAS Santa Ana - Municipal Limeño 1-0
Luis Ángel Firpo - Santa Tecla FC 0-3(0-2)

	Final Standings – Grupo A								
1.	CD Águila San Miguel	10	6	4	0	15	-	6	22
2.	Alianza FC San Salvador	10	6	1	3	18	-	12	19
3.	Jocoro FC	10	2	5	3	10	-	12	11
4.	Sonsonate FC	10	1	7	2	12	-	13	10
5.	CD Atlético Marte San Salvador	10	1	5	4	15	-	21	8
6.	AD Isidro Metapán Santa Ana	10	1	4	5	10	-	16	7

	Final Standings – Grupo B								
1.	CD FAS Santa Ana	10	6	2	2	15	-	10	20
2.	CD Municipal Limeño Santa Rosa de Lima	10	5	2	3	15	-	11	17
3.	Once Deportivo FC Ahuachapán	10	5	2	3	12	-	8	17
4.	CD Luis Ángel Firpo Usulután	10	3	3	4	8	-	11	12
5.	Santa Tecla FC	10	2	3	5	9	-	14	9
6.	AD Chalatenango	10	1	4	5	9	-	14	7

Top-4 of each group were qualified for the Torneo Apertura Play-offs.

Torneo Apertura Play-offs

Quarter-Finals [13-17.01.2021]

CD Luis Ángel Firpo Usulután - CD Águila San Miguel	0-2(0-0)	0-1(0-1)
Jocoro FC - CD Municipal Limeño Santa Rosa de Lima	0-0	2-1(1-1)
Sonsonate FC - CD FAS Santa Ana	0-1(0-1)	2-2(2-2)
Once Deportivo FC Ahuachapán - Alianza FC San Salvador	1-2(1-2)	1-3(1-1)

Semi-Finals [20-24.01.2021]

Jocoro FC - CD Águila San Miguel	1-0(1-0)	0-2(0-1)
Alianza FC San Salvador - CD FAS Santa Ana	3-0(2-0)	0-0

Final

31.01.2021, Estadio Cuscatlán, San Salvador; Attendance: 0
Referee: Iván Arcides Barton Cisneros
CD Águila San Miguel - Alianza FC San Salvador   0-3(0-1)
Águila: Benji Oldai Villalobos Segovia, Ronald Daniel Rodríguez Gomez, Andrés Felipe Quejada Murillo, Gerson Levi Mayén Villavicencio, José Santos Ortíz Ascencio, Fabricio Heriberto Alfaro Torres (75.Dixon Esau Rivas Cruz), Yan dos Santos Maciel (63.Marlon da Silva de Moura), Diego Elenilson Galdamez Coca (75.Víctor Vladimir García Campos), Marlon Emerson Trejo García, Kevin Noé Melara Mondragón, Nicolás Armando Muñoz Jarvis. Trainer: Ernesto Enrique Corti (Argentina).
Alianza: Mario Antonio González Martínez, Iván Roberto Mancia Ramírez, Rubén Eduardo Marroquín Meléndez, Jonathan David Jiménez Guzmán, Henry Javier Romero Ventura, Bryan Alexander Tamacas López (24.Cèsar Noè Flores Linares), Narciso Oswaldo Orellana, Juan Carlos Portillo Leal (89.Felipe Ponce Ramírez), Marvin Wilfredo Monterrosa Delzas, José Isaac Portillo Molina (89.Wilfredo Ulises Cienfuegos), Michell Mercado Martínez (68.Rodolfo Antonio Zelaya García). Trainer: Milton Antonio Meléndez Cornejo.
Goals: 0-1 Jonathan David Jiménez Guzmán (41), 0-2 Rodolfo Antonio Zelaya García (79), 0-3 Dixon Esau Rivas Cruz (84, own goal).

Torneo Apertura 2020 Winners: **Alianza FC San Salvador**

Best goalscorer Apertura 2020:
Nicolás Armando Muñoz Jarvis (PAN, CD Águila San Miguel) – 13 goals

Torneo Clausura 2021

Primera Fase / Group Stage - Results

Grupo occidental [14.02.-14.03.2021]
Isidro Metapán - FAS Santa Ana 2-1
Once Deportivo - Sonsonate FC 0-0
FAS Santa Ana - Sonsonate FC 4-1
Isidro Metapán - Once Deportivo 1-1
Sonsonate FC - Isidro Metapán 0-3(0-3)
Once Deportivo - FAS Santa Ana 3-1(3-1)
Sonsonate FC - Once Deportivo 0-1(0-0)
FAS Santa Ana - Isidro Metapán 0-1(0-0)
Once Deportivo - Isidro Metapán 1-0(0-0)
Sonsonate FC - FAS Santa Ana 2-1(2-0)
Isidro Metapán - Sonsonate FC 0-2(0-2)
FAS Santa Ana - Once Deportivo 0-0

Grupo central [13.02.-14.03.2021]
AD Chalatenango - Atlético Marte 3-1
Alianza FC - Santa Tecla FC 3-2
Atlético Marte - Santa Tecla FC 1-3
AD Chalatenango - Alianza FC 0-1
Alianza FC - Atlético Marte 3-2
Santa Tecla FC - AD Chalatenango 3-2
Santa Tecla FC - Alianza FC 0-3(0-0)
Atlético Marte - AD Chalatenango 0-0
Santa Tecla FC - Atlético Marte 1-0(1-0)
Alianza FC - AD Chalatenango 4-0(3-0)
Atlético Marte - Alianza FC 3-5(3-5)
AD Chalatenango - Santa Tecla FC 1-0(1-0)

Grupo oriental [13.02.-14.03.2021]
CD Águila - Municipal Limeño 1-1
Jocoro FC - Luis Ángel Firpo 1-2
CD Águila - Jocoro FC 3-1(1-1)
Municipal Limeño - Luis Ángel Firpo 1-1(0-0)
Jocoro FC - Municipal Limeño 0-0
Luis Ángel Firpo - CD Águila 1-0(1-0)
Luis Ángel Firpo - Jocoro FC 0-0
Municipal Limeño - CD Águila 1-2(0-1)
Jocoro FC - CD Águila 0-1(0-0)
Luis Ángel Firpo - Municipal Limeño 1-0(0-0)
CD Águila - Luis Ángel Firpo 0-0
Municipal Limeño - Jocoro FC 2-2(2-2)

Final Standings – occidental

1.	Once Deportivo FC Ahuachapán	6	3	3	0	7 - 2	12
2.	AD Isidro Metapán Santa Ana	6	3	1	2	5 - 4	10
3.	Sonsonate FC	6	2	1	3	5 - 9	7
4.	CD FAS Santa Ana	6	1	1	4	7 - 9	4

Final Standings – central

1.	Alianza FC San Salvador	6	6	0	0	19 - 7	18
2.	Santa Tecla FC	6	3	0	3	9 - 10	9
3.	AD Chalatenango	6	2	1	3	6 - 9	7
4.	CD Atlético Marte San Salvador	6	0	1	5	7 - 15	1

Final Standings – oriental

1.	CD Luis Ángel Firpo Usulután	6	3	3	0	5 - 2	12
2.	CD Águila San Miguel	6	3	2	1	7 - 4	11
3.	CD Municipal Limeño Santa Rosa de Lima	6	0	4	2	5 - 7	4
4.	Jocoro FC	6	0	3	3	4 - 8	3

Segunda Fase / Second Stage - Results

Grupo A [20.03.-01.05.2021]
Jocoro FC - Alianza FC 1-0
Atlético Marte - FAS Santa Ana 1-1
Once Deportivo - Luis Ángel Firpo 1-1(0-0)
Atlético Marte - Once Municipal 0-1(0-0)
FAS Santa Ana - Alianza FC 3-2(1-0)
Luis Ángel Firpo - Jocoro FC 2-0(1-0)
Jocoro FC - Atlético Marte 0-1(0-0)
Once Deportivo - FAS Santa Ana 3-1(1-0)
Alianza FC - Luis Ángel Firpo 1-0(0-0)
FAS Santa Ana - Luis Ángel Firpo 3-1(1-0)
Atlético Marte - Alianza FC 2-4(0-1)
Once Deportivo - Jocoro FC 0-0(0-0)
Luis Ángel Firpo - Atlético Marte 5-0(1-0)
Alianza FC - Once Deportivo 3-1(1-1)
Jocoro FC - FAS Santa Ana 1-1(0-0)
Alianza FC - Jocoro FC 4-0(1-0)
Luis Ángel Firpo - Once Deportivo 1-0(0-0)
FAS Santa Ana - Atlético Marte 4-3(1-2)
Jocoro FC - Luis Ángel Firpo 2-2(1-0)
Alianza FC - FAS Santa Ana 1-1(1-1)
Once Deportivo - Atlético Marte 1-1(1-1)
Luis Ángel Firpo - Alianza FC 1-2(0-2)
Atlético Marte - Jocoro FC 1-1(1-0)
FAS Santa Ana - Once Deportivo 2-3(1-1)
Alianza FC - Atlético Marte 1-2(0-1)
Jocoro FC - Once Deportivo 0-1(0-0)
Luis Ángel Firpo - FAS Santa Ana 0-0
Once Deportivo - Alianza FC 2-1(2-0)
Atlético Marte - Luis Ángel Firpo 1-1(0-0)
FAS Santa Ana - Jocoro FC 1-0(0-0)

Grupo B [20.03.-01.05.2021]
CD Águila - Isidro Metapán 0-2(0-1)
Santa Tecla FC - Municipal Limeño 1-1(0-0)
Sonsonate FC - AD Chalatenango 3-3(0-2)
CD Águila - Sonsonate FC 4-0(2-0)
AD Chalatenango - Municipal Limeño 1-0(1-0)
Isidro Metapán - Santa Tecla FC 1-2(0-1)
Santa Tecla FC - AD Chalatenango 1-4(0-4)
Sonsonate FC - Isidro Metapán 0-1(0-0)
Municipal Limeño - CD Águila 0-0
CD Águila - Santa Tecla FC 0-0
Sonsonate FC - Municipal Limeño 0-2(0-0)
Isidro Metapán - AD Chalatenango 1-0(0-0)
AD Chalatenango - CD Águila 0-0
Santa Tecla FC - Sonsonate FC 3-1(0-0)
Municipal Limeño - Isidro Metapán 2-1(0-1)
AD Chalatenango - Sonsonate FC 2-1(2-0)
Isidro Metapán - CD Águila 1-1(1-0)
Municipal Limeño - Santa Tecla FC 2-1(1-0)
Municipal Limeño - AD Chalatenango 3-0(3-0)
Santa Tecla FC - Isidro Metapán 3-1(1-0)
Sonsonate FC - CD Águila 0-1(0-0)
CD Águila - Municipal Limeño 1-1(0-0)
AD Chalatenango - Santa Tecla FC 1-1(1-0)
Isidro Metapán - Sonsonate FC 5-2(1-1)
AD Chalatenango - Isidro Metapán 0-4(0-1)
Municipal Limeño - Sonsonate FC 1-0(0-0)
Santa Tecla FC - CD Águila 1-1(1-1)
CD Águila - AD Chalatenango 2-1(1-1)
Isidro Metapán - Municipal Limeño 2-0(2-0)
Sonsonate FC - Santa Tecla FC 2-1(1-0)

Final Standings – Grupo A

1.	Once Deportivo FC Ahuachapán	10	5	3	2	13 - 10	18
2.	Alianza FC San Salvador	10	5	1	4	19 - 13	16
3.	CD FAS Santa Ana	10	4	4	2	17 - 15	16
4.	CD Luis Ángel Firpo Usulután	10	3	4	3	14 - 10	13
5.	CD Atlético Marte San Salvador	10	2	4	4	12 - 19	10
6.	Jocoro FC	10	1	4	5	5 - 13	7

Final Standings – Grupo B

1.	AD Isidro Metapán Santa Ana	10	6	1	3	19 - 10	19
2.	CD Municipal Limeño Santa Rosa de Lima	10	5	3	2	12 - 7	18
3.	CD Águila San Miguel	10	3	6	1	10 - 6	15
4.	Santa Tecla FC	10	3	4	3	14 - 14	13
5.	AD Chalatenango	10	3	3	4	12 - 16	12
6.	Sonsonate FC	10	1	1	8	9 - 23	4

Top-4 of each group were qualified for the Torneo Clausura Play-offs.

Torneo Clausura Play-offs

Quarter-Finals [05-09.05.2021]

Santa Tecla FC - Once Deportivo FC Ahuachapán	1-1(0-0)	2-1(0-0)
CD FAS Santa Ana - CD Municipal Limeño Santa Rosa de Lima	2-1(1-0)	1-2 aet; 4-2 pen
CD Luis Ángel Firpo Usulután - AD Isidro Metapán Santa Ana	1-0(0-0)	3-1(1-1)
CD Águila San Miguel - Alianza FC San Salvador	0-1(0-0)	1-2(1-0)

Semi-Finals [15-23.05.2021]

Santa Tecla FC - CD FAS Santa Ana	0-1(0-0)	1-0 aet; 2-4 pen
CD Luis Ángel Firpo Usulután - Alianza FC San Salvador	1-2(0-1)	1-0 aet; 4-5 pen

Final

30.05.2021, Estadio Cuscatlán, San Salvador; Attendance: n/a
Referee: Edgar Ramírez
CD FAS Santa Ana - Alianza FC San Salvador   **1-1(1-0,1-1,1-1); 4-3 on penalties**
FAS Santa Ana: Kévin Edenilson Carabantes Rivera, Ibsen Adalberto Castro Avelar, Roberto Leandro Chen Rodríguez, Edwin Mauricio Cuellar Linares, Andrés Alberto Flores Jaco, Erivan Stiven Flores Morales (99.Julio César Amaya Sibrián), Tomás Granitto Heesch (60.Guillermo Nicolás Stradella), Carlos Alberto Peña Rodríguez (Cap) (65.Dustin Clifman Corea Garay), Wilma Enrique Torres Peña (60.Brayan Balmore Landaverde Álvarez), Kévin Stiven Reyes Ortíz, Luís Arturo Peralta Ariño (99.Luis Alberto Perea Pérez). Trainer: Jorge Humberto Rodríguez Álvarez.
Alianza FC: Mario Antonio González Martínez, Henry Javier Romero Ventura, Rudy Geovanny Clavel Mendoza, Iván Roberto Mancia Ramírez, Jonathan David Jiménez Guzmán, Narciso Oswaldo Orellana, Marvin Wilfredo Monterroza Delzas (Cap) (118.Óscar Oswaldo Rodríguez Maldonado), José Isaac Portillo Molina (46.Rodolfo Antonio Zelaya García), Bryan Alexander Tamacas López (105.Óscar Elías Cerén Delgado), Juan Carlos Portillo Leal (85.Elvin Rolando Alvarado Sánchez), Michell Mercado Martínez. Trainer: Milton Antonio Meléndez Cornejo.
Goals: 1-0 Kévin Stiven Reyes Ortíz (39), 1-1 Edwin Mauricio Cuellar Linares (56 own goal).
Penalties: Brayan Balmore Landaverde Álvarez (saved); Iván Roberto Mancia Ramírez 0-1; Andrés Alberto Flores Jaco 1-1; Óscar Oswaldo Rodríguez Maldonado 1-2; Dustin Clifman Corea Garay 2-2; Rudy Geovanny Clavel Mendoza (missed); Kévin Stiven Reyes Ortíz (missed); Rodolfo Antonio Zelaya García 2-3; Luis Alberto Perea Pérez 3-3; Henry Javier Romero Ventura (missed); Roberto Leandro Chen Rodríguez (saved); Michell Mercado Martínez (missed); Ibsen Adalberto Castro Avelar 4-3; Elvin Rolando Alvarado Sánchez (saved).

Torneo Clausura 2021 Winners: **CD FAS Santa Ana**
Best goalscorer Clausura 2021: Rodolfo Antonio Zelaya García (Alianza FC San Salvador) – 11 goals

Aggregate Table 2020/2021

1.	Alianza FC San Salvador	32	22	3	7	70 - 35	69
2.	Once Deportivo FC Ahuachapán	32	16	9	7	39 - 29	57
3.	CD Águila San Miguel	32	14	12	6	39 - 24	54
4.	CD FAS Santa Ana	32	14	8	10	48 - 39	50
5.	CD Luis Ángel Firpo Usulután	32	12	11	9	32 - 27	47
6.	AD Isidro Metapán Santa Ana	32	13	7	12	49 - 40	46
7.	CD Municipal Limeño Santa Rosa de Lima	32	12	10	10	39 - 33	46
8.	Santa Tecla FC	32	9	10	13	38 - 48	37
9.	Jocoro FC	32	7	12	13	29 - 42	33
10.	AD Chalatenango	32	7	11	14	34 - 48	32
11.	Sonsonate FC (*Relegated*)	32	5	10	17	30 - 49	25
12.	CD Atlético Marte San Salvador	32	4	11	17	41 - 67	23

THE CLUBS 2020/2021

Please note: number of matches, subtitutes and goals from both Apertura and Clausura are including all Play-offs.

CLUB DEPORTIVO ÁGUILA SAN MIGUEL

Foundation date: February 15, 1926
Address: Bulevar Merliot, Poligono C No. 4, San Miguel
Stadium: Estadio „Juan Francisco Barraza", San Miguel (10,000)

THE SQUAD

	DOB	Ape M	(s)	G	Cla M	(s)	G
Goalkeepers:							
Benji Oldai Villalobos Segovia	15.07.1988	21		1	18		
Defenders:							
Reynaldo Adalberto Aparicio Romero	17.05.1993	9	(4)	1	3	(2)	
Fredy Ernesto Espinoza Cornejo	19.04.1992	3			8	(2)	
Kevin Antonio Mejía Berrios	08.06.1998		(11)				
Andrés Felipe Quejada Murillo (COL)	21.11.1985	19		2	17		1
Ronald Daniel Rodríguez Goméz	22.09.1998	12			15		1
Marlon Emerson Trejo García	19.10.1988	14			5	(1)	
Midfielders:							
Fabricio Heriberto Alfaro Torres	03.12.1990	4	(4)		11	(2)	
Bruno Kairon Santos Silva	23.09.1996	2	(6)	1	6	(6)	
Diego Elenilson Galdamez Coca	26.08.1994	19	(1)		14	(4)	1
Víctor Vladimir García Campos	15.06.1995	2	(11)		1	(14)	1
Edwin Oswaldo Lazo Valladares	16.06.1990	12	(1)		14		
Gerson Levi Mayén Villavicencio	09.02.1989	17	(1)	3	16	(1)	
Carlos Antonio Ortiz Ascencio	04.06.2000		(4)		1		
José Santos Ortíz Ascencio	22.01.1990	20			13	(3)	
Dixon Esau Rivas Cruz	08.11.1999	3	(17)		5	(9)	
Wilson Gilberto Rugamas Guardado	19.01.1990	17			1	(2)	
Luis Styven Vásquez Velásquez	29.10.2002				1		
Franklin Steven Torres						(3)	
Yan dos Santos Maciel (BRA)	24.03.1997	15	(2)	3	15	(2)	4
Forwards:							
Henry Geovany Argueta Geovany	01.06.1999					(6)	
Gerber Geuseppe Chávez	15.10.1997	4	(4)	1			
Marlon da Silva de Moura (BRA)	05.02.1990	3	(10)	2	8	(6)	4
Kevin Noé Melara Mondragón	12.10.1993	14	(4)		17		
Nicolás Armando Muñoz Jarvis (PAN)	21.12.1981	20	(1)	13	9	(6)	6
Kevin Leonel Sagastizado Galeas	23.09.1994	1	(6)				
Trainer:							
Hugo Norberto Coria Boianello (ARG)	01.04.1961	6					
[13.11.2020] Ernesto Enrique Corti (ARG)	21.03.1963	15					
[03.02.2021] Armando Osma Rueda (COL)	07.02.1961				18		

ALIANZA FÚTBOL CLUB SAN SALVADOR

Foundation date: October 12, 1958 (*as Atlético La Constancia*)
Address: Boulevard el Hipódromo, San Salvador
Stadium: Estadio Cuscatlán, San Salvador (44,313)

THE SQUAD

Name	DOB	Ape M	(s)	G	Cla M	(s)	G
Goalkeepers:							
Yimmy Rodrigo Cuéllar de León	20.10.1989	6			6		
Mario Antonio González Martínez	20.05.1997	15			15		
Defenders:							
Rudy Geovanny Clavel Mendoza	10.10.1996	11	(2)	1	13	(1)	1
Jorge Antonio Cruz Córtez	24.01.2000	1					
Mario Alberto Jacobo Segovia	02.08.1996	1			1		
Jonathan David Jiménez Guzmán	12.07.1992	17	(1)	1	15		
Israel Alexander Landaverde López	23.06.1994	4	(2)		7	(5)	
Iván Roberto Mancia Ramírez	19.12.1992	13	(1)		16		
Rubén Eduardo Marroquín Meléndez	15.10.1992	11	(3)		12	(2)	
Henry Javier Romero Ventura	17.10.1991	16		2	15	(1)	
Bryan Alexander Tamacas López	21.02.1995	14	(2)	3	16	(4)	2
Midfielders:							
Óscar Elías Cerén Delgado	26.10.1991				1	(11)	
Wilfredo Ulises Cienfuegos (USA)	10.02.1996	8	(10)	1		(8)	
Cèsar Noè Flores Linares	17.03.1996	9	(5)				
Álvaro José Monge			(1)				
Marvin Wilfredo Monterroza Delzas	03.03.1990	16	(1)	2	14	(1)	5
Narciso Oswaldo Orellana	28.01.1995	20		2	20		
Harold Daniel Osorio Moreno	20.08.2002					(1)	
Felipe Ponce Ramírez (MEX)	29.03.1988	5	(8)	5			
José Isaac Portillo Molina	08.11.1994	7	(4)	2	14	(5)	2
Juan Carlos Portillo Leal	28.12.1991	12	(2)	6	20	(1)	4
Óscar Oswaldo Rodríguez Maldonado	16.04.1995	3	(7)		4	(10)	
Forwards:							
Elvin Rolando Alvarado Sánchez	23.08.1998				10	(8)	3
Oswaldo Enrique Blanco Mancilla (COL)	21.05.1990	13	(2)	5			
José Enrique Contreras Estrada	01.02.1997	6	(7)	1			
Jorge Cristian Córdoba (ARG)	12.12.1987				11	(6)	6
Gerardo Maximiliano Freitas Talpamiz (URU)	04.03.1991	3	(5)	3			
Michell Mercado Martínez (COL)	01.01.1990	17	(3)	4	17	(4)	7
Luis Enrique Vásquez	04.01.2001	1	(2)				
Rodolfo Antonio Zelaya García	03.07.1988	2	(9)	4	4	(12)	11
Trainer:							
Juan Cortés Diéguez (ESP)	05.11.1983	14					
[27.12.2020] Milton Antonio Meléndez Cornejo	03.08.1967	7			21		

CLUB DEPORTIVO ATLÉTICO MARTE SAN SALVADOR

Foundation date: April 22, 1950
Address: *Not known*
Stadium: Estadio Cuscatlán, San Salvador (53,400)

THE SQUAD

	DOB	Ape M	(s)	G	Cla M	(s)	G
Goalkeepers:							
Rodrigo Emilio Artiga González	30.06.1999	1					
Matías Nahuel Coloca Lavandeira (ARG)	11.09.1985				13		
Rolando Ernesto Morales Hernández	01.03.1994	3			3		
Luis Norberto Tatuaca García (GUA)	06.07.1990	12					
Defenders:							
Argenis Orlando Alba Ramírez (COL)	02.04.1996	15		1	6	(4)	
Carlos Edgardo Anzora Domínguez	13.11.1992	2	(3)				
Diego Alejandro Chévez García	02.03.2000	15			16		1
José Alberto Guevara Somozo	24.02.1998	8	(2)		7	(3)	
José Mayky Henríquez Leal	04.12.1989	6	(4)		3	(2)	
Edgardo Arnulfo Mira Abrego (GUA)	10.03.1993	7	(6)				
José Bladimir Osorio Valladares	19.10.1988				11	(1)	
Yohalin Palacios Palacios (COL)	04.05.1988	2					
Marcos Ernesto Portillo Medina	26.05.1997				4		
Sebastián Rodríguez Viáfara (COL)	17.05.1997				6		
Midfielders:							
Deiber Yohan Ballesteros García (COL)	26.09.1993				9	(4)	2
Nelson Alexis Barrios Linares	23.06.1992					(3)	
Cristian Jeovanni Bernabé	22.02.1997	2	(1)		2	(1)	
Óscar Daniel Castillo					1	(7)	
Mauricio Josué Cerritos Saravia					4	(1)	
Diego José Chavarría Ramos	28.02.1990				8	(2)	
Héctor Ernesto Crespín Aguilar	02.02.1993	7	(2)		9	(1)	1
Mayer Andrés Gil Hurtado	07.09.2003				3		
Mauricio Armando Gómez Guzman	11.08.2000	2				(1)	
Mario Rigoberto González Acosta	13.10.1994	5	(3)				
Diego Gerardo Jiménez Hunter	25.10.1992	2	(4)				
Hugo Enrique López Martínez	29.11.1993	11				(1)	
Fernando Alfredo Montes Vásquez	17.08.1991	2	(3)				
Wilmar Jhonatan Novoa Alfaro	27.04.1995	10	(5)	3	16		1
José Isaac Portillo Molina	14.11.1999	16		2	13		2
Julio César Rivera Pineda		10	(3)	2	5	(2)	
Eduardo Álvaro Rodríguez Lloreda (COL)	28.07.1989	15		5			
Anthony Vladmir Roque Amaya	28.02.1996				14	(1)	2
Forwards:							
Kevin Armando Alvarenga Mejía						(3)	
Daniel Guzmán Miranda (MEX)	28.06.1992	9	(3)	4			
Jhonny Andrés Morán Chan	11.06.1994				7	(8)	4
Christian Alexander Rodríguez Vásquez	12.09.1995				2		
Edgar Geovany Valladares García		11	(5)	4	10	(6)	5
Eddy Alejandro Valle Ortíz	06.12.1993	1	(1)				
Fernando José Villalta Hernández	01.05.2000	2	(10)	1	4	(9)	1
Trainer:							
Cristian Eduardo Domizzi (ARG)	09.07.1969	16			16		

ASOCIACIÓN DEPORTIVO CHALATENANGO

Foundation date: 1930 (*as CD Alacranes*); re-founded July 10, 2017
Address: *Not known*
Stadium: Estadio "José Gregorio Martínez", Chalatenango (15,000)

THE SQUAD

	DOB	Ape M	(s)	G	Cla M	(s)	G
Goalkeepers:							
Oscar Daniel Arroyo Peña	28.01.1990	13			1		
Henry Edimar Hernández Cruz	04.01.1985				14		
Ernesto Antonio Paz Reina	26.01.1998	3					
Cristian Noel Rivera	29.10.2000				1		
Defenders:							
Álvaro Alexis Ardón Pereira	16.09.1995	10			3		
Jairo Vladimir González Romero					6	(1)	
Alejandro Ismael Henríquez Ferrufino	28.08.2002	2		1	6	(2)	
Fidel Ángel Jiménez Morales	29.01.1992	6	(3)		5	(1)	
Emerson Alexander Lalin Suazo (HON)	18.01.1994	15					
Miguel Ángel Lemus Ochoa	26.10.1993	15	(1)	3	14	(2)	
José Joél Ortega Rodríguez	13.02.1995	6	(3)		12	(1)	1
Félix Alexander Sánchez Paredes	16.07.1990	4					
Midfielders:							
Efraín Antonio Burgos Jr.	14.08.1988				4	(3)	
Saúl Ernesto Cabrera Moreno	22.08.1998				2	(7)	
Sergio Gabriel Córdoba Mejía (CRC)	21.12.1993	4	(1)				
Héctor Raúl Cruz Flores	08.12.1993	10	(1)		13		
Jairo Mauricio Henríquez Ferrufino	31.08.1993	15		3	13	(1)	
Kevin Alberto Hernández Juárez	20.05.1998	1	(1)		1	(1)	
José Rodrigo Herrera Guardado	08.05.1999	2	(9)	2	2	(4)	
Chevone Omelli Marsh (JAM)	25.02.1994				5	(5)	
Leonardo José Menjivar Peñate	24.10.2001	3	(2)			(6)	
Pedro Javier Orellana Orellana	11.01.1991	2	(3)				
Francisco Jacobo Posada	20.12.1997		(1)				
Andrés Enrique Prado Calderón	24.04.1997	1	(2)				
Henry Noé Reyes Martínez	03.04.1992	12			15		
Elías Ezequiel Rivas Muñoz	20.05.1998	9	(3)	1	5	(6)	3
Levin Sigfredo Rojas Vásquez	11.05.1999	2	(2)		1	(7)	
Jesús Everado Rubio Quintero (MEX)	24.12.1996				14		
Forwards:							
Craig Jeffrey Foster (JAM)	07.09.1991				16		6
Carlos Félix Gámez (MEX)	14.05.1991	2	(4)				
Brayan Josué Landaverde Rivera	01.04.1997	9	(7)		13	(2)	
Kemal Orlando Malcolm (JAM)	19.11.1989				10	(1)	8
Boris Vladimir Morales	13.08.1998	4	(3)	1			
Luis Javier Paradela Díaz (CUB)	21.01.1997	13	(1)	1			
José Angel Peña Carballo	10.12.1994	13	(2)	5			
Yonatan Alexander Pineda Torres	05.12.1997					(4)	
Douglas Moisés Rivas Marinero	03.09.1995					(3)	
Trainer:							
Juan Ramón Sánchez Paredes	01.09.1952	10					
[10.12.2020] Ricardo Raúl Montoya González (CRC)	07.11.1971	6			16		

CLUB DEPORTIVO FUTBOLISTAS ASOCIADOS SANTANECOS
SANTA ANA

Foundation date: February 16, 1947
Address: Calle Oriente No. 18c, Santa Ana
Stadium: Estadio „Óscar Alberto Quiteño", Santa Ana (15,000)

THE SQUAD	DOB	Ape M	(s)	G	Cla M	(s)	G
Goalkeepers:							
Kévin Edenilson Carabantes Rivera	20.03.1995	15			18		
Nicolás Alberto Pacheco Posada	07.04.1995	5			2		
Daniel Josael Saravia Rios	26.07.1999				1		
Defenders:							
Ibsen Adalberto Castro Avelar	24.10.1988	12			17	(2)	
Diego José Chávez Rivas	05.04.1997	11	(3)	2	7	(4)	
Roberto Leandro Chen Rodríguez (PAN)	24.05.1994				17		
Edwin Mauricio Cuellar Linares	17.06.1995	12	(3)		16		
Alexis Díaz					2		
Andrés Alberto Flores Jaco	20.01.1995	13	(1)		14	(1)	
Moisés Xavier García Orellana	26.06.1990	19			4		
Alberto Siliazar Henríquez	01.02.1999	5	(2)		3		
Rodolfo Huezo	14.08.2001	1					
Nestor Raúl Renderos López	10.09.1988	16			2	(2)	
Midfielders:							
Julio César Amaya Sibrián	29.03.1996	1	(16)		12	(7)	
Marvín Leonel Aranda Pérez	13.06.1999	10	(6)			(4)	
Walter Ernesto Ayala Chiguila	05.10.1997	3	(4)				
Dustin Clifman Corea Garay	21.03.1992				2	(14)	4
Erivan Stiven Flores Morales	28.09.1996	10	(3)	1	12	(4)	
Kevin Josué Garay	05.10.1998	2			1	(1)	
Mayer Andrés Gil Hurtado (COL)	07.09.1993	1	(3)				
Tomás Granitto Heesch	12.06.1993				17	(3)	
Brayan Balmore Landaverde Álvarez	27.05.1995	16	(2)	2	3	(4)	
Carlos Alberto Peña Rodríguez (MEX)	29.03.1990				19	(2)	4
Kévin Stiven Reyes Ortíz	28.08.1999				15	(4)	5
Josué Rivera Arévalo	09.05.1999		(1)				
Luis Fernando Rodríguez Barrios (PAR)	19.03.1993	6	(4)	2			
Forwards:							
Diego Daniel Areco Sayas (PAR)	05.11.1992	15	(5)	7			
Javier Israel Bolaños Figueroa	14.08.2001	4	(5)	1	1	(5)	
Raúl Eduardo Peñaranda Contreras (COL)	02.05.1991	4	(11)	3			
Luís Arturo Peralta Ariño (COL)	30.07.1992				16	(2)	5
Luis Alberto Perea Pérez (COL)	09.03.1986	6	(12)	2	6	(7)	2
Guillermo Nicolás Stradella (ARG)	06.12.1992	18	(2)	5	10	(11)	
Wilma Enrique Torres Peña	19.04.1994	15	(1)	2	14	(5)	8
Trainer:							
Jorge Humberto Rodríguez Álvarez	20.05.1971	20			21		

ASOCIACIÓN DEPORTIVA ISIDRO METAPÁN

Foundation date: September 29, 1950 (*as AD Isidro Menéndez*); re-founded June 2, 2000
Address: Avenida Benjamín Estrada Valiente y 1a. Calle Poniente, Metapán
Stadium: Estadio „Jorge 'Calero' Suárez", Metapán (10,000)

THE SQUAD	DOB	Ape M	(s)	G	Cla M	(s)	G
Goalkeepers:							
Érick David Alvarado Mejía	10.05.1994	1					
Óscar Enrique Pleitéz Mira	06.02.1993	13			15		
Luis Emilio Rivera Monroy	06.09.1997	2			3	(1)	
Defenders:							
Juan Alfredo Barahona Peña	12.02.1996	7	(2)	1	14	(2)	3
Julio Regino Cerritos Cañizales	16.07.1988	1					
Marvín Antonio Figueroa Monterrosa	12.03.1993	3			9	(4)	
Leonardo Francisco Incorvaia (ARG)	26.06.1992				14		1
Alexander Vidal Larín Hernández	27.06.1992	8	(1)	2			
Moisés Alexander Mejía Mejía	11.12.1994	10	(1)		3	(3)	1
Milton Alexander Molina Miguel	02.02.1989	15	(1)		15	(1)	1
José Gregorio Murcia Valle	21.10.1997	1				(3)	
Yeison Murillo Córdoba (COL)	30.11.1992	13					
Jaime Alexander Ortíz García	20.04.1994	2	(2)	1			
Midfielders:							
Christian Omar Aguilar Morales	14.07.2001	7	(4)	2	2	(9)	
Rudy Carlos Batres Valencia	09.11.1990	8	(1)		3	(9)	
Iván Alexander Castro Suazo	05.01.1995	9	(2)		8	(2)	
Walter Ernesto Ayala Chiguila	05.10.1997				17		3
Fernando Antonio Clavel Mendoza	28.09.1999		(1)			(4)	
Luis Antonio Figueroa	18.04.1999	1	(1)				
Cristian David Gil Hurtado (COL)	05.11.1996	3	(7)	1	5	(9)	3
Bayron Antonio López Acevedo	15.12.2000	10			17		1
Herbert Arnoldo Sosa Burgos	11.01.1990	13	(1)	2	16	(1)	2
Guillermo Andrés Vernetti (ARG)	17.04.1993				10	(8)	1
Kévin Edgardo Vidal Galdámez	28.06.2000	1					
Forwards:							
Fernando Gabriel Castillo Hernández	09.07.1997				14	(1)	1
Gerber Geuseppe Chávez	15.10.1997					(4)	1
Cristian David Cisneros Calderón	16.04.1994	2	(5)				
Carlos José García Morales	05.03.1995	5	(4)				
Jhon Emiro Machado Mosquera (COL)	01.01.1993	11	(1)	3	7	(1)	1
Marvin Roberto Márquez Joya	12.03.1998	3	(7)		10	(3)	3
Ricardo Ferreira da Silva „Ricardinho" (BRA)	31.12.1986	11	(4)	4			
Jomal Evans Jr. Williams (TRI)	28.04.1994	16		6	16	(1)	4
Trainer:							
Víctor Manuel Coreas Privado	30.03.1963	11					
[14.12.2020] José Oswaldo Figueroa	03.04.1963	5					
[09.01.2021] Juan Cortés Dieguez (ESP)	05.11.1983				18		

JOCORO FÚTBOL CLUB

Foundation date: May 19, 1991
Address: *Not known*
Stadium: Complejo Deportivo "Tierra de fuego", Jocoro (2,000)

THE SQUAD

Name	DOB	Ape M	Ape (s)	Ape G	Cla M	Cla (s)	Cla G
Goalkeepers:							
Héctor Wilfredo Carrillo Portillo	25.06.1994				3		
Felipe Enrique Amaya	03.11.1988	4	(1)				
José Manuel Gónzalez Hernández	06.10.1981	16			13		
Defenders:							
Arnulfo Beitar Córdoba (COL)	11.11.1988				10		1
Kevin Antonio Berrios	08.06.1998				3	(2)	
Edgar Remberto Campos Serrano	09.05.1983				8	(1)	
Elvis Donany Claros López	31.08.2000	15	(1)		10		
Guillermo Vladimir Fuentes Paz	30.11.2001		(1)				
José Salvador Galindo Turcio	21.09.1993	7	(5)		7	(1)	
David Moisés Hernández Villatoro	04.05.1987	9	(2)		2	(1)	
César Otoniel López Benítez	10.08.1992	8	(2)		5	(5)	
Alexis Vladimir Maravilla	29.12.1989	12	(1)		12		
Kevin Antonio Mejía Berrios	08.06.1998				2	(1)	
Nelson Oswaldo Moreno Arevalo	18.11.1994	13			13		
Eder Yenner Moscoso Arroyo (ECU)	20.05.1987	11		2			
Nelson Mauricio Pereira Argueta	02.10.1994	7	(3)				
Midfielders:							
Wilfredo Alexander Castro			(1)				
William Leonardo Guerrero Prins (COL)	06.09.1990				8	(3)	
Fredis Joel Hernández Villatoro	19.10.1991	5	(4)		8	(3)	1
Carlos Ovidio Lanza Martínez (HON)	15.05.1989	16		10	16		3
Kevin Zidane Martínez Ramos	04.06.1998	3	(5)		3	(3)	
Junior Jesús Padilla Zelaya (HON)	04.04.1992	12		1	14		1
Francisco Noé Reyes Navarro	14.12.1992	10	(6)				
Nelson Antonio Rodríguez Cruz		2	(2)				
Oscar Arnoldo Rodríguez Santos			(3)	1			
José Yuvini Salamanca Gutiérrez	22.05.1982	18	(2)	1	12	(3)	
Luis Enrique Salmerón Hernández	21.07.2002	4			1	(7)	
Roberto Carlos Sol González	08.05.1989	17	(2)	1	10	(4)	
Erick Enrique Villalobos Sorto	19.08.1995	1					
Forwards:							
Nelsón Esaú Alvarenga Hernández	01.01.1995	9	(5)		6	(1)	
Kelvin Isaías Argueta Portillo	24.10.1991	3	(2)		1	(1)	
Kevin Alexander Cruz Saravia	09.08.1997		(1)				
José David Díaz Ramos	20.05.1992				6	(4)	1
Santos Antonio Guzmán Villalta	23.05.1993				3	(9)	1
Roberto Carlos Hernández Mejicanos	01.12.1990	5	(8)	1			
Arnold Josué Meléndez Rivera (HON)	23.08.1995	13		4			
Trainer:							
Carlos Ernesto Romero Quintanilla	24.07.1966	20			16		

CLUB DEPORTIVO LUIS ÁNGEL FIRPO USULUTÁN

Foundation date: September 21, 1923
Address: Avenida Víctor Manuel Mejía Lara 5H, San Salvador
Stadium: Estadio "Sergio Torres Rivera", Usulután (10,000)

THE SQUAD

	DOB	Ape M	(s)	G	Cla M	(s)	G
Goalkeepers:							
Joel Ignacio Almeida Huerta (MEX)	29.01.1991				20		
Matías Nahuel Coloca Lavandeira (ARG)	11.09.1985	17					
Oscar Alexander Sánchez Cruz	24.05.1990	1				(1)	
Defenders:							
Mario Manuel Alfaro González	03.03.1996				15	(1)	1
Alexander José Amaya del Cid		1					
Lizandro Enmanuel Claros Saravias	25.01.1998	15		1	7	(5)	
Mario Enrique Martínez Rivera	10.04.1990	6	(2)				
Carlos Romero Monteagudo Alfaro	29.04.1985	9			8	(3)	
Tardelis Peña González (COL)	31.10.1988	17		1			
Jaime Alexander Ortíz García	20.04.1994				18	(1)	
Tardelis Peña González (COL)	31.10.1988				20		2
Denilson Vidal Rosales Ardon	17.08.1997	5	(1)				
Eduardo José Vigil Acosta	07.08.1996	17			20		2
Midfielders:							
Marcos David Aguilar			(1)				
Nelson Alberto Barahona Collins (PAN)	22.11.1987	11	(2)		17		1
José María Batres			(1)				
Diego José Chavarría Ramos	28.02.1990	12	(1)				
Francisco Abelardo Escobar Torres	05.07.1996	9	(2)		7	(2)	
Ever Alexander Flores López	03.01.1998	6	(6)		2	(7)	1
Christopher Felipe Gáleas	01.03.1993	8	(8)	1	2	(10)	
Marvin Hernández Ramos	07.07.1993	1	(2)				
José Jeremías Lemus	21.05.1999	3	(3)				
Alvaro Ramón Lizama Gavidia	24.05.1995				13	(3)	
William Enrique Mancía Bonilla	22.11.1987	11	(5)		2	(9)	
Gabriel Ernesto Núñez D´Alessandro (DOM)	24.01.1994	1					
Jefferson Audir Polio Argueta	13.04.1995	17		2	11	(3)	4
Luis Salmerón			(1)				
Forwards:							
Eber Edison Caicedo Peralta (ECU)	03.05.1991				13	(4)	5
Luis Ernesto Canales Belloso	17.03.1997	9	(3)	4	14	(3)	7
Cristian David Cisneros Calderón	16.04.1994				16		
Edgar Adonay Cruz Cruz	20.11.1993	6	(7)	1	8	(3)	1
Roberto Adonay Monge Herrera	08.08.1998					(9)	
Armando Enrique Polo Aguilar (PAN)	02.04.1990	9	(2)	2			
Daniel Vladimir Luna Melgar [†26.03.2021]	29.07.1996	3	(4)	1	1	(3)	
Frederick Counsellor Ongangan (NGA)	30.04.1993	3					
Kevin Leonel Sagastizado Galeas	23.09.1994				6	(4)	1
Fernando Obdulio Valladares Martínez	15.04.1990	1					
Julio César Torres Rivas						(1)	
Trainer:							
William Alexander Renderos Iraheta	03.10.1971	3					
[03.11.2020] Roberto Gamarra (ARG)	06.03.1958	15			20		

CLUB DEPORTIVO MUNICIPAL LIMEÑO

Foundation date: September 11, 1949
Address: *Not known*
Stadium: Estadio "Dr. José Ramón Flores Berríos", Santa Rosa de Lima (5,000)

THE SQUAD	DOB	M	Ape (s)	G	M	Cla (s)	G
Goalkeepers:							
Abiel Francisco Aguilera Alvarenga	29.08.1988	14			8		
Willian Ernesto Torres Peña	25.07.1985	4			10		
Defenders:							
Ever Alexander González Acosta	28.08.1998	10	(2)		4	(3)	
Arnulfo Beitar Córdoba (COL)	11.11.1988	13		1			
Edgar Remberto Campos Serrano	09.05.1983	2	(1)				
Walter Eliseo Guevara Canales	13.11.1992	4	(4)		9		1
Raúl Antonio Guzmán Romero	08.06.1997	3	(5)		3	(1)	
Blas Enoc Lizama Gavidia	11.04.1994	15			9	(3)	
Mario Ernesto Machado Salamanca	17.12.1990	13			8	(4)	
Luis Fernando Méndez Hernández	29.10.1997	14	(2)		16	(2)	
Elieser Yosimar Quiñones Quiñones (COL)	04.08.1988				14		1
Edwin Ernesto Sánchez Vigil	21.02.1990	10	(6)	5	4	(5)	
José Rómulo Villalobos Campos	01.09.1997				10	(1)	2
Midfielders:							
Meyson de Jesús Ascensio Capacho	06.02.1994	14	(3)	1	7	(6)	1
William Alfredo Canales Belloso	18.02.1995	14	(1)	1	9	(6)	2
Santos Geovany Cruz Alberto	24.08.2000				1	(1)	
Wilmer Rolando García Morán	25.10.2000		(1)				
Orlando José Martínez						(1)	
Kevin Ademir Pérez Galindo			(1)				
Fernando Javier Perla			(2)				
Ramón Adalberto Rodríguez Moreno	12.02.1997	15	(3)	1	13	(5)	2
Víctor Fabricio Torres	15.01.2001		(4)		2	(3)	1
Joel Alcides Turcios Mendoza	08.03.1998				2	(2)	
Jefferson Leonel Valladares					1		
Forwards:							
Harold Rafael Alas Rodríguez	19.09.1989	9	(8)	2	6	(6)	2
Robinson Aponza Carabili (COL)	11.04.1989				8	(6)	4
Carlos José García	05.03.1995				17		1
Samuel Esteban Giménez Cáceres (PAR)	10.02.1991	16	(1)	2			
Roberto Adonay Monge Herrera	08.08.1998		(1)				
Hugo Alexis Oviedo Jara (PAR)	14.12.1992	13	(1)	9	12	(5)	2
Kevin Arquímides Oviedo	18.05.1998	5	(7)		6	(4)	
Jeison Arley Quiñónez Angulo (COL)	17.09.1986		(8)	1			
Ever Leonel Rodríguez Moreno	12.02.1997	4	(6)		8	(4)	1
Ramón Antonio Viera López	30.08.1993	6	(7)		11	(4)	
Trainer:							
Álvaro Misael Alfaro Sánchez	06.01.1971	3					
[27.10.2020] Nelson Mauricio Ancheta Flores	30.07.1963	15			18		

ONCE DEPORTIVO FÚTBOL CLUB AHUACHAPÁN

Foundation date: August 20, 2019
Address: *Not known*
Stadium: Estadio "Arturo Simeón Magaña", Ahuachapán (5,000)

THE SQUAD

	DOB	Ape M	(s)	G	Cla M	(s)	G
Goalkeepers:							
Yonatan Daniel Guardado Girón	20.08.1996	15			18		
Ismael Antonio Valladares Merino	26.09.1986	3					
Defenders:							
Carlos Mauricio Arévalo Méndez	23.03.1988				7	(2)	
Luis Fernando Copete Murillo (NCA)	12.02.1989	15	(1)	2			
Jorge Antonio Cruz Córtez	24.01.2000				5	(2)	
Gerardo Alexander Guirola	21.06.1997	9	(2)		5	(1)	
Kevin Alexander Menjívar Henríquez	23.09.2000	13	(3)		12	(2)	1
Nahum Portilla						(1)	
Julio Enrique Sibrián Molina	05.05.1995	15			18		
Edgar Iván Solís Castillón (MEX)	05.03.1987				14		2
Dieter Eduardo Vargas Guzmán (MEX)	27.05.1993				18		1
José Rómulo Villalobos Campos	01.09.1997	5	(1)				
Midfielders:							
Óscar Ronaldo Almendárez Cañas	21.07.1997	2	(1)				
Gilberto Arnulfo Baires Hernández	01.04.1990	17	(1)			(10)	
Melvin Alberto Cartagena Portillo	30.07.1999	17			12	(1)	
Herberth Marcelo Díaz Rivas	19.04.2000	9	(6)	1	7	(4)	
Abdiel Anel Macea Molinar (PAN)	04.05.1991	9	(3)				
José Edin Méndez Jérez	26.10.1998		(1)				
Marvín Alexander Morales Andrade	10.12.1992	14	(2)		12	(3)	
José Rodolfo Orellana Berríos	01.06.1995		(3)			(1)	
Marvin Leonardo Piñón Polanco (MEX)	12.06.1991				3	(8)	
Anthony Vladmir Roque Amaya	28.02.1996	3	(6)				
José Rodrigo Vega Linares	31.05.1992		(1)				
Forwards:							
Elvin Rolando Alvarado Sánchez	23.08.1998	13	(3)	4			
Diego Josué Ascencio Mejía	15.05.1995	4	(1)	1	17		1
Fernando Gabriel Castillo Hernández	09.07.1997	15	(1)	3			
José Enrique Contreras Estrada	01.02.1997				14	(2)	1
Erick Alexander Guadrón Dubón	03.09.1997		(3)			(9)	1
José Manuel Iglesias Durán	30.07.1994	1					
Edgar Alejandro Medrano Ayarza (COL)	23.09.1994				18		7
Daley Yesid Mena Palomeque (COL)	07.02.1985	4	(8)	1			
Boris Vladimir Morales	13.08.1998					(6)	
Brayan Manrique Paz Ayala	14.11.1997	1	(7)	2			
David Antonio Rugamas Leiva	17.02.1990	14		8	18		7
Trainer:							
Bruno Martínez Silva (MEX)	01.06.1989	18			18		

SANTA TECLA FÚTBOL CLUB

Foundation date: January 15, 2007
Address: *Not known*
Stadium: Estadio Las Delicias, Santa Tecla (10,000)

THE SQUAD

	DOB	Ape M	(s)	G	Cla M	(s)	G
Goalkeepers:							
Jesús Alejandro Dautt Ramírez (MEX)	03.03.1990	12			19		
Wilberth Alberto Hernández Zavala	05.04.1994	4			1		
Erick Vega			(1)				
Defenders:							
Mario Manuel Alfaro González	03.03.1996	4	(3)				
Giovanni Ernesto Ávila	21.03.2000	12	(2)	1	18		
José Gerardo García Ramírez	31.05.1999	9			2		
Raúl Alexander González Tejada	27.03.1985				1	(2)	
Alexander Enrique Mendoza Rodas	04.06.1990	12		2	19		
Edgardo Arnulfo Mira Abrego (GUA)	10.03.1993				20		1
Óscar Antonio Paz Beltrán	14.03.1998	4	(6)		2	(16)	1
Maynor Enrique Serafín Pérez	14.01.1996	3	(3)		2	(1)	
Yosimar Elieser Quiñónes Sánchez (COL)	04.08.1988	8		1			
Josué Ernesto Santos Olivares	15.05.1996		(3)		2		
Walter Ernesto Torres Marroquín	19.08.1998	8	(3)		16	(2)	1
Midfielders:							
Iván Adalberto Barahona Díaz	01.08.1990	10	(4)	3	7	(3)	1
Ángel Alexander Callejas Lima	14.01.1999	2	(3)		3	(5)	
Marlon Ivan Cornejo Rivas	14.09.1993	12			18		3
Elmer Jonathán Escobar Hernández	19.02.1998	1					
William Gerardo Escobar Henríquez			(2)				
César Noé Flores Linares	17.03.1996				18	(1)	2
Álvaro Ramón Lizama Gavidia	24.05.1995	11	(2)	1			
Emerson Eugenio Mancía Bonilla	08.10.2000	2	(1)				
Cristian Fabián Oliveira Demello (URU)	20.01.1988				18	(1)	1
Josué David Pacheco Guevara	01.10.2000	2	(2)	1			
Fernando José Quintanilla Flores	02.01.1998	7	(7)		1	(12)	
Kévin Stiven Reyes Ortíz	28.08.1999	15		1			
Rodrigo José Rivera Sánchez	16.08.1993	15		2	14	(5)	
Eduardo Alauro Rodríguez Lloreda (COL)	28.07.1989				14	(4)	2
Luis Rodrigo Zetino						(1)	
Forwards:							
Diego Daniel Areco Sayas (PAR)	05.11.1992				4	(10)	2
Henry Geovany Argueta Geovany	01.06.1999		(1)				
José David Díaz Ramos	20.05.1992	15		3			
Carlos Alberto Flores Figueroa	13.08.1993	2	(5)		1		
Roberto Alexis González Montoya	25.03.1993				6	(13)	4
Santos Antonio Guzmán Villalta	23.05.1993	4	(7)				
Irvin Enrique Herrera Baires	30.08.1991				12	(3)	7
Aquiles Eliseo Méndez Fernández	14.06.1993		(4)				
Diego Alejandro Sánchez García	15.12.1999	2	(8)		2	(5)	2
Trainer:							
Juan Andrés Sarulyte (ARG)	18.04.1962	3					
[31.10.2020] Jaime Geovanni Medina Estrada	08.03.1980	13					
[25.01.2021] Rubén Fernando da Silva Echeverrito (URU)	11.04.1968				20		

SONSONATE FÚTBOL CLUB

Foundation date: March 2, 1948
Address: *Not known*
Stadium: Estadio "Ana Mercedes Campos", Sonsonate (9,000)

THE SQUAD

	DOB	Ape			Cla		
		M	(s)	G	M	(s)	G
Goalkeepers:							
Héctor Salvador Ramírez Carbajal	01.01.1995	16			10		
Gustavo Andrés Vega Monterrosa	01.01.1994	2			6		
Defenders:							
Alfredo Antonio Alvarado Lara	20.10.2000	1			2		
Carlos Mauricio Arévalo Méndez	23.03.1988	8	(1)				
Kévin Enrique Ayala Méndoza	15.07.1993	16		1	8		
Kévin Orlando Calderón Jérez	10.09.1993	7	(2)		12		1
Andrés Martín Lima Sánchez (URU)	09.01.1997				10	(1)	
Edson Sifredo Meléndez Reyes	17.09.1991	18		2	15		1
José Alberto Mondragón Mina (COL)	12.01.1994	8	(1)				
Alexis Mauricio Montes Renderos	01.06.1998	14		3			
Enner Francisco Orellana Velásquez	03.01.1995	8	(5)		15		1
Alexis Mauricio Montes Renderos	01.06.1998				11	(1)	1
Cristian Oswaldo Rivera					1		
Midfielders:							
Henry Geovanny Alvarenga Ramírez	15.05.1990	1	(9)	1	5	(3)	
René Amilcar Gómez Romero	08.01.1993	4	(5)		3	(6)	
Carlos Manuel Herrera Romero	23.01.1998	8	(8)		16		1
William Antonio Maldonado López	03.01.1990	15	(1)	2	4	(5)	
Jorge Luis Morán Rodas	10.04.1989	10	(3)		10	(6)	1
Jacobo Miguel Moreno Kattan	21.01.1997	14	(3)	1	15		2
Aldair Adilson Rivera Sánchez	01.06.1990	8	(3)		4	(10)	
Marcos Adonay Rodríguez Ochoa	10.08.1997	11	(5)	1	14	(1)	2
Sebastien Daniel Rondeau Rodríguez	19.01.2000		(2)				
Jonathan Alexander Ruano Murga	31.01.1998	1	(1)		1	(3)	
Marvin Aníbal Sandoval Contreras			(1)				
Anderson Javier Surio Portillo					1		
Forwards:							
David Alejandro Boquin (ARG)	23.04.1987	15		6			
Daniel Esteban Buitrago Tamayo (COL)	27.02.1991	7	(4)				
Levin Romeo Espinal Trejo	14.05.1998	1	(10)			(7)	
Roberto Alexis González Montoya	25.03.1993	4	(9)	1			
Ricardo Alexander Guevara Deras	10.10.1992						
Víctor Manuel Landazuri Díaz (COL)	04.03.1997				13		4
José Roberto Orellana	03.11.2000	1				(1)	
Trainer:							
Rubén Fernando da Silva Echeverrito (URU)	11.04.1968	18					
[29.01.21] Enrique Fabio Castromán Orellano (URU)					16		

SECOND LEVEL
Segunda División de El Salvador – Liga de Plata 2020/2021

Torneo Apertura 2020

Grupo occidental

1. AD Destroyer Puerto de La Libertad	31
2. CD Marte Soyapango	22
3. CD San Pablo Municipal San Pablo Tacachico	18
4. CD Titán Texistepeque	17
5. AD Santa Rosa Guachipilín	13
6. Municipal FC Juayúa	13
7. CSD Vendaval Apopa	9

Grupo oriental

1. CD Platense Zacatecoluca	27
2. CD Cacahuatique Ciudad Barrios	21
3. CD Fuerte San Francisco	18
4. CD Aspirante Jucuapa	17
5. CD Liberal Quelepa	13
6. CD Dragón San Miguel	11
7. CD Ilopaneco Ilopango	6

Top-4 of each group were qualified for the Torneo Apertura Play-offs.

Torneo Apertura Play-offs

Quarter-Finals [03-10.01.2021]

CD Titán Texistepeque - AD Destroyer Puerto de La Libertad	2-3	1-1
CD Marte Soyapango - CD San Pablo Municipal San Pablo Tacachico	2-1	1-2 aet 5-4 pen
CD Aspirante Jucuapa - CD Platense Zacatecoluca	0-1	0-0
CD Fuerte San Francisco - CD Cacahuatique Ciudad Barrios	1-0	0-2

Semi-Finals [17-24.01.2021]

CD Marte Soyapango - AD Destroyer Puerto de La Libertad	3-1	1-3 aet 2-4 pen
CD Cacahuatique Ciudad Barrios - CD Platense Zacatecoluca	1-2	1-1

Final [30.01.2021]

AD Destroyer Puerto de La Libertad - CD Platense Zacatecoluca	2-2 aet	5-6 pen

Torneo Apertura 2020 Champions: **CD Platense Zacatecoluca**

Torneo Clausura 2021

Grupo occidental

1. CD Titán Texistepeque	12	7	1	4	21	-	16	22
2. AD Destroyer Puerto de La Libertad	12	7	1	4	19	-	15	22
3. CD Marte Soyapango	12	6	2	4	17	-	13	20
4. CD San Pablo Municipal San Pablo Tacachico	12	5	4	3	23	-	20	19
5. Municipal FC Juayúa	12	5	2	5	20	-	16	17
6. AD Santa Rosa Guachipilín	12	4	0	8	16	-	23	12
7. CSD Vendaval Apopa	12	2	2	8	15	-	28	8

Grupo oriental

1. CD Platense Zacatecoluca	12	7	5	0	18	-	6	26
2. CD Aspirante Jucuapa	12	5	4	3	14	-	13	19
3. CD Fuerte San Francisco	12	4	5	3	13	-	11	17
4. CD Liberal Quelepa	12	5	2	5	20	-	19	17
5. CD Cacahuatique Ciudad Barrios	12	4	3	5	24	-	17	15
6. CD Dragón San Miguel	12	2	5	5	19	-	21	11
7. CD Ilopaneco Ilopango	12	2	2	8	8	-	29	8

Top-4 of each group were qualified for the Torneo Apertura Play-offs.

Torneo Clausura Play-offs

Quarter-Finals [16-23.05.2021]

CD San Pablo Municipal San Pablo Tacachico - CD Titán Texistepeque	3-0	0-1
CD Marte Soyapango - AD Destroyer Puerto de La Libertad	0-0	1-3
CD Liberal Quelepa - CD Platense Zacatecoluca	1-2	1-1
CD Fuerte San Francisco - CD Aspirante Jucuapa	1-1	1-1 aet
		7-6 pen

Semi-Finals [29.05.-06.06.2021]

CD San Pablo Municipal S. P. Tacachico - AD Destroyer Puerto de La Libertad	0-0	1-3
CD Fuerte San Francisco - CD Platense Zacatecoluca	1-0	0-2

Final [13.06.2021]

AD Destroyer Puerto de La Libertad - CD Platense Zacatecoluca	3-3 aet	4-3 pen

Torneo Clausura 2021 Champions: **AD Destroyer Puerto de La Libertad**

Promotion Final [20.06.2021]

AD Destroyer Puerto de La Libertad - CD Platense Zacatecoluca	1-2(0-0)

CD Platense Zacatecoluca promoted for the Primera División de Fútbol Profesional 2021/2022.

NATIONAL TEAM
INTERNATIONAL MATCHES 2020/2021

09.12.2020	Fort Lauderdale	United States - El Salvador	6-0(5-0)	(F)
25.03.2021	San Salvador	El Salvador - Grenada	2-0(1-0)	(WCQ)
28.03.2021	Willemstad	Montserrat - El Salvador	1-1(0-1)	(WCQ)
05.06.2021	Upper Bethlehem	US Virgin Islands - El Salvador	0-7(0-2)	(WCQ)
08.06.2021	San Salvador	El Salvador - Antigua and Barbuda	3-0(1-0)	(WCQ)
12.06.2021	Basseterre	Saint Kitts and Nevis - El Salvador	0-4(0-3)	(WCQ)
15.06.2021	San Salvador	El Salvador - Saint Kitts and Nevis	2-0(1-0)	(WCQ)
26.06.2021	Los Angeles	El Salvador - Guatemala	0-0	(F)
04.07.2021	Pula	Qatar - El Salvador	1-0(0-0)	(F)

09.12.2020, Friendly International
DRV PNK Stadium, Fort Lauderdale; Attendance: 0
Referee: Jose Raúl Torres Rivera (Puerto Rico)
UNITED STATES - EL SALVADOR   **6-0(5-0)**
SLV: Henry Edimar Hernández Cruz, Iván Roberto Mancia Ramírez, Rubén Eduardo Marroquín Meléndez (38.Bryan Alexander Tamacas López), Roberto Carlos Domínguez Fuentes, Darwin Adelso Cerén Delgado, Marvin Wilfredo Monterrosa Delzas (52.Pablo Oshan Punyed Dubon), Jonathan David Jiménez Guzmán (57.Alexander Vidal Larín Hernández), Narciso Oswaldo Orellana Guzmán, José David Díaz Ramos (38.Alexander Enrique Mendoza Rodas), Denis Omar Pineda Torres (70.Dustin Clifman Corea Garay), Joaquín Antonio Rivas Navarro (52.Andrés Alberto Flores Jaco). Trainer: Carlos Alberto de los Cobos Martínez (Mexico).

25.03.2021, 22nd FIFA World Cup Qualifiers, CONCACAF First Round
Estadio Cuscatlán, San Salvador
Referee: Kimbell Ward (Saint Kitts and Nevis)
EL SALVADOR - GRENADA   **2-0(1-0)**
SLV: Henry Edimar Hernández Cruz, Andrés Alberto Flores Jaco, Iván Roberto Mancia Ramírez, Julio Enrique Sibrián Molina (89.Roberto Carlos Domínguez Fuentes), Bryan Alexander Tamacas López, Gerson Levi Mayén Villavicencio, Andrés Alberto Flores Jaco (60.Diego Elenilson Galdámez Coca), Jaime Enrique Alas Morales (60.Jairo Mauricio Henríquez Ferrufino), Isaac Antonio Portillo Molina, David Antonio Rugamas Leiva (76.Dustin Clifman Corea Garay), Joaquín Antonio Rivas Navarro (72.Erick Alejandro Rivera). Trainer: Carlos Alberto de los Cobos Martínez (Mexico).
Goals: Gerson Levi Mayén Villavicencio (23), David Antonio Rugamas Leiva (46).

28.03.2021, 22nd FIFA World Cup Qualifiers, CONCACAF First Round
Stadion „Ergilio Hato", Willemstad
Referee: Ricangel de Leça (Aruba)
MONTSERRAT - EL SALVADOR   **1-1(0-1)**
SLV: Benji Oldai Villalobos Segovia, Andrés Alberto Flores Jaco, Iván Roberto Mancia Ramírez, Bryan Alexander Tamacas López (52.Ibsen Adalberto Castro Avelar), Roberto Carlos Domínguez Fuentes, Gerson Levi Mayén Villavicencio, Jaime Enrique Alas Morales (84.Julio Enrique Sibrián Molina), Rodrigo José Rivera Sánchez, Isaac Antonio Portillo Molina (56.Andrés Alberto Flores Jaco), David Antonio Rugamas Leiva (56.Dustin Clifman Corea Garay), Joaquín Antonio Rivas Navarro. Trainer: Hugo Ernesto Pérez Granados (United States).
Goal: David Antonio Rugamas Leiva (4).

05.06.2021, 22nd FIFA World Cup Qualifiers, CONCACAF First Round
Bethlehem Soccer Stadium, Upper Bethlehem; Attendance: 150
Referee: Ted Unkel (United States)
U.S. VIRGIN ISLANDS - EL SALVADOR **0-7(0-2)**
SLV: Mario Antonio González Martínez, Eriq Anthony Zavaleta Vanney, Bryan Alexander Tamacas López (74.Jairo Mauricio Henríquez Ferrufino), Alexander Vidal Larín Hernández, Darwin Adelso Cerén Delgado (59.Gerson Levi Mayén Villavicencio), Marvin Wilfredo Monterrosa Delzas, Juan Carlos Portillo Leal (74.Walmer Martínez), Isaac Antonio Portillo Molina, Ronald Daniel Rodríguez Goméz, Nelson Wilfredo Bonilla Sánchez (59.David Antonio Rugamas Leiva), Joaquín Antonio Rivas Navarro (46.Joshua Giovanni Pérez). Trainer: Hugo Ernesto Pérez Granados (United States).
Goals: Marvin Wilfredo Monterrosa Delzas (23), Juan Carlos Portillo Leal (31), David Antonio Rugamas Leiva (77), Joshua Giovanni Pérez (78), David Antonio Rugamas Leiva (82), Marvin Wilfredo Monterrosa Delzas (86), David Antonio Rugamas Leiva (90).

08.06.2021, 22nd FIFA World Cup Qualifiers, CONCACAF First Round
Estadio Cuscatlán, San Salvador
Referee: Keylor Antonio Herrera Villalobos (Costa Rica)
EL SALVADOR - ANTIGUA AND BARBUDA **3-0(1-0)**
SLV: Mario Antonio González Martínez, Eriq Anthony Zavaleta Vanney, Bryan Alexander Tamacas López (70.Roberto Carlos Domínguez Fuentes), Alexander Vidal Larín Hernández, Darwin Adelso Cerén Delgado, Marvin Wilfredo Monterrosa Delzas (81.Gerson Levi Mayén Villavicencio), Juan Carlos Portillo Leal (46.Walmer Martínez), Isaac Antonio Portillo Molina, Ronald Daniel Rodríguez Goméz, Nelson Wilfredo Bonilla Sánchez (60.David Antonio Rugamas Leiva), Joshua Giovanni Pérez (81.Jairo Mauricio Henríquez Ferrufino). Trainer: Hugo Ernesto Pérez Granados (United States).
Goals: Eriq Anthony Zavaleta Vanney (40), David Antonio Rugamas Leiva (68), Walmer Martínez (85).

12.06.2021, 22nd FIFA World Cup Qualifiers, CONCACAF Second Round
Warner Park, Basseterre
Referee: Kevin Morrison (Jamaica)
SAINT KITTS AND NEVIS - EL SALVADOR **0-4(0-3)**
SLV: Mario Antonio González Martínez, Eriq Anthony Zavaleta Vanney, Bryan Alexander Tamacas López, Alexander Vidal Larín Hernández, Darwin Adelso Cerén Delgado, Marvin Wilfredo Monterrosa Delzas, Ronald Daniel Rodríguez Goméz (86.José Rómulo Villalobos Campos), Melvin Adalberto Cartagena Portillo (76.Gerson Levi Mayén Villavicencio), David Antonio Rugamas Leiva (76.Nelson Wilfredo Bonilla Sánchez), Joaquín Antonio Rivas Navarro (46.Walmer Martínez), Joshua Giovanni Pérez (67.Juan Carlos Portillo Leal). Trainer: Hugo Ernesto Pérez Granados (United States).
Goals: David Antonio Rugamas Leiva (3), Joshua Giovanni Pérez (20), David Antonio Rugamas Leiva (27), Darwin Adelso Cerén Delgado (64 penalty).

15.06.2021, 22nd FIFA World Cup Qualifiers, CONCACAF Second Round
Estadio Cuscatlán, San Salvador
Referee: Keylor Herrera (Costa Rica)
EL SALVADOR - SAINT KITTS AND NEVIS **2-0(1-0)**
SLV: Mario Antonio González Martínez, Eriq Anthony Zavaleta Vanney, Bryan Alexander Tamacas López (81.Alexis Mauricio Montes Renderos), Alexander Vidal Larín Hernández, Darwin Adelso Cerén Delgado, Marvin Wilfredo Monterrosa Delzas (64.Miguel Ángel Ochoa Lemus), Jairo Mauricio Henríquez Ferrufino, Isaac Antonio Portillo Molina, Ronald Daniel Rodríguez Goméz (81.Roberto Carlos Domínguez Fuentes), David Antonio Rugamas Leiva (46.Nelson Wilfredo Bonilla Sánchez), Joshua Giovanni Pérez (64.Gerson Levi Mayén Villavicencio). Trainer: Hugo Ernesto Pérez Granados (United States).
Goals: Joshua Giovanni Pérez (24), Gerson Levi Mayén Villavicencio (87).

26.06.2021, Friendly International
Banc of California Stadium, Los Angeles (United States); Atendance: 0
Referee: Óscar Donaldo Moncada Godoy (Honduras)
EL SALVADOR - GUATEMALA   **0-0**
SLV: Mario Antonio González Martínez, Alexander Vidal Larín Hernández (82.Alexis Mauricio Montes Renderos), Bryan Alexander Tamacas López, Roberto Carlos Domínguez Fuentes, José Rómulo Villalobos Campos, Gerson Levi Mayén Villavicencio, Juan Carlos Portillo Leal (58.Jairo Mauricio Henríquez Ferrufino), Narciso Oswaldo Orellana Guzmán (82.Daniel Esteban Ríos), Isaac Antonio Portillo Molina, David Antonio Rugamas Leiva (76.Erick Alejandro Rivera), Joshua Giovanni Pérez., Trainer: Hugo Ernesto Pérez Granados (United States).

04.07.2021, Friendly International
Stadion "Aldo Drosina", Pula (Croatia); Atendance: 0
Referee: Ivan Bebek (Croatia)
QATAR - EL SALVADOR   **1-0(0-0)**
SLV: Mario Antonio González Martínez, Alexander Vidal Larín Hernández, Bryan Alexander Tamacas López, Roberto Carlos Domínguez Fuentes, Ronald Daniel Rodríguez Goméz, Darwin Adelso Cerén Delgado (71.Narciso Oswaldo Orellana Guzmán), Marvin Wilfredo Monterrosa Delzas (71.Walmer Martínez), Jairo Mauricio Henríquez Ferrufino (62.Armando Miguel Moreno Magaña), Isaac Antonio Portillo Molina, David Antonio Rugamas Leiva (62.Erick Alejandro Rivera), Joshua Giovanni Pérez (70.Juan Carlos Portillo Leal). Trainer: Hugo Ernesto Pérez Granados (United States).

NATIONAL TEAM PLAYERS 2020/2021

Name	DOB	Club
Goalkeepers		
Mario Antonio GONZÁLEZ Martínez	20.05.1997	*Alianza FC San Salvador*
Henry Edimar HERNÁNDEZ Cruz	04.01.1985	*CD Malacateco (GUA)*
Benji Oldai VILLALOBOS Segovia	15.07.1988	*CD Águila San Miguel*
Defenders		
Ibsen Adalberto CASTRO Avelar	24.10.1988	*CD FAS Santa Ana*
Roberto Carlos DOMÍNGUEZ Fuentes	09.05.1997	*Club Bolívar La Paz (BOL); 01.01.2021-> FK Partizani Tiranë (ALB)*
Andrés Alberto FLORES Jaco	20.01.1995	*CD FAS Santa Ana*
Alexander Vidal LARÍN Hernández	27.06.1992	*CSD Xelajú Mario Camposeco (GUA)*
Miguel Ángel Ochoa LEMUS	26.10.1993	*AD Chalatenango*
Iván Roberto MANCIA Ramírez	19.12.1992	*Alianza FC San Salvador*
Rubén Eduardo MARROQUÍN Meléndez	10.05.1992	*Alianza FC San Salvador*
Alexander Enrique MENDOZA Rodas	04.06.1990	*Santa Tecla FC*
Ronald Daniel RODRÍGUEZ Goméz	22.09.1998	*CD Águila San Miguel*
Julio Enrique SIBRIÁN Molina	17.07.1996	*Once Deportivo FC Ahuachapán*
Bryan Alexander TAMACAS López	21.02.1995	*Alianza FC San Salvador*
José Rómulo VILLALOBOS Campos	01.09.1997	*CD Municipal Limeño Santa Rosa de Lima*
Eriq Anthony ZAVALETA Vanney	02.08.1992	*Toronto FC (CAN)*

Midfielders

Name	Date	Club
Jaime Enrique ALAS Morales	30.07.1989	CSD Municipal Ciudad de Guatemala(GUA)
Melvin Adalberto CARTAGENA Portillo	30.07.1999	Once Deportivo FC Ahuachapán
Darwin Adelso CERÉN Delgado	31.12.1989	Houston Dynamo (USA)
Andrés Alexander FLORES Mejía	31.08.1990	Portland Timbers (USA)
Diego Elenilson GALDÁMEZ Coca	26.08.1994	CD Águila San Miguel
Jairo Mauricio HENRÍQUEZ Ferrufino	31.08.1993	AD Chalatenango
Jonathan David JIMÉNEZ Guzmán	12.07.1992	Alianza FC San Salvador
Gerson Levi MAYÉN Villavicencio	09.02.1989	CD Águila San Miguel
Marvin Wilfredo MONTERROSA Delzas	01.03.1991	Alianza FC San Salvador
Narciso Oswaldo ORELLANA Guzmán	28.01.1995	Alianza FC San Salvador
Denis Omar PINEDA Torres	10.08.1995	CD Técnico Universitario Ambato (ECU)
Isaac Antonio PORTILLO Molina	08.11.1994	Alianza FC San Salvador
Juan Carlos PORTILLO Leal	26.12.1991	Alianza FC San Salvador
Pablo Oshan PUNYED Dubon	18.04.1990	Víkingur Reykjavík (ISL)
Alexis Mauricio Montes RENDEROS	01.06.1998	Sonsonate FC
Daniel Esteban RÍOS	01.03.2003	Houston Dynamo (USA)
Rodrigo José RIVERA Sánchez	16.08.1993	Santa Tecla FC
Joaquín Antonio RIVAS Navarro	26.04.1992	FC Tulsa (USA)

Forwards

Name	Date	Club
Nelson Wilfredo BONILLA Sánchez	11.09.1990	Port FC Bangkok (THA)
Dustin Clifman COREA Garay	21.03.1992	Unattached; 24.02.2021-> CD FAS Santa Ana
José David DÍAZ Ramos	20.05.1993	Jocoro FC
Walmer MARTÍNEZ	17.08.1998	Hartford Athletic (USA)
Armando Miguel MORENO Magaña	10.09.1995	New Mexico United (USA)
Joshua Giovanni PÉREZ	21.01.1998	UD Ibiza-Eivissa (ESP)
Erick Alejandro RIVERA	10.10.1989	Club Aurora Cochabamba (BOL)
David Antonio RUGAMAS Leiva	17.02.1990	Once Deportivo FC Ahuachapán

National coaches

Name	Date
Carlos Alberto DE LOS COBOS Martínez (Mexico) [25.05.2018 – 21.04.2021]	10.12.1958
Hugo Ernesto PÉREZ Granados (United States) [from 23.04.2021]	08.11.1963

FRENCH GUIANA

The Country:	The FA:
Guyane (French Guiana)	Ligue de Football de Guyane
Capital: Cayenne (Prefecture)	B.P. 765 - Stade de Baduel, Cayenne
Surface: 83,534 km²	97322 Cedex
Population: 294,071 [2021]	Year of Formation: 1962
Time: UTC-3	Member of FIFA since: *not affiliated*
Independent since: *overseas region of France*	Member of CONCACAF since: 1964

NATIONAL TEAM RECORDS

First international match: 1946: French Guiana - Dutch Guyana 0-9
Most international caps: Rhudy Evens – 56 caps (since 2008)
Most international goals: Gary Pigrée – 16 goals / 20 caps (2012-2015)

CONCACAF GOLD CUP	
1991	Qualifiers
1993	Qualifiers
1996	Qualifiers
1998	Qualifiers
2000	Qualifiers
2002	Did not enter
2003	Did not enter
2005	Qualifiers
2007	Did not enter
2009	Did not enter
2011	Did not enter
2013	Qualifiers
2015	Qualifiers
2017	Final Tournament (Group Stage)
2019	Qualifiers
2021	Qualifiers

FIFA WORLD CUP	
1930	-
1934	-
1938	-
1950	-
1954	-
1958	-
1962	-
1966	-
1970	-
1974	-
1978	-
1982	-
1986	-
1990	-
1994	-
1998	-
2002	-
2006	-
2010	-
2014	-
2018	-

F.I.F.A. CONFEDERATIONS CUP 1992-2017

None

OLYMPIC FOOTBALL TOURNAMENTS 1900-2016

None

CCCF (Confederación Centroamericana y del Caribe de Fútbol) CHAMPIONSHIPS 1941-1961

None

CONCACAF CHAMPIONSHIPS 1963-1989

None

CONCACAF NATIONS LEAGUE

2019-2020	League B

CARIBBEAN CHAMPIONSHIPS 1989-2017

Year	Result	Year	Result
1989	Qualifiers	1999	Qualifiers
1991	Qualifiers	2001	Did not enter
1992	Qualifiers	2005	Qualifiers
1993	Qualifiers	2007	Did not enter
1994	Qualifiers	2008	Did not enter
1995	Final Tournament - Group Stage	2010	Did not enter
1996	Qualifiers	2012	Final Tournament - Group Stage
1997	Qualifiers	2014	Final Tournament - Group Stage
1998	Qualifiers	2017	Final Tournament - 3rd Place

FRENCH GUIANAN CLUB HONOURS IN CONCACAF CLUB COMPETITIONS:

CONCACAF Champions Cup / CONCACAF Champions League 1962-2020

None

CONCACAF League 2017-2020

None

Caribbean Club Championship 1997-2021

None

CONCACAF Cup Winners Cup 1991-1995*

None

Copa Interamericana 1968-1998*

None

*defunct competitions

NATIONAL COMPETITIONS
TABLE OF HONOURS

The first championship was held in 1912, but winners are not known until 1962/1963.

	CHAMPIONS	CUP WINNERS
1959/1960	*Not known*	AJ Saint-Georges Cayenne
1960/1961	*Not known*	*Not known*
1961/1962	*Not known*	*Not known*
1962/1963	Racing Club Cayenne	*Not known*
1963/1964	*Not known*	*Not known*
1964/1965	AJ Saint-Georges Cayenne	AJ Saint-Georges Cayenne
1965/1966	*Not known*	AJ Saint-Georges Cayenne
1966/1967	*Not known*	*Not known*
1967/1968	*Not known*	*Not known*
1968/1969	*Not known*	AJ Saint-Georges Cayenne
1969/1970	*Not known*	*Not known*
1970/1971	*Not known*	AJ Saint-Georges Cayenne
1971/1972	*Not known*	*Not known*
1972/1973	*Not known*	ASC Roura
1973/1974	*Not known*	AS Club Colonial Cayenne
1974/1975	*Not known*	AS Club Colonial Cayenne
1975/1976	*Not known*	Olympique de Cayenne
1976/1977	AS Club Colonial Cayenne	*Not known*
1977/1978	AS Club Colonial Cayenne	AS Club Colonial Cayenne
1978/1979	AS Club Colonial Cayenne	ASC Le Geldar Kourou
1979/1980	*Not known*	AJ Saint-Georges Cayenne
1980/1981	*Not known*	*Not known*
1981/1982	USL Montjoly	AS Club Colonial Cayenne
1982/1983	AJ Saint-Georges Cayenne	AJ Saint-Georges Cayenne
1983/1984	AJ Saint-Georges Cayenne	AJ Saint-Georges Cayenne
1984/1985	ASC Le Geldar Kourou	AJ Saint-Georges Cayenne
1985/1986	ASL Sport Guyanais Cayenne	*Not known*
1986/1987	*Not known*	*Not known*
1987/1988	ASC Le Geldar Kourou	*Not known*
1988/1989	ASC Le Geldar Kourou	*Not known*
1989/1990	SC Kouroucien	AJ Saint-Georges Cayenne
1990/1991	AS Club Colonial Cayenne	*Not known*
1991/1992	AS Club Colonial Cayenne	ASJ Mana
1992/1993	US Sinnamary	AS Club Colonial Cayenne
1993/1994	US Sinnamary	AS Club Colonial Cayenne
1994/1995	AS Jahouvey Mana	*Not known*
1995/1996	AS Club Colonial Cayenne	US Sinnamary
1996/1997	US Sinnamary	AS Club Colonial Cayenne
1997/1998	AS Jahouvey Mana	US Sinnamary
1998/1999	AJ Saint-Georges Cayenne	EF Iracoubo
1999/2000	AJ Saint-Georges Cayenne	AJ Saint-Georges Cayenne
2000/2001	ASC Le Geldar Kourou	AJ Saint-Georges Cayenne
2001/2002	AJ Saint-Georges Cayenne	US Sinnamary
2002/2003	US Matoury	AJ Saint-Georges Cayenne
2003/2004	ASC Le Geldar Kourou	AJ Saint-Georges Cayenne

2004/2005	ASC Le Geldar Kourou	US Matoury
2005/2006	US Matoury	US Macouria
2006/2007	US Macouria	ASC Le Geldar Kourou
2007/2008	ASC Le Geldar Kourou	Club Sportif et Culturel de Cayenne
2008/2009	ASC Le Geldar Kourou	ASC Le Geldar Kourou
2009/2010	ASC Le Geldar Kourou	Alianza FC San Salvador
2010/2011	US Matoury	US Matoury
2011/2012	US Matoury	US Matoury
2012/2013	ASC Le Geldar Kourou	US Matoury
2013/2014	US Matoury	ASC Le Geldar Kourou
2014/2015	Club Sportif et Culturel de Cayenne	US Matoury
2015/2016	US Matoury	US Matoury
2016/2017	US Matoury	*Competition not finished*
2017/2018	ASC Le Geldar Kourou	AS Étoile Matoury
2018/2019	ASC Agouado Apatou	AS Étoile Matoury
2019/2020	Olympique de Cayenne	*Competition abandoned*
2020/2021	*Competition not yet finished*	US Sinnamary

NATIONAL CHAMPIONSHIP
Division d'Honneur 2020/2021

The championship was interrupted in April 2021 due to COVID-19 pandemic.

Provisional tables based on the matches played:

Groupe A								
1. Olympique de Cayenne	11	6	1	4	25	-	15	30
2. AS Oyapock	9	6	0	3	22	-	17	27
3. Loyola OC	10	5	1	4	14	-	16	26
4. AS Étoile Matoury*	10	5	2	3	21	-	18	25
5. US Sinnamary**	10	4	2	4	16	-	13	23
6. AJ Saint-Georges Cayenne	9	3	3	3	16	-	16	21
7. ASC Kouroucien	10	2	2	6	16	-	24	18
8. ASC Agouado Apatou	7	1	1	5	11	-	22	11

*2 points deducted
**1 point deducted

Groupe B								
1. US Matoury	8	5	2	1	28	-	7	25
2. ASU Grand Santi Mana	5	5	0	0	11	-	4	20
3. ASC Le Geldar Kourou	6	3	1	2	10	-	7	16
4. CSC de Cayenne	9	1	2	6	7	-	19	14
5. ASC Arc en Ciel	7	2	0	5	11	-	21	13
6. ASC Ouest	6	2	1	3	9	-	14	13
7. ASC Rémire	5	1	2	2	7	-	11	10

Please note: the point system in French Guiana is 4 points for a win, 2 points for a draw and 1 point for a loss.

NATIONAL CUP
Coupe de Guyane Final 2020/2021

29.11.2020, Stade "Edmard Lama", Rémire-Montjoly
US Sinnamary - ASU Grand Santi Mana   **2-0(2-0)**
Goals: 1-0 Abionie Verlyno (21), 2-0 Jonel Lenso (43).

THE CLUBS

ASSOCIATION JEUNESSE DE SAINT-GEORGES
Year of Formation: 1968
Stadium: Stade "Georges Chaumet", Cayenne (7,000)

ASSOCIATION SPORTIVE ET CULTURELLE AGOUADO APATOU
Year of Formation: 1996
Stadium: Stade de Moutendé, Apatou (1,000)

ASSOCIATION SPORTIVE ET CULTURELLE KOUROUCIEN
Stadium: Stade de Bois-Chaudat, Kourou (2,850)

ASSOCIATION SPORTIVE ET CULTURELLE LE GELDAR KOUROU
Year of Formation: 1957
Stadium: Stade de Bois-Chaudat, Kourou (2,850)

ASSOCIATION SPORTIVE ÉTOILE MATOURY
Stadium: Stade Municipal, Matoury (2,353)

ASSOCIATION SPORTIVE OYAPOCK
Stadium: Stade Municipal, Saint-Georges-de-l'Oyapock (1,400)

ASSOCIATION SPORTIVE ET CULTURELLE RÉMIRE
Year of Formation: 1974
Stadium: Stade "Edmard Lama", Rémire-Montjoly (1,500)

ASSOCIATION SPORTIVE UNION GRAND SANTI MANA
Stadium: Stade "Guy Mariette", Mana (600)

CLUB SPORTIF ET CULTUREL DE CAYENNE
Stadium: Stade de Baduel, Cayenne (7,500)

OLYMPIQUE DE CAYENNE
Stadium: Stade "Georges Chaumet", Cayenne (7,000)

UNION SPORTIVE MATOURY
Stadium: Stade Municipal, Matoury (2,000)

UNION SPORTIVE SINNAMARY
Year of Formation: 1952
Stadium: Stade Omnisports, Sinnamary (2,500)

NATIONAL TEAM
INTERNATIONAL MATCHES 2020/2021

| 03.07.2021 | Fort Lauderdale | Cuba - French Guiana | 0-3 awarded | (GCQ) |
| 06.07.2021 | Fort Lauderdale | Trinidad and Tobago - French Guiana | 1-1; 8-7pen | (GCQ) |

03.07.2021, 16th CONCACAF Gold Cup Qualifiers, First Round
DRV PNK Stadium, Fort Lauderdale (United States); Attendance: 0
CUBA - FRENCH GUIANA   **0-3 (awarded)**
Please note: due to COVID-19 pandemic related travel and visa challenges, Cuba forfeited the match, a 3-0 win was awarded for French Guiana.

06.07.2021, 16th CONCACAF Gold Cup Qualifiers, Second Round
DRV PNK Stadium, Fort Lauderdale (United States); Attendance: 0
Referee: Ismail Elfath (United States)
TRINIDAD AND TOBAGO - FRENCH GUIANA   **1-1(1-1,1-1); 8-7 on penalties**
GYF: Simon Lugier, Ludovic Baal, Kévin Ramon Rimane, Grégory Lescot, Alain Mogès, Gary Gérard Marigard (88.Dylan Adam), Thomas Vancaeyezeele, Rhudy Evens, Calvin Soga (62.Carino Filbert Atchaliso Nkiére), Sloan Privat (85.Éric Alex), Arnold Abelenti (85.Jessy Marigard). Trainer: Thierry Albert De Neef (France).
Goal: Arnold Abelenti (44).
Penalties: Thomas Vancaeyezeele, Carino Filbert Atchaliso Nkiére, Rhudy Evens, Ludovic Baal, Alex Éric, Dylan Adam, Gary Gérard Marigard, Kévin Ramon Rimane (saved).

NATIONAL TEAM PLAYERS 2020/2021

Name	DOB	Club
Goalkeepers		
Simon LUGIER	02.08.1989	US Boulogne-sur-Mer (FRA)
Defenders		
Dylan ADAM	07.11.1998	AS Étoile Matoury
Ludovic BAAL	24.05.1986	Stade Brestois 29 (FRA)
Grégory LESCOT	10.05.1989	Vannes OC (FRA)
Gary Gérard MARIGARD	06.01.1988	Olympique Grande-Synthe (FRA)
Alain MOGES	22.07.1992	Angoulême-Soyaux Charante FC (FRA)
Kévin Ramon RIMANE	23.02.1991	AFC Hermannstadt Sibiu (ROU)
Midfielders		
Rhudy EVENS	13.02.1988	ASC Le Geldar Kourou
Calvin SOGA	18.01.1995	AJ Saint-Georges Cayenne
Thomas VANCAEYEZEELE	27.07.1994	San Diego Loyal SC (USA)
Forwards		
Arnold ABELENTI	09.09.1991	SO Romorantin (FRA)
Carino Filbert ATCHALISO Nkiére	14.02.1992	
Alex ÉRIC	21.09.1990	US Matoury
Jessy MARIGARD	22.10.1992	RFC Tournai (BEL)
Sloan PRIVAT	24.07.1989	Football Bourg-en-Bresse Péronnas 01 (FRA)
National coaches		
Thierry Albert DE NEEF (France)		27.10.1966

GRENADA

The Country:	The FA:
Grenada	Grenada Football Association
Capital: St. George's	Deco Building, P.O. Box 326 ST.,
Surface: 344 km²	St. George's
Population: 111,454 [2018]	Year of Formation: 1924
Time: UTC-4	Member of FIFA since: 1978
Independent since: 1974	Member of CONCACAF since: 1969

NATIONAL TEAM RECORDS

First international match:	21.11.1965, Kingstown (VIN): Dominica - Grenada 2-0
Most international caps:	Cassim Dorsette Langaigne – 72 caps (2004-2016)
Most international goals:	Ricky Charles – 37 goals / 71 caps (1995-2011)

CONCACAF GOLD CUP	
1991	Did not enter
1993	Qualifiers
1996	Qualifiers
1998	Qualifiers
2000	Qualifiers
2002	Qualifiers
2003	Qualifiers
2005	Qualifiers
2007	Qualifiers
2009	Final Tournament (Group Stage)
2011	Final Tournament (Group Stage)
2013	Qualifiers
2015	Qualifiers
2017	Qualifiers
2019	Qualifiers
2021	Final Tournament (*to be played*)

FIFA WORLD CUP	
1930	-
1934	-
1938	-
1950	-
1954	-
1958	-
1962	-
1966	-
1970	-
1974	-
1978	-
1982	Qualifiers
1986	*Withdrew*
1990	Did not enter
1994	Did not enter
1998	Qualifiers
2002	Qualifiers
2006	Qualifiers
2010	Qualifiers
2014	Qualifiers
2018	Qualifiers

F.I.F.A. CONFEDERATIONS CUP 1992-2017

None

OLYMPIC FOOTBALL TOURNAMENTS 1908-2016						
1908	-	1948	-	1972	-	1996	-
1912	-	1952	-	1976	-	2000	-
1920	-	1956	-	1980	-	2004	Qualifiers
1924	-	1960	-	1984	-	2008	Qualifiers
1928	-	1964	-	1988	-	2012	Qualifiers
1936	-	1968	-	1992	-	2016	Did not enter

CCCF (Confederación Centroamericana y del Caribe de Fútbol) CHAMPIONSHIPS 1941-1961
None

CONCACAF CHAMPIONSHIPS 1963-1989
None

CONCACAF NATIONS LEAGUE	
2019-2020	League B (*promoted to League A*)

CARIBBEAN CHAMPIONSHIPS 1989-2017			
1989	Final Tournament - Runners-up	1999	Final Tournament - Group Stage
1991	Did not enter	2001	Qualifiers
1992	Qualifiers	2005	Qualifiers
1993	Qualifiers	2007	Qualifiers
1994	Qualifiers	2008	Final Tournament - Runners-up
1995	Qualifiers	2010	Final Tournament - 4th Place
1996	Qualifiers	2012	Qualifiers
1997	Final Tournament - 4th Place	2014	Qualifiers
1998	Qualifiers	2017	Qualifiers

GRENADIAN CLUB HONOURS IN CONCACAF CLUB COMPETITIONS:

CONCACAF Champions Cup / CONCACAF Champions League 1962-2020
None

CONCACAF League 2017-2020
None

Caribbean Club Championship 1997-2021
None

CONCACAF Cup Winners Cup 1991-1995*
None

Copa Interamericana 1968-1998*
None

defunct competitions

NATIONAL COMPETITIONS
TABLE OF HONOURS

The first championship was held in 1924, but winners are not known until 1975.

	CHAMPIONS	CUP WINNERS*
1975/1976	Queens Park Rangers FC 1969 River Road	-
1977	*Not known*	-
1978	*Not known*	-
1979	*Not known*	-
1980	*Not known*	-
1981	*Not known*	-
1982	Queens Park Rangers FC 1969 River Road	-
1983	*Not known*	-
1984	Queens Park Rangers FC 1969 River Road	-
1985	*Not known*	-
1986	Carenage SC	-
1987	*Not known*	-
1988	*Not known*	-
1989	*Not known*	-
1990	*Not known*	-
1991	*Not known*	-
1992	*Not known*	-
1993	*Not known*	-
1994	Queens Park Rangers FC 1969 River Road	-
1995	Queens Park Rangers FC 1969 River Road	-
1996	Queens Park Rangers FC 1969 River Road	-
1997	Seven Seas Rock City	-
1998	Fontenoy United FC	Queens Park Rangers FC 1969 River Road
1999	St. Andrews Football League Grenville	*Not known*
2000	Grenada Boys Secondary School St. George's	Carenage SC
2001	Grenada Boys Secondary School St. George's	Hurricanes SC Victoria
2002	Queens Park Rangers FC 1969 River Road	*Not known*
2003	Hurricanes SC Victoria	Hurricanes SC Victoria
2004	*Championship abandoned*	*Not known*
2005	ASOMS Paradise FC Grenville	St. John's Sports
2006	Hurricanes SC Victoria	Hurricanes SC Victoria
2007	ASOMS Paradise FC Grenville	Fontenoy United FC
2008	Hurricanes SC Victoria	*No competition*
2009	*Championship abandoned*	Paradise FC International Grenville
2010	*Championship abandoned*	Eagles Super Strikers FC
2011	Hard Rock FC Plains	Hurricanes SC Victoria
2012	Hard Rock FC Plains	Paradise FC International Grenville
2013	Hard Rock FC Plains	Hard Rock FC Plains
2014	ASOMS Paradise FC Grenville	Hurricanes SC Victoria
2015	Hurricanes SC Victoria	Paradise FC International Grenville
2016	*Championship abandoned*	Paradise FC International Grenville
2017	*No competition*	Hurricanes SC Victoria
2017/2018	Hurricanes SC Victoria	*No competition*
2018/2019	Paradise FC International Grenville	Hard Rock FC Plains
2019/2020	*Championship abandoned*	FC Camerhogne (2019)
2020/2021	*No competition*	*No competition*

*called GFA Cup (1998-2007), Waggy T Super Knockout Cup (2009-2019).

2020	GFA CLUB CHAMPIONSHIP
	Hurricanes SC Victoria

NATIONAL CHAMPIONSHIP
Premier Division 2020/2021

No championship was played in 2020/2021.

GFA CLUB CHAMPIONSHIP
2020

This competition was played instead of regular league championship. Paradise FC International, last champions (2018/2019) refused to enter the competition.

Group Stage

Winner of each group were qualified for the Knock-out Stage.

Group A

1. Hurricanes SC Victoria	3	3	0	0	14 - 1	9
2. Queens Park Rangers FC 1969 River Road	3	2	0	1	14 - 7	6
3. St. Andrew's Football League	3	1	0	2	7 - 10	3
4. Tempe All Blacks	3	0	0	3	0 - 17	0

Group B

1. Grenada Boys Secondary School St. George's	3	2	1	0	13 - 2	7
2. FC Camerhogne	3	2	1	0	8 - 2	7
3. Sunjets United FC	2	0	0	2	1 - 7	0
4. Five Stars FC	2	0	0	2	1 - 12	0

Group C

1. Fontenoy United FC	3	3	0	0	9 - 2	9
2. Combined Northerners	3	2	0	1	13 - 3	6
3. Morne Jaloux SC	3	1	0	2	4 - 12	3
4. Mount Rich SC	3	0	0	3	1 - 10	0

Group D

1. Shamrock FC	2	2	0	0	10 - 2	6
2. Springs SC	2	1	0	1	4 - 8	3
3. Royal Grenada Police Force SC	2	0	0	2	1 - 5	0
4. Paradise FC International Grenville (*withdrew*)						

Group E

1. SAB Spartans SC	3	2	1	0	12 - 6	7
2. Happy Hill SC	3	2	0	1	10 - 7	6
3. Honved FC	3	1	0	2	11 - 10	3
4. St. David's FC	3	0	1	2	4 - 14	1

Group F

1. Eagles Super Strikers FC	3	3	0	0	14	-	7	9
2. Grenada U17	2	1	0	1	4	-	2	3
3. North Stars FC	3	1	0	2	4	-	7	3
4. Carenage SC	2	0	0	2	4	-	10	0

Group G

1. Hard Rock FC Plains	2	2	0	0	4	-	0	6
2. Grenada U20 Young Gunners	2	1	0	1	2	-	2	3
3. Christian Strikers SC	2	0	0	2	1	-	5	0

Group H

1. St. John's SC	3	3	0	0	28	-	2	9
2. Chantimelle FC	3	2	0	1	11	-	3	6
3. Mt. Horne FC	2	0	0	2	1	-	8	0
4. Bellevue Rangers FC	2	0	0	2	0	-	27	0

Knock-out Stage

Quarter-Finals [14-29.02.2020]

Fontenoy United FC - Shamrock FC	2-1	2-2
Hard Rock FC Plains - St. John's SC	1-1	3-2
Grenada Boys Secondary School St. George's - SAB Spartans SC	2-1	0-6
Hurricanes SC Victoria - Eagles Super Strikers FC	1-1	5-2

Semi-Finals [15-23.08.2020]

Hurricanes SC Victoria - Hard Rock FC Plains	3-1	4-4
Fontenoy United FC - SAB Spartans SC	4-3	3-3

Third Place Play-off [29.08.2020]

Hard Rock FC Plains - SAB Spartans SC	4-1

Final

29.08.2020, Kirani James Athletics Stadium, St. George's
Hurricanes SC Victoria - Fontenoy United FC — 3-1

2020 GFA Club Champions: **Hurricanes SC Victoria**

NATIONAL TEAM
INTERNATIONAL MATCHES 2020/2021

25.03.2021	San Salvador	El Salvador - Grenada	2-0(1-0)	(WCQ)
30.03.2021	St. George's	Grenada - U.S. Virgin Islands	1-0(1-0)	(WCQ)
04.06.2021	North Sound	Antigua and Barbuda - Grenada	1-0(1-0)	(WCQ)
08.06.2021	St. George's	Grenada - Montserrat	1-2(0-0)	(WCQ)

25.03.2021, 22nd FIFA World Cup Qualifiers, CONCACAF First Round
Estadio Cuscatlán, San Salvador
Referee: Kimbell Ward (Saint Kitts and Nevis)
EL SALVADOR - GRENADA   **2-0(1-0)**
GRN: Jason Kendell Belfon, Arthur Paterson, Kraig Nathaniel Noel-McLeod (75.Josh Patrick Gabriel), Tyrone Sterling, Moron Kemoni Phillip, Alexander Luke McQueen, Kwazim Jude Keron Theodore, Antonio Timothy German (72.Jamal Ray Charles), Ricky Steve Modeste (75.Saydrel Jude Lewis), Kharlton Belmar (65.Shavon Owner John-Brown), Kairo Ellis Mitchell. Trainer: Michael George Findlay (Canada).

30.03.2021, 22nd FIFA World Cup Qualifiers, CONCACAF First Round
"Kirani James" Athletic Stadium, St. George's
Referee: Sherwin Johnson (Guyana)
GRENADA - U.S. VIRGIN ISLANDS   **1-0(1-0)**
GRN: Jason Kendell Belfon, Arthur Paterson, Moron Kemoni Phillip (81.Steffon Abraham), Kwazim Jude Keron Theodore, Romar Frank, Irvine Smith, Josh Patrick Gabriel, Shavon Owner John-Brown, Kharlton Belmar (71.Joshua Otiamba Zion Isaac), Saydrel Jude Lewis (46.Leon Braveboy), Benjamin Ettienne (71.Chad Mark). Trainer: Michael George Findlay (Canada).
Goal: Saydrel Jude Lewis (33).

04.06.2021, 22nd FIFA World Cup Qualifiers, CONCACAF First Round
"Sir Vivian Richards" Stadium, North Sound
Referee: Francia María González Martínez (Mexico)
ANTIGUA AND BARBUDA - GRENADA   **1-0(1-0)**
GRN: Reice Jordan Charles-Cook, Aaron Jordan Pierre, Arthur Paterson, Tyrone Sterling, Kraig Nathaniel Noel-McLeod (85.Kwazim Jude Keron Theodore), Alexander Luke McQueen, Kwesi Paul, Antonio Timothy German (70.Dejon George Franklin Noel-Williams), Shavon Owner John-Brown, Kharlton Belmar (64.Ricardo de Niro German), Jamal Ray Charles (70.Kairo Ellis Mitchell). Trainer: Michael George Findlay (Canada).

08.06.2021, 22nd FIFA World Cup Qualifiers, CONCACAF First Round
"Kirani James" Athletic Stadium, St. George's; Attendance: 50
Referee: Adonai Escobedo González (Mexico)
GRENADA - MONTSERRAT   **1-2(0-0)**
GRN: Jason Kendell Belfon, Aaron Jordan Pierre, Arthur Paterson, Kwesi Paul, Tyrone Sterling, Kwazim Jude Keron Theodore (70.Steffon Adam Abraham), Romar Frank (46.Shavon Owner John-Brown), Ricardo de Niro German (57.Kairo Ellis Mitchell), Saydrel Jude Lewis (70.Kharlton Belmar), Dejon George Franklin Noel-Williams (57.Jamal Ray Charles), Benjamin Ettienne. Trainer: Michael George Findlay (Canada).
Goal: Saydrel Jude Lewis (58).

NATIONAL TEAM PLAYERS
2020/2021

Name	DOB	Club
Goalkeepers		
Jason Kendell BELFON	03.07.1990	*Williams Connection FC (TRI)*
Reice Jordan CHARLES-COOK	08.04.1994	*Welling United FC (ENG)*
Defenders		
Kraig Nathaniel NOEL-McLEOD	11.12.1999	*Maldon & Tiptree FC (ENG)*
Kwesi PAUL	07.11.1994	*Peachtree City MOBA (USA)*
Arthur J. PATERSON	31.01.1996	*Charleston Battery (USA)*
Aaron Jordan PIERRE	17.02.1993	*Shrewsbury Town FC (ENG)*
Tyrone STERLING	08.10.1987	*Concord Rangers FC (ENG)*
Midfielders		
Steffon Adam ABRAHAM	29.12.1999	*Paradise FC International*
Leon BRAVEBOY	13.01.1999	*Hard Rock FC*
Jamal Ray CHARLES	24.11.1995	*CD Real Sociedad Tocoa (HON)*
Romar FRANK	28.09.1996	*FC Camerhogne*
Josh Patrick GABRIEL	30.11.1999	*Grenada Boys Secondary School St. George's*
Shavon Owner JOHN-BROWN	13.04.1995	*New York Cosmos (USA)*
Chad MARK	07.12.1995	*Hard Rock FC*
Alexander Luke McQUEEN	24.03.1995	*Barnet FC (ENG)*
Moron Kemoni PHILLIP	19.03.1992	*Hurricanes SC Victoria*
Irvine SMITH	17.07.1989	*Paradise FC International*
Kwazim Jude Keron THEODORE	12.01.1996	*St. David's FC*
Forwards		
Kharlton BELMAR	01.12.1992	*Sacramento Republic (USA)*
Benjamin ETTIENNE	13.03.2003	*St. George Royal Cannons*
Antonio Timothy GERMAN	26.12.1991	*Persatuan Bola Sepak Polis Di-Raja Kuala Lumpur (MAS)*
Ricardo de Niro GERMAN	13.01.1999	*Crawley Town FC (ENG)*
Joshua Otiamba Zion ISAAC	28.10.2000	*Paradise FC International*
Saydrel Jude LEWIS	17.11.1997	*Paradise FC International*
Kairo Ellis MITCHELL	21.10.1997	*Chesterfield FC (ENG)*
Ricky Steve MODESTE	20.02.1988	*Dartford FC (ENG)*
Dejon George Franklin NOEL-WILLIAMS	22.02.1999	*CD Guadalajara (ESP)*
National coaches		
Michael George FINDLAY (Canada) [from 21.01.2021]		06.11.1963

GUADELOUPE

The Country:	The FA:
Guadeloupe	Ligue Guadeloupéenne de Football
Capital: Basse-Terre (Prefecture)	Rue De La Ville d'Orly - Bergevin
Surface: 1,628 km²	97110 Pointe-a-Pitre
Population: 395,700	Year of Formation: 1961
Time: UTC-4	Member of FIFA since: *not affiliated*
Independent since: *overseas region of France*	Member of CONCACAF since: 1964

NATIONAL TEAM RECORDS

First international match: 1934: Martinique - Guadeloupe 6-0
Most international caps: Jean-Luc Lambourde – 60 caps (since 2002)
Most international goals: Dominique Mocka – 17 goals / 37 caps (2002-2012)

CONCACAF GOLD CUP		FIFA WORLD CUP	
1991	Qualifiers	1930	-
1993	Qualifiers	1934	-
1996	Qualifiers	1938	-
1998	Qualifiers	1950	-
2000	Qualifiers	1954	-
2002	Qualifiers	1958	-
2003	Qualifiers	1962	-
2005	Qualifiers	1966	-
2007	Final Tournament (Semi-Finals)	1970	-
2009	Final Tournament (Quarter-Finals)	1974	-
2011	Final Tournament (Group Stage)	1978	-
2013	Qualifiers	1982	-
2015	Qualifiers	1986	-
2017	Qualifiers	1990	-
2019	Qualifiers	1994	-
2021	Final Tournament (*to be played*)	1998	-
		2002	-
		2006	-
		2010	-
		2014	-
		2018	-

F.I.F.A. CONFEDERATIONS CUP 1992-2017

None

OLYMPIC FOOTBALL TOURNAMENTS 1900-2016
None

CCCF (Confederación Centroamericana y del Caribe de Fútbol) CHAMPIONSHIPS 1941-1961
None

CONCACAF CHAMPIONSHIPS 1963-1989
None

CONCACAF NATIONS LEAGUE	
2019-2020	League C (*promoted to League B*)

CARIBBEAN CHAMPIONSHIPS 1989-2017			
1989	Final Tournament - Group Stage	1999	Final Tournament - Group Stage
1991	Qualifiers	2001	Qualifiers
1992	Final Tournament - Group Stage	2005	Qualifiers
1993	Qualifiers	2007	Final Tournament - 4th Place
1994	Final Tournament - 3rd Place	2008	Final Tournament - 3rd Place
1995	Qualifiers	2010	Final Tournament - Runners-up
1996	Did not enter	2012	Qualifiers
1997	Did not enter	2014	Qualifiers
1998	Qualifiers	2017	Qualifiers

GUADELOUPEAN CLUB HONOURS IN CONCACAF CLUB COMPETITIONS:

CONCACAF Champions Cup / CONCACAF Champions League 1962-2020
None

CONCACAF League 2017-2020
None

Caribbean Club Championship 1997-2021
None

CONCACAF Cup Winners Cup 1991-1995*
None

Copa Interamericana 1968-1998*
None

*defunct competitions

NATIONAL COMPETITIONS
TABLE OF HONOURS

The first championship was held in 1936/1937, but winners are not known until 1939/1940.

	CHAMPIONS	CUP WINNERS
1939/1940	AS Redoutable	*Not known*
1940/1941	*Not known*	*No competition*
1941/1942	AS Redoutable	Racing Club de Basse-Terre
1942/1943	*No competition*	*Competition not finished*
1943/1944	*No competition*	*No competition*
1944/1945	*No competition*	*No competition*
1945/1946	*No competition*	La Gauloise de Basse-Terre
1946/1947	*No competition*	Cygne Noir Basse-Terre
1947/1948	*No competition*	CS Moulien Le Moule
1948/1949	*No competition*	*No competition*
1949/1950	*No competition*	Red Star (*city not known*)
1950/1951	*No competition*	Racing Club de Basse-Terre
1951/1952	*Not known*	Racing Club de Basse-Terre
1952/1953	*Not known*	*No competition*
1953/1954	Arsenal Petit-Bourg	CS Moulien Le Moule
1954/1955	*Not known*	ASG Juventus de Sainte-Anne
1955/1956	*Not known*	Red Star (*city not known*)
1956/1957	*Not known*	CS Capesterrien
1957/1958	*Not known*	ASG Juventus de Sainte-Anne
1958/1959	*Not known*	Racing Club de Basse-Terre
1959/1960	*Not known*	Red Star (*city not known*)
1960/1961	*Not known*	AS Redoutable
1961/1962	*Not known*	CS Capesterrien
1962/1963	Cygne Noir Basse-Terre	Solidarité Scolaire SC Pointe-à-Pitre
1963/1964	*Not known*	Juventa (*city not known*)
1964/1965	*Not known*	*No competition*
1965/1966	*Not known*	*No competition*
1966/1967	ASG Juventus de Sainte-Anne	*No competition*
1967/1968	Racing Club de Basse-Terre	Juventa (*city not known*)
1968/1969	ASG Juventus de Sainte-Anne	Juventa (*city not known*)
1969/1970	Red Star (*city not known*)	Port-Louis
1970/1971	La Gauloise de Basse-Terre	ASG Juventus de Sainte-Anne
1971/1972	Cygne Noir Basse-Terre	CS Moulien Le Moule
1972/1973	ASG Juventus de Sainte-Anne	Solidarité Scolaire SC Pointe-à-Pitre
1973/1974	ASG Juventus de Sainte-Anne	CS Moulien Le Moule
1974/1975	ASG Juventus de Sainte-Anne	ASG Juventus de Sainte-Anne
1975/1976	ASG Juventus de Sainte-Anne	ASG Juventus de Sainte-Anne
1976/1977	*Not known*	L'Étoile de Morne-à-l'Eau
1977/1978	La Gauloise de Basse-Terre	ASG Juventus de Sainte-Anne
1978/1979	ASG Juventus de Sainte-Anne	L'Étoile de Morne-à-l'Eau
1979/1980	L'Étoile de Morne-à-l'Eau	JSC Mgte
1980/1981	L'Étoile de Morne-à-l'Eau	Jeunesse Trois-Rivières
1981/1982	L'Étoile de Morne-à-l'Eau	CS Capesterrien
1982/1983	*Not known*	Cygne Noir Basse-Terre
1983/1984	JS Capesterre Marie Galante	L'Étoile de Morne-à-l'Eau
1984/1985	CS Moulien Le Moule	L'Étoile de Morne-à-l'Eau

1985/1986	*Not known*	Solidarité Scolaire SC Pointe-à-Pitre
1986/1987	*Not known*	Siroco Abymes
1987/1988	Solidarité Scolaire SC Pointe-à-Pitre*	US Baie-Mahault
1988/1989	Zénith Morne-à-l'Eau	Zénith Morne-à-l'Eau
1989/1990	Solidarité Scolaire SC Pointe-à-Pitre	*No competition*
1990/1991	Solidarité Scolaire SC Pointe-à-Pitre	Racing Club de Basse-Terre
1991/1992	Solidarité Scolaire SC Pointe-à-Pitre	Solidarité Scolaire SC Pointe-à-Pitre
1992/1993	Solidarité Scolaire SC Pointe-à-Pitre	Solidarité Scolaire SC Pointe-à-Pitre
1993/1994	Jeunesse Trois-Rivières	Arsenal Petit-Bourg
1994/1995	Arsenal Petit-Bourg	*No competition*
1995/1996	L'Étoile de Morne-à-l'Eau	*No competition*
1996/1997	L'Étoile de Morne-à-l'Eau	*No competition*
1997/1998	L'Étoile de Morne-à-l'Eau	*No competition*
1998/1999	Racing Club de Basse-Terre	AJCS Terre-de-Haut
1999/2000	ASG Juventus de Sainte-Anne	AS Le Gosier
2000/2001	L'Étoile de Morne-à-l'Eau	Racing Club de Basse-Terre
2001/2002	L'Étoile de Morne-à-l'Eau	L'Étoile de Morne-à-l'Eau
2002/2003	Phare du Petit-Canal	*No competition*
2003/2004	Racing Club de Basse-Terre	Racing Club de Basse-Terre
2004/2005	AS Le Gosier	Rapid Club Petit-Canal
2005/2006	JS Vieux-Habitants	Amical Club Capesterre-de-Marie-Galante
2006/2007	L'Étoile de Morne-à-l'Eau	La Gauloise de Basse-Terre
2007/2008	Evolucas du Lamentin Petit-Bourg	CS Moulien Le Moule
2008/2009	CS Moulien Le Moule	Racing Club de Basse-Terre
2009/2010	JS Vieux-Habitants	CS Moulien Le Moule
2010/2011	CS Moulien Le Moule	Red Star Baie-Mahault
2011/2012	AJSS Les Saintes	USR Sainte-Rose
2012/2013	CS Moulien Le Moule	CS Moulien Le Moule
2013/2014	CS Moulien Le Moule	CS Moulien Le Moule
2014/2015	CS Moulien Le Moule	L'Étoile de Morne-à-l'Eau
2015/2016	USR Sainte-Rose	USC de Bananier
2016/2017	USR Sainte-Rose	CS Moulien Le Moule
2017/2018	CS Moulien Le Moule	L'Étoile de Morne-à-l'Eau
2018/2019	Amical Club Grand-Bourg de Marie Galante	US Baie-Mahaultienne
2019/2020	AS Le Gosier	CS Moulien Le Moule
2020/2021	*Championship suspended*	*Competition abandoned*

*moved later to Baie-Mahault.

NATIONAL CHAMPIONSHIP
Division d'Honneur 2020/2021

Please note: the point system in Guadeloupe is 4 points for a win, 2 points for a draw and 1 point for a loss.

Regular Stage

Groupe A

#	Team	P	W	D	L	GF	-	GA	Pts
1.	AS Le Gosier	16	12	4	0	38	-	14	56
2.	CS Moulien Le Moule	16	10	3	3	33	-	11	49
3.	Solidarité-Scolaire Baie-Mahault	16	8	3	5	27	-	22	43
4.	ASC Juventus de Sainte-Anne	16	7	4	5	19	-	16	41
5.	La Gauloise de Basse-Terre	16	6	4	6	15	-	18	38
6.	Stade Lamentinois	16	5	2	9	20	-	36	33
7.	Arsenal Club de Petit-Bourg	16	4	4	8	20	-	19	32
8.	Amical Club Grand-Bourg de Marie Galante	16	2	5	9	7	-	18	27
9.	CS Saint-François	16	2	3	11	15	-	40	25

Groupe B

#	Team	P	W	D	L	GF	-	GA	Pts
1.	ANJE Jeunesse Évolution Les Abymes	16	8	8	0	25	-	10	48
2.	Phare du Petit-Canal	16	9	5	2	25	-	11	48
3.	ASC Red Star Point-à-Pitre	16	8	2	6	27	-	21	42
4.	US Sainte-Rose	16	8	1	7	23	-	28	41
5.	US Baie-Mahaultienne	16	5	6	5	35	-	28	37
6.	JS Vieux Habitants	16	5	3	8	24	-	29	34
7.	AS Dynamo Le Moule	16	3	5	8	19	-	26	30
8.	AS Racing Club de Basse-Terre	16	3	6	7	18	-	26	30
9.	Centre Elite des Régions Françaises d'Amerique	16	3	4	9	24	-	41	29

Top-4 teams of each group were qualified for the Championship Round, while teams ranked 5-9 were qualified for the Relegation Round.

Both Relegation & Championship Round started on 27.03.2021, but only 2 Round were played and the championship was suspended due to COVID-19 pandemic.

NATIONAL CUP
Coupe de Guadeloupe Final 2020/2021

Competition abandoned due to Covid-19 pandemic.

THE CLUBS

AMICAL CLUB GRAND-BOURG DE MARIE GALANTE
Stadium: Stade „José Bade", Capesterre-de-Marie-Galante (1,500)

ARSENAL CLUB DE PETIT-BOURG
Stadium: Stade "Jean Naffer", Petit-Bourg (1,500)

ASOCCIATION NOUVELLE JEUNESSE ÉVOLUTION LES ABYMES
Stadium: Stade "René Serge Nabajoth", Les Abymes (7,500)

ASSOCIATION SPORTIVE DYNAMO LE MOULE
Stadium: Stade „Jacques Pontrémy", Le Moule (3,000)

ASSOCIATION SPORTIVE LE GOSSIER
Stadium: Stade Valette, Sainte-Anne (1,000)

CLUB SPORT SAINT-FRANÇOIS
Stadium: Stade "François-Xavier Durimel", Saint-François (1,000)

CLUB SPORTIF MOULIEN
Year of Formation: 1931
Stadium: Stade „Jacques Pontrémy", Le Moule (3,000)

JEUNESSE SPORTIVE DE VIEUX-HABITANTS
Stadium: Stade Municipal, Vieux-Habitants (5,000)

PHARE DU PETIT-CANAL
Stadium: Stade „Jacques Pontrémy", Le Moule (3,000)

SOLIDARITÉ-SCOLAIRE BAIE-MAHAULT
Stadium: Stade "Fiesque Duchesne", Baie-Mahault (5,000)

STADE LAMENTINOIS
Stadium: Stade "Germain Barbier", Lamentin (1,500)

UNION SPORTIVE BAIE-MAHAULTIENNE
Stadium: Stade "Fiesque Duchesne", Baie-Mahault (5,000)

UNION SPORTIVE SAINTE ROSE
Stadium: Stade de Desdonnes, Sainte-Rose (1,500)

NATIONAL TEAM
INTERNATIONAL MATCHES 2020/2021

23.06.2021	Fort-de-France	*Martinique - Guadeloupe*	*1-2(0-2)*	*(F)*
02.07.2021	Fort Lauderdale	*Guadeloupe - Bahamas*	*2-0(0-0)*	*(GCQ)*
06.07.2021	Fort Lauderdale	*Guatemala - Guadeloupe*	*1-1; 9-10 pen*	*(GCQ)*

23.06.2021, Friendly International
Stade Municipal "Pierre-Aliker", Fort-de-France; Attendance: 0
Referee: Nicolas Wassouf (Martinique)
MARTINIQUE - GUADELOUPE   **1-2(0-2)**
GPE: Yohan George Thuram-Ulien, Kelly Marvin Irep, Anthony Baron, Ronan Hauterville, Steve Solvet (87.Kévin Moeson), Mickaël David Alphonse (68.Dimitri Ramothe), Dimitri Kévin Cavaré, Morgan Michel Saint-Maximin (77.Kévin Edwing Malpon), Mavrick Annerose (83.Quentin Annette), Raphaël Sylvain Mirval (68.Luther Archimède), Matthias Jean Phaeton (76.Vikash Oyane Tillé). Trainer: Jocelyn Gaétan Angloma (France).
Goals: Ronan Hauterville (5), Steve Solvet (23).

02.07.2021, 16th CONCACAF Gold Cup Qualifiers, First Round
DRV PNK Stadium, Fort Lauderdale (United States); Attendance: 0
Referee: Reon Radix (Grenada)
GUADELOUPE - BAHAMAS   **2-0(0-0)**
GPE: Yohan George Thuram-Ulien, Anthony Baron, Mickaël David Alphonse (87.Kévin Moeson), Kelly Marvin Irep (59.Thomas Sébastien Pineau), Ronan Hauterville, Steve Solvet, Dimitri Kévin Cavaré, Morgan Michel Saint-Maximin (70.Kévin Edwing Malpon), Raphaël Sylvain Mirval (70.Luther Archimède), Matthias Jean Phaeton, Mavrick Annerose (86.Vikash Oyane Tillé). Trainer: Jocelyn Gaétan Angloma (France).
Goals: Matthias Jean Phaeton (61), Raphaël Sylvain Mirval (67).

06.07.2021, 16th CONCACAF Gold Cup Qualifiers, Second Round
DRV PNK Stadium, Fort Lauderdale (United States); Attendance: 0
Referee: Fernando Hernández Gómez (Mexico)
GUATEMALA - GUADELOUPE   **1-1(1-1,1-1); 9-10 on penalties**
GPE: Yohan George Thuram-Ulien, Anthony Baron, Mickaël David Alphonse, Kelly Marvin Irep (60.Thomas Sébastien Pineau), Steve Solvet, Ronan Hauterville, Dimitri Kévin Cavaré, Kévin Edwing Malpon (78.Quentin Annette), Morgan Michel Saint-Maximin (90.Kévin Moeson), Raphaël Sylvain Mirval (79.Mavrick Annerose), Matthias Jean Phaeton. Trainer: Jocelyn Gaétan Angloma (France).
Goal: Matthias Jean Phaeton (6).
Penalties: Dimitri Kévin Cavaré, Matthias Jean Phaeton, Anthony Baron (missed), Mavrick Annerose, Steve Solvet, Quentin Annette, Thomas Sébastien Pineau, Ronan Hauterville, Kévin Moeson, Mickaël David Alphonse (saved), Yohan George Thuram-Ulien, Dimitri Kévin Cavaré.

NATIONAL TEAM PLAYERS 2020/2021

Name	DOB	Club
Goalkeepers		
Yohan George THURAM-ULIEN	31.10.1988	*Amiens SC (FRA)*
Defenders		
Mickaël David ALPHONSE	12.07.1989	*Amiens SC (FRA)*
Anthony BARON	29.12.1992	*Stade Nyonnais (SUI)*
Dimitri Kévin CAVARÉ	05.02.1995	*FC Sion (SUI)*
Ronan HAUTERVILLE	21.11.1989	*Phare du Petit-Canal*
Kelly Marvin IREP	01.09.1995	*Enosis Neon Paralimni FC (CYP)*
Kévin MOESON	30.09.1997	*Solidarité-Scolaire Baie-Mahault*
Thomas Sébastien PINEAU	31.01.1991	*Solidarité-Scolaire Baie-Mahault*
Steve SOLVET	20.03.1996	*FC Sète (FRA)*
Midfielders		
Mavrick ANNEROSE	29.11.1995	*USR Sainte-Rose*
Quentin ANNETTE	13.01.1998	*Club Franciscain Le François (MTQ)*
Kévin Edwing MALPON	01.03.1996	*AS Le Gosier*
Dimitri RAMOTHE	08.09.1990	*Amical Club Grand-Bourg de Marie Galante*
Morgan Michel SAINT-MAXIMIN	02.08.1997	*Solidarité-Scolaire Baie-Mahault*
Vikash Oyane TILLE	26.11.1997	*CS Moulien Le Moule*
Forwards		
Luther ARCHIMÈDE	07.09.1999	*New York Red Bulls II (USA)*
Raphaël Sylvain MIRVAL	04.05.1996	*US Baie-Mahaultienne*
Matthias Jean PHAETON	08.01.2000	*En Avant Guingamp (FRA)*
National coaches		
Jocelyn Gaétan ANGLOMA (France) [from 28.12.2017]		07.08.1965

GUATEMALA

The Country:	The FA:
República de Guatemala (Republic of Guatemala) Capital: Ciudad de Guatemala Surface: 108,890 km² Population: 17,263,239 [2018] Time: UTC-6 Independent since: 1821	Federación Nacional de Fútbol de Guatemala 2a Calle 15-57, Zona 15 Boulevard Vista Hermosa, Ciudad Guatemala 01015 Year of Formation: 1919 Member of FIFA since: 1946 Member of CONCACAF since: 1961

NATIONAL TEAM RECORDS

First international match: 14.09.1921, Ciudad de Guatemala: Guatemala - Honduras 10-1
Most international caps: Carlos Humberto Ruíz Gutiérrez – 133 caps (1998-2016)
Most international goals: Carlos Humberto Ruíz Gutiérrez – 68 goals / 133 caps (1998-2016)

CONCACAF GOLD CUP	
1991	Final Tournament (Group Stage)
1993	Did not enter
1996	Final Tournament (4th Place)
1998	Final Tournament (Group Stage)
2000	Final Tournament (Group Stage)
2002	Final Tournament (Group Stage)
2003	Final Tournament (Group Stage)
2005	Final Tournament (Group Stage)
2007	Final Tournament (Quarter-Finals)
2009	Qualifiers
2011	Final Tournament (Quarter-Finals)
2013	Qualifiers
2015	Final Tournament (Group Stage)
2017	*Disqualified due to FIFA suspension*
2019	*Disqualified due to FIFA suspension*
2021	Qualifiers

FIFA WORLD CUP	
1930	-
1934	-
1938	-
1950	Did not enter
1954	Did not enter
1958	Qualifiers
1962	Qualifiers
1966	Did not enter
1970	Qualifiers
1974	Qualifiers
1978	Qualifiers
1982	Qualifiers
1986	Qualifiers
1990	Qualifiers
1994	Qualifiers
1998	Qualifiers
2002	Qualifiers
2006	Qualifiers
2010	Qualifiers
2014	Qualifiers
2018	*Disqualified due to FIFA suspension*

F.I.F.A. CONFEDERATIONS CUP 1992-2017

None

OLYMPIC FOOTBALL TOURNAMENTS 1908-2016

1908	-	1948	-	1972	Qualifiers	1996	Qualifiers
1912	-	1952	-	1976	FT/Group Stage	2000	Qualifiers
1920	-	1956	-	1980	Qualifiers	2004	Qualifiers
1924	-	1960	-	1984	Qualifiers	2008	Qualifiers
1928	-	1964	-	1988	FT/Group Stage	2012	Qualifiers
1936	-	1968	Quarter-Finals	1992	Qualifiers	2016	Qualifiers

CCCF (Confederación Centroamericana y del Caribe de Fútbol) CHAMPIONSHIPS 1941-1961
1943-1946-1948 (Runners-up), 1953 (3rd Place), 1955, 1961 (3rd Place)

CONCACAF CHAMPIONSHIPS 1963-1989
1963, 1965 (Runners-up), **1967 (Winners)**, 1969 (Runners-up), 1971, 1973, 1977, 1985, 1989

COPA AMÉRICA (invited as guests)
2016

CONCACAF NATIONS LEAGUE
2019-2020	League C (*promoted to League B*)

COPA CENTROAMERICANA (UNCAF NATIONS CHAMPIONSHIPS) 1991-2017

1991	Final Round - 3rd Place	2005	Final Round - 3rd Place
1993	Did not enter	2007	Final Round - 3rd Place
1995	Final Round - Runners-up	2009	Final Round - Group Stage
1997	Final Round - Runners-up	2011	Final Round - Group Stage
1999	Final Round - Runners-up	2013	Final Round - Group Stage
2001	**Final Round - Winners**	2014	Final Round - Runners-up
2003	Final Round - Runners-up	2017	Disqualified due to suspension

GUATEMALAN CLUB HONOURS IN CONCACAF CLUB COMPETITIONS:

CONCACAF Champions Cup / CONCACAF Champions League 1962-2020		
CSD Municipal Ciudad de Guatemala	1	1974
Comunicaciones FC Ciudad de Guatemala	1	1978

CONCACAF League 2017-2020
None

Caribbean Club Championship 1997-2021
None

CONCACAF Cup Winners Cup 1991-1995*
None

Copa Interamericana 1968-1998*
None

*defunct competitions

NATIONAL COMPETITIONS
TABLE OF HONOURS

	CHAMPIONS
	ERA AMATEUR
1919	Allies
1920	Hércules
1921	*No competition*
1922	Allies
1923	La Joya
1924	Escuela de Medicina[1]
1925	La Joya
1926	Escuela de Medicina
1927	Hércules
1928	Escuela de Medicina
1929	Escuela de Medicina
1930	Escuela de Medicina
1931	Escuela de Medicina
1932	Guatemala FC
1933	Escuela Politécnica
1934	Escuela Politécnica
1935	Cibeles
1936	Cibeles
1937	Quetzal
1938	CF Tipografía Nacional Ciudad de Guatemala
1939	CF Tipografía Nacional Ciudad de Guatemala
1940	CF Tipografía Nacional Ciudad de Guatemala
1941	Guatemala FC
	ERA PROFESIONAL
1942/1943	CSD Municipal Ciudad de Guatemala
1943	CF Tipografía Nacional Ciudad de Guatemala
1944/1945	CF Tipografía Nacional Ciudad de Guatemala
1947	CSD Municipal Ciudad de Guatemala
1950/1951	CSD Municipal Ciudad de Guatemala
1952/1953	CF Tipografía Nacional Ciudad de Guatemala
1954/1955	CSD Municipal Ciudad de Guatemala
1956	CSD Comunicaciones Ciudad de Guatemala
1957/1958	CSD Comunicaciones Ciudad de Guatemala
1959/1960	CSD Comunicaciones Ciudad de Guatemala
1961/1962	CSD Xelajú Mario Camposeco
1963/1964	CSD Municipal Ciudad de Guatemala
1964	Aurora FC Ciudad de Guatemala
1965/1966	CSD Municipal Ciudad de Guatemala
1966	Aurora FC Ciudad de Guatemala
1967/1968	Aurora FC Ciudad de Guatemala
1968/1969	CSD Comunicaciones Ciudad de Guatemala
1969/1970	CSD Municipal Ciudad de Guatemala
1970/1971	CSD Comunicaciones Ciudad de Guatemala
1971	CSD Comunicaciones Ciudad de Guatemala
1972	CSD Comunicaciones Ciudad de Guatemala
1973	CSD Municipal Ciudad de Guatemala

Año		Campeón
1974		CSD Municipal Ciudad de Guatemala
1975		Aurora FC Ciudad de Guatemala
1976		CSD Municipal Ciudad de Guatemala
1977		CSD Comunicaciones Ciudad de Guatemala
1978		Aurora FC Ciudad de Guatemala
1979/1980		CSD Comunicaciones Ciudad de Guatemala
1980		CSD Xelajú Mario Camposeco
1981		CSD Comunicaciones Ciudad de Guatemala
1982		CSD Comunicaciones Ciudad de Guatemala
1983		CSD Suchitepéquez
1984		Aurora FC Ciudad de Guatemala
1985/1986		CSD Comunicaciones Ciudad de Guatemala
1986		Aurora FC Ciudad de Guatemala
1987		CSD Municipal Ciudad de Guatemala
1988/1989		CSD Municipal Ciudad de Guatemala
1989/1990		CSD Municipal Ciudad de Guatemala
1990/1991		CSD Comunicaciones Ciudad de Guatemala
1991/1992		CSD Municipal Ciudad de Guatemala
1992/1993		Aurora FC Ciudad de Guatemala
1993/1994		CSD Municipal Ciudad de Guatemala
1994/1995		CSD Comunicaciones Ciudad de Guatemala
1995/1996		CSD Xelajú Mario Camposeco
1996/1997		CSD Comunicaciones Ciudad de Guatemala
1997/1998		CSD Comunicaciones Ciudad de Guatemala
1998/1999		CSD Comunicaciones Ciudad de Guatemala
1999/2000	Ape:	CSD Comunicaciones Ciudad de Guatemala
	Cla:	CSD Municipal Ciudad de Guatemala
2000/2001	Ape:	CSD Municipal Ciudad de Guatemala
	Cla:	CSD Comunicaciones Ciudad de Guatemala
2001/2002	Ape:	CSD Municipal Ciudad de Guatemala
	Cla:	CSD Municipal Ciudad de Guatemala
2002/2003	Ape:	CSD Comunicaciones Ciudad de Guatemala
	Cla:	CSD Comunicaciones Ciudad de Guatemala
2003/2004	Ape:	CSD Municipal Ciudad de Guatemala
	Cla:	CSD Cobán Imperial
2004/2005	Ape:	CSD Municipal Ciudad de Guatemala
	Cla:	CSD Municipal Ciudad de Guatemala
2005/2006	Ape:	CSD Municipal Ciudad de Guatemala
	Cla:	CSD Municipal Ciudad de Guatemala
2006/2007	Ape:	CSD Municipal Ciudad de Guatemala
	Cla:	CSD Xelajú Mario Camposeco
2007/2008	Ape:	CSD Jalapa FC
	Cla:	CSD Municipal Ciudad de Guatemala
2008/2009	Ape:	CSD Comunicaciones Ciudad de Guatemala
	Cla:	CSD Jalapa FC
2009/2010	Ape:	CSD Municipal Ciudad de Guatemala
	Cla:	CSD Municipal Ciudad de Guatemala
2010/2011	Ape:	CSD Comunicaciones Ciudad de Guatemala
	Cla:	CSD Comunicaciones Ciudad de Guatemala
2011/2012	Ape:	CSD Municipal Ciudad de Guatemala
	Cla:	CSD Xelajú Mario Camposeco
2012/2013	Ape:	CSD Comunicaciones Ciudad de Guatemala

	Cla:	CSD Comunicaciones Ciudad de Guatemala
2013/2014	Ape:	CSD Comunicaciones Ciudad de Guatemala
	Cla:	CSD Comunicaciones Ciudad de Guatemala
2014/2015	Ape:	CSD Comunicaciones Ciudad de Guatemala
	Cla:	CSD Comunicaciones Ciudad de Guatemala
2015/2016	Ape:	Antigua Guatemala FC
	Cla:	CSD Suchitepéquez
2016/2017	Ape:	Antigua Guatemala FC
	Cla:	CSD Municipal Ciudad de Guatemala
2017/2018	Ape:	Antigua Guatemala FC
	Cla:	CD Guastatoya
2018/2019	Ape:	CD Guastatoya
	Cla:	Antigua Guatemala FC
2019/2020	Ape:	CSD Municipal Ciudad de Guatemala
	Cla:	*Championship cancelled due to Covid-19 pandemic*
2020/2021	Ape:	CD Guastatoya
	Cla:	FC Santa Lucía Cotzumalguapa

[1]became Universidad de San Carlos Club de Fútbol in 1956.

Copa de Guatemala winners:
1944: Hospicio; 1951/52: CSD Comunicaciones Ciudad de Guatemala; 1955: CSD Comunicaciones Ciudad de Guatemala; 1956/57: International Railways of Central America (IRCA); 1958/59: Aurora FC Ciudad de Guatemala; 1960: CSD Municipal Ciudad de Guatemala; 1967: CSD Municipal Ciudad de Guatemala; 1972/73: CSD Xelajú Mario Camposeco; 1983: CSD Comunicaciones Ciudad de Guatemala; 1984/85: Juventud Retalteca; 1985-1991: *No competition*; 1991/92: CSD Comunicaciones Ciudad de Guatemala; 1992/93: Aurora FC Ciudad de Guatemala; 1993/94: CSD Suchitepéquez; 1994/95: CSD Municipal Ciudad de Guatemala; 1995/96: CSD Municipal Ciudad de Guatemala; 1996/97: Deportivo Amatitlán; 1997/98: CSD Suchitepéquez; 1998/99: CSD Municipal Ciudad de Guatemala; 2002: CSD Jalapa FC; 2003: CSD Municipal Ciudad de Guatemala; 2003/04: CSD Municipal Ciudad de Guatemala; 2005: CSD Jalapa FC; 2006: CSD Jalapa FC; 2009: CSD Comunicaciones Ciudad de Guatemala; 2010: CSD Xelajú Mario Camposeco.

NATIONAL CHAMPIONSHIP
Liga Nacional de Fútbol de Guatemala 2020/2021

Torneo Apertura 2020

Group Stage - Results

Grupo A (Suroccidente)

29.08.2020	Comunicaciones FC	-	CSD Xelajú Mario Camposeco	4-2(2-0)
30.08.2020	CD Iztapa	-	CD Malacateco	3-1(2-1)
	FC Santa Lucía Cotzumalguapa	-	Antigua Guatemala FC	0-1(0-1)
05.09.2020	CSD Xelajú Mario Camposeco	-	CD Iztapa	2-1(0-0)
06.09.2020	CD Malacateco	-	FC Santa Lucía Cotzumalguapa	1-2(1-2)
	Antigua Guatemala FC	-	Comunicaciones FC	1-1(1-1)
12.09.2020	CD Iztapa	-	Comunicaciones FC	1-1(0-1)
13.09.2020	CD Malacateco	-	Antigua Guatemala FC	2-1(1-1)
	FC Santa Lucía Cotzumalguapa	-	CSD Xelajú Mario Camposeco	0-1(0-1)
19.09.2020	Comunicaciones FC	-	FC Santa Lucía Cotzumalguapa	2-0(2-0)
	CD Iztapa	-	Antigua Guatemala FC	1-1(0-0)
20.09.2020	CSD Xelajú Mario Camposeco	-	CD Malacateco	1-1(1-0)
26.09.2020	CD Malacateco	-	Comunicaciones FC	1-0(1-0)
	FC Santa Lucía Cotzumalguapa	-	CD Iztapa	2-0(1-0)
27.09.2020	Antigua Guatemala FC	-	CSD Xelajú Mario Camposeco	2-1(1-0)
04.10.2020	CD Malacateco	-	CD Iztapa	1-3(1-0)
11.10.2020	FC Santa Lucía Cotzumalguapa	-	CD Malacateco	0-1(0-0)
	CD Iztapa	-	CSD Xelajú Mario Camposeco	5-0(2-0)
12.10.2020	Comunicaciones FC	-	Antigua Guatemala FC	2-1(1-1)
16.10.2020	Antigua Guatemala FC	-	CD Malacateco	0-1(0-1)
17.10.2020	Comunicaciones FC	-	CD Iztapa	3-0(2-0)
18.10.2020	CSD Xelajú Mario Camposeco	-	FC Santa Lucía Cotzumalguapa	0-0
24.10.2020	CD Malacateco	-	CSD Xelajú Mario Camposeco	2-1(1-0)
25.10.2020	Antigua Guatemala FC	-	CD Iztapa	3-1(3-1)
26.10.2020	FC Santa Lucía Cotzumalguapa	-	Comunicaciones FC	0-0
29.10.2020	CSD Xelajú Mario Camposeco	-	Antigua Guatemala FC	1-0(1-0)
31.10.2020	Comunicaciones FC	-	CD Malacateco	0-0
	CD Iztapa	-	FC Santa Lucía Cotzumalguapa	1-1(1-1)
25.11.2020	CSD Xelajú Mario Camposeco	-	Comunicaciones FC	3-1(1-1)
02.12.2020	Antigua Guatemala FC	-	FC Santa Lucía Cotzumalguapa	3-2(2-1)

Grupo B (Nororiente)

29.08.2020	CSD Sacachispas Chiquimula	-	CD Achuapa El Progreso	1-3(0-2)
	CSD Cobán Imperial	-	CSD Municipal	1-1(0-1)
30.08.2020	CD Guastatoya	-	Sanarate FC	1-1(0-1)
05.09.2020	CD Achuapa El Progreso	-	CSD Cobán Imperial	1-2(1-2)
	CSD Municipal	-	CD Guastatoya	2-1(0-1)
06.09.2020	Sanarate FC	-	CSD Sacachispas Chiquimula	1-1(0-0)
12.09.2020	CSD Cobán Imperial	-	CSD Sacachispas Chiquimula	2-1(2-0)
	CSD Municipal	-	Sanarate FC	5-0(3-0)
13.09.2020	CD Guastatoya	-	CD Achuapa El Progreso	2-2(1-2)
19.09.2020	CSD Cobán Imperial	-	Sanarate FC	2-0(0-0)

20.09.2020	CD Achuapa El Progreso	- CSD Municipal	1-0(0-0)
	CSD Sacachispas Chiquimula	- CD Guastatoya	2-1(2-1)
27.09.2020	CSD Municipal	- CSD Sacachispas Chiquimula	3-0(1-0)
	Sanarate FC	- CD Achuapa El Progreso	2-2(1-0)
	CD Guastatoya	- CSD Cobán Imperial	1-1(0-1)
04.10.2020	CD Achuapa El Progreso	- CSD Sacachispas Chiquimula	1-1(1-0)
10.10.2020	CSD Cobán Imperial	- CD Achuapa El Progreso	0-0
	CSD Sacachispas Chiquimula	- Sanarate FC	1-1(1-0)
	CD Guastatoya	- CSD Municipal	0-0
14.10.2020	CSD Municipal	- CSD Cobán Imperial	0-3 *awarded*
	Sanarate FC	- CD Guastatoya	1-2(0-1)
17.10.2020	CSD Sacachispas Chiquimula	- CSD Cobán Imperial	3-3(1-0)
18.10.2020	CD Achuapa El Progreso	- CD Guastatoya	0-1(0-0)
	Sanarate FC	- CSD Municipal	0-1(0-1)
24.10.2020	Sanarate FC	- CSD Cobán Imperial	1-0(1-0)
	CSD Municipal	- CD Achuapa El Progreso	3-1(2-0)
25.10.2020	CD Guastatoya	- CSD Sacachispas Chiquimula	3-3(0-1)
30.10.2020	CSD Sacachispas Chiquimula	- CSD Municipal	1-3(1-0)
31.10.2020	CSD Cobán Imperial	- CD Guastatoya	3-1(2-0)
01.11.2020	CD Achuapa El Progreso	- Sanarate FC	2-3(1-3)

Interzone Stage - Results

07.11.2020	FC Santa Lucía Cotzumalguapa	- CD Guastatoya	0-0
08.11.2020	Antigua Guatemala FC	- Sanarate FC	3-3(2-1)
	CSD Xelajú Mario Camposeco	- CD Achuapa El Progreso	2-0(1-0)
09.11.2020	CD Malacateco	- CSD Municipal	1-1(0-1)
	Comunicaciones FC	- CSD Sacachispas Chiquimula	4-0(1-0)
14.11.2020	CSD Sacachispas Chiquimula	- CD Iztapa	3-3(1-2)
15.11.2020	CD Achuapa El Progreso	- CD Malacateco	2-1(0-1)
18.11.2020	CD Iztapa	- CSD Cobán Imperial	1-0(0-0)
	CD Guastatoya	- CSD Xelajú Mario Camposeco	2-0(2-0)
21.11.2020	CD Iztapa	- Sanarate FC	4-1(1-1)
	FC Santa Lucía Cotzumalguapa	- CSD Sacachispas Chiquimula	2-0(0-0)
	CSD Xelajú Mario Camposeco	- CSD Cobán Imperial	0-0
22.11.2020	Comunicaciones FC	- CSD Municipal	2-1(0-0)
	Antigua Guatemala FC	- CD Achuapa El Progreso	2-0(1-0)
	CD Malacateco	- CD Guastatoya	2-0(2-0)
25.11.2020	CSD Cobán Imperial	- FC Santa Lucía Cotzumalguapa	2-0(1-0)
	CSD Municipal	- Antigua Guatemala FC	4-0(2-0)
28.11.2020	CSD Cobán Imperial	- CD Malacateco	2-1(2-0)
	CSD Sacachispas Chiquimula	- CSD Xelajú Mario Camposeco	2-1(0-1)
29.11.2020	CSD Municipal	- CD Iztapa	6-0(1-0)
	CD Achuapa El Progreso	- Comunicaciones FC	0-1(0-0)
	CD Guastatoya	- Antigua Guatemala FC	2-2(0-0)
05.12.2020	CD Malacateco	- CSD Sacachispas Chiquimula	2-0(1-0)
	CD Iztapa	- CD Achuapa El Progreso	0-1(0-0)
06.12.2020	FC Santa Lucía Cotzumalguapa	- CSD Municipal	0-2(0-0)
	Antigua Guatemala FC	- CSD Cobán Imperial	0-1(0-0)
07.12.2020	Comunicaciones FC	- CD Guastatoya	0-0
09.12.2020	Sanarate FC	- FC Santa Lucía Cotzumalguapa	2-3(1-2)
23.12.2020	Sanarate FC	- Comunicaciones FC	0-3(0-2)
25.12.2020	CSD Xelajú Mario Camposeco	- Sanarate FC	2-1(0-1)

28.12.2020	CSD Municipal	-	CSD Xelajú Mario Camposeco	1-0(1-0)
	CD Achuapa El Progreso	-	FC Santa Lucía Cotzumalguapa	1-0(1-0)
	CD Guastatoya	-	CD Iztapa	2-0(2-0)
	CSD Cobán Imperial	-	Comunicaciones FC	0-1(0-1)
	CSD Sacachispas Chiquimula	-	Antigua Guatemala FC	1-1(1-1)
	Sanarate FC	-	CD Malacateco	2-1(0-0)

Final Standings

Grupo A

1.	Comunicaciones FC Ciudad de Guatemala	16	9	5	2	25	-	10	32
2.	CD Malacateco	16	7	3	6	19	-	18	24
3.	CSD Xelajú Mario Camposeco	16	6	3	7	17	-	22	21
4.	Antigua Guatemala FC	16	5	5	6	21	-	23	20
5.	CD Iztapa	16	5	4	7	24	-	28	19
6.	FC Santa Lucía Cotzumalguapa	16	4	4	8	12	-	17	16

Grupo B

1.	CSD Municipal Ciudad de Guatemala	16	10	3	3	33	-	11	33
2.	CSD Cobán Imperial	16	8	5	3	22	-	12	29
3.	CD Guastatoya	16	4	8	4	19	-	19	20
4.	CD Achuapa El Progreso	16	5	4	7	17	-	21	19
5.	Sanarate FC	16	3	5	8	19	-	33	14
6.	CSD Sacachispas Chiquimula	16	2	7	7	20	-	34	13

Aggregate table / Tabla acumulada

1.	CSD Municipal Ciudad de Guatemala	16	10	3	3	33	-	11	33
2.	Comunicaciones FC Ciudad de Guatemala	16	9	5	2	25	-	10	32
3.	CSD Cobán Imperial	16	8	5	3	22	-	12	29
4.	CD Malacateco	16	7	3	6	19	-	18	24
5.	CSD Xelajú Mario Camposeco	16	6	3	7	17	-	22	21
6.	CD Guastatoya	16	4	8	4	19	-	19	20
7.	Antigua Guatemala FC	16	5	5	6	21	-	23	20
8.	CD Iztapa	16	5	4	7	24	-	28	19
9.	CD Achuapa El Progreso	16	5	4	7	17	-	21	19
10.	FC Santa Lucía Cotzumalguapa	16	4	4	8	12	-	17	16
11.	Sanarate FC	16	3	5	8	19	-	33	14
12.	CSD Sacachispas Chiquimula	16	2	7	7	20	-	34	13

Top-8 were qualified for the Torneo Apertura Play-offs.

Quarter-Finals [31.12.2020-17.01.2021]		
CSD Xelajú Mario Camposeco - CD Malacateco	1-0(1-0)	2-0(1-0)
CD Guastatoya - CSD Cobán Imperial	0-0	2-1(0-0)
CD Iztapa - CSD Municipal Ciudad de Guatemala	1-3(0-1)	1-3(0-2)
Antigua Guatemala FC - Comunicaciones FC Ciudad de Guatemala	0-0	3-0(2-0)

Semi-Finals [28-31.01.2021]		
Antigua Guatemala FC - CSD Municipal Ciudad de Guatemala*	1-1(1-0)	1-1(1-0)
CD Guastatoya - CSD Xelajú Mario Camposeco	1-1(0-1)	2-0(1-0)

*qualified on better record in regular season.

Championship Finals

04.02.2021, Estadio "David Cordón Hichos", Guastatoya; Attendance: 0
Referee: Bryan López Castellanos
CD Guastatoya - CSD Municipal Ciudad de Guatemala   2-1(2-1)
CD Guastatoya: Adrián Isaac de Lemos Calderón, Rubén Darío Morales Pereira, Omar Domínguez Palafox, Wilson Augusto Pineda Cornelio, Cristian Armin Reyes Hernández, Maximiliano Lombardi Rodríguez, Néstor Jucup Escobar (68.José Alberto Márquez Árdon), José Alfredo Corena Barboza, Marvin José Ceballos Flores (77.Aarón Navarro Cespedes), Luis Fernando Martínez Castellanos (68.Anderson Edgar Ortíz Falla), Luis Ángel Landín Cortés (77.Jorge Estuardo Vargas García). Trainer: William Fernando Coito Olivera (Uruguay).
Municipal: Víctor Rafael García Muníz, Carlos Eduardo Gallardo Nájera, Luis Enrique de León Valenzuela (63.Frank Edison de León Reyna), Héctor Osberto Moreira Pérez, Carlos Fernando Alvarado López (29.Alejandro Matías Díaz), José Alfredo Morales Concua, José Mario Rosales Marroquín, Jaime Enrique Alas Morales, Janderson Kione Pereira Rodrigues (78.John Roberth Méndez Sánchez), José Carlos Martínez Navas, Ramiro Iván Rocca (78.Rudy Ronaldo Barrientos Reyes). Trainer: Sebastián Alejandro Bini (Argentina).
Goals: 1-0 José Alfredo Corena Barboza (3), 2-0 Luis Fernando Martínez Castellanos (14), 2-1 Ramiro Iván Rocca (19).

07.02.2021, Estadio "Manuel Felipe Carrera", Ciudad de Guatemala; Attendance: 0
Referee: Walter Alexander López Castellanos
CSD Municipal Ciudad de Guatemala - CD Guastatoya   1-1(1-1)
Municipal: Víctor Rafael García Muníz, Carlos Eduardo Gallardo Nájera, Héctor Osberto Moreira Pérez, José Alfredo Morales Concua (65.Rudy Ronaldo Barrientos Reyes), José Mario Rosales Marroquín (87.Manuel Estuardo López Rodas), Frank Edison de León Reyna (56.John Roberth Méndez Sánchez), Jaime Enrique Alas Morales, Janderson Kione Pereira Rodrigues (87.Carlos Fernando Alvarado López), José Carlos Martínez Navas, Alejandro Matías Díaz, Ramiro Iván Rocca. Trainer: Sebastián Alejandro Bini (Argentina).
CD Guastatoya: Adrián Isaac de Lemos Calderón, Rubén Darío Morales Pereira, Omar Domínguez Palafox, Wilson Augusto Pineda Cornelio, José Alfredo Corena Barboza, Néstor Jucup Escobar (46.José Alberto Márquez Árdon), Maximiliano Lombardi Rodríguez, Marvin José Ceballos Flores (60.Aarón Navarro Cespedes), Cristian Armin Reyes Hernández (34.Uzias Bernabé Hernández Farfán), Luis Fernando Martínez Castellanos (88.Fredy Gustavo Orellana García), Luis Ángel Landín Cortés (46.Jorge Estuardo Vargas García). Trainer: William Fernando Coito Olivera (Uruguay).
Goals: 0-1 Omar Domínguez Palafox (6), 1-1 Néstor Jucup Escobar (8).

Torneo Apertura 2020 Champions: **CD Guastatoya**

Best goalscorer Torneo Apertura 2020:
Ramiro Iván Rocca (ARG, CSD Municipal Ciudad de Guatemala) – 22 goals

Torneo Clausura 2021

Group Stage - Results

Grupo A (Suroccidente)

20.02.2021	CD Iztapa	- CD Malacateco	1-1(0-0)
21.02.2021	FC Santa Lucía Cotzumalguapa	- Antigua Guatemala FC	1-0(1-0)
	Comunicaciones FC	- CSD Xelajú Mario Camposeco	3-2(3-2)
27.02.2021	Antigua Guatemala FC	- Comunicaciones FC	1-2(1-1)
	CD Malacateco	- FC Santa Lucía Cotzumalguapa	0-0
28.02.2021	CSD Xelajú Mario Camposeco	- CD Iztapa	2-1(2-1)
03.03.2021	CD Iztapa	- Comunicaciones FC	3-3(2-2)
	CD Malacateco	- Antigua Guatemala FC	2-0(0-0)
	FC Santa Lucía Cotzumalguapa	- CSD Xelajú Mario Camposeco	0-0
06.03.2021	CD Iztapa	- Antigua Guatemala FC	5-2(3-1)
	Comunicaciones FC	- FC Santa Lucía Cotzumalguapa	3-1(3-1)
07.03.2021	CSD Xelajú Mario Camposeco	- CD Malacateco	0-0
10.03.2021	Antigua Guatemala FC	- CSD Xelajú Mario Camposeco	1-1(1-1)
	CD Malacateco	- Comunicaciones FC	0-3(0-3)
	FC Santa Lucía Cotzumalguapa	- CD Iztapa	3-1(3-1)
13.03.2021	CSD Xelajú Mario Camposeco	- Comunicaciones FC	0-1(0-0)
14.03.2021	CD Malacateco	- CD Iztapa	1-1(1-0)
	Antigua Guatemala FC	- FC Santa Lucía Cotzumalguapa	0-0
30.03.2021	CD Iztapa	- CSD Xelajú Mario Camposeco	1-0(1-0)
31.03.2021	FC Santa Lucía Cotzumalguapa	- CD Malacateco	1-0(0-0)
01.04.2021	Comunicaciones FC	- Antigua Guatemala FC	0-0
04.04.2021	Antigua Guatemala FC	- CD Malacateco	1-2(0-0)
	CSD Xelajú Mario Camposeco	- FC Santa Lucía Cotzumalguapa	0-1(0-0)
	Comunicaciones FC	- CD Iztapa	5-0(4-0)
07.04.2021	CD Malacateco	- CSD Xelajú Mario Camposeco	0-0
	Antigua Guatemala FC	- CD Iztapa	3-2(1-1)
	FC Santa Lucía Cotzumalguapa	- Comunicaciones FC	0-0
10.04.2021	CD Iztapa	- FC Santa Lucía Cotzumalguapa	2-0(2-0)
11.04.2021	CSD Xelajú Mario Camposeco	- Antigua Guatemala FC	3-0(3-0)
	Comunicaciones FC	- CD Malacateco	1-0(1-0)

Grupo B (Nororiente)

20.02.2021	CSD Sacachispas Chiquimula	- CD Achuapa El Progreso	1-0(1-0)
21.02.2021	CSD Cobán Imperial	- CSD Municipal	1-0(1-0)
	CD Guastatoya	- Sanarate FC	5-1(5-1)
27.02.2021	CSD Municipal	- CD Guastatoya	0-1(0-1)
28.02.2021	CD Achuapa El Progreso	- CSD Cobán Imperial	2-1(0-0)
	Sanarate FC	- CSD Sacachispas Chiquimula	0-0
03.03.2021	CSD Cobán Imperial	- CSD Sacachispas Chiquimula	2-2(0-2)
	CD Guastatoya	- CD Achuapa El Progreso	3-0(1-0)
	CSD Municipal	- Sanarate FC	3-1(1-1)
06.03.2021	CSD Cobán Imperial	- Sanarate FC	2-0(0-0)
	CSD Sacachispas Chiquimula	- CD Guastatoya	0-1(0-1)
07.03.2021	CD Achuapa El Progreso	- CSD Municipal	1-2(1-2)
10.03.2021	Sanarate FC	- CD Achuapa El Progreso	2-1(2-1)

	CD Guastatoya	- CSD Cobán Imperial	1-1(1-1)
	CSD Municipal	- CSD Sacachispas Chiquimula	1-2(1-2)
13.03.2021	CD Achuapa El Progreso	- CSD Sacachispas Chiquimula	2-1(1-1)
	CSD Municipal	- CSD Cobán Imperial	2-0(1-0)
14.03.2021	Sanarate FC	- CD Guastatoya	3-2(2-2)
31.03.2021	CSD Cobán Imperial	- CD Achuapa El Progreso	3-2(2-0)
	CSD Sacachispas Chiquimula	- Sanarate FC	2-1(0-1)
01.04.2021	CD Guastatoya	- CSD Municipal	0-0
	CSD Sacachispas Chiquimula	- CSD Cobán Imperial	1-2(1-0)
04.04.2021	CD Achuapa El Progreso	- CD Guastatoya	1-0(1-0)
	Sanarate FC	- CSD Municipal	2-1(1-1)
07.04.2021	Sanarate FC	- CSD Cobán Imperial	0-0
	CD Guastatoya	- CSD Sacachispas Chiquimula	3-0(1-0)
	CSD Municipal	- CD Achuapa El Progreso	3-0(2-0)
10.04.2021	CSD Cobán Imperial	- CD Guastatoya	0-1(0-1)
	CSD Sacachispas Chiquimula	- CSD Municipal	0-3(0-2)
11.04.2021	CD Achuapa El Progreso	- Sanarate FC	2-2(0-1)

Interzone Stage - Results

14.04.2021	CSD Cobán Imperial	- CD Iztapa	2-2(0-2)
	CD Achuapa El Progreso	- CSD Xelajú Mario Camposeco	1-1(1-0)
	Sanarate FC	- Antigua Guatemala FC	1-1(1-0)
	CD Guastatoya	- FC Santa Lucía Cotzumalguapa	1-1(0-0)
	CSD Municipal	- CD Malacateco	3-0(1-0)
	CSD Sacachispas Chiquimula	- Comunicaciones FC	1-0(0-0)
17.04.2021	CD Iztapa	- CSD Sacachispas Chiquimula	4-0(1-0)
	FC Santa Lucía Cotzumalguapa	- CSD Cobán Imperial	1-1(0-1)
	Comunicaciones FC	- Sanarate FC	3-0(1-0)
18.04.2021	Antigua Guatemala FC	- CSD Municipal	1-1(1-1)
	CD Malacateco	- CD Achuapa El Progreso	1-0(1-0)
	CSD Xelajú Mario Camposeco	- CD Guastatoya	1-1(1-0)
21.04.2021	CSD Cobán Imperial	- CSD Xelajú Mario Camposeco	0-0
	CD Achuapa El Progreso	- Antigua Guatemala FC	1-2(0-0)
	Sanarate FC	- CD Iztapa	1-1(1-0)
	CD Guastatoya	- CD Malacateco	0-0
	CSD Municipal	- Comunicaciones FC	0-1(0-0)
	CSD Sacachispas Chiquimula	- FC Santa Lucía Cotzumalguapa	1-2(1-0)
24.04.2021	CD Iztapa	- CSD Municipal	0-0
	FC Santa Lucía Cotzumalguapa	- Sanarate FC	1-0(1-0)
25.04.2021	Antigua Guatemala FC	- CD Guastatoya	0-0
	CD Malacateco	- CSD Cobán Imperial	0-0
	CSD Xelajú Mario Camposeco	- CSD Sacachispas Chiquimula	3-1(0-1)
	Comunicaciones FC	- CD Achuapa El Progreso	2-1(0-1)
28.04.2021	Sanarate FC	- CSD Xelajú Mario Camposeco	1-1(1-0)
	CD Achuapa El Progreso	- CD Iztapa	0-3(0-0)
	CSD Cobán Imperial	- Antigua Guatemala FC	4-2(1-0)
	CD Guastatoya	- Comunicaciones FC	2-0(1-0)
	CSD Municipal	- FC Santa Lucía Cotzumalguapa	2-1(0-1)
	CSD Sacachispas Chiquimula	- CD Malacateco	2-1(2-1)
02.05.2021	Antigua Guatemala FC	- CSD Sacachispas Chiquimula	1-1(0-0)
	Comunicaciones FC	- CSD Cobán Imperial	1-1(0-0)
	CD Iztapa	- CD Guastatoya	2-2(1-1)
	CD Malacateco	- Sanarate FC	0-1(0-1)

FC Santa Lucía Cotzumalguapa	-	CD Achuapa El Progreso			0-2(0-0)
CSD Xelajú Mario Camposeco	-	CSD Municipal			0-3(0-1)

Final Standings

Grupo A

1. Comunicaciones FC Ciudad de Guatemala	16	10	4	2	28	-	12	34
2. FC Santa Lucía Cotzumalguapa	16	6	6	4	13	-	13	24
3. CD Iztapa	16	5	7	4	29	-	25	22
4. CSD Xelajú Mario Camposeco	16	3	8	5	14	-	15	17
5. CD Malacateco	16	3	7	6	8	-	14	16
6. Antigua Guatemala FC	16	2	7	7	15	-	26	13

Grupo B

1. CD Guastatoya	16	7	7	2	23	-	10	28
2. CSD Municipal Ciudad de Guatemala	16	8	3	5	24	-	11	27
3. CSD Cobán Imperial	16	5	8	3	20	-	17	23
4. Sanarate FC	16	4	6	6	16	-	25	18
5. CSD Sacachispas Chiquimula	16	5	3	8	15	-	26	18
6. CD Achuapa El Progreso	16	4	2	10	16	-	27	14

Tabla acumulada

1. Comunicaciones FC Ciudad de Guatemala	16	10	4	2	28	-	12	34
2. CD Guastatoya	16	7	7	2	23	-	10	28
3. CSD Municipal Ciudad de Guatemala	16	8	3	5	24	-	11	27
4. FC Santa Lucía Cotzumalguapa	16	6	6	4	13	-	13	24
5. CSD Cobán Imperial	16	5	8	3	20	-	17	23
6. CD Iztapa	16	5	7	4	29	-	25	22
7. Sanarate FC	16	4	6	6	16	-	25	18
8. CSD Sacachispas Chiquimula	16	5	3	8	15	-	26	18
9. CSD Xelajú Mario Camposeco	16	3	8	5	14	-	15	17
10. CD Malacateco	16	3	7	6	8	-	14	16
11. CD Achuapa El Progreso	16	4	2	10	16	-	27	14
12. Antigua Guatemala FC	16	2	7	7	15	-	26	13

Top-8 were qualified for the Torneo Clausura Play-offs.

Quarter-Finals [05-09.05.2021]

Sanarate FC - CD Guastatoya	2-0(2-0)	1-4(0-0)
CSD Sacachispas Chiquimula - Comunicaciones FC Ciudad de Guatemala	0-1(0-1)	0-1(0-0)
CD Iztapa - CSD Municipal Ciudad de Guatemala	3-1(1-0)	0-0
CSD Cobán Imperial - FC Santa Lucía Cotzumalguapa	1-1(1-0)	0-3(0-2)

Semi-Finals [12-16.05.2021]

CD Iztapa - Comunicaciones FC Ciudad de Guatemala	2-2(1-1)	1-1(1-0)
FC Santa Lucía Cotzumalguapa - CD Guastatoya	1-0(1-0)	2-1(0-1)

Finals

20.05.2021, Estadio Municipal, Santa Lucía Cotzumalguapa; Attendance: 9,000
Referee: Walter Alexander López Castellanos
FC Santa Lucía Cotzumalguapa - Comunicaciones FC Ciudad de Guatemala   4-0(3-0)
Santa Lucía: Braulio César Linares Ortíz, Emerson Manfredy Cabrera Melgar (71.Kevin Alejandro Ávila Alvizuris), Santos Israel Crisanto García, Thales Douglas Moreira Possas, William Roberto Amaya Gordillo, Jonathan Rafael Velásquez (72.Erwin Armando Morales Hernández), Rafael da Roza Moreira "Rafinha" (58.Nelson Enrique Miranda Nery), Diego Samuel Ruiz Golón, Manfred Noé Icuté Fuentes, Isaác Acuña Sánchez (50.Mynor Rodolfo Asencio Trejo), Romario Luiz da Silva "Romarinho". Trainer: Mario Francisco Acevedo Ruiz (Nicaragua).
Comunicaciones: Kevin Jorge Amilcar Moscoso Mayén, Michael Umaña Corrales, Alexander Robinson Delgado (67.Nicolás Samayoa Pacheco), José Carlos Pinto Samayoa [*sent off 75*], Rodrigo Saravia Samayoa (46.Stheven Adán Robles Ruiz), José Manuel Contreras y Contreras, Óscar Alexander Santis Cayax (67.Pablo Nicolás Royón Silvera), Jorge Eduardo Aparicio Grijalva, Kevin Josué Grijalva González (46.Manfred Russell Russell), Junior Alberto Lacayo Róchez (46.Rafael Andrés Lezcano Montero), Agustín Enrique Herrera Osuna. Trainer: Mauricio Antonio Tapia (Argentina).
Goals: 1-0 Diego Samuel Ruiz Golón (12), 2-0 Romario Luiz da Silva "Romarinho" (29), 3-0 Isaác Acuña Sánchez (38), 4-0 Romario Luiz da Silva "Romarinho" (88).

23.05.2021, Estadio "Doroteo Guamuch Flores", Ciudad de Guatemala; Attendance: 0
Referee: Mario Alberto Escobar Toca
Comunicaciones FC Ciudad de Guatemala - FC Santa Lucía Cotzumalguapa   5-2(2-0)
Comunicaciones: Kevin Jorge Amilcar Moscoso Mayén, Nicolás Samayoa Pacheco, Michael Umaña Corrales, Alexander Robinson Delgado, José Manuel Contreras y Contreras, Óscar Alexander Santis Cayax (79.Allen José Yanes Pinto), Stheven Adán Robles Ruiz (79.Fredy William Thompson León), Jorge Eduardo Aparicio Grijalva (68.Rodrigo Saravia Samayoa), Rafael Andrés Lezcano Montero (36.Junior Alberto Lacayo Róchez), Agustín Enrique Herrera Osuna, Pablo Nicolás Royón Silvera (68.Lynner Oneal García Mejía). Trainer: Mauricio Antonio Tapia (Argentina).
Santa Lucía: Braulio César Linares Ortíz, Emerson Manfredy Cabrera Melgar (78.Nelson Enrique Miranda Nery), Santos Israel Crisanto García, Thales Douglas Moreira Possas, William Roberto Amaya Gordillo [*sent off 85*], Rafael da Roza Moreira "Rafinha", Jonathan Rafael Velásquez (46.Erwin Armando Morales Hernández), Diego Samuel Ruiz Golón (46.Isaác Acuña Sánchez), Manfred Noé Icuté Fuentes, Anllel de Jesus Porras Conejo (46.Mynor Rodolfo Asencio Trejo), Romario Luiz da Silva "Romarinho". Trainer: Mario Francisco Acevedo Ruiz (Nicaragua).
Goals: 1-0 Junior Alberto Lacayo Róchez (39), 2-0 Stheven Adán Robles Ruiz (45+2), 3-0 Pablo Nicolás Royón Silvera (46), 4-0 Junior Alberto Lacayo Róchez (54), 5-0 Junior Alberto Lacayo Róchez (73), 5-1 Thales Douglas Moreira Possas (90+1), 5-2 Nelson Enrique Miranda Nery (90+3).
Please note: Jorge Eduardo Aparicio Grijalva was sent off on the bench (90).

Torneo Clausura 2021 Champions: **FC Santa Lucía Cotzumalguapa**

Best goalscorer Torneo Clausura 2021:
Luis Ángel Landín Cortés (MEX, CD Guastatoya) &
Nicolás Iván Martínez Vargas (ARG, CD Achuapa El Progreso) – both 10 goals

Tabla Anual 2020/2021

1.	Comunicaciones FC Ciudad de Guatemala	32	19	9	4	53 - 22	66
2.	CSD Municipal Ciudad de Guatemala	32	19	6	7	58 - 19	63
3.	CSD Cobán Imperial	32	12	13	7	39 - 30	49
4.	CD Guastatoya	32	11	15	6	42 - 29	48
5.	CD Iztapa	32	10	11	11	53 - 53	41
6.	CD Malacateco	32	10	10	12	27 - 32	40
7.	FC Santa Lucía Cotzumalguapa	32	10	10	12	25 - 30	40
8.	CSD Xelajú Mario Camposeco	32	9	11	12	31 - 37	38
9.	Antigua Guatemala FC	32	7	12	13	36 - 49	33
10.	CD Achuapa El Progreso	32	9	6	17	33 - 48	33
11.	Sanarate FC (*Relegated*)	32	7	11	14	35 - 58	32
12.	CSD Sacachispas Chiquimula (*Relegated*)	32	7	10	15	35 - 60	31

THE CLUBS 2020/2021

Please note: number of matches, subtitutes and goals are including Apertura/Clausura and all Play-offs.

CLUB DEPORTIVO ACHUAPA EL PROGRESO

Foundation date: 1932
Address: *Not known*
Stadium: Estadio Municipal "Manuel Ariza", El Progreso (1,500)

THE SQUAD

	DOB	Ape M	(s)	G	Cla M	(s)	G
Goalkeepers:							
Brandon Gustavo Dávila López	22.08.1996	2			12		
Eder Alexander García Castillo		2			4		
Iván Waldemar Pacheco Hernández	23.03.1992	12					
Defenders:							
Rony Ismael Barrera Ovando	20.11.1994	5	(5)		13	(1)	
Carlos Estuardo Herrera Velásquez	27.03.1988					(1)	
Bryan Manolo Lemus	01.04.1994	13	(2)	1	6		
David Isaac López Bernal	08.06.1998	7			4	(1)	
Hamilton López	26.10.1983				5	(2)	
Juliano Rangel de Andrade (BRA)	04.04.1984	15		2	10		
Tobit Mareano Vásquez Barrientos	10.04.1994	13	(3)		12	(1)	
Midfielders:							
Gerardo Alberto Arias Gaytán	18.11.1985				11	(1)	
Juan Luis Cardona Luna	24.04.1993	15		2	13	(2)	1
Juan Carlos Escobar Aguilar		4	(3)				
Ribix Aldair García Ramírez	14.10.1994	14			10	(1)	
Juan Manuel Klug Ramírez	19.01.1995	4	(2)	2	2	(10)	
Rodrigo Darío Ligorria (ARG)	07.09.1988	8	(5)	1			
Eisner Iván Loboa Balanta (COL)	17.05.1987	1	(2)				
Edgar Alejandro Macal Razuleu	05.12.1990	7	(6)	1	12	(4)	1
Kleyman Darwrin Toribio Moscoso Mejía	21.07.1998				4	(5)	1
Kevin Alberto Navas Flores						(1)	
Marlon José Negrete Martínez (COL)	01.09.1986				13	(1)	2
Donald Darío Paz Cordón	24.05.1997	2					

Ronald Alldayr Regalado Kress	12.10.1996				7	(5)	
Jorge Rigoberto Ticurú de Paz	01.07.1993	2	(3)				
Sergio Alejandro Trujillo Herrera	19.11.1987	5	(6)				
Joshua Alexander Vargas Drummond (HON)	29.11.1994				13	(1)	

Forwards:

César Dimas Chinchilla Divas		8	(5)	1	3	(11)	
Jorge Estuardo Escobar Váldez		1	(3)		4	(2)	
Mario Raúl Hernández Pocasangre	01.12.1996	13	(2)	4	1	(6)	
Kléber William da Silva Pereira (BRA)	21.08.1992	2	(2)	2			
Gerson Danilo Lima Bonilla	10.11.1992	7					
José Javier Longo Ordóñez	24.05.1994	5	(6)		3	(8)	
Nicolás Iván Martínez Vargas (ARG)	19.03.1991				14	(2)	10
Helder Estuardo Orantes González			(2)				
Diego Alejandro Palma Molina	19.10.1995		(2)				
William Enrique Palacios González (COL)	29.07.1994	9		1			

Trainer:

Irvin Aquiles Olivares Barrera		11	
[09.11.2020] Marlon Iván León y León	03.03.1967	5	11
[18.04.2021] Sergio Enrique Pardo Valenzuela (CHI)	24.02.1948		5

ANTIGUA GUATEMALA FÚTBOL CLUB

Foundation date: 1958
Address: *Not known*
Stadium: Estadio Pensativo, Antigua Guatemala (10,000)

THE SQUAD

	DOB	Ape M	(s)	G	Cla M	(s)	G
Goalkeepers:							
Víctor Manuel Ayala González	08.05.1989	19			10		
Luis José Morán Varela	04.02.1998	1			6		
Defenders:							
José Agustín Ardón Castellanos	20.01.2000	8		1	7	(2)	1
Oscar Antonio Castellanos Santos	18.01.2000				8	(4)	
Kervin René García Sandoval	07.12.1990	8	(6)				
Moises Edwardo Hernández Moralez	05.03.1992	15	(1)		15		
Cristian Alexander Jiménez Martínez	26.04.1995	5	(9)	1	11	(4)	
José Antonio Mena Alfaro (CRC)	02.02.1989	17			16		
Allan Ricardo Miranda Albertazzi (CRC)	28.05.1987	10	(6)				
Midfielders:							
Pablo Andrés Aguilar Palacios	21.02.1995	10	(4)	3			
Jairo Randolfo Arreola Silva	20.09.1985	15	(2)	2	10	(3)	2
Kevin Eduardo Arriola García	03.08.1991	6	(9)	1			
Randy Yormein Chirino Serrano (CRC)	16.01.1996				5	(1)	
Marco Leonel Dominguez-Ramírez (CAN)	25.02.1996	15	(1)	1	11	(1)	
José Miguel Gálvez Ruiz	24.05.1999					(1)	
Kervin René García Sandoval	07.12.1990				7		
Emmanuel Giovani Hernández Neri (MEX)	04.01.1993	15	(2)	2			
Kener Hairon Lemus Méndez	09.02.1994	9	(8)		8	(2)	
Carlos Anselmo Mejía del Cid	13.11.1991				7	(5)	1
Jesús Andrés Mora Castañeda	25.11.1998					(2)	
Christian Omar Ojeda Ramírez	18.03.1996	9	(7)		7	(4)	
Vidal Alexander Paz Sagché	24.06.1997	1	(10)			(2)	
John-Paul Rochford (TRI)	05.01.2000					(1)	
Marlon Renato Sequén Suruy	23.06.1993	7	(3)		6	(7)	
Forwards:							
Robin Osvaldo Betancourth Cue	25.11.1991	19	(1)	6			
Luis Genaro Castillo Martínez (MEX)	25.05.1993				6	(2)	3
Joseph Christopher Cox Goods (PAN)	25.06.1994				4	(2)	2
Oliver Alexander Díaz Choma	04.01.1998		(3)				
Ever Arsenio Guzmán Zavala (MEX)	15.03.1988				5	(4)	
Josué Isaac Martínez Areas (CRC)	25.03.1990	12	(4)	5	13	(2)	4
Nicolás Iván Martínez Vargas (ARG)	19.03.1991	10	(4)	4			
Juan David Osorio Tobón (COL)	06.06.1990	8			12		
Cayo Henrique Ribeiro Lopes (BRA)	06.11.1999	1	(5)				
Deyner Padilla Toro (PAN)					2	(13)	2
Trainer:							
Juan Antonio Torres Servín (MEX)	15.07.1968	10					
[11.11.2020] Jeffrey Michael Korytoski (USA)	1977	10			4		
[07.03.2021] Roberto Montoya López (MEX)	10.10.1965				12		

CLUB SOCIAL Y DEPORTIVO COBÁN IMPERIAL

Foundation date: August 1, 1936
Address: *Not known*
Stadium: Estadio "José Ángel Rossi", Cobán (12,000)

THE SQUAD

	DOB	M	Ape (s)	G	M	Cla (s)	G
Goalkeepers:							
José De Jesús Calderón Frías (PAN)	14.08.1985				11		
Derby Rafael Carrillo Berduo (USA)	19.09.1987	1					
Mario José Mendoza Oliva	22.07.1998				7		
Kevin Jorge Amilcar Moscoso Mayén	13.06.1993	17					
Defenders:							
Yeltsin Delfino Álvarez Castro	02.11.1994	13	(3)	3	7	(10)	2
César Raúl Calderón Hernández	25.06.1996	3	(10)		7	(5)	
Alexander Enemias Cifuentes Santos	22.01.1990	1	(3)				
Allan Ricardo Miranda Albertazzi (CRC)	28.05.1987				12	(1)	
Erwin Armando Morales Hernández	29.05.1985	13	(1)				
José Andrés Ruiz Rumph	30.05.1996	8	(4)		14	(4)	
Jorge Luis Sotomayor (ARG)	29.03.1988	17			17		
Elías Enoc Vásquez Prera	18.06.1992	12	(1)	1	7	(1)	
Midfielders:							
Pedro Manuel Alejandro Altán Hernández	04.06.1997	10	(5)	2	9	(4)	3
Kevin Eduardo Arriola García	03.08.1991				6	(9)	1
Ángel Rubén Cabrera Noriega	10.02.1996	16	(1)		12	(4)	2
Carlos Joaquín Antonio Flores Leiva		6			1		
Alejandro Miguel Galindo	05.03.1992				11	(2)	
Victor Eduardo Guay Sanchez (GLP)	03.10.1994	13	(3)	1	10	(7)	1
Janderson Kione Pereira Rodrigues (BRA)	18.02.1989				18		4
Enrique Haroldo Klug Sand	01.04.1990	3	(8)		2	(1)	
Byron Javier Leal Ramírez	24.03.1994	16	(1)		7	(7)	
Eddy Estuardo Revolorio Guzmán	26.03.2000	1					
Juan Carlos Silva Maya (MEX)	06.02.1988	9	(4)	1			
Eduardo Beltrán Soto Barrios	03.03.1990	15	(1)	1	18		
Marcelo Leonel Vidal (ARG)	15.01.1991	3	(2)				
Forwards:							
Robin Osvaldo Betancourth Cue	25.11.1991				17	(1)	4
Lauro Ramón Cazal (PAR)	23.03.1986	12	(4)	6			
Bladimir Yovany Díaz Saavedra (COL)	10.07.1992				4	(12)	4
Edi Danilo Guerra Pérez	11.12.1987	4	(9)	1			
Hárim Enrique Quezada Gámez	17.10.1997	5	(10)	3			
Edin Franzue Rivas Leal	07.06.2000				1	(5)	
Trainer:							
Rafael Ernesto Díaz Aitkenhead	27.06.1981	18			6		
[25.03.2021] Enrique Ernesto Corti (ARG)	21.03.1963				12		

COMUNICACIONES FÚTBOL CLUB CIUDAD DE GUATEMALA

Foundation date: August 16, 1949
Address: 10a. Avenida 18-02, Zona 10 (Centro Comercial Prisa II Nivel, Oficina 202), Ciudad de Guatemala
Stadium: Estadio "Doroteo Guamuch Flores", Ciudad de Guatemala (30,000)

THE SQUAD

	DOB	Ape M	(s)	G	Cla M	(s)	G
Goalkeepers:							
José de Jesús Calderón Frías (PAN)	14.08.1985	10					
Kevin Jorge Amilcar Moscoso Mayén	13.06.1993				15		
Fredy Alexander Pérez Chacón	09.12.1994	8			7		
Defenders:							
José Alfredo Corena Barboza (COL)	29.09.1992				11	(3)	4
Gerardo Arturo Gordillo Olivero	17.08.1994	6	(2)				
Rafael Humberto Morales de León	06.04.1988	14		2	15		2
José Manuel Murillo Morán (PAN)	24.02.1995	7	(7)	1			
José Carlos Pinto Samayoa	16.06.1993	16			15	(1)	
Alexander Robinson Delgado (CRC)	21.11.1988				12	(2)	
Nicolás Samayoa Pacheco	02.08.1995	2	(3)		9	(4)	1
Michael Umaña Corrales (CRC)	16.07.1982	13			16	(1)	2
Allen José Yanes Pinto	04.07.1997	7			6	(6)	
Midfielders:							
Pablo Andres Aguilar Palacios	21.02.1995				4	(11)	
Jorge Eduardo Aparicio Grijalva	21.11.1992	8	(5)	1	13	(3)	
Carlos Mauricio Castrillo Alonzo	16.05.1985	2	(3)		1		
Brayan Estuardo Chajón Juárez	25.06.1997		(3)				
Deiveth Alejandro Chinchilla Castañeda	09.08.2000		(1)				
José Manuel Contreras y Contreras	19.01.1986	10	(4)		12	(6)	1
Alejandro Miguel Galindo	05.03.1992	9	(1)				
Lynner Oneal García Mejía	07.05.2000					(1)	
Carlos Anselmo Mejía del Cid	13.11.1991	4	(7)	1			
Oscar Denilson Mejía Del Cid	16.01.1999	1					
Stheven Adán Robles Ruiz	12.11.1995	13	(5)		11	(6)	2
Richard Francisco Rodríguez Reyes	12.01.1998		(1)				
Manfred Russell Russell (CRC)	23.09.1988	9	(8)	1	6	(9)	
Óscar Alexander Santis Cayax	25.03.1999	6	(9)	5	18	(2)	5
Rodrigo Saravia Samayoa	22.02.1993	14	(1)	1	13	(7)	
Fredy William Thompson León	02.06.1982	2	(2)		3	(5)	
Forwards:							
Dewinder Deesmith Bradley Gómez	21.07.1994	2	(6)	1	3	(4)	
Bladimir Yovany Díaz Saavedra (COL)	10.07.1992	1	(9)	2			
Kevin Josué Grijalva González	09.01.1995	3	(2)	1	6		
Agustín Enrique Herrera Osuna (MEX)	22.03.1985	13	(2)	6	17	(5)	7
Junior Alberto Lacayo Róchez (HON)	19.08.1995				10	(11)	6
Rafael Andrés Lezcano Montero (CRC)	05.05.1990	18		3	13	(7)	4
Pablo Nicolás Royón Silvera (URU)	28.01.1991				6	(10)	4
Trainer:							
Mauricio Antonio Tapia (ARG)	20.08.1970	18			22		

CLUB DEPORTIVO GUASTATOYA

Foundation date: 2010
Address: *Not known*
Stadium: Estadio "David Cordón Hichos", Guastatoya (3,100)

THE SQUAD	DOB	Ape M	(s)	G	Cla M	(s)	G
Goalkeepers:							
Adrián Isaac de Lemos Calderón (CRC)	13.10.1982	22			19		
Erwin Josualdo Rodríguez Hernández	03.08.1991				1		
Defenders:							
José Alfredo Corena Barboza (COL)	29.09.1992	21		2			
Omar Domínguez Palafox (MEX)	13.04.1988	20		2	17		1
Walter Estuardo García Duarte	28.10.1991	4	(2)		2	(3)	
José Alberto Márquez Árdon	06.08.1988	13	(5)		10	(1)	
Rubén Darío Morales Pereira	04.06.1987	16			11	(1)	2
Manuel Enrique Moreno Ordóñez	18.06.1992				11		1
Aarón Navarro Cespedes (CRC)	29.05.1987	10	(8)		13	(3)	
Wilson Augusto Pineda Cornelio	25.09.1993	20			18	(1)	2
Oscar Obed Josadac Pinto Velásquez		2	(1)				
Midfielders:							
Marvin José Ceballos Flores	22.04.1992	17	(2)	4	13	(2)	1
Nixsón Wilfredo Flores Reyes	13.05.1993				9	(4)	
Samuel Enrique Garrido Arriaza	03.06.1999	2			1	(6)	
Uzias Bernabé Hernández Farfán	20.07.1997	9	(7)		7	(6)	
Néstor Jucup Escobar	26.02.1989	12	(6)		6	(1)	
Maximiliano Lombardi Rodríguez (URU)	11.05.1987	11		2	18		4
Oscar Denilson Mejía Del Cid	16.01.1999				3	(10)	
Carlos Daniel Orellana Orellana	14.04.1999				1	(6)	2
Fredy Gustavo Orellana García	08.08.1990		(8)			(4)	
Anderson Edgar Ortíz Falla	07.11.2001	6	(11)	1	4	(2)	2
Cristian Armin Reyes Hernández	05.12.1991	10	(2)		3	(6)	
Edgardo Luis Ruiz Benítez (COL)	17.05.1995				2	(8)	
Wagner Herderson Josué Sagastume Morales	18.11.2000	1					
Denilson Ariel Sánchez Muñoz	25.06.1999				15	(4)	
Jorge Estuardo Vargas García	26.02.1993	15	(6)	5	10	(4)	
Forwards:							
Luis Ángel Landín Cortés (MEX)	23.07.1986	19	(2)	5	16	(1)	10
Luis Fernando Martínez Castellanos	14.12.1991	8	(9)	4	10	(3)	3
Kevin Alexander Norales Quezada	26.01.1992	1	(3)				
William Zapata Brand (COL)	28.04.1988	3	(4)	1			
Trainer:							
Fabricio Javier Benítez Píriz	11.06.1975	10					
[01.11.2020] William Fernando Coito Olivera (URU)		12			20		

CLUB DEPORTIVO IZTAPA

Foundation date: *Not known*
Address: *Not known*
Stadium: Estadio Municipal Morón, Iztapa (3,000)

THE SQUAD	DOB	Ape M	(s)	G	Cla M	(s)	G
Goalkeepers:							
José Carlos García Mendez	16.02.1993				3		
Elder Alexander Hernández Barrios	14.05.1995	5					
Liborio Vicente Sánchez Ledesma (MEX)	09.10.1989	13					
Luis Norberto Tatuaca García Luis Tatuaca	06.07.1990				17		
Defenders:							
Sergio Danilo Azurdia López	17.07.1989	12	(1)		5		
Emerson Manfredy Cabrera Melgar	15.02.1991	8	(4)	1			
José Luis Castillejos Ruiz	24.02.1995					(2)	
Alexander Enemías Cifuentes Santos	22.01.1990				12	(5)	
Roberto Javier Cóbar Gil	15.10.1989	7	(1)				
Julián Antonio de Jesús Priego	23.09.1987	9	(1)	2	14	(5)	
Eliseo Díaz Ortíz	17.07.1990	6	(8)		15	(2)	1
Nicolás Adrián Foglia (ARG)	07.10.1986				18		2
Fredy David López Galindo	07.07.1992				8	(10)	1
Germán Ariel Niz (ARG)	23.03.1996	4					
Wilson Leonel Pineda Barillas	25.09.1993					(4)	
Jordan Hakeem Smith Wint (CRC)	23.04.1991	13			19		3
Antony Marcelo Torres Cordero	19.08.1994	7	(2)		1	(1)	
Midfielders:							
Christian Alexander Albizures García	05.02.1995				16	(4)	3
Nelson Adonais Ávila Ramos		1					
Grimaldo Ronal Oswaldo Berrios Santiago	11.08.2000					(1)	
Julio Enrique Fajardo López	03.02.1997	12	(5)	2			
Josué Odir Flores Palencia (SLV)	13.05.1988	15	(3)	4			
Lynner O'Neal García Mejía	07.05.2000	2	(11)	2			
Elder Leonel Gómez Chávez	14.05.1995		(1)		1	(2)	
Néstor Migdael Grajeda Lima	20.08.1988	13					
Cristian Daniel Guerra Hernández	27.06.1995	14	(1)		18		
Jonathan Winibacker López Mejicano	10.05.1988	16	(1)	1			
Andrés Alejandro Quiñonez Alcerro	26.06.1996	1	(5)				
Edwin Retolaza Durán	11.02.1999					(1)	
Pedro Julio Samayoa Moreno	25.07.1985	14	(1)	1	17	(2)	2
Elvis Naaman Zamora Ruano			(1)		1	(6)	
Forwards:							
Waldemar Jesús Acosta Ferreira (URU)	25.08.1986	7	(7)				
Carlos Kamiani Félix Suenaga (MEX)	05.01.1985	17	(1)	11	16	(1)	6
Nelson Iván García García	23.03.1999	2	(6)	2	11	(9)	8
Edi Danilo Guerra Pérez	11.12.1987				6	(9)	1
Cristian Alexis Hernández (ARG)	24.08.1995				17	(3)	8
Kevin Alexander Norales	26.01.1992				5	(9)	
Trainer:							
Ramiro Augusto Cepeda Alvarado	25.04.1975	18			20		

CLUB DEPORTIVO MALACATECO MALACATÁN

Foundation date: September 8, 1962
Address: *Not known*
Stadium: Estadio Santa Lucia, Malacatán (5,500)

THE SQUAD

	DOB	Ape M	(s)	G	Cla M	(s)	G
Goalkeepers:							
Jonathan Josué Dávila Cifuentes	18.02.1993	3			1		
Henry Edimar Hernández Cruz (SLV)	04.01.1985	15					
Walter Emilio Maldonado López					1		
Rubén Darío Silva Silva (URU)	19.02.1992				14		
Defenders:							
Víctor Efrain Armas López	08.12.1995	3	(6)				
Wilmer Menfil Barrios Matias	23.06.1993				7	(2)	
Carlos Arturo De León García	31.03.1999	3	(2)		4	(3)	
Fredy David López Galindo	07.07.1992	13	(3)	2			
Elmer Antonio Morales Asencio (MEX)	18.12.2000	1	(2)		3	(1)	
Orlando Enrique Osorio Mondul (COL)	28.01.1990	15			15		
Kevin Emanuel Ruiz García	18.05.1995	13			12	(1)	
Midfielders:							
César Eduardo Archila	30.07.1993	7	(7)	1	9	(5)	1
Bainer Elí Barrios Delgado	19.03.1994	10	(4)	1	6	(3)	
Franclin Noelí Barrios Delgado	24.06.1992					(1)	
Sixto Ubaldo Betancourt Véliz	16.05.1992	16			13		
Raúl Fernando Calderón Hernández	09.03.1993	9	(5)		15		
Maynor Iván de León Reyna	24.10.1990	7	(6)				
Jorge Ignacio Gatgens Quirós (CRC)	23.07.1988	10	(3)	1	2		
Wilson Ariel Godoy Gudiel	06.09.1987					(1)	
Wilson Alberto López González	06.09.1987	9					
José Guillermo Ochoa de León	03.02.2001	1	(5)	1	5	(9)	
Mynor Jobely Pop Solval	01.11.1986	16	(1)	1	16		
Kevin Estuardo Ramírez Siguenza	01.08.2002		(3)		1	(4)	
Durban Leonardo Reyes Vásquez	29.04.1997	7	(7)		13		
Oliver Alexander Rodas	06.02.1998				5	(11)	1
Jorge Alberto Sánchez Laparra	08.05.1991	10	(4)	1			
José Alfredo Sánchez Barquero (CRC)	20.05.1987	3	(4)		13		
Esteban Sierra (COL)	07.07.2000					(2)	
Wilton Murilo de Freitas Silva (BRA)	19.09.1996		(2)				
Forwards:							
Pedro Federico Báez Benítez (PAR)	15.01.1997	16		8			
Jahir Alejandro Barraza Flores (MEX)	17.09.1990	6		2	3	(2)	1
Santiago Castillo Gómez (COL)					5	(3)	1
Lauro Ramón Cazal (PAR)	23.03.1986				13	(2)	4
Wilson Alberto López González	30.07.1994		(1)				
Mauro Ronaldo Portillo Arroyo	14.07.1995	5	(9)	1			
Edward Santeliz de la Roca	18.06.1987					(6)	
Anderson Omar Villagran Villagran	10.05.2003					(3)	
Trainer:							
Ronald Gómez Gómez (CRC)	24.01.1975	18			16		

CLUB SOCIAL Y DEPORTIVO MUNICIPAL
CIUDAD DE GUATEMALA

Foundation date: May 17, 1936
Address: 2a Calle 15-95, Zona 13, Ciudad de Guatemala
Stadium: Estadio "Manuel Felipe Carrera" [El Trébol], Ciudad de Guatemala (7,500)

THE SQUAD

	DOB	M	Ape (s)	G	M	Cla (s)	G
Goalkeepers:							
Víctor Rafael García Muníz (URU)	08.12.1989	19			3		
Kenderson Alessandro Navarro Hernández	25.02.2002	3			15		
Defenders:							
Carlos Fernando Alvarado López	14.02.1999	9	(8)	1	6	(5)	
Luis Enrique de León Valenzuela	14.11.1995	15	(3)		7	(3)	
Carlos Eduardo Gallardo Nájera	08.04.1984	20			14	(1)	1
Manuel Estuardo López Rodas	26.04.1990	11	(6)		8	(2)	1
Steve Eduardo Makuka Pereyra (URU)	26.11.1994				17		
José Alfredo Morales Concua	03.12.1996	13	(4)		17	(1)	1
Héctor Osberto Moreira Pérez	27.12.1987	13	(2)	1			
Eric Payeras (USA)	04.10.1999	1					
Midfielders:							
Jaime Enrique Alas Morales (SLV)	30.07.1989	21		1	9	(2)	1
Rudy Ronaldo Barrientos Reyes	01.03.1999	17	(3)	1	13	(4)	
Brandon Andrés de León Ramos	30.09.1993	4	(7)		5	(2)	
Frank Edison de León Reyna	26.12.1994	10	(7)	2	7	(7)	1
Janderson Kione Pereira Rodrigues (BRA)	18.02.1989	18	(1)	5			
John Roberth Méndez Sánchez	24.06.1999	3	(12)	2	14	(4)	2
Carlos Antonio Monterroso Cruz	26.06.1996	1					
José Mario Rosales Marroquín	24.06.1993	19	(2)	1	15	(1)	
Luis Pedro Rosas Cabrera	07.06.1999	3	(9)		4	(10)	
Forwards:							
Gustavo Ezequiel Britos (ARG)	20.02.1990				11	(1)	9
Erick Alejandro Castro	24.04.2001		(1)				
Alejandro Matías Díaz (ARG)	27.05.1989	12	(5)	3	9	(5)	2
José Daniel Franco Aldana	21.10.2001					(2)	
José Carlos Martínez Navas	10.10.1997	12	(8)	4	16	(2)	6
Hárim Enrique Quezada Gámez	17.10.1997				2	(12)	1
Edwin Orlando Rivas Tambito	08.01.1992				6	(3)	
Ramiro Iván Rocca (ARG)	21.11.1988	18	(3)	22			
Trainer:							
Sebastián Alejandro Bini (ARG)	21.12.1979	22			18		

CLUB SOCIAL Y DEPORTIVO SACACHISPAS CHIQUIMULA

Foundation date: June 15, 1949
Address: *Not known*
Stadium: Estadio Las Victorias, Chiquimula (9,500)

THE SQUAD

	DOB	Ape M	(s)	G	Cla M	(s)	G
Goalkeepers:							
Luis Rolando Lucero Escobar	08.09.1990	5					
Christian Alejandro Mendoza Oliva	12.06.1992					(1)	
Johnny Alexander Navarro Ortega	06.08.1994	11	(1)				
Mynor Roberto Padilla Zúñiga	09.07.1993				18		
Defenders:							
Wilmer Menfil Barrios Matías	23.06.1993	13	(1)				
Edwin Arturo Chacón Alonso	22.11.1983	8			13	(1)	3
Denilson Luis Antonio Hernández Coronado	12.08.1997	7	(3)	1			
Rigoberto Benabi Hernández Chong		8	(3)	1	17		
Jamal Michael Jack (TRI)	17.12.1987	11	(2)	1			
José Manuel Lémus Ruíz	05.11.1992				17		
Jesús Jonathan Lozano Santiago (COL)	08.12.1993				10	(4)	
Luis Herminio Pérez Villeda	23.08.1994	11	(3)		3	(13)	
Alex Nolberto Pozuelas Morales		1	(4)				
Rolman Santiago Sandoval Recinos	05.11.1983	9			4	(2)	
Pablo Ademar Solórzano Recinos	04.03.1988				6	(5)	
Manuel Antonio Soto Archila	30.05.1986				5	(2)	
Midfielders:							
Egidio Raúl Arévalo Ríos (URU)	01.01.1982				18		
Sergio Antonio Casasola Segura	28.11.1990	2					
Brayan Omar Castañeda Bantos						(3)	
Nery Gerardo Cifuentes Pinto	16.01.2000	5	(9)				
Frederico Da Silva Moreira Marques (BRA)	11.09.1990		(2)				
Franklin Eduardo García	03.06.1994				2	(2)	
Allan Vinicio López Castañeda	13.11.1997	6	(3)		17		1
Daniel Marroquín Bardales	24.09.1994	7	(2)				
Esteban Marroquín Bardales	28.04.1999	1	(1)				
Carlos Roberto Montepeque Orellana	15.12.1994	4	(10)	2			
Herberth Amaniel Morales Solis	05.10.1992	1	(4)				
Ronald Alldayr Regalado Kress	12.10.1996	14					
Marco Tulio Rivas Pérez	20.04.1991	14		1	18		
Edgardo Luis Ruiz Benítez (COL)	17.05.1995	12	(2)	2			
José Alfredo Sánchez Barquero (CRC)	20.05.1987				12	(4)	
André Musa Solorzano Abed	10.07.1994		(1)		3		
Forwards:							
Cristian Alvarado Aliaga	12.09.1996	3	(9)	1			
Diego Francisco Ávila Murillo (ECU)	15.11.1993	10		3	15	(2)	6
Edsón Hernández Marroquin					1		1
Omar Alberto López Guzmán (MEX)	27.06.1989	13		8			
Andy Alessandro Palencia García	12.05.2002				1	(7)	1
Mauro Ronaldo Portillo	14.07.1995					(3)	
Leandro Gastón Rodríguez (ARG)	01.05.1987				18		3
Trainer:							
Érick Fernando González Rodríguez		8					
[19.10.2020] Alejandro Javier Larrea (URU)	05.12.1966	8			5		

[11.03.2021] Diego Adolfo Cerutti Stalder (ARG)   02.12.1971 | 13

SANARATE FÚTBOL CLUB
Foundation date: October 1, 1958
Address: *Not known*
Stadium: Estadio Municipal de Sanarate, Sanarate (3,000)

THE SQUAD

	DOB	Ape M	(s)	G	Cla M	(s)	G
Goalkeepers:							
Bryan Alejandro Mejía	01.07.1995				1		
Iván Waldemar Pacheco Hernández	29.03.1992				10		
Manuel Alejandro Sosa Rivera	05.04.1987	16			7		
Defenders:							
Kevyn Stuars Aguilar de León	14.04.1997	13		1	15	(3)	1
Tomás Castillo Pacheco	07.04.1991				2	(3)	
Nixon Wilfredo Flores Reyes	13.05.1993	14	(1)				
Charles Williams Martínez Viscaya (VEN)	19.04.1994				16	(1)	7
Néstor Fernando Martínez Norales	13.03.1981				2		
Dilan Noé Palencia Gereda	26.06.2001	11					
Kevin Daniel Palencia Conde	09.09.1995	6	(1)		4	(2)	
Yoisel Piedra Guillén (CUB)	27.03.1994	11			17		
Oscar Obed Josadac Pinto Velásquez (ARG)					4	(9)	1
Midfielders:							
Jhonnatan Mauricio Álvarez Lima			(2)			(3)	
Diego Andrés Archila			(2)				
Albert Ismael Barrientos Salazar	01.07.1994				3	(7)	
Juan Carlos Castañeda Verbena		1	(1)				
William Jehú Fajardo Montenegro					1	(9)	1
Jorge Alfredo Herrera Arriaza			(3)				
Sergio Manolo Jucup Escobar	08.09.1985	11	(3)				
Anderson Estuardo Molina Carrillo	10.04.2004	3	(6)			(3)	
José Javier Morales Mangandid	10.11.1997	12	(1)				
Jonathan Alexis Morán Urizar	18.10.1997	5	(9)		10	(3)	
Orlando Javier Moreira Ferreira (PAR)	04.05.1992				17		1
Marlon José Negrete Martínez (COL)	01.09.1986	11		6			
Nery Rodolfo Oliva Vásquez	24.04.1989				8		
Dilan Noé Palencia Gereda	26.06.2001				15	(3)	
Luis Carlos Ramírez Marroquín	25.11.1994	8	(3)				
Aslinn Enzi Rodas De León	07.10.1992	15		1	18		1
Juan José Rodas Carias			(1)				
Luis Guillermo Rodas Juárez	04.12.1990				10	(2)	
Carlos Yuliani Santos Vargas	03.08.2003					(5)	
Otto Geovani Tatuaca Álvarez	23.11.1998	4	(5)				
Forwards:							
Leandro Aníbal Bazán (ARG)	30.03.1990				3		2
César Alexis Canario (ARG)	18.08.1987	14		7	6	(3)	
William Jehú Fajardo Montenegro	26.01.2001	1	(8)				
Osmar Danibel López Zúñiga	04.11.1987				14	(3)	2
Christopher Rodolfo Ramírez Ulrich	08.01.1994	11	(1)	2	15	(3)	3
Edin Franzué Rivas Leal	07.06.2000	9	(5)	2			
Trainer:							
Carlos Gabriel Castillo y Castillo	20.12.1971	16					
[14.01.2021] Matías Tatangelo (ARG)	27.09.1985				18		

FÚTBOL CLUB SANTA LUCÍA COTZUMALGUAPA

Foundation date: 1992 / Refounded 2014
Address: *Not known*
Stadium: Estadio Municipal, Santa Lucía Cotzumalguapa (9,000)

THE SQUAD

	DOB	Ape M	(s)	G	Cla M	(s)	G
Goalkeepers:							
José Carlos García Méndez	16.02.1993	4					
Braulio César Linares Ortíz (USA)	29.01.1996	11			21		
Edín Edivaldo Valiente Flores	08.09.1987	1	(1)		1		
Defenders:							
Emerson Manfredy Cabrera Melgar	15.02.1991				9	(3)	
Santos Israel Crisanto García (HON)	20.09.1994	11		2	21	(1)	
Miguel Ángel Farfán Díaz	21.03.1988		(8)			(1)	
Jorge Melecio Matul de León	04.11.1993	8			7		
Brayan Morales Granados	15.06.1995	7	(5)	1	4	(4)	
Erwin Armando Morales Hernández	29.05.1985				2	(4)	
William Omar Ramírez Vásquez	21.04.1991	8	(1)				
José Eduardo Salazar Menéndez	22.02.1991	1	(1)				
Diego Rolando Santis Cayax	13.07.2002	5	(4)		2	(6)	
Thales Douglas Moreira Possas (BRA)	15.08.1990	16		1	21		1
Midfielders:							
Isaác Acuña Sánchez (MEX)	18.08.1989				5	(5)	3
William Roberto Amaya Gordillo	29.06.1995	1	(3)		7	(5)	
Kevin Alejandro Ávila Alvizuris	08.05.1994	9	(1)		16	(3)	
José Javier del Águila Martínez	07.03.1991	4	(3)		12	(4)	
Sérgio Iván González Girón		4			3		
Manfred Noé Icuté Fuentes	20.04.1988	15		1	14	(7)	1
Rafael da Roza Moreira "Rafinha" (BRA)	11.10.1988	14			18		1
Carlo Stefano Rodríguez Lara						(1)	
Diego Samuel Ruiz Golón	14.02.1992	12	(1)	4	8	(8)	4
Alexander Fernando Sican Ortíz	01.01.1970		(1)				
Jonathan Rafael Velásquez	24.06.1993	5	(4)		17	(3)	4
Forwards:							
Mynor Rodolfo Asencio Trejo	27.11.1986	2	(10)	1	8	(9)	
Mario Andrés Calero Luna			(2)				
Denis Lima de Assis (BRA)	29.12.1989	1	(1)				
Jean Theodoro Sobrinho (BRA)	25.02.1993	4	(5)				
Kendel Omar Herrarte Mayen	06.04.1992	13			11	(7)	
Cristian Jeyson Lima Cruz	02.10.1992	1	(6)				
Nelson Enrique Miranda Nery	21.12.1990	7	(5)	1	3	(11)	1
Anllel de Jesus Porras Conejo (CRC)	25.12.1990				17	(3)	4
Romario Luiz da Silva "Romarinho" (BRA)	05.03.1990	12	(4)		15	(4)	7
Trainer:							
Sergio Augusto Guevara González	07.07.1973	16					
[05.01.2021] Mario Francisco Acevedo Ruiz (NCA)	12.07.1972				22		

CLUB SOCIAL Y DEPORTVO XELAJÚ MARIO CAMPOSECO QUETZALTENANGO

Foundation date: February 24, 1942
Address: 1a. Calle y 14 Avenida, Zona 3, Quetzaltenango
Stadium: Estadio „Escolar Mario Camposeco", Quetzaltenango (11,000)

THE SQUAD

	DOB	Ape M	(s)	G	Cla M	(s)	G
Goalkeepers:							
Nery Estuardo Lobos Mejía	15.04.1990	5	(1)		3	(1)	
David Andrés Monsalve (CAN)	21.12.1988	15			13		
Defenders:							
José Eduardo Castañeda Barrios	26.09.1994	11	(4)		10	(4)	
Oscar Antonio Castellanos Santos	18.01.2000	18					
Tomás Castillo Pacheco	07.04.1991	6	(1)				
Carlos Salvador Pablo Renato Estrada Santos	12.09.1997				15		
Edwin Haroldo Fuentes Leal	22.02.1991	8	(8)		2	(2)	
Javier Alberto González del Aguila	27.04.1998	13	(1)		16		1
Rodolfo Rafael González Ruiz	04.03.1985	6			3	(2)	
Alexander Vidal Larín Hernández (SLV)	27.06.1992				10	(2)	1
Héctor Osberto Moreira Pérez	27.12.1987				11	(1)	
Jeffrey Payeras (USA)	16.10.1993	3	(1)		3	(1)	
Midfielders:							
Cristian Alexander Albizures García	06.02.1995	13	(3)	1			
Gerardo Alberto Arias Gaytán	18.11.1985	14	(1)				
Cristian David Castillo Hernández			(1)		12	(3)	2
Nery Gerardo Cifuentes Pinto	16.01.2000					(1)	
Dustin Clifman Corea Garay (SLV)	21.03.1992	3	(1)				
Maynor Iván de León Reyna	24.10.1990				12		
Josué Odir Flores Palencia (SLV)	13.05.1988				12	(4)	1
Yordin Noé Hernández Gramajo	24.08.1996				5	(4)	
Francisco Javier López Rodrígez	16.05.2002		(2)		1	(1)	
Víctor Alexis Matta Calderón	16.03.1990	9	(4)	1	3	(9)	
Pablo Jesús Mingorance (ARG)	02.11.1989	15	(3)	2	8	(5)	2
Fredy Fernando Ruano Garzona	29.03.1990	9	(4)				
Widvin Gabriel Tebalán Sicó	11.09.2000	2	(6)				
Joshua Ramiro Ubico Pyle	13.06.1999	9	(6)	2			
Juan Antonio Yax García (HON)	23.07.1988	13	(4)		5	(2)	
Forwards:							
Elmer William Cardoza Herrera	29.07.2002		(1)		1	(3)	
Mario César Castellanos Pinelo	19.05.1982	1	(11)				
Francisco Eliomar Rodrigues Farias "Léo Bahia" (BRA)	19.05.1991		(2)		7	(5)	1
Wilber Mauricio Pérez Medrano	26.09.1988	12	(8)	5	9	(4)	4
Edwin Orlando Rivas Tambito	08.01.1992	14	(3)	1			
Israel Silva Matos De Souza (BRA)	24.06.1981	19		9	8	(7)	
Esnaydi Zuñiga y Zúñiga	12.10.1999	2	(5)		7	(7)	
Trainer:							
Walter Enrique Claverí Alvarado	24.11.1957	14					
[09.12.2020] Marco Antonio Morales Muralles		6			6		
[02.02.2021] Gustavo Darío Machaín Uhalde (URU)	19.09.1965				8		
[05.04.2021] Marco Antonio Morales Muralles					2		

SECOND LEVEL
Primera División de Ascenso 2020/2021

Torneo Apertura 2020

Grupo A (Occidente)
1.	Deportivo San Pedro FC	8	3	4	1	12	-	5	13
2.	CD Marquense San Marcos	8	3	4	1	8	-	5	13
3.	CSD Xinabajul-Huehue	8	3	2	3	8	-	7	11
4.	Quiché FC	8	1	4	3	2	-	7	7
5.	Plataneros La Blanca	8	1	4	3	6	-	12	7

Grupo B (Suroccidente)
1.	CSD Puerto San José	8	3	4	1	11	-	6	13
2.	CSD Sololá	8	4	1	3	11	-	12	13
3.	CSD Suchitepéquez	8	3	3	2	13	-	6	12
4.	CD Coatepecano IB	8	2	3	3	4	-	7	9
5.	CSD Nueva Concepción	8	1	3	4	8	-	16	6

Grupo C (Centro-Sur)
1.	CD Naranjeros Escuintla Siquinalá	8	4	4	0	9	-	2	16
2.	Aurora FC Ciudad de Guatemala	8	3	2	3	8	-	8	11
3.	FC Chimaltenango	8	3	2	3	4	-	4	11
4.	CD Petapa	8	2	3	3	7	-	7	9
5.	Comunicaciones FC "B" Ciud. de Guatemala	8	2	1	5	6	-	13	7

Grupo D (Centro-Oriente-Norte)
1.	CSD Mixco	8	7	0	1	18	-	8	21
2.	CSD Mictlán	8	3	3	2	8	-	7	12
3.	CSD Sayaxché	8	3	1	4	11	-	13	10
4.	CSD Zacapa	8	2	2	4	7	-	10	8
5.	CSD Carchá	8	1	2	5	7	-	13	5

Top-2 of each group were qualified for the Play-offs.

Play-offs

Quarter-Finals [02-05.12.2020]
CSD Mictlán - CD Naranjeros Escuintla Siquinalá	2-1	3-1
Aurora FC Ciudad de Guatemala - CSD Mixco	0-0	1-1
CD Marquense San Marcos - CSD Puerto San José	1-1	0-1
CSD Sololá - Deportivo San Pedro FC	1-0	1-2

Semi-Finals [09-13.12.2020]
CSD Mictlán - CSD Sololá	1-0	0-1
Aurora FC Ciudad de Guatemala - CSD Puerto San José	2-0	0-0

Final [17-20.12.2020]
Aurora FC Ciudad de Guatemala - CSD Sololá	1-0	2-1

Torneo Apertura 2020 Winners: **Aurora FC Ciudad de Guatemala**

Torneo Clausura 2021

Grupo A (Occidente)

1.	Quiché FC	8	5	1	2	9 - 6	16
2.	Plataneros La Blanca	8	3	2	3	13 - 12	11
3.	CSD Xinabajul-Huehue	8	3	2	3	8 - 7	11
4.	CD Marquense San Marcos	8	3	2	3	10 - 11	11
5.	Deportivo San Pedro FC	8	1	3	4	5 - 9	6

Grupo B (Suroccidente)

1.	CSD Nueva Concepción	8	4	3	1	10 - 7	15
2.	CSD Suchitepéquez	8	3	3	2	10 - 7	12
3.	CD Coatepecano IB	8	3	2	3	9 - 8	11
4.	CSD Sololá	8	2	3	3	6 - 6	9
5.	CSD Puerto San José	8	0	5	3	3 - 10	5

Grupo C (Centro-Sur)

1.	Comunicaciones FC "B" Ciud. de Guatemala	8	5	2	1	14 - 4	17
2.	FC Chimaltenango	8	3	4	1	7 - 6	13
3.	Aurora FC Ciudad de Guatemala	8	3	3	2	8 - 6	12
4.	CD Naranjeros Escuintla Siquinalá	8	3	1	4	9 - 7	10
5.	CD Petapa	8	1	0	7	5 - 20	3

Grupo D (Centro-Oriente-Norte)

1.	CSD Mictlán	8	4	4	0	11 - 6	16
2.	CSD Mixco	8	4	2	2	10 - 5	14
3.	CSD Zacapa	8	3	2	3	6 - 4	11
4.	CSD Carchá	8	2	1	5	7 - 16	7
5.	CSD Sayaxché	8	1	3	4	6 - 9	6

Top-2 of each group were qualified for the Play-offs.

Play-offs

Quarter-Finals [21-25.04.2021]

FC Chimaltenango - Quiché FC	1-1	0-1
CSD Xinabajul-Huehue - Comunicaciones FC "B" Ciudad de Guatemala	0-0	1-3
CSD Mixco - CSD Nueva Concepción	1-1	0-4
CSD Suchitepéquez - CSD Mictlán	2-1	0-5

Semi-Finals [28.04.-02.05.2021]

Quiché FC - CSD Mictlán	2-1	1-1
CSD Nueva Concepción - Comunicaciones FC "B" Ciudad de Guatemala	2-3	2-1

Final [06-09.05.2021]

CSD Nueva Concepción - Quiché FC	1-0	0-2

Torneo Clausura 2021 Winners: **Quiché FC**

Promotion Play-off [15.05.2021]

Quiché FC - CSD Sololá	1-1
Aurora FC Ciudad de Guatemala - CSD Nueva Concepción	0-1

CSD Sololá and **CSD Nueva Concepción** promoted for next season's Liga Nacional de Fútbol.

NATIONAL TEAM
INTERNATIONAL MATCHES 2020/2021

30.09.2020	Ciudad de México	Mexico - Guatemala	3-0(3-0)	(F)
06.10.2020	Managua	Nicaragua - Guatemala	0-0	(F)
15.11.2020	Ciudad de Guatemala	Guatemala - Honduras	2-1(1-0)	(F)
23.01.2021	Ciudad de Guatemala	Guatemala - Puerto Rico	1-0(0-0)	(F)
24.02.2021	Ciudad de Guatemala	Guatemala - Nicaragua	1-0(0-0)	(F)
24.03.2021	Ciudad de Guatemala	Guatemala - Cuba	1-0(0-0)	(WCQ)
27.03.2021	Willemstad	British Virgin Islands - Guatemala	0-3(0-2)	(WCQ)
04.06.2021	Ciudad de Guatemala	Guatemala - Saint Vincent and the Grenadines	10-0(5-0)	(WCQ)
08.06.2021	Willemstad	Curaçao - Guatemala	0-0	(WCQ)
26.06.2021	Los Angeles	El Salvador - Guatemala	0-0	(F)
02.07.2021	Fort Lauderdale	Guatemala - Guyana	4-0(1-0)	(GCQ)
06.07.2021	Fort Lauderdale	Guatemala - Guadeloupe	1-1; 9-10p	(GCQ)

30.09.2020, Friendly International
Estadio Azteca, Ciudad de México; Attendance: 0
Referee: Fernando Hernández Gómez (Mexico)
MEXICO - GUATEMALA   **3-0(3-0)**
GUA: Ricardo Antonio Jérez Figueroa, Carlos Eduardo Gallardo Nájera, Gerardo Arturo Gordillo, José Carlos Pinto Samayoa, Alejandro Miguel Galindo (74.Christopher Rodolfo Ramírez Ulrich), Jorge Eduardo Aparicio Grijalva (78.Rodrigo Saravia Samayoa), Marco Leonel Domínguez-Ramírez (46.Rudy Ronaldo Barrientos Reyes), Luis Enrique de León Valenzuela, Stheven Adán Robles Ruiz (59.Eduardo Beltrán Soto Barrios), Antonio de Jesús López Amenábar (59.Jairo Randolfo Arreola Silva), Luis Fernando Martínez Castellanos (78.Jorge Estuardo Vargas García). Trainer: Marvin Amarini Villatoro de León.

06.10.2020, Friendly International
Estadio Nacional de Fútbol de Nicaragua, Managua; Attendance: 0
Referee: Nitzar Antonio Sandoval Chávez (Nicaragua)
NICARAGUA - GUATEMALA   **0-0**
GUA: Kevin Jorge Amílcar Moscoso Mayén, Moisés Hernández Hernández (82.Luis Enrique de León Valenzuela), Gerardo Arturo Gordillo, José Carlos Pinto Samayoa, Wilson Augusto Pineda Cornelio, Jairo Randolfo Arreola Silva (76.Christopher Rodolfo Ramírez Ulrich), Alejandro Miguel Galindo (59.Darwin Gregorio Lom Moscoso), Jorge Eduardo Aparicio Grijalva, Rodrigo Saravia Samayoa, Rudy Ronaldo Barrientos Reyes (59.Jorge Estuardo Vargas García), Antonio de Jesús López Amenábar. Trainer: Marvin Amarini Villatoro de León.

15.11.2020, Friendly International
Estadio "Doroteo Guamuch Flores", Ciudad de Guatemala; Attendance: 0
Referee: Mario Alberto Escobar Toca (Guatemala)
GUATEMALA - HONDURAS   **2-1(1-0)**
GUA: Ricardo Antonio Jérez Figueroa, Moisés Hernández Hernández, José Carlos Pinto Samayoa, Luis Enrique de León Valenzuela (80.Jairo Randolfo Arreola Silva), Stheven Adán Robles Ruiz, José Alberto Márquez Árdon (73.Christian Daniel Guerra Hernández), Rudy Ronaldo Barrientos Reyes, Kervin René García Sandoval, Antonio de Jesús López Amenábar (87.Marvin José Ceballos Flores), Luis Fernando Martínez Castellanos (80.Jorge Estuardo Vargas García), Darwin Gregorio Lom Moscoso (72.Harim Enrique Quezada Gámez). Trainer: Marvin Amarini Villatoro de León.
Goals: Darwin Gregorio Lom Moscoso (24, 66 penalty).

23.01.2021, Friendly International
Estadio "Doroteo Guamuch Flores", Ciudad de Guatemala; Attendance: 0
Referee: Bryan Lopez Castellanos (Guatemala)
GUATEMALA - PUERTO RICO **1-0(0-0)**
GUA: Kevin Jorge Amílcar Moscoso Mayén, Moisés Hernández Hernández (46.Stheven Adán Robles Ruiz), Sixto Ubaldo Betancourt Véliz, Wilson Augusto Pineda Cornelio, Yeltsin Delfino Álvarez Castro (68.Robin Osvaldo Betancourth Cué), Óscar Antonio Castellanos Santos, Nicholas Rittmeyer (59.Marvin José Ceballos Flores), Rodrigo Saravia Samayoa, Rudy Ronaldo Barrientos Reyes, Christopher Rodolfo Ramírez Ulrich (46.Pablo Andrés Aguilar Palacios), Darwin Gregorio Lom Moscoso (68.José Carlos Martínez Navas). Trainer: Marvin Amarini Villatoro de León.
Goal: Darwin Gregorio Lom Moscoso (67).

24.02.2021, Friendly International
Estadio "Doroteo Guamuch Flores", Ciudad de Guatemala; Attendance: 0
Referee: Sergio Armando Reyna Moller (Guatemala)
GUATEMALA - NICARAGUA **1-0(0-0)**
GUA: Kevin Jorge Amílcar Moscoso Mayén, Moisés Hernández Hernández, José Carlos Pinto Samayoa, Allen José Yanes Pinto, Óscar Antonio Castellanos Santos (82.Pablo Andrés Aguilar Palacios), Stheven Adán Robles Ruiz, Óscar Alexander Santís Cayax (71.Nicholas Rittmeyer), Rodrigo Saravia Samayoa, Rudy Ronaldo Barrientos Reyes (61.José Alberto Márquez Árdon), José Carlos Martínez Navas (61.Marvin José Ceballos Flores), Darwin Gregorio Lom Moscoso (71.Robin Osvaldo Betancourth Cué). Trainer: Marvin Amarini Villatoro de León.
Goal: Nicholas Rittmeyer (90+4).

24.03.2021, 22nd FIFA World Cup Qualifiers, CONCACAF First Round
Estadio "Doroteo Guamuch Flores", Ciudad de Guatemala
Referee: Benjamin Pineda Ávila (Costa Rica)
GUATEMALA - CUBA **1-0(0-0)**
GUA: Nicholas George Hagen Godoy, Moisés Hernández Hernández, Gerardo Arturo Gordillo, José Carlos Pinto Samayoa, Allen José Yanes Pinto (46.Wilson Augusto Pineda Cornelio), Stheven Adán Robles Ruiz, Rodrigo Saravia Samayoa (63.José Manuel Contreras), José Alberto Márquez Árdon, Antonio de Jesús López Amenábar (88.Nicholas Rittmeyer), Luis Fernando Martínez Castellanos (63.Marvin José Ceballos Flores), Darwin Gregorio Lom Moscoso (75.José Carlos Martínez Navas). Trainer: Marvin Amarini Villatoro de León.
Goal: Luis Fernando Martínez Castellanos (60).

27.03.2021, 22nd FIFA World Cup Qualifiers, CONCACAF First Round
Stadion „Ergilio Hato", Willemstad (Curaçao)
Referee: Óscar Donaldo Moncada (Honduras)
BRITISH VIRGIN ISLANDS - GUATEMALA **0-3(0-2)**
GUA: Ricardo Antonio Jérez Figueroa, Moisés Hernández Hernández, Gerardo Arturo Gordillo, José Carlos Pinto Samayoa, José Manuel Contreras (76.Robin Osvaldo Betancourth Cué), Marvin José Ceballos Flores (64.Óscar Alexander Santís Cayax), Nicholas Rittmeyer (76.Rudy Ronaldo Barrientos Reyes), Stheven Adán Robles Ruiz, José Alberto Márquez Árdon (35.Rodrigo Saravia Samayoa), Antonio de Jesús López Amenábar Darwin Gregorio Lom Moscoso (64.José Carlos Martínez Navas). Trainer: Marvin Amarini Villatoro de León.
Goals: Darwin Gregorio Lom Moscoso (21), Moisés Hernández Hernández (44), Robin Osvaldo Betancourth Cué (81).

04.06.2021, 22nd FIFA World Cup Qualifiers, CONCACAF First Round
Estadio "Doroteo Guamuch Flores", Ciudad de Guatemala; Attendance: n/a
Referee: Erick Moisés Lezama Pavón (Nicaragua)
GUATEMALA - SAINT VINCENT AND THE GRENADINES   10-0(5-0)
GUA: Nicholas George Hagen Godoy, Moisés Hernández Hernández (64.John Roberth Méndez Sánchez), Gerardo Arturo Gordillo, José Carlos Pinto Samayoa, Matan Peleg, Stheven Adán Robles Ruiz, Óscar Alexander Santís Cayax (46.Robin Osvaldo Betancourth Cué), Rodrigo Saravia Samayoa, Rudy Ronaldo Barrientos Reyes (79.José Carlos Martínez Navas), Luis Fernando Martínez Castellanos (63.Marvin José Ceballos Flores), Darwin Gregorio Lom Moscoso (46.Jorge Estuardo Vargas García). Trainer: Marvin Amarini Villatoro de León.
Goals: Darwin Gregorio Lom Moscoso (2), Rudy Ronaldo Barrientos Reyes (12), Óscar Alexander Santís Cayax (16), Moisés Hernández Hernández (33 penalty), Gerardo Arturo Gordillo (41), Luis Fernando Martínez Castellanos (52), Robin Osvaldo Betancourth Cué (66), Marvin José Ceballos Flores (79 penalty), Jorge Estuardo Vargas García (85), John Roberth Méndez Sánchez (89).

08.06.2021, 22nd FIFA World Cup Qualifiers, CONCACAF First Round
Stadion „Ergilio Hato", Willemstad; Attendance: 3,000
Referee: Armando Villareal (United States)
CURAÇAO - GUATEMALA   0-0
GUA: Nicholas George Hagen Godoy, Moisés Hernández Hernández, José Carlos Pinto Samayoa, Matan Peleg (78.Jorge Estuardo Vargas García), Stheven Adán Robles Ruiz, Óscar Alexander Santís Cayax (78.Marvin José Ceballos Flores), Rodrigo Saravia Samayoa (65.Marco Leonel Domínguez-Ramírez), Rudy Ronaldo Barrientos Reyes, Kervin René García Sandoval, Luis Fernando Martínez Castellanos (88.José Carlos Martínez Navas), Darwin Gregorio Lom Moscoso (65.Robin Osvaldo Betancourth Cué). Trainer: Marvin Amarini Villatoro de León.

26.06.2021, Friendly International
Banc of California Stadium, Los Angeles (United States); Atendance: 0
Referee: Óscar Donaldo Moncada Godoy (Honduras)
EL SALVADOR - GUATEMALA   0-0
GUA: Nicholas George Hagen Godoy, Moisés Hernández Hernández, José Carlos Pinto Samayoa, Matan Peleg, José Andrés Ruiz Rumph (46.Rodrigo Saravia Samayoa), Jorge Estuardo Vargas García (80.Darwin Gregorio Lom Moscoso), Marco Leonel Domínguez-Ramírez, Stheven Adán Robles Ruiz, Kervin René García Sandoval (81.Wilson Augusto Pineda Cornelio), Luis Fernando Martínez Castellanos (64.Marvin José Ceballos Flores), José Carlos Martínez Navas (46.Robin Osvaldo Betancourth Cué). Trainer: Marvin Amarini Villatoro de León.

02.07.2021, 16th CONCACAF Gold Cup Qualifiers, First Round
DRV PNK Stadium, Fort Lauderdale (United States); Attendance: 0
Referee: Juan Gabriel Calderón (Costa Rica)
GUATEMALA - GUYANA   4-0(1-0)
GUA: Nicholas George Hagen Godoy, Moisés Hernández Hernández, Gerardo Arturo Gordillo, José Carlos Pinto Samayoa, Matan Peleg (60.Wilson Augusto Pineda Cornelio), Jairo Randolfo Arreola Silva (60.Jorge Estuardo Vargas García), Marvin José Ceballos Flores (John Roberth Méndez Sánchez), Marco Leonel Domínguez-Ramírez, Stheven Adán Robles Ruiz (73.José Andrés Ruiz Rumph), Luis Fernando Martínez Castellanos, Darwin Gregorio Lom Moscoso (78.José Carlos Martínez Navas). Trainer: Marvin Amarini Villatoro de León.
Goals: Reiss James Greenidge (21 own goal), Luis Fernando Martínez Castellanos (35), Darwin Gregorio Lom Moscoso (45+2), José Carlos Martínez Navas (57).

06.07.2021, 16th CONCACAF Gold Cup Qualifiers, Second Round
DRV PNK Stadium, Fort Lauderdale (United States); Attendance: 0
Referee: Fernando Hernández Gómez (Mexico)
GUATEMALA - GUADELOUPE **1-1(1-1,1-1); 9-10 on penalties**
GUA: Nicholas George Hagen Godoy (Ricardo Antonio Jérez Figueroa), Moisés Hernández Hernández, Gerardo Arturo Gordillo, José Carlos Pinto Samayoa, Matan Peleg, Marvin José Ceballos Flores, Marco Leonel Domínguez-Ramírez (70.Rudy Ronaldo Barrientos Reyes), Stheven Adán Robles Ruiz (87.Wilson Augusto Pineda Cornelio), Luis Fernando Martínez Castellanos (87.Óscar Alexander Santís Cayax), José Carlos Martínez Navas, Darwin Gregorio Lom Moscoso (70.Rodrigo Saravia Samayoa). Trainer: Marvin Amarini Villatoro de León.
Goal: Luis Fernando Martínez Castellanos (17).
Penalties: Marvin José Ceballos Flores (missed), José Carlos Martínez Navas, Óscar Alexander Santís Cayax, Rudy Ronaldo Barrientos Reyes, Moisés Hernández Hernández, Wilson Augusto Pineda Cornelio, José Carlos Pinto Samayoa, Rodrigo Saravia Samayoa, Matan Peleg, Gerardo Arturo Gordillo (saved), Ricardo Antonio Jérez Figueroa, Marvin José Ceballos Flores (missed).

NATIONAL TEAM PLAYERS 2020/2021

Name	DOB	Club
Goalkeepers		
Nicholas George HAGEN Godoy	02.08.1996	*Sabail FK Bakı (AZE)*
Ricardo Antonio JEREZ Figueroa	04.02.1986	*CD Alianza Petrolera Barrancabermeja (COL)*
Kevin Jorge Amílcar MOSCOSO Mayén	13.06.1999	*CSD Cobán Imperial; 24.01.2021-> Comunicaciones FC Ciudad de Guatemala*
Defenders		
Sixto Ubaldo BETANCOURT Véliz	16.05.1992	*CD Malacateco*
Óscar Antonio CASTELLANOS Santos	18.01.2000	*CSD Xelajú Mario Camposeco; 08.02.2021-> Antigua Guatemala FC*
Carlos Eduardo GALLARDO Nájera	08.04.1984	*CSD Municipal Ciudad de Guatemala*
Kervin René GARCÍA Sandoval	07.12.1990	*Antigua Guatemala FC*
Gerardo Arturo GORDILLO	17.08.1994	*Comunicaciones FC Ciudad de Guatemala; 08.01.2021-> CCD Universidad Técnica de Cajamarca (PER)*
Moisés HERNÁNDEZ Hernández	05.03.1992	*Antigua Guatemala FC*
Matan PELEG	11.11.1993	*Hapoel Nof HaGalil FC (ISR)*
Wilson Augusto PINEDA Cornelio	23.09.1993	*CD Guastatoya*
José Carlos PINTO Samayoa	16.06.1993	*Comunicaciones FC Ciudad de Guatemala*
Eduardo Beltrán SOTO Barrios	03.03.1990	*CSD Cobán Imperial*
Allen José YANES Pinto	04.07.1997	*Comunicaciones FC Ciudad de Guatemala*

Midfielders

Pablo Andrés AGUILAR Palacios	21.02.1995	Antigua Guatemala FC; 04.02.2021-> Comunicaciones FC Ciudad de Guatemala
Yeltsin Delfino ÁLVAREZ Castro	02.11.1994	CSD Cobán Imperial
Jorge Eduardo APARICIO Grijalva	21.11.1992	Comunicaciones FC Ciudad de Guatemala
Rudy Ronaldo BARRIENTOS Reyes	01.03.1999	CSD Municipal Ciudad de Guatemala
Marvin José CEBALLOS Flores	22.04.1992	CD Guastatoya
José Manuel CONTRERAS	19.01.1986	Comunicaciones FC Ciudad de Guatemala
Luis Enrique DE LEÓN Valenzuela	14.11.1995	CSD Municipal Ciudad de Guatemala
Marco Leonel DOMÍNGUEZ-RAMÍREZ	25.02.1996	Antigua Guatemala FC
Alejandro Miguel GALINDO	05.03.1992	Comunicaciones FC Ciudad de Guatemala
Christian Daniel GUERRA Hernández	27.01.1995	CD Iztapa
José Alberto MÁRQUEZ Ardon	06.03.1985	CD Guastatoya
John Roberth MÉNDEZ Sánchez	24.06.1999	CSD Municipal Ciudad de Guatemala
Christopher Rodolfo RAMÍREZ Ulrich	08.01.1994	CSD Sanarate FC
Nicholas RITTMEYER	13.10.1993	Charleston Battery (USA)
Stheven Adán ROBLES Ruiz	12.11.1995	Comunicaciones FC Ciudad de Guatemala
José Andrés RUIZ Rumph	30.05.1996	CSD Cobán Imperial
Óscar Alexander SANTIS Cayax	25.03.1999	Comunicaciones FC Ciudad de Guatemala
Rodrigo SARAVIA Samayoa	22.02.1993	Comunicaciones FC Ciudad de Guatemala
Jorge Estuardo VARGAS García	26.02.1993	CD Guastatoya

Forwards

Jairo Randolfo ARREOLA Silva	20.09.1985	Antigua Guatemala FC
Robin Osvaldo BETANCOURTH Cué	25.11.1991	Antigua Guatemala FC; 07.02.2021-> CSD Cobán Imperial
Darwin Gregorio LOM Moscoso	14.07.1997	Chattanooga FC (USA); 01.12.2020-> Unattached; 24.03.2021-> California United Strikers FC Orange County (USA)
Antonio de Jesús LÓPEZ Amenábar	10.04.1997	CF América Ciudad de México (MEX)
José Carlos MARTÍNEZ Navas	10.10.1997	CSD Municipal Ciudad de Guatemala
Luis Fernando MARTÍNEZ Castellanos	14.12.1991	CD Guastatoya
Harim Enrique QUEZADA Gámez	17.10.1997	CSD Cobán Imperial

National coaches

Marvin Amarini VILLATORO de León [from 09.03.2018]		06.05.1985

GUYANA

The Country:	The FA:
Co-operative Republic of Guyana	Guyana Football Federation
Capital: Georgetown	Lot 17 Dadanawa Street Section „K",
Surface: 214,999 km²	Campbellville P.O. Box 10727, Georgetown
Population: 743,700 [2019]	Year of Formation: 1902
Time: UTC-4	Member of FIFA since: 1970
Independent since: 1966	Member of CONCACAF since: 1961

NATIONAL TEAM RECORDS

First international match: 28.01.1921: Surinam - British Guyana 1-2
Most international caps: Walter Moore – 77 caps (since 2004)
Most international goals: Nigel Codrington – 18 goals / 26 caps (2001-2010)

CONCACAF GOLD CUP	
1991	Qualifiers
1993	Qualifiers
1996	Qualifiers
1998	Did not enter
2000	Qualifiers
2002	Qualifiers
2003	Qualifiers
2005	*Withdrew*
2007	Qualifiers
2009	Qualifiers
2011	Qualifiers
2013	Qualifiers
2015	Qualifiers
2017	Qualifiers
2019	Final Tournament (Group Stage)
2021	Qualifiers

FIFA WORLD CUP	
1930	-
1934	-
1938	-
1950	-
1954	-
1958	-
1962	-
1966	-
1970	-
1974	Did not enter
1978	Did not enter
1982	Qualifiers
1986	Qualifiers
1990	Qualifiers
1994	Qualifiers
1998	Qualifiers
2002	*Suspended by FIFA*
2006	Qualifiers
2010	Qualifiers
2014	Qualifiers
2018	Qualifiers

F.I.F.A. CONFEDERATIONS CUP 1992-2017

None

OLYMPIC FOOTBALL TOURNAMENTS 1908-2016

1908	-	1948	-	1972	Did not enter	1996	Qualifiers
1912	-	1952	-	1976	Did not enter	2000	Qualifiers
1920	-	1956	-	1980	Did not enter	2004	Qualifiers
1924	-	1960	-	1984	Did not enter	2008	Qualifiers
1928	-	1964	-	1988	Qualifiers	2012	Qualifiers
1936	-	1968	-	1992	Did not enter	2016	Qualifiers

CCCF (Confederación Centroamericana y del Caribe de Fútbol) CHAMPIONSHIPS 1941-1961
None

CONCACAF CHAMPIONSHIPS 1963-1989
1971

CONCACAF NATIONS LEAGUE
2019-2020	League B

CARIBBEAN CHAMPIONSHIPS 1989-2017

1989	Did not enter	1999	Qualifiers
1991	Final Tournament - 4th Place	2001	Qualifiers
1992	Qualifiers	2005	*Withdrew*
1993	Qualifiers	2007	Final Tournament - Group Stage
1994	Qualifiers	2008	Qualifiers
1995	Qualifiers	2010	Final Tournament - Group Stage
1996	Did not enter	2012	Qualifiers
1997	Qualifiers	2014	Qualifiers
1998	Qualifiers	2017	Qualifiers

GUYANESE CLUB HONOURS IN CONCACAF CLUB COMPETITIONS:

CONCACAF Champions Cup / CONCACAF Champions League 1962-2020
None

CONCACAF League 2017-2020
None

Caribbean Club Championship 1997-2021
None

CONCACAF Cup Winners Cup 1991-1995*
None

Copa Interamericana 1968-1998*
None

*defunct competitions

NATIONAL COMPETITIONS
TABLE OF HONOURS

	CHAMPIONS	CUP WINNERS
1990	Santos FC Georgetown	-
1991	Santos FC Georgetown	Milerock FC Linden
1992	*No competition*	Eagles United Linden
1993	*No competition*	Botafogo Linden
1994	Western Tigers FC Georgetown	Camptown Georgetown
1995	Milerock Linden	Topp XX Linden

1996	Omai Gold Seekers	Beacon's Georgetown
1997	Topp XX Linden	Topp XX Linden
1997/1998	-	Milerock FC Linden
1998/1999	Santos FC Georgetown	Doc's Khelwalaas Trinidad
1999/2000	*No competition*	Topp XX Linden
2000/2001	Conquerors Georgetown	Topp XX Linden
2001/2002	*No competition*	Real Victoria Kings East Demerara
2002/2003	*No competition*	Conquerors Georgetown
2003/2004	*No competition*	Camptown Georgetown
2004/2005	*No competition*	Conquerors Georgetown
2005/2006	*No competition*	Topp XX Linden
2006/2007	*No competition*	Joe Public FC Trinidad
2007/2008	*No competition*	Alpha United FC Providence
2008/2009	*No competition*	Pele FC Georgetown
2009/2010	Alpha United FC Providence	Western Tigers FC Georgetown
2010/2011	Alpha United FC Providence	Alpha United FC Providence
2012	Alpha United FC Providence	Caledonian AIA Malabar (Trinidad and Tobago)
2013	Alpha United FC Providence	Buxton United East Coast Demerara
2013/2014	Alpha United FC Providence	Wismar/Christianburg SS
2014/2015	*No competition*	Slingerz FC
2015/2016	Slingerz FC Vergenoegen	*No competition*
2016/2017	Guyana Defence Force Georgetown	*No competition*
2017/2018	Fruta Conquerors FC Georgetown	*No competition*
2019	Fruta Conquerors FC Georgetown	*No competition*
2020	*No competition*	*No competition*

Note: the championship tournament was called NBIC Championship (1990-1991 & 1998-2000), Carib League (1994-1997) and National Football League (since 2000).

NATIONAL CHAMPIONSHIP
GFF Elite League 2020

The championship was not played due to COVID-19 pandemic.

NATIONAL TEAM
INTERNATIONAL MATCHES 2020/2021

25.03.2021	San Cristóbal	Trinidad and Tobago - Guyana	3-0(3-0)	(WCQ)
30.03.2021	Santo Domingo	Guyana - Bahamas	4-0(1-0)	(WCQ)
04.06.2021	Basseterre	Saint Kitts and Nevis - Guyana	3-0(2-0)	(WCQ)
08.06.2021	Georgetown	Guyana - Puerto Rico	0-2(0-2)	(WCQ)
02.07.2021	Fort Lauderdale	Guatemala - Guyana	4-0(1-0)	(GCQ)

25.03.2021, 22nd FIFA World Cup Qualifiers, CONCACAF First Round
Estadio Panamericano, San Cristóbal (Dominican Republic)
Referee: Randy Encarnacion Solano (Dominican Republic)
TRINIDAD AND TOBAGO - GUYANA 3-0(3-0)
GUY: Akeil Kayode Clarke, Matthew Anthony Briggs, Kadell Ebony Daniel, Samuel Peter Cox, Trayon Denzil Bobb (71.Pernell Anthony Schultz), Terence Owen Vancooten, Miquel Howard Hugh Scarlett (56.Bayli Alexander Spencer-Adams), Callum Kyle Harriott (76.Kelsey The First Benjamin), Daniel Jeran Wilson, Keanu Marqheal Marsh-Brown (56.Jobe Caesar), Emery Welshman. Trainer: Márcio Máximo Barcellos (Brazil).

30.03.2021, 22nd FIFA World Cup Qualifiers, CONCACAF First Round
Estadio Olímpico "Félix Sánchez", Santo Domingo (Dominican Republic)
Referee: Sergio Armando Reyna Moller (Guatemala)
GUYANA - BAHAMAS 4-0(1-0)
GUY: Kai John Oliver McKenzie-Lyle, Matthew Anthony Briggs, Kadell Ebony Daniel, Samuel Peter Cox, Trayon Denzil Bobb (78.Nathan Daniel Moriah-Welsh), Terence Owen Vancooten, Miquel Howard Hugh Scarlett (82.Nicholai Andrews), Callum Kyle Harriott (70.Omari Glasgow), Daniel Jeran Wilson (82.Jobe Caesar), Keanu Marqheal Marsh-Brown (70.Pernell Anthony Schultz), Emery Welshman. Trainer: Márcio Máximo Barcellos (Brazil).
Goals: Terence Owen Vancooten (8), Kadell Ebony Daniel (54), Omari Glasgow (75), Emery Welshman (81).

04.06.2021, 22nd FIFA World Cup Qualifiers, CONCACAF First Round
Warner Park, Basseterre
Referee: Ricangel de Leça (Aruba)
SAINT KITTS AND NEVIS - GUYANA 3-0(2-0)
GUY: Kai John Oliver McKenzie-Lyle, Matthew Anthony Briggs, Bayli Alexander Spencer-Adams (46.Jobe Caesar), Stephen Winston Duke-McKenna (69.Kelsey The First Benjamin), Liam Gordon, Pernell Anthony Schultz (74.Osafa Simpson), Terence Owen Vancooten, Miquel Howard Hugh Scarlett, Daniel Jeran Wilson, Keanu Marqheal Marsh-Brown (80.Nathan Daniel Moriah-Welsh), Omari Glasgow (46.Trayon Denzil Bobb). Trainer: Márcio Máximo Barcellos (Brazil).

08.06.2021, 22nd FIFA World Cup Qualifiers, CONCACAF First Round
Warner Park, Basseterre (Saint Kitts and Nevis)
Referee: Ismael Cornejo Meléndez (El Salvador)
GUYANA - PUERTO RICO 0-2(0-2)
GUY: Kai John Oliver McKenzie-Lyle, Matthew Anthony Briggs, Liam Gordon, Terence Owen Vancooten, Miquel Howard Hugh Scarlett (46.Nicholai Andrews), Stephen Winston Duke-McKenna, Jobe Caesar (55.Javier George), Osafa Simpson (31.Nathan Daniel Moriah-Welsh), Daniel Jeran Wilson (65.Marcus Wilson), Keanu Marqheal Marsh-Brown, Omari Glasgow (65.Kelsey The First Benjamin). Trainer: Márcio Máximo Barcellos (Brazil).

03.07.2021, 16th CONCACAF Gold Cup Qualifiers, First Round
DRV PNK Stadium, Fort Lauderdale (United States); Attendance: 0
Referee: Juan Gabriel Calderón (Costa Rica)
GUATEMALA - GUYANA   **4-0(1-0)**
GUY: Kai John Oliver McKenzie-Lyle, Matthew Anthony Briggs, Reiss James Greenidge (76.Trayon Denzil Bobb), Stephen Winston Duke-McKenna, Nicholai Andrews, Terence Owen Vancooten, Jobe Caesar, Nathan Daniel Moriah-Welsh (62.Javier George), Daniel Jeran Wilson (57.Omari Glasgow), Keanu Marqheal Marsh-Brown [*sent off 40*], Emery Welshman (77.Sheldon Lawrence Holder). Trainer: Márcio Máximo Barcellos (Brazil).

NATIONAL TEAM PLAYERS 2020/2021		
Name	**DOB**	**Club**
Goalkeepers		
Akeil Kayode CLARKE	25.10.1988	*Fruta Conquerors FC Georgetown*
Kai John Oliver McKENZIE-LYLE	30.11.1997	*Cambridge United FC (ENG)*
Defenders		
Nicholai ANDREWS	03.11.2002	*Santos FC Georgetown*
Matthew Anthony BRIGGS	06.03.1991	*Vejle BK (DEN)*
Kadell Ebony DANIEL	03.06.1994	*Kingstonian FC (ENG)*
Liam GORDON	15.05.1999	*Dagenham & Redbridge FC (ENG)*
Reiss James GREENIDGE	08.02.1996	*Bolton Wanderers FC (ENG)*
Miquel Howard Hugh SCARLETT	27.09.2000	*Colchester United FC (ENG)*
Pernell Anthony SCHULTZ	07.04.1994	*Morvant Caledonia United (TRI)*
Bayli Alexander SPENCER-ADAMS	26.06.2001	*Dover Athletic FC (ENG)*
Terence Owen VANCOOTEN	29.12.1997	*Stevenage FC (ENG)*
Marcus WILSON	19.04.2002	*Santos FC Georgetown*
Midfielders		
Kelsey The First BENJAMIN	08.05.1990	*Georgetown FC*
Trayon Denzil BOBB	05.01.1993	*Uitvlugt Warriors FC*
Samuel Peter COX	10.10.1990	*Hampton & Richmond Borough FC (ENG)*
Stephen Winston DUKE-McKENNA	17.08.2000	*Queens Park Rangers FC London FC (ENG)*
Javier GEORGE	27.01.2001	*Stade Beaucairois (FRA)*
Omari GLASGOW	22.11.2003	*Fruta Conquerors FC Georgetown*
Nathan Daniel MORIAH-WELSH	18.03.2002	*AFC Bournemouth (ENG)*
Osafa SIMPSON	07.09.2002	*Guyana Defence Force Georgetown*
Daniel Jeran WILSON	01.11.1993	*Police FC Georgetown*
Forwards		
Jobe CAESAR	1999	*Guyana Defence Force Georgetown*
Callum Kyle HARRIOTT	04.03.1994	*Colchester United FC (ENG)*
Sheldon Lawrence HOLDER	30.09.1991	*Morvant Caledonia United (TRI)*
Keanu Marqheal MARSH-BROWN	10.08.1992	*Wrexham AFC (WAL)*
Emery WELSHMAN	09.11.1991	*Hapoel Ra'anana AFC (ISR)*
National coaches		
MÁRCIO MÁXIMO Barcellos (Brazil) [from 21.08.2019]		29.04.1962

HAITI

The Country:	The FA:
République d'Haïti (Republic of Haiti)	Fédération Haïtienne de Football
Capital: Port-au-Prince	Stade „Sylvio Cator"
Surface: 27,751 km²	Rue Oswald Durand, Port-au-Prince
Population: 11,439,646 [2018]	Year of Formation: 1904
Time: UTC-5	Member of FIFA since: 1934
Independent since: 1825	Member of CONCACAF since: 1961

NATIONAL TEAM RECORDS

First international match: 22.03.1925, Port-au-Prince: Haiti - Jamaica 1-2
Most international caps: Pierre Richard Bruny – 95 caps (1998-2010)
Most international goals: Emmanuel Sannon – 37 goals / 65 caps (1970-1981)

CONCACAF GOLD CUP	
1991	Qualifiers
1993	Did not enter
1996	Did not enter
1998	*Withdrew*
2000	Final Tournament (Group Stage)
2002	Final Tournament (Quarter-Finals)
2003	Qualifiers
2005	Qualifiers
2007	Final Tournament (Group Stage)
2009	Final Tournament (Quarter-Finals)
2011	Qualifiers
2013	Final Tournament (Group Stage)
2015	Final Tournament (Quarter-Finals)
2017	Qualifiers
2019	Final Tournament (Semi-Finals)
2021	Final Tournament (*to be played*)

FIFA WORLD CUP	
1930	-
1934	Qualifiers
1938	Did not enter
1950	Did not enter
1954	Qualifiers
1958	Did not enter
1962	Did not enter
1966	Did not enter
1970	Qualifiers
1974	Final Tournament (Group Stage)
1978	Qualifiers
1982	Qualifiers
1986	Qualifiers
1990	Did not enter
1994	Qualifiers
1998	Qualifiers
2002	Qualifiers
2006	Qualifiers
2010	Qualifiers
2014	Qualifiers
2018	Qualifiers

F.I.F.A. CONFEDERATIONS CUP 1992-2017
None

OLYMPIC FOOTBALL TOURNAMENTS 1908-2016

1908	-	1948	-	1972	Did not enter	1996	Did not enter
1912	-	1952	-	1976	Did not enter	2000	Qualifiers
1920	-	1956	-	1980	Qualifiers	2004	Qualifiers
1924	-	1960	-	1984	Did not enter	2008	Qualifiers
1928	-	1964	-	1988	Did not enter	2012	Qualifiers
1936	-	1968	Qualifiers	1992	Qualifiers	2016	Qualifiers

CCCF (Confederación Centroamericana y del Caribe de Fútbol) CHAMPIONSHIPS 1941-1961

1957 (Winners), 1961 (Runners-up)

CONCACAF CHAMPIONSHIPS 1963-1989

1965, 1967, 1971 (Runners-up), **1973 (Winners)**, 1977 (Runners-up), 1981, 1985

COPA AMÉRICA (invited as guests)

2016

CONCACAF NATIONS LEAGUE

2019-2020	League A (*relegated to League B*)

CARIBBEAN CHAMPIONSHIPS 1989-2017

1989	Did not enter	1999	Final Tournament - Group Stage
1991	Qualifiers	2001	Final Tournament - Runners-up
1992	Did not enter	2005	Qualifiers
1993	Did not enter	2007	**Final Tournament - Winners**
1994	Final Tournament - Group Stage	2008	Final Tournament - Group Stage
1995	Did not enter	2010	Qualifiers
1996	Final Tournament - Group Stage	2012	Final Tournament - 3rd Place
1997	Qualifiers	2014	Final Tournament - 3rd Place
1998	Final Tournament - 3rd Place	2017	Qualifiers

HAITIAN CLUB HONOURS IN CONCACAF CLUB COMPETITIONS:

CONCACAF Champions Cup / CONCACAF Champions League 1962-2020

Racing Club Haïtien Port-au-Prince	1	1963
Violette Athletic Club Port-au-Prince	1	1984

CONCACAF League 2017-2020

None

Caribbean Club Championship 1997-2021

None

CONCACAF Cup Winners Cup 1991-1995*

None

Copa Interamericana 1968-1998*

None

*defunct competitions

NATIONAL COMPETITIONS
TABLE OF HONOURS

	CHAMPIONS
1937/1938	Racing Club Haïtien Port-au-Prince
1939	Violette AC Port-au-Prince
1940	Hatüey Bacardi Club Port-au-Prince
1941	Racing Club Haïtien Port-au-Prince
1942/1943	Etoile Haïtienne Port-au-Prince
1943	Arsenal FC
1944	Etoile Haïtienne Port-au-Prince
1945	Hatüey Bacardi Club Port-au-Prince
1946	Racing Club Haïtien Port-au-Prince
1947	Racing Club Haïtien Port-au-Prince
1948	Excelsior AC Port-au-Prince
1949	*Competition not finished*
1950	Excelsior AC Port-au-Prince
1951	Excelsior AC Port-au-Prince
1952/1953	Aigle Noir AC Port-au-Prince
1953/1954	Racing Club Haïtien Port-au-Prince
1954	*No competition*
1955	Aigle Noir AC Port-au-Prince
1956	Jeunesse Pétion-Ville
1957	Violette AC Port-au-Prince
1958	Racing Club Haïtien Port-au-Prince
1959	*No competition*
1960	*No competition*
1961	Etoile Haïtienne Port-au-Prince
1962	Racing Club Haïtien Port-au-Prince
1963	*No competition*
1964	*No competition*
1965	*No competition*
1966	*No competition*
1967	*No competition*
1968	Violette AC Port-au-Prince
1969	Racing Club Haïtien Port-au-Prince
1970	Aigle Noir AC Port-au-Prince
1971	Don Bosco FC Pétion-Ville
1972	*No competition*
1973	*No competition*
1974	*No competition*
1975	*No competition*
1976	*No competition*
1977	*No competition*
1978	*No competition*
1979	*No competition*
1980	*No competition*
1981	*No competition*
1982	*No competition*
1983	Violette AC Port-au-Prince
1984	*No competition*

1985	No competition	
1986	No competition	
1987	No competition	
1987/1988	Not known	
1988/1989	FICA Cap-Haïtien	
1989/1990	FICA Cap-Haïtien	
1990/1991	FICA Cap-Haïtien	
1991/1992	Competition not finished	
1992/1993	Tempête FC Saint-Marc	
1993/1994	FICA Cap-Haïtien	
1994/1995	Violette AC Port-au-Prince	
1996	Racing FC Gônaïves	
1997	AS Capoise Cap-Haïtien	
1998	FICA Cap-Haïtien	
1999	Violette AC Port-au-Prince	
2000	Racing Club Haïtien Port-au-Prince	
2001	FICA Cap-Haïtien	
2002	Ou:	Roulado Le Gônaïves
	Fe:	Racing Club Haïtien Port-au-Prince
2003	Ou:	Don Bosco FC Pétion-Ville
	Fe:	Roulado Le Gônaïves
2004	No competition	
2004/2005	Ou:	AS Mirebalais
	Fe:	Baltimore SC Saint-Marc
2005/2006	Baltimore SC Saint-Marc	
2007	Ou:	Baltimore SC Saint-Marc
	Fe:	AS Cavaly Léogâne
2008	Ou:	Tempête FC Saint-Marc
	Fe:	Racing FC Gônaïves
2009	Ou:	Tempête FC Saint-Marc
	Fe:	Racing Club Haïtien Port-au-Prince
2010	Ou:	Tempête FC Saint-Marc
	Fe:	Victory SC Port-au-Prince
2011	Ou:	Baltimore SC Saint-Marc
	Fe:	Tempête FC Saint-Marc
2012	Valencia de Léogâne	
2013	AS Mirebalais	
2014	Ou:	América FC des Cayes
	Fe:	Don Bosco FC Pétion-Ville
2015	Ou:	Don Bosco FC Pétion-Ville
	Cl:	FICA Cap-Haïtien
2016	Ou:	Racing FC Gônaïves
	Cl:	FICA Cap-Haïtien
2017	Ou:	Real Hope FA Cap-Haïtien
	Cl:	AS Capoise Cap-Haïtien
2018	Ou:	AS Capoise Cap-Haïtien
	Cl:	Don Bosco FC Pétion-Ville
2019	Ou:	Arcahaie FC
	Cl:	Championship abandoned
2020	Ou:	Championship cancelled
	Cl:	Championship cancelled

2020/2021	Ou:	Violette AC Port-au-Prince
	Cl:	*Not yet finished*

Ou=Championnat Ouverture (1st half-Season);
Fe / Cl =Championnat Fermeture / Clôture (2nd half-Season)

Coupe d'Haïti (Coupe Vincent) winners:
1932: Union des Sociétés Artibonitiennes; 1937/38: AS Capoise Cap Haïtien; 1939: Violette AC Port-au-Prince; 1941: Racing Club Haïtien; 1942: Excelsior Athletic Club; 1944: Racing Club Haïtien; 1947: Hatüey Bacardi Club Port-au-Prince; 1950: Excelsior Athletic Club; 1951 Violette AC Port-au-Prince; 1954: Victory Sportif Club; 1960: Aigle Noir AC Port-au-Prince; 1962: Victory Sportif Club; 2010: Victory SC Port-au-Prince; 2011: AS Capoise Cap-Haïtien.

Super Huit winners:
2006: Baltimore SC Saint-Marc; 2007: Tempête FC Saint-Marc; 2008: AS Mirebalais; 2009: AS Capoise Cap-Haïtien; 2010: Aigle Noir AC Port-au-Prince; 2011: AS Capoise Cap-Haïtien; 2012: Tempête FC Saint-Marc; 2013: Baltimore SC Saint-Marc; 2014: América FC des Cayes.

NATIONAL CHAMPIONSHIP
Championnat National Division 1 Ligue Haïtienne 2020

Série d'Ouverture

The championship was cancelled after 4 Rounds due to COVID-19 pandemic.

Série de Clôture

The championship was cancelled due to transition to autumn-spring rhythm.

NATIONAL CHAMPIONSHIP
Championnat National Division 1 Ligue Haïtienne 2020/2021

Série d'Ouverture 2020

1.	Arcahaie FC	17	9	3	5	20	-	10	30
2.	Baltimore SC Saint-Marc	17	8	6	3	12	-	5	30
3.	Triomphe de Liancourt FC	17	9	3	5	17	-	15	30
4.	AS Capoise Cap-Haïtien	17	7	6	4	16	-	12	27
5.	Racing Club Haïtien Port-au-Prince	17	8	3	6	17	-	14	27
6.	Violette AC Port-au-Prince	17	5	10	2	18	-	13	25
7.	AS Cavaly Léogâne	17	7	4	6	16	-	14	25
8.	América FC des Cayes	17	7	4	6	16	-	15	25
9.	Real Hope FA Cap-Haïtien	17	6	5	6	21	-	15	23
10.	Tempête FC Saint-Marc	17	6	4	7	18	-	15	22
11.	FC Juventus des Cayes	17	6	4	7	12	-	16	22
12.	US Rivartibonitienne	17	5	5	7	15	-	22	20
13.	Don Bosco FC Pétion-Ville	17	4	7	6	20	-	21	19
14.	Ouanaminthe FC	17	4	6	7	11	-	18	18
15.	Cosmopolites SC Port-au-Prince	17	4	6	7	13	-	23	18
16.	FICA Cap-Haïtien	17	2	11	4	17	-	16	17
17.	Racing FC Gônaïves	17	3	7	7	12	-	18	16
18.	AS Mirebalais	17	2	8	7	10	-	19	14

Top-2 qualified for the Semi-Finals; Teams ranked 3-6 qualified for the Quarter-Finals.

Quarter-Finals [23-27.12.2020]

Racing Club Haïtien Port-au-Prince - AS Capoise Cap-Haïtien	2-3	1-1
Violette AC Port-au-Prince - Triomphe de Liancourt FC	3-0	1-2

Semi-Finals [30.12.2020-03.01.2021]

AS Capoise Cap-Haïtien - Arcahaie FC	0-0	0-0 aet; 0-2 pen
Violette AC Port-au-Prince - Baltimore SC Saint-Marc	1-0	1-0

Finals [06-10.01.2021]

Violette AC Port-au-Prince - Arcahaie FC	2-1
Arcahaie FC - Violette AC Port-au-Prince	0-3

2020 Série d'Ouverture Champions: **Violette AC Port-au-Prince**

Série de Clôture 2021

The competition was started on 04.04.2021, but was not finished until this yearbook went to print.

THE CLUBS

AMÉRICA DES CAYES
Year of Formation: 1973
Stadium: Parc de Foot Land des Gabions des Cayes, Les Cayes (2,000)

ARCAHAIE FOOTBALL CLUB
Year of Formation: n/a
Stadium: Parc Saint-Yves, Arcahaie (1,000)

ASSOCIACION SPORTIF CAVALY LÉOGÂNE
Year of Formation: 1975
Stadium: Stade „Sylvio Cator", Léogâne (10,500)

ASSOCIATION SPORTIVE CAPOISE CAP-HAÏTIEN
Year of Formation: 1930
Stadium: Parc Saint-Victor, Cap-Haïtien (7,500)

ASSOCIATION SPORTIVE MIREBALAIS
Year of Formation: 2000
Stadium: Parc "Nelson Petit-Frère", Mirebalais (2,000)

BALTIMORE SPORTIF CLUB SAINT-MARC
Year of Formation: 1974
Stadium: Parc Levelt, Saint-Marc (5,500)

COSMOPOLITES SPORTS CLUB PORT-AU-PRINCE
Year of Formation: 2015
Stadium: Stade „Sylvio Cator", Port-au-Prince (10,000)

DON BOSCO FOOTBALL CLUB de PÉTIONVILLE
Year of Formation: 1963
Stadium: Stade de Pétionville, Pétionville (5,000)

FOOTBALL CLUB JUVENTUS DES CAYES
Year of Formation: 2006
Stadium: Parc Larco, Les Cayes (n/a)

FOOTBALL INTER CLUB ASSOCIATION CAP-HAÏTIEN
Year of Formation: 1972
Stadium: Parc Saint-Victor, Cap-Haïtien (7,500)

OUANAMINTHE FOOTBALL CLUB
Year of Formation: 2011
Stadium: Parc Notre Dame de Vapor, Ouanaminthe (1,000)

RACING CLUB HAÏTIEN PORT-AU PRINCE
Year of Formation: 1923
Stadium: Stade „Sylvio Cator", Port-au-Prince (10,000)

RACING FOOTBALL CLUB GÔNAÏVES
Year of Formation: 1962
Stadium: Parc "Stenio Vincent", Gônaïves (3,000)

RÉAL HOPE FOOTBALL ACADEMY CAP-HAÏTIEN
Year of Formation: 2014
Stadium: Parc Saint-Victor, Cap-Haïtien (7,500)

TEMPÊTE FOOTBALL CLUB SAINT-MARC
Year of Formation: 1970
Stadium: Parc Levelt, Saint-Marc (10,000)

TRIOMPHE DE LIANCOURT FOOTBALL CLUB
Year of Formation: n/a
Stadium: Parc Mercinus Deslouches, Liancourt (1,000)

VIOLETTE ATHLETIC CLUB PORT-AU-PRINCE
Year of Formation: 1918
Stadium: Stade „Sylvio Cator", Port-au-Prince (10,000)

NATIONAL TEAM
INTERNATIONAL MATCHES 2020/2021

25.03.2021	Port-au-Prince	Haiti - Belize	2-0(0-0)	(WCQ)
05.06.2021	Providenciales	Turks and Caicos Islands - Haiti	0-10(0-5)	(WCQ)
08.06.2021	Port-au-Prince	Haiti - Nicaragua	1-0(0-0)	(WCQ)
12.06.2021	Port-au-Prince	Haiti - Canada	0-1(0-1)	(WCQ)
15.06.2021	Bridgeview	Canada - Haiti	3-0(0-0)	(WCQ)
02.07.2021	Fort Lauderdale	Haiti - Saint Vincent and the Grenadines	6-1(3-1)	(GCQ)
06.07.2021	Fort Lauderdale	Haiti - Bermuda	4-1(3-0)	(GCQ)

25.03.2021, 22nd FIFA World Cup Qualifiers, CONCACAF First Round
Stade "Sylvio Cator", Port-au-Prince
Referee: Walter Alexander López Castellanos (Guatemala)
HAITI - BELIZE   **2-0(0-0)**
HAI: Johnathan Placide, Mechack Jérôme, Ricardo Adé Kat, Steven Séance, Ashkanov Appollon (63.Christiano François), Soni Mustivar, Wild-donald Guerrier, Bryan Alceus, Hervé Bazile, Louicius Don Deedson (63.Duckens Moses Nazon), Daniel Jamesley (46.Steeven Issa Saba). Trainer: Jean-Jacques Pierre.
Goals: Ricardo Adé Kat (50), Steven Séance (80).

05.06.2021, 22nd FIFA World Cup Qualifiers, CONCACAF First Round
TCIFA National Academy, Providenciales
Referee: Diego Montaño Robles (Mexico)
TURKS AND CAICOS ISLANDS - HAITI   **0-10(0-5)**
HAI: Johnathan Placide, Kévin Pierre Lafrance, Stéphane Lambese, Jeppe Friborg Simonsen (65.Louicius Don Deedson), Alex Junior Christian (65.Ashkanov Appollon), James Geffrard, Derrick Buckley Etienne Jr., Bryan Alceus (65.Soni Mustivar), Hervé Bazile (46.Mikaël Gabriel Cantave), Carnejy Antoine, Duckens Moses Nazon (53.Frantzdy Pierrot). Trainer: Jean-Jacques Pierre.
Goals: Duckens Moses Nazon (27, 30, 34, 37), Carnejy Antoine (42), Jeppe Friborg Simonsen (53), Frantzdy Pierrot (75), Carnejy Antoine (83), Frantzdy Pierrot (87, 90).

08.06.2021, 22nd FIFA World Cup Qualifiers, CONCACAF First Round
Stade "Sylvio Cator", Port-au-Prince
Referee: Kevin Morrison (Jamaica)
HAITI - NICARAGUA   **1-0(0-0)**
HAI: Johnathan Placide, Kévin Pierre Lafrance, Ricardo Adé Kat, Stéphane Lambese (73.Louicius Don Deedson), Jeppe Friborg Simonsen, Alex Junior Christian, Soni Mustivar (24.James Geffrard), Derrick Buckley Etienne Jr. (73.Mikaël Gabriel Cantave [*sent off 88*]), Bryan Alceus, Duckens Moses Nazon (59.Carnejy Antoine), Frantzdy Pierrot. Trainer: Jean-Jacques Pierre.
Goal: Derrick Buckley Etienne Jr. (63).

12.06.2021, 22nd FIFA World Cup Qualifiers, CONCACAF Second Round
Stade "Sylvio Cator", Port-au-Prince
Referee: John Francis Pitti Hernández (Panama)
HAITI - CANADA   **0-1(0-1)**
HAI: Johnathan Placide, Kévin Pierre Lafrance (46.Leverton Pierre), Ricardo Adé Kat, Stéphane Lambese (66.Carlens Arcus), Jeppe Friborg Simonsen (78.Hervé Bazile), Alex Junior Christian, James Geffrard, Derrick Buckley Etienne Jr. (66.Duckens Moses Nazon), Bryan Alceus, Carnejy Antoine (46.Steeven Issa Saba), Frantzdy Pierrot. Trainer: Jean-Jacques Pierre.

15.06.2021, 22nd FIFA World Cup Qualifiers, CONCACAF Second Round
SeatGeek Stadium, Bridgeview (United States)
Referee: Rubiel Vasquez (United States)
CANADA - HAITI   **3-0(0-0)**
HAI: Josué Duverger, Kévin Pierre Lafrance, Ricardo Adé Kat, Carlens Arcus, Jeppe Friborg Simonsen, Bryan Alceus (86.Louicius Don Deedson), Leverton Pierre, Steeven Issa Saba (78.Stéphane Lambese), Hervé Bazile (46.Derrick Buckley Etienne Jr.), Duckens Moses Nazon, Frantzdy Pierrot. Trainer: Jean-Jacques Pierre.

02.07.2021, 16th CONCACAF Gold Cup Qualifiers, First Round
DRV PNK Stadium, Fort Lauderdale (United States); Attendance: 0
Referee: Oshane Nation (Jamaica)
HAITI - SAINT VINCENT AND THE GRENADINES   **6-1(3-1)**
HAI: Josué Duverger, Ricardo Adé Kat, Carlens Arcus (75.Stéphane Lambese), Alex Junior Christian (66.Martin Expérience), James Geffrard (66.Kévin Pierre Lafrance), Derrick Buckley Etienne Jr. (81.Zachary Herivaux), Bryan Alceus, Leverton Pierre, Carnejy Antoine, Duckens Moses Nazon, Frantzdy Pierrot (81.Ronaldo Damus). Trainer: Jean-Jacques Pierre.
Goals: Duckens Moses Nazon (26 penalty), Frantzdy Pierrot (33), Derrick Buckley Etienne Jr. (37 penalty), Duckens Moses Nazon (59), Jahvin Sutherland (72 own goal), Carnejy Antoine (90).

06.07.2021, 16th CONCACAF Gold Cup Qualifiers, Second Round
DRV PNK Stadium, Fort Lauderdale (United States); Attendance: 0
Referee: Iván Arcides Barton Cisneros (El Salvador)
HAITI - BERMUDA   **4-1(3-0)**
HAI: Brian Sylvestre, Ricardo Adé Kat, Carlens Arcus, James Geffrard, Martin Expérience, Derrick Buckley Etienne Jr. (82.Zachary Herivaux), Bryan Alceus, Leverton Pierre (62.Kévin Pierre Lafrance), Carnejy Antoine (81.Stéphane Lambese), Duckens Moses Nazon, Frantzdy Pierrot (54.Ronaldo Damus). Trainer: Jean-Jacques Pierre.
Goals: Frantzdy Pierrot (23, 28, 34), Duckens Moses Nazon (87 penalty).

NATIONAL TEAM PLAYERS 2020/2021

Name	DOB	Club

Goalkeepers

Josué DUVERGER	27.04.2000	Vitória FC Setúbal (POR)
Johnathan PLACIDE	29.01.1988	FC Tsarsko Selo Sofia (BUL)
Brian SYLVESTRE	19.12.1992	Miami FC (USA)

Defenders

Ricardo ADÉ Kat	21.05.1990	Mushuc Runa SC Ambato (ECU)
Ashkanov APPOLLON	03.04.1991	San Diego 1904 FC (USA)
Carlens ARCUS	28.06.1996	AJ Auxerre (FRA)
Alex Junior CHRISTIAN	05.12.1993	FC Atyrau (KAZ)
Martin EXPÉRIENCE	09.03.1999	US Avranches (FRA)
James GEFFRARD	26.08.1994	HFX Wanderers FC Halifax (CAN)
Mechack JÉRÔME	21.04.1990	El Paso Locomotive (USA)
Kévin Pierre LAFRANCE	13.01.1990	AEK Larnaca FC (CYP)
Stéphane LAMBESE	10.05.1995	US Orléans Loiret Football (FRA)
Steven SÉANCE	20.02.1992	US Avranches Mont Saint Michel (FRA)
Jeppe Friborg SIMONSEN	21.11.1995	Sønderjysk Elitesport (DEN)

Midfielders

Bryan ALCEUS	01.02.1996	CS Gaz Metan Mediaş (ROU)
Hervé BAZILE	18.03.1990	Le Havre AC (FRA)
Mikaël Gabriel CANTAVE	25.10.1996	CP Villarrobledo (ESP)
Derrick Buckley ETIENNE Jr.	25.11.1996	Columbus Crew (USA)
Wild-donald GUERRIER	31.03.1989	Apollon Limassol FC (CYP)
Zachary HERIVAUX	01.02.1996	Birmingham Legion (USA)
Soni MUSTIVAR	12.02.1990	Nea Salamis Famagusta FC (CYP)
Leverton PIERRE	09.03.1998	USL Dunkerque (FRA)
Steeven Issa SABA	24.02.1993	Violette AC Port-au-Prince

Forwards

Carnejy ANTOINE	27.07.1991	US Orléans Loiret Football (FRA)
Ronaldo DAMUS	12.09.1999	Orange County SC (USA)
Louicius Don DEEDSON	11.02.2001	Hobro IK (DEN)
Christiano FRANÇOIS	17.07.1993	Miami FC (USA)
Daniel JAMESLEY	19.10.1996	Universidad O&M FC Santo Domingo (DOM)
Duckens Moses NAZON	07.04.1994	Sint-Truidense VV (BEL)
Frantzdy PIERROT	29.03.1995	En Avant Guingamp (FRA)

National coaches

Jean-Jacques PIERRE [from 11.03.2021]		23.01.1981

HONDURAS

The Country:	The FA:
República de Honduras (Republic of Honduras) Capital: Tegucigalpa Surface: 112,492 km² Population: 9,587,522 [2018] Time: UTC-6 Independent since: 1821	Federación Nacional Autónoma de Fútbol de Honduras Col. Florencia Norte, Edificio Plaza America, Ave. Roble 1 y 2 Nivel, Tegucigalpa 504 Year of Formation: 1951 Member of FIFA since: 1951 Member of CONCACAF since: 1961

NATIONAL TEAM RECORDS

First international match: 14.09.1921, Ciudad de Guatemala: Guatemala - Honduras 10-1
Most international caps: Maynor Alexis Figueroa Róchez – 168 caps (since 2003)
Most international goals: Carlos Alberto Pavón Plummer – 57 goals / 101 caps (1993-2010)

CONCACAF GOLD CUP

1991	Final Tournament (Runners-up)
1993	Final Tournament (Group Stage)
1996	Final Tournament (Group Stage)
1998	Final Tournament (Group Stage)
2000	Final Tournament (Quarter-Finals)
2002	Qualifiers
2003	Final Tournament (Group Stage)
2005	Final Tournament (Semi-Finals)
2007	Final Tournament (Quarter-Finals)
2009	Final Tournament (Semi-Finals)
2011	Final Tournament (Semi-Finals)
2013	Final Tournament (Semi-Finals)
2015	Final Tournament (Group Stage)
2017	Final Tournament (Quarter-Finals)
2019	Final Tournament (Group Stage)
2021	Final Tournament (*to be played*)

FIFA WORLD CUP

Year	Result
1930	-
1934	-
1938	-
1950	-
1954	Did not enter
1958	Did not enter
1962	Qualifiers
1966	Qualifiers
1970	Qualifiers
1974	Qualifiers
1978	Did not enter
1982	Final Tournament (Group Stage)
1986	Qualifiers
1990	Qualifiers
1994	Qualifiers
1998	Qualifiers
2002	Qualifiers
2006	Qualifiers
2010	Final Tournament (Group Stage)
2014	Final Tournament (Group Stage)
2018	Qualifiers

F.I.F.A. CONFEDERATIONS CUP 1992-2017

None

OLYMPIC FOOTBALL TOURNAMENTS 1908-2016							
1908	-	1948	-	1972	Did not enter	1996	Did not enter
1912	-	1952	-	1976	Qualifiers	2000	FT/Group Stage
1920	-	1956	-	1980	Did not enter	2004	Qualifiers
1924	-	1960	-	1984	Qualifiers	2008	FT/Group Stage
1928	-	1964	-	1988	Qualifiers	2012	Quarter-Finals
1936	-	1968	*Withdrew*	1992	Qualifiers	2016	FT/4th Place

CCCF (Confederación Centroamericana y del Caribe de Fútbol) CHAMPIONSHIPS 1941-1961
1946, 1953 (Runners-up), 1955 (3rd Place), 1957 (3rd Place), 1960 (3rd Place)
CONCACAF CHAMPIONSHIPS 1963-1989
1963, 1967 (3rd Place), 1971, 1973, **1981 (Winners)**, 1985 (Runners-up)
COPA AMÉRICA
2001 (3rd Place)

CONCACAF NATIONS LEAGUE	
2019-2020	League A

COPA CENTROAMERICANA (UNCAF NATIONS CHAMPIONSHIPS) 1991-2017			
1991	Final Round - Runners-up	2005	Final Round - Runners-up
1993	**Final Round - Winners**	2007	Final Round - Group Stage
1995	**Final Round - Winners**	2009	Final Round - 3rd Place
1997	Final Round - 4th Place	2011	**Final Round - Winners**
1999	Final Round - 3rd Place	2013	Final Round - Runners-up
2001	Final Round - Group Stage	2014	Final Round - 5th Place
2003	Final Round - 4th Place	2017	**Final Round - Winners**

HONDURAN CLUB HONOURS IN CONCACAF CLUB COMPETITIONS:

CONCACAF Champions Cup / CONCACAF Champions League 1962-2020		
Club Deportivo Olimpia Tegucigalpa	2	1972, 1988
CONCACAF League 2017-2020		
None		
Caribbean Club Championship 1997-2021		
None		
CONCACAF Cup Winners Cup 1991-1995*		
None		
Copa Interamericana 1968-1998*		
None		

*defunct competitions

NATIONAL COMPETITIONS
TABLE OF HONOURS

	CHAMPIONS
	Liga Amateur de Honduras
1947/1948	CD Victoria La Ceiba
1948/1949	CD Hibueras La Lima
1949/1950	CD Motagua
1950/1951	Club Sula de La Lima
1951/1952	CD Abacá
1952/1953	*No competition*
1953/1954	*No competition*
1954/1955	CD Federal Tegucigalpa
1955/1956	CD Hibueras La Lima
1956/1957	CD Olimpia Tegucigalpa
1957/1958	CD Olimpia Tegucigalpa
1958/1959	CD Olimpia Tegucigalpa
1959/1960	*No competition*
1960/1961	CD Olimpia Tegucigalpa
1961/1962	CD Vida
1962/1963	CD Olimpia Tegucigalpa
1963/1964	CD Olimpia Tegucigalpa
1964/1965	*No competition*
	Liga Nacional de Fútbol de Honduras (LINAFUTH)
1965/1966	CD Platense Puerto Cortés
1966/1967	CD Olimpia Tegucigalpa
1967/1968	CD Olimpia Tegucigalpa
1968/1969	CD Motagua Tegucigalpa
1969/1970	CD Olimpia Tegucigalpa
1970/1971	CD Motagua Tegucigalpa
1971/1972	CD Olimpia Tegucigalpa
1972/1973	*Competition abandoned*
1973	CD Motagua Tegucigalpa
1974	Real CD España San Pedro Sula
1975	Real CD España San Pedro Sula
1976	Real CD España San Pedro Sula
1977	CD Olimpia Tegucigalpa
1978/1979	CD Motagua Tegucigalpa
1979	CD Marathón San Pedro Sula
1980	Real CD España San Pedro Sula
1981	CDS Vida La Ceiba
1982	CD Olimpia Tegucigalpa
1983	CDS Vida La Ceiba
1984	CD Olimpia Tegucigalpa
1985	CD Marathón San Pedro Sula
1986	CD Olimpia Tegucigalpa
1987	CD Olimpia Tegucigalpa
1988	Real CD España San Pedro Sula
1989/1990	CD Olimpia Tegucigalpa
1990/1991	Real CD España San Pedro Sula
1991/1992	CD Motagua Tegucigalpa

1992/1993		CD Olimpia Tegucigalpa
1993/1994		Real CD España San Pedro Sula
1994/1995		CD Victoria La Ceiba
1995/1996		CD Olimpia Tegucigalpa
1996/1997		CD Olimpia Tegucigalpa
1997/1998	Ape:	CD Motagua Tegucigalpa
	Cla:	CD Motagua Tegucigalpa
1999		CD Olimpia Tegucigalpa
1999/2000	Ape:	CD Motagua Tegucigalpa
	Cla:	CD Motagua Tegucigalpa
2000/2001	Ape:	CD Olimpia Tegucigalpa
	Cla:	CD Platense Puerto Cortés
2001/2002	Ape:	CD Motagua Tegucigalpa
	Cla:	CD Marathón San Pedro Sula
2002/2003	Ape:	CD Olimpia Tegucigalpa
	Cla:	CD Marathón San Pedro Sula
2003/2004	Ape:	Real CD España San Pedro Sula
	Cla:	CD Olimpia Tegucigalpa
2004/2005	Ape:	CD Marathón San Pedro Sula
	Cla:	CD Olimpia Tegucigalpa
2005/2006	Ape:	CD Olimpia Tegucigalpa
	Cla:	CD Olimpia Tegucigalpa
2006/2007	Ape:	CD Motagua Tegucigalpa
	Cla:	Real CD España San Pedro Sula
2007/2008	Ape:	CD Marathón San Pedro Sula
	Cla:	CD Olimpia Tegucigalpa
2008/2009	Ape:	CD Marathón San Pedro Sula
	Cla:	CD Olimpia Tegucigalpa
2009/2010	Ape:	CD Marathón San Pedro Sula
	Cla:	CD Olimpia Tegucigalpa
2010/2011	Ape:	Real CD España San Pedro Sula
	Cla:	CD Motagua Tegucigalpa
2011/2012	Ape:	CD Olimpia Tegucigalpa
	Cla:	CD Olimpia Tegucigalpa
2012/2013	Ape:	CD Olimpia Tegucigalpa
	Cla:	CD Olimpia Tegucigalpa
2013/2014	Ape:	Real CD España San Pedro Sula
	Cla:	CD Olimpia Tegucigalpa
2014/2015	Ape:	CD Motagua Tegucigalpa
	Cla:	CD Olimpia Tegucigalpa
2015/2016	Ape:	CD Honduras El Progreso
	Cla:	CD Olimpia Tegucigalpa
2016/2017	Ape:	CD Motagua Tegucigalpa
	Cla:	CD Motagua Tegucigalpa
2017/2018	Ape:	Real CD España San Pedro Sula
	Cla:	CD Marathón San Pedro Sula
2018/2019	Ape:	FC Motagua Tegucigalpa
	Cla:	FC Motagua Tegucigalpa
2019/2020	Ape:	CD Olimpia Tegucigalpa
	Cla:	*Championship cancelled due to Covid-19 pandemic*
2020/2021	Ape:	CD Olimpia Tegucigalpa
	Cla:	CD Olimpia Tegucigalpa

Copa Honduras winners:
1992: Real CD España San Pedro Sula; 1993: Real Maya Deportivo Danlí; 1994: CD Marathón San Pedro Sula; 1995: CD Olimpia Tegucigalpa; 1996: CD Platense Puerto Cortés; 1997: CD Platense Puerto Cortés.

NATIONAL CHAMPIONSHIP
Liga Nacional de Fútbol de Honduras 2020/2021

Torneo Apertura 2020

Regular Stage - Results

Round 1 [26.09.-03.10.2020]
Lobos de la UPNFM - FC Motagua 2-3(1-2)
Real CD España - CD Olimpia 1-1(0-0)
Real Sociedad - Real de Minas 0-0
CDS Vida - CD Platense 3-3(2-1)
Honduras Progreso - CD Marathón 1-1(1-1)

Round 2 [07.10.2020]
CD Platense - Real CD España 1-0(1-0)
Real Sociedad - Lobos de la UPNFM 2-3(2-0)
CD Marathón - FC Motagua 1-2(0-0)
Honduras Progreso - CDS Vida 1-1(1-1)
CD Olimpia - Real de Minas 0-0

Round 3 [10-11.10.2020]
CDS Vida - CD Marathón 0-1(0-0)
Real de Minas - CD Platense 1-1(0-0)
CD Olimpia - Lobos de la UPNFM 3-1(1-1)
FC Motagua - Real Sociedad 2-1(2-1)
Real CD España - Honduras Progreso 5-0(2-0)

Round 4 [14-15.10.2020]
CD Marathón - Real CD España 3-0(2-0)
Lobos de la UPNFM - Real de Minas 2-2(0-2)
CDS Vida - Real Sociedad 1-0(0-0)
CD Platense - Honduras Progreso 0-0
FC Motagua - CD Olimpia 0-0

Round 5 [18.10.2020]
CD Platense - CD Marathón 0-1(0-0)
Real Sociedad - CD Olimpia 0-2(0-0)
Real de Minas - FC Motagua 0-3(0-0)
Real CD España - CDS Vida 0-3(0-1)
Honduras Progreso - Lobos UPNFM 2-3(0-0)

Round 6 [05-06.12.2020]
CD Marathón - Honduras Progreso 4-0(2-0)
Real de Minas - Real Sociedad 2-1(1-1)
FC Motagua - Lobos de la UPNFM 0-1(0-1)
CD Platense - CDS Vida 1-0(0-0)
CD Olimpia - Real CD España 1-0(0-0)

Round 7 [24-25.10.2020]
Real de Minas - CD Olimpia 2-3(1-1)
Lobos de la UPNFM - Real Sociedad 1-1(1-1)
CDS Vida - Honduras Progreso 4-1(1-1)
FC Motagua - CD Marathón 1-1(1-0)
Real CD España - CD Platense 3-2(1-0)

Round 8 [28.10.2020]
CD Marathón - CDS Vida 0-2(0-0)
Real Sociedad - FC Motagua 1-5(0-2)
CD Platense - Real de Minas 3-2(1-1)
Lobos de la UPNFM - CD Olimpia 1-1(0-1)
Honduras Progreso - Real CD España 0-3(0-0)

Round 9 [31.10.-01.11.2020]
Real de Minas - Lobos de la UPNFM 1-1(0-1)
Honduras Progreso - CD Platense 1-1(1-1)
CD Olimpia - FC Motagua 2-1(1-0)
Real Sociedad - CDS Vida 1-6(1-2)
Real CD España - CD Marathón 0-1(0-1)

Round 10 [21-23.11.2020]
CDS Vida - Real CD España 2-2(1-1)
FC Motagua - Real de Minas 2-1(0-0)
CD Marathón - CD Platense 3-0(2-0)
CD Olimpia - Real Sociedad 5-0(3-0)
Lobos UPNFM - Honduras Progreso 0-1(0-0)

Round 11 [25-26.11.2020]	Round 12 [28-29.11.2020]
Real Sociedad - CD Platense 2-3(2-1)	CD Marathón - Real Sociedad 5-0(3-0)
Lobos de la UPNFM - CD Marathón 0-2(0-1)	CDS Vida - Real de Minas 3-1(2-1)
Real CD España - Real de Minas 1-1(1-0)	CD Olimpia - Honduras Progreso 5-0(4-0)
CD Olimpia - CDS Vida 1-0(1-0)	Real CD España - FC Motagua 0-1(0-1)
Honduras Progreso - FC Motagua 0-5(0-3)	CD Platense - Lobos de la UPNFM 1-1(0-0)

Round 13 [14-15.11.2020]	Round 14 [12.12.2020]
Real de Minas - CD Marathón 2-0(1-0)	CD Marathón - CD Olimpia 1-3(1-1)
Honduras Progreso - Real Sociedad 1-2(0-1)	Real de Minas - Honduras Progreso 3-4(3-2)
Lobos UPNFM - Real CD España 1-1(0-1)	CDS Vida - Lobos de la UPNFM 0-3(0-1)
CD Platense - CD Olimpia 2-3(2-2)	FC Motagua - CD Platense 5-0(2-0)
FC Motagua - CDS Vida 3-0(2-0)	Real Sociedad - Real CD España 1-2(0-1)

Final Standings – Grupo A

1. CD Marathón San Pedro Sula	14	8	2	4	24 - 11	26
2. CDS Vida La Ceiba	14	6	3	5	25 - 18	21
3. CD Platense Puerto Cortés	14	4	5	5	18 - 25	17
4. Real CD España San Pedro Sula	14	4	4	6	18 - 18	16
5. CD Honduras El Progreso	14	2	4	8	12 - 37	10

Final Standings – Grupo B

1. CD Olimpia Tegucigalpa	14	10	4	0	30 - 9	34
2. FC Motagua Tegucigalpa	14	10	2	2	33 - 10	32
3. CD Lobos de la UPN Francisco Morazán Tegucigalpa	14	4	6	4	20 - 20	18
4. CD Real de Minas Tegucigalpa	14	2	6	6	18 - 24	12
5. CD Real Sociedad Tocoa	14	1	2	11	12 - 38	5

Winners of both groups were qualfied for the Group Stage Finals and also for the Play-off Semi-Finals, while teams ranked second and third were qualified for the Quarter-Finals.

Apertura Play-offs

Group Stage Finals [23-27.12.2020]

CD Marathón San Pedro Sula - CD Olimpia Tegucigalpa	3-1(0-0)	0-1(0-0)

CD Marathón San Pedro Sula were qualified for the Torneo Apertura Finals / Finalisima.

Quarter-Finals / Repechajes [17-23.12.2020]

CD Lobos de la UPN Francisco Morazán Tegucigalpa - CDS Vida La Ceiba	1-3(0-2)	1-5(1-3)
CD Platense Puerto Cortés - FC Motagua Tegucigalpa	2-4(1-2)	1-0(1-0)

Semi-Finals [30.12.-03.01.2021]

CDS Vida La Ceiba - CD Olimpia Tegucigalpa	0-0	0-3(0-2)
FC Motagua Tegucigalpa - CD Marathón San Pedro Sula	2-0(1-0)	2-1(2-1)

Finals [06-10.01.2021]

FC Motagua Tegucigalpa - CD Olimpia Tegucigalpa   1-3(0-3)   0-0
CD Olimpia Tegucigalpa were qualified for the Torneo Apertura Finals / Finalisima.

Championship Finals / Finalisima

14.01.2021, Estadio Nacional, Tegucigalpa; Attendance: 0
Referee: Héctor Said Martínez Sorto
CD Olimpia Tegucigalpa - CD Marathón San Pedro Sula   **2-0(2-0)**
Olimpia: Edrick Eduardo Menjívar Jonhnson, Jonathan Josué Paz Hernández, Maylor Alberto Nuñez Flores, Javier Arnaldo Portillo Martínez (46.Samuel Arturo Córdova Howe), Johnny Harold Leverón Uclés, Deybi Aldair Flores Flores, José Alejandro Reyes Cerna (46.German Noe Mejía Briceño), Edwin Alexander Rodríguez Castillo (86.Marvin Javier Bernárdez García), Eddie Gabriel Hernández Padilla, Jerry Ricardo Bengtson Bodden (82.Justin Arboleda Buenaños), José Mario Pinto Paz (68.Josmán Alexander Figueroa Arzú). Trainer: Pedro Antonio Troglio (Argentina).
Marathón: Denovan Galileo Torres Pérez, Cristian Yaffet Moreira Güity, Mathías Sebastián Techera Pizarro, Luis Fernando Garrido Garrido (61.Axel Moisés Motiño Rivera), John Paul Suazo Caballero, Allan Alexander Banegas Murillo, Kervin Fabián Arriaga Villanueva, Edwin Solani Solano Martínez (90.Carlos Iván García Castillo), Luis Fernando Vega Cillacorta, Marlon Roberto Ramírez Arauz (70.Selvin Rolando Guevara Casco), Bruno Volpi. Trainer: Héctor Vargas Baldús (Argentina).
Goals: 1-0 Eddie Gabriel Hernández Padilla (46), 2-0 Jerry Ricardo Bengtson Bodden (72).

17.01.2021, Estadio "Yankel Rosenthal", San Pedro Sula; Attendance: 0
Referee: Héctor Francisco Rodríguez Hernández
CD Marathón San Pedro Sula - CD Olimpia Tegucigalpa   **0-1(0-1)**
Marathón: Denovan Galileo Torres Pérez, Mathías Sebastián Techera Pizarro, Luis Fernando Garrido Garrido, John Paul Suazo Caballero (63.Cristian Neptali Calix Alvarado; 71.Axel Moisés Motiño Rivera), Allan Alexander Banegas Murillo, Kervin Fabián Arriaga Villanueva, Frelys Edilson López Saravia (46.Yaudel Lahera García), Edwin Solani Solano Martínez, Luis Fernando Vega Cillacorta, Marlon Roberto Ramírez Arauz (51.Selvin Rolando Guevara Casco), Bruno Volpi [*sent off 85*]. Trainer: Héctor Vargas Baldús (Argentina).
Olimpia: Edrick Eduardo Menjívar Jonhnson, Johnny Harold Leverón Uclés, Samuel Arturo Córdova Howe (71.Ever Gonzalo Alvarado Sandoval), Jonathan Josué Paz Hernández, Maylor Alberto Nuñez Flores, Deybi Aldair Flores Flores, German Noe Mejía Briceño, Edwin Alexander Rodríguez Castillo (85.Michaell Anthony Chirinos López), Eddie Gabriel Hernández Padilla, Jerry Ricardo Bengtson Bodden (64.Justin Arboleda Buenaños), José Mario Pinto Paz (64.Josmán Alexander Figueroa Arzú). Trainer: Pedro Antonio Troglio (Argentina).
Goal: 0-1 Justin Arboleda Buenaños (72).

Torneo Apertura 2020 Champions: **CD Olimpia Tegucigalpa**

Best goalscorer Torneo Apertura 2020:
Román Rubilio Castillo Álvarez (FC Motagua Tegucigalpa),
Jerry Ricardo Bengtson Bodden (CD Olimpia Tegucigalpa),
Carlos Roberto Bernárdez García (BLZ, CD Platense Puerto Cortés) – all 10 goals

Torneo Clausura 2021

Regular Stage - Results

Round 1 [16-17.02.2021]
Lobos de la UPNFM - FC Motagua 1-2(1-0)
Honduras Progreso - CD Marathón 1-1
Real Sociedad - Real de Minas 1-1(1-0)
CDS Vida - CD Platense 2-2(1-1)
Real CD España - CD Olimpia 1-2(1-1)

Round 2 [20-24.02.2021]
CD Marathón - FC Motagua 0-1(0-1)
CD Olimpia - Real de Minas 2-0(0-0)
Honduras Progreso - CDS Vida 0-0
Real Sociedad - Lobos de la UPNFM 1-1(1-1)
CD Platense - Real CD España 2-2(1-1)[07.04.]

Round 3 [24.02.2021]
Real de Minas - CD Platense 1-4(1-4)
FC Motagua - Real Sociedad 2-0(2-0)
CDS Vida - CD Marathón 0-1(0-0)
CD Olimpia - Lobos de la UPNFM 5-1(2-1)
Real CD España - Honduras Progreso 1-0(0-0)

Round 4 [27-28.02.2021]
CD Marathón - Real CD España 1-2(0-2)
Lobos de la UPNFM - Real de Minas 2-0(1-0)
CDS Vida - Real Sociedad 2-2(1-0)
FC Motagua - CD Olimpia 1-2(1-2)
CD Platense - Honduras Progreso 0-4(0-2)

Round 5 [03-04.03.2021]
Real de Minas - FC Motagua 0-3(0-2)
Real Sociedad - CD Olimpia 2-2(1-2)
CD Platense - CD Marathón 5-3(5-1)
Honduras Progreso - Lobos UPNFM 0-3(0-3)
Real CD España - CDS Vida 0-0

Round 6 [06-07.03.2021]
Real de Minas - Real Sociedad 0-0
CD Marathón - Honduras Progreso 1-1(0-0)
FC Motagua - Lobos de la UPNFM 3-1(2-0)
CD Platense - CDS Vida 2-2(2-1)
CD Olimpia - Real CD España 1-0(0-0)

Round 7 [10-11.03.2021]
CDS Vida - Honduras Progreso 1-1(0-1)
Real de Minas - CD Olimpia 0-3(0-3)
FC Motagua - CD Marathón 2-0(1-0)
Real CD España - CD Platense 4-0(2-0)
Lobos UPNFM - Real Socied. 1-2(0-1) [28.03.]

Round 8 [16-17.03.2021]
CD Marathón - CDS Vida 1-2(0-2)
CD Platense - Real de Minas 1-1(0-0)
Lobos de la UPNFM - CD Olimpia 2-1(1-0)
Honduras Progreso - Real CD España 1-1(1-1)
Real Sociedad - FC Motagua 3-3(1-1) [07.04.]

Round 9 [21.03.2021]
Real de Minas - Lobos de la UPNFM 0-3(0-1)
Real CD España - CD Marathón 2-2(1-1)
Real Sociedad - CDS Vida 2-4(0-1)
Honduras Progreso - CD Platense 2-2(0-2)
CD Olimpia - FC Motagua 0-0

Round 10 [31.03.-03.04.2021]
Lobos UPNFM - Honduras Progreso 0-2(0-1)
CD Marathón - CD Platense 1-0(1-0)
FC Motagua - Real de Minas 2-2(0-0)
CDS Vida - Real CD España 2-3(1-2)
CD Olimpia - Real Sociedad 3-1(2-1)

Round 11 [09-11.04.2021]
CD Marathón - Lobos de la UPNFM 1-1(1-1)
CD Platense - Real Sociedad 1-1(0-0)
CDS Vida - CD Olimpia 0-3(0-2)
Real de Minas - Real CD España 0-0
FC Motagua - Honduras Progreso 5-2(2-1)

Round 12 [17.04.2021]
Real Sociedad - CD Marathón 1-1(0-1)
Real de Minas - CDS Vida 2-2(1-1)
Lobos de la UPNFM - CD Platense 0-0
Honduras Progreso - CD Olimpia 0-5(0-3)
FC Motagua - Real CD España 1-0(0-0)

Round 13 [21-22.04.2021]
CD Marathón - Real de Minas 3-2(2-0)
Real Sociedad - Honduras Progreso 3-1(2-0)
CDS Vida - FC Motagua 1-1(0-1)
CD Olimpia - CD Platense 5-0(2-0)
Real CD España - Lobos d.l. UPNFM 1-1(0-0)

Round 14 [28.04.2021]
CD Olimpia - CD Marathón 2-1(0-0)
Honduras Progreso - Real de Minas 5-2(3-1)
Lobos de la UPNFM - CDS Vida 3-1(1-0)
CD Platense - FC Motagua 2-3(0-1)
Real CD España - Real Sociedad 0-0

Final Standings – Grupo A								
1. Real CD España San Pedro Sula	14	4	7	3	17	-	13	19
2. CD Honduras El Progreso	14	3	6	5	20	-	25	15
3. CDS Vida La Ceiba	14	2	8	4	19	-	23	14
4. CD Marathón San Pedro Sula	14	3	5	6	17	-	22	14
5. CD Platense Puerto Cortés	14	2	6	6	20	-	33	12

Final Standings – Grupo B								
1. CD Olimpia Tegucigalpa	14	11	2	1	36	-	9	35
2. FC Motagua Tegucigalpa	14	9	4	1	29	-	14	31
3. CD Lobos de la UPN Francisco Morazán Tegucigalpa	14	5	4	5	20	-	19	19
4. CD Real Sociedad Tocoa	14	3	8	3	21	-	21	17
5. CD Real de Minas Tegucigalpa	14	0	6	8	11	-	31	6

Winners of both groups were qualfied for the Play-off Semi-Finals, while teams ranked second and third were qualified for the Quarter-Finals.

Clausura Play-offs

Group Stage Finals [01-05.05.2021]
Real CD España San Pedro Sula - CD Olimpia Tegucigalpa   0-0   1-2(1-2)
CD Olimpia Tegucigalpa were qualified for the Torneo Clausura Finals / Finalisima.

Quarter-Finals / Repechajes [01-05.05.2021]
CD Lobos de la UPN Francisco Morazán Tegucigalpa - CD Honduras El Progreso   3-2(2-1)   0-4(0-2)
CDS Vida La Ceiba - FC Motagua Tegucigalpa   1-1(1-1)   0-3(0-0)

Semi-Finals [08-12.05.2021]
CD Honduras El Progreso - CD Olimpia Tegucigalpa   0-0   0-7(0-4)
FC Motagua Tegucigalpa - Real CD España San Pedro Sula   1-0(1-0)   0-1 aet; 7-6 pen

Championship Finals / Finalisima

16.05.2021, Estadio Nacional, Tegucigalpa; Attendance: 0
Referee: Armando Isai Castro Oviedo
FC Motagua Tegucigalpa - CD Olimpia Tegucigalpa   2-1(1-0)
Motagua: Jonathan Felipe Rougier, Juan Pablo Montes Montes, Marcelo Antonio Pereira Rodríguez, Wesly Roberto Decas, Raúl Marcelo Santos Colindres, Héctor Enrique Castellanos Villatoro (77.Oscar Alberto García Fernández), Juan Ángel Delgado Murillo, Carlos Roberto Fernández Martínez (77.Josué Isaias Villafranca Quiñónez), Gonzalo Martín Klusener (70.Iván Edgardo López Cano), Matías Alejandro Galvaliz (67.Walter Joel Martínez Betanco), Roberto Moreira Aldana (77.Kevin Josué López Maldonado). Trainer: Diego Martín Vásquez Castro (Argentina).
Olimpia: Edrick Eduardo Menjívar Jonhnson, Elvin Oliva Casildo [*sent off 71*], Ever Gonzalo Alvarado Sandoval (46.José Antonio García Robledo), Edwin Alexander Rodríguez Castillo [*sent off 78*], Maylor Alberto Nuñez Flores, Johnny Harold Leverón Uclés, Deybi Aldair Flores Flores [*sent off 90*], German Noe Mejía Briceño, Justin Arboleda Buenaños (87.Eddie Gabriel Hernández Padilla), Jerry Ricardo Bengtson Bodden (74.Jonathan Josué Paz Hernández), Michael Anthony Chirinos López (83.Mayron Ariel Flores Zavala). Trainer: Pedro Antonio Troglio (Argentina).
Goals: 1-0 Roberto Moreira Aldana (35 penalty), 1-1 Jerry Ricardo Bengtson Bodden (56), 2-1 Josué Isaias Villafranca Quiñónez (90+2 penalty).

19.05.2021, Estadio Nacional, Tegucigalpa; Attendance: 0
Referee: Héctor Said Martínez Sorto
CD Olimpia Tegucigalpa - FC Motagua Tegucigalpa   1-0(1-0,1-0,1-0); 4-3 on penalties
Olimpia: Edrick Eduardo Menjívar Jonhnson, José Antonio García Robledo, Ever Gonzalo Alvarado Sandoval, Jorge Daniel Álvarez Rodas (68.Mayron Ariel Flores Zavala), Maylor Alberto Nuñez Flores, Johnny Harold Leverón Uclés, German Noe Mejía Briceño (87.Brayan Antonio Beckeles), Justin Arboleda Buenaños (68.Eddie Gabriel Hernández Padilla), José Mario Pinto Paz (86.Marvin Javier Bernárdez García), Jerry Ricardo Bengtson Bodden, Michaell Anthony Chirinos López (76.Josmán Alexander Figueroa Arzú). Trainer: Pedro Antonio Troglio (Argentina).
Motagua: Jonathan Felipe Rougier, Juan Pablo Montes Montes, Marcelo Antonio Pereira Rodríguez, Wesly Roberto Decas, Raúl Marcelo Santos Colindres, Héctor Enrique Castellanos Villatoro, Juan Ángel Delgado Murillo (46.Walter Joel Martínez Betanco), Carlos Roberto Fernández Martínez (61.Oscar Alberto García Fernández), Gonzalo Martín Klusener (61.Josué Isaias Villafranca Quiñónez), Matías Alejandro Galvaliz (61.Kevin Josué López Maldonado), Roberto Moreira Aldana. Trainer: Diego Martín Vásquez Castro (Argentina).
Goal: 1-0 Jerry Ricardo Bengtson Bodden (44).
Penalties: Roberto Moreira Aldana (saved); Ever Gonzalo Alvarado Sandoval 1-0; Oscar Alberto García Fernández 1-1; Johnny Harold Leverón Uclés (saved); Wesly Roberto Decas 1-2; Eddie Gabriel Hernández Padilla 2-2; Josué Isaias Villafranca Quiñónez 2-3; Mayron Ariel Flores Zavala 3-3; Walter Joel Martínez Betanco (saved); Jerry Ricardo Bengtson Bodden 4-3.

Torneo Clausura 2021 Champions: **CD Olimpia Tegucigalpa**

Best goalscorer Torneo Clausura 2021:
Jerry Ricardo Bengtson Bodden (CD Olimpia Tegucigalpa) – 14 goals

Aggregate Table 2020/2021

1.	CD Olimpia Tegucigalpa	28	21	6	1	66 - 18	69
2.	FC Motagua Tegucigalpa	28	19	6	3	62 - 24	63
3.	CD Marathón San Pedro Sula	28	11	7	10	41 - 33	40
4.	CD Lobos de la UPN Francisco Morazán Tegucigalpa	28	9	10	9	40 - 39	37
5.	Real CD España San Pedro Sula	28	8	11	9	35 - 31	35
6.	CDS Vida La Ceiba	28	8	11	9	44 - 41	35
7.	CD Platense Puerto Cortés	28	6	11	11	38 - 58	29
8.	CD Honduras El Progreso	28	5	10	13	32 - 62	25
9.	CD Real Sociedad Tocoa	28	4	10	14	33 - 59	22
10.	CD Real de Minas Tegucigalpa (*Relegated*)	28	2	12	14	29 - 55	18

THE CLUBS 2020/2021

Please note: number of matches, subtitutes and goals are including Apertura+Clausura+all Play-offs.

CLUB DEPORTIVO HONDURAS EL PROGRESO

Foundation date: 1965
Address: *Not known*
Stadium: Estadio "Humberto Micheletti", El Progreso (5,000)

THE SQUAD

	DOB	Ape M	(s)	G	Cla M	(s)	G
Goalkeepers:							
José Omar García Marín	28.02.2000	1					
Kevin Vance Hernández Kirkconnell	21.12.1985	13			1		
José Alberto Mendoza Posas	21.07.1989				17		
Defenders:							
Romário Efraín Cavachuela Gómez	09.01.1995	4	(2)				
Hilder Geovany Colón Alvarez	06.04.1989	11			14		
Roberto Carlos Díaz	13.02.2001				1	(5)	
Miguel Ángel Herrera Martínez (COL)	17.06.1988	5					
Bryan Arturo Johnson Sacasa	09.10.1989				7	(5)	2
Jorge Roberto Saldivar Granado	16.09.1984	5					
Selvin Ariel Tinoco Maldonado	14.02.1991	6	(1)				
Arnaldo Ibrahin Urbina Torres	04.11.1995	9			17	(1)	
Midfielders:							
Oslín Antonio Acevedo Orellana	11.04.2002		(2)				
Carlos Alvarado	28.07.1996	1	(1)				
José Miguel Barreto Pérez (URU)	09.02.1993				17		
Jesús Marcelo Canales Cálix	06.01.1991	12	(1)	2	9	(8)	1
Juan Ángel Delgado Murillo	21.07.1992	9	(1)	1			
Yunni Dolmo	02.02.2001	3			4	(6)	1
Oscar Gregory González Vargas	23.05.1996	3	(2)		18		1
Rolman Fabier González Gallardo	15.09.1997		(1)				
Maverick Josue Hernández Flores	17.02.1999	1	(1)				
Samuel Enríque Lucas Arana	07.11.1996	5	(6)	1	2	(5)	
Eduardo Maldonado	04.03.1994	10	(2)		11	(4)	
Eduardo Martínez	01.06.1998	1	(1)				
Janier Isaí Martinez	09.02.2002					(1)	
Franklyn Joel Morales Martínez	13.02.1988					(1)	
Axel Efrain Padilla Cáceres	26.01.2001		(2)				
Jairo Daniel Puerto Herrera	28.12.1988				15		
José Daniel Quiróz Portillo	26.05.1997				9	(5)	
Cristian Sacaza	18.08.1998	9	(3)	1	15	(1)	1
Óscar Leonardo Salas Miranda	30.11.1993				8	(9)	
Axel Soto	08.03.2001	3	(1)				
Forwards:							
Rafael Enrique Agámez Valencia (COL)	26.08.1994	7	(3)		16		9
Erick Salvador Andino Portillo	21.07.1989	10	(3)	2			
Davis Bladimir Argueta Zambrano	15.05.1996	1					
Yerson Gutiérrez Cuenca (COL)	20.01.1994	10	(2)	3			
Julián Martínez (COL)	13.04.1989	3					
Walter Julián Martínez Ramos	24.03.1982	3	(2)		1	(4)	
José Alejandro Morales Hernández	24.09.1999		(1)				
Yeison Mauricio Mosquera Mosquera (COL)	13.01.1997	9	(1)	1			

| Eduardo Matías Rotondi (ARG) | 29.01.1992 | | 16 | (2) | 10 |

Trainer:		
Mauro German Reyes Cuéllar	19.11.1966	8
David Fúnez [Caretaker]		1
Washington Fernando Araújo Recarey (URU)	23.02.1972	5		18

CLUB DEPORTIVO MARATHÓN SAN PEDRO SULA
Foundation date: November 25, 1925
Address: 27 Avenida, entre 7 y 8 Calle, Colonia San Carlos de Sula, San Pedro Sula
Stadium: Estadio "General Francisco Morazán", San Pedro Sula (20,000)

THE SQUAD

	DOB	Ape			Cla		
		M	(s)	G	M	(s)	G
Goalkeepers:							
Luis Enrique Ortíz Hernández	23.01.1998	2					
Denovan Galileo Torres Pérez	04.10.1989	18			14		
Defenders:							
Brayan Josué Castillo Arzú	05.06.1998				5	(3)	
Wilmer Crisanto Casildo	19.09.1989				11	(1)	
Carlos Iván García Castillo	29.09.1998		(2)		6		
Emilio Arturo Izaguirre Giron	10.05.1986				13	(1)	
Bryan Arturo Johnson Sacasa	09.10.1989	14		1			
José Carlos López Perdomo	22.10.1993	2	(3)		4	(1)	
Cristian Yaffet Moreira Güity	21.05.2000	7	(8)		4		
Michael Otoniel Osorio Morales	10.09.1994	3	(1)				
Carlos Alberto Perdomo Martínez	01.07.1989	1	(4)				
Walter Adrián Ramírez Pineda	22.09.2000		(2)	1	6	(1)	
Mikel Noe Santos Castillo	27.04.1999	1	(2)		5	(3)	
Mathías Sebastián Techera Pizarro (URU)	16.02.1992	17		1	11		
Midfielders:							
Kervin Fabián Arriaga Villanueva	05.01.1998	17		4	6	(1)	1
Allan Alexander Banegas Murillo	04.10.1994	17		2			
Cristian Neptali Calix Alvarado	09.09.1999	8	(5)	1	1	(3)	
Luis Fernando Garrido Garrido	05.11.1990	14	(2)		6		
Selvin Rolando Guevara Casco	15.02.1999	5	(6)		4	(2)	
Kevin John Hoyos Manzur (USA)	25.02.1993				7	(5)	4
Axel Moisés Motiño Rivera	02.11.2000	2	(6)		4	(5)	
Edwin Solani Solano Martínez	25.01.1996	17		4	10	(4)	3
John Paul Suazo Caballero	07.10.1995	18			7	(3)	
Luis Fernando Vega Cillacorta	28.02.2002	16	(2)	2	7	(2)	
Forwards:							
Carlo Yaír Costly Molina	18.07.1982				1	(9)	4
Yaudel Lahera García (CUB)	09.02.1991	6	(6)	2			
Yaudel Lahera García (CUB)	09.02.1991				6	(2)	
Frelys Edilson López Saravia	01.03.1995	2	(6)		1	(4)	
Jeffry Eyeri Miranda Miguel	03.09.2002		(3)		1	(2)	
Ryduan Palermo (ARG)	24.07.1996	7	(6)	2	4	(6)	2
Marlon Roberto Ramírez Arauz	17.04.1994	9	(3)		7	(3)	1
José Enrique Vigil Lobo	26.04.1999	1	(6)	1	3		1
Bruno Volpi (ARG)	23.06.1993	16	(3)	7			
Trainer:							
Héctor Vargas Baldús (ARG)	15.03.1959	20			14		

FÚTBOL CLUB MOTAGUA TEGUCIGALPA

Foundation date: August 29, 1928
Address: Colonia Jardines de Toncontín, Comayaguela, Tegucigalpa
Stadium: Estadio „Tiburcio Carías Andino", Tegucigalpa (35,000)

THE SQUAD

	DOB	Ape M	(s)	G	Cla M	(s)	G
Goalkeepers:							
Hugo Donaldo Caballero Mejía	05.01.1997					(1)	
Marlon Javier Licona López	09.02.1991	4			2		
Jonathan Felipe Rougier (ARG)	29.10.1987	16			18		
Defenders:							
Marvin Alcides Ávila Ardon	09.03.2002					(1)	
Harrison Robel Bernárdez Caballero	14.05.1997	1					
Félix Joan Crisanto Velásquez	09.09.1990	1	(3)				
Wilmer Crisanto Casildo	24.06.1989	3	(7)				
Wesly Roberto Decas	11.08.1999	15			11		
Omar Josué Elvir Casco	28.09.1989	15	(3)		9	(2)	2
Albert Fabricio Galindo Zavala	21.10.2000				3		
Elmer Alexander Guity Centeno	24.10.1996				1	(2)	
Emilio Arturo Izaguirre Giron	10.05.1986	10	(5)				
Christopher Áaron Meléndez Suazo	25.11.1997	17	(2)	1	10		1
Juan Pablo Montes Montes	26.12.1985	4			14		
Jonathan Adid Núñez García	26.11.2001	7	(3)		3	(2)	1
Danilo Palacios	11.06.2001		(1)				
Marcelo Antonio Pereira Rodríguez	27.05.1995	9		1	17		
Diego Fernando Rodríguez López	06.11.1995				5	(1)	
Midfielders:							
Héctor Enrique Castellanos Villatoro	28.12.1992	12	(2)	1	8	(2)	
Juan Ángel Delgado Murillo	21.07.1992				11	(3)	1
Ariel Armando Flores Baquedano	18.05.2001					(1)	
Oscar Alberto García Fernández	16.05.1990				3	(6)	1
Juan Ramón Gómez Martínez	03.04.2000		(4)				
Iván Edgardo López Cano	05.10.1990				6	(11)	3
Reinieri Joel Mayorquín Gámez	13.07.1989	4	(7)		1	(2)	1
Jesse Antonio Moncada Matute	05.01.1990				1	(9)	1
Bayron Edimar Dionicio Méndez	04.07.1988	1	(3)	1		(3)	
Sergio Salvador Peña Zelaya	09.05.1987	9	(7)	1	4	(4)	1
Raúl Marcelo Santos Colindres	02.08.1992	12	(1)		11	(1)	
Forwards:							
Arnol Daniel Álvarez Martínez	19.01.2001		(1)				
Eduardo Alonso Arriola Jr.					2		
Román Rubilio Castillo Álvarez	26.11.1991	13	(1)	10			
Carlos Roberto Fernández Martínez	17.02.1992				11	(7)	2
Matías Alejandro Galvaliz (ARG)	06.06.1989	12	(5)		15	(3)	2
Gonzalo Martín Klusener (ARG)	21.10.1983	11	(8)	8	8	(8)	4
Kevin Josué López Maldonado	03.02.1996	15	(3)	6	7	(7)	2
Walter Joel Martínez Betanco	26.03.1991	15	(4)	2	12	(5)	2
Roberto Moreira Aldana (PAR)	06.05.1987	9	(8)	6	19		7
Marco Tulio Vega Ordoñez	14.04.1987	5	(8)	4	8	(6)	4
Josué Isaias Villafranca Quiñónez	16.12.1999					(8)	1
Trainer:							
Diego Martín Vásquez Castro (ARG)	03.07.1971	20			20		

CLUB DEPORTIVO OLIMPIA TEGUCIGALPA

Foundation date: June 12, 1912
Address: Calle de atras antiguo Cine Maya, Casa No. 2017, Colonia Palmira, Tegucigalpa
Stadium: Estadio „Tiburcio Carías Andino", Tegucigalpa (35,000)

THE SQUAD

	DOB	Ape M	(s)	G	Cla M	(s)	G
Goalkeepers:							
Harold Geovanny Fonseca Baca	08.10.1993	5					
Edrick Eduardo Menjívar Jonhson	01.03.1993	17			19		
José Rafael Zúñiga Euceda	13.05.1990				1		
Defenders:							
Ever Gonzalo Alvarado Sandoval	30.01.1992	4		1	11	(2)	
Jorge Daniel Álvarez Rodas	28.01.1998	10	(3)	1	2	(4)	
Brayan Antonio Beckeles	28.11.1985				1	(8)	1
José Arnaldo Cañete Prieto (PAR)	19.03.1996	1					
Samuel Arturo Córdova Howe	01.10.1988	7	(6)	1	7		
Josmán Alexander Figueroa Arzú		1	(8)		5	(10)	
José Antonio García Robledo	21.09.1998				7	(2)	2
Elvin Oliva Casildo	24.10.1997	11	(1)	2	10		
André Daniel Orellana Leverón	11.03.2002	4	(1)				
Jonathan Josué Paz Hernández	18.06.1995	15			8	(1)	1
Javier Arnaldo Portillo Martínez	10.06.1981	10	(1)		2	(2)	
Edwin Alexander Rodríguez Castillo	25.09.1999	16	(3)	1	9	(3)	1
Midfielders:							
Allan Alexander Banegas Murillo	04.10.1993				4	(2)	
Deybi Aldair Flores Flores	16.06.1996	20	(1)		17		
Mayron Ariel Flores Zavala	09.07.1996		(5)		1	(3)	
Leonardo Matías Garrido (ARG)	02.02.1986	3	(8)	1		(7)	
Pedro Ramón González Martínez	13.02.2002	1	(1)				
Johnny Harold Leverón Uclés	07.02.1990	15	(1)		17	(1)	1
Cristian Omar Maidana (ARG)	24.01.1987	1	(1)			(1)	
Axel Jamir Maldonado Manzanares	24.07.2001					(1)	
German Noe Mejía Briceño	01.10.1994	5	(4)		16	(2)	
Maylor Alberto Nuñez Flores	05.07.1996	19	(2)	1	17		
Carlos Enrique Pineda López	23.09.1997	7	(4)				
José Alejandro Reyes Cerna	05.11.1997	3	(9)	2			
Forwards:							
Ezequiel Lucas Aguirre (ARG)	08.01.1992				5	(7)	2
Justin Arboleda Buenaños (COL)	18.09.1992	12	(8)	7	13	(4)	8
Jerry Ricardo Bengtson Bodden	08.04.1987	16	(4)	10	17	(1)	14
Marvin Javier Bernárdez García	05.02.1995	8	(7)	1	2	(8)	
Michaell Anthony Chirinos López	17.06.1995	9	(3)	3	18		6
Eddie Gabriel Hernández Padilla	27.02.1991	8	(3)	7	3	(7)	4
José Mario Pinto Paz	27.09.1997	9	(7)		7	(7)	3
Diego Antonio Reyes Sandoval	13.01.1990	5	(6)	2	1	(6)	1
Trainer:							
Pedro Antonio Troglio (ARG)	28.07.1965	22			20		

CLUB DEPORTIVO PLATENSE PUERTO CORTÉS

Foundation date: July 4, 1960
Address: Planta Baja Estadio Excelsior, Puerto Cortés
Stadium: Estadio Excélsior, Puerto Cortés (10,000)

THE SQUAD

	DOB	Ape M	(s)	G	Cla M	(s)	G
Goalkeepers:							
Bruno Arquel Aleman Herrera	02.06.2000	1					
José Mariano Pineda Suazo	19.10.1987	15			14		
Defenders:							
Jesús Alberto Araya Chambers (PAN)	03.01.1996	1					
Rony Adolfo Cambell Reaños	16.08.1999	1					
Luis Gabriel Castro Pardo (COL)	28.07.1985	1					
Anthony Aldair Cervantes Pavón	10.08.1998	9	(2)		3		
Antony Martínez		2	(3)		1		
Marcos Lionzo Martínez Álvarez	08.11.1995	11			10		
José David Montoya Johnson	15.11.1999				2	(2)	
César Antonio Oseguera Raudales	20.07.1990	10	(1)	2	12	(1)	
Cristian Enrique Padilla Turcios	19.08.1999	1	(3)		2	(6)	
Aldair Simanca Peña (COL)	04.07.1998				4	(2)	
Richard Zuñiga	05.05.2000	2	(7)	1		(3)	
Midfielders:							
Marlon José Alvarenga Morales	27.09.1999	1					
Edgar Anthony Álvarez Reyes	18.01.1980	1					
Héctor Javier Aranda Medina	27.03.1997				8	(3)	
Víctor René Araúz Calderón	22.04.1996	12		2	10		
Isaac Rosell Arias	23.03.2001					(1)	
Henry Arony Ayala Martínez	31.01.1996	3					
Ilce Fernando Barahona Castillo	27.09.1998	11	(1)	1	9	(1)	1
Orbin Asiel Cabrera Morales	25.06.1995	1	(2)			(1)	
Dabirson Antonio Castillo Sánchez	25.09.1996	13	(1)	2	13		1
Joseph Samuel Cunningham Crisanto	20.08.1996	1	(2)				
Ángel Domínguez		2	(1)				
José Domínguez	29.07.2001				11	(2)	1
Luis Ricauter Jaramillo (PAN)	25.04.1988	11	(1)				
Mauro Daniel Leiva (ARG)	25.05.1995	1	(7)				
Brayan Fernando Martínez Pérez	16.07.1993	10	(1)				
Julio Javier Moncada Bogran	06.10.1994	1	(5)		2	(4)	
Hesller Morales		4	(3)	1	2	(6)	
Sergio Murillo Carabalí (PAN)	12.05.1994					(1)	
Denilson David Nuñez Martínez	24.05.1999	1	(1)		1		
Hesller Ortíz	12.05.1995	2					
Osbed Alberto Pérez Norales	03.02.2000	2			2	(1)	
Brayan Fabricio Reyes Colón	27.09.1991				4	(2)	
Edson Rocha		2	(3)				
Jeancarlo Jassyr Vargas Drummond	16.05.1998	5	(2)	2	2	(2)	
Joshua Alexander Vargas Drummond	29.11.1994	7					
Ángel Gustavo Velásquez Rodríguez	30.10.1999	5	(3)			(2)	
Mateo Zapata Ortíz	20.09.1994				1	(4)	
Forwards:							
Carlos Roberto Bernárdez García (BLZ)	28.12.1992	14	(1)	10	6	(2)	3
Aldo Yohan Fajardo Maldonado	13.11.1997	4	(2)		12	(1)	3

281

Yerson Gutiérrez Cuenca (COL)	20.01.1994			12	(1)	7
Nicolás Pedro Lugli (ARG)	09.07.1996	7	(3)			
Byron Miguel Rodríguez Nelson	26.08.1997		(2)	6	(8)	3
Henry Adonis Romero Velásquez	12.08.1996			5	(7)	2
Carlos Ugarte	02.08.2002	1				

Trainer:

Jhon Jairo López Taborda (COL)	10.03.1968	16	14

CLUB DEPORTIVO REAL DE MINAS TEGUCIGALPA
Foundation date: 2012
Address: *Not known*
Stadium: Estadio „Marcelo Tinoco", Danlí (5,000)

THE SQUAD

	DOB	M	Ape (s)	G	M	Cla (s)	G
Goalkeepers:							
Julani Kyle Archibald (SKN)	18.05.1991	10			14		
Gerson Nahamán Argueta Dubón	10.03.1991	4					
Defenders:							
Dylan Jerome Andrade Bodden	08.03.1998	7			8	(2)	
Harrison Robel Bernárdez Caballero	14.05.1997				10	(2)	
Klifox Onel Bernárdez Valerio	18.09.1994	9			12	(1)	1
Roney Bernárdez Caballero	19.06.2002	1	(3)	1	1	(6)	1
Bryan Ariel Castro Murillo	05.03.1991				6		
José Antonio García Robledo	21.09.1998	12					
Elison David Rivas Mejia	20.11.1999				6	(4)	
Diego Fernando Rodríguez López	06.11.1995	13		8			
Luis Ismael Santos Alvarado	05.03.1996	9	(1)		13		
Midfielders:							
Manuel Isaac Aguirre Iscoa			(1)				
Jorge Alberto Almendarez Rodríguez	07.02.1999		(1)		1		
Darwin Rolando Andino Mendoza	27.03.1999	9	(2)	1	2	(1)	
Axel Barrios	28.08.2003				3	(1)	1
Henry Misael Guity Bernárdez	24.06.1996				1	(2)	1
Sebastián José Colón (COL)	25.06.1998	8		2	1	(3)	
Alex Mauricio Corrales Osorto	29.03.1993	1					
Alex Reiniery Cubas Pacheco	22.06.1994	2	(2)				
Edder Gerardo Delgado Zerón	20.11.1986				11		2
Harry Duarte			(1)				
Oscar Alberto García Fernández	16.05.1990	11	(1)	3			
Henry Misael Guity Bernárdez	24.06.1996					(2)	
Jack Eudardo Jean-Baptiste Cruz	20.12.1999	8	(1)		8	(3)	
Kevin Rafael Johnson Escamilla	11.09.1995					(4)	
Everson Jared López Bonilla	03.11.2000		(1)				
David Alberto Mendoza Escobar	22.12.1991	13			10		
Mario Ernesto Moncada Arguijo	29.07.1998		(2)		3	(5)	
Jesse Antonio Moncada Matute	05.01.1990	9	(3)	2			
William Moncada	30.10.1991	1			10	(2)	1
Nelson José Muñoz García	07.06.1993	3	(1)				
Joshua Franshua Nieto Matamoros	03.09.1994				7	(1)	3
Wilker Witty Ordoñez	06.11.2001	1	(1)				
Aldo Josué Oviedo Gallardo	07.01.1990	10		1	6	(5)	
Yeison Adonis Oyuela Aguilar	1999	2	(2)				

Edgar Palma			(3)			
Jairo Joel Rivas Zuniga	29.07.2001		(2)		(3)	
Rodrigo Rodríguez Duarte	20.06.2004			1	(3)	
Cristhian Sierra		1				

Forwards:

Erick Salvador Andino Portillo	21.07.1989			5	(4)	1
Axel Barrio	28.08.2003	3				
Marvin Leonel Cálix Antúnez	06.03.1992			1	(4)	
Jonathan Capacho Zambrano (COL)	22.01.1998	2	(3)			
David Fernando Fonseca Alemán		1	(1)			
Foslyn Eggerton Grant Valladares	04.10.1998			9	(3)	
Tahir Karanha Omari Hanley (SKN)	05.05.1997				(1)	
Kevin Andrés Maradiaga Berrantes	19.01.1994			5	(1)	
César Miguel Romero Moncada	19.01.1999	4	(2)			

Trainer:

José Antonio Hernández Pérez (ESP)	19.02.1981	-			
Harold Yépez Peña (COL)	02.07.1975	3			
José Israel Canales		11		4	
Reynaldo Antonio Tilguath Flores	04.08.1979			10	

REAL CLUB DEPORTIVO ESPAÑA
SAN PEDRO SULA

Foundation date: July 14, 1929
Address: 27 Avenida 28 y 31 Calle, Colonia Luisiana, San Pedro Sula
Stadium: Estadio „General Francisco Morazán", San Pedro Sula (18,000)

THE SQUAD

	DOB	Ape M	(s)	G	Cla M	(s)	G
Goalkeepers:							
José Omar García Marín	28.02.2000					(1)	
Luís Aurelio López Fernández	13.09.1993	11			14		
Michael Alexandru Perelló Lopez	11.07.1998	3			4		
Defenders:							
Steven Jared Bonilla Rodríguez	10.05.2002	1					
Maycol Alfredo Figueroa Arteaga	11.08.2001				1		
Franco Valentin Flores (ARG)	28.05.1993				12	(1)	
Franklin Geovany Flores Sacaza	18.05.1996	12			17		1
Junior García					1		
Carlos Alberto Mejía Cruz	23.03.1997	12	(2)		4		
Getsel Ramón Montes Escobar	23.06.1996	8			15	(2)	
Pablo Nicolás Pírez Montes (URU)	08.01.1990	6	(1)				
Elison David Rivas Mejia	20.11.1999	1	(3)				
Henry Sánchez	05.01.2002		(1)				
Matías Fernando Soto de Freitas (URU)	23.04.1991	5	(1)	1			
Allans Josué Vargas Murillo	25.09.1993	11		1	13	(1)	1
Midfielders:							
Arnold Barahona	10.02.2000					(2)	
Jhon Hendric Benavídez Banegas	26.12.1995	9	(1)		11	(1)	
Miguel Ángel Carrasco Reyes	10.06.2003	3	(1)		6	(3)	
Gerson Aldair Chávez Suazo	31.01.2000	10	(2)		12	(1)	
Santiago Nicolás Correa Parodi (URU)	27.07.1990	8	(2)				
Devron Kyber García Ducker	17.02.1996	9			10	(3)	
Eric Junior García (SLV)	16.10.1999	2	(1)				

Samuel Gómez (USA)	06.08.1996				2	(1)	
Iván Edgardo López Cano	05.10.1990	11	(2)	2			
Jorge Jalil López Delgado	14.08.1999	1					
Mario Roberto Martínez Hernández	30.07.1989	10	(3)	4	13	(3)	2
Yeisón Fernando Mejía Zelaya	18.01.1998				11	(4)	1
Daniel Alcides Meléndez Mejía	09.04.2002					(2)	
Wisdom Niiayitey Quaye July	08.04.1998				6	(4)	
José Daniel Quiróz Portillo	26.05.1997		(7)				
José Alejandro Reyes Cerna	05.11.1997				10	(3)	
Henry Sánchez	05.01.2002				1	(2)	

Forwards:

Jorge Alfredo Castrillo	28.07.2002		(3)	1		(1)	
Maikel Antonio García Bardales	11.04.1999	2	(4)	1	7	(5)	1
Rony Darío Martínez Almendarez	16.10.1987	5	(8)	2			
Patrick Oneal Palacios Martínez	29.01.2000					(4)	
Ramiro Iván Rocca (ARG)	22.11.1988				16		8
Omar Arnulfo Rosas Salomón (MEX)	06.08.1993				5	(7)	2
Ángel Gabriel Tejeda Escobar	01.06.1991	6	(3)	4			
Delis Matías Vargas Blanco (URU)	25.10.1994	3	(2)		1	(1)	
Darixon Eniel Vuelto Pérez	15.01.1998	5	(7)	2	6	(7)	

Trainer:

Ramiro Martínez (URU)	31.08.1966	10
Edgarson Emilson Soto Fajardo	20.10.1964	4
Raúl Erasto Gutiérrez Jacobo (MEX)	16.10.1966	18

CLUB DEPORTIVO REAL SOCIEDAD TOCOA

Foundation date: August 16, 1988
Address: *Not known*
Stadium: Estadio "Francisco Martínez Durón", Tocoa (10,000)

THE SQUAD

	DOB	Ape M	(s)	G	Cla M	(s)	G
Goalkeepers:							
Juan Pablo Domínguez (ARG)	17.02.1992				1		
Obed Isrrael Enamorado Palacios	15.09.1985	8			9		
William Andrés Robledo Rivas	10.12.1990	4					
Wilson David Urbina Contreas	08.08.1998	2	(1)		4		
Defenders:							
Bréyner Bonilla Montaño (COL)	21.07.1986				10		1
Sonny Renán Fernández Ávila	03.04.1995				10		
Henry Adalberto Figueroa Alonzo	28.12.1992	1					
Dilmer Alberto Gutiérrez Castillo	24.05.1986	6	(1)		10	(1)	
Yeer Lisandro Gutiérrez Miguel	24.08.1992	6	(3)	1			
Kenneth Zenon Hernández Álvarez	26.05.1997				1	(2)	
Deyron Martínez	20.12.1999				1	(2)	
Edgar Samir Martínez	29.08.1989	4					
Robbie Edward Matute Pandy	20.11.1987	10	(1)		5	(4)	
Daniel Rocha	12.11.1999				1		
José Danilo Tobías Chávez	20.01.1992				13	(1)	2
Ricky Joél Zapata Mejía	23.11.1997	3	(1)		9	(1)	
Midfielders:							
Christian Josué Altamirano Metzgen	26.11.1989				10	(2)	4
Michel Emilson Antúnez Zelaya	23.06.1993	3			4	(1)	

Desther Ventura Ávila Martínez					1	(1)	
José Canales	25.07.1996	4	(3)		5	(2)	
Kendrick Armando Carcamo Tatun	27.04.1994		(1)			(2)	1
Jorge Chávez		1	(3)				
Henry Raúl Clark Peña	10.06.1985	8	(1)				
Jorge Aarón Claros Juárez	08.01.1986				10	(2)	
Wilmer Daniel Fuentes Alvarenga	21.04.1992	4	(3)		9	(3)	
Deyron Martínez	20.12.1999	6	(2)	1			
Maynor Matute		2	(1)				
Yeisón Fernando Mejía Zelaya	18.01.1998	8	(2)				
Oliver David Morazán Torres	05.01.1988	14		3			
Jesús Alberto Munguía Fernández	26.07.1991	4	(1)				
Abel Isaías Olariaga (ARG)	10.12.1986	9		1			
Enuar Iván Salgado Vega	25.06.1991	3	(1)		5		

Forwards:

Kemsie Rickie Abbott Bodden	08.12.1994	4	(2)		4	(1)	
Clinton Guadalupe Arzú Suazo	12.12.1995				1	(7)	
Pablo César Arzú Castillo	31.10.1990		(4)				
Jamal Ray Charles (GRN)	24.11.1995	12	(2)	1			
Jonatan Eduardo Corzo (ARG)	18.12.1992				4	(6)	1
Alex Noel Martínez Bulnes	20.06.1905	4	(2)	1			
Christian Samir Martínez Centeno	08.09.1990	3			4	(2)	
Rony Darío Martínez Almendarez	16.10.1987				14		8
Patrick Lonnie McLaughlin Batis			(1)				
Dany Antonio Mejía Rivera	21.01.1997	3	(1)			(3)	
Osman Leonel Melgares Munguía	27.11.1986	5	(2)	4	1	(6)	1
Eliaquim Ariel Navarro Floresq	31.01.2001	4	(1)				
Maykel Alejandro Reyes Azcuy (CUB)	04.03.1993				3	(6)	
Brayan Rivera	05.10.1996	2			4		
Henry Adonis Romero Velásquez	12.08.1996	2	(6)				
Bryan Rosales	05.10.1998				1		
Henry Alfredo Vivas Cuero (COL)	18.09.1994	5	(2)				
Willsy Neven Wood Aguilera	02.10.1995					(5)	

Trainer:

Carlos Humberto Martínez Pineda	19.10.1965	5			
Adrián García Padilla (ESP)	08.12.1980	6			
Carlos Ramón Tábora Hernández	30.01.1965	3		4	
Héctor Ramón Castellón Fernández	31.08.1960			10	

CLUB DEPORTIVO LOBOS DE LA UNIVERSIDAD PEDAGÓGICA NACIONAL FRANCISCO MORAZÁN TEGUCIGALPA

Foundation date: August 10, 2010
Address: *Not known*
Stadium: Estadio „Tiburcio Carías Andino", Tegucigalpa (35,000)

THE SQUAD	DOB	Ape M	(s)	G	Cla M	(s)	G
Goalkeepers:							
Jordy Josué Castro Martínez	10.04.2000	5					
Bryan Fernando Cruz Ramirez	23.07.1995	1					
Celio Antonio Valladares Ávila	02.05.1989	10			16		
Defenders:							
Pablo Cacho		6	(2)				
Marco Antonio Godoy Vallecillo	06.06.1999	4	(4)		10	(1)	
Axel Daniel Gómez Guzmán	28.06.2000	12			7		
Elmer Alexander Guity Centeno	24.10.1996	2	(3)				
Lesvin Fernando Medina Almendares	26.08.1993	9		1	11		
Ronal Gustavo Montoya Sierra	04.07.1990	14		1	13		2
Michael Otoniel Osorio Morales	10.09.1994				9	(1)	3
Eduard Enrique Reyes Guiza	30.08.1997	11			4		
Jason Sánchez		6		2	9		
Lázaro Alejandro Yánez Martínez	03.08.1989	1	(2)				
Midfielders:							
Luis Daniel Álvarez	25.01.2003					(4)	
Luis Fernando Argeñal Padilla	09.12.1997	5	(1)		15		1
Elix Daniel Gómez Coello	14.08.2002					(1)	
Kevin Andrés Maradiaga Berrantes	19.01.1994	1					
Víctor Alfonso Moncada Ramírez	24.02.1990	7	(9)	4			
Erick Josué Peña Paz	26.08.1996	1	(1)				
Carlos Alberto Róchez Crisanto	18.02.1995	10	(5)	3	10	(5)	4
Kenneth Ulloa		2	(4)	1			
Hilder Eduardo Torres Guatemala	14.04.1995				7	(4)	
Christopher Jared Urmeneta Flores	25.08.1994	10	(1)		7	(2)	
Edgar Enrique Vásquez Mejía	23.11.1998	2	(3)		6	(4)	
Forwards:							
Leonardo Alejandro Bodden Castro	01.10.1994				2	(2)	
Ted Bodden	21.04.2001	6	(2)	1			
Sendel Eduardo Cruz López	13.12.1998	5	(2)		8	(3)	1
Jerrick Arturo Díaz Matute	17.02.1989				3	(8)	1
Samuel Elvir Suniga	25.04.2001	4	(5)	1	9	(5)	2
Rembrandt Adán Flores Bonilla	12.05.1997	1	(9)		1	(6)	
Jason Garay García	05.06.1998	5	(1)				
César Alberto Guillén Clark	27.10.1996				8	(8)	3
Junior Alberto Lacayo Róchez	19.08.1995	12	(1)	1			
Juan Ramón Mejía Erazo	01.08.1988	11		4	9	(6)	4
Arnold Josué Meléndez Rivera	23.08.1995				4	(6)	1
Kilmar Aldair Peña Oseguera	09.03.1997	5	(5)	1			
Jairo Róchez Crisanto	05.04.1991	8	(1)	2	8	(4)	1
Roy Stephen Rodríguez Medina (PER)	08.12.2003					(3)	
Trainer:							
José Salomón Nazar Ordóñez	07.09.1953	16			16		

CLUB DEPORTIVO Y SOCIAL VIDA LA CEIBA

Foundation date: October 14, 1940
Address: 3ra. Etapa No 0-10, La Ceiba
Stadium: Estadio „Nilmo Edwards", La Ceiba (20,000)

THE SQUAD

	DOB	Ape M	(s)	G	Cla M	(s)	G
Goalkeepers:							
Cristian Yesid Arroyave Copete (COL)	05.07.1995				5		
Ricardo Gabriel Canales Lanza	30.05.1982	4			1		
Roberto Josué López Díaz	23.04.1995				10		
José Alberto Mendoza Posas	21.07.1989	14					
Defenders:							
Bryan Josué Bernárdez Barrios	24.05.1994				7	(2)	1
Darwin Geovany Diego Mejía	14.07.1999	2					
Jeffri Gilberto Flores Fernández	04.08.1994	6	(2)		3		
Raymond Jafet Guity López		1					
Carlos Eduardo Meléndez Rosales	08.12.1997	15		6	9	(1)	2
Joel Isai Membreño Villamil	13.10.2001					(2)	1
Brian Alberto Osorto Melgar	30.10.2001		(1)				
Eduardo Rivera	12.10.2001					(4)	
Michael Rosales	27.01.2002	7	(1)		4	(5)	
Carlos Alfredo Sánchez Sánchez	22.08.1990	16	(1)	1	15		1
José David Velásquez Colón	08.12.1989	13		1	16		1
Midfielders:							
Alexander Maximino Aguilar Ayala	23.07.1987	16		6	15		2
Carlos Horacio Argueta Ramos	25.06.1995	13	(2)	1	4	(4)	
Guillermo Rafael Chavasco Martínez (URU)	09.07.1991				5	(1)	1
José Alberto Escalante Rapalo	29.05.1995	14	(1)		7		
Ederson Ariel Fúnez Fúnes	25.06.2004		(3)			(4)	
Jonathan Mazzola (ARG)	30.04.1991	7	(6)				
Denis Javier Meléndez Rosales	22.06.1995	18		2	13		
Luis Fernando Meléndez Rosales	26.01.2000	3	(4)		2	(7)	1
Julián Andrés Mendoza Blanco (COL)	11.09.1993				1	(1)	
Oliver David Morazán Torres	05.01.1988				11	(3)	
Danilo Palacios	11.06.2001				13	(2)	
Luis Enrique Palma Oseguera	17.01.2000	16		9	10		4
Maykel Antonio Pavón Fernández	12.05.1999					(1)	
Wisdom Niiayitey Quaye July	08.04.1998	16		2			
Roger Alexander Sander Bodden Jr.	16.08.1999	2	(4)		5	(9)	
Dayron Suazo	21.02.1999	3	(3)		4	(3)	
Hilder Eduardo Torres Guatemala	14.04.1995	4	(7)	1			
Forwards:							
Cristián Ernesto Alessandrini (ARG)	27.05.1985		(4)				
Mauro Sergio Bustamante (ARG)	23.06.1991					(1)	
Juan Ramón Contreras Díaz	21.01.1999		(9)				
Foslyn Eggerton Grant Valladares	04.10.1998	3	(1)				
César Alberto Guillén Clark	27.10.1996	4	(10)	1			
Iverson Oneal Jiménez Sacaza	02.03.2003				1	(1)	1
Ronald Alberto Maradiaga	30.11.2002	1	(1)			(1)	
Limberth Pérez	22.08.2000				1	(3)	
Ángel Gabriel Tejeda Escobar	01.06.1991				14	(2)	4
Trainer:							

Ramón Enrique Maradiaga Chávez	30.11.1954	9	
Nerlin Alexis Membreño Flores	24.01.1972	9	11
Fernando Manuel Mendes Mira (POR)	02.04.1962		5

NATIONAL TEAM
INTERNATIONAL MATCHES 2020/2021

10.10.2020	Comayagua	Honduras - Nicaragua	1-1(0-1)	(F)
15.10.2020	Ciudad de Guatemala	Guatemala - Honduras	2-1(1-0)	(F)
24.03.2021	Zhodzina	Belarus - Honduras	1-1(1-1)	(F)
28.03.2021	Thessaloníki	Greece - Honduras	2-1(1-1)	(F)
03.06.2021	Denver	Honduras - United States	0-1(0-0)	(CNL)
06.06.2021	Denver	Honduras - Costa Rica	2-2; 5-4 p	(CNL)
12.06.2021	Atlanta	Mexico - Honduras	0-0	(F)

10.10.2020, Friendly International
Estadio "Carlos Miranda", Comayagua; Attendance: 0
Referee: Óscar Donaldo Moncada (Honduras)
HONDURAS - NICARAGUA   **1-1(0-1)**
HON: Luis Aurelio López Fernández, Emilio Arturo Izaguirre Girón, Jonathan Josué Paz Hernández, Marcelo Antonio Pereira Rodríguez, Raúl Marcelo Santos Colindres (76.Edwin Solany Solano Martínez), Héctor Enrique Castellanos Villatoro (46.Jorge Daniel Álvarez Rodas), Jhow Hendric Benavídez Banegas, Kevin Josué López Maldonado (66.Ilce Fernando Barahona Castillo), Carlos Enrique Pineda López (76.Kervin Fabián Arriaga Villanueva), Edwin Alexander Rodríguez Castillo (46.Darixon Eniel Vuelto Pérez), Román Rubilio Castillo Álvarez (72.Juan Ramón Mejía Erazo).
Trainer: Fabián Coito Machado (Uruguay).
Goal: Jonathan Josué Paz Hernández (90+2).

15.10.2020, Friendly International
Estadio "Doroteo Guamuch Flores", Ciudad de Guatemala; Attendance: 0
Referee: Mario Alberto Escobar Toca (Guatemala)
GUATEMALA - HONDURAS   **2-1(1-0)**
HON: Luis Aurelio López Fernández, Maynor Alexis Figueroa Róchez, Franklin Geovany Flores Sacaza (62.Omar Josué Elvir Casco), Denil Omar Maldonado Munguía, Alexander Agustín López Rodríguez, Raúl Marcelo Santos Colindres (46.Jhow Hendric Benavídez Banegas), Ilce Fernando Barahona Castillo (79.Marcelo Antonio Pereira Rodríguez), Carlos Enrique Pineda López (62.Óscar Boniek García Ramírez), Darixon Eniel Vuelto Pérez (79.Edwin Alexander Rodríguez Castillo), Douglas Francisco Martínez Juárez (46.Juan Ramón Mejía Erazo), Jonathan Josué Rubio Toro. Trainer: Fabián Coito Machado (Uruguay).
Goal: Alexander Agustín López Rodríguez (68 penalty).

24.03.2021, Friendly International
Torpedo Stadium, Zhodzina; Attendance: 425
Referee: Aleksey Matyunin (Russia)
BELARUS - HONDURAS   **1-1(1-1)**
HON: Edrick Eduardo Menjívar Jonhson, Maynor Alexis Figueroa Róchez, Kevin Javier Álvarez Hernández (87.Maylor Alberto Núñez Flores), Marcelo Antonio Pereira Rodríguez, Diego Fernando Rodríguez López, Alexander Agustín López Rodríguez (82.Bryan Josué Acosta Ramos), Deybi Aldair Flores, Brayan Josué Velásquez Moya, Jerry Ricardo Bengtson Bodden (88.Jorge Renan Benguché Ramírez), Alberth Josué Elis Martínez, Jonathan Josué Rubio Toro (73.Walter Joel Martínez Betanco).
Trainer: Fabián Coito Machado (Uruguay).
Goal: Alexander Agustín López Rodríguez (45).

28.03.2021, Friendly International
Stádio Toumba, Thessaloníki; Attendance: 0
Referee: Urs Schnyder (Switzerland)
GREECE - HONDURAS   **2-1(1-1)**
HON: Edrick Eduardo Menjívar Jonhnson, Maynor Alexis Figueroa Róchez, Kevin Javier Álvarez Hernández, Maylor Alberto Núñez Flores (46.Kevin Josué López Maldonado), Marcelo Antonio Pereira Rodríguez, Diego Fernando Rodríguez López, Alfredo Antonio Mejía Escobar (65.Jonathan Josué Rubio Toro), Bryan Josué Acosta Ramos (65.Alexander Agustín López Rodríguez), Deybi Aldair Flores, Jerry Ricardo Bengtson Bodden (66.Brayan Josué Velásquez Moya), Alberth Josué Elis Martínez. Trainer: Fabián Coito Machado (Uruguay).
Goal: Diego Fernando Rodríguez López (41).

03.06.2021, 1st CONCACAF Nations League, Semi-Finals
Empower File at Mile High Stadium, Denver; Attendance: 34,451
Referee: Oshane Nation (Jamaica)
HONDURAS - UNITED STATES   **0-1(0-0)**
HON: Luis Aurelio López Fernández, Maynor Alexis Figueroa Róchez, Kevin Javier Álvarez Hernández, Marcelo Antonio Pereira Rodríguez (74.Óscar Boniek García Ramírez), Diego Fernando Rodríguez López (65.Éver Gonzalo Álvarado Sandoval), Alexander Agustín López Rodríguez (64.Bryan Josué Acosta Ramos), Deybi Aldair Flores, Rigoberto Manuel Rivas Vindel (74.Jhow Hendric Benavídez Banegas), Anthony Rubén Lozano Colón, Alberth Josué Elis Martínez, Jonathan Josué Rubio Toro (64.Edwin Alexander Rodríguez Castillo). Trainer: Fabián Coito Machado (Uruguay).

06.06.2021, 1st CONCACAF Nations League, Third Place Play-off
Empower Field at Mile High Stadium, Denver (United States); Attendance: 37,648
Referee: Reon Radix (Grenada)
HONDURAS - COSTA RICA   **2-2(0-1,2-2,2-2); 5-4 on penalties**
HON: Luis Aurelio López Fernández, Maynor Alexis Figueroa Róchez, Kevin Javier Álvarez Hernández, Marcelo Antonio Pereira Rodríguez, Diego Fernando Rodríguez López (78.Éver Gonzalo Álvarado Sandoval), Bryan Josué Acosta Ramos, Deybi Aldair Flores, Rigoberto Manuel Rivas Vindel (46.Alexander Agustín López Rodríguez), Edwin Alexander Rodríguez Castillo (78.Jonathan Josué Rubio Toro), Anthony Rubén Lozano Colón (63.Jorge Renan Benguché Ramírez), Alberth Josué Elis Martínez. Trainer: Fabián Coito Machado (Uruguay).
Goals: Edwin Alexander Rodríguez Castillo (48), Alberth Josué Elis Martínez (80).
Penalties: Alexander Agustín López Rodríguez, Alberth Josué Elis Martínez, Jorge Renan Benguché Ramírez, Jonathan Josué Rubio Toro (saved), Bryan Josué Acosta Ramos, Éver Gonzalo Álvarado Sandoval.

12.06.2021, Friendly International
Mercedes-Benz Stadium, Atlanta; Attendance: 70,072
Referee: Ted Unkel (United States)
MEXICO - HONDURAS   **0-0**
HON: Luis Aurelio López Fernández (61.Alex Nahíd Güity Barrios), Maynor Alexis Figueroa Róchez, Kevin Javier Álvarez Hernández, Marcelo Antonio Pereira Rodríguez, Diego Fernando Rodríguez López (68.Éver Gonzalo Álvarado Sandoval), Alexander Agustín López Rodríguez (69.Kervin Fabián Arriaga Villanueva), Bryan Josué Acosta Ramos, Deybi Aldair Flores (85.Óscar Boniek García Ramírez), Edwin Alexander Rodríguez Castillo, Walter Joel Martínez Betanco (69.Jonathan Josué Rubio Toro), Jorge Renan Benguché Ramírez (86.Rigoberto Manuel Rivas Vindel). Trainer: Fabián Coito Machado (Uruguay).

NATIONAL TEAM PLAYERS
2020/2021

Name	DOB	Club
Goalkeepers		
Alex Nahíd GÜITY Barrios	20.07.1997	*CD Olimpia Tegucigalpa*
Luis Aurelio LÓPEZ Fernández	13.09.1993	*Real CD España San Pedro Sula*
Edrick Eduardo MENJÍVAR Jonhson	01.03.1993	*CD Olimpia Tegucigalpa*
Defenders		
Éver Gonzalo ÁLVARADO Sandoval	30.11.1992	*CD Olimpia Tegucigalpa*
Kevin Javier ÁLVAREZ Hernández	03.08.1996	*IFK Norrköping (SWE)*
Omar Josué ELVIR Casco	28.09.1989	*FC Motagua Tegucigalpa*
Maynor Alexis FIGUEROA Róchez	02.05.1983	*Houston Dynamo (USA)*
Franklin Geovany FLORES Sacaza	18.05.1996	*Real CD España San Pedro Sula*
Emilio Arturo IZAGUIRRE Girón	10.05.1986	*FC Motagua Tegucigalpa*
Denil Omar MALDONADO Munguía	26.05.1998	*Everton de Viña del Mar (CHI)*
Maylor Alberto NÚÑEZ Flores	05.07.1996	*CD Olimpia Tegucigalpa*
Jonathan Josué PAZ Hernández	18.06.1995	*CD Olimpia Tegucigalpa*
Marcelo Antonio PEREIRA Rodríguez	27.05.1995	*FC Motagua Tegucigalpa*
Diego Fernando RODRÍGUEZ López	06.11.1995	*FC Motagua Tegucigalpa*
Raúl Marcelo SANTOS Colindres	03.08.1992	*FC Motagua Tegucigalpa*
Midfielders		
Bryan Josué ACOSTA Ramos	24.11.1993	*FC Dallas (USA)*
Jorge Daniel ÁLVAREZ Rodas	28.01.1998	*CD Olimpia Tegucigalpa*
Kervin Fabián ARRIAGA Villanueva	05.01.1998	*CD Marathón San Pedro Sula*
Ilce Fernando BARAHONA Castillo	27.09.1998	*CD Platense Puerto Cortés*
Jhow Hendric BENAVÍDEZ Banegas	26.12.1995	*Real CD España San Pedro Sula*
Héctor Enrique CASTELLANOS Villatoro	28.12.1992	*FC Motagua Tegucigalpa*
Deybi Aldair FLORES	16.06.1996	*CD Olimpia Tegucigalpa*
Óscar Boniek GARCÍA Ramírez	04.09.1984	*Houston Dynamo (USA)*
Alexander Agustín LÓPEZ Rodríguez	05.06.1992	*Liga Deportiva Alajuelense (CRC)*
Kevin Josué LÓPEZ Maldonado	03.02.1996	*FC Motagua Tegucigalpa*
Walter Joel MARTÍNEZ Betanco	26.03.1991	*FC Motagua Tegucigalpa*
Alfredo Antonio MEJÍA Escobar	03.04.1990	*APO Levadiakos (GRE)*
Carlos Enrique PINEDA López	23.09.1997	*CD Olimpia Tegucigalpa*
Rigoberto Manuel RIVAS Vindel	31.07.1998	*Reggina 1914 (ITA)*
Edwin Alexander RODRÍGUEZ Castillo	25.09.1999	*CD Olimpia Tegucigalpa*
Edwin Solany SOLANO Martínez	25.01.1996	*CD Marathón San Pedro Sula*
Brayan Josué VELÁSQUEZ Moya	19.10.1992	*CD Primeiro de Agosto Luanda (ANG)*

Forwards		
Jerry Ricardo BENGTSON Bodden	08.04.1987	*CD Olimpia Tegucigalpa*
Jorge Renan BENGUCHÉ Ramírez	21.05.1996	*Boavista FC Porto (POR)*
Román Rubilio CASTILLO Álvarez	26.11.1991	*FC Motagua Tegucigalpa*
Alberth Josué ELIS Martínez	16.02.1996	*Boavista FC Porto (POR)*
Anthony Rubén LOZANO Colón	25.04.1993	*Cádiz CF (ESP)*
Douglas Francisco MARTÍNEZ Juárez	05.06.1997	*Real Salt Lake (USA)*
Juan Ramón MEJÍA Erazo	01.08.1988	*CD Lobos UPNFM Tegucigalpa*
Jonathan Josué Rubio TORO	21.10.1996	*GD Chaves (POR)*
Darixon Eniel VUELTO Pérez	15.01.1998	*Real CD España San Pedro Sula*

National coaches		
Fabián COITO Machado (Uruguay) [from 14.02.2019]		17.03.1967

JAMAICA

The Country:	The FA:
Jamaica	Jamaica Football Federation
Capital: Kingston	20 St. Lucia Crescent, Kingston 5
Surface: 11,100 km²	Year of Formation: 1910
Population: 2,726,667 [2018]	Member of FIFA since: 1962
Time: UTC-5	Member of CONCACAF since: 1965
Independent since: 1962	

NATIONAL TEAM RECORDS

First international match: 22.03.1925, Port-au-Prince: Haiti - Jamaica 1-2
Most international caps: Ian Goodison – 128 caps (1996-2009)
Most international goals: Luton Shelton – 35 goals / 75 caps (2004-2013)

CONCACAF GOLD CUP		FIFA WORLD CUP	
1991	Final Tournament (Group Stage)	1930	-
1993	Final Tournament (3rd Place)	1934	-
1996	Qualifiers	1938	-
1998	Final Tournament (4th Place)	1950	-
2000	Final Tournament (Group Stage)	1954	-
2002	Qualifiers	1958	-
2003	Final Tournament (Quarter-Finals)	1962	-
2005	Final Tournament (Quarter-Finals)	1966	Qualifiers
2007	Qualifiers	1970	Qualifiers
2009	Final Tournament (Group Stage)	1974	*Withdrew*
2011	Final Tournament (Quarter-Finals)	1978	Qualifiers
2013	Qualifiers	1982	Did not enter
2015	Final Tournament (Runners-up)	1986	*Withdrew*
2017	Final Tournament (Runners-up)	1990	Qualifiers
2019	Final Tournament (Semi-Finals)	1994	Qualifiers
2021	Final Tournament (*to be played*)	1998	Final Tournament (Group Stage)
		2002	Qualifiers
		2006	Qualifiers
		2010	Qualifiers
		2014	Qualifiers
		2018	Qualifiers

F.I.F.A. CONFEDERATIONS CUP 1992-2017

None

OLYMPIC FOOTBALL TOURNAMENTS 1908-2016

1908	-	1948	-	1972	Qualifiers	1996	Qualifiers
1912	-	1952	-	1976	Qualifiers	2000	Qualifiers
1920	-	1956	-	1980	Qualifiers	2004	Qualifiers
1924	-	1960	-	1984	Qualifiers	2008	Qualifiers
1928	-	1964	-	1988	Qualifiers	2012	Qualifiers
1936	-	1968	-	1992	Qualifiers	2016	Qualifiers

CCCF (Confederación Centroamericana y del Caribe de Fútbol) CHAMPIONSHIPS 1941-1961
None

CONCACAF CHAMPIONSHIPS 1963-1989
1963, 1967, 1969, 1971

COPA AMÉRICA (invited as guests)
2016

CONCACAF NATIONS LEAGUE

2019-2020	League B (*promoted to League A*)

CARIBBEAN CHAMPIONSHIPS 1989-2017

1989	Qualifiers	1999	Final Tournament - Semi-Finals
1991	**Final Tournament - Winners**	2001	Final Tournament - Group Stage
1992	Final Tournament - Runners-up	2005	**Final Tournament - Winners**
1993	Final Tournament - Runners-up	2007	Qualifiers
1994	Qualifiers	2008	**Final Tournament - Winners**
1995	Final Tournament - Group Stage	2010	**Final Tournament - Winners**
1996	Final Tournament - Group Stage	2012	Final Tournament - Group Stage
1997	Final Tournament - 3rd Place	2014	**Final Tournament - Winners**
1998	**Final Tournament - Winners**	2017	Final Tournament - Runners-up

JAMAICAN CLUB HONOURS IN CONCACAF CLUB COMPETITIONS:

CONCACAF Champions Cup / CONCACAF Champions League 1962-2020
None

CONCACAF League 2017-2020
None

Caribbean Club Championship 1997-2021

Harbour View FC Kingston	2	2004, 2007
Portmore United FC	1	2005

CONCACAF Cup Winners Cup 1991-1995*
None

Copa Interamericana 1968-1998*
None

*defunct competitions

NATIONAL COMPETITIONS
TABLE OF HONOURS

	CHAMPIONS	CUP WINNERS[1]
1973/1974	Santos FC Kingston	-
1974/1975	Santos FC Kingston	-
1975/1976	Santos FC Kingston	-

1976/1977	Santos FC Kingston	-
1977/1978	Arnett Gardens FC Kingston	-
1978/1979	*Championship abandoned*	-
1979/1980	Santos FC Kingston	-
1980/1981	Cavalier FC Kingston	-
1981/1982	*No competition*	-
1982/1983	Tivoli Gardens FC Kingston	-
1983/1984	Boys' Town FC Kingston	-
1984/1985	Jamaica Defence Force Kingston	-
1985/1986	Boys' Town FC Kingston	-
1986/1987	Seba United FC Montego Bay	-
1987/1988	Wadadah FC Montego Bay	-
1988/1989	Boys' Town FC Kingston	-
1989/1990	Reno FC Savannah del Mar	-
1990/1991	Reno FC Savannah del Mar	Olympic Gardens
1991/1992	Wadadah FC Montego Bay	Seba United FC Montego Bay
1992/1993	Hazard United FC May Pen	Olympic Gardens
1993/1994	Violet Kickers FC Montego Bay	Harbour View FC Kingston
1994/1995	Reno FC Savannah del Mar	Reno FC Savannah del Mar
1995/1996	Violet Kickers FC Montego Bay	Reno FC Savannah del Mar
1996/1997	Seba United FC Montego Bay	Naggo's Head FC Portmore
1997/1998	Waterhouse FC Kingston	Harbour View FC Kingston
1998/1999	Tivoli Gardens FC Kingston	Tivoli Gardens FC Kingston
1999/2000	Harbour View FC Kingston	Hazard United FC May Pen
2000/2001	Arnett Gardens FC Kingston	Harbour View FC Kingston
2001/2002	Arnett Gardens FC Kingston	Harbour View FC Kingston
2002/2003	Hazard United FC May Pen	Hazard United FC May Pen
2003/2004	Tivoli Gardens FC Kingston	Waterhouse FC Kingston
2004/2005	Portmore United FC	Portmore United FC
2005/2006	Waterhouse FC Kingston	Tivoli Gardens FC Kingston
2006/2007	Harbour View FC Kingston	Portmore United FC
2007/2008	Portmore United FC	Waterhouse FC Kingston
2008/2009	Tivoli Gardens FC Kingston	Boys' Town FC Kingston
2009/2010	Harbour View FC Kingston	Boys' Town FC Kingston
2010/2011	Tivoli Gardens FC Kingston	Tivoli Gardens FC Kingston
2011/2012	Portmore United FC	*No competition*
2012/2013	Harbour View FC Kingston	Waterhouse FC Kingston
2013/2014	Montego Bay United FC	Reno FC Savannah del Mar
2014/2015	Arnett Gardens FC Kingston	*No competition*
2015/2016	Montego Bay United FC	*No competition*
2016/2017	Arnett Gardens FC Kingston	*No competition*
2017/2018	Portmore United FC	*No competition*
2018/2019	Portmore United FC	*No competition*
2019/2020	*Competition cancelled*	*No competition*
2020/2021	*No competition*	*No competition*

[1] The FA Cup competition was called JNBS Federation Cup (1990/91-2003/04), Red Stripe Champions Cup (2004/05-2006/07), City of Kingston Champions Cup (2007/08), Flow Champions Cup (2008/09-2012/13) and JFF Champions Cup (since 2013/14).

NATIONAL CHAMPIONSHIP
Red Stripe Premier League 2020/2021

No competition was played due to COVID-19 pandemic.

NATIONAL TEAM
INTERNATIONAL MATCHES 2020/2021

14.11.2020	Riyadh	Saudi Arabia - Jamaica	3-0(1-0)	(F)
17.11.2020	Riyadh	Saudi Arabia - Jamaica	1-2(1-1)	(F)
25.03.2021	Wiener Neustadt	United States - Jamaica	4-1(1-0)	(F)
07.06.2021	Miki	Jamaica - Serbia	1-1(0-1)	(F)

14.11.2020, Friendly International
"Prince Faisal bin Fahd" Stadium, Riyadh; Attendance: 0
Referee: Ahmed Eisa Mohamed Darwish (United Arab Emirates)
SAUDI ARABIA - JAMAICA   **3-0(1-0)**
JAM: Dwayne St. Aubyn Miller, Kemar Michael Lawrence, Gregory Alex Leigh, Damion Onandi Lowe, Daniel Anthony Johnson (70.Michael Anthony James Hector), Kevon Lambert, Lamar Walker (62.Tyreek Anthony Magee), Jahshaun Mustaf Anglin (46.Ravel Ryan Morrison), Kemal Orlando Malcolm (78.Chavany Shaunjay Willis), Kaheem Anthony Parris (46.Bobby Armani Decordova-Reid), Norman Odale Campbell (46.Leon Patrick Bailey Butler). Trainer: Theodore Whitmore.

17.11.2020, Friendly International
"Prince Faisal bin Fahd" Stadium, Riyadh; Attendance: 0
Referee: Yahya Mohammed Ali Hassan Al Mulla (United Arab Emirates)
SAUDI ARABIA - JAMAICA   **1-2(1-1)**
JAM: Dwayne St. Aubyn Miller (46.Amal Monte Knight), Oniel David Fisher, Michael Anthony James Hector, Gregory Alex Leigh, Damion Onandi Lowe, Ravel Ryan Morrison (90.Jahshaun Mustaf Anglin), Daniel Anthony Johnson, Bobby Armani Decordova-Reid (68.Tyreek Anthony Magee), Javon Romario East, Leon Patrick Bailey Butler (82.Kevon Lambert), Norman Odale Campbell (62.Kemar Michael Lawrence). Trainer: Theodore Whitmore.
Goals: Daniel Anthony Johnson (34), Javon Romario East (64).

25.03.2021, Friendly International
Wiener Neustadt Stadion, Wiener Neustadt (Austria); Attendance: 0
Referee: Christian-Petru Ciochirca (Austria)
UNITED STATES - JAMAICA   **4-1(1-0)**
JAM: Jeadine Shemar White, Adrian Joseph Mariappa, Liam Simon Moore, Michael Anthony James Hector, Amari'i Kyren Bell, Ethan Rupert Pinnock (64.Curtis Anthony Tilt), Ricardo Wayne Morris (55.Chavany Shaunjay Willis), Kasey Remel Palmer (86.Renaldo Wellington), Kevaughn Isaacs (55.Omar Duke Holness), Andre Anthony Gray (86.Jabari Akil Yero Hylton), Jamal Akua Lowe (72.John Luca Levee). Trainer: Theodore Whitmore.
Goal: Damion Onandi Lowe (70).

07.06.2021, Friendly International
Miki Athletic Stadium, Miki (Japan); Attendance: 0
Referee: Yudai Yamamoto (Japan)
JAMAICA - SERBIA   **1-1(0-1)**
JAM: Dennis Taylor, Adrian Joseph Mariappa, Liam Simon Moore, Oniel David Fisher, Damion Onandi Lowe (72.Ravel Ryan Morrison), Amari'i Kyren Bell, Wesley Nathan Hylton Harding, Devon Chesterton Williams (86.Kevon Lambert), Blair Sebastian Turgott (67.Kemal Orlando Malcolm), Andre Anthony Gray (79.Curtis Anthony Tilt), Javon Romario East. Trainer: Theodore Whitmore.
Goal: Andre Anthony Gray (29).

NATIONAL TEAM PLAYERS 2020/2021

Name	DOB	Club
Goalkeepers		
Amal Monte KNIGHT	19.11.1993	*FC Tucson (USA)*
Dwayne St. Aubyn MILLER	14.07.1987	*Syrianska FC Södertälje (SWE)*
Dennis TAYLOR	05.05.1990	*Humble Lions FC York*
Jeadine Shemar WHITE	07.07.2000	*Cavalier Soccer Club Kingston*
Defenders		
Amari'i Kyren BELL	05.05.1994	*Blackburn Rovers FC (ENG)*
Oniel David FISHER	22.11.1991	*Washington DC United (USA); 15.02.2021-> Los Angeles Galaxy (USA)*
Michael Anthony James HECTOR	19.07.1972	*Fulham FC London (ENG)*
Kemar Michael LAWRENCE	17.09.1992	*RSC Anderlecht Bruxelles (BEL)*
Gregory Alex LEIGH	30.09.1994	*Aberdeen FC (SCO)*
Damion Onandi LOWE	03.02.1983	*El-Ittihad El-Iskandary Alexandria (EGY)*
Adrian Joseph MARIAPPA	03.10.1986	*Bristol City FC (ENG)*
Liam Simon MOORE	31.01.1993	*Reading FC (ENG)*
Ethan Rupert PINNOCK	29.05.1993	*Brentford FC (ENG)*
Renaldo WELLINGTON	03.03.1999	*Montego Bay United*
Midfielders		
Jahshaun Mustaf ANGLIN	06.05.2001	*Harbour View FC Kingston*
Wesley Nathan Hylton HARDING	20.10.1996	*Rotherham United FC (ENG)*
Omar Duke HOLNESS	13.03.1994	*Darlington FC (ENG)*
Kevaughn ISAACS	12.01.1996	*Mount Pleasant Football Academy Saint Ann*
Daniel Anthony JOHNSON	08.10.1992	*Preston North End FC (ENG)*
Kevon LAMBERT	22.03.1997	*Phoenix Rising FC (USA)*
John Luca LEVEE	21.02.1997	*Harbour View FC Kingston*
Tyreek Anthony MAGEE	27.10.1999	*KAS Eupen (BEL)*
Ricardo Wayne MORRIS	11.02.1992	*Portmore United FC*
Ravel Ryan MORRISON	02.02.1993	*ADO Den Haag (NED); 09.01.2021-> Unattached*
Kasey Remel PALMER	09.11.1996	*Bristol City FC (ENG)*
Kaheem Anthony PARRIS	06.01.2000	*NK Krka (SVN)*
Curtis Anthony TILT	04.08.1991	*Wigan Athletic FC (ENG)*

Blair Sebastian TURGOTT	22.05.1994	*Östersunds FK (SWE)*
Lamar WALKER	05.12.1999	*Portmore United FC*
Devon Chesterton WILLIAMS	08.04.1992	*Miami FC (USA)*

Forwards

Leon Patrick BAILEY Butler	09.08.1997	*TSV Bayer 04 Leverkusen (GER)*
Norman Odale CAMPBELL	24.11.1999	*FK Grafičar Beograd (SRB)*
Bobby Armani DECORDOVA-REID	02.02.1993	*Fulham FC London (ENG)*
Javon Romario EAST	22.03.1995	*AD San Carlos Ciudad Quesada (CRC); 31.12.2020-> Santos de Guápiles FC (CRC)*
Andre Anthony GRAY	26.06.1991	*Watford FC (ENG)*
Jabari Akil Yero HYLTON	15.11.1998	*University of West Indies FC Kingston*
Jamal Akua LOWE	21.07.1994	*Swansea City AFC (WAL)*
Kemal Orlando MALCOLM	19.11.1989	*Arnett Gardens FC Kingston; 24.02.2021-> AD Chalatenango (SLV)*
Chavany Shaunjay WILLIS	17.09.1997	*Portmore United FC*

National coaches

| Theodore WHITMORE [from 01.01.2017] | | 05.08.1972 |

MARTINIQUE

The Country:	The FA:
Martinique	Ligue de Football de Martinique
Capital: Fort-de-France	2 Rue Saint John Perse, Morne Tartenson
Surface: 1,128 km²	B.P. 307, 97203 Fort de France
Population: 375,053 [2021]	Year of Formation: 1953
Time: UTC-4	Member of FIFA since: *not affiliated*
Independent since: *overseas region of France*	Member of CONCACAF since: 1983

NATIONAL TEAM RECORDS

First international match: 11.02.1931, Fort-de-France: Martinique - Barbados 2-3
Most international caps: Daniel Julien Hérelle – 77 caps (since 2006)
Most international goals: Kévin Marius Parsemain – 35 goals / 55 caps (since 2008)

CONCACAF GOLD CUP		FIFA WORLD CUP	
1991	Qualifiers	1930	-
1993	Final Tournament (Group Stage)	1934	-
1996	Qualifiers	1938	-
1998	Qualifiers	1950	-
2000	Qualifiers	1954	-
2002	Final Tournament (Quarter-Finals)	1958	-
2003	Final Tournament (Group Stage)	1962	-
2005	Qualifiers	1966	-
2007	Qualifiers	1970	-
2009	Qualifiers	1974	-
2011	Qualifiers	1978	-
2013	Final Tournament (Group Stage)	1982	-
2015	Qualifiers	1986	-
2017	Final Tournament (Group Stage)	1990	-
2019	Final Tournament (Group Stage)	1994	-
2021	Final Tournament (*to be played*)	1998	-
		2002	-
		2006	-
		2010	-
		2014	-
		2018	-

F.I.F.A. CONFEDERATIONS CUP 1992-2017
None

OLYMPIC FOOTBALL TOURNAMENTS 1900-2016	
None	

CCCF (Confederación Centroamericana y del Caribe de Fútbol) CHAMPIONSHIPS 1941-1961	
None	

CONCACAF CHAMPIONSHIPS 1963-1989	
None	

CONCACAF NATIONS LEAGUE	
2019-2020	League A

CARIBBEAN CHAMPIONSHIPS 1989-2017			
1989	Qualifiers	1999	Qualifiers
1991	Final Tournament - Group Stage	2001	Final Tournament - 3rd Place
1992	Final Tournament - 3rd Place	2005	Qualifiers
1993	**Final Tournament - Winners**	2007	Final Tournament - Group Stage
1994	Final Tournament - Runners-up	2008	Qualifiers
1995	Qualifiers	2010	Final Tournament - Group Stage
1996	Final Tournament - 3rd Place	2012	Final Tournament - 4th Place
1997	Final Tournament - Group Stage	2014	Final Tournament - Group Stage
1998	Final Tournament - Group Stage	2017	Final Tournament - 4th Place

MARTINIQUE CLUB HONOURS IN CONCACAF CLUB COMPETITIONS:

CONCACAF Champions Cup / CONCACAF Champions League 1962-2020
None

CONCACAF League 2017-2020
None

Caribbean Club Championship 1997-2021
None

CONCACAF Cup Winners Cup 1991-1995*
None

Copa Interamericana 1968-1998*
None

*defunct competitions

NATIONAL COMPETITIONS TABLE OF HONOURS		
	CHAMPIONS	**CUP WINNERS**
1919	Intrépide Fort-de-France	-
1920	Club Colonial de Fort-de-France	-
1921	Club Colonial de Fort-de-France	-
1922	Club Colonial de Fort-de-France	-
1923	Club Colonial de Fort-de-France	-
1924	Club Colonial de Fort-de-France	-
1925	Intrépide Fort-de-France	-
1926	Club Colonial de Fort-de-France	-
1927	Golden Star de Fort-de-France	-
1928	Golden Star de Fort-de-France	-
1929	Golden Star de Fort-de-France	-

1930	Club Colonial de Fort-de-France	-
1931	Club Colonial de Fort-de-France	-
1932	Stade Spiritain Saint-Esprit	-
1933	Intrépide Fort-de-France	-
1934	*Championship annulled*	-
1935	Club Colonial de Fort-de-France	-
1936	Golden Star de Fort-de-France	-
1937	Golden Star de Fort-de-France	-
1938	Club Colonial de Fort-de-France	-
1939	Golden Star de Fort-de-France	-
1940	Club Colonial de Fort-de-France	-
1941	Club Colonial de Fort-de-France	-
1942	Club Colonial de Fort-de-France	-
1943	Club Colonial de Fort-de-France	-
1944	Gauloise Trinité	-
1945	Good Luck de Fort-de-France	-
1946	Aigle Sportif de Fort-de-France	-
1947	Aigle Sportif de Fort-de-France	-
1948	Golden Star de Fort-de-France	-
1949	Club Colonial de Fort-de-France	-
1950	Gauloise Trinité	-
1951	Gauloise Trinité	-
1952	Golden Star de Fort-de-France	-
1953	Golden Star de Fort-de-France	Golden Star de Fort-de-France
1954	Golden Star de Fort-de-France	Club Franciscain Le François
1955	Gauloise Trinité	Club Colonial de Fort-de-France
1956	Golden Star de Fort-de-France	Good Luck de Fort-de-France
1957	Good Luck de Fort-de-France	Golden Star de Fort-de-France
1958	Golden Star de Fort-de-France	Golden Star de Fort-de-France
1959	Golden Star de Fort-de-France	Club Colonial de Fort-de-France
1960	Stade Spiritain Saint-Esprit	US Le Robert
1961	Stade Spiritain Saint-Esprit	US Le Robert
1962	Golden Star de Fort-de-France	Club Colonial de Fort-de-France
1963	Assaut de Saint-Pierre	Golden Star de Fort-de-France
1964	Club Colonial de Fort-de-France	Assaut de Saint-Pierre
1965	Club Colonial de Fort-de-France	Assaut de Saint-Pierre
1966	Assaut de Saint-Pierre	Assaut de Saint-Pierre
1967	Assaut de Saint-Pierre	Assaut de Saint-Pierre
1968	Assaut de Saint-Pierre	Assaut de Saint-Pierre
1969	-	Club Franciscain Le François
1969/1970	Eclair Rivière Salée	Golden Star de Fort-de-France
1970/1971	Club Franciscain Le François	*Competition annulled*
1971/1972	CS Vauclinois Le Vauclin	*Competition annulled*
1972/1973	Club Colonial de Fort-de-France	Good Luck de Fort-de-France
1973/1974	Assaut de Saint-Pierre	Good Luck de Fort-de-France
1974/1975	CS Vauclinois Le Vauclin	*Not known*
1975/1976	AS Samaritaine Sainte-Marie	*Not known*
1976/1977	Golden Star de Fort-de-France	CS Case-Pilote
1977/1978	Renaissance Sainte Anne	Racing Club Rivière-Pilote
1978/1979	Renaissance Sainte Anne	Good Luck de Fort-de-France
1979/1980	Renaissance Sainte Anne	Club Colonial de Fort-de-France
1980/1981	Gauloise Trinité	Racing Club Rivière-Pilote

1981/1982	AS Samaritaine Sainte-Marie	*Not known*
1982/1983	Racing Club Rivière-Pilote	*Not known*
1983/1984	L'Aiglon du Lamentin	*Not known*
1984/1985	Olympique de Marin	*Not known*
1985/1986	Golden Star de Fort-de-France	Club Franciscain Le François
1986/1987	Excelsior de Schoelcher	Club Franciscain Le François
1987/1988	Excelsior de Schoelcher	*Not known*
1988/1989	Excelsior de Schoelcher	*Not known*
1989/1990	US Marinoise	Club Franciscain Le François
1990/1991	L'Aiglon du Lamentin	*Not known*
1991/1992	L'Aiglon du Lamentin	*Not known*
1992/1993	US Le Robert	*Not known*
1993/1994	Club Franciscain Le François	*Not known*
1994/1995	US Marinoise	L'Aiglon du Lamentin
1995/1996	Club Franciscain Le François	L'Aiglon du Lamentin
1996/1997	Club Franciscain Le François	Rapid Club Le Lorrain
1997/1998	L'Aiglon du Lamentin	Club Franciscain Le François
1998/1999	Club Franciscain Le François	Club Franciscain Le François
1999/2000	Club Franciscain Le François	Assaut de Saint-Pierre
2000/2001	Club Franciscain Le François	Club Franciscain Le François
2001/2002	Club Franciscain Le François	Club Franciscain Le François
2002/2003	Club Franciscain Le François	Club Franciscain Le François
2003/2004	Club Franciscain Le François	Club Franciscain Le François
2004/2005	Club Franciscain Le François	Club Franciscain Le François
2005/2006	Club Franciscain Le François	CS Case-Pilote
2006/2007	Club Franciscain Le François	Club Franciscain Le François
2007/2008	Racing Club Rivière-Pilote	Club Franciscain Le François
2008/2009	Club Franciscain Le François	L'Aiglon du Lamentin
2009/2010	Racing Club Rivière-Pilote	CS Case-Pilote
2010/2011	Club Colonial de Fort-de-France	Racing Club Rivière-Pilote
2011/2012	Racing Club Rivière-Pilote	Club Franciscain Le François
2012/2013	Club Franciscain Le François	Racing Club Rivière-Pilote
2013/2014	Club Franciscain Le François	Club Colonial de Fort-de-France
2014/2015	Golden Lion FC de Saint-Joseph	Club Franciscain Le François
2015/2016	Golden Lion FC de Saint-Joseph	Golden Lion FC de Saint-Joseph
2016/2017	Club Franciscain Le François	AS Samaritaine Sainte-Marie
2017/2018	Club Franciscain Le François	Club Franciscain Le François
2018/2019	Club Franciscain Le François	Golden Lion FC de Saint-Joseph
2019/2020	AS Samaritaine Sainte-Marie	*Competition abandoned*
2020/2021	*Competition apparently abandoned*	*No competition*

NATIONAL CHAMPIONSHIP
Championnat National - Division d'Honneur / Trophée "Gérard Janvion" 2020/2021

Note: in the Martinique Championship, there are 4 points for a win, 2 points for a draw and 1 point for a loss!

Regular Stage

Groupe A

1. Golden Lion FC de Saint-Joseph	14	13	0	1	42	-	11	53
2. AS Samaritaine Sainte-Marie	14	9	3	2	28	-	8	44
3. Racing Club Saint-Joseph	14	5	6	3	19	-	18	35
4. Assaut FC Saint-Pierre	14	6	1	7	18	-	22	33
5. US Le Robert	14	5	2	7	17	-	26	31
6. Club Olympique Trénelle Fort-de-France	14	3	3	8	22	-	22	26
7. Union des Jeunes Monnérot Robert	14	2	5	7	18	-	39	25
8. Golden Star de Fort-de-France	14	1	4	9	16	-	34	21

Groupe B

1. Club Franciscain Le François	14	12	0	2	42	-	10	50
2. Club Colonial de Fort-de-France	14	11	1	2	33	-	13	48
3. L'Essor-Préchotain Le Prêcheur	14	9	1	4	25	-	22	42
4. L'Aiglon du Lamentin	14	8	2	4	26	-	12	40
5. Rapid Club du Lorrain	14	3	3	8	16	-	28	26
6. Racing Club Rivière-Pilote	14	2	4	8	7	-	21	23
7. New Star Ducos	14	2	2	10	13	-	33	22
8. L'Olympique du Marin	14	1	3	10	7	-	30	20

Top-3 of each group were qualified for the Championship Round, while teams ranked 4-8 were qualified for the Relegation Round.

The championship was interrupted due to COVID-19 pandemic and was not continued until the end of June 2021.

NATIONAL CUP
Coupe de Martinique Final 2020/2021

Competition abandoned due to Covid-19 pandemic.

THE CLUBS

L'AIGLON DU LAMENTIN
Year of Formation: 1905
Stadium: Stade „Georges Gratiant", Lamentin (8,500)

ASSAUT FOOTBALL CLUB SAINT-PIERRE
Stadium: Stade "Paul Pierre-Charles", Saint-Pierre (3,000)

ASSOCIATION SPORTIVE SAMARITAINE SAINTE-MARIE
Year of Formation: 1920
Stadium: Stade Xercès-Louis à l'Union, Sainte-Marie (400)

CLUB COLONIAL DE FORT-DE-FRANCE
Year of Formation: 1906
Stadium: Stade d'Honneur de Dillon, Fort-de-France (16,300)

CLUB FRANCISCAIN LE FRANÇOIS
Year of Formation: 1936
Stadium: Stade Municipal François, Le François (5,000)

CLUB OLYMPIQUE TRÉNELLE FORT-DE-FRANCE
Stadium: Stade Municipal "Pierre-Aliker", Fort-de-France (18,000)

L'ESSOR-PRÉCHOTAIN LE PRÊCHEUR
Stadium: Stade „Albert Joyau", Le Prêcheur (2,000)

GOLDEN LION FOOTBALL CLUB DE SAINT-JOSEPH
Stadium: Stade "Henri Murano", Saint-Joseph (2,000)

GOLDEN STAR DE FORT-DE-FRANCE
Year of Formation: 1905
Stadium: Stade Municipal "Pierre-Aliker", Fort-de-France (18,000)

NEW STAR DE DUCOS FOOTBALL CLUB
Stadium: Stade Municipal "Max Soron", Ducos (1,000)

L'OLYMPIQUE DU MARIN
Stadium: Stade „Roger Bonaro", Le marin (2,500)

RACING CLUB RIVIÈRE-PILOTE
Year of Formation: 1961
Stadium: Stade En Camée, Rivière-Pilote (3,000)

RACING CLUB SAINT JOSEPH
Stadium: Stade "Henri Murano", Saint-Joseph (2,000)

RAPID CLUB DU LORRAIN
Stadium: Stade "Joseph Pernock", Le Lorrain (1,500)

UNION DES JEUNES MONNÉROT ROBERT
Stadium: Stade "Georges Spitz", Le Robert (2,000)

UNION SPORTIVE LE ROBERT
Year of Formation: 1903
Stadium: Stade "Georges Spitz", Le Robert (2,000)

NATIONAL TEAM
INTERNATIONAL MATCHES 2020/2021

23.06.2021   Fort-de-France   Martinique - Guadeloupe   1-2(0-2)   (F)

23.06.2021, Friendly International
Stade Municipal "Pierre-Aliker", Fort-de-France; Attendance: 0
Referee: Nicolas Wassouf (Martinique)
MARTINIQUE - GUADELOUPE   **1-2(0-2)**
MTQ: Arnaud Emile Benoit Huygues des Etages (46.Gilles Meslien), Jean-Claude Junior Michalet, Sébastien Antoine Crétinoir, Karl Vitulin, Yordan Louis Olivier Thimon (59.Christof Érick Marie Jougon), Romario Barthéléry (83.Florian Goma), Yann Grégory Thimon (82.Norman Igor Grelet), Daniel Hérelle, Stéphane Ludovic Abaul, Grégory Pastel (88.Emmanuel Rivière), Johnny Daniel Marajo (82.Enrick Reuperné). Trainer: Mario Bocaly.
Goal: Johnny Marajo (73).

NATIONAL TEAM PLAYERS 2020/2021

Goalkeepers

Name	DOB	Club
Arnaud Emile Benoit HUYGUES DES ETAGES	30.12.1985	*L'Aiglon du Lamentin*
Gilles MESLIEN	17.06.1989	*Golden Lion FC de Saint-Joseph*

Defenders

Name	DOB	Club
Romano Roland BARTHÉLÉRY	24.06.1994	*Golden Lion FC de Saint-Joseph*
Sébastien Antoine CRÉTINOIR	12.02.1986	*Golden Lion FC de Saint-Joseph*
Florian GOMA	21.01.2001	*AS Samaritaine Sainte-Marie*
Jean-Claude Junior MICHALET	08.04.2000	*Golden Lion FC de Saint-Joseph*
Yordan Louis Olivier THIMON	19.09.1996	*Club Franciscain Le François*
Karl VITULIN	15.01.1991	*AS Samaritaine Sainte-Marie*

Midfielders

Name	DOB	Club
Stéphane Ludovic ABAUL	23.11.1991	*Club Franciscain Le François*
Norman Igor GRELET	14.07.1993	*Golden Lion FC de Saint-Joseph*
Daniel HERELLE	17.10.1988	*Golden Lion FC de Saint-Joseph*
Christof Érick Marie JOUGON	10.07.1995	*Club Franciscain Le François*
Johnny Daniel MARAJO	21.10.1993	*Club Franciscain Le François*
Yann Grégory THIMON	01.01.1990	*Club Franciscain Le François*

Forwards

Name	DOB	Club
Grégory PASTEL	18.09.1990	*Racing Club Rivière-Pilote*
Enrick REUPERNE	03.08.1998	*L'Aiglon du Lamentin*
Emmanuel RIVIÈRE	03.03.1990	*FC Crotone (ITA)*

National coaches

Name		DOB
Mario BOCALY [from 07.12.2017]		28.07.1978

MEXICO

The Country:	The FA:
Estados Unidos Mexicanos (United Mexican States) Capital: Ciudad de México Surface: 1,972,550 km² Population: 126,014,024 [2020] Time: UTC-8 to -6 Independent since: 1810	Federación Mexicana de Fútbol Asociación Avenida Arboleda 101, Ex Hacienda Santín, San Mateo Otzacatipan, C.P. 50210 Toluca Year of Formation: 1927 Member of FIFA since: 1929 Member of CONCACAF since: 1961

NATIONAL TEAM RECORDS

First international match: 01.01.1923, Ciudad de Guatemala: Guatemala - Mexico 2-3
Most international caps: Luis Claudio Suárez Sánchez – 177 caps (1992-2006)
Most international goals: Javier Hernández Balcázar – 52 goals / 109 caps (since 2009)

CONCACAF GOLD CUP		FIFA WORLD CUP	
1991	Final Tournament (3rd Place)	1930	Final Tournament (Group Stage)
1993	**Final Tournament (Winners)**	1934	Qualifiers
1996	**Final Tournament (Winners)**	1938	*Withdrew*
1998	**Final Tournament (Winners)**	1950	Final Tournament (Group Stage)
2000	Final Tournament (Quarter-Finals)	1954	Final Tournament (Group Stage)
2002	Final Tournament (Quarter-Finals)	1958	Final Tournament (Group Stage)
2003	**Final Tournament (Winners)**	1962	Final Tournament (Group Stage)
2005	Final Tournament (Quarter-Finals)	1966	Final Tournament (Group Stage)
2007	Final Tournament (Runners-up)	1970	Final Tournament (Quarter-Finals)
2009	**Final Tournament (Winners)**	1974	Qualifiers
2011	**Final Tournament (Winners)**	1978	Final Tournament (Group Stage)
2013	Final Tournament (Semi-Finals)	1982	Qualifiers
2015	**Final Tournament (Winners)**	1986	Final Tournament (Quarter-Finals)
2017	Final Tournament (Semi-Finals)	1990	Banned by FIFA
2019	**Final Tournament (Winners)**	1994	Final Tournament (2nd Round of 16)
2021	Final Tournament (*to be played*)	1998	Final Tournament (2nd Round of 16)
		2002	Final Tournament (2nd Round of 16)
		2006	Final Tournament (2nd Round of 16)
		2010	Final Tournament (2nd Round of 16)
		2014	Final Tournament (2nd Round of 16)
		2018	Final Tournament (2nd Round of 16)

F.I.F.A. CONFEDERATIONS CUP 1992-2017

1995 (3rd Place), 1997 (Group Stage), **1999 (Winners)**, 2001 (Group Stage), 2005 (Semi-Finals), 2013 (Group Stage), 2017 (4th Place)

OLYMPIC FOOTBALL TOURNAMENTS 1908-2016						
1908	-	1948	FT-1/8 Finals	1972	FT/2nd Round	1996	Quarter-Finals
1912	-	1952	*Withdrew*	1976	FT/Group Stage	2000	Qualifiers
1920	-	1956	*Withdrew*	1980	Qualifiers	2004	FT/Group Stage
1924	-	1960	Qualifiers	1984	Qualifiers	2008	Qualifiers
1928	FT-1/8 Finals	1964	FT/Group Stage	1988	Qualifiers	2012	**Winners**
1936	-	1968	FT/4th Place	1992	FT/Group Stage	2016	FT/Group Stage

CCCF (Confederación Centroamericana y del Caribe de Fútbol) CHAMPIONSHIPS 1941-1961
None
CONCACAF CHAMPIONSHIPS 1963-1989
1963, **1965 (Winners)**, 1967 (Runners-up), 1969, **1971 (Winners)**, 1973 (3rd Place), **1977 (Winners)**, 1981 (3rd Place)
NAFC (North American Football Confederation) CHAMPIONSHIPS 1947-1991
1947 & 1949 (Winners), 1990 (Runners-up), **1991 (Winners)**
COPA AMÉRICA
1993 (Runners-up), 1995, 1997 & 1999 (3rd Place), 2001 (Runners-up), 2004, 2007 (3rd Place), 2011, 2015, 2016

CONCACAF NATIONS LEAGUE	
2019-2020	League A

MEXICAN CLUB HONOURS IN CONCACAF CLUB COMPETITIONS:

CONCACAF Champions Cup / CONCACAF Champions League 1962-2020		
Club de Fútbol América Ciudad de México	7	1977, 1987, 1990, 1992, 2006, 2014/2015, 2015/2016
Cruz Azul FC Ciudad de México	6	1969, 1970, 1971, 1996, 1997, 2013/2014
Club de Fútbol Pachuca	5	2002, 2007, 2008, 2009/2010, 2016/2017
Club de Fútbol Monterrey	4	2010/2011, 2011/2012, 2012/2013, 2019
Club Universidad Nacional (UNAM) Ciudad de México	3	1980, 1982, 1989
Deportivo Toluca Fútbol Club	2	1968, 2003
Atlante Fútbol Club Cancún	2	1983, 2008/2009
Club Deportivo Guadalajara S.A.	2	1962, 2018
Puebla Futbol Club	1	1991
Club Deportivo Cachorros de la Universidad de Guadalajara	1	1978
Atlético Español Fútbol Club Ciudad de México	1	1975
Necaxa Club de Fútbol	1	1999
CF Tigres de la Universidad Autónoma de Nuevo León	1	2020
CONCACAF League 2017-2020		
None		
Caribbean Club Championship 1997-2021		
None		
CONCACAF Cup Winners Cup 1991-1995*		
Club de Futbol Monterrey	1	1993
Necaxa Club de Fútbol	1	1994
Club de Futbol Estudiantes Tecos UAG	1	1995

Copa Interamericana 1968-1998*		
Club de Fútbol América Ciudad de México	2	1977, 1990
Club Universidad Nacional (UNAM) Ciudad de México	1	1980

*defunct competitions

NATIONAL COMPETITIONS
TABLE OF HONOURS

CHAMPIONS
THE AMATEUR ERA

1902/1903	Orizaba AC
1903/1904	Mexico Cricket Club
1904/1905	Pachuca AC[1]
1905/1906	Reforma AC Ciudad de México
1906/1907	Reforma AC Ciudad de México
1907/1908	British FC Ciudad de México
1908/1909	Reforma AC Ciudad de México
1919/1910	Reforma AC Ciudad de México
1910/1911	Reforma AC Ciudad de México
1911/1912	Reforma AC Ciudad de México
1912/1913	México FC Ciudad de México
1913/1914	Real España Club Ciudad de México
1914/1915	Real España Club Ciudad de México
1915/1916	Real España Club Ciudad de México
1916/1917	Real España Club Ciudad de México
1917/1918	Pachuca AC
1918/1919	Real España Club Ciudad de México
1919/1920	Real España Club Ciudad de México (Liga Nacional) Pachuca AC (Liga Mexicana)
1920/1921	Real España Club Ciudad de México (Liga Nacional) Germania FV Ciudad de México (Liga Mexicana)
1921/1922	Real España Club Ciudad de México
1922/1923	Asturias FC Ciudad de México
1923/1924	Real España Club Ciudad de México
1924/1925	CF América Ciudad de México
1925/1926	CF América Ciudad de México
1926/1927	CF América Ciudad de México
1927/1928	CF América Ciudad de México
1928/1929	CD Marte Ciudad de México
1929/1930	Real España Club Ciudad de México
1930/1931	*No competition*
1931/1932	Atlante FC Ciudad de México[2]
1932/1933	Necaxa CF Aguascalientes
1933/1934	Real España Club Ciudad de México
1934/1935	Necaxa CF Aguascalientes
1935/1936	Real España Club Ciudad de México
1936/1937	Necaxa CF Aguascalientes
1937/1938	Necaxa CF Aguascalientes
1938/1939	Asturias FC Ciudad de México
1939/1940	Real España Club Ciudad de México
1940/1941	Atlante FC Ciudad de México

1941/1942	Real España Club Ciudad de México
1942/1943	CD Marte Ciudad de México
THE PROFESSIONAL ERA	
1943/1944	Asturias FC Ciudad de México
1944/1945	Real España Club Ciudad de México
1945/1946	Tiburones Rojos de Veracruz
1946/1947	Atlante FC Ciudad de México
1947/1948	CSD León
1948/1949	CSD León
1949/1950	Tiburones Rojos de Veracruz
1950/1951	CSD Atlas Guadalajara
1951/1952	CSD León
1952/1953	Tampico Madero FC
1953/1954	CD Marte Ciudad de México
1954/1955	CD Zacatepec
1955/1956	CSD León
1956/1957	CD Guadalajara
1957/1958	CD Zacatepec
1958/1959	CD Guadalajara
1959/1960	CD Guadalajara
1960/1961	CD Guadalajara
1961/1962	CD Guadalajara
1962/1963	CD Oro Guadalajara
1963/1964	CD Guadalajara
1964/1965	CD Guadalajara
1965/1966	CF América Ciudad de México
1966/1967	Deportivo Toluca FC
1967/1968	Deportivo Toluca FC
1968/1969	CDSC Cruz Azul Ciudad de México
1969/1970	CD Guadalajara
México'70	CDSC Cruz Azul Ciudad de México
1970/1971	CF América Ciudad de México
1971/1972	CDSC Cruz Azul Ciudad de México
1972/1973	CDSC Cruz Azul Ciudad de México
1973/1974	CDSC Cruz Azul Ciudad de México
1974/1975	Deportivo Toluca FC
1975/1976	CF América Ciudad de México
1976/1977	Club Universidad Nacional Ciudad de México[3]
1977/1978	CF Tigres de la Universidad Autónoma de Nuevo León
1978/1979	CDSC Cruz Azul Ciudad de México
1979/1980	CDSC Cruz Azul Ciudad de México
1980/1981	Club Universidad Nacional Ciudad de México
1981/1982	CF Tigres de la Universidad Autónoma de Nuevo León
1982/1983	Puebla FC
1983/1984	CF América Ciudad de México
1984/1985	CF América Ciudad de México
Prode 85	CF América Ciudad de México
México'86	CF Monterrey
1986/1987	CD Guadalajara
1987/1988	CF América Ciudad de México
1988/1989	CF América Ciudad de México
1989/1990	Puebla FC

Temporada		Campeón
1990/1991		Club Universidad Nacional Ciudad de México
1991/1992		CSD León
1992/1993		Atlante FC Ciudad de México
1993/1994		CD Estudiantes Tecos de la UAG
1994/1995		Necaxa CF Aguascalientes
1995/1996		Necaxa CF Aguascalientes
1996/1997	Inv:	FC Santos Laguna Torreón
	Ver:	CD Guadalajara
1997/1998	Inv:	CDSC Cruz Azul Ciudad de México
	Ver:	Deportivo Toluca FC
1998/1999	Inv:	Necaxa CF Aguascalientes
	Ver:	Deportivo Toluca FC
1999/2000	Inv:	CF Pachuca
	Ver:	Deportivo Toluca FC
2000/2001	Inv:	Club Atlético Monarcas Morelia
	Ver:	FC Santos Laguna Torreón
2001/2002	Inv:	CF Pachuca
	Ver:	CF América Ciudad de México
2002/2003	Ape:	Deportivo Toluca FC
	Cla:	CF Monterrey
2003/2004	Ape:	CF Pachuca
	Cla:	Club Universidad Nacional Ciudad de México
2004/2005	Ape:	Club Universidad Nacional Ciudad de México
	Cla:	CF América Ciudad de México
2005/2006	Ape:	Deportivo Toluca FC
	Cla:	CF Pachuca
2006/2007	Ape:	CD Guadalajara
	Cla:	CF Pachuca
2007/2008	Ape:	Atlante FC Cancún
	Cla:	FC Santos Laguna Torreón
2008/2009	Ape:	Deportivo Toluca FC
	Cla:	CF Pachuca
2009/2010	Ape:	CF Monterrey
	Cla:	Deportivo Toluca FC
2010/2011	Ape:	CF Monterrey
	Cla:	Club Universidad Nacional Ciudad de México
2011/2012	Ape:	CF Tigres de la Universidad Autónoma de Nuevo León
	Cla:	Club Santos Laguna Torreón
2012/2013	Ape:	Club Tijuana Xoloitzcuintles de Caliente
	Cla:	CF América Ciudad de México
2013/2014	Ape:	Club León
	Cla:	Club León
2014/2015	Ape:	CF América Ciudad de México
	Cla:	Club Santos Laguna Torreón
2015/2016	Ape:	CF Tigres de la Universidad Autónoma de Nuevo León
	Cla:	CF Pachuca
2016/2017	Ape:	CF Tigres de la Universidad Autónoma de Nuevo León
	Cla:	CD Guadalajara
2017/2018	Ape:	CF Tigres de la Universidad Autónoma de Nuevo León
	Cla:	Club Santos Laguna Torreón
2018/2019	Ape:	CF América Ciudad de México
	Cla:	CF Tigres de la Universidad Autónoma de Nuevo León

2019/2020	Ape:	CF Monterrey
	Cla:	*Competition cancelled*
2020/2021	Ape:	Club León
	Cla:	Cruz Azul FC Ciudad de México

Inv= Invierno (Winter); Ver= Verano (Summer)
[1] became later Pachuca CF
[2] the club was relocated at the start of the 2007/2008 season to Cancún.
[3] knwon as Pumas de la UNAM

LIST OF CUP WINNERS

Copa Tower
1907/08: Pachuca AC; 1908/09: Reforma AC Ciudad de México; 1909/10: Reforma AC Ciudad de México; 1910/11: British FC Ciudad de México; 1911/12: Pachuca AC; 1912/13: *No competition*;1913/14: México FC Ciudad de México; 1914/15: Real España Club Ciudad de México; 1915/16: Rovers FC México; 1916/17: Real España Club Ciudad de México; 1917/18: Real España Club Ciudad de México; 1918/19: Real España Club Ciudad de México.
Copa Eliminatoria
1919/20: *No competition*; 1920/21: México FC Ciudad de México; 1921/22: Asturias FC Ciudad de México; 1922/23: Asturias FC Ciudad de México; 1923/24: Asturias FC Ciudad de México; 1924/25: Necaxa CF Aguascalientes; 1925/26: Necaxa CF Aguascalientes; 1926 to 1932: *No competition*.
Copa México
1932/33: Necaxa CF Aguascalientes; 1933/34: Asturias FC Ciudad de México; 1934/35: *No competition*; 1935/36: Necaxa CF Aguascalientes; 1936/37: Asturias FC Ciudad de México; 1937/38: CF América Ciudad de México; 1938/39: Asturias FC Ciudad de México; 1939/40: Asturias FC Ciudad de México; 1940/41: Asturias FC Ciudad de México; 1941/42: Atlante FC Ciudad de México; 1942/43: UD Moctezuma de Orizaba; 1943/44: Real España Club Ciudad de México; 1944/45: Puebla FC; 1945/46: CSD Atlas Guadalajara; 1946/47: UD Moctezuma de Orizaba; 1947/48: Tiburones Rojos de Veracruz; 1948/49: CSD León; 1949/50: CSD Atlas Guadalajara; 1950/51: Atlante FC Ciudad de México; 1951/52: Atlante FC Ciudad de México; 1952/53: Puebla FC; 1953/54: CF América Ciudad de México; 1954/55: CF América Ciudad de México; 1955/56: Deportivo Toluca FC; 1956/57: CD Zacatepec; 1957/58: CSD León; 1958/59: CD Zacatepec; 1959/60: Necaxa CF Aguascalientes; 1960/61: Tampico Madero FC; 1961/62: CSD Atlas Guadalajara; 1962/63: CD Guadalajara; 1963/64: CF América Ciudad de México; 1964/65: CF América Ciudad de México; 1965/66: Necaxa CF Aguascalientes; 1966/67: CSD León; 1967/68: CSD Atlas Guadalajara; 1968/69: CDSC Cruz Azul Ciudad de México; 1969/70: CD Guadalajara; 1970/71: CSD León; 1971/72: CSD León; 1972/73: *No competition*; 1973/74: CF América Ciudad de México; 1974/75: Club Universidad Nacional Ciudad de México; 1975/76: CF Tigres de la Universidad Autónoma de Nuevo León; 1976 to 1987: *No competition*; 1987/88: Puebla FC; 1988/89: Deportivo Toluca FC; 1989/90: Puebla FC; 1990/91: CD Universidad de Guadalajara; 1991/92: CF Monterrey; 1992 to 1994: *No competition*; 1994/95: Necaxa CF Aguascalientes; 1995/96: CF Tigres de la Universidad Autónoma de Nuevo León; 1996/97: CDSC Cruz Azul Ciudad de México;

Copa MX

2012	Apertura	CSD Dorados de Sinaloa
2013	Clausura	CDSC Cruz Azul Ciudad de México
2013	Apertura	Club Atlético Monarcas Morelia
2014	Clausura	CF Tigres de la Universidad Autónoma de Nuevo León
2014	Apertura	Club Santos Laguna Torreón
2015	Clausura	Puebla FC
2015	Apertura	CD Guadalajara
2016	Clausura	CD Tiburones Rojos de Veracruz
2016	Apertura	Querétaro FC

2017	Clausura	CD Guadalajara
2017	Apertura	CF Monterrey
2018	Clausura	ID Necaxa Aguascalientes
2018	Apertura	Cruz Azul FC Ciudad de México
2019	Clausura	CF América Ciudad de México
2019/2020	CF Monterrey	
2020/2021	*Competition postponed due to Covid-19 pandemic*	

NATIONAL CHAMPIONSHIP
Primera División de México - Liga BBVA MX 2020/2021

Torneo Guard1anes Apertura 2020

Results

Round 1 [24-28.07.2020]
ID Necaxa - Tigres UANL 0-3(0-2)
CD Guadalajara - Club León 0-0
Club Tijuana - Atlas Guadalajara 3-1(1-1)
Cruz Azul - Santos Laguna 2-0(1-0)
Club UNAM - Querétaro FC 3-2(1-0)
Atlético de San Luis - FC Juárez 1-1(1-0)
CF Pachuca - CF América 1-2(0-0)
Mazatlán FC - Club Puebla 1-4(1-1)
CF Monterrey - Deportivo Toluca 3-1(2-0)

Round 2 [31.07.-03.08.2020]
Club Puebla - Cruz Azul 1-1(0-0)
FC Juárez - ID Necaxa 1-0(0-0)
Tigres UANL - CF Pachuca 1-1(0-0)
CF América - Club Tijuana 4-0(1-0)
Deportivo Toluca - Atlético San Luis 3-2(2-1)
Querétaro FC - Mazatlán FC 1-1(0-0)
Santos Laguna - CD Guadalajara 2-0(1-0)
Atlas Guadalajara - Club UNAM 1-2(0-1)
Club León - CF Monterrey 1-0(0-0)

Round 3 [06-09.08.2020]
CF Pachuca - Querétaro FC 1-0(1-0)
Club Tijuana - Tigres UANL 0-0
ID Necaxa - CF América 1-1(0-1)
Mazatlán FC - Deportivo Toluca 2-1(2-1)
Cruz Azul - Club León 2-0(1-0)
CF Monterrey - Santos Laguna 2-2(1-1)
CD Guadalajara - Club Puebla 0-1(0-0)
Club UNAM - FC Juárez 1-1(0-0)
Atlético San Luis - Atlas Guadalajara 1-1(1-1)

Round 4 [11-13.08.2020]
ID Necaxa - Mazatlán FC 1-0(1-0)
CF Pachuca - Club León 0-1(0-0)
Tigres UANL - Club Puebla 2-1(2-0)
Querétaro FC - Cruz Azul 1-0(1-0)
FC Juárez - CD Guadalajara 0-2(0-0)
Club UNAM - CF Monterrey 1-1(1-0)
Club Tijuana - Atlético de San Luis 0-2(0-1)
Atlas Guadalajara - Deportivo Toluca 1-2(1-1)
CF América - Santos Laguna 3-1(3-0)

Round 5 [14-17.08.2020]
Club Puebla - CF Pachuca 0-1(0-0)
CD Guadalajara - Atlético de San Luis 2-2(0-0)
Cruz Azul - FC Juárez 3-2(1-1)
Mazatlán FC - Club UNAM 0-0
CF Monterrey - ID Necaxa 1-1(0-0)
Deportivo Toluca - Tigres UANL 3-2(1-1)
Santos Laguna - Atlas Guadalajara 0-0
Querétaro FC - CF América 4-1(1-0)
Club León - Club Tijuana 2-1(0-1)

Round 6 [21-24.08.2020]
ID Necaxa - Santos Laguna 2-1(0-1)
FC Juárez - Club León 0-0
Atlas Guadalajara - Querétaro FC 1-0(1-0)
Tigres UANL - Club UNAM 1-1(0-0)
CF América - CF Monterrey 1-3(0-2)
Deportivo Toluca - CD Guadalajara 1-0(0-0)
Atlético de San Luis - Cruz Azul 1-3(1-2)
Club Tijuana - Club Puebla 1-0(1-0)
CF Pachuca - Mazatlán FC 4-3(2-1)

Round 7 [28-31.08.2020]
Club Puebla - Deportivo Toluca 4-1(2-1)
Mazatlán FC - Tigres UANL 1-1(0-0)
Atlético de San Luis - CF América 1-2(1-1)
CD Guadalajara - CF Pachuca 0-0
Cruz Azul - ID Necaxa 3-0(1-0)
Club UNAM - Club Tijuana 3-0(1-0)
Santos Laguna - Querétaro FC 2-1(1-1)
CF Monterrey - FC Juárez 2-1(0-1)
Club León - Atlas Guadalajara 2-1(2-1)

Round 8 [02-05.09.2020]
CF América - Mazatlán FC 3-1(0-0)
Querétaro FC - Deportivo Toluca 4-1(2-0)
CF Pachuca - Atlético de San Luis 3-1(2-0)
ID Necaxa - Club León 0-2(0-1)
Club Tijuana - CF Monterrey 2-1(1-1)
FC Juárez - Santos Laguna 1-1(0-0)
Club UNAM - Club Puebla 4-1(2-1)
Atlas Guadalajara - Cruz Azul 1-0(0-0)
Tigres UANL - CD Guadalajara 1-3(0-1)

Round 9 [08-09.09.2020]
Atlético de San Luis - ID Necaxa 2-1(0-1)
Deportivo Toluca - FC Juárez 0-1(0-0)
CF Monterrey - Atlas Guadalajara 1-1(0-0)
CD Guadalajara - Querétaro FC 1-1(1-0)
Club Puebla - CF América 2-3(2-0)
Club León - Tigres UANL 1-1(1-0)
Cruz Azul - CF Pachuca 1-0(0-0)
Mazatlán FC - Club Tijuana 1-0(1-0)
Santos Laguna - Club UNAM 1-2(0-1)

Round 10 [11-14.09.2020]
ID Necaxa - CD Guadalajara 1-2(0-0)
FC Juárez - Club Puebla 1-0(1-0)
Atlas Guadalajara - Mazatlán FC 1-1(0-0)
Tigres UANL - Santos Laguna 2-0(1-0)
CF América - Deportivo Toluca 1-1(1-1)
Club UNAM - Atlético de San Luis 3-0(1-0)
Querétaro FC - Club León 2-3(0-1)
Club Tijuana - Cruz Azul 1-2(1-0)
CF Pachuca - CF Monterrey 1-1(0-1)

Round 11 [18-21.09.2020]
ID Necaxa - Club Puebla 0-1(0-1)
Mazatlán FC - Cruz Azul 2-3(1-1)
Atlas Guadalajara - CF Pachuca 0-1(0-0)
Tigres UANL - Querétaro FC 3-0(0-0)
CF América - CD Guadalajara 1-0(1-0)
Deportivo Toluca - Santos Laguna 1-2(0-1)
Atlético de San Luis - CF Monterrey 1-2(1-2)
Club León - Club UNAM 2-0(1-0)
Club Tijuana - FC Juárez 2-1(1-1) [30.09.]

Round 12 [24-27.09.2020]
CF Pachuca - Deportivo Toluca 0-0
Club Puebla - Querétaro FC 3-3(1-2)
FC Juárez - Atlas Guadalajara 0-1(0-1)
CD Guadalajara - Mazatlán FC 2-1(2-1)
Club UNAM - ID Necaxa 1-1(0-1)
CF Monterrey - Tigres UANL 0-2(0-1)
Atlético de San Luis - Club León 0-2(0-1)
Cruz Azul - CF América 0-0
Santos Laguna - Club Tijuana 2-0(2-0) [11.10.]

Round 13 [02-04.10.2020]
Club Puebla - Santos Laguna 0-2(0-2)
Club León - Mazatlán FC 2-1(0-0)
Atlas Guadalajara - ID Necaxa 0-1(0-0)
Tigres UANL - Atlético de San Luis 3-0(0-0)
CF América - Club UNAM 2-2(1-1)
Deportivo Toluca - Cruz Azul 2-0(1-0)
FC Juárez - CF Pachuca 1-1(0-1)
Querétaro FC - CF Monterrey 1-2(0-0)
Club Tijuana - CD Guadalajara 0-0

Round 14 [15-19.10.2020]
Atlético de San Luis - Querétaro FC 2-1(1-0)
ID Necaxa - Club Tijuana 2-0(1-0)
Mazatlán FC - FC Juárez 3-2(3-1)
CF Monterrey - Club Puebla 3-1(2-0)
CD Guadalajara - Atlas Guadalajara 3-2(2-0)
Cruz Azul - Tigres UANL 0-2(0-0)
Club UNAM - Deportivo Toluca 1-0(0-0)
Santos Laguna - CF Pachuca 1-1(1-1)
Club León - CF América 3-2(2-2)

Round 15 [23-26.10.2020]
Club Puebla - Club León 1-2(0-0)
Querétaro FC - ID Necaxa 0-1(0-1)
Tigres UANL - FC Juárez 1-1(0-0)
Mazatlán FC - CF Monterrey 1-2(0-2)
CF América - Atlas Guadalajara 1-0(0-0)
Deportivo Toluca - Club Tijuana 2-0(2-0)
CD Guadalajara - Cruz Azul 0-2(0-1)
Santos Laguna - Atlético de San Luis 2-1(1-1)
CF Pachuca - Club UNAM 1-1(1-1)

Round 16 [29.10.-02.11.2020]
Atlético de San Luis - Mazatlán FC 0-5(0-5)
ID Necaxa - Deportivo Toluca 3-2(1-1)
Club Tijuana - CF Pachuca 0-2(0-1)
FC Juárez - Querétaro FC 1-0(0-0)
Atlas Guadalajara - Club Puebla 0-1(0-1)
Club UNAM - CD Guadalajara 2-2(1-2)
CF Monterrey - Cruz Azul 1-0(0-0)
CF América - Tigres UANL 3-1(1-0)
Club León - Santos Laguna 2-1(0-1)

Round 17 [06-08.11.2020]
Club Puebla - Atlético de San Luis 1-0(1-0)
FC Juárez - CF América 1-1(1-0)
CD Guadalajara - CF Monterrey 3-1(0-1)
CF Pachuca - ID Necaxa 0-1(0-0)
Tigres UANL - Atlas Guadalajara 1-1(1-0)

Cruz Azul - Club UNAM 1-2(0-0)
Deportivo Toluca - Club León 2-2(1-1)
Santos Laguna - Mazatlán FC 4-0(0-0)
Querétaro FC - Club Tijuana 2-2(1-0)

Final Standings

1.	Club León	17	12	4	1	27 - 14	40
2.	Club Universidad Nacional Ciudad de México	17	8	8	1	29 - 17	32
3.	CF América Ciudad de México	17	9	5	3	31 - 22	32
4.	Cruz Azul FC Ciudad de México	17	9	2	6	23 - 16	29
5.	CF Monterrey	17	8	5	4	26 - 21	29
6.	CF Tigres de la Universidad Autónoma de Nuevo León	17	7	7	3	27 - 16	28
7.	CD Guadalajara	17	7	5	5	20 - 17	26
8.	Club Santos Laguna Torreón	17	7	4	6	24 - 20	25
9.	CF Pachuca	17	6	7	4	18 - 14	25
10.	ID Necaxa Aguascalientes	17	7	3	7	16 - 20	24
11.	Deportivo Toluca FC	17	6	3	8	23 - 28	21
12.	Club Puebla	17	6	2	9	22 - 25	20
13.	FC Juárez	17	4	7	6	16 - 19	19
14.	Mazatlán FC	17	4	4	9	24 - 31	16
15.	Club Tijuana Xoloitzcuintles de Caliente	17	4	3	10	12 - 27	15
16.	CSD Atlas Guadalajara	17	3	5	9	13 - 20	14
17.	Querétaro FC	17	3	4	10	23 - 28	13
18.	Club Atlético de San Luis	17	3	2	12	16 - 35	11

Top-4 teams were qualified for the 2020 Torneo Guard1anes Apertura Liguilla Quarter-Finals, while teams ranked 5-12 were qualified for the 2020 Torneo Guard1anes Apertura Liguilla Reclassification.

2020 Torneo Guard1anes Apertura Liguilla

Reclassification [21-22.11.2020]
CF Monterrey - Club Puebla 2-2(1-0) 2-4 pen
CF Tigres de la Universidad Autónoma de Nuevo León - Deportivo Toluca FC 2-1(2-0)
CD Guadalajara - ID Necaxa Aguascalientes 1-0(0-0)
Club Santos Laguna Torreón - CF Pachuca 0-3(0-1)

Quarter-Finals [25-29.11.2020]		
Club Puebla - Club León	2-1(2-1)	0-2(0-2)
CF Pachuca - Club Universidad Nacional Ciudad de México	0-1(0-1)	0-0
CD Guadalajara - CF América Ciudad de México	1-0(0-0)	2-1(1-0)
CF Tigres de la Un. Autónoma de Nuevo León - Cruz Azul FC Ciudad de México	1-3(0-1)	1-0(0-0)

Semi-Finals [02-06.12.2020]		
CD Guadalajara - Club León	1-1(0-1)	0-1(0-1)
Cruz Azul FC Cd. de México - Club Universidad Nacional Ciudad de México*	4-0(3-0)	0-4(0-3)

*advanced into the finals having better record in the regular season.

Torneo Guard1anes Apertura Finals

10.12.2020, Estadio Olímpico Universitario, Ciudad de México; Attendance: 0
Referee: Fernando Hernández Gómez
Club Universidad Nacional Ciudad de México - Club León   **1-1(0-0)**
Club UNAM: Julio José González Vela Alvizu, Alan Mozo Rodríguez, Manuel Alejandro Mayorga Almaráz, Johan Felipe Vásquez Ibarra, Nicolás Omar Freire, Andrés Iniestra Vázquez Mellado (Cap), Leonel López González (77.Erik Antonio Lira Méndez), Juan Pablo Vigón Cham, Juan Ignacio Dinenno De Cara, Juan Manuel Iturbe Arévalos (52.Carlos Gutiérrez Estefa), Carlos Gabriel González Espínola (85.Jerónimo Rodríguez Guemes). Trainer: Andrés Luciano Lillini (Argentina).
Club León: Rodolfo Cota Robles, Andrés Felipe Mosquera Guardia, Fernando Navarro Morán (90+2.José de Jesús Godínez Navarro), William José Tesillo Gutiérrez, Jaine Stiven Barreiro Solis, José Iván Rodríguez Rebollar (67.José David Ramírez García), Luis Arturo Montes Jiménez (Cap), Ángel Israel Mena Delgado, Jean David Meneses Villarroel (83.Juan Ignacio González Ibarra), Pedro Jesús Aquino Sánchez, Joel Nathaniel Campbell Samuels (46.Emmanuel Gigliotti). Trainer: Marcos Ignacio Ambriz Espinoza.
Goals: 1-0 Carlos Gabriel González Espínola (71), 1-1 Emmanuel Gigliotti (88).

13.12.2020, Estadio León, León; Attendance: 0
Referee: Jorge Antonio Pérez Durán
Club León - Club Universidad Nacional Ciudad de México   **2-0(1-0)**
Club León: Rodolfo Cota Robles, Andrés Felipe Mosquera Guardia, Fernando Navarro Morán (86.José de Jesús Godínez Navarro), William José Tesillo Gutiérrez, Juan Ignacio González Ibarra (Cap), Luis Arturo Montes Jiménez, Ángel Israel Mena Delgado (14.Joel Nathaniel Campbell Samuels; 79.José Iván Rodríguez Rebollar), Jean David Meneses Villarroel Yairo (79.Yesid Moreno Berrío), Pedro Jesús Aquino Sánchez, José David Ramírez García, Emmanuel Gigliotti (86.Nicolás Sosa Sánchez). Trainer: Marcos Ignacio Ambriz Espinoza.
Club UNAM: Alfredo Talavera Díaz, Alan Mozo Rodríguez, Manuel Alejandro Mayorga Almaráz, Johan Felipe Vásquez Ibarra (58.Favio Enrique Álvarez), Nicolás Omar Freire, Andrés Iniestra Vázquez Mellado (Cap), Carlos Gutiérrez Estefa (38.Juan Manuel Iturbe Arévalos), Leonel López González (69.Erik Antonio Lira Méndez), Juan Pablo Vigón Cham, Juan Ignacio Dinenno De Cara, Carlos Gabriel González Espínola. Trainer: Andrés Luciano Lillini (Argentina).
Goals: 1-0 Emmanuel Gigliotti (11), 2-0 Yairo Yesid Moreno Berrío (82).

2020 Torneo Guard1anes Apertura Champions: **Club León**

Best goalscorer Torneo Guard1anes Apertura 2020 (only regular season):
Jonathan Javier Rodríguez Portillo (URU, Cruz Azul FC Ciudad de México) –12 goals

Torneo Guard1anes Clausura 2021

Results

Round 1 [08-11.01.2021]
Club Puebla - CD Guadalajara 1-1(1-0)
Club Tijuana - Club UNAM 0-0
Mazatlán FC - ID Necaxa 3-2(2-1)
Atlas Guadalajara - CF Monterrey 0-2(0-2)
Tigres UANL - Club León 2-0(1-0)
CF América - Atlético de San Luis 2-1(1-0)
Deportivo Toluca - Querétaro FC 3-1(2-1)
Santos Laguna - Cruz Azul 1-0(0-0)
CF Pachuca - FC Juárez 1-1(0-1)

Round 2 [15-18.01.2021]
ID Necaxa - Atlético de San Luis 1-0(0-0)
FC Juárez - Club Tijuana 0-0
CD Guadalajara - Deportivo Toluca 1-1(1-1)
Cruz Azul - Club Puebla 0-1(0-1)
CF Monterrey - CF América 1-0(1-0)
Club UNAM - Mazatlán FC 3-0(1-0)
Santos Laguna - Tigres UANL 2-0(0-0)
Querétaro FC - Atlas Guadalajara 1-0(0-0)
Club León - CF Pachuca 0-0

Round 3 [21-26.01.2021]
Atlético de San Luis - CD Guadalajara 3-1(2-0)
Club Puebla - Club Tijuana 0-1(0-1)
Mazatlán FC - Santos Laguna 0-0
Atlas Guadalajara - Tigres UANL 0-2(0-1)
Deportivo Toluca - ID Necaxa 2-0(1-0)
Querétaro FC - Club UNAM 2-0(2-0)
CF Pachuca - Cruz Azul 0-1(0-0)
CF América - FC Juárez 2-0(1-0)
CF Monterrey - Club León 1-1(0-1) [10.03.]

Round 4 [28.01.-02.02.2021]
Tigres UANL - ID Necaxa 1-1(1-1)
Mazatlán FC - CF Pachuca 1-0(1-0)
CD Guadalajara - FC Juárez 1-2(0-2)
Cruz Azul - Querétaro FC 4-1(3-1)
Club Tijuana - Deportivo Toluca 3-2(3-1)
Club UNAM - Atlas Guadalajara 0-0
Santos Laguna - CF América 1-1(0-1)
Club León - Atlético de San Luis 3-1(0-0)
Club Puebla - CF Monterrey 0-0

Round 5 [04-08.02.2021]
Atlético de San Luis - Club Tijuana 2-2(1-2)
Querétaro FC - CF Pachuca 3-1(2-0)
ID Necaxa - Cruz Azul 0-2(0-2)
Atlas Guadalajara - Santos Laguna 1-1(0-1)
CF América - Club Puebla 1-0(0-0)
CF Monterrey - Club UNAM 1-0(1-0)
Deportivo Toluca - Mazatlán FC 4-1(3-0)
Club León - CD Guadalajara 1-3(0-2)
FC Juárez - Tigres UANL 2-3(0-0) [14.04.]

Round 6 [12-17.02.2021]
Club Puebla - FC Juárez 4-0(2-0)
Club Tijuana - Club León 2-0(1-0)
Mazatlán FC - Atlético de San Luis 0-3(0-2)
CD Guadalajara - ID Necaxa 2-2(1-1)
CF América - Querétaro FC 2-1(1-1)
Deportivo Toluca - Club UNAM 1-0(0-0)
Santos Laguna - CF Monterrey 1-0(0-0)
CF Pachuca - Atlas Guadalajara 0-1(0-1)
Tigres UANL - Cruz Azul 0-2(0-1)

Round 7 [18-22.02.2021]
Atlético de San Luis - Santos Laguna 1-0(1-0)
ID Necaxa - CF Monterrey 1-1(0-1)
FC Juárez - Mazatlán FC 1-0(0-0)
Cruz Azul - Deportivo Toluca 3-2(2-2)
Atlas Guadalajara - CF América 3-0 Wert.
Club UNAM - Club León 0-1(0-0)
Querétaro FC - Club Puebla 1-1(0-0)
Tigres UANL - Club Tijuana 3-2(2-0)
CF Pachuca - CD Guadalajara 1-1(0-1)

Round 8 [25-28.02.2021]
Atlético de San Luis - Tigres UANL 2-2(1-1)
Club Puebla - ID Necaxa 1-0(0-0)
Mazatlán FC - Querétaro FC 3-0(2-0)
Deportivo Toluca - Atlas Guadalajara 0-0
CF América - CF Pachuca 2-0(2-0)
Club León - Cruz Azul 0-1(0-0)
CF Monterrey - Club Tijuana 1-1(1-0)
Santos Laguna - FC Juárez 3-2(2-0)
CD Guadalajara - Club UNAM 2-1(2-1)

Round 9 [02-04.03.2021]
Atlas Guadalajara - Atlético San Luis 3-1(1-1)
Tigres UANL - Deportivo Toluca 0-1(0-0)
Club León - Club Puebla 1-2(1-0)
FC Juárez - CF Monterrey 1-6(1-2)
Querétaro FC - CD Guadalajara 2-2(1-1)
Cruz Azul - Mazatlán FC 1-0(0-0)
Club Tijuana - CF América 0-2(0-0)
ID Necaxa - CF Pachuca 2-2(1-1)
Club UNAM - Santos Laguna 1-0(0-0)

Round 10 [05-08.03.2021]
Atlético de San Luis - Deportivo Toluca 0-0
Club Puebla - Tigres UANL 1-1(1-1)
Atlas Guadalajara - FC Juárez 2-0(1-0)
CF América - Club León 2-1(1-1)
CF Monterrey - Querétaro FC 2-1(2-1)
Mazatlán FC - CD Guadalajara 1-1(1-1)
Santos Laguna - ID Necaxa 3-1(1-0)
Club UNAM - Cruz Azul 0-1(0-0)
CF Pachuca - Club Tijuana 2-1(2-1)

Round 11 [12-15.03.2021]
Club Puebla - Atlas Guadalajara 0-1(0-0)
FC Juárez - Club UNAM 1-1(1-0)
Tigres UANL - Mazatlán FC 1-2(0-1)
Cruz Azul - CF Monterrey 1-0(1-0)
Club Tijuana - Santos Laguna 0-1(0-1)
Deportivo Toluca - CF Pachuca 0-2(0-0)
Querétaro FC - Atlético de San Luis 2-1(2-0)
CD Guadalajara - CF América 0-3(0-1)
Club León - ID Necaxa 3-1(2-0)

Round 12 [18-21.03.2021]
CF Pachuca - Tigres UANL 1-0(0-0)
ID Necaxa - FC Juárez 1-0(0-0)
Mazatlán FC - CF América 0-1(0-0)
Atlético de San Luis - Club UNAM 0-1(0-0)
Cruz Azul - Atlas Guadalajara 3-2(1-1)
Club Tijuana - Querétaro FC 3-1(3-1)
Deportivo Toluca - Club Puebla 4-4(1-0)
Santos Laguna - Club León 1-2(1-1)
Monterrey - CD Guadalajara 1-2(0-1) [21.04.]

Round 13 [02-04.04.2021]
Club Puebla - Mazatlán FC 3-1(1-1)
FC Juárez - Cruz Azul 0-1(0-0)
Atlas Guadalajara - Club Tijuana 1-0(1-0)
CF América - ID Necaxa 2-1(1-1)
CF Monterrey - Atlético de San Luis 2-0(0-0)
Club UNAM - CF Pachuca 2-2(0-1)
CD Guadalajara - Santos Laguna 1-1(0-1)
Querétaro FC - Tigres UANL 0-1(0-1)
Club León - Deportivo Toluca 2-1(0-1)

Round 14 [09-12.04.2021]
ID Necaxa - Club UNAM 0-1(0-0)
FC Juárez - Atlético de San Luis 2-1(1-0)
Atlas Guadalajara - Club León 1-3(0-1)
Cruz Azul - CD Guadalajara 1-0(0-0)
Tigres UANL - CF América 1-3(0-1)
Deportivo Toluca - CF Monterrey 1-2(0-0)
Querétaro FC - Santos Laguna 0-1(0-0)
Club Tijuana - Mazatlán FC 2-3(2-1)
CF Pachuca - Club Puebla 1-3(0-1)

Round 15 [16-19.04.2021]
ID Necaxa - Querétaro FC 0-0
Mazatlán FC - Atlas Guadalajara 0-0
Atlético de San Luis - Club Puebla 1-4(0-1)
CD Guadalajara - Club Tijuana 2-0(0-0)
CF América - Cruz Azul 1-1(1-0)
Club UNAM - Tigres UANL 0-0
Santos Laguna - Deportivo Toluca 3-1(2-0)
CF Monterrey - CF Pachuca 0-1(0-0)
Club León - FC Juárez 2-0(0-0)

Round 16 [23-26.04.2021]
Club Puebla - Club UNAM 0-0
Club Tijuana - ID Necaxa 1-0(0-0)
Mazatlán FC - Club León 4-3(1-2)
Cruz Azul - Atlético de San Luis 3-2(2-1)
Atlas Guadalajara - CD Guadalajara 0-1(0-0)
Tigres UANL - CF Monterrey 2-1(1-1)
Deportivo Toluca - CF América 3-1(2-0)
Querétaro FC - FC Juárez 1-0(0-0)
CF Pachuca - Santos Laguna 1-0(0-0)

Round 17 [29.04.-02.05.2021]
Atlético de San Luis - CF Pachuca 1-5(1-2)
ID Necaxa - Atlas Guadalajara 1-5(1-2)
FC Juárez - Deportivo Toluca 1-0(0-0)
CD Guadalajara - Tigres UANL 0-0
Club León - Querétaro FC 2-1(1-0)

Cruz Azul - Club Tijuana 1-1(1-0)
CF Monterrey - Mazatlán FC 1-0(1-0)
Santos Laguna - Club Puebla 0-0
Club UNAM - CF América 0-1(0-0)

Final Standings

1.	Cruz Azul FC Ciudad de México	17	13	2	2	26	-	11	41
2.	CF América Ciudad de México	17	12	2	3	26	-	14	38
3.	Club Puebla	17	7	7	3	25	-	14	28
4.	CF Monterrey	17	8	4	5	22	-	13	28
5.	Club Santos Laguna Torreón	17	7	5	5	18	-	13	26
6.	Club León	17	8	2	7	25	-	23	26
7.	CSD Atlas Guadalajara	17	7	4	6	20	-	15	25
8.	CF Pachuca	17	6	5	6	20	-	19	23
9.	CD Guadalajara	17	5	8	4	21	-	21	23
10.	CF Tigres de la Universidad Autónoma de Nuevo León	17	6	5	6	19	-	20	23
11.	Deportivo Toluca FC	17	6	4	7	26	-	24	22
12.	Querétaro FC	17	6	3	8	19	-	25	21
13.	Mazatlán FC	17	6	3	8	19	-	26	21
14.	Club Tijuana Xoloitzcuintles de Caliente	17	5	5	7	19	-	21	20
15.	Club Universidad Nacional Ciudad de México	17	4	6	7	10	-	12	18
16.	FC Juárez	17	4	3	10	13	-	29	15
17.	Club Atlético de San Luis	17	3	3	11	20	-	33	12
18.	ID Necaxa Aguascalientes	17	2	5	10	14	-	29	11

Top-4 teams were qualified for the 2020 Torneo Guard1anes Clausura Liguilla Quarter-Finals, while teams ranked 5-12 were qualified for the 2020 Torneo Guard1anes Clausura Liguilla Reclassification.

2020 Torneo Guard1anes Clausura Liguilla

Reclassification [08-09.05.2021]

Club Santos Laguna Torreón - Querétaro FC	5-0(2-0)	
CSD Atlas Guadalajara - CF Tigres de la Universidad Autónoma de Nuevo León	1-0(0-0)	
Club León - Deportivo Toluca FC	2-2 aet	2-4 pen
CF Pachuca - CD Guadalajara	4-2(0-1)	

Quarter-Finals [12-16.05.2021]

Deportivo Toluca FC - Cruz Azul FC Ciudad de México	2-1(1-1)	1-3(1-1)
CSD Atlas Guadalajara - Club Puebla*	1-0(0-0)	0-1(0-0)
CF Pachuca - CF América Ciudad de México	3-1(1-1)	2-4(1-2)
Club Santos Laguna Torreón - CF Monterrey	2-1(0-1)	1-1(0-1)

*advanced to the semi-finals having better record in the regular season.

Semi-Finals [19-23.05.2021]

CF Pachuca - Cruz Azul FC Ciudad de México	0-0	0-1(0-0)
Club Santos Laguna Torreón - Club Puebla	3-0(2-0)	0-1(0-0)

Torneo Guard1anes Clausura Finals

27.05.2021, Estadio Corona, Torreón; Attendance: 14,577
Referee: Fernando Guerrero Ramírez
Club Santos Laguna Torreón - Cruz Azul FC Ciudad de México   0-1(0-0)
Santos Laguna: Carlos Acevedo López (Cap), Carlos Emilio Orrantía Treviño (82.Jesús Antonio Isijara Rodríguez), Félix Torres Caicedo, Matheus Doria Macedo, Omar Antonio Campos Chagoya, Fernando Gorriarán Fontes (76.Santiago Rene Muñoz Robles), Alan Jhosué Cervantes Martín del Campo, Juan Ferney Otero Tovar, Diego Alfonso Valdés Contreras, Eduar Ayrton Preciado García (76.Andrés Felipe Ibargüen García), Eduardo Daniel Aguirre Lara (87.Ignacio Alejandro Jeraldino Gil). Trainer: Guillermo Jorge Almada Alves (Uruguay).
Cruz Azul: José de Jesús Corona Rodríguez (Cap), Juan Marcelo Escobar Chena, Pablo César Aguilar Benítez, Julio César Domínguez Juárez, Adrián Alexei Aldrete Rodríguez (86.Santiago Tomás Giménez), José Ignacio Rivero Segade (70.Walter Iván Alexis Montoya), Luis Francisco Romo Barrón (76.Elías Hernán Hernández Jacuinde), Rafael Baca Miranda, Victor Yoshimar Yotún Flores (70.Orbelín Pineda Alvarado), Guillermo Matías Fernández (77.José Joaquín Martínez Valadez), Jonathan Javier Rodríguez Portillo. Trainer: Juan Máximo Reynoso Guzmán (Peru).
Goal: 0-1 Luis Francisco Romo Barrón (71).

30.05.2021, Estadio Azteca, Ciudad de México; Attendance: 21,016
Referee: Fernando Hernández Gómez
Cruz Azul FC Ciudad de México - Club Santos Laguna Torreón   1-1(0-1)
Cruz Azul: José de Jesús Corona Rodríguez (Cap), Juan Marcelo Escobar Chena, Pablo César Aguilar Benítez, Julio César Domínguez Juárez, José Ignacio Rivero Segade (82.Walter Iván Alexis Montoya), Luis Francisco Romo Barrón, Rafael Baca Miranda, Guillermo Matías Fernández (61.Adrián Alexei Aldrete Rodríguez), Roberto Carlos Alvarado Hernández (46.Santiago Tomás Giménez), Orbelín Pineda Alvarado (46.Víctor Yoshimar Yotún Flores), Jonathan Javier Rodríguez Portillo (86.José Joaquín Martínez Valadez). Trainer: Juan Máximo Reynoso Guzmán (Peru).
Santos Laguna: Carlos Acevedo López (Cap), Carlos Emilio Orrantía Treviño, Félix Torres Caicedo, Matheus Doria Macedo, Omar Antonio Campos Chagoya, Fernando Gorriarán Fontes (55.Ronaldo de Jesús Prieto Ramírez), Alan Jhosué Cervantes Martín del Campo, Juan Ferney Otero Tovar (77.Jesús Alberto Ocejo Zazueta), Diego Alfonso Valdés Contreras, Eduar Ayrton Preciado García (69.Andrés Felipe Ibargüen García), Eduardo Daniel Aguirre Lara (68.Santiago Rene Muñoz Robles). Trainer: Guillermo Jorge Almada Alves (Uruguay).
Goals: 0-1 Diego Alfonso Valdés Contreras (37), 1-1 Jonathan Javier Rodríguez Portillo (51).

2021 Torneo Guard1anes Clausura Champions: **Cruz Azul FC Ciudad de México**

Best goalscorer Torneo Guard1anes Clausura 2021 (only regular season):
Alexis Pedro Canelo (ARG, Deportivo Toluca FC) – 11 goals

Relegation Table 2020/2021

The team which will be relegated is determined on average points taking into account results of the last six seasons (Apertura & Clausura 2018/2019, Apertura & Clausura 2019/2020 and Apertura & Clausura 2020/2021).

Pos	Team	2018/19 P	2019/20 P	2020/21 P	Total P	M	Aver
1.	CF América Ciudad de México	62	65	70	197	103	1.9126
2.	Cruz Azul FC Ciudad de México	66	58	70	194	103	1.8738
3.	Club León	59	62	66	187	103	1.8155
4.	CF Tigres de la UA de Nuevo León	66	60	51	177	103	1.7184
5.	Club Santos Laguna Torreón	52	66	51	169	103	1.6408
6.	CF Monterrey	60	41	57	158	103	1.5340
7.	Club UNAMl Ciudad de México	47	57	40	154	103	1.4951
8.	CF Pachuca	52	47	48	147	103	1.4272
9.	CD Guadalajara	38	50	49	137	103	1.3301
10.	Club Puebla	44	42	48	134	103	1.3010
11.	Deportivo Toluca FC	51	34	43	128	103	1.2427
12.	Querétaro FC	37	55	34	126	103	1.2233
13.	ID Necaxa Aguascalientes	43	45	35	123	103	1.1942
14.	Mazatlán FC	38	45	37	120	103	1.1650
15.	Club Tijuana Xoloitz. de Caliente	35	40	35	120	103	1.1650
16.	FC Juárez	39	39	34	112	103	1.0874
17.	CSD Atlas Guadalajara	30	34	39	106	103	1.0291
18.	Club Atlético de San Luis	-	41	23	64	69	0.9275

Please note: the promotion and relegation between Liga MX and Liga de Expansión MX was suspended, however, the coefficient table will be used to establish the payment of fines that will be used for the development of the clubs of the silver circuit. Per Article 24 of the competition regulations, the last three positioned teams in the coefficient table have to pay as follows: 120 million in the last place; 70 million the penultimate; and 50 million will be paid by the sixteenth team in the table.

Aggregate Table 2020/2021

1.	Cruz Azul FC Ciudad de México	34	22	4	8	49 - 27	70
2.	CF América Ciudad de México	34	21	7	6	57 - 36	70
3.	Club León	34	20	6	8	52 - 37	66
4.	CF Monterrey	34	16	9	9	48 - 34	57
5.	CF Tigres de la Universidad Autónoma de Nuevo León	34	13	12	9	46 - 36	51
6.	Club Santos Laguna Torreón	34	14	9	11	42 - 33	51
7.	Club Universidad Nacional Ciudad de México	34	12	14	8	39 - 29	50
8.	CD Guadalajara	34	12	13	9	41 - 38	49
9.	Club Puebla	34	13	9	12	47 - 39	48
10.	CF Pachuca	34	12	12	10	38 - 33	48
11.	Deportivo Toluca FC	34	12	7	15	49 - 52	43
12.	CSD Atlas Guadalajara	34	10	9	15	33 - 35	39
13.	Mazatlán FC	34	10	7	17	43 - 57	37
14.	Club Tijuana Xoloitzcuintles de Caliente	34	9	8	17	31 - 48	35
15.	ID Necaxa Aguascalientes	34	9	8	17	30 - 49	35
16.	Deportivo Toluca FC	34	9	7	18	42 - 53	34
17.	FC Juárez	34	8	10	16	29 - 48	34
18.	Club Atlético de San Luis	34	6	5	23	36 - 68	23

THE CLUBS 2020/2021

Please note: matches and goals in both Liguillas (Apertura & Clausura) included.

CLUB DE FÚTBOL AMÉRICA CIUDAD DE MÉXICO

Foundation date: October 12, 1916
Address: Calle del Toro No. 100, Col. Ex Hacienda de Coapa Delegación Coyoacán, México DFCP 14390
Stadium: Estadio Azteca, Ciudad de México (87,000

THE SQUAD

	DOB	M	Ape (s)	G	M	Cla (s)	G
Goalkeepers:							
Oscar Francisco Jiménez Fabela	12.10.1988	3			2		
Francisco Guillermo Ochoa Magaña	13.07.1985	16			17		
Defenders:							
Paul Nicolás Aguilar Rojas	06.03.1986	4	(2)				
Víctor Emanuel Aguilera (ARG)	11.06.1989	11	(1)	4	14	(2)	3
Sebastián Enzo Cáceres Ramos (URU)	18.02.1999	14	(1)		16		
Bryan Colula Alarcón	06.04.1996				1	(1)	
Jesús Alonso Escoboza Lugo	22.01.1993	5	(6)			(4)	
Luis Fernando Fuentes Vargas	14.09.1986	10			19		1
Ramón Juárez del Castillo	09.05.2001	5	(3)		2		
Luis Ricardo Reyes Moreno	03.04.1991	8	(2)				
Jorge Eduardo Sánchez Ramos	10.12.1997	15		1	18		
Jordan Jesús Silva Díaz	30.07.1994				2	(2)	
Bruno Amílcar Valdez (PAR)	06.10.1992	6		1	4		
Midfielders:							
Pedro Jesús Aquino Sánchez (PER)	13.04.1995				13	(2)	3
Nicolás Benedetti Roa (COL)	25.04.1997	5	(4)	1	1	(3)	
Santiago Cáseres (ARG)	25.02.1997	11	(5)				
Francisco Sebastián Córdova Reyes	12.06.1997	18	(1)	5	10	(2)	2
Sergio Ismael Díaz Velázquez (PAR)	05.03.1998	1	(6)				
Álvaro Fidalgo Fernández (ESP)	09.04.1997				11	(1)	
Fernando Rubén González Pineda	27.01.1994	6	(6)				
Mauro Alberto Laínez Leyva	09.05.1996				17	(2)	1
Antonio de Jesús López Amenábar	10.04.1997	3	(5)		3	(5)	
Alan Medina Camacho	19.08.1997					(6)	
Santiago Naveda Lara	16.04.2001				9	(10)	1
Alfonso Emilio Sánchez Castillo	16.06.1994	1	(6)		2	(1)	
Richard Rafael Sánchez Guerrero (PAR)	29.03.1996	18		2	12	(3)	3
Leonardo Gabriel Suárez (ARG)	30.03.1996	6	(5)	1	9	(7)	2
Forwards:							
Giovani Álex dos Santos Ramírez	11.05.1989	7	(4)	1	3	(4)	1
Andrés Felipe Ibargüen García (COL)	07.05.1992	2	(5)				
Henry Josué Martín Mex	18.11.1992	14	(5)	8	11	(4)	8
Roger Beyker Martínez Tobinson (COL)	23.06.1994	6	(5)	1	9	(9)	6
Federico Sebastián Viñas Barboza (URU)	30.06.1998	14	(2)	6	4	(13)	1
Trainer:							
Miguel Ernesto Herrera Aguirre	18.03.1978	19					
[01.01.2021] Santiago Hernán Solari Poggio	07.10.1976				19		

CLUB SOCIAL Y DEPORTIVO ATLAS GUADALAJARA

Foundation date: August 15, 1916
Address: Avenida Patria Colomo No. 2300, Lomos del Bosque 45110, Guadalajara
Stadium: Estadio Jalisco, Guadalajara (56,713

THE SQUAD

	DOB	Ape M	(s)	G	Cla M	(s)	G
Goalkeepers:							
José Santiago Hernández García	01.05.1997	1					
Camilo Andrés Vargas Gil (COL)	09.03.1989	16			20		
Defenders:							
José Javier Abella Fanjul	10.02.1994	13			1	(4)	
Gaddi Axel Aguirre Ledesma	31.03.1996				1		
Jesús Alberto Angulo Uriarte	30.01.1998	15			16		
Diego Armando Barbosa Zaragoza	25.09.1996	3	(1)		19	(1)	
Germán Andrés Conti (ARG)	03.06.1994	14		1			
Armando Escobar Díaz	27.08.1993		(1)				
Martín Hugo Nervo (ARG)	06.01.1991	17			19		
Luis Ricardo Reyes Moreno	03.04.1991				4	(3)	
Anderson Santamaría Bardales (PER)	10.01.1992	1	(1)		18		1
Brayton Josué Vázquez Vélez	05.03.1998	1	(3)		2	(1)	
Midfielders:							
Luciano Federico Acosta (ARG)	31.05.1994	13	(2)	2	4	(4)	
Pablo González Díaz	07.07.1992				2	(7)	
Alex Renato Ibarra Mina (ECU)	20.01.1991	10	(3)	2	15	(1)	2
Víctor Ignacio Malcorra (ARG)	24.07.1987	17		4	17	(3)	1
Ángel Jeremy Márquez Castañeda	21.06.2000	5	(3)		18	(1)	1
Edyairth Alberto Ortega Alatorre	23.01.1997		(8)			(2)	
Alan Neftaly Reyes Martínez	11.06.2001		(3)				
Lorenzo Enrique Reyes Vicencio	13.06.1991	16					
Aldo Paúl Rocha González	06.11.1992				20		3
Edgar Zaldivar Valverde	17.10.1996	7		1		(7)	1
Forwards:							
Milton Joel Caraglio Lugo (ARG)	01.12.1988				18	(2)	1
Marcelo Javier Correa (ARG)	23.10.1992	15	(1)	1	3	(9)	
Julio César Furch (ARG)	29.07.1989					(7)	2
Brayan Eduardo Garnica Cortéz	27.05.1996				1		
Jonathan Ozziel Herrera Morales	23.05.2001	1	(6)		3	(11)	3
Jesús Antonio Isijara Rodríguez	26.09.1989	15	(1)				
Ignacio Alejandro Jeraldino Gil (CHI)	06.12.1995	6	(11)	1			
Jairo Ezequiel Mungaray López	23.01.2001		(2)				
Ían Jairo Misael Torres Ramírez	05.07.2000	1	(7)		18	(1)	4
Christopher Brayan Trejo Morantes	02.12.1999		(6)		1	(9)	
Trainer:							
Rafael Puente Del Río	31.01.1979	3					
[10.08.2020] Rubén Duarte Casillas	01.04.1967	2					
[23.08.2020] Diego Martín Cocca Pera (ARG)	11.02.1972	12			20		

CLUB ATLÉTICO DE SAN LUIS

Foundation date: May 28, 2013
Address: Malaquitas #1030, esq. con Av. Coral, 78399 San Luis Potosí
Stadium: Estadio "Alfonso Lastras", San Luis Potosí (25,709

THE SQUAD

	DOB	Ape M	(s)	G	Cla M	(s)	G
Goalkeepers:							
Carlos Felipe Rodríguez Rangel	03.04.1989	7			2		
Axel Wilfredo Werner (ARG)	28.02.1996	10			15		
Defenders:							
Ventura Alvarado Aispuro (USA)	16.08.1992	12			1		
Enrique López Fernández „Cadete" (ESP)	24.06.1994	9	(2)				
Matías Ezequiel Catalán (ARG)	19.08.1992	11	(3)	1			
Dionicio Manuel Escalante Moreno	12.05.1990	5	(4)		7	(1)	
Uziel Amin García Martínez	09.04.2001	2					
Ramiro Gabriel González Hernández (ARG)	21.11.1990	14		3	17		2
Juan Manuel Izquierdo Viana (URU)	04.07.1997				4		
Luis Fernando León Bermeo (ECU)	11.04.1993	5	(1)				
Rodrigo Javier Noya García (ARG)	31.01.1990	9	(3)		8		
Jesús Fernando Piñuelas Sandoval	27.03.1998				4	(3)	
Luis Gerardo Ramírez Flores	06.03.1996				2	(1)	
Midfielders:							
Federico Gino Acevedo Fagúndez (URU)	26.02.1993				4	(5)	
Juan David Castro Ruíz	21.12.1991	8	(7)		14	(1)	2
Ricardo Chávez Soto	19.11.1994				12	(3)	
Jhon Fredy Duque Arias (COL)	04.06.1992				5	(1)	
Luis Felipe Gallegos Leiva (CHI)	03.12.1991		(2)		8	(3)	2
Felipe De Jesús García Hernández	30.03.1999		(1)				
Ricardo Gibran García Martínez	30.01.2000		(2)				
Javier Güemez López	17.10.1991				17		
Pablo César López Martínez	07.01.1998	7	(4)		1	(2)	
Camilo Sebastián Mayada Mesa (URU)	08.01.1991	15			14		
Renato Mendoza Navarro	15.07.1996		(2)				
David Rodríguez Uribe	05.05.2002				2	(2)	
Jorge Alberto Sánchez López	14.02.1993	12	(3)			(6)	
Forwards:							
Pablo Edson Barrera Acosta	21.06.1987	14	(2)	1	8	(5)	
Damián Iván Batallini (ARG)	24.06.1996				13	(3)	
Germán Berterame (ARG)	13.11.1998	16		5	12	(2)	3
Walter Antonio Castillo Salazar	22.10.1997		(1)			(2)	
Nicolás Alejandro Ibáñez (ARG)	23.08.1994	11	(1)	3	17		10
Anderson Andrés Julio Santos (ECU)	31.05.1996	4	(7)			(1)	
Lucas Giuliano Passerini (ARG)	16.07.1994					(10)	
Diego Iván Pineda Juárez	08.04.1995	3	(9)			(3)	
Mauro Daniel Quiroga (ARG)	07.12.1989	13	(2)	3			
Trainer:							
Guillermo Alejandro Vázquez Herrera	25.05.1967	16					
[31.10.2020] Luis Francisco García Llamas	04.04.1964	1					
[23.11.2020] Leonel Rocco Herrera (URU)	18.09.1966				17		

CRUZ AZUL FÚTBOL CLUB CIUDAD DE MÉXICO

Foundation date: January 5, 1947
Address: Avenida San Pablo No. 100, La Noria 16030, Xochimilco, Ciudad de México
Stadium: Estadio Azteca / Azul, Ciudad de México (87,000 / 35,000

THE SQUAD

	DOB	Ape M	(s)	G	Cla M	(s)	G
Goalkeepers:							
José de Jesús Corona Rodríguez	26.01.1981	20			21		
Sebastián Jurado Roca	28.09.1997	1			2		
Defenders:							
Pablo César Aguilar Benítez (PAR)	02.04.1987	7			15	(5)	1
Adrián Alexei Aldrete Rodríguez	14.06.1988	20			10	(5)	1
Julio César Domínguez Juárez	08.11.1987	18		1	22		
Juan Marcelo Escobar Chena (PAR)	03.07.1995	20		3	20	(1)	2
Jaiber Jiménez Ramírez	07.01.1995				2		
Igor Lichnovsky Osorio (CHI)	07.03.1994	11					
José Joaquín Martínez Valadez	22.02.1987	2	(5)		10	(9)	
Josué Emmanuel Reyes Santacruz	10.12.1997	6	(1)		1	(1)	
Luis Francisco Romo Barrón	05.06.1995	20		3	18	(1)	3
Midfielders:							
Roberto Carlos Alvarado Hernández	07.09.1998	9	(6)	1	16	(5)	3
Brayan Dennys Angulo Tenorio (ECU)	30.11.1995				5	(8)	3
Rafael Baca Miranda	11.09.1989	13	(2)	1	20	(2)	
Jonathan Darwin Borja Colorado (ECU)	05.04.1994		(3)				
Josué Misael Domínguez González	27.10.1999	1	(11)			(4)	
Guillermo Matías Fernández (ARG)	11.10.1991				15	(4)	3
Alexis Hazael Gutiérrez Torres	26.02.2000	1	(7)	1		(2)	
Elías Hernán Hernández Jacuinde	29.04.1988	8	(7)		4	(14)	2
Walter Iván Alexis Montoya (ARG)	21.07.1993				3	(11)	
Orbelín Pineda Alvarado	24.03.1996	19		2	16	(6)	2
José Ignacio Rivero Segade (URU)	10.04.1992	12	(7)		15	(4)	
Víctor Yoshimar Yotún Flores (PER)	07.04.1990	9	(7)	1	11	(12)	
Forwards:							
Milton Joel Caraglio Lugo (ARG)	01.12.1988	3	(6)				
Alex Stik Castro Giraldo (COL)	08.03.1994	1	(1)				
Santiago Tomás Giménez	18.04.2001	10	(8)	4	9	(9)	2
Jonathan Javier Rodríguez Portillo (URU)	06.07.1993	20		13	18	(3)	11
Trainer:							
Robert Dante Siboldi Badiola (URU)	24.09.1965	21					
[14.12.2020] Luis Armando González Bejarano	16.11.1968	-					
[02.01.2021] Juan Máximo Reynoso Guzmán (PER)	28.12.1969				23		

CLUB DEPORTIVO GUADALAJARA S.A.

Foundation date: May 8, 1906
Address: Avenida Aviación No. 3800, Colonia San Juan Ocotán 45019, Zapopan, Guadalajara
Stadium: Estadio Akron, Guadalajara (49,850

THE SQUAD

	DOB	Ape M	(s)	G	Cla M	(s)	G
Goalkeepers:							
Raúl Manolo Gudiño Vega	22.04.1996	13			11		
José Antonio Rodríguez Romero	04.07.1992	9			7		
Defenders:							
Antonio Briseño Vázquez	05.02.1994	4	(7)		9	(4)	
Cristian Yonathan Calderón del Real	24.05.1997	10	(7)	4	2	(7)	
José Antonio Madueña López	29.05.1990		(2)				
Manuel Alejandro Mayorga Almaráz	29.05.1997				8	(2)	2
Hiram Ricardo Mier Alanís	25.08.1989	22			9		
Luis Alejandro Olivas Salcedo	10.02.2000		(1)		5		
Miguel Ángel Ponce Briseño	12.04.1989	15	(4)		11	(2)	2
Jesús Enrique Sánchez García	31.08.1989	22			16	(2)	1
Gilberto Sepúlveda López	04.02.1999	19	(1)		13	(2)	
Midfielders:							
Jesús Ricardo Angulo Uriarte	20.02.1997	13	(8)	4	13	(5)	3
Carlos Uriel Antuna Romero	21.08.1997	17	(3)	4	16	(2)	2
Fernando Beltrán Cruz	08.05.1998	11	(7)		4	(11)	
Isaác Brizuela Muñoz	28.08.1990	21		2	15	(2)	1
Carlos Ernesto Cisneros Barajas	30.08.1993					(2)	
Sergio Adrián Flores Reyes	12.02.1995				1	(9)	
Javier Eduardo López Ramírez	17.09.1994		(9)				
Óscar Uriel Macías Mora	09.07.1998		(1)				
Jesús Antonio Molina Granados	29.03.1988	20		2	17		3
Zahid Yibram Muñoz López	29.01.2001		(1)			(1)	
Alan Eduardo Torres Villanueva	19.02.2000	3	(6)		10	(6)	
José Juan Vázquez Gómez	14.03.1988	5	(5)				
Dieter Daniel Villalpando Pérez	04.08.1991	2	(9)				
Forwards:							
Ronaldo Cisneros Morell	08.01.1997	1	(6)				
César Saúl Huerta Valera	03.12.2000				1	(8)	
José Juan Macías Guzmán	22.09.1999	16	(1)	6	13	(3)	6
Sebastián Martínez Vidrio	06.01.2001	2	(1)				
Oribe Peralta Morones	12.01.1984	2	(8)		1	(2)	
Ernesto Alexis Vega Rojas	25.11.1997	12	(2)	2	15	(3)	2
Adrián Eduardo Villalobos Orozco	12.11.1997		(1)				
Ángel Zaldívar Caviedes	08.02.1994	3	(3)	1	1	(12)	1
Trainer:							
Luis Fernando Tena Garduño	20.01.1958	3					
[09.08.2020; Caretaker] Marcelo Michel Leaño	14.02.1987	1					
[13.08.2020] Víctor Manuel Vucetich Rojas	25.06.1955	18			18		

FÚTBOL CLUB JUÁREZ

Foundation date: May 29, 2015
Address: Calle Henry Dunant 5150 Progresista, 32310 Ciudad Juárez, Chihuahua
Stadium: Estadio Olímpico "Benito Juárez", Ciudad Juárez (19,703

THE SQUAD

	DOB	Ape M	(s)	G	Cla M	(s)	G
Goalkeepers:							
Enrique Eduardo Palos Reyes	31.05.1986	7			10		
Edmundo Iván Vázquez Mellado Pérez	14.12.1982	10			7		
Defenders:							
Alberto Joshimar Acosta Alvarado	26.02.1988	7	(2)		9		
Elio Castro Guadarrama	26.07.1988		(1)		1	(2)	
Luis Donaldo Hernández González	02.02.1998	1	(5)				
Luis Alberto López López	25.08.1993	8			12	(2)	
Hedgardo Marín Arroyo	21.02.1993	3			10		
Alan Omar Mendoza López	28.09.1993	6	(6)		3	(1)	
Maximiliano Martín Olivera de Andrea (URU)	05.03.1992	14		1			
Luis Alberto Pavez Muñoz (CHI)	17.09.1995				8	(4)	1
Pol García Tena (ESP)	18.02.1995				7	(3)	
Bruno Sebastián Romo Rojas (CHI)	20.05.1989	14	(1)				
Víctor Gustavo Velázquez Ramos (PAR)	17.04.1991	17		1	16	(1)	2
Midfielders:							
Blas Esteban Armoa Núñez (PAR)	03.02.2000	4	(4)		1	(3)	
Francisco Contreras Báez	16.05.1999	4	(1)		5	(4)	1
José Joaquín Esquivel Martínez	07.01.1998	4	(2)		13	(2)	
Marco Jhonfai Fabián de la Mora	21.07.1989	9	(1)		11	(3)	
Martín Luis Galván Romo	14.02.1993	1	(5)		1	(1)	1
Ariel Matías García (ARG)	22.10.1991				13	(2)	2
Andrés Iniesta Vázquez Mellado	11.03.1996				5	(6)	
Jefferson Alfredo Intriago Mendoza (ECU)	04.06.1996	13			12		
William Gabriel Mendieta Pintos (PAR)	09.01.1989	1	(6)		3	(5)	1
Francisco Javier Nevarez Pulgarin	03.12.2000	1	(2)		3		
Martín Ernesto Rabuñal Rey (URU)	22.04.1994	8	(1)				
Carlos Iván Rosel Bermont	31.08.1995		(4)		2	(6)	
Flavio Jesús Santos Carrillo	03.01.1987	13	(4)		10	(5)	
Jesús Eduardo Zavala Castañeda	21.07.1987	9	(4)			(3)	
Forwards:							
Eryc Leonel Castillo Arroyo (ECU)	05.02.1995	7	(5)	2	5	(4)	
Ayron Del Valle Rodríguez (COL)	27.01.1989				7	(6)	
Mauro Raúl Fernández (ARG)	31.03.1989	6	(4)				
Dario Lezcano Mendoza (PAR)	30.06.1990	13	(2)	10	13		5
Víctor Omar Mañón Barrón	06.02.1992	2	(2)				
Brian Alejandro Rubio Rodríguez	09.11.1996	5	(5)	2		(4)	
Trainer:							
Gabriel Esteban Caballero Schiker	05.02.1971	17					
[30.11.2020] Luis Fernando Tena Garduño	20.01.1958				10		
[17.03.2021] Luis Alfonso Sosa Cisneros	05.10.1967				7		

CLUB LEÓN FÚTBOL CLUB

Foundation date: August 20, 1944
Address: Boulevard Adolfo López Mateos 1810, Colonia La Martinica, 37500 León de los Aldamas
Stadium: Estadio León „Nou Camp", León de Aldamas - 31,297

THE SQUAD

	DOB	M	Ape (s)	G	M	Cla (s)	G
Goalkeepers:							
Alfonso Blanco Antúnez	31.07.1987	3			4		
Rodolfo Cota Robles	03.07.1987	20			14		
Defenders:							
Jaine Stiven Barreiro Solis (COL)	19.06.1994	22			15	(2)	1
Gil Giovanni Burón Morales	11.06.1994	2			3	(2)	
Juan Ignacio González Ibarra	08.07.1984	1	(6)				
Pedro Hernández García	31.10.2000				3	(2)	
Andrés Felipe Mosquera Guardia (COL)	20.02.1990	8	(3)		11	(4)	
Fernando Navarro Morán	18.04.1989	19	(1)	4	8	(3)	1
Osvaldo Rodríguez del Portal	10.09.1996	5	(7)		11	(4)	1
William José Tesillo Gutiérrez (COL)	02.02.1990	22			14		
Midfielders:							
Fidel Daniel Ambríz González	21.03.2003	1	(1)		1	(1)	1
Pedro Jesús Aquino Sánchez (PER)	13.04.1995	16	(4)				
Santiago Colombatto (ARG)	17.01.1997				9	(1)	1
Fernando Rubén González Pineda	27.01.1994				7	(4)	
Ángel Israel Mena Delgado (ECU)	21.01.1988	20	(1)	9	11	(5)	8
Jean David Meneses Villarroel (CHI)	16.03.1993	18	(3)	5	15	(3)	2
Luis Arturo Montes Jiménez	15.05.1986	23		4	11	(2)	1
Yairo Yesid Moreno Berrío (COL)	04.04.1995	13	(1)	2	8	(4)	
Iván Fernando Ochoa Chávez	13.08.1996		(1)				
José David Ramírez García	14.12.1995	16	(3)		15	(3)	
José Iván Rodríguez Rebollar	17.06.1996	8	(9)		5	(2)	
Jesse Zamudio García	08.03.1999		(3)				
Forwards:							
Joel Nathaniel Campbell Samuels (CRC)	26.06.1992	7	(14)	1	10	(6)	1
Víctor Alejandro Dávila Zavala (CHI)	04.11.1997				13	(3)	7
Emmanuel Gigliotti (ARG)	20.05.1987	19	(2)	7	7	(4)	2
José de Jesús Godínez Navarro	20.01.1997		(4)		2	(7)	
Armando León Reséndez	18.01.2000	1	(4)				
Juan Pablo Israel Rangel Quintana	21.01.2000					(1)	
Nicolás Sosa Sánchez (URU)	06.04.1996	9	(7)		1	(3)	
Trainer:							
Marcos Ignacio Ambriz Espinoza	07.02.1965	23			18		

CLUB DE FÚTBOL MONTERREY

Foundation date: June 28, 1945
Address: Avenida Revolución No. 846-B, Colonia Jardín Español, 64820 Monterrey
Stadium: Estadio BBVA Bancomer, Monterrey (53,500

THE SQUAD

	DOB	M	Ape (s)	G	M	Cla (s)	G
Goalkeepers:							
Luis Alberto Cárdenas López	15.09.1993	3			1		
Hugo Alfonso González Durán	01.08.1990	15			18		
Defenders:							
Jesús Daniel Gallardo Vasconcelos	15.08.1994	12	(2)		18		
Edson Antonio Gutiérrez Moreno	19.01.1996	3			1	(1)	
Miguel Arturo Layún Prado	25.06.1988	8	(9)		10	(5)	
John Stefan Medina Ramírez (COL)	14.06.1992	13		1	10	(1)	
César Jasib Montes Castro	24.02.1997	14			14	(2)	
Adrián Mora Barraza	15.08.1997				1		
Daniel Alexis Parra Durán	20.07.1999	2	(7)	1			
Luis Gustavo Sánchez Saucedo	03.05.2000		(1)		1	(1)	
Nicolás Gabriel Sánchez (ARG)	04.02.1986	18		6	8	(1)	
Sebastián Ignacio Vegas Orellana (CHI)	04.12.1996	13	(3)	1	16		1
Midfielders:							
José Alfonso Alvarado Pérez	15.03.2000		(6)		1	(9)	1
Eric David Cantú Guerrero	28.02.1999	1	(3)		1	(1)	
Arturo Alfonso González González	05.09.1994	4	(8)	1	17	(2)	2
Jonathan Alexander González Mendoza (USA)	13.04.1999		(7)		2	(3)	
Claudio Matías Kranevitter (ARG)	21.05.1993	9	(8)		11	(7)	
Maximiliano Eduardo Meza (ARG)	15.12.1992	10	(7)	2	17	(2)	5
Celso Fabián Ortíz Gamarra (PAR)	26.01.1989	13	(3)		9	(8)	
Carlos Alberto Rodríguez Gómez	03.01.1997	14	(2)	1	15	(4)	
Ángel Eduardo Zapata Praga	03.02.2001	2	(3)				
Forwards:							
Rogelio Gabriel Funes Mori (ARG)	05.03.1991	16	(2)	6	15	(1)	9
Avilés Hurtado Herrera (COL)	20.04.1987	5	(3)	2	5	(9)	
Vincent Petrus Anna Sebastiaan Janssen (NED)	15.06.1994	7	(5)	2	9	(4)	5
Aké Arnaud Loba (CIV)	01.04.1998	7	(1)	4	3	(7)	1
Shayr Mohamed González	04.04.2000	1	(2)				
Dorlan Mauricio Pabón Ríos (COL)	24.01.1988	8	(3)	1	6	(7)	
Trainer:							
Antonio Ricardo Mohamed Matijevich (ARG)	02.04.1970	18					
[07.12.2020] Javier Aguirre Onandía	01.12.1958				19		

MAZATLÁN FÚTBOL CLUB

Foundation date: June 2, 2020
Address: Av. Munich, Fraccionamiento Pradera Dorada, Mazatlán, Sinaloa, C.P. 00000
Stadium: Estadio Mazatlán, Mazatlán (25,000

THE SQUAD

Name	DOB	Ape M	(s)	G	Cla M	(s)	G
Goalkeepers:							
Miguel Ángel Fraga Licona	03.09.1987	11					
Ricardo Daniel Gutiérrez Hernández	17.06.1997	2			3	(1)	
Carlos Sebastián Sosa Silva (URU)	19.08.1986	4					
Nicolas Vikonis Moreau (URU)	06.04.1984				14		
Defenders:							
Nicolás Andrés Díaz Huincales (CHI)	20.05.1999	14		2	12		2
Gonzalo Alejandro Jara Reyes (CHI)	29.08.1985	6	(3)				
Israel Sabdi Jiménez Ñáñez	13.08.1989	6			14	(2)	
José Enrique Ortíz Córtes (COL)	16.11.1998	15	(1)		12	(1)	
Jorge Antonio Padilla Leal	06.09.1993	11	(5)		2	(8)	
Luis Gabriel Rey Mejía	14.09.2002					(1)	
Salvador Rodríguez Morales	06.08.2001				3	(1)	
Carlos Alonso Vargas Tenorio	14.02.1999	3	(4)		13	(1)	1
Efraín Velarde Calvillo	18.04.1986	13	(1)		5	(3)	
Néstor Vicente Vidrio Serrano	22.03.1989				12	(3)	
Midfielders:							
Daniel Guadalupe Amador Osuna	22.03.1997				5	(3)	
Ulises Israel Cardona Carrillo	13.11.1998					(3)	
Giovanni Augusto Oliveira Cardoso (BRA)	05.09.1989				11	(4)	4
Luis Ángel Mendoza Escamilla	03.02.1990	14	(3)	1	11	(5)	
Roberto Ismael Meráz Bernal	04.08.1999	4	(4)		7	(4)	
Rodrigo Javier Millar Carvajal (CHI)	03.11.1981	2	(4)		4	(4)	
Iván Jared Moreno Fuguemann	17.01.1998		(1)			(2)	
Mario Humberto Osuna	20.08.1988	11	(3)	2	6	(5)	
Manuel Pérez Ruiz	18.03.1993		(2)		1	(3)	
Cándido Saúl Ramírez Montes	05.06.1993	2	(8)		5	(3)	
Lorenzo Enrique Reyes Vicencio (CHI)	13.06.1991				8	(1)	
Aldo Paúl Rocha González	06.11.1992	15	(1)	1			
Walter Gael Sandoval Contreras	05.11.1995				8	(6)	
Jorge Luis Valdivia Toro	19.10.1983	1	(2)				
Forwards:							
Sagir David Arce Chávez (USA)	15.02.2002		(1)				
Fernando Luís Aristeguieta de Luca (VEN)	09.04.1992	8	(8)	4	11	(4)	3
César Saúl Huerta Valera	03.12.2000	15	(2)	3			
Miguel Ángel Sansores Sánchez	28.04.1991	9	(6)	3			
Camilo da Silva Sanvezzo (BRA)	21.07.1988	7	(4)	8	15	(1)	5
Ricardo Marín Sánchez	18.03.1998		(1)			(2)	
Michael Jhon Ander Rangel Valencia (COL)	08.03.1991				5	(6)	4
Martín Vladimir Rodríguez Torrejon (CHI)	05.08.1994	14	(3)				
Trainer:							
Juan Francisco Palencia Hernández	28.04.1973	13					
[06.10.2020] Tomás Juan Boy Espinoza	28.06.1951	4			17		

IMPULSORA DEL DEPORTIVO NECAXA S.A.

Foundation date: August 21, 1923
Address: Boulevard Juan Pablo II No. 1301, Colonia La Cantera, 20180 Aguascalientes
Stadium Estadio Victoria, Aguascalientes (25,994

THE SQUAD

	DOB	Ape M	(s)	G	Cla M	(s)	G
Goalkeepers:							
Sebastián Andrés Fassi Álvarez	19.05.1993	3					
Edgar Adolfo Hernández Téllez	27.08.1982				6	(1)	
Luis Ángel Malagón Velázquez	02.03.1997	15			11		
Defenders:							
Jorge Luis Aguilar Miranda (PAR)	04.02.1993				4	(2)	
Ricardo Chávez Soto	19.11.1994	10	(2)				
Mario Humberto de Luna Saucedo	05.01.1988	4	(6)		9	(3)	
Idekel Alberto Domínguez Rodríguez	02.06.2000	15			15		
Jairo Daniel González Fajardo	27.02.1992	1	(1)		8		
Julio César González Trinidad (PAR)	28.06.1992	18			14		
Carlos Alberto Guzmán Fonseca	19.05.1994	1				(1)	
Alán Isidro Montes Castro	26.10.2000		(1)				
Jair Pereira Rodríguez	07.07.1986	4	(2)		5	(1)	
Raúl Martín Sandoval Zavala	18.01.2000	2	(3)		3	(5)	
Unai Bilbao Arteta (ESP)	04.02.1994	18		3	17		
Midfielders:							
Francisco Javier Acuña Víctor	19.01.1988					(1)	
Alejandro Andrade Rivera	16.08.2001		(3)		6	(3)	
Fernando David Arce Juárez (USA)	27.11.1996	9	(4)	1	4	(5)	
Claudio Andrés Baeza Baeza (CHI)	23.12.1993	14	(1)	1			
David Cabrera Pujol	07.09.1989	16	(2)	2	14		
Bryan Andrés Carvallo Utreras (CHI)	15.09.1996					(6)	
Yerko Bastián Leiva Lazo (CHI)	14.06.1998	1	(2)			(5)	
Waldo Emilio Madrid Quezada	25.08.2003					(1)	
Kevin Bryan Mercado Mina (ECU)	28.01.1995				5	(6)	
Alejandro Zendejas Saavedra	07.02.1998	11	(4)	3	17		2
Forwards:							
Rodrigo Sebastián Aguirre Soto (URU)	01.10.1994				3	(3)	
Martín Barragán Negrete	14.07.1991	5	(11)		12	(5)	3
Bryan Aarón Casas Roque	21.10.2004					(2)	
José Antonio Cobián Ruíz	14.09.1998	2	(5)				
Juan Antonio Delgado Baeza (CHI)	05.03.1993	14	(2)		12	(1)	2
Ian González Nieto (ESP)	11.02.1993	11	(4)	3	10	(6)	3
Daniel López Pinedo	12.07.2000				1	(5)	1
Oscar Manuel Millán Garduño	15.07.2001		(2)				
Lucas Giuliano Passerini (ARG)	16.07.1994	14	(2)	3			
Joao Leandro Rodríguez González (COL)	19.05.1996	5	(3)				
Maximiliano Nahuel Salas (ARG)	01.12.1997	5	(11)		11	(5)	2
Trainer:							
Luis Alfonso Sosa Cisneros	05.10.1967	8					
[06.09.2020] José Guadalupe Cruz Núñez	22.11.1967	10			11		
[19.03.2021] Guillermo Alejandro Vázquez Herrera	25.05.1967				6		

CLUB DE FÚTBOL PACHUCA

Foundation date: November 28, 1901
Address: Libramiento Circuito de la Concépción, Colonia La Concepción, 42060 Pachuca de Soto
Stadium Estadio „Miguel Hidalgo", Pachuca (27,512

THE SQUAD

	DOB	Ape M	(s)	G	Cla M	(s)	G
Goalkeepers:							
Carlos Agustín Moreno Luna	29.01.1998				1	(1)	
Franco Luis Torgnascioli Lagreca (URU)	24.08.1990	1					
Óscar Alfredo Ustari (ARG)	03.07.1986	19			21		
Defenders:							
Daniel Alonso Aceves Patiño	28.03.2001		(1)				
Kevin Nahin Álvarez Campos	15.01.1999	14	(3)		18	(3)	1
Gustavo Daniel Cabral (ARG)	14.10.1985	19			22		2
Matías Ezequiel Catalán (ARG)	19.08.1992				7	(10)	
Benjamín Galindo Cruz	10.03.1999	1					
Emmanuel García Vaca	28.12.1989	4	(4)		7		
Josué Gómez del Rosal	06.07.1999	1	(2)				
Miguel Ángel Herrera Equihua	03.04.1989	2	(3)		5	(9)	
René López Aburto	04.01.2002		(1)				
Óscar Fabián Murillo Murillo (COL)	18.04.1988	19		2	17	(1)	2
Rodrigo Salinas Dorantes	09.05.1988	8	(3)				
Miguel Ángel Tapias Davila	09.01.1997				1	(2)	
Midfielders:							
Erick Germain Aguirre Tafolla	23.02.1997	15		1	21		2
Luis Gerardo Chávez Magallón	15.01.1996	20			17	(3)	2
Francisco Antonio Figueroa Díaz	13.06.1999	4	(4)		8	(5)	
Víctor Alfonso Guzmán Guzmán	03.02.1995	9	(5)	5	6	(6)	
Jorge Daniel Hernández Govea	10.06.1989	8			6	(7)	
Romario Andrés Ibarra Mina (ECU)	24.09.1994	4	(5)		5	(5)	2
Jahaziel Marchand Herrera	28.09.2001				1	(1)	
Efraín Orona Zavala	22.02.1999	2	(7)			(4)	
Kevin Ariel Ortega Mercado	04.01.2002	1					
Edgar Felipe Pardo Castro (COL)	17.08.1990	12	(5)	1	17	(3)	1
Víctor Ismael Sosa (ARG)	18.01.1987	10	(8)	3	15	(5)	3
Forwards:							
Luis Angel Calzadilla Santillán	14.01.2000		(1)			(1)	
Victor Alejandro Dávila Zavala	04.11.1997	14	(4)	5			
Roberto Carlos De La Rosa González	04.01.2000	9	(7)	2	10	(9)	6
Bryan Alonso González Olivan	10.04.2003		(2)		2	(2)	
Colin Kâzım-Richards (TUR)	26.08.1986	1	(3)	1			
Hárold Santiago Mosquera Caicedo (COL)	07.02.1995				2	(7)	
Eduardo Mustre Torres	21.01.2003		(1)				
Roberto Antonio Nurse Anguiano (PAN)	16.12.1983	3	(7)		6	(5)	1
Mauro Daniel Quiroga (ARG)	07.12.1989				7	(9)	2
Leonardo Javier Ramos (ARG)	21.08.1989	3	(5)				
Erick Daniel Sánchez Ocegueda	20.07.1999	15	(4)		20	(2)	4
Cristian Souza España (URU)	28.08.1995	2	(5)	1			
Trainer:							
Paulo César Pezzolano Suárez (URU)	25.04.1983	20			22		

CLUB DE FÚTBOL PUEBLA

Foundation date: October 6, 1968
Address: Boulevard Gustavo Díaz Ordaz No. 3915, Colonia San Baltazar, 72550 Puebla
Stadium: Estadio Cuauhtémoc, Puebla (51,726

THE SQUAD

	DOB	Ape M	(s)	G	Cla M	(s)	G
Goalkeepers:							
Jesús Iván Rodríguez Trujillo	21.05.1993	4				(1)	
Antony Domingo Silva Cano (PAR)	27.02.1984				21		
Nicolas Vikonis Moreau (URU)	06.04.1984	16					
Defenders:							
Brayan Alexis Angulo León (COL)	02.11.1989	15	(3)	1			
Maximiliano Javier Araújo Vilches (URU)	15.02.2000		(4)		12	(9)	2
Daniel Arreola Argüello	08.10.1985	12		1			
George Ulises Corral	18.07.1990	14	(2)	1	19		
Emanuel Gularte Méndez (URU)	30.09.1997	7	(3)		10	(3)	1
Lucas Jaques Varone Maia (BRA)	23.02.1993				3	(5)	
Jesús Arturo Paganoni Peña	24.09.1988	1	(1)		1	(2)	
Maximiliano Perg Schneider (URU)	16.09.1991	19			17		1
Juan Pablo Segovia González (ARG)	21.03.1989				18	(1)	1
Ivo Saúl Vázquez Serrano	16.10.2000					(1)	
Néstor Vicente Vidrio Serrano	22.03.1989	8	(8)				
Midfielders:							
Clifford Aboagye (GHA)	11.02.1995				1	(3)	
Daniel Aguilar Muñoz	06.02.1998	4	(4)		8	(7)	1
Daniel Álvarez López	22.07.1994	7	(8)	2	3	(17)	4
Alejandro Saúl Chumacero Bracamonte (BOL)	22.04.1991	3	(4)				
Diego Eduardo de Buen Juárez	03.07.1991				3	(6)	
Pablo González Díaz	07.07.1992	17	(3)	2			
Osvaldo David Martínez Arce (PAR)	08.04.1986	7	(7)	3			
Israel Reyes Romero	23.05.2000	4			13	(2)	
Salvador Reyes Chávez	04.05.1998	13	(3)	1	21		2
Javier Alván Salas Salazar	20.08.1993	17			20		
Forwards:							
Alan Jesús Acosta Montañez	19.12.1996		(4)				
Bernardo Nicolás Cuesta (ARG)	20.12.1988	3	(8)	1			
Amaury Gabriel Escoto Ruíz	30.11.1992	7	(11)	3	4	(14)	
Omar Andrés Fernández Frasica (COL)	11.02.1993	18	(2)	2	20		
Gustavo Henrique Ferrareis (BRA)	02.01.1996					(11)	
Eduardo Herrera Aguirre	25.07.1988		(7)				
Guillermo Martínez Ayala	15.03.1995					(11)	1
Santiago Gabriel Ormeño Zayas	04.02.1994	12	(4)	7	18	(2)	10
Ángel Manuel Robles Guerrero	18.11.2001					(1)	
Christian Alejandro Tabó Hornos (URU)	23.11.1993	12	(3)	1	19		3
Trainer:							
Juan Máximo Reynoso Guzmán (PER)	28.12.1969	20					
[01.01.2021] Nicolás Ricardo Larcamón	11.08.1984				21		

QUERÉTARO FÚTBOL CLUB

Foundation date: July 8, 1950
Address: Prol. Luis Vega y Monroy 409-4, Colonia Balaustradas, 76079 Querétaro
Stadium: Estadio Corregidora, Querétaro - 35,575

THE SQUAD

	DOB	Ape M	(s)	G	Cla M	(s)	G
Goalkeepers:							
Gil Esaul Alcalá Barba	29.07.1992	14			11		
Eduardo Bravo Avila	18.02.1991	3					
Gerardo Daniel Ruiz Barragán	05.09.1985				5		
Luis Carlos Villegas García	07.07.2001				2		
Defenders:							
Daniel Ángel Cervantes Fraire	28.06.1990	15		1	12	(1)	
José Alexis Doldán Aquino (PAR)	27.02.1997	3	(1)		14		1
Aristeo García Moreno	19.02.1999					(2)	
Alfonso Luna Islas	23.01.1990	13					
Hugo Alejandro Magallanes Silveira (URU)	26.08.1997				5	(4)	
Omar Israel Mendoza Martín	28.10.1988				15		
Juan Pablo Meza Tepezano	13.08.1993	1	(2)		4	(1)	
Julio César Nava García	29.12.1989	5	(5)				
Martín Rea Zuccotti (URU)	13.11.1997	6	(2)		5	(2)	
Julián Alberto Velázquez (ARG)	23.10.1990	11		1			
Erik Vera Franco	24.03.1992	11	(1)		8	(1)	
Irving Mauro Zurita García	27.09.1991	7	(5)				
Midfielders:							
Omar Arellano Riverón	18.06.1987	3	(8)	1			
Joshua Antonio Canales Hernández (HON)	20.07.2000					(1)	
Kevin Rafael Escamilla Moreno	21.02.1994	4	(5)		10	(6)	
José Jesús Gurrola Castro	15.04.1998				4	(7)	1
Javier Eduardo Ibarra de la Rosa	06.02.1998	2	(1)		2	(3)	
Fernando Madrigal González	12.11.1991	17		2	18		1
Jefferson Antonio Montero Vite (ECU)	01.09.1989				8	(5)	
Gonzalo Montes Calderini (URU)	22.12.1994	13	(2)		10	(5)	1
Arturo Adolfo Palma Cisneros	16.01.2001				2	(3)	
Kevin Federik Ramírez Dutra (URU)	01.04.1994	14	(3)	3	13	(3)	2
Francisco Israel Rivera Dávalos	23.09.1994	1	(4)				
Luis Antonio Valencia Mosquera (ECU)	04.08.1985				15		1
Forwards:							
Nicolás Gabriel Albarracín Basil (URU)	11.06.1993	1	(1)				
Jonathan Enrique Betancourt Mina (ECU)	14.02.1995	4	(7)				
Francisco da Costa Aragão "Chico" (BRA)	05.05.1995		(3)		4	(6)	1
Jonathan David dos Santos Duré (URU)	18.04.1992				4	(4)	
Joe Gallardo Camacho (USA)	01.01.1998				1	(6)	1
Omar Islas Hernández	13.04.1996	9	(4)	4			
Jonathan Ezequiel Perlaza Leiva (ECU)	13.09.1997	1	(3)				
José Alfredo Ramírez Espino	29.08.2000		(1)			(5)	
Alejandro Rivero López	14.01.2000					(1)	
Ángel Baltazar Sepúlveda Sánchez	15.02.1991	16	(1)	3	18		6
David Alejandro Salazar Zepeda	05.08.1991		(1)				
Sebastián Sosa Sánchez (URU)	13.03.1994	2	(8)	1			
Hugo Gabriel Silveira Pereira (URU)	23.05.1993	11	(1)	6	8	(8)	3
Trainer:							

| Álex Diego Tejado | | 01.07.1985 | 15 | | | | |
| [27.10.2020] Héctor Altamirano Escudero | | 17.03.1977 | 2 | | 18 | | |

CLUB SANTOS LAGUNA TORREÓN

Foundation date: September 4, 1983
Address: Calle Alberto Swain No. 13, Colonia Zona Industrial, 27019 Torreón
Stadium: Estadio Corona, Torreón (29,237

THE SQUAD

	DOB	Ape M	(s)	G	Cla M	(s)	G
Goalkeepers:							
Carlos Acevedo López	19.04.1996	18			24		
Defenders:							
Gerardo Daniel Arteaga Zamora	07.09.1998	1					
Jonathan Alejandro Díaz Rivas	11.05.1999	1	(2)		3		
Matheus Doria Macedo (BRA)	08.11.1994	17		1	24		2
Ismael Govea Solorzano	20.02.1997	1			3	(3)	
Areli Betsiel Hernández Huerta	22.12.1994	2					
Hugo Isaác Rodríguez de la O	08.06.1990	16		2	2	(3)	
Félix Torres Caicedo (ECU)	11.01.1997	5			22		1
Josécarlos Van Rankin Galland	14.05.1993	13	(1)	2			
Midfielders:							
David Alfredo Andrade Gómez	09.07.1993	14		1	4	(1)	
Omar Antonio Campos Chagoya	20.07.2002				18	(2)	1
Jordan Carrillo Rodríguez	30.11.2001		(4)			(2)	
Alan Jhosué Cervantes Martín del Campo	17.01.1998	15	(2)		23		
Edgar Games González	20.02.2001	2			2	(1)	
Fernando Gorriarán Fontes (URU)	27.11.1994	17		4	20	(1)	3
Andrés Felipe Ibargüen García (COL)	07.05.1992				4	(14)	
Jesús Antonio Isijara Rodríguez	26.09.1989				9	(6)	
Adrián Lozano Magallanes	08.05.1999	2	(5)			(5)	
Carlos Emilio Orrantía Treviño	01.02.1991	2	(8)		13	(6)	
Juan Ferney Otero Tovar (COL)	26.05.1995				23		3
Ronaldo de Jesús Prieto Ramírez	03.03.1997		(4)		12	(5)	1
Ulises Rivas Gilio	25.01.1996	6	(2)				
Diego Alfonso Valdés Contreras (CHI)	30.01.1994	11	(2)		10	(2)	3
Forwards:							
Eduardo Daniel Aguirre Lara	03.08.1998	7	(6)		14	(10)	8
Julio César Furch (ARG)	29.07.1989	16	(2)	5			
Brayan Eduardo Garnica Cortéz	27.05.1996	11	(2)	1			
Jair Alejandro González Romo	04.03.2002	2	(2)				
Ignacio Alejandro Jeraldino Gil (CHI)	06.12.1995				4	(13)	
Santiago Rene Muñoz Robles	14.08.2002		(1)		11	(7)	3
Jesús Alberto Ocejo Zazueta	16.06.1998		(6)		8	(12)	1
Raúl Octavio Rivero Falero (URU)	24.01.1992	11	(3)	3			
Walter Gael Sandoval Contreras	05.11.1995	8	(6)	3			
Eduar Ayrton Preciado García (ECU)	17.07.1994				11		3
Trainer:							
Guillermo Jorge Almada Alves (URU)	18.06.1969	18			24		

CLUB DE FÚTBOL TIGRES
DE LA UNIVERSIDAD AUTÓNOMA DE NUEVO LEÓN

Foundation date: March 7, 1960
Address: Puerta 13, Colonia Ciudad Universitaria, 66451 San Nicolás de los Garza
Stadium: Estadio Universitario, San Nicolás, Nuevo León (41,615

THE SQUAD

	DOB	M	Ape (s)	G	M	Cla (s)	G
Goalkeepers:							
Carlos Gustavo Galindo De La Rosa	07.04.2000	2					
Nahuel Ignacio Guzmán (ARG)	10.08.1986	16			18		
Miguel René Ortega Rodríguez	13.04.1995	2					
Defenders:							
Hugo Ayala Castro	31.03.1987	12	(2)		3		
Aldo Jafid Cruz Sánchez	24.09.1997				6		
Francisco Javier Meza Palma (COL)	29.08.1991	18		1	4	(4)	
Diego Antonio Reyes Rosales	19.09.1992	7	(2)		13	(1)	3
Luis Alfonso Rodríguez Alanís	21.01.1991	17	(1)	2	11		
Carlos Joel Salcedo Hernández	29.09.1993	13	(2)		17		1
Juan José Sánchez Purata	09.01.1998		(3)			(3)	
Eduardo Santiago Tercero Méndez	06.05.1996		(4)				
Jorge Emmanuel Torres Nilo	16.01.1988		(6)				
Francisco Eduardo Venegas Moreno	16.07.1998		(1)		2	(2)	
Midfielders:							
Javier Ignacio Aquino Carmona	11.02.1990	18			15		
Erick Alejandro Ávalos Alejo	21.04.2000				2	(3)	
Jesús Alberto Dueñas Manzo	16.03.1989	19	(1)	1	12	(1)	
Leonardo Cecilio Fernández López (URU)	08.11.1998	8	(5)	1	3	(6)	
Raymundo de Jesús Fulgencio Román	12.02.2000		(5)		2	(3)	
Guido Hernán Pizarro Demestri (ARG)	26.02.1990	18		1	18		
Rafael de Souza Pereira "Rafael Carioca" (BRA)	18.06.1989	18			15		
Jordan Steeven Sierra Flores (ECU)	23.04.1997	1	(5)		1	(3)	
Forwards:							
André-Pierre Christian Gignac (FRA)	05.12.1985	20		13	15		3
Carlos Gabriel González Espínola (PAR)	04.02.1993				15	(1)	4
Nicolás Federico López Alonso (URU)	01.10.1993	3	(8)	6	7	(6)	6
Julián Andrés Quiñones Quiñones (COL)	24.03.1997	8	(7)	1	4	(5)	1
Luis Enrique Quiñones García (COL)	26.06.1991	13	(1)	1	15	(1)	1
Eduardo Jesús Vargas Rojas (CHI)	20.11.1989	7	(7)	3			
Trainer:							
Ricardo Ferretti de Oliveira (BRA)	22.02.1954	20			18		

CLUB TIJUANA XOLOITZCUINTLES DE CALIENTE

Foundation date: January 14, 2007
Address: Avenida Márquez de León, Zona Río, 22320 Tijuana
Stadium: Estadio Caliente, Tijuana (27,333

THE SQUAD

	DOB	Ape M	(s)	G	Cla M	(s)	G
Goalkeepers:							
Benny Díaz	15.12.1998				2	(1)	
Jonathan Emmanuel Orozco Martínez	12.05.1986	17			15		
Defenders:							
Jorge Luis Aguilar Miranda (PAR)	04.02.1993	7	(1)				
Bryan Alexis Angulo León (COL)	02.11.1989	9	(6)	3	17		
Miguel Ángel Barbieri (ARG)	24.08.1993	12					
Bryan Colula Alarcón	06.04.1996	2					
Aldo Jafid Cruz Sánchez	24.09.1997	6	(5)				
Jaime Gómez Valencia	17.07.1993	9	(4)	1	2	(11)	
Víctor Andrés Guzmán Olmedo	07.03.2002	16			13		
Gonzalo Alejandro Jara Reyes (CHI)	29.08.1985				13		
Vladimir Eduardo Loroña Aguilar	16.11.1998	6	(1)	1	15	(1)	
Jordan Jesús Silva Díaz	30.07.1994	7	(2)				
Eduardo Santiago Tercero Méndez	06.05.1996				7	(1)	
Julián Alberto Velázquez (ARG)	23.10.1990				1	(1)	
Midfielders:							
Clifford Aboagye (GHA)	11.02.1995	4	(5)				
Kevin Alexander Balanta Lucumí (COL)	28.04.1997	6	(3)				
David Matías Barbona (ARG)	22.02.1995	5	(4)		14	(2)	1
Miler Alejandro Bolaños Reascos (ECU)	01.06.1990	4		1			
Edwin Andrés Cardona Bedoya (COL)	08.12.1992		(1)				
Jordi Cortizo de la Piedra	30.06.1996	8	(8)	2	2	(8)	
Luis Javier Gamíz Ávila	04.04.2000	5	(2)			(3)	
Edgar Iván López Rodríguez	21.04.1999	9	(6)	1	1	(11)	2
Fidel Francisco Martínez Tenorio (ECU)	15.02.1990				12	(5)	8
Esteban Andrés Pavez Suazo (CHI)	01.05.1990				15		
Jordan Lenín Rezabala Anzules (ECU)	29.02.2000	2	(5)				
Christian Hernando Rivera Cuéllar (COL)	14.01.1996	8	(5)		15	(2)	
Marcel Alejandro Ruiz Suárez	26.10.2000	10	(3)		1	(9)	
Junior Nazareno Sornoza Moreira (ECU)	28.01.1994				14	(2)	
Forwards:							
Christian Eduardo Castillo Leyva	31.07.2003					(1)	
Fabián Andrés Castillo Sánchez (COL)	17.06.1992	15	(2)	2	5	(11)	2
Mauro Alberto Laínez Leyva	09.05.1996	12	(2)				
Luís Leal dos Anjos (STP)	29.05.1987	3	(4)				
Mauro Andrés Manotas Páez (COL)	15.07.1995				16	(1)	5
Ariel Gerardo Nahuelpán Osten (ARG)	15.10.1987	4					
Miguel Ángel Sansores Sánchez	28.04.1991				7	(8)	1
Gerson Romario Vázquez Ogara	12.11.2001		(3)	1		(3)	
Paolo Yrizar Martín del Campo	06.08.1997	1	(2)				
Trainer:							
Pablo Adrián Guede Barrirero (ARG)	12.11.1974	17			14		
[14.04.2021] Ildefonso Mendoza Segovia	21.09.1975				1		
[19.04.2021] Robert Dante Siboldi Badiola (URU)	24.09.1965				2		

335

DEPORTIVO TOLUCA FÚTBOL CLUB

Foundation date: February 12, 1917
Address: Calle Felipe Villanueva No. 300, Colonia San Bernardino, 50080 Toluca de Lerdo
Stadium: Estadio „Nemesio Díez", Toluca (30,000

THE SQUAD						
	DOB	\multicolumn{3}{c}{Ape}	\multicolumn{3}{c}{Cla}
		M	(s)	G	M	(s)	G
Goalkeepers:							
Luis Manuel García Palomera	31.12.1992	17			16		
Alfredo Saldívar Medina	09.02.1990	1			4		
Defenders:							
Miguel Ángel Barbieri (ARG)	24.08.1993				19		2
Aníbal Hernán Chalá Ayoví (ECU)	09.05.1996	2					
Diego González Hernández	14.05.1996	14	(1)	1			
Raúl López Gómez	23.02.1993	18			10	(8)	1
Jonatan Ramón Maidana (ARG)	29.07.1985	9	(3)	1			
Adrián Mora Barraza	15.08.1997	12	(3)				
Oscar Haret Ortega Gatica	19.05.2000	6		1	4	(7)	
Jorge Alejandro Rodríguez Hernández	03.09.2001					(4)	
Rodrigo Salinas Dorantes	09.05.1988				11	(4)	
Brandon Guadalupe Sartiaguin Godoy	21.02.2000	7	(1)	1		(2)	
Gastón Sauro (ARG)	23.02.1990	12		1		(1)	
Jorge Emmanuel Torres Nilo	16.01.1988				20		1
Midfielders:							
Claudio Andrés Baeza Baeza (CHI)	23.12.1993				20		
Kevin Castañeda Vargas	28.10.1999		(13)		13	(4)	3
Javier Güemez López	17.10.1991	11	(3)	1			
Giovanny de Jesús León Salazar	08.02.2000		(2)				
Pablo Nicolás López de León (URU)	08.10.1996	1	(4)			(2)	
João Jimmy Plata Cotera (ECU)	01.03.1992	1	(6)			(8)	1
Diego Rigonato Rodrigues (BRA)	09.03.1988		(1)		17	(1)	1
Antonio Ríos Martínez	24.10.1988	10	(2)		3	(4)	
Alan Omar Rodríguez Ortíz	20.03.1996		(1)			(1)	
Rubens Oscar Sambueza (ARG)	01.01.1984	17	(1)	3	18	(1)	1
José Juan Vázquez Gómez	14.03.1988				20		
William Fernando da Silva (BRA)	20.11.1986	15	(1)	1		(2)	
Forwards:							
Diego Abella Calleja	22.10.1998	2	(4)				
Iván Emmanuel Acero Rodríguez	01.07.2000		(1)				
Alexis Pedro Canelo (ARG)	03.02.1992	12	(1)	6	20		14
Carlos Ernesto Cisneros Barajas	30.08.1993	3	(3)				
Michael Steveen Estrada Martínez (ECU)	07.04.1996	11	(6)	4	17	(3)	7
Alan Medina Camacho	19.08.1997	9	(6)	1			
Enrique Luis Triverio (ARG)	31.12.1988	8	(9)	1	4	(15)	
Isaias Violante Romero	20.10.2003		(2)			(3)	
Paolo Yrizar Martín del Campo	06.08.1997				4	(3)	
Trainer:							
José Manuel de la Torre Menchaca	13.11.1965	12					
[07.10.2020] Carlos Adrián Morales Higuera	06.09.1979	6					
[01.12.2020] Rolando Hernán Cristante Mandarino (ARG)	16.09.1969				20		

CLUB UNIVERSIDAD NACIONAL (UNAM) CIUDAD DE MÉXICO

Foundation date: August 28, 1954
Address: Calle Totonacas No. 560, Colonia Ajusco, 4300 Delegación Coyoacán, Ciudad de México
Stadium: Estadio Olímpico Universitario, Ciudad de México (68,954

THE SQUAD

	DOB	Ape M	(s)	G	Cla M	(s)	G
Goalkeepers:							
Julio José González Vela Alvizu	23.04.1991	8	(1)		1		
Alfredo Talavera Díaz	18.09.1982	15			16		
Defenders:							
Nicolás Omar Freire (ARG)	18.02.1994	21		1	17		
Manuel Alejandro Mayorga Almaráz	29.05.1997	17	(2)	1			
Alan Mozo Rodríguez	05.04.1997	17	(3)		12	(1)	
Luis Fernando Quintana Vega	03.02.1992	6	(1)		2		
Jesús Andrés Rivas Gutiérrez	29.10.2002	4	(1)		3	(1)	
Johan Felipe Vásquez Ibarra	22.10.1998	22	(1)	1	16		
Midfielders:							
Favio Enrique Álvarez (ARG)	23.01.1993	14	(2)	2	10	(5)	
José Antonio Cobián Ruíz	14.09.1998					(2)	
Amaury García Moreno	19.12.2001	2	(3)		1	(3)	
Ángel García Hernández	01.09.2000					(12)	
Carlos Gutiérrez Estefa	05.02.1999	15	(6)		15	(2)	1
Andrés Iniestra Vázquez Mellado	11.03.1996	13	(3)	1			
Erik Antonio Lira Méndez	08.05.2000	12	(7)		15	(2)	
Leonel López González	24.05.1994	5	(4)		3	(6)	
Gerardo Moreno Cruz	29.11.1993		(3)			(2)	
Jerónimo Rodríguez Guemes	24.03.1999	5	(3)		12	(1)	
Sebastián Saucedo Mondragón (USA)	22.01.1997	2	(3)		4	(3)	1
Juan Pablo Vigón Cham	20.07.1991	14	(3)	4	17		1
Facundo Federico Waller Martiarena (URU)	09.04.1997	6	(10)		14	(3)	1
Forwards:							
Juan Ignacio Dinenno De Cara (ARG)	29.08.1994	23		12	12	(1)	4
Brian Eduardo Figueroa Flores	28.05.1999		(4)				
Carlos Gabriel González Espínola (PAR)	04.02.1993	20	(2)	7			
Juan Manuel Iturbe Arévalos (PAR)	04.06.1993	12	(10)	2	3	(10)	
Bryan Mendoza Cruz	08.09.1997		(9)	1		(4)	
Emanuel Montejano Arroyo	12.07.2001				4	(2)	1
Jacob Eduardo Morales Zenon	22.03.1999					(1)	
Gabriel Arturo Torres Tejada (PAN)	31.10.1988				10	(1)	1
Trainer:							
Andrés Luciano Lillini (ARG)	13.08.1974	23			17		

SECOND LEVEL
Liga de Expansión MX 2020/2021

Torneo Guard1anes Apertura 2020

Regular Stage

1.	Celaya FC	15	9	5	1	21 - 10	35
2.	Atlante FC Ciudad de México	15	9	1	5	25 - 14	32
3.	Cimarrones de Sonora FC Hermosillo	15	9	1	5	25 - 16	30
4.	Club Atlético Morelia	15	7	5	3	24 - 18	29
5.	Cancún FC	15	7	3	5	19 - 14	27
6.	Tampico Madero FC	15	6	5	4	14 - 12	26
7.	CD Mineros de Zacatecas	15	6	5	4	24 - 19	25
8.	Tepatitlán FC	15	6	5	4	20 - 15	24
9.	CD Tapatío Guadalajara	15	5	6	4	20 - 14	22
10.	Tlaxcala FC	15	5	3	7	13 - 22	20
11.	Venados FC Yucatán Mérida	15	4	4	7	14 - 21	17
12.	Pumas Tabasco Villahermosa	15	3	5	7	20 - 30	17
13.	CSD Dorados de Sinaloa Culiacán	15	3	5	7	18 - 27	16
14.	Club Leones Negros de la Universidad de Guadalajara	15	3	4	8	17 - 21	15
15.	Alebrijes de Oaxaca FC	15	4	1	10	15 - 25	15
16.	CF Correcaminos de la Universidad Autónoma de Tamaulipas (UAT) Ciudad Victoria	15	3	4	8	17 - 28	13

Stage Winner advanced to the Semi-Finals, runners-up advanced to the Quarter-Finals, while teams ranked 3-12 were qualified for the 2020 Apertura Liguilla Reclassification.

2020 Apertura Liguilla

Reclassification [24-26.11.2020]

Cimarrones de Sonora FC Hermosillo - Pumas Tabasco Villahermosa	2-3(1-0)	
Club Atlético Morelia - Venados FC Yucatán Mérida	1-0(0-0)	
Cancún FC - Tlaxcala FC	1-2(0-2)	
Tampico Madero FC - CD Tapatío Guadalajara	0-0 aet	5-3 pen
CD Mineros de Zacatecas - Tepatitlán FC	1-0(0-0)	

Quarter-Finals [02-06.12.2020]

Pumas Tabasco Villahermosa - Atlante FC Ciudad de México*	1-1(0-1)	0-0
Tlaxcala FC - Club Atlético Morelia	0-2(0-2)	0-3(0-3)
CD Mineros de Zacatecas - Tampico Madero FC	2-1(1-1)	0-3(0-3)

Semi-Finals [09-12.12.2020]

Tampico Madero FC - Celaya FC	1-0(1-0)	2-2(1-1)
Club Atlético Morelia - Atlante FC Ciudad de México*	1-1(1-0)	0-0

*advanced to the semi-finals having better record in the regular season.

Final [17-20.12.2020]

Tampico Madero FC - Atlante FC Ciudad de México	1-1(1-0)
Atlante FC Ciudad de México - Tampico Madero FC	2-3(0-0,1-2)

2020 Torneo Guard1anes Apertura Champions: **Tampico Madero FC**

Torneo Guard1anes Clausura 2021

1.	Club Atlético Morelia	15	9	2	4	26	-	19	33
2.	Celaya FC	15	6	7	2	19	-	11	28
3.	Cimarrones de Sonora FC Hermosillo	15	6	8	1	20	-	11	27
4.	CD Mineros de Zacatecas	15	7	3	5	21	-	21	27
5.	CD Tapatío Guadalajara	15	6	4	5	14	-	14	24
6.	Tepatitlán FC	15	6	4	5	13	-	19	24
7.	Atlante FC Ciudad de México	15	6	4	5	18	-	12	23
8.	Cancún FC	15	6	3	6	15	-	17	21
9.	CSD Dorados de Sinaloa Culiacán	15	3	9	3	15	-	16	20
10.	Tlaxcala FC	15	5	4	6	15	-	17	20
11.	Alebrijes de Oaxaca FC	15	4	7	4	24	-	24	19
12.	Venados FC Yucatán Mérida	15	3	8	4	15	-	16	18
13.	Pumas Tabasco Villahermosa	15	4	3	8	14	-	19	18
14.	Tampico Madero FC	15	3	7	5	11	-	12	16
15.	CF Correcaminos de la Universidad Autónoma de Tamaulipas (UAT) Ciudad Victoria	15	3	4	8	16	-	20	14
16.	Club Leones Negros de la Universidad de Guadalajara	15	2	5	8	11	-	19	12

Stage Winner advanced to the Semi-Finals, runners-up advanced to the Quarter-Finals, while teams ranked 3-12 were qualified for the 2020 Clausura Liguilla Reclassification.

2021 Clausura Liguilla

Reclassification [20-22.04.2021]

Cimarrones de Sonora FC Hermosillo - Venados FC Yucatán Mérida	2-2 aet	4-3 pen
CD Mineros de Zacatecas - Alebrijes de Oaxaca FC	6-0(2-0)	
Tepatitlán FC - CSD Dorados de Sinaloa Culiacán	1-1 aet	4-2 pen
Atlante FC Ciudad de México - Cancún FC	2-1(1-1)	
CD Tapatío Guadalajara - Tlaxcala FC	1-0(1-0)	

Quarter-Finals [27.04.-02.05.2021]

Atlante FC Ciudad de México - Celaya FC	2-0(0-0)	3-3(2-1)
Tepatitlán FC - Cimarrones de Sonora FC Hermosillo	2-0(0-0)	4-1(1-1)
CD Tapatío Guadalajara - CD Mineros de Zacatecas	0-1(0-0)	1-2(1-0)

Semi-Finals [04-08.05.2021]

Atlante FC Ciudad de México - Club Atlético Morelia	0-1(0-1)	1-1(1-1)
Tepatitlán FC - CD Mineros de Zacatecas	3-0(0-0)	1-1(0-1)

Final [12-15.05.2021]	
Tepatitlán FC - Club Atlético Morelia	1-0(0-0)
Club Atlético Morelia - Tepatitlán FC	2-2(2-1)

2021 Torneo Guard1anes Clausura Champions: **Tepatitlán FC**

Relegation Table 2020/2021

The team which will be relegated is determined on average points taking into account results of the last six seasons (Apertura & Clausura 2018/2019, Apertura & Clausura 2019/2020 and Apertura & Clausura 2020/2021).

Pos	Team	2018/19 P	2019/20 P	2020/21 P	Total P	Total M	Aver
1.	CD Mineros de Zacatecas	60	34	47	138	77	1.8387
2.	Atlante FC Ciudad de México	47	31	50	128	77	1.7097
3.	Cimarrones de Sonora FC Hermosillo	47	23	54	124	77	1.5806
4.	Club Atlético Morelia	35	32	55	122	77	1.5333
5.	Tepatitlán FC	-	-	45	45	30	1.5294
6.	CD Tapatío Guadalajara	-	-	43	43	30	1.5000
7.	Celaya FC	26	25	57	108	77	1.4000
8.	Tampico Madero FC	0	29	39	68	49	1.3387
9.	Alebrijes de Oaxaca FC	41	27	32	100	77	1.3065
10.	Tlaxcala FC	-	-	37	37	30	1.2258
11.	CSD Dorados de Sinaloa Culiacán	42	19	32	93	77	1.2097
12.	Cancún FC	27	16	45	88	77	1.2000
13.	Club Leones Negros de la Universidad de Guadalajara	35	28	24	87	77	1.1451
14.	CF Correcaminos de la Universidad Autónoma de Tamaulipas (UAT) Ciudad Victoria	32	26	26	84	77	1.0806
15.	Venados FC Yucatán Mérida	29	21	33	83	77	1.0645
16.	Pumas Tabasco Villahermosa	-	-	29	29	30	0.9333

Please note: the promotion and relegation between Liga de Expansión MX and Third Level was suspended, however, the coefficient table will be used to establish the payment of fines that will be used for the development of the clubs of the silver circuit. Per Article 24 of the competition regulations, the last three positioned teams in the coefficient table have to pay as follows: 1,5 million in the last place; 1 million the penultimate; and 500,000 will be paid by the sixteenth team in the table.

The subsidiary clubs (Pumas Tabasco Villahermosa and CD Tapatío Guadalajara), in addition to the two guests of the Premier League (Tepatitlán FC and Tlaxcala FC) are exempt from paying the fine, however, if a team of those mentioned finishes in those positions, there will be not counted in the table and that fine will not be paid by any other team.

NATIONAL TEAM
INTERNATIONAL MATCHES 2020/2021

30.09.2020	Ciudad de México	Mexico - Guatemala	3-0(3-0)	(F)
07.10.2020	Amsterdam	Netherlands - Mexico	0-1(0-0)	(F)
13.10.2020	Den Haag	Mexico - Algeria	2-2(1-1)	(F)
14.11.2020	Wiener Neustadt	Mexico - Korea Republic	3-2(0-1)	(F)
17.11.2020	Graz	Japan - Mexico	0-2(0-0)	(F)
27.03.2021	Cardiff	Wales - Mexico	1-0(1-0)	(F)
30.03.2021	Wiener Neustadt	Costa Rica - Mexico	0-1(0-0)	(F)
29.05.2021	Arlington	Mexico - Iceland	2-1(0-1)	(F)
03.06.2021	Denver	Mexico - Costa Rica	0-0; 5-4 pen	(CNL)
06.06.2021	Denver	United States - Mexico	3-2(1-1,2-2)	(CNL)
12.06.2021	Atlanta	Mexico - Honduras	0-0	(F)
30.06.2021	Nashville	Mexico - Panama	3-0(1-0)	(F)
03.07.2021	Los Angeles	Mexico - Nigeria	4-0(2-0)	(F)

30.09.2020, Friendly International
Estadio Azteca, Ciudad de México; Attendance: 0
Referee: Fernando Hernández Gómez (Mexico)
MEXICO - GUATEMALA   **3-0(3-0)**
MEX: Hugo Alfonso González Durán, Luis Alfonso Rodríguez Alanís (61.Jorge Eduardo Sánchez Ramos), Carlos Joel Salcedo Hernández, César Jasib Montes Castro (78.Gilberto Sepúlveda López), Luis Francisco Romo Barrón, Orbelín Pineda Alvarado, Jesús Daniel Gallardo Vasconcelos (61.Miguel Arturo Layún Prado), Francisco Sebastián Córdova Reyes (70.Fernando Beltrán Cruz), Carlos Alberto Rodríguez Gómez, Carlos Uriel Antuna Romero (61.Roberto Carlos Alvarado Hernández), Henry Josué Martín Mex (70.Ernesto Alexis Vega Rojas). Trainer: Gerardo Daniel Martino (Argentina).
Goals: Henry Josué Martín Mex (6), Orbelín Pineda Alvarado (28), Francisco Sebastián Córdova Reyes (36).

07.10.2020, Friendly International
"Johan Cruijff" Arena, Amsterdam; Attendance: 0
Referee: Srđan Jovanović (Serbia)
NETHERLANDS - MEXICO   **0-1(0-0)**
MEX: Alfredo Talavera Díaz, Héctor Alfredo Moreno Herrera (87.Néstor Alejandro Araujo Razo), Luis Alfonso Rodríguez Alanís, César Jasib Montes Castro, Edson Omar Álvarez Velázquez (77.Luis Francisco Romo Barrón), José Andrés Guardado Hernández (62.Jonathan dos Santos Ramírez), Héctor Miguel Herrera López (81.Omar Nicolás Govea García), Rodolfo Gilbert Pizarro Thomas (63.Orbelín Pineda Alvarado), Jesús Daniel Gallardo Vasconcelos, Jesús Manuel Corona Ruíz, Raúl Alonso Jiménez Rodríguez (77.Henry Josué Martín Mex). Trainer: Gerardo Daniel Martino (Argentina).
Goal: Raúl Alonso Jiménez Rodríguez (60 penalty).

13.10.2020, Friendly International
Cars Jeans Stadion, Den Haag (Netherlands); Attendance: 0
Referee: Hendrikus Sebastian "Bas" Nijhuis (Netherlands)
MEXICO - ALGERIA   **2-2(1-1)**
MEX: Rodolfo Cota Robles, Héctor Alfredo Moreno Herrera (49.Gilberto Sepúlveda López), Néstor Alejandro Araujo Razo, Jorge Eduardo Sánchez Ramos, Luis Francisco Romo Barrón (73.Alan Pulido Izaguirre), Héctor Miguel Herrera López, Jonathan dos Santos Ramírez (64.José Andrés Guardado Hernández), Rodolfo Gilbert Pizarro Thomas (64.Diego Lainez Leyva), Jesús Daniel Gallardo Vasconcelos, Jesús Manuel Corona Ruíz, Raúl Alonso Jiménez Rodríguez. Trainer: Gerardo Daniel Martino (Argentina).
Goals: Jesús Manuel Corona Ruíz (43), Diego Lainez Leyva (86).

14.11.2020, Friendly International
Wiener Neustadt Stadion, Wiener Neustadt (Austria); Attendance: 0
Referee: Harald Lechner (Austria)
MEXICO - KOREA REPUBLIC **3-2(0-1)**
MEX: Hugo Alfonso González Durán, Héctor Alfredo Moreno Herrera, Luis Alfonso Rodríguez Alanís (68.Jorge Eduardo Sánchez Ramos), Carlos Joel Salcedo Hernández (83.Néstor Alejandro Araujo Razo), Edson Omar Álvarez Velázquez, Jesús Daniel Gallardo Vasconcelos, Francisco Sebastián Córdova Reyes (54.Orbelín Pineda Alvarado), Carlos Alberto Rodríguez Gómez, Jesús Manuel Corona Ruíz (54.Carlos Uriel Antuna Romero), Raúl Alonso Jiménez Rodríguez, Hirving Rodrigo Lozano Bahena (83.Rodolfo Gilbert Pizarro Thomas). Trainer: Gerardo Daniel Martino (Argentina).
Goals: Raúl Alonso Jiménez Rodríguez (67), Carlos Uriel Antuna Romero (69), Carlos Joel Salcedo Hernández (70).

17.11.2020, Friendly International
Merkur-Arena, Graz (Austria); Attendance: n/a
Referee: Manuel Schüttengruber (Austria)
JAPAN - MEXICO **0-2(0-0)**
MEX: Francisco Guillermo Ochoa Magaña, Héctor Alfredo Moreno Herrera, Néstor Alejandro Araujo Razo, Jorge Eduardo Sánchez Ramos, Luis Francisco Romo Barrón, Rodolfo Gilbert Pizarro Thomas (89.Diego Lainez Leyva), Orbelín Pineda Alvarado (64.Carlos Uriel Antuna Romero), Jesús Daniel Gallardo Vasconcelos (46.Luis Alfonso Rodríguez Alanís), Carlos Alberto Rodríguez Gómez (46.Edson Omar Álvarez Velázquez), Raúl Alonso Jiménez Rodríguez (64.Henry Josué Martín Mex), Hirving Rodrigo Lozano Bahena (82.Roberto Carlos Alvarado Hernández). Trainer: Gerardo Daniel Martino (Argentina).
Goals: Raúl Alonso Jiménez Rodríguez (63), Hirving Rodrigo Lozano Bahena (68).

27.03.2021, Friendly International
Cardiff City Stadium, Cardiff; Attendance: 0
Referee: Ian McNabb (Northern Ireland)
WALES - MEXICO **1-0(1-0)**
MEX: Francisco Guillermo Ochoa Magaña, Luis Alfonso Rodríguez Alanís (61.Rodolfo Gilbert Pizarro Thomas), Carlos Joel Salcedo Hernández, César Jasib Montes Castro, Edson Omar Álvarez Velázquez (83.Diego Lainez Leyva), José Andrés Guardado Hernández (62.Jorge Eduardo Sánchez Ramos), Héctor Miguel Herrera López, Orbelín Pineda Alvarado (78.Jonathan dos Santos Ramírez), Jesús Daniel Gallardo Vasconcelos (79.Gerardo Daniel Arteaga Zamora), Jesús Manuel Corona Ruíz, Hirving Rodrigo Lozano Bahena. Trainer: Gerardo Daniel Martino (Argentina).

30.03.2021, Friendly International
Wiener Neustadt Stadion, Wiener Neustadt (Austria); Attendance: 0
Referee: Christian-Petru Ciochirca (Austria)
COSTA RICA - MEXICO **0-1(0-0)**
MEX: Alfredo Talavera Díaz, Héctor Alfredo Moreno Herrera, Carlos Joel Salcedo Hernández, Jorge Eduardo Sánchez Ramos, Luis Francisco Romo Barrón, Gerardo Daniel Arteaga Zamora, Jonathan dos Santos Ramírez (68.Héctor Miguel Herrera López), Rodolfo Gilbert Pizarro Thomas (65.Diego Lainez Leyva), Érick Gabriel Gutiérrez Galaviz (68.Orbelín Pineda Alvarado), Jesús Manuel Corona Ruíz (81.Efraín Álvarez), Hirving Rodrigo Lozano Bahena. Trainer: Gerardo Daniel Martino (Argentina).
Goal: Hirving Rodrigo Lozano Bahena (89).

29.05.2021, Friendly International
AT&T Stadium, Arlington (United States); Attendance: 44,892
Referee: Ted Unkel (United States)
MEXICO - ICELAND **2-1(0-1)**
MEX: Alfredo Talavera Díaz, Héctor Alfredo Moreno Herrera, Carlos Joel Salcedo Hernández (63.Héctor Miguel Herrera López), Jesús Daniel Gallardo Vasconcelos (63.Hirving Rodrigo Lozano Bahena), Jorge Eduardo Sánchez Ramos (64.Gerardo Daniel Arteaga Zamora), José Andrés Guardado Hernández, Carlos Alberto Rodríguez Gómez (63.Néstor Alejandro Araujo Razo), Edson Omar Álvarez Velázquez, Carlos Uriel Antuna Romero, Diego Lainez Leyva (81.Luis Alfonso Rodríguez Alanís), Henry Josué Martín Mex. Trainer: Gerardo Daniel Martino (Argentina).
Goals: Hirving Rodrigo Lozano Bahena (73, 78).

03.06.2021, 1st CONCACAF Nations League, Semi-Finals
Empower Field at Mile High Stadium, Denver (United States); Attendance: 34,451
Referee: Bryan López Castellanos (Guatemala)
MEXICO - COSTA RICA **0-0; 5-4 on penalties**
MEX: Francisco Guillermo Ochoa Magaña, Héctor Alfredo Moreno Herrera, Néstor Alejandro Araujo Razo, Gerardo Daniel Arteaga Zamora (68.Jesús Daniel Gallardo Vasconcelos), José Andrés Guardado Hernández (58.Luis Francisco Romo Barrón), Héctor Miguel Herrera López (78.Orbelín Pineda Alvarado), Edson Omar Álvarez Velázquez, Carlos Uriel Antuna Romero, Diego Lainez Leyva (58.Luis Alfonso Rodríguez Alanís), Henry Josué Martín Mex (58.Alan Pulido Izaguirre), Hirving Rodrigo Lozano Bahena. Trainer: Gerardo Daniel Martino (Argentina).
Penalties: Carlos Uriel Antuna Romero (missed), Hirving Rodrigo Lozano Bahena, Orbelín Pineda Alvarado, Alan Pulido Izaguirre, Luis Francisco Romo Barrón, Jesús Daniel Gallardo Vasconcelos.

06.06.2021, 1st CONCACAF Nations League, Final
Empower Field at Mile High Stadium, Denver; Attendance: 34,451
Referee: Bryan López Castellanos (Guatemala)
UNITED STATES - MEXICO **3-2(1-1,2-2)**
MEX: Francisco Guillermo Ochoa Magaña, Héctor Alfredo Moreno Herrera (100.Carlos Joel Salcedo Hernández), Luis Alfonso Rodríguez Alanís, Néstor Alejandro Araujo Razo, Jesús Daniel Gallardo Vasconcelos, Héctor Miguel Herrera López (100.José Andrés Guardado Hernández), Carlos Alberto Rodríguez Gómez (66.Luis Francisco Romo Barrón), Edson Omar Álvarez Velázquez (117.Orbelín Pineda Alvarado), Carlos Uriel Antuna Romero (78.Diego Lainez Leyva), Jesús Manuel Corona Ruíz (66.Henry Josué Martín Mex), Hirving Rodrigo Lozano Bahena. Trainer: Gerardo Daniel Martino (Argentina).
Goals: Jesús Manuel Corona Ruíz (2), Diego Lainez Leyva (79).

12.06.2021, Friendly International
Mercedes-Benz Stadium, Atlanta; Attendance: 70,072
Referee: Ted Unkel (United States)
MEXICO - HONDURAS **0-0**
MEX: Rodolfo Cota Robles, Héctor Alfredo Moreno Herrera (87.Érick Gabriel Gutiérrez Galaviz), Osvaldo Rodríguez del Portal, Jorge Eduardo Sánchez Ramos, Gerardo Daniel Arteaga Zamora, Orbelín Pineda Alvarado (70.Carlos Uriel Antuna Romero), Carlos Alberto Rodríguez Gómez, Edson Omar Álvarez Velázquez, Luis Francisco Romo Barrón, Alan Pulido Izaguirre (69.Henry Josué Martín Mex), Jesús Manuel Corona Ruíz (46.Diego Lainez Leyva). Trainer: Gerardo Daniel Martino (Argentina).

30.06.2021, Friendly International
Nissan Stadium, Nashville; Attendance: 30,386
Referee: Kevin Morrison (Jamaica)
MEXICO - PANAMA   **3-0(1-0)**
MEX: Francisco Guillermo Ochoa Magaña, César Jasib Montes Castro (65.Jesús Alberto Angulo Uriarte), Jorge Eduardo Sánchez Ramos, Johan Felipe Vásquez Ibarra, Érick Germáin Aguirre Tafolla, Francisco Sebastián Córdova Reyes (46.José Joaquín Esquivel Martínez), Carlos Alberto Rodríguez Gómez (64.Roberto Carlos Alvarado Hernández), Luis Francisco Romo Barrón (89.Fernando Beltrán Cruz), Diego Lainez Leyva (74.Carlos Uriel Antuna Romero), Henry Josué Martín Mex, Ernesto Alexis Vega Rojas (74.Jesús Ricardo Angulo Uriarte). Trainer: Gerardo Daniel Martino (Argentina).
Goals: D. Lainez (21), C. Montes (57), H. Martín (90+1).

03.07.2021, Friendly International
Memorial Coliseum, Los Angeles; Attendance: 30,386
Referee: Oliver Amet Vergara Rodríguez (Panama)
MEXICO - NIGERIA   **4-0(2-0)**
MEX: Alfredo Talavera Díaz, Luis Alfonso Rodríguez Alanís (79.Kevin Nahin Álvarez Campos), Carlos Joel Salcedo Hernández (79.Jesús Daniel Gallardo Vasconcelos), Osvaldo Rodríguez del Portal, Edson Omar Álvarez Velázquez, Gilberto Sepúlveda López, Héctor Miguel Herrera López 67.(Jonathan dos Santos Ramírez), Érick Gabriel Gutiérrez Galaviz (81.Alan Josué Cervantes Martín del Campo), Rogelio Gabriel Funes Mori (66.Orbelín Pineda Alvarado), Jesús Manuel Corona Ruíz (66.Efraín Álvarez), Hirving Rodrigo Lozano Bahena. Trainer: Gerardo Daniel Martino (Argentina).
Goals: H. Herrera (2), R. Funes Mori (4), H. Herrera (52), J. dos Santos (78).

NATIONAL TEAM PLAYERS 2020/2021		
Name	**DOB**	**Club**
Goalkeepers		
Rodolfo COTA Robles	03.07.1987	*Club León*
Hugo Alfonso GONZÁLEZ Durán	01.08.1990	*CF Monterrey*
Francisco Guillermo OCHOA Magaña	13.07.1985	*CF América Ciudad de México*
Alfredo TALAVERA Díaz	18.09.1982	*Club UNAM Ciudad de México*
Defenders		
Érick Germáin AGUIRRE Tafolla	23.02.1997	*CF Pachuca*
Kevin Nahin ÁLVAREZ Campos	15.01.1999	*CF Pachuca*
Jesús Alberto ANGULO Uriarte	30.01.1998	*Atlas FC Guadalajara*
Néstor Alejandro ARAUJO Razo	29.08.1991	*RC Celta de Vigo (ESP)*
Gerardo Daniel ARTEAGA Zamora	07.09.1998	*KRC Genk (BEL)*
José Joaquín ESQUIVEL Martínez	07.01.1998	*FC Juárez*
Miguel Arturo LAYÚN Prado	25.06.1988	*CF Monterrey*
César Jasib MONTES Castro	24.02.1997	*CF Monterrey*
Héctor Alfredo MORENO Herrera	17.01.1988	*Al-Gharafa SC Al Rayyan (QAT)*
Luis Alfonso RODRÍGUEZ Alanís	21.01.1991	*CF Tigres de la UA de Nuevo León*
Osvaldo RODRÍGUEZ del Portal	12.09.1996	*Club León*
Luis Francisco ROMO Barrón	05.06.1995	*Cruz Azul FC Ciudad de México*
Carlos Joel SALCEDO Hernández	29.09.1993	*CF Tigres de la UA de Nuevo León*
Jorge Eduardo SÁNCHEZ Ramos	10.12.1997	*CF América Ciudad de México*
Gilberto SEPÚLVEDA López	04.02.1999	*CD Guadalajara*
Johan Felipe VÁSQUEZ Ibarra	22.10.1998	*Club UNAM Ciudad de México*

Midfielders

Roberto Carlos ALVARADO Hernández	07.09.1998	*Cruz Azul FC Ciudad de México*
Edson Omar ÁLVAREZ Velázquez	24.10.1997	*AFC Ajax Amsterdam (NED)*
Efraín ÁLVAREZ	19.06.2002	*Los Angeles Galaxy (USA)*
Jesús Ricardo ANGULO Uriarte	20.02.1997	*CD Guadalajara*
Carlos Uriel ANTUNA Romero	21.08.1997	*CD Guadalajara*
Fernando BELTRÁN Cruz	08.05.1998	*CD Guadalajara*
Alan Josué CERVANTES Martín del Campo	17.01.1998	*Club Santos Laguna Torréon*
Francisco Sebastián CÓRDOVA Reyes	12.06.1997	*CF América Ciudad de México*
Jonathan DOS SANTOS Ramírez	26.04.1990	*Los Angeles Galaxy (USA)*
Jesús Daniel GALLARDO Vasconcelos	15.08.1994	*CF Monterrey*
Omar Nicolás GOVEA García	18.01.1996	*SV Zulte Waregem (BEL)*
José Andrés GUARDADO Hernández	28.09.1986	*Real Betis Balompié Sevilla (ESP)*
Érick Gabriel GUTIÉRREZ Galaviz	15.06.1995	*PSV Eindhoven (NED)*
Héctor Miguel HERRERA López	19.04.1990	*Club Atlético de Madrid (ESP)*
Diego LAINEZ Leyva	09.06.2000	*Real Betis Balompié Sevilla (ESP)*
Orbelín PINEDA Alvarado	24.03.1996	*Cruz Azul FC Ciudad de México*
Rodolfo Gilbert PIZARRO Thomas	15.02.1994	*CIF Inter Miami (USA)*
Carlos Alberto RODRÍGUEZ Gómez	03.01.1997	*CF Monterrey*

Forwards

Jesús Manuel CORONA Ruíz	06.01.1993	*FC do Porto (POR)*
Rogelio Gabriel FUNES Mori	05.03.1991	*CF Monterrey*
Raúl Alonso JIMÉNEZ Rodríguez	05.05.1991	*Wolverhampton Wanderers FC (ENG)*
Hirving Rodrigo LOZANO Bahena	30.07.1995	*SSC Napoli (ITA)*
Henry Josué MARTÍN Mex	18.11.1992	*CF América Ciudad de México*
Alan PULIDO Izaguirre	08.03.1991	*Sporting Kansas City (USA)*
Ernesto Alexis VEGA Rojas	25.11.1997	*CD Guadalajara*

National coaches

Gerardo Daniel MARTINO (Argentina) [from 07.01.2019]	20.11.1962

MONTSERRAT

The Country:	The FA:
Montserrat	Montserrat Football Association
Capital: Plymouth	P.O. Box 505, 1250 Blakes, Plymouth
Surface: 102 km²	Year of Formation: 1994
Population: 4,649 [2019]	Member of FIFA since: 1996
Time: UTC-4	Member of CONCACAF since: 1994
Independent since: *British overseas territory*	

NATIONAL TEAM RECORDS

First international match: 10.05.1991: Saint Lucia - Montserrat 3-0
Most international caps: Not known
Most international goals: Not known

CONCACAF GOLD CUP	
1991	Qualifiers
1993	Did not enter
1996	Qualifiers
1998	Did not enter
2000	Qualifiers
2002	Qualifiers
2003	*Withdrew*
2005	Qualifiers
2007	Did not enter
2009	Did not enter
2011	Qualifiers
2013	Qualifiers
2015	Qualifiers
2017	Did not enter
2019	Qualifiers
2021	Qualifiers

FIFA WORLD CUP	
1930	-
1934	-
1938	-
1950	-
1954	-
1958	-
1962	-
1966	-
1970	-
1974	-
1978	-
1982	-
1986	-
1990	-
1994	-
1998	Did not enter
2002	Qualifiers
2006	Qualifiers
2010	Qualifiers
2014	Qualifiers
2018	Qualifiers

F.I.F.A. CONFEDERATIONS CUP 1992-2017

None

OLYMPIC FOOTBALL TOURNAMENTS 1900-2016

None

CCCF (Confederación Centroamericana y del Caribe de Fútbol) CHAMPIONSHIPS 1941-1961

None

CONCACAF CHAMPIONSHIPS 1963-1989

None

CONCACAF NATIONS LEAGUE

2019-2020	League B

CARIBBEAN CHAMPIONSHIPS 1989-2017

Year	Result	Year	Result
1989	Did not enter	1999	Qualifiers
1991	Qualifiers	2001	Qualifiers
1992	Qualifiers	2005	Qualifiers
1993	Did not enter	2007	Did not enter
1994	Qualifiers	2008	Did not enter
1995	Qualifiers	2010	Qualifiers
1996	Did not enter	2012	Qualifiers
1997	Did not enter	2014	Qualifiers
1998	Did not enter	2017	Did not enter

MONTSERRATIAN CLUB HONOURS IN CONCACAF CLUB COMPETITIONS:

CONCACAF Champions Cup / CONCACAF Champions League 1962-2020

None

CONCACAF League 2017-2020

None

Caribbean Club Championship 1997-2021

None

CONCACAF Cup Winners Cup 1991-1995*

None

Copa Interamericana 1968-1998*

None

*defunct competitions

NATIONAL COMPETITIONS
TABLE OF HONOURS

	CHAMPIONS
1995/1996	Royal Montserrat Police Force
1996/1997	*Championship cancelled*
1997/1998	*No championship*
1998/1999	*No championship*
2000	Royal Montserrat Police Force
2001	Royal Montserrat Police Force
2002/2003	Royal Montserrat Police Force
2004	Ideal SC Brades
2005	*No championship*
2006	*No championship*
2007	*No championship*
2008	*No championship*
2009	*No championship*
2010	*No championship*
2011	*No championship*
2012	*No championship*
2013	*No championship*
2014	*No championship*
2015	*No championship*
2016	Royal Montserrat Police Force FC
2017	*Not known*
2018	*Not known*
2019	*Not known*
2020	*Not known*

NATIONAL CHAMPIONSHIP 2020

No results and final tables available.

NATIONAL TEAM
INTERNATIONAL MATCHES 2020/2021

24.03.2021	Willemstad	Antigua and Barbuda - Montserrat	2-2(2-2)	(WCQ)
28.03.2021	Willemstad	Montserrat - El Salvador	1-1(0-1)	(WCQ)
02.06.2021	San Cristóbal	Montserrat - U.S. Virgin Islands	4-0(1-0)	(WCQ)
08.06.2021	St. George's	Grenada - Montserrat	1-2(0-0)	(WCQ)
02.07.2021	Fort Lauderdale	Trinidad and Tobago - Montserrat	6-1(3-0)	(GCQ)

24.03.2021, 22nd FIFA World Cup Qualifiers, CONCACAF First Round
Stadion „Ergilio Hato", Willemstad (Curaçao)
Referee: Melvin Orlando Matamoros (Honduras)
ANTIGUA AND BARBUDA - MONTSERRAT   **2-2(2-2)**
MSR: Corrin Alex Brooks-Meade, Craig Michael Braham-Barrett, Michael Williams (66.Dean Mason), Joseph Terrence Taylor, Alex Craig James Dyer (83.Bradley Maurice Woods-Garness), James Richard Comley, Rohan Greg Ince, Brandon Comley, Jamie Paul Allen, Spencer James Andrew Weir-Daley (46.Matthew Robert Whichelow), Lyle James Alfred Taylor. Trainer: William Donachie (Scotland).
Goals: Lyle James Alfred Taylor (7 penalty, 22).

28.03.2021, 22nd FIFA World Cup Qualifiers, CONCACAF First Round
Stadion „Ergilio Hato", Willemstad
Referee: Ricangel de Leça (Aruba)
MONTSERRAT - EL SALVADOR   **1-1(0-1)**
MSR: Corrin Alex Brooks-Meade, Nathan Lewis Pond, Craig Michael Braham-Barrett, Joseph Terrence Taylor, James Richard Comley, Matthew Robert Whichelow, Dean Mason (78.Alex Craig James Dyer), Rohan Greg Ince (20.Kaleem Strawbridge-Simon), Jamie Paul Allen, Brandon Comley, Lyle James Alfred Taylor. Trainer: William Donachie (Scotland).
Goal: Lyle James Alfred Taylor (89).

02.06.2021, 22nd FIFA World Cup Qualifiers, CONCACAF First Round
Estadio Panamericano, San Cristóbal (Dominican Republic)
Referee: Selvin Brown Chavarria (Honduras)
MONTSERRAT - U.S. VIRGIN ISLANDS   **4-0(1-0)**
MSR: Nicholas Taylor Mills Greaves, Nathan Lewis Pond, Craig Michael Braham-Barrett, Donervon Joseph Daniels, Joseph Terrence Taylor, James Richard Comley, Rohan Greg Ince (88.Alex Craig James Dyer), Jamie Paul Allen (81.Kaleem Strawbridge-Simon), Matthew Anthony Willock (60.Adrian Lewis Clifton), Brandon Comley, Lyle James Alfred Taylor. Trainer: William Donachie (Scotland).
Goals: Nathan Lewis Pond (39), Rohan Greg Ince (60), Adrian Lewis Clifton (67, 83).

08.06.2021, 22nd FIFA World Cup Qualifiers, CONCACAF First Round
Kirani James Athletic Stadium, St. George's; Attendance: 50
Referee: Adonai Escobedo González (Mexico)
GRENADA - MONTSERRAT   **1-2(0-0)**
MSR: Corrin Alex Brooks-Meade, Nathan Lewis Pond, Craig Michael Braham-Barrett, Joseph Terrence Taylor (59.Jernade Ronnel Meade), James Richard Comley, Dean Mason, Rohan Greg Ince, Jamie Paul Allen, Matthew Anthony Willock (59.Adrian Lewis Clifton), Lyle James Alfred Taylor, Kaleem Strawbridge-Simon (71.Alex Craig James Dyer). Trainer: William Donachie (Scotland).
Goals: Lyle James Alfred Taylor (85, 87 penalty).

02.07.2021, 16th CONCACAF Gold Cup Qualifiers, First Round
DRV PNK Stadium, Fort Lauderdale (United States); Attendance: 0
Referee: Bryan Hamed López Castellanos (Guatemala)
TRINIDAD AND TOBAGO - MONTSERRAT　　　　　　　　　　**6-1(3-0)**
MSR: Corrin Alex Brooks-Meade, Nathan Lewis Pond, Craig Michael Braham-Barrett, Joseph Terrence Taylor (46.Kaleem Strawbridge-Simon), Alex Craig James Dyer (46.Spencer James Andrew Weir-Daley), James Richard Comley, Dean Mason (85.Matthew Anthony Willock), Rohan Greg Ince, Jamie Paul Allen, Brandon Comley (46.Jernade Ronnel Meade), Lyle James Alfred Taylor. Trainer: William Donachie (Scotland).
Goal: Lyle James Alfred Taylor (55).

NATIONAL TEAM PLAYERS 2020/2021

Name	DOB	Club
Goalkeepers		
Corrin Alex BROOKS-MEADE	19.03.1988	*Oroklini-Troulloi FC 2020*
Nicholas TAYLOR Mills Greaves	20.08.1991	*Erith Town FC (ENG)*
Defenders		
Craig Michael BRAHAM-BARRETT	01.09.1988	*Dartford FC (ENG)*
Donervon Joseph DANIELS	24.11.1993	*Crewe Alexandra FC (ENG)*
Jernade Ronnel MEADE	25.10.1992	*Dartford FC (ENG)*
Nathan Lewis POND	05.01.1985	*AFC Fylde (ENG)*
Joseph Terrence "Joey" TAYLOR	18.08.1997	*Staines Town FC (ENG)*
Michael WILLIAMS	05.02.1988	*Rushall Olympic FC (ENG)*
Midfielders		
Adrian Lewis CLIFTON	12.12.1988	*Dagenham & Redbridge FC (ENG)*
Brandon COMLEY	18.11.1995	*Bolton Wanderers FC (ENG)*
James Richard COMLEY	24.01.1991	*Maidenhead United FC (ENG)*
Alex Craig James DYER	11.06.1990	*Wealdstone FC (ENG)*
Rohan Greg INCE	08.11.1992	*Maidenhead United FC (ENG)*
Dean MASON	28.02.1989	*Hayes & Yeading United FC (ENG)*
Kaleem STRAWBRIDGE-SIMON	08.07.1996	*Welling United FC (ENG)*
Matthew Robert WHICHELOW	28.09.1991	*Unattached*
Matthew Anthony WILLOCK	20.08.1996	*Gillingham FC (ENG)*
Forwards		
Jamie Paul ALLEN	25.05.1995	*FC Halifax Town (ENG)*
Lyle James Alfred TAYLOR	29.03.1990	*Nottingham Forest FC (ENG)*
Spencer James Andrew WEIR-DALEY	05.08.1985	*AFC Rushden & Diamonds (ENG)*
Bradley Maurice WOODS-GARNESS	27.06.1986	*Bedford Town FC (ENG)*
National coaches		
William DONACHIE (Scotland) [from 01.07.2018]		05.10.1951

NICARAGUA

The Country:	The FA:
República de Nicaragua (Republic of Nicaragua) Capital: Managua Surface: 130,373 km² Population: 6,486,201 [2019] Time: UTC-6	Federación Nicaragüense de Fútbol Porton Principal del Hospital Bautista, Cuadra Abajo 1, Cuadra al Sur y 1/2 Cuadra Abajo, Apartado Postal 976, Managua Year of Formation: 1931 Member of FIFA since: 1950 Member of CONCACAF since: 1961

NATIONAL TEAM RECORDS

First international match: 01.05.1929, San Salvador: El Salvador - Nicaragua 9-0
Most international caps: Josué Abraham Quijano Potosme – 70 caps (since 2011)
Most international goals: Juan Ramón Barrera Pérez – 21 goals / 63 caps (since 2009)

CONCACAF GOLD CUP	
1991	Qualifiers
1993	Qualifiers
1996	Qualifiers
1998	Qualifiers
2000	Qualifiers
2002	Qualifiers
2003	Qualifiers
2005	Qualifiers
2007	Qualifiers
2009	Final Tournament (Group Stage)
2011	Qualifiers
2013	Qualifiers
2015	Qualifiers
2017	Final Tournament (Group Stage)
2019	Final Tournament (Group Stage)
2021	Qualifiers

FIFA WORLD CUP	
1930	-
1934	-
1938	-
1950	Did not enter
1954	Did not enter
1958	Did not enter
1962	Did not enter
1966	Did not enter
1970	Did not enter
1974	Did not enter
1978	Did not enter
1982	Did not enter
1986	Did not enter
1990	Did not enter
1994	Qualifiers
1998	Qualifiers
2002	Qualifiers
2006	Qualifiers
2010	Qualifiers
2014	Qualifiers
2018	Qualifiers

F.I.F.A. CONFEDERATIONS CUP 1992-2017

None

OLYMPIC FOOTBALL TOURNAMENTS 1908-2016								
1908	-	1948	-	1972	Did not enter	1996	Did not enter
1912	-	1952	Did not enter	1976	Qualifiers	2000	Qualifiers
1920	-	1956	Did not enter	1980	Did not enter	2004	Qualifiers
1924	-	1960	Did not enter	1984	Did not enter	2008	Qualifiers
1928	-	1964	Did not enter	1988	Did not enter	2012	Qualifiers
1936	-	1968	Did not enter	1992	Did not enter	2016	Qualifiers

CCCF (Confederación Centroamericana y del Caribe de Fútbol) CHAMPIONSHIPS 1941-1961
1941, 1943, 1946, 1951 (3rd Place), 1953, 1961

CONCACAF CHAMPIONSHIPS 1963-1989
1963, 1965, 1967, 1971

CONCACAF NATIONS LEAGUE	
2019-2020	League B

COPA CENTROAMERICANA (UNCAF NATIONS CHAMPIONSHIPS) 1991-2017			
1991	Preliminary Round	2005	Final Round - Group Stage
1993	Preliminary Round	2007	Final Round - 6th Place
1995	Preliminary Round	2009	Final Round - 5th Place
1997	Final Round - Group Stage	2011	Final Round - 6th Place
1999	Final Round - Group Stage	2013	Final Round - Group Stage
2001	Final Round - Group Stage	2014	Final Round - 6th Place
2003	Final Round - 6th Place	2017	Final Round - 5th Place

NICARAGUAN CLUB HONOURS IN CONCACAF CLUB COMPETITIONS:

CONCACAF Champions Cup / CONCACAF Champions League 1962-2020
None

CONCACAF League 2017-2020
None

Caribbean Club Championship 1997-2021
None

*CONCACAF Cup Winners Cup 1991-1995**
None

*Copa Interamericana 1968-1998**
None

*defunct competitions

NATIONAL COMPETITIONS
TABLE OF HONOURS

	CHAMPIONS
1933	Alas Managua FC
1934	Club Atlético Managua FC
1935	*No competition*
1936	*No competition*
1937	*No competition*
1938	*No competition*
1939	Lido FC Managua
1940	Diriangén FC Diriamba

1941	Diriangén FC Diriamba
1942	Diriangén FC Diriamba
1943	Diriangén FC Diriamba
1944	Diriangén FC Diriamba
1945	Diriangén FC Diriamba
1946	Ferrocarril FC Managua
1947	Colegio C-A FC
1948	Ferrocarril FC Managua
1949	Diriangén FC Diriamba
1950	Aduana Managua FC
1951	Aduana Managua FC
1952	*No competition*
1953	Diriangén FC Diriamba
1954	La Salle FC
1955	Aduana Managua FC
1956	Diriangén FC Diriamba
1957	*No competition*
1958	Club Atlético Managua FC
1959	Diriangén FC Diriamba
1960	La Nica FC
1961	Santa Cecilia FC
1962	*No competition*
1963	*No competition*
1964	*No competition*
1965	Santa Cecilia FC
1966	Flor de Caña FC
1967	Flor de Caña FC
1968	Universidad Centroamericana FC Managua
1969	Diriangén FC Diriamba
1970	Diriangén FC Diriamba
1971	Santa Cecilia FC
1972	Santa Cecilia FC
1973	Santa Cecilia FC
1974	Diriangén FC Diriamba
1975	Universidad Centroamericana FC Managua
1976	Universidad Centroamericana FC Managua
1977	Universidad Centroamericana FC Managua
1978	*No competition*
1979	*No competition*
1980	Bufalos Rivas FC
1981	Diriangén FC Diriamba
1982	Diriangén FC Diriamba
1983	Diriangén FC Diriamba
1984	Deportivo Masaya
1985	América Managua FC
1986	Deportivo Masaya
1987	Diriangén FC Diriamba
1988	América Managua FC
1989	Diriangén FC Diriamba
1990	América Managua FC
1991	Real Estelí FC
1992	Diriangén FC Diriamba

1993	Juventus Managua FC
1994	Juventus Managua FC
1994/1995	Diriangén FC Diriamba
1995/1996	Diriangén FC Diriamba
1996/1997	Diriangén FC Diriamba
1997/1998	Deportivo Walter Ferretti Managua
1998/1999	Real Estelí FC
1999/2000	Diriangén FC Diriamba
2000/2001	Deportivo Walter Ferretti Managua
2001/2002	Club Deportivo Jalapa
2002/2003	Real Estelí FC
2003/2004	Ape: Real Estelí FC
	Cla: Real Estelí FC
2004/2005	Diriangén FC Diriamba
2005/2006	Diriangén FC Diriamba
2006/2007	Real Estelí FC
2007/2008	Real Estelí FC
2008/2009	Real Estelí FC
2009/2010	Real Estelí FC
2010/2011	Real Estelí FC
2011/2012	Real Estelí FC
2012/2013	Real Estelí FC
2013/2014	Real Estelí FC
2014/2015	CD Walter Ferretti Managua
2015/2016	Real Estelí FC
2016/2017	Real Estelí FC
2017/2018	Ape: CD Walter Ferretti Managua
	Cla: Diriangén FC Diriamba
2018/2019	Ape: Managua FC
	Cla: Real Estelí FC
2019/2020	Ape: Real Estelí FC
	Cla: Real Estelí FC
2020/2021	Ape: Real Estelí FC
	Cla: Diriangén FC Diriamba

Copa Nicaragua Winners:
1966: *Not known*; 1983: Deportivo Masaya; 1984: San Marcos FC; 1985: *Not known*; 1991: Real Estelí FC; 1995: San Marcos FC; 1996: Diriangén FC Diriamba; 1997: Diriangén FC Diriamba; 2005: Deportivo Masatepe.

NATIONAL CHAMPIONSHIP
Primera División de Nicaragua 2020/2021

Torneo Apertura 2020

First Stage - Results

Round 1 [01-02.08.2020]
Managua FC - CD Junior 2-0(0-0)
Real Estelí - CD Ocotal 2-1(0-0)
Walter Ferretti - Real Madriz 3-1(1-1)
Diriangén FC - Chinandega FC 2-0(1-0)
ART Municipal - Juventus FC 1-0(0-0)

Round 2 [08-09.08.2020]
Real Madriz - Diriangén FC 1-1(1-1)
Juventus FC - Walter Ferretti 1-3(1-1)
CD Junior - ART Municipal 1-0(0-0)
Chinandega FC - Real Estelí 1-5(0-2)
CD Ocotal - Managua FC 5-0(2-0)

Round 3 [12-13.08.2020]
Diriangén FC - Juventus FC 1-0(0-0)
Walter Ferretti - ART Municipal 0-0
Real Estelí - Real Madriz 2-0(1-0)
Managua FC - Chinandega FC 1-0(0-0)
CD Ocotal - CD Junior 3-1(1-0)

Round 4 [15-16.08.2020]
Real Madriz - Managua FC 0-2(0-0)
Juventus FC - Real Estelí 1-4(1-3)
Chinandega FC - CD Ocotal 4-2(1-0)
ART Municipal - Diriangén FC 2-0(2-0)
CD Junior - Walter Ferretti 0-4(0-1)

Round 5 [22-23.08.2020]
Diriangén FC - Walter Ferretti 0-1(0-0)
Managua FC - Juventus FC 0-1(0-0)
Real Estelí - ART Municipal 2-1(0-1)
Chinandega FC - CD Junior 2-2(0-0)
CD Ocotal - Real Madriz 1-1(0-1)

Round 6 [29-30.08.2020]
CD Junior - Diriangén FC 1-1(0-0)
ART Municipal - Managua FC 1-0(0-0)
Walter Ferretti - Real Estelí 0-0
Real Madriz - Chinandega FC 0-1(0-0)
Juventus FC - CD Ocotal 1-0(1-0)

Round 7 [05-06.09.2020]
Real Estelí - Diriangén FC 1-0(1-0)
Managua FC - Walter Ferretti 1-2(1-0)
Chinandega FC - Juventus FC 3-2(1-1)
Real Madriz - CD Junior 1-1(1-0)
CD Ocotal - ART Municipal 0-0

Round 8 [12-13.09.2020]
Walter Ferretti - CD Ocotal 2-0(2-0)
CD Junior - Real Estelí 0-0
Diriangén FC - Managua FC 0-0
ART Municipal - Chinandega FC 1-1(0-0)
Juventus FC - Real Madriz 1-0(1-0)

Round 9 [19-20.09.2020]
CD Ocotal - Diriangén FC 1-0(0-0)
Managua FC - Real Estelí 3-4(0-2)
Juventus FC - CD Junior 1-1(0-1)
Chinandega FC - Walter Ferretti 2-2(0-0)
Real Madriz - ART Municipal 3-0(1-0)

Round 10 [26-27.09.2020]
CD Junior - Managua FC 2-2(1-1)
CD Ocotal - Real Estelí 0-1(0-1)
Chinandega FC - Diriangén FC 1-3(0-1)
Real Madriz - Walter Ferretti 2-2(0-1)
Juventus FC - ART Municipal 2-2(1-1)

Round 11 [30.09.2020]
Managua FC - CD Ocotal 2-2(1-0)
ART Municipal - CD Junior 1-0(1-0)
Diriangén FC - Real Madriz 3-1(2-1)
Walter Ferretti - Juventus FC 0-1(0-0)
Real Estelí - Chinandega FC 3-0(1-0)

Round 12 [17-18.10.2020]
ART Municipal - Walter Ferretti 3-0(1-0)
CD Junior - CD Ocotal 1-0(0-0)
Real Madriz - Real Estelí 1-0(0-0)
Juventus FC - Diriangén FC 3-1(1-0)
Chinandega FC - Managua FC 0-0 [11.11.]

Round 13 [23-25.10.2020]
Real Estelí - Juventus FC 3-0(1-0)
Diriangén FC - ART Municipal 1-1(0-1)
Walter Ferretti - CD Junior 1-0(0-0)
CD Ocotal - Chinandega FC 1-2(0-2)
Managua FC - Real Madriz 0-1(0-0)

Round 14 [28-29.10.2020]
CD Junior - Chinandega FC 0-1(0-0)
ART Municipal - Real Estelí 1-0(0-0)
Juventus FC - Managua FC 2-3(1-2)
Walter Ferretti - Diriangén FC 0-1(0-0)
Real Madriz - CD Ocotal 0-1(0-0)

Round 15 [31.10.-01.11.2020]
Real Estelí - Walter Ferretti 1-1(1-1)
Managua FC - ART Municipal 3-1(1-1)
Diriangén FC - CD Junior 3-2(2-0)
Chinandega FC - Real Madriz 1-1(0-0)
CD Ocotal - Juventus FC 0-0

Round 16 [07-08.11.2020]
Juventus FC - Chinandega FC 5-1(3-1)
CD Junior - Real Madriz 2-2(0-2)
Walter Ferretti - Managua FC 4-2(3-1)
Diriangén FC - Real Estelí 2-2(0-1)
ART Municipal - CD Ocotal 2-0(1-0) [11.11.]

Round 17 [14-15.11.2020]
Real Madriz - Juventus FC 1-1(1-0)
CD Ocotal - Walter Ferretti 2-0(1-0)
Chinandega FC - ART Municipal 1-1(0-1)
Real Estelí - CD Junior 1-1(0-1)
Managua FC - Diriangén FC 3-4(2-1)

Round 18 [19.11.2020]
Real Estelí - Managua FC 1-0(0-0)
Diriangén FC - CD Ocotal 6-1(1-0)
CD Junior - Juventus FC 1-1(0-1)
Walter Ferretti - Chinandega FC 4-0(2-0)
ART Municipal - Real Madriz 2-1(0-1)

Final Standings

1.	Real Estelí FC	18	11	5	2	32 - 13	38
2.	CD Walter Ferretti Managua	18	9	5	4	29 - 17	32
3.	ART Municipal Jalapa	18	8	6	4	20 - 15	30
4.	Diriangén FC Diriamba	18	8	5	5	29 - 21	29
5.	Juventus FC Managua	18	6	5	7	23 - 25	23
6.	Chinandega FC	18	5	6	7	21 - 35	21
7.	CD Ocotal	18	5	4	9	20 - 25	19
8.	Managua FC	18	5	4	9	24 - 30	19
9.	Real Madriz FC Somoto	18	3	7	8	17 - 24	16
10.	CD Junior de Managua	18	2	9	7	16 - 26	15

Top-2 teams qualified for the Semi-Finals, while teams ranked 3-6 were qualified for the Quarter-Finals.

Apertura Play-offs

Quarter-Finals / Repechajes [22.11.2020]
ART Municipal Jalapa - Chinandega FC 0-2(0-2)
Diriangén FC Diriamba - Juventus FC Managua 2-0(2-0)

Semi-Finals [28.11.-06.12.2020]
Diriangén FC Diriamba - CD Walter Ferretti Managua 3-2(0-2) 3-1(2-0)
Chinandega FC - Real Estelí FC 2-2(0-1) 0-1(0-1)

Championship Finals

13.12.2020, Estadio „Cacique Diriangén", Diriamba; Attendance: 0
Referee: Erick Lezama
Diriangén FC Diriamba - Real Estelí FC **0-0**
Diriangén: Justo Llorente Collado, Erick José Téllez Fonseca, Josué Calderón (62.Agner Jonathan Acuña Álvarez), Erick Mendoza Fariñas, Jason Eliézer Coronel Martínez, Misael Álvarez, José Bernardo Laureiro Alves, Alexis Damián Ramos (86.Jonathan Alexander Zapata Palacios), Luis Fernando Coronel Martínez, Maycon de Jesus Santana, Jeffrey Misael Chávez López. Trainer: Flavio Rego Da Silva (Brazil).
Real Estelí: Rodrigo Pérez Romo, Rodrigo José Bronzatti, Marlon Andrés López Moreno, Josué Abraham Quijano Potosme, Manuel Rosas Arreola (69.Óscar Acevedo), Oscar Renan López, Juan Ramón Barrera Pérez, Luis Alberto Acuña (77.Jorge Andrés Betancur Bustamante), Richard Andrés Rodríguez Alvéz, Henry García, Edgar Josué Castillo Bellorin (46.Brandon Ayerdis). Trainer: Holver Flores.

20.12.2020, Estádio Nacional, Managua; Attendance: 0
Referee: Nitzar Antonio Sandoval Chávez
Real Estelí FC - Diriangén FC Diriamba **1-0(0-0)**
Real Estelí: Rodrigo Pérez Romo, Rodrigo José Bronzatti, Josué Abraham Quijano Potosme, Manuel Rosas Arreola, Óscar Acevedo [*sent off on the bench 82*] (71.Francisco Esteban Paz), Juan Ramón Barrera Pérez, Yohn Géiler Mosquera Martínez, Richard Andrés Rodríguez Alvéz, Harold Medina, Henry García (78.Carlos Alberto Chavarria Rodríguez), Jorge Andrés Betancur Bustamante (80.Luis Alfredo López). Trainer: Holver Flores.
Diriangén: Justo Llorente Collado, Erick José Téllez Fonseca, Josué Calderón (46.Alexander Zúñiga), Jason Eliézer Coronel Martínez (85.Víctor Armando Parrales Espinoza), Erick Mendoza Fariñas (76.Agner Jonathan Acuña Álvarez), Misael Álvarez, José Bernardo Laureiro Alves, Alexis Damián Ramos, Luis Fernando Coronel Martínez, Maycon de Jesus Santana, Jeffrey Misael Chávez López. Trainer: Flavio Rego Da Silva (Brazil).
Goal: 1-0 Manuel Rosas Arreola (68).

Torneo Apertura 2020 Winners: **Real Estelí FC**

Best goalscorer Apertura 2020: Juan Ramón Barrera Pérez (Real Estelí FC) – 13 goals

Torneo Clausura 2021

First Stage - Results

Round 1 [23-24.01.2021]
CD Junior - Managua FC 1-3(0-1)
Juventus FC - ART Municipal 3-1
Real Madriz - Walter Ferretti 1-1(1-1)
Chinandega FC - Diriangén FC 0-3(0-1)
CD Ocotal - Real Estelí 0-1(0-0)

Round 2 [27-28.01.2021]
Managua FC - CD Ocotal 3-0(2-0)
ART Municipal - CD Junior 1-1(0-1)
Diriangén FC - Real Madriz 4-0(0-0)
Walter Ferretti - Juventus FC 1-0(0-0)
Chinandega FC - Real Estelí 2-4(0-3)

Round 3 [31.01.-01.02.2021]
ART Municipal - Walter Ferretti 2-0(2-0)
CD Junior - CD Ocotal 0-0
Juventus FC - Diriangén FC 1-0(0-0)
Chinandega FC - Managua FC 1-1(0-1)
Real Madriz - Real Estelí 0-1(0-0)

Round 4 [03-04.02.2021]
Managua FC - Real Madriz 4-1(0-1)
Diriangén FC - ART Municipal 2-0(0-0)
CD Ocotal - Chinandega FC 0-0
Walter Ferretti - CD Junior 2-0(2-0)
Juventus FC - Real Estelí 0-1(0-0)

Round 5 [06-07.02.2021]
CD Junior - Chinandega FC 2-1(1-0)
Real Madriz - CD Ocotal 1-2(0-1)
Walter Ferretti - Diriangén FC 2-0(2-0)
Juventus FC - Managua FC 0-5(0-2)
ART Municipal - Real Estelí 2-1(1-0)

Round 6 [10-11.02.2021]
Managua FC - ART Municipal 5-2(4-2)
CD Ocotal - Juventus FC 1-0(0-0)
Diriangén FC - CD Junior 2-0(0-0)
Walter Ferretti - Real Estelí 0-1(0-0)
Chinandega FC - Real Madriz 1-2(1-2)

Round 7 [13-14.02.2021]
ART Municipal - CD Ocotal 3-3(0-1)
Diriangén FC - Real Estelí 1-0(1-0)
Walter Ferretti - Managua FC 2-1(0-1)
Juventus FC - Chinandega FC 1-3(0-1)
CD Junior - Real Madriz 1-0(0-0)

Round 8 [17-18.02.2021]
Managua FC - Diriangén FC 1-3(0-1)
CD Ocotal - Walter Ferretti 3-0(1-0)
Real Estelí - CD Junior 7-0(1-0)
Chinandega FC - ART Municipal 1-1(0-0)
Real Madriz - Juventus FC 2-1(1-0)

Round 9 [27-28.02.2021]
ART Municipal - Real Madriz 4-1(1-1)
Walter Ferretti - Chinandega FC 5-1(3-1)
Real Estelí - Managua FC 1-1(0-1)
Diriangén FC - CD Ocotal 0-1(0-1)
CD Junior - Juventus FC 1-2(0-0)

Round 10 [06-07.03.2021]
Walter Ferretti - Real Madriz 2-0(1-0)
Real Estelí - CD Ocotal 1-1(0-0)
Managua FC - CD Junior 3-1(2-0)
ART Municipal - Juventus FC 1-0(0-0)
Diriangén FC - Chinandega FC 3-0(1-0)

Round 11 [13-14.03.2021]
Real Madriz - Diriangén FC 1-2(0-1)
CD Junior - ART Municipal 2-1(0-1)
Real Estelí - Chinandega FC 4-1(2-0)
Juventus FC - Walter Ferretti 1-2(1-0)
CD Ocotal - Managua FC 1-0(1-0)

Round 12 [31.03.2021]
Walter Ferretti - ART Municipal 4-0(0-0)
CD Ocotal - CD Junior 2-1(2-0)
Diriangén FC - Juventus FC 4-2(2-1)
Real Estelí - Real Madriz 0-3 *awarded*
Managua FC - Chinandega FC 3-1(2-1)

Round 13 [09-14.04.2021]
CD Junior - Walter Ferretti 1-1(1-0)
Chinandega - CD Ocotal 2-1(1-1)
ART Municipal - Diriangén FC 0-2(0-0)
Real Madriz - Managua FC 1-0(0-0)
Real Estelí - Juventus FC 4-0(3-0) [22.04.]

Round 14 [17-19.04.2021]
CD Ocotal - Real Madriz 1-1(0-1)
Diriangén FC - Walter Ferretti 1-1(1-0)
Chinandega - CD Junior 2-1(1-0)
Managua FC - Juventus FC 4-1(1-0)
Real Estelí - ART Municipal 1-0(0-0)

Round 15 [24-25.04.2021]
CD Junior - Diriangén FC 0-1(0-0)
Real Madriz - Chinandega 2-0(0-0)
Juventus FC - CD Ocotal 3-1(2-0)
ART Municipal - Managua FC 2-2(1-2)
Real Estelí - Walter Ferretti 2-1(1-1)

Round 16 [28-29.04.2021]
Real Madriz - CD Junior 1-2(0-0)
Real Estelí - Diriangén FC 3-0(2-0)
Managua FC - Walter Ferretti 3-1(1-0)
Chinandega - Juventus FC 0-0
CD Ocotal - ART Municipal 2-0(1-0)

Round 17 [01-02.05.2021]
Diriangén FC - Managua FC 4-1(3-1)
CD Junior - Real Estelí 0-2(0-0)
Juventus FC - Real Madriz 0-0
ART Municipal - Chinandega 1-1(0-1)
Walter Ferretti - CD Ocotal 1-0(1-0)

Round 18 [05-06.05.2021]
Real Madriz - ART Municipal 1-0(1-0)
Chinandega - Walter Ferretti 0-3(0-3)
Juventus FC - CD Junior 2-2(2-2)
Managua FC - Real Estelí 1-0(0-0)
CD Ocotal - Diriangén FC 3-4(1-0)

Final Standings

1.	Diriangén FC Diriamba	18	13	1	4	36 - 16	40
2.	Real Estelí FC	18	12	2	4	34 - 13	38
3.	Managua FC	18	10	3	5	41 - 23	33
4.	CD Walter Ferretti Managua	18	10	3	5	29 - 17	33
5.	CD Ocotal	18	7	5	6	22 - 21	26
6.	Real Madriz FC Somoto	18	6	3	9	18 - 26	21
7.	ART Municipal Jalapa	18	4	5	9	21 - 32	17
8.	CD Junior de Managua	18	4	4	10	16 - 33	16
9.	Juventus FC Managua	18	4	3	11	17 - 33	15
10.	Chinandega FC	18	3	5	10	17 - 37	14

Top-2 teams were qualified for the Semi-Finals, while teams ranked 3-6 were qualified for the Quarter-Finals / Repechajes.

Clausura Play-offs

Quarter-Finals / Repechajes [09.05.2021]
CD Walter Ferretti Managua - CD Ocotal   3-0(0-0)
Managua FC - Real Madriz FC Somoto   1-0(0-0)

Semi-Finals [12-16.05.2021]
CD Walter Ferretti Managua - Diriangén FC Diriamba   1-0(0-0)   0-3(0-1)
Managua FC - Real Estelí FC   3-1(0-1)   2-4(0-1)

Finals

22.05.2021, Estádio Nacional, Managua; Attendance: 0
Referee: Tatiana Guzmán Alguera
Managua FC - Diriangén FC Diriamba   **0-2(0-0)**
Managua: Erly Rolando Méndez Ocampo, Christiam Quinto, Wesner Antonio De Trinidad (54.Darwin Contreras), Rigoberto Fuentes Galeano, Márcio Leandro Barbosa da Silveira, Kevin José Serapio Oviedo, Ulises Emanuel Pozo Jiménez (67.Nahúm Elieth Peralta Arce), Agenor Báez Cano, Lucas Michel dos Santos Oliveira, Edward Enrique Morillo Jimenéz, Miguel Ángel Guerrero Bustos (54.Pablo Gállego Lardiés). Trainer: Emilio Aburto.
Diriangén: Justo Llorente Collado, Erick José Téllez Fonseca, Erick Mendoza Fariñas (84.David Emmanuel Jarquin Salazar), Jeffrey Misael Chávez López (82.Alexander Zúñiga), Yohn Géiler Mosquera Martínez, Jason Eliézer Coronel Martínez, Josué Calderón (46.Jaime José Moreno Ciorciari), Robinson Luiz da Silva, José Bernardo Laureiro Alves, Luis Fernando Coronel Martínez, Maycon de Jesus Santana. Trainer: Flavio Rego Da Silva (Brazil).
Goals: 0-1 Robinson Luiz da Silva (65), 0-2 Robinson Luiz da Silva (69).

29.05.2021, Estadio „Cacique Diriangén", Diriamba; Attendance: 0
Referee: Nitzar Antonio Sandoval Chávez
Diriangén FC Diriamba - Managua FC   **1-1(1-0)**
Diriangén: Justo Llorente Collado, Erick José Téllez Fonseca, Erick Mendoza Fariñas, Jeffrey Misael Chávez López (48.Jaime José Moreno Ciorciari), Yohn Géiler Mosquera Martínez, Jason Eliézer Coronel Martínez (85.Marel Álvarez), Josué Calderón (76.Tulio López González), Robinson Luiz da Silva, José Bernardo Laureiro Alves, Luis Fernando Coronel Martínez, Maycon de Jesus Santana [*sent off 86*]. Trainer: Flavio Rego Da Silva (Brazil).
Managua: Erly Rolando Méndez Ocampo, Rigoberto Fuentes Galeano (75.Ulises Emanuel Pozo Jiménez), Márcio Leandro Barbosa da Silveira, Kevin José Serapio Oviedo, Agenor Báez Cano, Danilo Zuñiga Araúz, Nahúm Elieth Peralta Arce (58.Darwin Contreras), Pablo Gállego Lardiés, Lucas Michel dos Santos Oliveira, Edward Enrique Morillo Jimenéz, Miguel Ángel Guerrero Bustos. Trainer: Emilio Aburto.
Goals: 1-0 Maycon de Jesus Santana (40), 1-1 Edward Enrique Morillo Jimenéz (81).

Torneo Clausura 2021 Winners: **Diriangén FC Diriamba**
Best goalscorer Clausura 2021: Lucas Michel dos Santos Oliveira (BRA, Managua FC) – 16 goals

Aggregate Table 2020/2021

1.	Real Estelí FC	36	23	7	6	66 - 26	76
2.	Diriangén FC Diriamba	36	21	6	9	65 - 37	69
3.	CD Walter Ferretti Managua	36	19	8	9	58 - 34	65
4.	ART Municipal Jalapa	36	16	11	13	41 - 47	59
5.	Managua FC	36	15	7	14	65 - 53	52
6.	CD Ocotal	36	12	9	15	42 - 46	45
7.	Juventus FC Managua	36	10	8	18	40 - 58	38
8.	Real Madriz FC Somoto	36	9	10	17	35 - 50	37
9.	Chinandega FC (*Promotion/Relegation Play-Off*)	36	8	11	17	38 - 72	35
10.	CD Junior de Managua (*Relegated*)	36	6	13	17	32 - 59	31

Relegation Play-offs [20-26.06.2021]

H6H Export Sébaco FC - Chinandega FC   2-0(1-0)   3-3(0-1)

THE CLUBS 2020/2021

Please note: number of matches, subtitutes and goals are including Apertura + Clausura + Play-offs!

ART MUNICIPAL JALAPA

Year of Formation: 2011
Stadium: Estadio "Alejandro Ramos Turcio", Jalapa (2,000)

THE SQUAD

	DOB	Ape M	(s)	G	Cla M	(s)	G
Goalkeepers:							
Fredman Castillo	21.09.1990	2			11		
Henry Alberto Maradiaga Galeano	05.02.1990	17			7		
Defenders:							
Adolfo Colindres	11.06.1996	15			11	(1)	1
Marcos García	02.05.1998	15			9	(2)	2
Marlon José Medina García	06.03.1985	18		1	14	(2)	1
Edder Jesus Mondragón Garcia (MEX)	15.11.1992	16		3	10	(2)	
Eddy Nicoya	18.05.2001	8	(3)		11	(2)	2
Gersan Ramos Medina		2	(7)		3	(5)	
Delvin David Siles	27.09.1995	8	(4)		1	(1)	
Bismarck Antonio Véliz Gómez	10.09.1993	11	(2)		11	(1)	1
Midfielders:							
Jeffrey Alfonso Araica Hernández	18.01.1990	3	(5)		7	(8)	
Acner Arvizu Blandon						(1)	
Luis Borge		18	(1)	1	4	(1)	
Mario Briones	03.09.2000	1			12		
José Carlos Gutiérrez					11		
Mykael Antonio Montiel	27.01.1990	15			8	(1)	
Manuel Rocha	03.01.1999				1		
Rony Talavera Duarte	08.05.1994		(3)			(2)	
Forwards:							
Edry Centeno	19.04.2001	10	(4)	1	17		2
Gabriel de Oliveira Coelho (BRA)	22.02.1993	13	(1)	1			
Luis Manuel Galeano Molina	15.10.1991	13	(1)	7	14	(1)	5
Kevin Gutiérrez					2		
Hexell López	09.01.2000		(6)		4	(4)	
Harling Moreno	08.04.1997	4			2	(6)	1
Ronaldo Luis Pabón Arévalo (COL)	03.02.1998	6	(8)	2			
Yeiner Vivas (COL)	28.12.1994				12	(5)	2
Brayan Xavier Zuñiga Ortéz (HON)	01.12.1995	14	(2)	4	16	(1)	4
Trainer:							
Carlos Javier Martino (ARG)	20.05.1975	19			18		

CHINANDEGA FÚTBOL CLUBE

Year of Formation: 1975
Stadium: Estadio "Efraín Tijerino Mazariego" / Estadio La Veranera, Chinandega (8,000 / 800)

THE SQUAD

	DOB	Ape M	(s)	G	Cla M	(s)	G
Goalkeepers:							
Mashuel Aaron Amador Álvarez	05.12.1993	5			1		
Brayan de Jesús Cañate Orozco (COL)	12.09.1994	16	(1)		17		
Defenders:							
Ervin José Aguirre	17.03.1991	19			14		
Cristian Manuel Cabria Julio	25.05.1992	20		2	13		3
Gerson Castillo						(1)	
Mario Huete						(2)	
Daniel Rodríguez	25.07.1999	20		1	11	(1)	
Nasser Iván Valverde Baltodano	04.01.1993	1	(5)				
Kevin Venerio	28.06.1999	11	(2)	1	14		1
Midfielders:							
Erick Alberto Alcázar Iriarte (COL)	20.09.1987	12	(6)	8	14	(3)	4
Ariacny Abnel Alvarado Pineda	15.07.1984	15	(1)		12	(2)	
Lester José Espinoza Morán	23.09.1987	19			17		1
José Luis Loaisiga Acosta	24.06.1995	12	(3)		9	(4)	
Yadder López						(1)	
Alejandro Meléndez	16.05.2001		(1)				
Pedro Méndez	04.12.2001	1			2		
José Ángel Molina Ramírez	21.04.1989	8	(2)		5	(1)	1
Edgar Olaguez Urbina (MEX)	11.07.1997				10	(5)	2
Roberto Rodríguez		18		1	17		
Jorge Vega	20.03.1997	1					
Francisco Zeledón	05.07.2000	3				(3)	
Forwards:							
Francisco Acosta						(1)	
Marlon Rafael Barrios Pérez (COL)	12.12.1986	5	(7)	2			
Lesther Francisco Bonilla Miranda	01.04.1992		(1)		5	(2)	
Óscar García	18.01.1993				3	(2)	1
Kevin Gómez					4	(2)	
Josué Benjamín Gutiérrez Medrano	15.08.1994	3	(7)	1	2	(3)	
Jessie Jafett López Hogson	24.10.1990		(2)				
Erling Morán	24.12.1984	9	(4)	2	15	(1)	3
Jorge Nuñez	26.02.1994		(1)				
Wilson Osorio						(4)	
Eulises Ezequiel Pavón Alvarado	06.01.1993	11	(5)	2			
Duver Quiñones (COL)	18.06.1998	20		4	13	(3)	
José Torres	22.01.1995	1	(7)				
Luis Manuel Zeledón Oporta	30.01.1994	1					
Trainer:							
Reyna Espinoza		21			18		

DIRIANGÉN FÚTBOL CLUB DIRIAMBA

Year of Formation: 1917
Stadium: Estadio „Cacique Diriangén", Diriamba (7,500)

THE SQUAD	DOB	Ape M	(s)	G	Cla M	(s)	G
Goalkeepers:							
Ronaldo Espinoza	03.07.1999	5			3		
Justo Llorente Collado	27.02.1994	18			19		
Defenders:							
Marel Álvarez (HON)	19.08.1995	3			8	(5)	
Misael Álvarez	13.09.2000	18		3			
Kevin González Chavarría	23.02.1995	7	(2)				
Jeffrey Misael Chávez López	10.02.1997				17		
Kevin González Chavarría	23.02.1995				3	(3)	
David Emmanuel Jarquin Salazar	07.06.1997	8	(1)		7	(4)	1
Erick Mendoza Fariñas	23.04.1993	17	(2)		14	(4)	
Daron Patterson	04.09.2003	2					
Erick José Téllez Fonseca	28.01.1989	13			19		
Anyelo Velásquez	22.12.2004	2			1		
Midfielders:							
Abner Jonathan Acuña Álvarez	05.03.1997	4	(11)	2	3	(9)	1
Josué Calderón	30.05.2002	11			20		1
Jason Eliézer Coronel Martínez	06.10.1993	14			17	(1)	
Marcelo Cruz	05.03.2001	2					
Mario Dávila	07.11.1997				3		
Elyin Hernández	07.03.2000	7	(3)		3	(2)	
Jeremias Hurtado		2					
Tulio López González	22.02.1996	9	(3)	1	3	(7)	
Yohn Géiler Mosquera Martínez (COL)	15.04.1989				18		2
Carlos Muñoz					1		
Jonathan Pacheco (ARG)	08.05.1992				3		1
Víctor Armando Parrales Espinoza	06.04.1991	5	(7)	1			
Pedro Augusto Dos Santos Souza "Pedrinho" (BRA)	21.11.1991	16	(3)			(1)	
Bryant Román	13.05.2001	1	(2)				
Cristofer Sánchez Jarquin		1					
Jonathan Alexander Zapata Palacios	03.10.1994	4	(5)		5	(1)	
Forwards:							
Cristóbal Ramón Aragón Sánchez	27.01.1999	1	(4)				
Josué Arias Téllez	05.02.2002	3					
Jeffrey Misael Chávez López	10.02.1997	15	(2)				
Luis Fernando Coronel Martínez	25.02.1997	19	(2)	8	13	(6)	3
Álvaro Nadyr Hernández Sevilla	20.10.1999	2					
José Bernardo Laureiro Alves (URU)	02.02.1992	19	(1)	5	16	(2)	5
Maycon de Jesus Santana (BRA)	11.07.1992	15	(3)	8	20		13
Jaime José Moreno Ciorciari	30.03.1995				12	(4)	5
Alexis Damián Ramos (ARG)	13.04.1989	6	(4)	6			
Robinson Luiz da Silva (BRA)	26.04.1985				14	(4)	7
Amilkar Talavera	13.11.1996					(2)	
Alexander Zúñiga	23.03.2001	4	(8)			(11)	2
Trainer:							
Flavio Rego Da Silva (BRA)	10.06.1973	23			22		

CORPORACIÓN DEPORTIVA JUNIOR DE MANAGUA

Year of Formation: 2016
Stadium: Estadio Nacional de Fútbol de Nicaragua, Managua (20,000)

THE SQUAD

	DOB	Ape M	(s)	G	Cla M	(s)	G
Goalkeepers:							
Lester José Acevedo García	20.03.1992				6		
Jeremy Espinoza	13.05.2001	8			2		
Kevin Sánchez Muñoz	13.06.1994	4					
Diedrich Erwing Téllez Cuevas	31.10.1984	6			10		
Defenders:							
Carlos Brenes	25.05.1992				11		
Steven Cáceres	14.09.1994	18		3	17		1
Cyril Alexander Errington Rodríguez (SLV)	30.03.1992				4		
Wesly Gómez	21.03.1997	11					
Ronald López	23.04.2001	7	(2)	1	15		
Estarling Gabriel Mercado Acuña	25.11.1999				13	(3)	
Samuel Alexander Padilla	19.12.2001	11	(2)		3	(3)	1
Wilder Alfredo Wilson Pérez	01.07.2000	13	(1)	2			
Midfielders:							
José Antonia Carrion Mayorga	20.03.1989	2					
Stward Castillo	10.02.2000	1	(2)		14		
Mike Cruz	19.07.1994	6	(5)	1			
Luis Gaitan	19.01.1998	12	(3)		9	(2)	
Fernando García					1		
Joshua Guadamuz					1	(1)	
Carlos Alexei Membreño Callejas	19.12.1988	10	(2)				
Bismarck René Montiel Avalos	05.03.1995	18		2	15	(1)	5
Olsztyn Eliezer Reyes	16.05.1997	16			12	(3)	5
Yuran Rodríguez Galeano		6	(1)		2		
Bryant Román	13.05.2001				1	(6)	
Oscar Soto	05.03.1998	4	(3)	1	8	(3)	
Marcos Antonio Zambrana García	31.08.1993	1			10	(4)	
Forwards:							
Cristóbal Ramón Aragón Sanchez	27.01.1999				4	(4)	1
José Baltodano	15.09.1994	4	(5)	1			
Adolfo Bermúdez	06.12.1995				1	(5)	
Pedro Espinoza	31.05.1998		(3)				
Francisco González	16.08.1998				1		
José González	25.07.1994		(5)		3	(5)	
Luis Gutiérrez	19.02.1995	1	(4)	2	5	(2)	
Álvaro Nadyr Hernández Sevilla	20.10.1999				14	(1)	1
Eduardo Narváez	02.11.1999	9	(7)		4	(5)	
Cristian Ortega		2	(1)				
Juan Carlos Rosales	18.12.1991	10	(4)	2	1		
Francisco Sánchez		7		1	4		
Isaac Sequeira	17.10.1999	11	(2)		7	(1)	
Jhonson Ugarte						(1)	1
Trainer:							
Tyron Manuel Acevedo Selva	12.07.1978	18			18		

JUVENTUS FÚTBOL CLUB MANAGUA

Year of Formation: 1977
Stadium: Estadio "Arnoldo y Matty Chávez", Managua (2,000)

THE SQUAD

	DOB	Ape M	(s)	G	Cla M	(s)	G
Goalkeepers:							
Denillson Javier Gutiérrez Narvaez	14.05.1999	5	(1)				
Alyer López	16.05.1999	14			18		
Defenders:							
Julio Barrios					2		
Julio Ricardo Bernàrdez Barrios (HON)	27.06.1989				6	(1)	
Carlos Brenes	25.05.1992		(1)				
Jason Domingo Casco Juárez	13.02.1990	7					
William España	26.02.1993	6	(5)		17		
Bosco Gabriel García Mojica	27.10.1994	14			10	(1)	
Diego León	19.07.1996	2					
Henry Mayorga	15.08.2000	13	(1)		8	(1)	
Alexander Moreno (PAR)		9		1	9	(1)	1
Rafael Vieira Moreira (BRA)	15.08.1988	15		1	18		
Aldryn Ramírez	13.01.1995	3			1	(3)	
Midfielders:							
Junior Noel Arteaga Pineda	09.12.1999	17		6	12	(1)	1
Engel Balladares	03.09.2001	1					
Damie Bolaños Mayorga	21.10.2000	7	(1)		3	(3)	
Leonardo Bonilla	03.09.2002	9		1	8	(2)	
David Andrés Castrillón Tamayo (COL)	18.05.1994				13	(3)	3
Christian Euseda Giron		5	(3)				
Emanuel García	12.08.1997	2	(15)		11	(6)	1
Carlos Guevara	14.04.1999				3	(3)	
Francisco Hernández	06.10.1995	4					
Elmer Antonio Mejía Rodríguez (HON)	23.06.1978	12		2			
Néstor Olivares	29.08.2002				7	(1)	
Jorjavio Ríos	12.02.2000	3	(1)		2		
Marvin Robles	01.10.2001				1		
Cristopher Rodríguez	01.02.1992	9	(2)	3	16	(1)	2
Forwards:							
Adrian Chavarria					4	(5)	4
Carlos Félix Gámez (MEX)	14.05.1991				7	(1)	1
Jorge García Hurtado	27.08.1998	3	(2)	1			
Carlos Fernando Guardado Valdez	26.11.2000	8	(2)	2	2	(2)	1
Fernando Salvador Insaurralde Cantero (PAR)	05.06.1995	10	(3)				
Cesar Lacayo	22.05.1997	2	(2)	1			
Patrick Luna	09.08.1997	3	(3)		4	(4)	
Allan Mercado	22.02.1998	5	(1)	1			
Elmer Pastrán	18.10.2000	5	(7)	4	8	(6)	2
Ulises Antonio Rayo López	12.01.1994	2	(3)				
Mario Solórzano	26.06.2001	7	(3)		2	(1)	
Francisco Vallecillo	20.10.2002	7			6		
Trainer:							
Óscar Blanco		19			18		

MANAGUA FÚTBOL CLUB

Year of Formation: 2006
Stadium: Estadio Nacional de Fútbol de Nicaragua, Managua (20,000)

THE SQUAD

	DOB	Ape M	(s)	G	Cla M	(s)	G
Goalkeepers:							
Lester José Acevedo García	20.03.1992	11					
Gustavo Silva Pires (BRA)	16.03.1992				8		
Erly Rolando Méndez Ocampo	19.05.1988	7			15	(1)	
Defenders:							
Modesto Efren Agurcia Gutiérrez	01.06.1998	1	(5)				
Justing Cano					8		1
Wesner Antonio De Trinidad	10.11.1995	13	(2)		14	(1)	
Rigoberto Fuentes Galeano	11.02.1990	15	(2)	2	18	(3)	
Doslin García						(1)	
Marcos Francisco Gonzalez Ojeda (PAR)	15.07.1995	8	(1)				
Andy Josué Herrera	15.04.1997	3	(1)				
Márcio Leandro Barbosa da Silveira (BRA)	13.07.1988				20		2
Camphers Pérez	13.05.1998	10	(2)		12	(1)	
Christiam Quinto	17.01.2001	8	(1)		11	(3)	
Jonathan Sánchez	01.11.2001	3					
Midfielders:							
Agenor Báez Cano	18.12.1997	5	(5)		15	(4)	3
Darwin Contreras	03.08.2000				6	(7)	
Isaac Correa					1		
Jeremy Cuarezma	28.05.2000	4	(2)		4	(4)	
Nahúm Elieth Peralta Arce	21.10.1994	9	(2)	2	13	(6)	5
Ulises Emanuel Pozo Jiménez	22.02.1992	14	(1)		6	(9)	
Kevin José Serapio Oviedo	09.04.1996	15	(1)	1	20	(1)	1
Danilo Zuñiga Araúz	04.06.1997	14	(3)	4	13	(5)	2
Forwards:							
Brayan Josué Castillo Arzú (HON)	05.06.1998	2	(4)	1			
Leandro Figueroa (ARG)	28.03.1993	11	(4)				
Pablo Gállego Lardiés (ESP)	01.10.1993	16	(1)	9	12	(8)	6
Miguel Ángel Guerrero Bustos	06.08.2001	15	(2)	2	15	(3)	3
Lucas Michel dos Santos Oliveira (BRA)	10.04.1994				21	(1)	16
Ricardo Mendieta Dolmos	18.01.1995	6	(8)	2		(3)	1
Edward Enrique Morillo Jimenéz (VEN)	28.07.1995				19	(4)	7
Salomón Palacios	12.12.2000		(2)		2	(2)	
Diego Peláez Silva (ESP)	18.05.1989	8	(1)				
Trainer:							
Emilio Aburto		18			23		

CLUB DEPORTIVO OCOTAL

Year of Formation: 2002
Stadium: Estadio "Roy Fernando Bermúdez", Ocotal (3,000)

THE SQUAD

	DOB	Ape M	(s)	G	Cla M	(s)	G
Goalkeepers:							
Sebastián Alzáte (COL)					5		
Kenet Bautista	23.10.1999	4	(1)		14		
Ricky Inestroza	14.06.1998	1					
Carlos Didier Mosquera Murillo (COL)	23.06.1991	13					
Defenders:							
Jorge Ellis	07.12.1992	13			1		
Jaime Rafael Fernández García	14.08.1995	1		1			
Alvaro Figueroa	17.03.1998	12		1	13	(1)	1
Allan Gutiérrez (HON)	12.01.1992	6	(3)				
Manuel Salvador Gutiérrez Castro	20.01.1987	10	(1)				
Junior Lanuza	30.06.1984	9	(1)	1			
Jermar López					2		
Guillermo Alfonso Meléndez Vargas (COL)	15.11.1994	3					
Joel Isaac Obando	20.11.2000	11	(2)		13	(1)	1
Gabriel Eduardo Ortíz Jiménez (HON)	09.02.1998				13	(3)	1
Keveen Alberto Torres Urbina	19.05.1998				6	(4)	
Doriam Velasquez	14.07.1998	9			7		
Midfielders:							
Wilson Aleman					1		
Edwin Álvarez (HON)		15		4		(1)	
Jareck Cáceres	10.01.2003	16	(1)	3	16	(2)	3
Walter Chávez (HON)		14	(2)	5	1		
Leyvin Cruz	07.10.1995				1	(2)	
Kevin Noe Meraz Arias (HON)	29.06.1993	1					
Norlan Martínez						(1)	
Jonathan Enrique Moncada Zeledón	03.01.1998	12		1			
Josué Morales	03.03.2000				7	(6)	
Ariel Iván Rodríguez Alvarado	07.01.1999	3			3	(1)	
Pablo Rodríguez	14.06.2000				8	(2)	
Saddys Alexander Sandoval Fletes	16.02.1992	1	(5)				
Maberin Urtecho	01.10.1997	1					
Francisco Valdivia	08.01.1998				8	(2)	
Victor Zavala	18.12.1994	16			17		
Forwards:							
Diego Arismendi (COL)	17.09.1997				11	(3)	4
Daniel Cadena Sánchez	09.02.1987				13	(2)	4
Juan Manuel Cervellón	11.03.2002	2	(1)			(1)	
Víctor Escoto	08.03.1999	1					
Carlos Gómez			(3)				
Bancy Hernández		8	(7)		18		2
Yomar Yasir Martínez Herrera	25.11.1999		(10)	1	2	(6)	
Ismael Antonio Mendieta Dolmo	20.02.2001	13	(2)	3	8	(4)	2
Jeimar Renteria (COL)					7	(6)	2
Daniel Salvador Reyes Avellán	21.07.1990	2	(5)				
Leonardo Tercero		1	(1)				
Angel Gustavo Velásquez Rodríguez (HON)	24.06.1993				14		2

Trainer:		
Marcos Rivera	18	
[01.2021] Mario José Alfaro Mercado		19

REAL ESTELÍ FÚTBOL CLUB

Year of Formation: 1960
Stadium: Estadio Independencia, Estelí (4,800)

THE SQUAD

	DOB	Ape M	(s)	G	Cla M	(s)	G
Goalkeepers:							
Denver Fox	24.04.1996	9			12		
Jeann Francisco Iglesias	27.11.2003	2					
Rodrigo Pérez Romo (ESP)	23.10.1991	11			1		
Álvaro Gabriel Rezzano (ARG)	07.07.1994				7	(1)	
Defenders:							
Óscar Acevedo	18.03.1997	14	(3)	1	13	(1)	1
Rodrigo José Bronzatti (BRA)	06.12.1986	9	(1)	1	12	(1)	1
Cristian Mauriel Gutiérrez Peralta	06.01.1993	12		1	1	(3)	
Engels Rizo López	11.05.1995					(1)	
Luis Alfredo López	11.09.1998	6	(6)		4	(3)	1
Oscar Renan López	27.02.1992	10	(1)		13	(1)	
Francisco Esteban Paz	07.08.1982	4	(5)		7	(6)	
Josué Abraham Quijano Potosme	10.03.1991	16	(2)	2	16	(1)	
Manuel Rosas Arreola	14.10.1983	17	(2)	1	13	(1)	
Midfielders:							
Luis Alberto Acuña (ARG)	20.01.1989	10	(7)	3	7	(10)	2
Brandon Ayerdis	11.09.1999	10	(7)	5	1	(5)	1
Jorge Andrés Betancur Bustamante (COL)	19.08.1991	13	(4)	1	16	(3)	
Henry García	03.08.1991	14	(3)	1	10	(1)	2
Marlon Andrés López Moreno	02.11.1992	8	(4)		12		
Harold Medina	30.01.2002	11	(2)	1	8		
Fernando Mercado (MEX)	04.12.1994	4	(3)				
Yohn Géiler Mosquera Martínez (COL)	15.04.1989	15		1			
Senga Nicolás Kata Martínez "Niko Kata" (EQG)	15.01.1993				5	(4)	
Ayel Palacios	22.03.2002	1					
Richard Andrés Rodríguez Alvéz	13.07.1992	18	(1)	2	19		3
Vítor Silva Honorato "Vítor Faísca" (BRA)	16.04.1989				11	(2)	5
Forwards:							
Juan Ramón Barrera Pérez	02.05.1989	19		13	14	(4)	11
Keylon Batiz	01.02.1996				9		5
Edgar Josué Castillo Bellorin	21.05.2002	6		1	3	(1)	
Carlos Alberto Chavarria Rodríguez	02.05.1994	3	(3)	1	6	(8)	7
Alexis Lennin Somarriba Vargas	11.05.1994		(7)	1			
Trainer:							
Holver Flores		22			20		

REAL MADRIZ FÚTBOL CLUB SOMOTO

Year of Formation: 1996
Stadium: Estadio Solidaridad "Augusto Cesar Mendoza", Somoto (3,000)

THE SQUAD

	DOB	Ape M	(s)	G	Cla M	(s)	G
Goalkeepers:							
Erick Alemán	25.01.1984	3					
Josúe Ernesto Álvarez Nárvaez	08.07.1997	11			3		
Anderson Calderón	16.02.2001				3		
Pablo Hernández					13		
Ronaldo Ruíz	10.12.1997	4					
Defenders:							
Modesto Efrén Agurcia	01.06.1998				8	(5)	1
Carlos Gámez						(3)	
Axel Hernández	30.11.2000	1	(1)		3	(5)	
Kevin Hernández						(3)	
Jonathan Lopéz Gallo	07.08.1992	13	(2)		18		2
Jamilton Moreno Cruz	18.09.1996	15				(2)	
Joel Abraham Obando	20.11.2000		(1)				
Nicolas Romario Quiñones	03.06.1995	1	(2)				
Jaffeth Alexander Salgado	19.09.1995	8	(3)	1	4	(4)	
Roger Trujillo	02.07.1996	14	(1)	1	2		
Midfielders:							
Randy Benavides	26.12.1991	17	(1)		19		
Alvaro Noé Bermúdez Mendoza	22.09.1990	9	(1)		11	(2)	
Edwin Leonel Castro Ríos (HON)	01.03.1995				11	(5)	5
Kevin Felipe Castro Cárdenas (COL)	01.02.1999				18	(1)	2
Kevin Espinoza	06.03.2000	3	(6)	1	1	(1)	
Ramón Eduardo Estrada Díaz	30.12.2000	18			16		
Nicanor Garcias					1	(1)	
Eliazar Jonathan Hernández Inestroza	11.08.1995		(1)		1		
Jaret Martínez	03.12.1999	2	(1)				
Criss Ocampo	05.08.2002		(1)				
Brayan Enrique Ortíz Mojica (COL)	16.04.1997	15	(1)	1			
Alberto Sebastián Paredes Cáceres (HON)					18		1
Omar Alfredo Pozo Alfaro	27.08.2000	1	(5)		5	(4)	
Bryan Rodríguez			(1)				
Waldner Isaí Vásquez Pineda	20.03.2002	14			17		
Forwards:							
Héctor Bryann Ardón Euceda (HON)	09.03.1995	5	(4)	1			
Dennis Berger	09.12.1998	4	(2)				
Lester Duván Bordas	07.08.1994		(1)				
Kivian Enoc Díaz	08.03.2000	5	(4)	1	10	(4)	
Roris Espinoza	14.04.1997	6	(7)	2	16	(2)	1
Daniel Ortega Salazar	24.10.2001	2	(1)		3	(2)	
Deibyn Reyes	01.07.1993	12		5	8	(6)	3
Francisco Vargas (COL)	27.02.1997	15	(2)	4			
Trainer:							
Carlos Matamoros		18					
[01.2021] Ronaldo Alvarado					19		

CLUB DEPORTIVO WALTER FERRETTI MANAGUA
Year of Formation: 1987
Stadium: Estadio Nacional de Fútbol de Nicaragua, Managua (20,000)

THE SQUAD	DOB	Ape M	(s)	G	Cla M	(s)	G
Goalkeepers:							
Denis Jesús Espinoza Camacho	25.08.1983	18			20		
Esdras Israel González Rodríguez	29.12.1992	2			1		
Defenders:							
Jason Antonio Castellón García	24.01.1992	12	(3)	1	15	(5)	
Raúl Ernesto Davila	04.05.2000	3	(8)				
Henry Gamez		2	(1)		2		
Melvin Ramón Hernández	26.04.1994	8	(3)		19	(1)	2
René David Huete Moncada	05.06.1995	14		3	8	(3)	1
Roberto Miranda	12.09.2000	1	(7)			(3)	
Henry Niño Gómez	03.10.1997	13	(2)		9	(2)	1
Alejandro Hernán Tapia Campos	28.03.1993	11			20		1
Midfielders:							
Hayder Rubén Calero	19.09.1997	12	(4)		15	(4)	1
Christiano Roberto Fernandes de Lima (BRA)	31.07.1985	20		6			
Marvin David Fletes	12.11.1997	18			19	(1)	2
Jonathan Enrique Moncada Zeledon	03.01.1998				14	(3)	
Bryan Muñoz		3	(1)				
Sergio Javier Nápoles Saucedo (MEX)	23.11.1989				15	(2)	5
César Pulido						(1)	
Diego Alejandro Rosales Pineda (HON)	31.10.1998	7	(3)	1			
Wilmer Vásquez	20.10.1990					(1)	
Forwards:							
Cristhian Flores Rivas	27.08.1996	12	(4)	3	6	(5)	4
Dshon Forbes	09.07.1997	17	(1)	11	9	(2)	6
Bryan Antonio García Sirias	21.08.1995	3	(9)		16	(2)	2
Taufic Eduardo Guarch Rubio (MEX)	04.10.1991	19		4			
Osler Josué Mendoza Murillo	29.10.1997	1			2		1
Chris Patterson	20.08.2002					(3)	
Alexis Lennin Somarriba Vargas	11.05.1994				11	(5)	1
Anderson Josué Treminio Hulse	17.04.1997		(5)		1	(5)	
Ezequiel Ugalde	19.09.2001	14	(3)	1	16	(3)	2
Fernando Villalpando Domínguez (MEX)	02.09.1996	10	(1)	2	13	(5)	4
Trainer:							
Henry Urbina		22			21		

NATIONAL TEAM
INTERNATIONAL MATCHES 2020/2021

06.10.2020	Managua	Nicaragua - Guatemala	0-0	(F)
10.10.2020	Comayagua	Honduras - Nicaragua	1-1(0-1)	(F)
24.02.2021	Ciudad de Guatemala	Guatemala - Nicaragua	1-0(0-0)	(F)
27.03.2021	San Cristóbal	Turks and Caicos Islands - Nicaragua	0-7(0-3)	(WCQ)
04.06.2021	Managua	Nicaragua - Belize	3-0(1-0)	(WCQ)
08.06.2021	Port-au-Prince	Haiti - Nicaragua	1-0(0-0)	(WCQ)

06.10.2020, Friendly International
Estadio Nacional de Fútbol de Nicaragua, Managua; Attendance: 0
Referee: Nitzar Antonio Sandoval Chávez (Nicaragua)
NICARAGUA - GUATEMALA 0-0
NCA: Denis Jesús Espinoza Camacho, Jason Antonio Castellón García (63.Josué Abraham Quijano Potosme), Manuel Rosas Arreola, Cristian Mauriel Gutiérrez Peralta, René David Huete Moncada, Marlon Andrés López Moreno (66.Kevin José Serapio Oviedo), Juan Ramón Barrera Pérez, Richard Andrés Rodríguez Alvéz, Carlos Alberto Chavarría Rodríguez (88.Brandon Josué Ayerdis), Henry Antonio García Orozco (88.Luis Alfredo López), Dshon Forbes (63.Ricardo Mendieta). Trainer: Juan Vita (Argentina).

10.10.2020, Friendly International
Estadio "Carlos Miranda", Comayagua; Attendance: 0
Referee: Óscar Donaldo Moncada (Honduras)
HONDURAS - NICARAGUA 1-1(0-1)
NCA: Denis Jesús Espinoza Camacho, Josué Abraham Quijano Potosme, Manuel Rosas Arreola, Cristian Mauriel Gutiérrez Peralta, René David Huete Moncada [*sent off 17*], Richard Andrés Rodríguez Alvéz (76.Harold Medina), Renato Punyed Dubón (24.Kevin José Serapio Oviedo), Carlos Alberto Chavarría Rodríguez (46.Ricardo Mendieta), Henry Antonio García Orozco (76.Luis Alfredo López), Dshon Forbes (21.Marvin David Fletes), Brandon Josué Ayerdis (75.Luis Manuel Galeano Molina). Trainer: Juan Vita (Argentina).
Goal: Carlos Alberto Chavarría Rodríguez (40).

24.02.2021, Friendly International
Estadio "Doroteo Guamuch Flores", Ciudad de Guatemala; Attendance: 0
Referee: Sergio Armando Reyna Moller (Guatemala)
GUATEMALA - NICARAGUA 1-0(0-0)
NCA: Denis Jesús Espinoza Camacho, Josué Abraham Quijano Potosme, Manuel Rosas Arreola (57.Alejandro Hernán Tapia Campos), Kevin José Serapio Oviedo (66.Henry Niño Gómez), Melvin Ramón Hernández, Marvin David Fletes, Juan Ramón Barrera Pérez, Nahúm Elieth Peralta Arce (57.Carlos Alberto Chavarría Rodríguez), Richard Andrés Rodríguez Alvéz, Henry Antonio García Orozco (67.Danilo Zúñiga Arauz), Jaime José Moreno Ciorciari (79.Daniel Cadena Sánchez). Trainer: Juan Vita (Argentina).

27.03.2021, 22nd FIFA World Cup Qualifiers, CONCACAF First Round
Estadio Panamericano, San Cristóbal (Dominican Republic)
Referee: William Anderson (Puerto Rico)
TURKS AND CAICOS ISLANDS - NICARAGUA   **0-7(0-3)**
NCA: Denis Jesús Espinoza Camacho, Luis Fernando Copete Murillo (21.Manuel Rosas Arreola), Josué Abraham Quijano Potosme, Jason Telémaco Ingram Oporta (55.Franklin Geovany Flores Sacaza), Marvin David Fletes, Juan Ramón Barrera Pérez (68.Dshon Forbes), Richard Andrés Rodríguez Alvéz, Danilo Zúñiga Arauz (55.Matías Moldskred Belli), Carlos Alberto Chavarría Rodríguez (68.Ezequiel Ugalde), Ariagner Steven Smith Medina, Byron Bonilla Martínez. Trainer: Juan Vita (Argentina).
Goals: Juan Ramón Barrera Pérez (3), Ariagner Steven Smith Medina (8, 45+2), Marvin David Fletes (46), Juan Ramón Barrera Pérez (59), Dshon Forbes (78), Matías Moldskred Belli (87).

04.06.2021, 22nd FIFA World Cup Qualifiers, CONCACAF First Round
Estadio Nacional, Managua
Referee: Nelson Alcides Salgado Trujillo (Honduras)
NICARAGUA - BELIZE   **3-0(1-0)**
NCA: Denis Jesús Espinoza Camacho, Franklin Geovany Flores Sacaza, Luis Fernando Copete Murillo (59.Melvin Ramón Hernández), Josué Abraham Quijano Potosme, Kevin José Serapio Oviedo, Marvin David Fletes, Juan Ramón Barrera Pérez (65.Henry Antonio García Orozco), Richard Andrés Rodríguez Alvéz (74.Brandon Josué Ayerdis), Carlos Alberto Chavarría Rodríguez, Jaime José Moreno Ciorciari (74.Danilo Zúñiga Arauz), Byron Bonilla Martínez (60.Matías Moldskred Belli). Trainer: Juan Vita (Argentina).
Goals: Richard Andrés Rodríguez Alvéz (25), Byron Bonilla Martínez (46), Juan Ramón Barrera Pérez (51).

08.06.2021, 22nd FIFA World Cup Qualifiers, CONCACAF First Round
Stade "Sylvio Cator", Port-au-Prince
Referee: Kevin Morrison (Jamaica)
HAITI - NICARAGUA   **1-0(0-0)**
NCA: Denis Jesús Espinoza Camacho, Franklin Geovany Flores Sacaza (89.Danilo Zúñiga Arauz), Luis Fernando Copete Murillo, Josué Abraham Quijano Potosme (46.Henry Niño Gómez), Kevin José Serapio Oviedo [*sent off 83*], Marvin David Fletes, Juan Ramón Barrera Pérez, Richard Andrés Rodríguez Alvéz, Carlos Alberto Chavarría Rodríguez (80.Brandon Josué Ayerdis), Jaime José Moreno Ciorciari, Byron Bonilla Martínez (60.Matías Moldskred Belli). Trainer: Juan Vita (Argentina).

NATIONAL TEAM PLAYERS
2020/2021

Name	DOB	Club
Goalkeepers		
Denis Jesús ESPINOZA Camacho	25.08.1983	CD Walter Ferretti Managua
Defenders		
Jason Antonio CASTELLÓN García	24.01.1992	CD Walter Ferretti Managua
Luis Fernando COPETE Murillo	12.02.1989	Club Independiente Petrolero Sucre (BOL)
Marvin David FLETES	12.11.1997	CD Walter Ferretti Managua
Cristian Mauriel GUTIÉRREZ Peralta	06.01.1993	Real Estelí FC
Melvin Ramón HERNÁNDEZ	26.04.1994	CD Walter Ferretti Managua
René David HUETE Moncada	05.06.1995	CD Walter Ferretti Managua
Jason Telémaco INGRAM Oporta	20.08.1997	Santos de Guápiles FC (CRC)
Luis Alfredo LÓPEZ	11.09.1998	Real Estelí FC
Henry NIÑO Gómez	03.10.1997	CD Walter Ferretti Managua
Josué Abraham QUIJANO Potosme	10.03.1991	Real Estelí FC
Manuel ROSAS Arreola	14.10.1983	Real Estelí FC
Alejandro Hernán TAPIA Campos	28.03.1993	CD Walter Ferretti Managua
Midfielders		
Juan Ramón BARRERA Pérez	02.05.1989	Real Estelí FC
Daniel CADENA Sánchez	09.02.1987	CD Ocotal
Henry Antonio GARCÍA Orozco	21.07.1990	Real Estelí FC
Harold MEDINA	30.01.2002	Real Estelí FC
Marlon Andrés LÓPEZ Moreno	02.11.1992	Real Estelí FC
Matías MOLDSKRED Belli	12.08.1997	IK Start Kristiansand (NOR)
Nahúm Elieth PERALTA Arce	21.10.1994	Managua FC
Renato PUNYED Dubón	22.08.1995	Nybergsund IL (NOR)
Richard Andrés RODRÍGUEZ Alvéz	13.07.1992	CD Santani San Estanislao (PAR)
Kevin José SERAPIO Oviedo	09.04.1996	Managua FC
Danilo ZÚNIGA Arauz	04.06.1997	Managua FC
Forwards		
Brandon Josué AYERDIS	11.09.1999	Real Estelí FC
Byron BONILLA Martínez	30.08.1993	CS Cartaginés Deportiva SA (CRC)
Daniel CADENA Sánchez	09.02.1987	CD Ocotal
Carlos Alberto CHAVARRÍA Rodríguez	02.05.1994	Real Estelí FC
Dshon FORBES	09.07.1997	CD Walter Ferretti Managua
Luis Manuel GALEANO Molina	15.10.1994	ART Municipal Jalapa
Ricardo MENDIETA	18.01.1995	Managua FC
Jaime José MORENO Ciorciari	30.03.1995	Diriangén FC Diriamba
Ariagner Steven Smith Medina	13.12.1998	FC Sputnik Rechitsa (BLR)
Ezequiel UGALDE	19.09.2001	CD Walter Ferretti Managua
National coaches		
Juan VITA (Argentina) [from 30.08.2020]		11.05.1987

PANAMA

The Country:	The FA:
República de Panamá (Republic of Panama)	Federación Panameña de Fútbol
Capital: Ciudad de Panamá	Ciudad Deportiva "Irving Saladino", Juan Díaz,
Surface: 75,157 km²	Apartado 0835-394–Zona 10, Ciudad de Panamá
Population: 4,176,869 [2018]	Year of Formation: 1937
Time: UTC-5	Member of FIFA since: 1938
Independent since: 1821	Member of CONCACAF since: 1961

NATIONAL TEAM RECORDS

First international match: 28.07.1937, Cali (COL): Panama - Mexico 2-2
Most international caps: Gabriel Enrique Gómez Girón – 149 caps (2003-2018)
Most international goals: Luis Carlos Tejada Hansell – 43 goals / 107 caps (since 2001)

CONCACAF GOLD CUP		FIFA WORLD CUP	
1991	Qualifiers	1930	-
1993	Final Tournament (Group Stage)	1934	-
1996	Qualifiers	1938	Did not enter
1998	Qualifiers	1950	Did not enter
2000	Did not enter	1954	Did not enter
2002	Qualifiers	1958	Did not enter
2003	Qualifiers	1962	Did not enter
2005	Final Tournament (Runners-up)	1966	Did not enter
2007	Final Tournament (Quarter-Finals)	1970	Did not enter
2009	Final Tournament (Quarter-Finals)	1974	Did not enter
2011	Final Tournament (Semi-Finals)	1978	Qualifiers
2013	Final Tournament (Runners-up)	1982	Qualifiers
2015	Final Tournament (3rd Place)	1986	Qualifiers
2017	Final Tournament (Quarter-Finals)	1990	Qualifiers
2019	Final Tournament (Quarter-Finals)	1994	Qualifiers
2021	Final Tournament (*to be played*)	1998	Qualifiers
		2002	Qualifiers
		2006	Qualifiers
		2010	Qualifiers
		2014	Qualifiers
		2018	Qualifiers

F.I.F.A. CONFEDERATIONS CUP 1992-2017

None

OLYMPIC FOOTBALL TOURNAMENTS 1908-2016

1908	-	1948	-	1972	Qualifiers	1996	Qualifiers
1912	-	1952	-	1976	Did not enter	2000	Qualifiers
1920	-	1956	-	1980	Qualifiers	2004	Qualifiers
1924	-	1960	-	1984	Did not enter	2008	Qualifiers
1928	-	1964	Qualifiers	1988	Qualifiers	2012	Qualifiers
1936	-	1968	Did not enter	1992	Qualifiers	2016	Qualifiers

CCCF (Confederación Centroamericana y del Caribe de Fútbol) CHAMPIONSHIPS 1941-1961

1941, 1946, 1948 (3rd Place), **1951 (Winners)**, 1953, 1957, 1961

CONCACAF CHAMPIONSHIPS 1963-1989

1963, 1967, 1969

COPA AMÉRICA (invited as guests)

2016

CONCACAF NATIONS LEAGUE

2019-2020	League A

COPA CENTROAMERICANA (UNCAF NATIONS CHAMPIONSHIPS) 1991-2017

1991	Preliminary Round	2005	Final Round - Group Stage
1993	Final Round - 3rd Place	2007	Final Round - Runners-up
1995	Final Round - Group Stage	2009	**Final Round - Winners**
1997	Final Round - Group Stage	2011	Final Round - 3rd Place
1999	Did not enter	2013	Final Round - Group Stage
2001	Final Round - 4th Place	2014	Final Round - 3rd Place
2003	Final Round - Group Stage	2017	Final Round - Runners-up

PANAMIAN CLUB HONOURS IN CONCACAF CLUB COMPETITIONS:

CONCACAF Champions Cup / CONCACAF Champions League 1962-2020
None

CONCACAF League 2017-2020
None

Caribbean Club Championship 1997-2021
None

*CONCACAF Cup Winners Cup 1991-1995**
None

*Copa Interamericana 1968-1998**
None

*defunct competitions

NATIONAL COMPETITIONS
TABLE OF HONOURS

The first edition of the Panamanian Championship was always played in 1951, San José FC was the first winners. Unfortunately, there are no data available about the winners between 1952 and 1988.

	CHAMPIONS
1988	CD Plaza Amador Ciudad de Panamá
1989	Tauro FC Ciudad de Panamá
1990	CD Plaza Amador Ciudad de Panamá

1991	Tauro FC Ciudad de Panamá	
1992	CD Plaza Amador Ciudad de Panamá	
1993	AFC Euro Kickers Ciudad de Panamá	
1994/1995	San Francisco FC La Chorrera	
1995/1996	San Francisco FC La Chorrera	
1996/1997	Tauro FC Ciudad de Panamá	
1997/1998	Tauro FC Ciudad de Panamá	
1998/1999	CD Árabe Unido Ciudad de Colón	
1999/2000	Tauro FC Ciudad de Panamá	
2000/2001	Panamá Viejo FC Ciudad de Panamá	
2001	CD Árabe Unido Ciudad de Colón	
2002	CD Plaza Amador Ciudad de Panamá	
2003	Tauro FC Ciudad de Panamá	
2004	CD Árabe Unido Ciudad de Colón	
2005	CD Plaza Amador Ciudad de Panamá	
2006	San Francisco FC La Chorrera	
2007	Ape:	Tauro FC Ciudad de Panamá
	Cla:	San Francisco FC La Chorrera
2008	Ape:	San Francisco FC La Chorrera
	Cla:	CD Árabe Unido Ciudad de Colón
2009	Ape:	San Francisco FC La Chorrera
2009/2010	Ape:	CD Árabe Unido Ciudad de Colón
	Cla:	CD Árabe Unido Ciudad de Colón
2010/2011	Ape:	Tauro FC Ciudad de Panamá
	Cla:	San Francisco FC La Chorrera
2011/2012	Ape:	Chorrillo FC Ciudad de Panamá
	Cla:	Tauro FC Ciudad de Panamá
2012/2013	Ape:	CD Árabe Unido Ciudad de Colón
	Cla:	AdF Sporting San Miguelito
2013/2014	Ape:	Tauro FC Ciudad de Panamá
	Cla:	Chorrillo FC Ciudad de Panamá
2014/2015	Ape:	San Francisco FC La Chorrera
	Cla:	CD Árabe Unido Ciudad de Colón
2015/2016	Ape:	CD Árabe Unido Ciudad de Colón
	Cla:	CD Plaza Amador Ciudad de Panamá
2016/2017	Ape:	CD Árabe Unido Ciudad de Colón
	Cla:	Tauro FC Ciudad de Panamá
2017/2018	Ape:	Chorrillo FC Ciudad de Panamá
	Cla:	CA Independiente La Chorrera
2018/2019	Ape:	Tauro FC Ciudad de Panamá
	Cla:	CA Independiente La Chorrera
2019	Ape:	Tauro FC Ciudad de Panamá
2020	Ape:	*Championship cancelled due to COVID-19 pandemic*
	Cla:	CA Independiente La Chorrera

	Copa Panamá
2015	San Francisco FC La Chorrera
2016/2017	Santa Gema FC Arraiján
2017/2018	*No competition*

NATIONAL CHAMPIONSHIP
Liga Panameña de Fútbol / Liga Cable Onda 2020

Torneo Apertura 2020

First Stage - Results

Round 1 [25-26.01.2020]
Tauro FC - Árabe Unido 2-1(0-1)
Atlético Chiriquí - San Francisco FC 0-2(0-0)
CA Independiente - Alianza FC 1-0(1-0)
Sporting S. Miguelito - Costa del Este 2-0(2-0)
CD Plaza Amador - CD Universitario 1-1(1-0)

Round 2 [31.01.-01.02.2020]
Costa del Este - CA Independiente 0-0
San Francisco FC - CD Plaza Amador 6-3(4-1)
CD Universitario - Atlético Chiriquí 2-0(0-0)
Sporting San Miguelito - Árabe Unido 0-1(0-0)
Alianza FC - Tauro FC 1-2(0-1)

Round 3 [07-09.02.2020]
Árabe Unido - CD Plaza Amador 2-0(1-0)
CA Independiente - Tauro FC 1-3(0-0)
Atlético Chiriquí - Sporting San Miguelito 0-0
Alianza FC - San Francisco FC 2-1(2-0)
Costa del Este - CD Universitario 2-3(0-2)

Round 4 [14-16.02.2020]
Árabe Unido - CA Independiente 0-1(0-0)
Sporting San Miguelito - Alianza FC 1-0(1-0)
Tauro FC - Costa del Este 1-0(0-0)
San Francisco FC - CD Universitario 0-2(0-1)
CD Plaza Amador - Atlético Chiriquí 1-0(1-0)

Round 5 [19-20.02.2020]
CA Independiente - San Francisco FC 1-1(0-1)
Costa del Este - Atlético Chiriquí 1-0(0-0)
CD Universitario - Tauro FC 0-0
CD Plaza Amador - Sporting San Mig. 2-0(0-0)
Alianza FC - Árabe Unido 0-2(0-1)

Round 6 [28.02.-01.03.2020]
San Francisco FC - Sporting San Miguelito 0-0
CD Universitario - CA Independiente 3-2(1-2)
Atlético Chiriquí - Árabe Unido 2-3(1-1)
Tauro FC - CD Plaza Amador 2-2(0-1)
Costa del Este - Alianza FC 1-1(0-0)

Round 7 [03.03.2020]
CD Plaza Amador - CA Independiente 0-0
Árabe Unido - Costa del Este 1-0(1-0)
Alianza FC - Atlético Chiriquí 2-0(1-0)
Sporting San Miguelito - CD Universitario 0-0
San Francisco FC - Tauro FC 1-0(0-0)

Round 8 [07-08.03.2020]
CD Universitario - Árabe Unido 1-0(1-0)
CA Independiente - Sporting San Mig. 1-1(0-0)
Atlético Chiriquí - Tauro FC 0-2(0-0)
Alianza FC - CD Plaza Amador 1-0(0-0)
Costa del Este - San Francisco FC 1-0(0-0)

On 17.03.2020, Liga Panameña de Fútbol cancelled the championship due to COVID-19 pandemic. No title was awarded.

Standings at cancellation

1.	CD Universitario Penonomé	8	5	3	0	12	-	5	18
2.	Tauro FC Ciudad de Panamá	8	5	2	1	12	-	6	17
3.	CD Árabe Unido Ciudad de Colón	8	5	0	3	10	-	6	15
4.	San Francisco FC La Chorrera	8	3	2	3	11	-	9	11
5.	AdF Sporting San Miguelito	8	2	4	2	4	-	4	10
6.	CA Independiente La Chorrera	8	2	4	2	7	-	8	10
7.	Alianza FC Ciudad de Panamá	8	3	1	4	7	-	8	10
8.	CD Plaza Amador Ciudad de Panamá	8	2	3	3	9	-	12	9
9.	Costa del Este FC Ciudad de Panamá	8	2	2	4	5	-	8	8
10.	CD Atlético Chiriquí David	8	0	1	7	2	-	13	1

Torneo Clausura 2020

First Stage - Results

Round 1 [22-25.10.2020]
Tauro FC - Árabe Unido 1-1(0-0)
San Francisco FC - Atlético Chiriquí 1-1(1-0)
Costa del Este - Sporting San Mig. 2-1(1-0)
CD Plaza Amador - CD Universitario 0-0
CA Independiente - Alianza FC 1-1(0-0)

Round 2 [29-31.10.2020]
Árabe Unido - Sporting San Miguelito 1-2(1-1)
Alianza FC - Tauro FC 2-2(0-0)
CA Independiente - Costa del Este 2-0(1-0)
CD Plaza Amador - San Francisco FC 0-0
Atlético Chiriquí - CD Universitario 0-0

Round 3 [06-08.11.2020]
Sporting San Miguelito - Atlético Chiriquí 0-0
Costa del Este - CD Universitario 3-0(2-0)
CD Plaza Amador - Árabe Unido 0-2(0-1)
Tauro FC - CA Independiente 0-3(0-1)
San Francisco FC - Alianza FC 0-0

Round 4 [12-14.11.2020]
Atlético Chiriquí - CD Plaza Amador 1-2(1-2)
Tauro FC - Costa del Este 0-0
CD Universitario - San Francisco FC 0-1(0-0)
Árabe Unido - CA Independiente 2-0(1-0)
Alianza FC - Sporting San Miguelito 1-0(0-0)

Round 5 [18-19.11.2020]
Árabe Unido - Atlético Chiriquí 0-0
CA Independiente - CD Universitario 4-0(1-0)
Sporting San Mig. - San Francisco FC 1-2(0-1)
CD Plaza Amador - Tauro FC 0-1(0-0)
Costa del Este - Alianza FC 1-1(1-0)

Round 6 [21-22.11.2020]
CD Universitario - Tauro FC 1-4(1-2)
Sporting San Mig. - CDPlaza Amador 0-1(0-0)
Atlético Chiriquí - Costa del Este 3-3(2-1)
Alianza FC - Árabe Unido 5-2(4-1)
San Francisco FC - CA Independiente 1-1(0-0) [01.12.]

Round 7 [24-25.11.2020]
Universitario - Sporting San Miguelito 1-4(1-4)
Atlético Chiriquí - Alianza FC 1-2(0-1)
Costa del Este - Árabe Unido 1-1(0-0)
CA Independiente - CD Plaza Amador 0-0
Tauro FC - San Francisco FC 1-0(0-0) [04.12.]

Round 8 [28-29.11.2020]
CA Independiente - Atlético Chiriquí 2-0(1-0)
San Francisco FC - Árabe Unido 3-0(2-0)
Tauro FC - Sporting San Miguelito 1-2(1-0)
Alianza FC - CD Universitario 0-0
Costa del Este - CD Plaza Amador 1-1(0-0)

Round 9 [07.12.2020]
Sporting San Mig. - CA Independiente 0-2(0-1)
Árabe Unido - CD Universitario 2-1(1-0)
Atlético Chiriquí - Tauro FC 0-1(0-1)
CD Plaza Amador - Alianza FC 1-0(1-0)
San Francisco FC - Costa del Este 0-0

	Final Standings							
1.	CA Independiente La Chorrera	9	5	3	1	15 - 4	18
2.	Tauro FC Ciudad de Panamá	9	4	3	2	11 - 9	15
3.	Alianza FC Ciudad de Panamá	9	3	5	1	12 - 8	14
4.	San Francisco FC La Chorrera	9	3	5	1	8 - 4	14
5.	CD Plaza Amador Ciudad de Panamá	9	3	4	2	5 - 5	13
6.	Costa del Este FC Ciudad de Panamá	9	2	6	1	11 - 9	12
7.	CD Árabe Unido Ciudad de Colón	9	3	3	3	11 - 13	12
8.	AdF Sporting San Miguelito	9	3	1	5	10 - 11	10
9.	CD Atlético Chiriquí David	9	0	5	4	6 - 11	5
10.	CD Universitario Penonomé	9	0	3	6	3 - 18	3

Top-2 teams qualified for the Semi-Finals, while teams ranked 3-6 were qualified for the Quarter-Finals.

Quarter-Finals [10-11.12.2020]	
Alianza FC Ciudad de Panamá - Costa del Este FC Ciudad de Panamá	1-4(0-2)
San Francisco FC La Chorrera - CD Plaza Amador Ciudad de Panamá	1-0(0-0)

Semi-Finals [13-17.12.2020]		
Costa del Este FC Ciudad de Panamá - CA Independiente La Chorrera	1-2(1-1)	0-0
San Francisco FC La Chorrera - Tauro FC Ciudad de Panamá	2-0(1-0)	2-2(0-1)

Final

20.12.2020, Estadio "Agustín 'Muquita' Sánchez", La Chorrera; Attendance: 0
Referee: Oliver Amet Vergara Rodríguez
CA Independiente La Chorrera - San Francisco FC La Chorrera   3-1(1-0)
Independiente: José Carlos Guerra, Azmahar Anibal Ariano Navarro, Francisco Javier Vence Gómez, Omar Federico Córdoba Quintero, Jiovany Javier Ramos Díaz, Juan Alberto González Pineda (76.Alexis Venancio Palacios Curley), Dionisio Bernal Asprilla, Joseph Yeramid Rosales Erazo (90.Rafael Águila Rodríguez), Martin Morán, Alfredo Horacio Stephens Francis, José Fajardo Nelson. Trainer: Francisco Perlo (Venezuela).
San Francisco: Eric Hughes Guevara, Martín Antonio Gómez Rodríguez (76.Jean Carlos Sánchez Rose), Roderick Alonso Miller Molina, Roberto Leandro Chen Rodríguez, Francisco Antonio Palacios Alleyne, Manuel Alexander Vargas Moreno (77.Víctor Manuel Ávila Reyes), Jhamal Adonis Rodríguez Thomas, Luis Aurelio Pereira Lewis (60.Wesley Alberto Cabrera Duarte), Jorge Luis Serrano Francis (60.Isidoro Joamir Hinestroza Hernández), Jair Ibrahim Catuy Arosemena, Cristian David Zúñiga Pino (60.José Luis Garcés Rivera). Trainer: Gonzálo Soto Cortázar (Colombia).
Goals: 1-0 Azmahar Anibal Ariano Navarro (21), 2-0 Alfredo Horacio Stephens Francis (60 penalty), 2-1 (89), 3-1 Alfredo Horacio Stephens Francis (90+5 penalty).

Torneo Clausura 2020 Champions: **CA Independiente La Chorrera**

Best goalscorer Clausura 2020:
Alfredo Horacio Stephens Francis (CA Independiente La Chorrera) – 7 goals

THE CLUBS 2020

Please note: number of matches, subtitutes and goals are including Clausura + Play-offs.

ALIANZA FÚTBOL CLUB CIUDAD DE PANAMÁ

Foundation date: March 2, 1963
Address: Via Transistmica, Zona 5, 0816-04943 Chilibre
Stadium: Estadio "Rommel Fernández Gutiérrez", Ciudad de Panamá (32,000)

THE SQUAD

	DOB	M	(s)	G
Goalkeepers:				
Alvaro Montenegro	21.07.1996	5		
Reynaldo Polo Carcamo	21.08.1991	5	(1)	
Defenders:				
Eduardo Antonio Anderson Gómez	01.03.2001	4		
Rolando Gumbs			(1)	
Eduardo Alberto Mena García	02.11.1999	5		
Santiago Arturo Rodríguez Salinas	07.04.1995	2	(4)	
Abdiel Sealy	09.11.1995	9		
Midfielders:				
Maurício Castaño Grisales (COL)	06.12.1993	9		
Maikell Kediaer Díaz Pérez	16.02.2000	2	(3)	
Alexander González Moreno	14.12.1994	7	(2)	1
José Guillermo Rivas Rodríguez	04.07.1995	6	(1)	
Manuel Axel Rodríguez Edwards	09.04.1998	4	(4)	
Jovani Francisco Welch López	07.12.1999	4	(2)	
Forwards:				
Abdiel Abrego	09.08.1997		(6)	1
Jahir Antonio Alvarado Avila		1		
Marlon Anel Ávila Aldeano	27.02.1993	4	(4)	
Ricaurte Hekeem Barsallo Towshned	05.09.1994	9		2
Alcides Díaz	18.10.2001	7	(1)	1
Jordan Joel Girón Rivas	21.12.2000	4	(3)	
Fernando Ameth Guerrero Arroyo	27.05.1998		(3)	
Azarías Londoño	21.06.2001	3	(2)	2
César Augusto Medina Mejía	10.04.1980	5	(2)	3
Héctor Manuel Peñaloza Sánchez	18.02.1989	3	(3)	1
Rolando Rodríguez		5		
Rudy Anthony Yearwood Ramos	28.09.1995	7	(2)	2
Trainer:				
Cecilio Garcés	08.07.1974	10		

CLUB DEPORTIVO ÁRABE UNIDO CIUDAD DE COLÓN

Foundation date: April 28, 1994
Address: Calle Las Gladiolas Casa B-25, Colón
Stadium: Estadio „Armando Dely Valdés", Ciudad de Colón (4,000)

THE SQUAD

	DOB	M	(s)	G
Goalkeepers:				
Aldo Alexis Ciel Rodríguez	03.12.1997	1		
José Ariel Kelly	05.07.1992	8		
Defenders:				
Emmanuel Santiago Ceballos Rodríguez			(2)	
Cristopher Denzel Cragwell Sjogreen	26.06.2001	6		
Armando Dely	21.05.2001	2		
Gilberto Hernández Bultrón	26.06.1997	9		1
Soyell Isiah Trejos Tesis	19.04.2000	1	(1)	
Alejandro Alonso Yearwood Francis	29.04.1996	3	(1)	
Midfielders:				
Chamell Gernell Asprilla Alarcón	11.08.1998	3	(3)	
Rubén Baruco Aguilar	12.04.1999	5		
Gabriel Enrique Brown Martínez	17.05.1998	6		
Edgar Daniel Cunningham McKay	02.10.2000	3	(4)	1
Jael Jair Garibaldi Ríos		1	(1)	
José Del Carmen Garibaldi Salazar	28.05.1997	8	(1)	
Jorge Antonio Grant Daley	21.11.1997	1	(2)	
Jaime Juvenal Harrison Danies	29.10.2003	1	(3)	
Emanuel Mena Alveo	07.08.1995	7		
Kemuel Aurelio Patrick James	11.01.2000	2		
Juan Gerardo Villalobos de la Espada		1		
Forwards:				
Efraín Bristan Niño	20.01.1999	1	(1)	2
Joseph Christopher Cox Goods	25.06.1994	8	(1)	3
Rodolfo Ernesto Ford Gondola	09.09.1997	6	(2)	1
Ernie Antonio Mares Medina	05.01.1998	2	(1)	
Jean Carlos Navarro	20.04.2002	3	(4)	
Erick Eleazar Rodríguez Martínez	07.08.1994	6	(2)	1
Everardo Ernesto Rose Clarke	23.07.1999	3	(3)	
Carlos Daniel Small Cardenas	13.03.1995	2	(5)	1
Trainer:				
Julio Antonio Medina III Morales	14.07.1976	9		

CLUB DEPORTIVO ATLÉTICO CHIRIQUÍ DAVID

Foundation date: June 18, 2002
Address: Avenida Obaldia, David
Stadium: Estadio San Cristóbal, David (2,890)

THE SQUAD	DOB	M	(s)	G
Goalkeepers:				
Edward Isahit Chacón Mojica	25.09.1991	3		
José Ricardo Cubilla Nuñez	11.02.1995	6	(1)	
Defenders:				
Porfirio Ávila Aguilar	19.01.1990	9		
Raúl Antonio Guerra	25.05.1995	8		1
Daniel Alberto Ortega Jurado	09.10.1995		(5)	
José Arturo Ortega Jercovic	01.12.1999	2	(2)	
Yeison Yahir Ortega Lu	30.10.2001	9		1
Amilcar Amador Quiroz Gaitan	04.07.1990	9		
Midfielders:				
Isaac Alvarado	01.07.2002		(1)	
Edgar Alonso Aparicio Rutenelly	03.12.1996	4	(2)	2
Raymond Barnes	06.10.1998	3	(2)	
Michael Casazola Alvarado	27.04.1993	8		
Jonathan Geovani Cedeño Delgado	14.09.1995	1	(2)	
José Agustin Gómez Rodríguez	19.01.1991	8		1
Jonathan Smith González Candanedo	05.05.1994	1	(5)	
Alan Miranda Hurtado	15.05.2001	1	(3)	
Javier Enríque Rivera Castillo	17.03.1998	8		1
Jorge Enrique Samudio Torres	23.09.1992	9		
Geovanny Oscar Tascón Atencio	15.07.1997	1	(2)	
Zabdiel Jose Vega Ortega	02.06.2001	1		
Forwards:				
Miguel Ángel Saavedra Cazasola	20.03.1993	8		
Trainer:				
Patricio Sampó (ARG)		9		

COSTA DEL ESTE FÚTBOL CLUB CIUDAD DE PANAMÁ

Foundation date: 2008 (*as Santos FC La Chorrera*)
Address: *Not known*
Stadium: Estadio Maracaná, Ciudad de Panamá (5,500)

THE SQUAD

	DOB	M	(s)	G
Goalkeepers:				
Kevin Melgar Cárdenas	19.11.1992	3		
César Jair Samudio Murillo	23.03.1994	9		
Defenders:				
Joseph Josué Gil Rodríguez	09.05.1991	12		
Yair Fernando Jaén Reina	16.03.1997	8	(2)	5
José Fernando López Pisciotti	27.05.1999	6	(3)	
Rodrigo Ariel Melgarejo Ferreira	23.05.2002	2	(4)	
Luis Alberto Mendoza Macías	14.04.1984	6	(1)	
Ángel Gabriel Ortega Ricord	29.10.2000		(2)	
Gabriel Emiliano Pusula Coronel (ARG)	23.01.1997	11	(1)	1
Eric Enrique Vásquez Martínez	08.01.1988	10		
Midfielders:				
Alcides De los Ríos Girón	06.06.1993	6	(2)	
Pedro Ernesto Jeanine Portillo	04.09.1993	12		
José Antonio Múñoz Riquelme	15.01.1993	5	(3)	
Yoameth Astero Murillo Cedeño	07.11.2001	4	(3)	
Christian Ruíz		1		
Rodrigo Tello Rojas	13.08.1983	1	(2)	
César Augusto Yanis Velasco	28.01.1996	8	(1)	2
Forwards:				
Rubén Walter Barrow Hansell	28.04.1995		(3)	
Luis Antonio Hurtado White	07.09.1992		(3)	
Josué Manuel Luna Barnett	11.03.2001	1	(1)	
Valentín Enríque Pimentel Armuelles	30.05.1991	12		3
Edson de Sousa Samms Record	27.03.1995	5	(5)	1
Ernesto Arturo Sinclair Chávez	10.05.1989	4	(6)	2
Daniel Fernando Vargas Campbell	24.11.1995	2	(3)	
Adonis Aldhair Villanueva Carvajal	02.08.1994	3	(3)	1
Reymundo Enrique Williams Araúz	17.01.2004	1	(3)	1
Trainer:				
Julio Infante (VEN)		12		

CLUB ATLÉTICO INDEPENDIENTE DE LA CHORRERA
Foundation date: 1982
Address: Calle 4ta Norte, Barrio Colón, La Chorrera
Stadium: Estadio "Agustín 'Muquita' Sánchez", La Chorrera (3,040)

THE SQUAD

	DOB	M	(s)	G
Goalkeepers:				
José Carlos Guerra	12.09.1994	10		
Eddie Roberts Chifundo	10.05.1994	2	(1)	
Defenders:				
Azmahar Anibal Ariano Navarro	14.01.1991	6	(1)	1
Davis Abdiel Contreras White	09.12.2001		(2)	
Omar Federico Córdoba Quintero	13.06.1994	11		
Juan Alberto González Pineda	17.10.1991	5	(5)	
Juan Carlos Hernández Ávila	12.04.1996	1	(1)	
Jordy Enrique Meléndez Acosta	25.09.1994	4	(1)	3
Jiovany Javier Ramos Díaz	26.01.1997	11		1
Kevin Joel Record Machore	16.08.2000		(1)	
Francisco Javier Vence Gómez	11.04.1992	11		1
Midfielders:				
Rafael Águila Rodríguez	29.01.1997	8	(3)	
Dionisio Bernal Asprilla	01.05.1996	8	(2)	
Omar Ezequiel Browne Zuñiga	03.05.1994		(3)	1
Elías Linares	29.01.1996	1	(1)	
Manuel Morán Velásquez	20.11.1997		(4)	
Martin Morán	30.08.2001	11		
Andrés Alejandro Peñalba Martínez	08.07.1997	2	(3)	
Eric Emanuel Pinto Rodríguez	08.12.2002		(3)	
Joseph Yeramid Rosales Erazo (HON)	06.11.2000	6	(4)	
Leonel Triana	04.09.1992	2	(4)	1
Forwards:				
Andrick Joel Edwards Ríos	12.04.1999		(3)	
José Fajardo Nelson	18.08.1993	9	(1)	3
Alexis Venancio Palacios Curley	10.06.1995	9	(2)	1
Guido Adalberto Rouse Luzcando	04.03.1996	3	(5)	1
Alfredo Horacio Stephens Francis	25.12.1994	12		7
Trainer:				
Francisco Perlo (VEN)	16.05.1987	12		

CLUB DEPORTIVO PLAZA AMADOR CIUDAD DE PANAMÁ

Foundation date: 1955
Address: Edificio Via España 120, Balboa, Ciudad de Panamá
Stadium: Estadio Maracaná, Ciudad de Panamá (5,500)

THE SQUAD

	DOB	M	(s)	G
Goalkeepers:				
Jaime Antonio de Gracia Cortes	11.05.1996	10		
Defenders:				
Omar Enrique Alba Burrowes		1		
Guillermo Josúe Benítez Espinoza	05.03.1999	10		
Emanuel Raphael Chanis Muñoz	21.12.1998	8		
Manuel Antonio Gamboa	05.02.1999	9		
José Matos	08.03.2002		(1)	
Jesús Andrés West Salazar	19.06.1999	6		
Midfielders:				
Ricardo Enrique Buitrago Medina	03.10.1985	9	(1)	
Jonathan Antonio Ceceña Stephenson	01.03.1999	7	(3)	1
Mauro Javier Cedeño Crosthwaite	05.02.2001	2	(3)	
Carlos Alejandro Escobar Smith	11.05.1999	3	(1)	
Abdul Gadiel Knight Ceballos	17.01.2002	6	(1)	
Joel Francisco Lara Garibaldo		3	(3)	
Ovidio López		2	(4)	
Francisco Javier Narbón Cuadra	11.02.1995	10		
Alberto Quiñones Robledo	26.05.1997	3	(3)	
Michael Rodríguez Santiago	09.01.2001	1	(1)	
Omar Rodrigo Valencia Arauz		1	(4)	
Rodolfo Alejandro Vega Iguala		7	(1)	
Forwards:				
Daniel Ali Arévalo Arrocha	21.04.2001		(2)	
Leandro Alexander Ávila Santamaría	22.03.1998	7	(1)	2
Alberto Aaron Saldaña Rodríguez	23.05.2000	1	(3)	
Luis Carlos Tejada Hansell	28.03.1982	4	(4)	2
Trainer:				
Jorge Luis Dely Valdés	12.03.1967	10		

SAN FRANCISCO FÚTBOL CLUB LA CHORRERA

Foundation date: 1971
Address: Plaza Banco General, Calle 50 y Avenida Aquilino de la Guardia, Mezzanine, San Francisco
Stadium: Estadio "Agustín 'Muquita' Sánchez", La Chorrera (3,040)

THE SQUAD

	DOB	M	(s)	G
Goalkeepers:				
Samuel Melquicidec Castañeda Villareal	09.01.1994	5		
Eric Hughes Guevara	11.07.1986	8		
Defenders:				
Ismael Betegón	27.05.2001	2	(1)	
Roberto Leandro Chen Rodríguez	24.05.1994	13		1
Martín Antonio Gómez Rodríguez	14.05.1989	5	(1)	
Roderick Alonso Miller Molina	03.04.1992	11		
Francisco Antonio Palacios Alleyne	23.03.1991	10		
Jean Carlos Sánchez Rose	13.08.1999	4	(5)	
Midfielders:				
Víctor Manuel Ávila Reyes	17.08.1998	1	(7)	2
Wesley Alberto Cabrera Duarte	20.11.1998	2	(6)	
Ángel Daniel Castillo Whinttington	12.03.2002	4	(2)	
Luis Aurelio Pereira Lewis	13.09.1995	11	(1)	
Aimar Ariel Rodríguez Gil		2	(4)	1
Jhamal Adonis Rodríguez Thomas	28.01.1995	10	(1)	2
Jorge Luis Serrano Francis	19.01.1998	9	(4)	1
Manuel Alexander Vargas Moreno	19.01.1991	9	(3)	
Forwards:				
Jair Ibrahim Catuy Arosemena	28.01.1992	12		3
Sergio Cunningham Torres	01.04.1994	3	(2)	1
Abdiel Anel Garcés Díaz	07.01.2001	2	(2)	
José Luis Garcés Rivera	06.05.1981	3	(4)	
Isidoro Joamir Hinestroza Hernández	11.09.1997	2	(8)	2
Fernando Vidal Mena González	08.08.1990	7	(1)	1
Generik Ronaldo Robinson Brown	24.04.2005		(4)	
Ervin Vladimir Zorrilla Pérez	14.05.1996	1	(2)	
Cristian David Zúñiga Pino (COL)	07.05.1992	7	(2)	
Trainer:				
Gonzálo Soto Cortázar (COL)	26.01.1993	13		

ACADEMIA DE FÚTBOL SPORTING SAN MIGUELITO

Foundation date: 1989
Address: Altos de Santa Maria, San Miguelito
Stadium: Estadio "Profesor Javier Cruz García", Ciudad de Panamá (700)

THE SQUAD

	DOB	M	(s)	G
Goalkeepers:				
Álex Raúl Rodríguez Ledezma	05.08.1990	9		
Defenders:				
Chamir Dupuy Shreeves	14.05.1996	7		
Kevin Omar Galván López	10.03.1996	6	(2)	
Emmanuel Isaias Gómez Hernández	17.05.2000	4	(1)	
Chin Jossue Hormechea Hoy	12.05.1996	7	(1)	
Kadir José Hurtado Lorenzo	01.06.2001	5	(1)	1
Carlos Antonio Lambert Cerna	24.11.2000	3	(1)	
Yojad Rivera Rodríguez	01.08.1992	6		
Andrés Felipe Rodríguez Gordon (COL)	11.06.1995	2	(1)	
Midfielders:				
Gabriel Chiari De León	07.06.1993	2	(4)	
Gabriel Enrique Gómez Girón	29.05.1984	8		
Jesús Abraham Murillo Gudiño	14.08.2001		(1)	
Josué Joel Núñez	20.07.2000	1		
Harold Rodríguez		1		
Richard David Rodríguez González	25.12.1995	7	(2)	2
Marcos Aníbal Sánchez Mullins	23.12.1989	2	(5)	
Stiben Camilo Santos	14.01.1998	3	(1)	
Darío Daniel Wright Filos	25.04.1994	3		
Forwards:				
Ricardo Mauricio Clarke Hamilton	27.09.1992	5	(4)	3
Alexis Corpas Jordan	30.08.1994	5	(2)	1
Jesús Gabriel Delgado Singh	29.07.2001	2	(1)	
Ronaldo Antonio Dinolis Rodríguez	17.11.1994	4	(2)	1
Diomedes Lucero	26.12.2004		(2)	
Yaír Yoel Rentería	24.05.1990	1	(1)	1
Tomás Abdiel Rodríguez Mena	09.03.1999	5	(3)	1
Alexander Santimateo	04.09.2002		(2)	
Joel Antonio Suira Prescott	12.03.2001	1	(4)	
Trainer:				
Dorian López (COL)		9		

TAURO FÚTBOL CLUB

Foundation date: 1984
Address: Calle Francisco Filos, Pedregal, Ciudad de Panamá
Stadium: Estadio "Rommel Fernández Gutiérrez", Ciudad de Panamá (32,000)

THE SQUAD

	DOB	M	(s)	G
Goalkeepers:				
Jorginho Antonio Frías Bethancourt	21.03.2001	4		
Celino Hinojosa	25.03.2000	7	(1)	
Defenders:				
Iván Alejandro Anderson Hernández	24.11.1997	9	(1)	
Luis Yohan Asprilla	28.05.2001	2	(2)	
Giancarlos Moreno Estrada	22.07.2002	5	(3)	
Gerardo Omar Negrete Caballero (COL)	14.09.1992	6		
Luis Carlos Ovalle Victoria	07.09.1988	1	(4)	
Richard Amed Peralta Robledo	20.09.1993	11		3
Midfielders:				
Misael Acosta Labrador	19.07.1998	8		1
Rolando Vicente Botello Garibaldo	20.11.1991	10		
Edilson Denilson Carrasquilla Alcazar	06.06.2002	6	(3)	
Jonnathan Alonso García De Paredes	07.02.1998	7	(1)	
Axel Antonio McKenzie Morales	10.07.1999	1	(1)	
Victor Medina	18.02.2001	8	(3)	2
Rigoberto Niño Cabrera	03.06.1991	4		
Cristian Josué Quintero Carvajal	23.05.1997	2	(6)	
Justin Alberto Simons Samaniego	19.09.1997	3		
Ernesto Emanuel Walker Willis	09.02.1999	2	(4)	
Javir Kadir White Quintero	08.02.2003		(1)	
Forwards:				
Edwin Enrique Aguilar Samaniego	07.08.1985	4	(2)	4
Azael Mauricio Brown Espada	09.07.2001	2	(2)	
Jorge Samuel Clement Gutiérrez	12.02.2000	6	(2)	
Ismael Díaz de León	12.05.1997	1	(5)	1
Saed Ismael Díaz de León	23.06.1999	3	(3)	
Omar Alexander Hinestroza González	27.06.1994	7	(1)	1
Aaron Joel Lowis Christie	12.09.2002		(3)	
Diego Ezequiel Valanta Del Busto	08.09.2000	2	(4)	1
Trainer:				
Rafael Loreto Mea Vitali (VEN)	16.02.1975	3		
Javier Ainstein (ARG)	12.01.1983	8		

CLUB DEPORTIVO UNIVERSITARIO PENOMONÉ

Foundation date: 1974
Address: *Not known*
Stadium: Estadio "Virgilio Tejeira Andrión", Penomoné (900)

THE SQUAD

	DOB	M	(s)	G
Goalkeepers:				
Juan Carlos Loaiza Iguala	29.06.1998	6	(1)	
Óscar Emilio McFarlane Ortega	29.11.1980	3	(1)	
Defenders:				
Rolando Antonio Algandona Tejada	12.04.1989	8		
Kevin Omar Calderón Chávez	07.09.2000	2	(2)	
Imanol Sadad Ortega Rodríguez			(1)	
Samir José Ramírez Headley	27.04.1997	7		
Manuel Vicente Torres Morales	25.11.1978	7		
Osvaldo José Valencia Chambers	19.03.2003	2		
Carlos Shalom Zuñiga Hurtado	18.10.2000	1	(7)	
Midfielders:				
Jadir Jossuelo Anaya Morris	10.03.1997		(1)	
Ricardo Guardia Ávila	04.02.1997		(1)	
Jean Carlos Castillo Racero	19.02.2002		(4)	
Abdiel Alexander Castro Castillo	21.06.2002	6		
Nilson Daniel Espinosa Saldaña	21.05.1995	6	(2)	
Carlos Alberto Gutiérrez	14.03.1995	8		1
Yair José Hurtado Lorenzo	08.01.1995	3	(4)	
Lilio Mena Lewis	10.08.2001	4		1
Roberto Antonio Meneses Mclean	10.03.1999	2	(2)	
Jean Carlos Montenegro Martínez	01.05.1999	9		
Marlon Josué Navas Torrero	25.10.2001	1		
Sergio Vidal Ramírez Chávez	12.11.2000	8	(1)	
César Augusto Reyna Valladares	16.03.1998	2	(1)	
Elio Aldair Valdez	22.01.2000	1		
Forwards:				
Abdel Concepcion Aguilar Andrade	17.01.1998	6	(1)	
Eduardo Gabriel Aparicio Gutíerrez	15.10.2003	2	(1)	
Alfonso Manuel Machado Quintero	12.05.2000	2	(1)	
Sergio Jordan Moreno Aparicio	28.07.1992	3	(3)	1
Trainer:				
Sir Gary Stempel Powell (ENG)	15.12.1957	9		

SECOND LEVEL
Liga Nacional de Ascenso 2020

The second level was cancelled due to COVID-19 pandemic.
Herrera FC (called earlier Azuero FC) and **Veraguas CD** were promoted to First Level 2021.

NATIONAL TEAM
INTERNATIONAL MATCHES 2020/2021

10.10.2020	San José	Costa Rica - Panama	0-1(0-0)	(F)
13.10.2020	San José	Costa Rica - Panama	0-1(0-1)	(F)
13.11.2020	Graz	Japan - Panama	1-0(0-0)	(F)
16.11.2020	Wiener Neustadt	United States - Panama	6-2(3-1)	(F)
28.01.2021	Ciudad de Panamá	Panama - Serbia	0-0	(F)
25.03.2021	Santo Domingo	Panama - Barbados	1-0(0-0)	(WCQ)
28.03.2021	Santo Domingo	Dominica - Panama	1-2(0-1)	(WCQ)
05.06.2021	Ciudad de Panamá	Anguilla - Panama	0-13(0-4)	(WCQ)
08.06.2021	Ciudad de Panamá	Panama - Dominican Republic	3-0(1-0)	(WCQ)
12.06.2021	Ciudad de Panamá	Panama - Curaçao	2-1(0-0)	(WCQ)
15.06.2021	Willemstad	Curaçao - Panama	0-0	(WCQ)
30.06.2021	Nashville	Mexico - Panama	3-0(1-0)	(F)

10.10.2020, Friendly International
Estadio Nacional, San José; Attendance: 0
Referee: Keylor Antonio Herrera Villalobos (Costa Rica)
COSTA RICA - PANAMA 0-1(0-0)
PAN: José de Jesus Calderón Frias, Harold Oshkaly Cummings Segura, Francisco Antonio Palacios Alleyne, Jiovany Javier Ramos Díaz, Alexander González Moreno (59.Víctor Alfredo Griffith Mullins), José Manuel Murillo Morán (86.Ernesto Emanuel Walker Willis), Miguel Elías Camargo Cañizales (73.César Augusto Yanis Velasco), Alejandro Alonso Yearwood Francis, Abdiel Armando Ayarza Cocanegra, Diego Ezequiel Valanta Del Busto (46.Diego Ezequiel Valanta Del Busto), Cécilio Alfonso Waterman Ruiz (60.José Fajardo Nelson). Trainer: Thomas Christiansen Tarín (Denmark).
Goal: Abdiel Armando Ayarza Cocanegra (90+1).

13.10.2020, Friendly International
Estadio Nacional, San José; Attendance: 0
Referee: Juan Gabriel Calderón Pérez (Costa Rica)
COSTA RICA - PANAMA 0-1(0-1)
PAN: Luis Ricardo Mejía Cajar, Harold Oshkaly Cummings Segura, Richard Amed Peralta Robledo, Francisco Antonio Palacios Alleyne, Miguel Elías Camargo Cañizales (61.Cécilio Alfonso Waterman Ruiz), César Augusto Yanis Velasco (81.Víctor Manuel Medina Cunningham), Alejandro Alonso Yearwood Francis, Víctor Alfredo Griffith Mullins (90+3.Alexander González Moreno), Abdiel Armando Ayarza Cocanegra, Diego Ezequiel Valanta Del Busto (89.Jiovany Javier Ramos Díaz), José Fajardo Nelson (75.Ernesto Emanuel Walker Willis). Trainer: Thomas Christiansen Tarín (Denmark).
Goal: Abdiel Armando Ayarza Cocanegra (38).

13.11.2020, Friendly International
Merkur-Arena, Graz (Austria); Attendance: 0
Referee: Christian-Petru Ciochirca (Austria)
JAPAN - PANAMA 1-0(0-0)
PAN: Luis Ricardo Mejía Cajar [*sent off 78*], Harold Oshkaly Cummings Segura, Óscar Antonio Linton Bethancourt, Michael Amir Murillo Bermúdez, Andrés Alberto Andrade Cedeño, César Augusto Yanis Velasco (71.Diego Ezequiel Valanta Del Busto), Adalberto Eliécer Carrasquilla Alcázar, Víctor Alfredo Griffith Mullins (61.Armando Enrique Cooper Whitaker), Abdiel Armando Ayarza Cocanegra (81.Orlando Mosquera), Gabriel Arturo Torres Tejada (81.José Fajardo Nelson), Édgar Joel Bárcenas Herrera (71.Omar Ezequiel Browne Zuñiga). Trainer: Thomas Christiansen Tarín (Denmark).

16.11.2020, Friendly International
Wiener Neustadt Stadion, Wiener Neustadt (Austria); Attendance: 0
Referee: Harald Lechner (Austria)
UNITED STATES - PANAMA   **6-2(3-1)**
PAN: Orlando Mosquera, Óscar Antonio Linton Bethancourt, Fidel Escobar Mendieta, Michael Amir Murillo Bermúdez, Armando Enrique Cooper Whitaker (75.Abdiel Armando Ayarza Cocanegra), Adalberto Eliécer Carrasquilla Alcázar (55.Víctor Alfredo Griffith Mullins), Alejandro Alonso Yearwood Francis (55.Andrés Alberto Andrade Cedeño), Diego Ezequiel Valanta Del Busto (75.Omar Ezequiel Browne Zuñiga), Eduardo Antonio Guerrero Lozcano (46.Gabriel Arturo Torres Tejada), José Fajardo Nelson, Juan David Tejada Londono (46.César Augusto Yanis Velasco). Trainer: Thomas Christiansen Tarín (Denmark).
Goals: José Fajardo Nelson (8, 79).

28.01.2021, Friendly International
Estadio Olímpico "Rommel Fernández Gutiérrez", Ciudad de Panamá; Attendance: 0
Referee: Ameth Ariel Sánchez Pinzón (Panama)
PANAMA - SERBIA   **0-0**
PAN: Luis Ricardo Mejía Cajar, Roderick Alonso Miller Molina, Francisco Javier Vence Gómez, José Manuel Murillo Morán (87.Jean Carlos Rodríguez Quiñones), Francisco Antonio Palacios Alleyne, Jiovany Javier Ramos Díaz, Misael Acosta Labrador (58.Romeesh Nathaniel Ivey Belgravey), César Augusto Yanis Velasco (89.Rodolfo Alejandro Vega Iguala), Víctor Alfredo Griffith Mullins, Jair Ibrahim Catuy Arosemena (82.Yair Fernando Jaén Reina), Ismael Díaz De León (69.Andrés Alejandro Peñalba Martínez). Trainer: Thomas Christiansen Tarín (Denmark).

25.03.2021, 22nd FIFA World Cup Qualifiers, CONCACAF First Round
Estadio Olímpico "Félix Sánchez", Santo Domingo (Dominican Republic)
Referee: Nima Saghafi (United States)
PANAMA - BARBADOS   **1-0(0-0)**
PAN: Orlando Mosquera, Érick Javier Davis Grajales, Harold Oshkaly Cummings Segura, Michael Amir Murillo Bermúdez, Andrés Alberto Andrade Cedeño (71.José Fajardo Nelson), Aníbal Cesis Godoy Lemus, Adalberto Eliécer Carrasquilla Alcázar (46.César Augusto Yanis Velasco), José Rodríguez (79.José Manuel Murillo Morán), Abdiel Armando Ayarza Cocanegra (46.Miguel Elías Camargo Cañizales), Gabriel Arturo Torres Tejada (65.Jair Ibrahim Catuy Arosemena), Édgar Joel Bárcenas Herrera. Trainer: Thomas Christiansen Tarín (Denmark).
Goal: Jair Ibrahim Catuy Arosemena (82).

28.03.2021, 22nd FIFA World Cup Qualifiers, CONCACAF First Round
Estadio Olímpico "Félix Sánchez", Santo Domingo (Dominican Republic)
Referee: Marco Antonio Ortíz Nava (Mexico)
DOMINICA - PANAMA   **1-2(0-1)**
PAN: Orlando Mosquera, Érick Javier Davis Grajales, Harold Oshkaly Cummings Segura, Andrés Alberto Andrade Cedeño, Cesar Rodolfo Blackman Camarena, Aníbal Cesis Godoy Lemus (64.Víctor Alfredo Griffith Mullins), Miguel Elías Camargo Cañizales (46.Adalberto Eliécer Carrasquilla Alcázar), César Augusto Yanis Velasco (86.Abdiel Armando Ayarza Cocanegra), José Rodríguez (25.José Fajardo Nelson), Jair Ibrahim Catuy Arosemena (64.Gabriel Arturo Torres Tejada), Édgar Joel Bárcenas Herrera. Trainer: Thomas Christiansen Tarín (Denmark).
Goals: Briel Thomas (28 own goal), José Fajardo Nelson (86).

05.06.2021, 22nd FIFA World Cup Qualifiers, CONCACAF First Round
Estadio Nacional "Rod Carew", Ciudad de Panamá
Referee: Sergio Armando Reyna Moller (Guatemala)
ANGUILLA - PANAMA 0-13(0-4)
PAN: José de Jesus Calderón Frías, Adolfo Abdiel Machado, Richard Amed Peralta Robledo, Omar Federico Córdoba Quintero, Francisco Antonio Palacios Alleyne, Armando Enrique Cooper Whitaker (46.César Augusto Yanis Velasco), Miguel Elías Camargo Cañizales (71.Abdiel Armando Ayarza Cocanegra), Carlos Miguel Harvey Cesneros (46.Víctor Alfredo Griffith Mullins), Gabriel Arturo Torres Tejada, Cécilio Alfonso Waterman Ruiz (71.Jair Ibrahim Catuy Arosemena), Diego Ezequiel Valanta Del Busto (46.Alberto Abdiel Quintero Medina). Trainer: Thomas Christiansen Tarín (Denmark).
Goals: Armando Enrique Cooper Whitaker (7, 18), Diego Ezequiel Valanta Del Busto (32), Gabriel Arturo Torres Tejada (35 penalty), Tafari Smith (48 own goal), Cécilio Alfonso Waterman Ruiz (51), Gabriel Arturo Torres Tejada (54), Miguel Elías Camargo Cañizales (58), Gabriel Arturo Torres Tejada (71), Jair Ibrahim Catuy Arosemena (73), Gabriel Arturo Torres Tejada (84 penalty), Alberto Abdiel Quintero Medina (85), Francisco Antonio Palacios Alleyne (90).

08.06.2021, 22nd FIFA World Cup Qualifiers, CONCACAF First Round
Estadio Nacional "Rod Carew", Ciudad de Panamá
Referee: Walter Alexander Agustín López Rodríguez Castellanos (Guatemala))
PANAMA - DOMINICAN REPUBLIC 3-0(1-0)
PAN: Luis Ricardo Mejía Cajar, Érick Javier Davis Grajales (63.Adolfo Abdiel Machado), Harold Oshkaly Cummings Segura, Michael Amir Murillo Bermúdez, Andrés Alberto Andrade Cedeño, Alberto Abdiel Quintero Medina (61.César Augusto Yanis Velasco), Aníbal Cesis Godoy Lemus, Miguel Elías Camargo Cañizales (46.Édgar Joel Bárcenas Herrera), Adalberto Eliécer Carrasquilla Alcázar, Eduardo Antonio Guerrero Lozcano (46.José Luis Rodríguez Francis), José Fajardo Nelson (69.Cécilio Alfonso Waterman Ruiz). Trainer: Thomas Christiansen Tarín (Denmark).
Goals: Aníbal Cesis Godoy Lemus (8), Édgar Joel Bárcenas Herrera (67), Cécilio Alfonso Waterman Ruiz (86).

12.06.2021, 22nd FIFA World Cup Qualifiers, CONCACAF Second Round
Estadio Nacional, Ciudad de Panamá; Attendance: 7,000
Referee: Jaime Herrera Bonilla (El Salvador)
PANAMA - CURAÇAO 2-1(0-0)
PAN: Luis Ricardo Mejía Cajar, Érick Javier Davis Grajales, Harold Oshkaly Cummings Segura, Michael Amir Murillo Bermúdez, Andrés Alberto Andrade Cedeño, Alberto Abdiel Quintero Medina (73.Armando Enrique Cooper Whitaker), Aníbal Cesis Godoy Lemus, Adalberto Eliécer Carrasquilla Alcázar (84.Víctor Alfredo Griffith Mullins), José Luis Rodríguez Francis (57.César Augusto Yanis Velasco), Gabriel Arturo Torres Tejada (57.Cécilio Alfonso Waterman Ruiz), Édgar Joel Bárcenas Herrera. Trainer: Thomas Christiansen Tarín (Denmark).
Goals: Alberto Abdiel Quintero Medina (55), Cécilio Alfonso Waterman Ruiz (77).

15.06.2021, 22nd FIFA World Cup Qualifiers, CONCACAF Second Round
Stadion „Ergilio Hato", Willemstad
Referee: Marco Antonio Ortíz Nava (Mexico)
CURAÇAO - PANAMA 0-0
PAN: Luis Ricardo Mejía Cajar, Érick Javier Davis Grajales, Harold Oshkaly Cummings Segura, Francisco Antonio Palacios Alleyne (86.Adolfo Abdiel Machado), Andrés Alberto Andrade Cedeño, Alberto Abdiel Quintero Medina, Aníbal Cesis Godoy Lemus, Adalberto Eliécer Carrasquilla Alcázar, José Luis Rodríguez Francis (76.César Augusto Yanis Velasco), Édgar Joel Bárcenas Herrera (76.Abdiel Armando Ayarza Cocanegra), José Fajardo Nelson (59.Cécilio Alfonso Waterman Ruiz). Trainer: Thomas Christiansen Tarín (Denmark).

30.06.2021, Friendly International
Nissan Stadium, Nashville; Attendance: 30,386
Referee: Kevin Morrison (Jamaica)
MEXICO - PANAMA   **3-0(1-0)**
PAN: José de Jesus Calderón Frias, Adolfo Abdiel Machado, Érick Javier Davis Grajales, Richard Amed Peralta Robledo (46.Andrés Alberto Andrade Cedeño), Omar Federico Córdoba Quintero (46.Alberto Abdiel Quintero Medina), Francisco Antonio Palacios Alleyne, Aníbal Cesis Godoy Lemus, Miguel Elías Camargo Cañizales (46.César Augusto Yanis Velasco), Víctor Alfredo Griffith Mullins (46.Adalberto Eliécer Carrasquilla Alcázar), Jorman Israel Aguilar Bustamante (60.Gabriel Arturo Torres Tejada), José Fajardo Nelson (74.Cécilio Alfonso Waterman Ruiz). Trainer: Thomas Christiansen Tarín (Denmark).

NATIONAL TEAM PLAYERS 2020/2021

Name	DOB	Club
Goalkeepers		
José de Jesus CALDERÓN Frias	14.08.1985	*CSD Cobán Imperial (GUA)*
Luis Ricardo MEJÍA Cajar	16.03.1991	*Club Nacional de Football Montevideo (URU); 01.01.2021-> Unattached; 03.04.2021-> CA Fénix Montevideo (URU)*
Orlando MOSQUERA	25.12.1994	*Boluspor Kulübü (TUR)*
Defenders		
Andrés Alberto ANDRADE Cedeño	16.10.1998	*Linzer ASK (AUT)*
Cesar Rodolfo BLACKMAN Camarena	02.04.1998	*FC DAC 1904 Dunajská Streda (SVK)*
Omar Federico CÓRDOBA Quintero	13.06.1994	*CA Independiente La Chorrera*
Harold Oshkaly CUMMINGS Segura	01.03.1992	*Club Unión Española Santiago (CHI); 28.01.2021-> Club Always Ready La Paz (BOL)*
Érick Javier DAVIS Grajales	31.03.1991	*FC DAC 1904 Dunajská Streda (SVK)*
Fidel ESCOBAR Mendieta	09.01.1995	*AD Alcorcón (ESP)*
Óscar Antonio LINTON Bethancourt	29.01.1993	*Sliema Wanderers FC (MLT)*
Adolfo Abdiel MACHADO	14.02.1985	*AD San Carlos Ciudad Quesada (CRC)*
Roderick Alonso MILLER Molina	03.04.1992	*San Francisco FC La Chorrera*
Michael Amir MURILLO Bermúdez	11.02.1996	*RSC Anderlecht Bruxelles (BEL)*
Francisco Antonio PALACIOS Alleyne	23.03.1991	*San Francisco FC La Chorrera*
Richard Amed PERALTA Robledo	20.09.1993	*Tauro FC Ciudad de Panamá*
Jiovany Javier RAMOS Díaz	26.01.1997	*CA Independiente La Chorrera*
Francisco Javier VENCE Gómez	11.04.1992	*CA Independiente La Chorrera*
Alejandro Alonso YEARWOOD Francis	29.04.1996	*CD Árabe Unido Ciudad de Colón*

Midfielders		
Misael ACOSTA Labrador	19.07.1998	*Tauro FC Ciudad de Panamá*
Abdiel Armando AYARZA Cocanegra	12.09.1992	*CS Cienciano Cuzco (PER)*
Omar Ezequiel BROWNE Zuñiga	03.05.1994	*CA Independiente La Chorrera*
Miguel Elías CAMARGO Cañizales	05.09.1993	*Deportivo Táchira FC San Cristóbal (VEN); 01.01.2021-> AD Pasto (COL); 19.05.2021 -> CD Independiente Medellín (COL)*
Armando Enrique COOPER Whitaker	26.11.1987	*Hapoel Tel Aviv FC (ISR); 19.01.2021-> Maccabi Petah Tikva FC (ISR)*
Adalberto Eliécer CARRASQUILLA Alcázar	28.11.1998	*FC Cartagena (ESP)*
Aníbal Cesis GODOY Lemus	10.02.1990	*Nashville SC (USA)*
Alexander GONZÁLEZ Moreno	14.12.1994	*Alianza FC Ciudad de Panamá*
Víctor Alfredo GRIFFITH Mullins	12.12.2000	*Santos de Guápiles FC (CRC); 01.01.2021-> Unattached; 03.03.2021-> CD Árabe Unido Ciudad de Colón*
Eduardo Antonio GUERRERO Lozcano	21.02.2000	*Maccabi Tel Aviv FC (ISR)*
Carlos Miguel HARVEY Cesneros	03.02.2000	*Los Angeles Galaxy (USA)*
Romeesh Nathaniel IVEY Belgravey	14.07.1994	*CD Alianza Petrolera Barrancabermeja (COL)*
Yair Fernando JAÉN Reina	16.03.1997	*Costa del Este FC Ciudad de Panamá*
Víctor Manuel MEDINA Cunningham	18.02.2001	*Tauro FC Ciudad de Panamá*
José Manuel MURILLO Morán	24.02.1995	*Comunicaciones FC Ciudad de Guatemala (GUA); 25.01.2021-> CD Plaza Amador Ciudad de Panamá*
Andrés Alejandro PEÑALBA Martínez	08.07.1997	*Herrera FC*
Alberto Abdiel QUINTERO Medina	18.12.1987	*Club Universitario de Deportes Lima (PER)*
José Luis RODRÍGUEZ Francis	19.06.1997	*CD Lugo (ESP)*
Rodolfo Alejandro VEGA Iguala	12.06.2003	*CD Plaza Amador Ciudad de Panamá*
Ernesto Emanuel WALKER Willis	09.02.1999	*Tauro FC Ciudad de Panamá*
César Augusto YANIS Velasco	28.01.1996	*Costa del Este FC Ciudad de Panamá*

Forwards		
Jorman Israel AGUILAR Bustamante	11.09.1994	*AD San Carlos Ciudad Quesada (CRC); 18.01.2021-> Sport Boys Association Callao (PER)*
Édgar Joel BÁRCENAS Herrera	23.10.1993	*Girona FC (ESP)*
Jair Ibrahim CATUY Arosemena	28.01.1992	*CD Universitario Penonomé*
Ismael DÍAZ De León	12.05.1997	*Tauro FC Ciudad de Panamá*
José FAJARDO Nelson	18.08.1993	*CA Independiente La Chorrera; 04.01.2021 -> 9 de Octubre FC Guayaquil (ECU)*
Juan David TEJADA London	14.01.1997	*Tampa Bay Rowdies (USA)*
Gabriel Arturo TORRES Tejada	31.10.1988	*CARE Independiente del Valle Sangolquí (ECU); 31.01.2021-> Club UNAM Ciudad de México (MEX)*
Diego Ezequiel VALANTA Del Busto	08.09.2000	*Tauro FC Ciudad de Panamá*
Cécilio Alfonso WATERMAN Ruiz	13.04.1991	*CD Universidad de Concepción (CHI); 27.03.3021-> Everton de Viña del Mar(CHI)*

National coaches		
Thomas CHRISTIANSEN Tarín (Denmark) [from 22.07.2020]		11.03.1973

PUERTO RICO

The Country:	The FA:
Estado Libre Asociado de Puerto Rico (Commonwealth of Puerto Rico) Capital: San Juan Surface: 9,104 km² Population: 3,285,874 [2020] Time: UTC-4 Independent since: 1898	Federación Puertorriqueña de Fútbol Calle Los Angeles Final Plaza de Santurce Apartado Postal 367557, San Juan 00936 Year of Formation: 1940 Member of FIFA since: 1960 Member of CONCACAF since: 1960

NATIONAL TEAM RECORDS

First international match: 12.11.1940: Cuba - Puerto Rico 1-1
Most international caps: Héctor Omar Ramos Lebron – 36 caps (since 2010)
Most international goals: Héctor Omar Ramos Lebron – 18 goals / 36 caps (since 2010)

CONCACAF GOLD CUP	
1991	Did not enter
1993	Did not enter
1996	Qualifiers
1998	Did not enter
2000	Qualifiers
2002	Qualifiers
2003	Did not enter
2005	Qualifiers
2007	Did not enter
2009	Did not enter
2011	Qualifiers
2013	Qualifiers
2015	Qualifiers
2017	Qualifiers
2019	Qualifiers
2021	Qualifiers

FIFA WORLD CUP	
1930	-
1934	-
1938	-
1950	-
1954	-
1958	-
1962	Did not enter
1966	Did not enter
1970	Did not enter
1974	Qualifiers
1978	Did not enter
1982	Did not enter
1986	Qualifiers
1990	Qualifiers
1994	Qualifiers
1998	Qualifiers
2002	Qualifiers
2006	Did not enter
2010	Qualifiers
2014	Qualifiers
2018	Qualifiers

F.I.F.A. CONFEDERATIONS CUP 1992-2017

None

OLYMPIC FOOTBALL TOURNAMENTS 1900-2016
1992 (Qualifiers), 2008 (Qualifiers), 2016 (Qualifiers)

CCCF (Confederación Centroamericana y del Caribe de Fútbol) CHAMPIONSHIPS 1941-1961
None

CONCACAF CHAMPIONSHIPS 1963-1989
None

CONCACAF NATIONS LEAGUE	
2019-2020	League C

CARIBBEAN CHAMPIONSHIPS 1989-2017

1989	Did not enter	1999	Qualifiers
1991	Qualifiers	2001	Qualifiers
1992	Did not enter	2005	Qualifiers
1993	Final Tournament - Group Stage	2007	Did not enter
1994	Qualifiers	2008	Did not enter
1995	Qualifiers	2010	Qualifiers
1996	Did not enter	2012	Qualifiers
1997	*Withdrew*	2014	Qualifiers
1998	Qualifiers	2017	Qualifiers

PUERTO RICAN CLUB HONOURS IN CONCACAF CLUB COMPETITIONS:

CONCACAF Champions Cup / CONCACAF Champions League 1962-2020		
None		

CONCACAF League 2017-2020		
None		

Caribbean Club Championship 1997-2021		
Puero Rico Islanders FC Bayamón	2	2010, 2011

CONCACAF Cup Winners Cup 1991-1995*		
None		

Copa Interamericana 1968-1998*		
None		

*defunct competitions

NATIONAL COMPETITIONS
TABLE OF HONOURS

	CHAMPIONS
	Asociación de Fútbol de Puerto Rico
1996	*Not known*
	Liga Mayor de Fútbol
1997	Leones Maunabo
1998	Islanders San Juan
1999	Islanders San Juan
2000	Vaqueros Bayamón
2001	Islanders San Juan
2002	Vaqueros Bayamón
2003	Sporting Carolina

2004	Sporting San Lorenzo
2005	Real Quintana San Juan
Campeonato Nacional de Fútbol	
2005	Fraigcomar Río Piedras
2006	Fraigcomar Río Piedras
2007	Fraigcomar Río Piedras
Puerto Rico Soccer League	
2008	Sevilla FC Juncos
2009	Bayamón FC
2010	CA River Plate Puerto Rico Ponce
Liga Nacional de Fútbol de Puerto Rico	
2011	FC Leones de Ponce
2012	Bayamón FC
2013	Sevilla FC Puerto Rico Juncos
2014	Yabuco Sual FC Yabucoa
2015	Criollos de Caguas FC
2016	*Season cancelled*
2017	Global Premier Soccer Puerto Rico
2018/2019	Metropolitan Football Academy San Juan
2019/2020	*Competition suspended*
2020/2021	*No competition*

NATIONAL CHAMPIONSHIP
Liga Nacional de Fútbol de Puerto Rico 2020/2021

The championship was cancelled due to COVID-19 pandemic.

NATIONAL TEAM
INTERNATIONAL MATCHES 2020/2021

19.01.2021	Santo Domingo	Dominican Republic - Puerto Rico	0-1(0-1)	(F)
23.01.2021	Ciudad de Guatemala	Guatemala - Puerto Rico	1-0(0-0)	(F)
24.03.2021	San Cristóbal	Saint Kitts and Nevis - Puerto Rico	1-0(1-0)	(WCQ)
28.03.2021	Mayagüez	Puerto Rico - Trinidad and Tobago	1-1(0-0)	(WCQ)
02.06.2021	Mayagüez	Puerto Rico - Bahamas	7-0(4-0)	(WCQ)
08.06.2021	Georgetown	Guyana - Puerto Rico	0-2(0-2)	(WCQ)

19.01.2021, Friendly International
Estadio Olímpico "Félix Sánchez", Santo Domingo; Attendance: 0
Referee: Randy Encarnación (Dominican Republic)
DOMINICAN REPUBLIC - PUERTO RICO   **0-1(0-1)**
PUR: Cody Matthew Laurendi, Callum Blu Stretch, Daniel Rosario, Nicolás Javier Cardona Ruiz, Raúl González III, Darren Scott Ríos, Devin Vega (80.Isaac Emmanuel Angking), Sidney Adam Rivera, Alec Díaz (80.Wilfredo Rivera Cepeda), Jaden Servania, Kevin Javier Hernández Hernández (69.Juan Ignacio O'Neill De Corral). Trainer: Elgy Fabricio Morales Herrera.
Goal: Sidney Adam Rivera (45+1 penalty).

23.01.2021, Friendly International
Estadio "Doroteo Guamuch Flores", Ciudad de Guatemala; Attendance: 0
Referee: Bryan Lopez Castellanos (Guatemala)
GUATEMALA - PUERTO RICO   **1-0(0-0)**
PUR: Cody Matthew Laurendi, Callum Blu Stretch, Daniel Rosario, Nicolás Javier Cardona Ruiz, Raúl González III (62.Jan Carlos Mateo Delgado), Darren Scott Ríos (31.Giovanni Padrón), Devin Vega (64.Kevin Javier Hernández Hernández), Juan Ignacio O'Neill De Corral, Sidney Adam Rivera (63.Isaac Emmanuel Angking), Alec Díaz (63.Wilfredo Rivera Cepeda), Jaden Servania. Trainer: Elgy Fabricio Morales Herrera.

24.03.2021, 22nd FIFA World Cup Qualifiers, CONCACAF First Round
Estadio Panamericano, San Cristóbal (Dominican Republic)
Referee: Randy Encarnacion Solano (Dominican Republic)
SAINT KITTS AND NEVIS - PUERTO RICO   **1-0(1-0)**
PUR: Cody Matthew Laurendi, Daniel Rosario, Nicolás Javier Cardona Ruiz (72.Rodolfo Eduardo Sulia Herrera), Raúl González III, Darren Scott Ríos (72.Juan Ignacio O'Neill De Corral), Devin Vega, Isaac Emmanuel Angking (69.Wilfredo Rivera Cepeda), Gerald Jadiel Díaz Agrait, Ricardo Emmanuel Rivera De León, Sidney Adam Rivera (89.Alec Díaz), Jaden Servania (89.Jan Carlos Mateo Delgado). Trainer: David Sarachan (United States).

28.03.2021, 22nd FIFA World Cup Qualifiers, CONCACAF First Round
Mayagüez Athletics Stadium, Mayagüez
Referee: Adonai Escobedo González (Mexico)
PUERTO RICO - TRINIDAD AND TOBAGO   **1-1(0-0)**
PUR: Cody Matthew Laurendi, Daniel Rosario, Nicolás Javier Cardona Ruiz, Raúl González III (87.Eli Robert Carr), Darren Scott Ríos, Devin Vega (87.Giovanni Padrón), Isaac Emmanuel Angking (71.Alec Díaz), Gerald Jadiel Díaz Agrait (63.Jaden Servania), Juan Ignacio O'Neill De Corral, Sidney Adam Rivera (63.Ricardo Emmanuel Rivera De León), Wilfredo Rivera Cepeda. Trainer: David Sarachan (United States).
Goal: Ricardo Emmanuel Rivera De León (71).

02.06.2021, 22nd FIFA World Cup Qualifiers, CONCACAF First Round
Mayagüez Athletics Stadium, Mayagüez
Referee: Tori Penso (United States)

PUERTO RICO - BAHAMAS   **7-0(4-0)**

PUR: Joel Serrano Mercado, Zarek Chase Valentin, Nicolás Javier Cardona Ruiz, Raúl González III (67.Rodolfo Eduardo Sulia Herrera), Darren Scott Ríos, Devin Vega (64.Jaden Servania), Isaac Emmanuel Angking (74.Jordan Saling), Gerald Jadiel Díaz Agrait, Juan Ignacio O'Neill De Corral, Ricardo Emmanuel Rivera De León (64.Lester Hayes III), Wilfredo Rivera Cepeda (64.Daniel Rosario). Trainer: David Sarachan (United States).

Goals: Gerald Jadiel Díaz Agrait (3), Ricardo Emmanuel Rivera De León (13), Isaac Emmanuel Angking (31), Ricardo Emmanuel Rivera De León (43 penalty), Devin Vega (62), Jaden Servania (66), Lester Hayes III (90+2).

08.06.2021, 22nd FIFA World Cup Qualifiers, CONCACAF First Round
Warner Park, Basseterre (Saint Kitts and Nevis)
Referee: Ismael Cornejo Meléndez (El Salvador)

GUYANA - PUERTO RICO   **0-2(0-2)**

PUR: Joel Serrano Mercado, Zarek Chase Valentin, Nicolás Javier Cardona Ruiz, Raúl González III, Darren Scott Ríos (87.Rodolfo Eduardo Sulia Herrera), Devin Vega (87.Kevin Javier Hernández Hernández), Isaac Emmanuel Angking (64.Jaden Servania), Gerald Jadiel Díaz Agrait, Juan Ignacio O'Neill De Corral, Ricardo Emmanuel Rivera De León (64.Lester Hayes III), Wilfredo Rivera Cepeda (79.Eli Robert Carr). Trainer: David Sarachan (United States).

Goals: Wilfredo Rivera Cepeda (12), Isaac Emmanuel Angking (25 penalty).

NATIONAL TEAM PLAYERS 2020/2021

Name	DOB	Club
Goalkeepers		
Cody Matthew LAURENDI	15.08.1988	*Oklahoma City Energy (USA)*
Joel Serrano MERCADO	17.05.1999	*Mercy Mavericks (USA)*
Defenders		
Nicolás Javier CARDONA Ruiz	11.02.1999	*UB Conquense (ESP); 22.02.2021-> Hartford Athletic (USA)*
Daniel ROSARIO	10.04.2002	*Orlando Academy (USA)*
Callum Blu STRETCH	19.09.1999	*Indiana Hoosiers (USA)*
Rodolfo Eduardo SULIA Herrera	08.08.2002	*Metropolitan Football Academy San Juan*
Zarek Chase VALENTIN	06.08.1991	*Houston Dynamo (USA)*
Midfielders		
Isaac Emmanuel ANGKING	24.01.2000	*Unattached*
Eli Robert CARR	19.01.2001	*Longwood Lancers (USA)*
Gerald Jadiel DÍAZ Agrait	29.03.1999	*Vilamarxant CF (ESP)*
Raúl GONZÁLEZ III	03.10.1994	*Memphis 901 FC (USA)*
Jan Carlos MATEO Delgado	31.01.2003	*GPS Puerto Rico*
Juan Ignacio O'NEILL De Corral	12.07.1998	*Santa Clara Broncos (USA)*
Darren Scott RÍOS	14.10.1995	*Satélite Norte Santa Cruz (BOL)*
Wilfredo RIVERA Cepeda	14.10.2003	*Orlando City SC (USA)*
Devin VEGA	11.12.1998	*Unattached*
Forwards		
Alec DÍAZ	07.12.2001	*Tacoma Defiance (USA)*
Lester HAYES III	19.09.1993	*El Palo FC (ESP)*
Kevin Javier HERNÁNDEZ Hernández	17.07.1999	*Satélite Norte Santa Cruz (BOL)*
Giovanni PADRÓN	15.04.1998	*Nashville Knights (USA)*
Ricardo Emmanuel RIVERA De León	17.04.1997	*Vilamarxant CF (ESP)*
Sidney Adam RIVERA	15.11.1993	*Bangladesh Police FC Dhākā (BAN)*
Jordan SALING	15.03.1996	*Unattached*
Jaden SERVANIA	16.07.2001	*Birmingham Legion (USA)*
National coaches		
Elgy Fabricio MORALES Herrera [25.05.2019 – 24.02.2021]		21.09.1975
David SARACHAN (United States) [from 24.02.2021]		07.06.1954

SAINT KITTS AND NEVIS

The Country:	The FA:
Federation of Saint Kitts and Nevis	St. Kitts and Nevis Football Association
Capital: Basseterre	Lozack Road, P.O. Box 465, Basseterre
Surface: 261 km²	Year of Formation: 1932
Population: 52,441 [2018]	Member of FIFA since: 1992
Time: UTC-4	Member of CONCACAF since: 1990
Independent since: 1983	

NATIONAL TEAM RECORDS

First international match: 18.08.1938: Saint Kitts and Nevis – Grenada 2-4
Most international caps: Thrizen Jahl Leader – 76 caps (since 2004)
Most international goals: Keith Jerome Gumbs Tukijo – 24 goals / 41 caps (1993-2011)

CONCACAF GOLD CUP		FIFA WORLD CUP	
1991	Qualifiers	1930	-
1993	Qualifiers	1934	-
1996	Qualifiers	1938	-
1998	Qualifiers	1950	-
2000	Qualifiers	1954	-
2002	Qualifiers	1958	-
2003	Qualifiers	1962	-
2005	Qualifiers	1966	-
2007	Qualifiers	1970	-
2009	Qualifiers	1974	-
2011	Qualifiers	1978	-
2013	Qualifiers	1982	-
2015	Qualifiers	1986	-
2017	Qualifiers	1990	-
2019	Qualifiers	1994	Did not enter
2021	Qualifiers	1998	Qualifiers
		2002	Qualifiers
		2006	Qualifiers
		2010	Qualifiers
		2014	Qualifiers
		2018	Qualifiers

F.I.F.A. CONFEDERATIONS CUP 1992-2017

None

OLYMPIC FOOTBALL TOURNAMENTS 1908-2016							
1908	-	1948	-	1972	-	1996	-
1912	-	1952	-	1976	-	2000	Qualifiers
1920	-	1956	-	1980	-	2004	Qualifiers
1924	-	1960	-	1984	-	2008	Qualifiers
1928	-	1964	-	1988	-	2012	Qualifiers
1936	-	1968	-	1992	-	2016	Qualifiers

CCCF (Confederación Centroamericana y del Caribe de Fútbol) CHAMPIONSHIPS 1941-1961
None
CONCACAF CHAMPIONSHIPS 1963-1989
None

CONCACAF NATIONS LEAGUE	
2019-2020	League B (*relegated to League C*)

CARIBBEAN CHAMPIONSHIPS 1989-2017			
1989	Qualifiers	1999	Final Tournament - Group Stage
1991	Qualifiers	2001	Final Tournament - Group Stage
1992	Qualifiers	2005	Qualifiers
1993	Final Tournament - 4th Place	2007	Qualifiers
1994	Qualifiers	2008	Qualifiers
1995	Qualifiers	2010	Qualifiers
1996	Final Tournament - Group Stage	2012	Qualifiers
1997	Final Tournament - Runners-up	2014	Qualifiers
1998	Qualifiers	2017	Qualifiers

SAINT KITTS AND NEVIS CLUB HONOURS IN CONCACAF CLUB COMPETITIONS:

CONCACAF Champions Cup / CONCACAF Champions League 1962-2020
None
CONCACAF League 2017-2020
None
Caribbean Club Championship 1997-2021
None
CONCACAF Cup Winners Cup 1991-1995*
None
Copa Interamericana 1968-1998*
None

**defunct competitions*

NATIONAL COMPETITIONS
TABLE OF HONORS – SAINT KITTS

	CHAMPIONS	CUP WINNERS
1980	Village Superstars FC Basseterre	-
1981	Newtown United FC Basseterre	-
1982	*Not known*	-
1983	*Not known*	-
1984	Newtown United FC Basseterre	-
1985	*Not known*	-
1986	Garden Hotspurs FC Basseterre	-
1987	Newtown United FC Basseterre	-
1988	Newtown United FC Basseterre	-
1989	Newtown United FC Basseterre	-
1990	Garden Hotspurs FC Basseterre	-
1991	Village Superstars FC Basseterre	-
1992	Newtown United FC Basseterre	-
1993	Newtown United FC Basseterre	-
1994	Garden Hotspurs FC Basseterre	-
1995	Newtown United FC Basseterre	-
1996	Newtown United FC Basseterre	-
1997	Newtown United FC Basseterre	-
1998	Newtown United FC Basseterre	-
1999	St. Paul's United FC Basseterre	-
2000/2001	Garden Hotspurs FC Basseterre	-
2001/2002	Cayon Rockets	Cayon Rockets
2002/2003	Village Superstars FC Basseterre	Village Superstars FC Basseterre
2003/2004	Newtown United FC Basseterre	Village Superstars FC Basseterre
2004/2005	Village Superstars FC Basseterre	*Not known*
2005/2006	Village Superstars FC Basseterre	*Not known*
2006/2007	Newtown United FC Basseterre	Newtown United FC Basseterre
2007/2008	Newtown United FC Basseterre	-
2008/2009	St. Paul's United FC Basseterre	-
2009/2010	Newtown United FC Basseterre	-
2010/2011	Village Superstars FC Basseterre	Village Superstars FC Basseterre
2011/2012	Newtown United FC Basseterre	St. Paul's United FC Basseterre
2012/2013	Conaree FC	Conaree FC
2013/2014	St. Pauls United FC Basseterre	Newtown United FC Basseterre
2014/2015	St. Pauls United FC Basseterre	Conaree FC
2015/2016	Cayon FC	Garden Hotspurs FC Basseterre
2016/2017	Cayon FC	Village Superstars FC Champsville
2017/2018	Village Superstars FC Champsville	Cayon FC
2018/2019	*Championship abandoned*	Newtown United FC
2019/2020	St. Pauls United Strikers FC Basseterre	St. Pauls United Strikers FC Basseterre

NATIONAL COMPETITIONS
TABLE OF HONORS - NEVIS

	CHAMPIONS	CUP WINNERS
2003/2004	Bath United	-
2004/2005	Fitness Pioneers	-
2005/2006	Harris United	-
2006/2007	Bath United	Harris United
2007/2008	SL Horsford Highlights FC	BA SSG Strikers Stoney Grove
2008/2009	SL Horsford Highlights FC	BA SSG Strikers Stoney Grove
2009/2010	BA SSG Strikers Stoney Grove	BA SSG Strikers Stoney Grove
2010/2011	Bath United	SL Horsford Highlights International
2011/2012	*Not held*	*Not known*
2012/2013	*Not held*	Bath United
2013/2014	SL Horsford Highlights FC	*Not known*
2014/2015	*Not held*	*Not known*
2015/2016	*Not held*	SL Horsford Highlights International
2016/2017	SL Horsford Highlights International	*Not held*
2017/2018	*Championship abandoned*	Pioneers FC
2018/2019	*Championship abandoned*	*Not held*
2019/2020	Youth of the Future	*Not held*

NATIONAL CHAMPIONSHIP
SKNFA Digicel Premier League 2021

The championship started on 19.02.2021 due to transition to autumn-spring rhythm.
Results and final tables will be presented in next year's yearbook.

NATIONAL TEAM
INTERNATIONAL MATCHES 2020/2021

24.03.2021	San Cristóbal	Saint Kitts and Nevis - Puerto Rico	1-0(1-0)	(WCQ)
27.03.2021	Nassau	Bahamas - Saint Kitts and Nevis	0-4(0-1)	(WCQ)
04.06.2021	Basseterre	Saint Kitts and Nevis - Guyana	3-0(2-0)	(WCQ)
08.06.2021	San Cristóbal	Trinidad and Tobago - Saint Kitts and Nevis	2-0(1-0)	(WCQ)
12.06.2021	Basseterre	El Salvador - Saint Kitts and Nevis	0-4(0-3)	(WCQ)
15.06.2021	San Salvador	Saint Kitts and Nevis - El Salvador	2-0(1-0)	(WCQ)

24.03.2021, 22nd FIFA World Cup Qualifiers, CONCACAF First Round
Estadio Panamericano, San Cristóbal (Dominican Republic)
Referee: Randy Encarnacion Solano (Dominican Republic)
SAINT KITTS AND NEVIS - PUERTO RICO   **1-0(1-0)**
SKN: Julani Kyle Archibald, Ordell Brian Flemming, Andre Maurice Keith Burley, Kimaree Brian Alister Rogers (65.Keithroy Junior Royston Freeman), Lois Paul Maynard, Gerard Geron Agustus Williams, Raheem Somersall (60.Theo Jay Wharton), Yohannes Menelik Battice Mitchum, Vinceroy Desron Nelson, Omari Shaquil Jabari Sterling-James (65.Tishan Tajahni Hanley), Rowan Earl Anthony Liburd. Trainer: Leonardo Martins Neiva (Brazil).
Goal: Vinceroy Desron Nelson (42).

27.03.2021, 22nd FIFA World Cup Qualifiers, CONCACAF First Round
"Thomas Robinson" Stadium, Nassau
Referee: Óscar Macías Romo (Mexico)
BAHAMAS - SAINT KITTS AND NEVIS   **0-4(0-1)**
SKN: Julani Kyle Archibald, Ordell Brian Flemming, Andre Maurice Keith Burley, Keithroy Junior Royston Freeman (87.Tahir Hanley), Kimaree Brian Alister Rogers (87.Niquan Phipps), Lois Paul Maynard, Gerard Geron Agustus Williams, Raheem Somersall (89.Malique Roberts), Yohannes Menelik Battice Mitchum, Vinceroy Desron Nelson (77.Raheem O'Niel Francis), Rowan Earl Anthony Liburd (77.Omari Shaquil Jabari Sterling-James). Trainer: Leonardo Martins Neiva (Brazil).
Goals: Keithroy Junior Royston Freeman (25), Kimaree Brian Alister Rogers (51 penalty), Keithroy Junior Royston Freeman (65), Omari Shaquil Jabari Sterling-James (82).

04.06.2021, 22nd FIFA World Cup Qualifiers, CONCACAF First Round
Warner Park, Basseterre
Referee: Ricangel de Leça (Aruba)
SAINT KITTS AND NEVIS - GUYANA   **3-0(2-0)**
SKN: Julani Kyle Archibald, Thrizen Jahl Leader (77.Malique Roberts), Ordell Brian Flemming, Keithroy Junior Royston Freeman (77.Rowan Earl Anthony Liburd), Gerard Geron Agustus Williams, Romaine Theodore Sawyers (86.Vinceroy Desron Nelson), Theo Jay Wharton (46.Andre Maurice Keith Burley), Lois Paul Maynard, Raheem Somersall (77.Yohannes Menelik Battice Mitchum), Harrison Andreas Panayiotou, Omari Shaquil Jabari Sterling-James. Trainer: Leonardo Martins Neiva (Brazil).
Goals: Keithroy Junior Royston Freeman (9 penalty, 36), Romaine Theodore Sawyers (67).

08.06.2021, 22nd FIFA World Cup Qualifiers, CONCACAF First Round
"Estadio Olímpico "Félix Sánchez", Santo Domingo (Dominican Republic)
Referee: Randy Encarnacion Solano (Dominican Republic)
TRINIDAD AND TOBAGO - SAINT KITTS AND NEVIS   **2-0(1-0)**
SKN: Clifford Samuel, Ordell Brian Flemming, Andre Maurice Keith Burley, Romaine Theodore Sawyers, Theo Jay Wharton (41.Yohannes Menelik Battice Mitchum), Lois Paul Maynard, Gerard Geron Agustus Williams (86.Malique Roberts), Raheem Somersall (86.Kalonji Clarke), Harrison Andreas Panayiotou, Omari Shaquil Jabari Sterling-James (68.Tiquanny Williams), Rowan Earl Anthony Liburd (68.Vinceroy Desron Nelson). Trainer: Leonardo Martins Neiva (Brazil).

12.06.2021, 22nd FIFA World Cup Qualifiers, CONCACAF Second Round
Warner Park, Basseterre
Referee: Kevin Morrison (Jamaica)
EL SALVADOR - SAINT KITTS AND NEVIS   **0-4(0-3)**
SKN: Julani Kyle Archibald, Thrizen Jahl Leader, Ordell Brian Flemming (39.Vinceroy Desron Nelson), Keithroy Junior Royston Freeman, Romaine Theodore Sawyers, Gerard Geron Agustus Williams, Lois Paul Maynard, Raheem Somersall (62.Rowan Earl Anthony Liburd), Yohannes Menelik Battice Mitchum, Harrison Andreas Panayiotou (80.Tiquanny Williams), Omari Shaquil Jabari Sterling-James (62.Tahir Hanley). Trainer: Leonardo Martins Neiva (Brazil).

15.06.2021, 22nd FIFA World Cup Qualifiers, CONCACAF Second Round
Estadio Cuscatlán, San Salvador
Referee: Keylor Herrera (Costa Rica)
SAINT KITTS AND NEVIS - EL SALVADOR   **2-0(1-0)**
SKN: Julani Kyle Archibald, Thrizen Jahl Leader (79.Raheem O'Niel Francis), Andre Maurice Keith Burley, Ordell Brian Flemming, Keithroy Junior Royston Freeman, Petrez Williams (46.Theo Jay Wharton), Gerard Geron Agustus Williams, Romaine Theodore Sawyers (79.Xavier French), Yohannes Menelik Battice Mitchum, Harrison Andreas Panayiotou (46.Tiquanny Williams), Vinceroy Desron Nelson (60.Rowan Earl Anthony Liburd). Trainer: Leonardo Martins Neiva (Brazil).

NATIONAL TEAM PLAYERS
2020/2021

Name	DOB	Club

Goalkeepers

Julani Kyle ARCHIBALD	18.05.1991	*Real Minas de Tegucigalpa (HON)*
Clifford SAMUEL	13.01.1990	*Conaree FC*

Defenders

Andre Maurice Keith BURLEY	10.09.1999	*Hungerford Town FC (ENG)*
Ordell Brian FLEMMING	16.09.1993	*Village Superstars FC Champsville*
Xavier FRENCH	14.05.1997	*Saddlers United FC Basseterre*
Thrizen Jahl LEADER	03.07.1984	*St. Pauls United Strikers FC Basseterre*
Malique ROBERTS	01.08.2001	*Cayon Rockets FC*
Petrez WILLIAMS	18.06.2000	*St. Pauls United Strikers FC Basseterre*

Midfielders

Kalonji CLARKE	15.02.2001	*St. Pauls United Strikers FC Basseterre*
Raheem O'Niel FRANCIS	28.05.1996	*Village Superstars FC Champsville*
Lois Paul MAYNARD	22.01.1989	*Stockport County FC (ENG)*
Yohannes Menelik Battice MITCHUM	06.04.1998	*Newtown United FC*
Kimaree Brian Alister ROGERS	14.01.1994	*Village Superstars FC Champsville*
Romaine Theodore SAWYERS	02.11.1991	*West Bromwich Albion FC (ENG)*
Raheem SOMERSALL	05.07.1997	*South Georgia Tormenta (USA)*
Omari Shaquil Jabari STERLING-JAMES	15.09.1993	*Kidderminster Harriers FC (ENG)*
Theo Jay WHARTON	15.11.1994	*Barry Town United FC (WAL)*
Gerard Geron Agustus WILLIAMS	04.06.1988	*Cayon Rockets FC*

Forwards

Keithroy Junior Royston FREEMAN	16.10.1993	*St. Pauls United Strikers FC Basseterre*
Tahir HANLEY	05.05.1997	*Real Minas de Tegucigalpa (HON)*
Tishan Tajahni HANLEY	22.08.1990	*Allentown United (USA)*
Rowan Earl Anthony LIBURD	28.08.1992	*Billericay Town FC (ENG)*
Vinceroy Desron NELSON	10.01.1996	*St. Pauls United Strikers FC Basseterre*
Harrison Andreas PANAYIOTOU	28.10.1994	*Aldershot Town FC (ENG)*
Niquan PHIPPS		*Saddlers United FC Basseterre*
Tiquanny WILLIAMS	10.09.1991	*United Old Road Jets*

National coaches

Leonardo Martins NEIVA "Léo Neiva" (Brazil) [from 17.02.2021]	10.12.1977

SAINT LUCIA

The Country:	The FA:
Saint Lucia	St. Lucia Football Association
Capital: Castries	Barnard Hill, P.O. Box 255, Castries
Surface: 620 km²	Year of Formation: 1979
Population: 184,401 [2021]	Member of FIFA since: 1988
Time: UTC-4	Member of CONCACAF since: 1965
Independent since: 1979	

NATIONAL TEAM RECORDS	
First international match:	18.06.1989, Kingston: Jamaica - Saint Lucia 1-1
Most international caps:	Kurt Frederick – 44 caps (since 2010)
Most international goals:	Earl Jude Jean – 20 goasl / 23 caps (1990-2004)

CONCACAF GOLD CUP		FIFA WORLD CUP	
1991	Qualifiers	1930	-
1993	Qualifiers	1934	-
1996	Qualifiers	1938	-
1998	Qualifiers	1950	-
2000	Qualifiers	1954	-
2002	Qualifiers	1958	-
2003	Qualifiers	1962	-
2005	Qualifiers	1966	-
2007	Qualifiers	1970	-
2009	Did not enter	1974	-
2011	Qualifiers	1978	-
2013	Qualifiers	1982	Did not enter
2015	Qualifiers	1986	Did not enter
2017	Did not enter	1990	Did not enter
2019	Qualifiers	1994	Qualifiers
2021	Qualifiers	1998	Qualifiers
		2002	Qualifiers
		2006	Qualifiers
		2010	Qualifiers
		2014	Qualifiers
		2018	Qualifiers

F.I.F.A. CONFEDERATIONS CUP 1992-2017
None

OLYMPIC FOOTBALL TOURNAMENTS 1908-2016

2016 (Qualifiers)

CCCF (Confederación Centroamericana y del Caribe de Fútbol) CHAMPIONSHIPS 1941-1961

None

CONCACAF CHAMPIONSHIPS 1963-1989

None

CONCACAF NATIONS LEAGUE

2019-2020	League B (*relegated to League C*)

CARIBBEAN CHAMPIONSHIPS 1989-2017

Year	Result	Year	Result
1989	Qualifiers	1999	Qualifiers
1991	Final Tournament - 3rd Place	2001	Qualifiers
1992	Qualifiers	2005	Qualifiers
1993	Final Tournament - Group Stage	2007	Qualifiers
1994	Did not enter	2008	Did not enter
1995	Final Tournament - Group Stage	2010	Qualifiers
1996	Qualifiers	2012	Qualifiers
1997	Qualifiers	2014	Qualifiers
1998	Qualifiers	2017	Did not enter

SAINT LUCIAN CLUB HONOURS IN CONCACAF CLUB COMPETITIONS:

CONCACAF Champions Cup / CONCACAF Champions League 1962-2020

None

CONCACAF League 2017-2020

None

Caribbean Club Championship 1997-2021

None

CONCACAF Cup Winners Cup 1991-1995*

None

Copa Interamericana 1968-1998*

None

defunct competitions

NATIONAL COMPETITIONS
TABLE OF HONOURS

	CHAMPIONS	CUP WINNERS
1980	Dames SC Vieux Fort	-
1981	Uptown Rebels Vieux Fort	-
1982	*Not known*	-
1983	*Not known*	-
1984	*Not known*	-
1985	*Not known*	-
1986	*Not known*	-
1987	*Not known*	-
1988	*Not known*	-
1989	*Not known*	-
1990	*Not known*	-

1991	*Not known*	-
1992	*Not known*	-
1993	*Not known*	-
1994	*Not known*	-
1995	*Not known*	-
1996	*Not known*	-
1997	Pioneers FC Castries	-
1998	Rovers United Mabouya Valley	Mabouya Valley
1999	Roots Alley Ballers Vieux Fort	Roots Alley Ballers Vieux Fort
2000	Roots Alley Ballers Vieux Fort	Rovers United Mabouya Valley
2001	VSADC Castries	VSADC Castries
2002	VSADC Castries	VSADC Castries
2003/2004	Roots Alley Ballers Vieux Fort	18 Plus Dennery
2004/2005	Northern United Gros Islet	Northern United Gros Islet
2005/2006	Canaries FC	Elite Challengers Soufrière
2006/2007	GYSO Soufrière	Northern United Gros Islet
2007/2008	GYSO Soufrière	-
2008	Aux Lyons United Mabouya Valley	*No competition*
2009	Roots Alley Ballers Vieux Fort	Dennery Aux-Lyons
2010	Northern United All Stars Gros Islet	*Final game abandoned*
2011	VSADC Castries	*No competition*
2012	VSADC Castries	*No competition*
2013	Big Players FC Marchand	Marchand FC
2014	Aux Lyons United Mabouya Valley	*No competition*
2015	Gros Islet	*No competition*
2016	Survivals FC Mabouya Valley	*No competition*
2017	Northern United Gros Islet	*No competition*
2018	Platinum FC Vieux Fort	Marchand FC
2019	Platinum FC Vieux Fort	Gros Islet
2020	*Championship cancelled*	*Competition cancelled*

NATIONAL CHAMPIONSHIP
Saint Lucia FA First Division 2020

The championship was cancelled after 2 Rounds on 18.03.2020, due to COVID-19 pandemic

NATIONAL CUP
FA Island Cup Final 2019

The competition was cancelled due to COVID-19 pandemic

NATIONAL TEAM
INTERNATIONAL MATCHES 2020/2021

Saint Lucia was drawn into Group E of the 22nd FIFA World Cup Qualifiers, CONCACAF First Round, but withdrew before playing.

SAINT MARTIN

The Country:	The FA:
Collectivité de Saint-Martin (Collectivity of Saint Martin) Capital: Marigor Surface: 53,2 km² Population: 34,065 [2018] Time: UTC-4 Independent since: *overseas region of France*	Comité de Football du Saint-Martin Sandy-Ground Stade Albertic Richards P.O. Box 811, Cedex, Saint-Martin 97059 Year of Formation: 1986 Member of FIFA since: *not affiliated* Member of CONCACAF since: 2002

NATIONAL TEAM RECORDS

First international match: 01.11.1994: Antigua and Barbuda - Saint-Martin 2-1
Most international caps: Not known
Most international goals: Not known

CONCACAF GOLD CUP	
1991	Did not enter
1993	Did not enter
1996	Did not enter
1998	Did not enter
2000	Qualifiers
2002	Qualifiers
2003	Qualifiers
2005	Qualifiers
2007	Qualifiers
2009	Qualifiers
2011	Qualifiers
2013	Qualifiers
2015	Did not enter
2017	*Withdrew*
2019	Qualifiers
2021	Qualifiers

FIFA WORLD CUP	
1930	-
1934	-
1938	-
1950	-
1954	-
1958	-
1962	-
1966	-
1970	-
1974	-
1978	-
1982	-
1986	-
1990	-
1994	-
1998	-
2002	-
2006	-
2010	-
2014	-
2018	-

F.I.F.A. CONFEDERATIONS CUP 1992-2017

None

OLYMPIC FOOTBALL TOURNAMENTS 1900-2016
None

CCCF (Confederación Centroamericana y del Caribe de Fútbol) CHAMPIONSHIPS 1941-1961
None

CONCACAF CHAMPIONSHIPS 1963-1989
None

NAFC (North American Football Confederation) CHAMPIONSHIPS 1947-1991

CONCACAF NATIONS LEAGUE	
2019-2020	League C

CARIBBEAN CHAMPIONSHIPS 1989-2017			
1989	Did not enter	1999	Qualifiers
1991	Did not enter	2001	Qualifiers
1992	Did not enter	2005	Qualifiers
1993	Did not enter	2007	Qualifiers
1994	Did not enter	2008	Qualifiers
1995	Did not enter	2010	Qualifiers
1996	Did not enter	2012	Qualifiers
1997	Did not enter	2014	Did not enter
1998	Did not enter	2017	*Withdrew*

SAINT-MARTIN CLUB HONOURS IN CONCACAF CLUB COMPETITIONS:

CONCACAF Champions Cup / CONCACAF Champions League 1962-2020
None

CONCACAF League 2017-2020
None

Caribbean Club Championship 1997-2021
None

CONCACAF Cup Winners Cup 1991-1995*
None

Copa Interamericana 1968-1998*
None

**defunct competitions*

NATIONAL COMPETITIONS
TABLE OF HONOURS

The territory of Saint Martin consists of two islands: Saint Martin (the French part of this island, shared with the Dutch territory of Sint-Maarten) and Saint Barthélémy; both having a separate championship.

	CHAMPIONS	
	SAINT-MARTIN	SAINT-BARTHÉLÉMY
1970/1971	Junior Stars Marigot	
1971/1972	Junior Stars Marigot	
1972/1973	Junior Stars Marigot	
1973/1974	Saint-Louis Stars Sandy Ground	
1974/1975	Saint-Louis Stars Sandy Ground	
1975/1976	Saint-Louis Stars Sandy Ground	
1976/1977	Saint-Louis Stars Sandy Ground	
1977/1978	Saint-Louis Stars Sandy Ground	
1978/1979	Saint-Louis Stars Sandy Ground	
1979/1980	Junior Stars Marigot	
1980/1981	Junior Stars Marigot	
1981/1982	Saint-Louis Stars Sandy Ground	
1982/1983	Saint-Louis Stars Sandy Ground	
1983/1984	Saint-Louis Stars Sandy Ground	
1984/1985	Saint-Louis Stars Sandy Ground	
1985/1986	Junior Stars Marigot	
1986/1987	Saint-Louis Stars Sandy Ground	
1987/1988	Saint-Louis Stars Sandy Ground	
1988/1989	Saint-Louis Stars Sandy Ground	
1989/1990	Junior Stars Marigot	
1990/1991	Junior Stars Marigot	
1991/1992	Saint-Louis Stars Sandy Ground	
1992/1993	Saint-Louis Stars Sandy Ground	
1993/1994	Saint-Louis Stars Sandy Ground	
1994/1995	Saint-Louis Stars Sandy Ground	
1995/1996	Saint-Louis Stars Sandy Ground	
1996/1997	Saint-Louis Stars Sandy Ground	
1997/1998	Jah Rebels	-
1998/1999	Jah Rebels	-
1999/2000	Junior Stars Marigot	-
2000/2001	Sporting Club	-
2001/2002	Orléans Attackers FC Quartier-d'Orleans	-
2002/2003	Junior Stars Marigot	-
2003/2004	Juventus de Saint-Martin	FC Gustavia
2004/2005	Orléans Attackers FC Quartier-d'Orleans	FC Beach-Hôtel
2005/2006	Orléans Attackers FC Quartier-d'Orleans	FC Beach-Hôtel*
2006/2007	Orléans Attackers FC Quartier-d'Orleans	Amical FC Beach-Hôtel
2007/2008	Orléans Attackers FC Quartier-d'Orleans	AS Portuguese Saint-Barthélémy
2008/2009	ASC Saint-Louis Stars Sandy Ground	AS Portuguese Saint-Barthélémy
2009/2010	Orléans Attackers FC Quartier-d'Orleans	AS Portuguese Saint-Barthélémy
2010/2011	Junior Stars Marigot	AS Portuguese Saint-Barthélémy
2011/2012	FC Concordia Marigot	Amical FC Beach-Hôtel

413

2012/2013	Orléans Attackers FC Quartier-d'Orleans	Ouanalao FC
2013/2014	Junior Stars Marigot	Ouanalao FC
2014/2015	Orléans Attackers FC Quartier-d'Orleans	FC Gustavia
2015/2016	FC Concordia Marigot	FC Gustavia
2016/2017	FC Marigot Saint-Martin	AS Portuguese Saint-Barthélémy
2017/2018	*No competition*	FC Arawak
2018/2019	*Championship abandoned*	AS Portuguese Saint-Barthélémy
2019/2020	*No competition*	*No competition*
2020/2021	FC Concordia Marigot	Team FWI

*became Amical FC Beach-Hôtel in 2006.

NATIONAL CHAMPIONSHIP

Ligue de Saint-Martin 2020/2021

1.	**FC Concordia Marigot**	10	7	2	1	26 - 10		33
2.	Phoenicks	10	7	2	1	23 - 12		33
3.	Junior Stars Marigot	10	6	2	2	24 - 17		30
4.	Orléans Attackers FC Quartier-d'Orleans	10	2	2	6	15 - 19		18
5.	ASC Saint-Louis Stars Sandy Ground	10	1	2	7	17 - 26		15
6.	Flamingo Quartier-d'Orleans	10	2	0	8	5 - 26		9

Ligue de Saint Barthélémy 2020/2021

1.	**Team FWI**	8	5	3	0	26 - 11		18
2.	FC Arawak	8	4	1	3	20 - 12		13
3.	FC Gustavia	8	4	1	3	18 - 12		13
4.	Diables Rouges	7	1	2	4	7 - 19		5
5.	AS Portuguese Saint-Barthélémy	7	1	1	5	9 - 26		4

NATIONAL CUP

Coupe de Saint-Martin Final 2020/2021

Informations are not available

Coupe de Noël Saint Barthélémy Final 2020/2021

Informations are not available

NATIONAL TEAM
INTERNATIONAL MATCHES 2020/2021

No international activities for the Saint Martin national team during the 2020/2021 season.

SAINT VINCENT AND THE GRENADINES

The Country:	The FA:
Saint Vincent and the Grenadines	Saint Vincent and the Grenadines Football Federation
Capital: Kingstown	Corner of Grenville & Higginson Street,
Surface: 389 km²	P.O. Box 1278, Kingstown
Population: 110,211 [2018]	Year of Formation: 1979
Time: UTC-4	Member of FIFA since: 1988
Independent since: 1979	Member of CONCACAF since: 1986

NATIONAL TEAM RECORDS

First international match:	1948: Saint Vincent and the Grenadines - Trinidad and Tobago 1-2
Most international caps:	Shandel Samuel – 63 caps (2001-2016)
	Kendall Velox – 63 caps (1992-2008)
Most international goals:	Shandel Samuel – 33 goals / 63 caps (2001-2016)

CONCACAF GOLD CUP	
1991	Did not enter
1993	Qualifiers
1996	Final Tournament (Group Stage)
1998	Qualifiers
2000	Qualifiers
2002	Qualifiers
2003	Did not enter
2005	Qualifiers
2007	Qualifiers
2009	Qualifiers
2011	Qualifiers
2013	Qualifiers
2015	Qualifiers
2017	Qualifiers
2019	Qualifiers
2021	Qualifiers

FIFA WORLD CUP	
1930	-
1934	-
1938	-
1950	-
1954	-
1958	-
1962	-
1966	-
1970	-
1974	-
1978	-
1982	-
1986	-
1990	Did not enter
1994	Qualifiers
1998	Qualifiers
2002	Qualifiers
2006	Qualifiers
2010	Qualifiers
2014	Qualifiers
2018	Qualifiers

F.I.F.A. CONFEDERATIONS CUP 1992-2017

None

OLYMPIC FOOTBALL TOURNAMENTS 1908-2016							
1908	-	1948	-	1972	-	1996	Qualifiers
1912	-	1952	-	1976	-	2000	Qualifiers
1920	-	1956	-	1980	-	2004	Did not enter
1924	-	1960	-	1984	-	2008	Qualifiers
1928	-	1964	-	1988	-	2012	Qualifiers
1936	-	1968	-	1992	-	2016	Qualifiers

CCCF (Confederación Centroamericana y del Caribe de Fútbol) CHAMPIONSHIPS 1941-1961
None

CONCACAF CHAMPIONSHIPS 1963-1989
1989

CONCACAF NATIONS LEAGUE	
2019-2020	League B

CARIBBEAN CHAMPIONSHIPS 1989-2017			
1989	Final Tournament - Group Stage	1999	Qualifiers
1991	Did not enter	2001	Qualifiers
1992	Final Tournament - Group Stage	2005	Qualifiers
1993	Final Tournament - Group Stage	2007	Final Tournament - Group Stage
1994	Qualifiers	2008	Qualifiers
1995	Final Tournament - Runners-up	2010	Qualifiers
1996	Final Tournament - Group Stage	2012	Qualifiers
1997	Qualifiers	2014	Qualifiers
1998	Qualifiers	2017	Qualifiers

SAINT VINCENT AND THE GRENADINES CLUB HONOURS IN CONCACAF CLUB COMPETITIONS:

CONCACAF Champions Cup / CONCACAF Champions League 1962-2020
None

CONCACAF League 2017-2020
None

Caribbean Club Championship 1997-2021
None

CONCACAF Cup Winners Cup 1991-1995*
None

Copa Interamericana 1968-1998*
None

defunct competitions

NATIONAL COMPETITIONS TABLE OF HONOURS

1998/1999	Camdonia Chelsea SC Lowmans
1999/2000	*No competition*
2000/2001	*No competition*
2001/2002	*No competition*
2002/2003	*No competition*
2003/2004	Hope International FC Kingstown
2004/2005	Universal Mufflers Samba FC

2005/2006	Hope International FC Kingstown
2006/2007	*No competition*
2007/2008	*No competition*
2008/2009	*No competition*
2009/2010	Avenues United FC Kingstown
2010/2011	Avenues United FC Kingstown
2011/2012	Avenues United FC Kingstown
2012/2013	*No competition*
2013/2014	BESCO Pastures United FC
2014/2015	Hope International FC Kingstown
2016	System 3 FC Kingstown
2017	Avenues United FC Kingstown
2018/2019	BESCO Pastures United FC Layou
2019/2020	Hope International FC Kingstown
2020/2021	*Championship cancelled*

NATIONAL CHAMPIONSHIP
SVGFF Club Championship 2019/2020

The 2019/2020 championship was suspended from 11.03. to 11.08.2020, due to COVID-19 pandemic. You will find here the final table to complete missed datas from last year's yearbook.

1.	**Hope International FC Kingstown**	22	16	2	4	61	-	30	50
2.	North Leeward Predators FC Chateaubelair	22	14	4	4	53	-	23	46
3.	System 3 FC Kingstown	22	14	3	5	67	-	34	45
4.	Je Belle's FC	22	13	4	5	46	-	26	43
5.	BESCO Pastures United FC Layou	22	11	2	9	43	-	41	35
6.	Sion Hill FC	22	8	5	9	41	-	40	29
7.	Avenues United FC Kingstown	22	7	6	9	36	-	41	27
8.	Awesome FC	22	7	5	10	22	-	47	26
9.	SV United (*Relegated*)	22	7	3	12	33	-	38	24
10.	Camdonia Chelsea SC Lowmans (*Relegated*)	22	5	2	15	30	-	59	17
11.	Bequia United FC Port Elizabeth (*Relegated*)	22	5	2	15	30	-	66	17
12.	Greiggs FC (*Relegated*)	22	4	4	14	44	-	61	16

Promoted for the 2020/2021 season: Layou FC, Largo Height FC.

NATIONAL CHAMPIONSHIP
SVGFF Club Championship 2020/2021

The 2019/2020 championship was suspended on 19.12.2020 after 4 Rounds (pandemic reasons). Later, on 04.06.2021, the Championship was cancelled due to COVID-19 pandemic.

NATIONAL TEAM
INTERNATIONAL MATCHES 2020/2021

25.03.2021	Willemstad	Curaçao - Saint Vincent and the Grenadines	5-0(4-0)	(WCQ)
30.03.2021	Willemstad	Saint Vincent and the Grenadines - British Virgin Islands	3-0(2-0)	(WCQ)
04.06.2021	Ciudad de Guatemala	Guatemala - Saint Vincent and the Grenadines	10-0(5-0)	(WCQ)
08.06.2021	St. George's	Saint Vincent and the Grenadines - Cuba	0-1(0-0)	(WCQ)
02.07.2021	Fort Lauderdale	Haiti - Saint Vincent and the Grenadines	6-1(3-1)	(GCQ)

25.03.2021, 22nd FIFA World Cup Qualifiers, CONCACAF First Round
Stadion „Ergilio Hato", Willemstad
Referee: Benjamin Pineda Ávila (Costa Rica)
CURAÇAO - SAINT VINCENT AND THE GRENADINES   5-0(4-0)
VIN: Dwaine Peters Sandy, Jahvin Darren Tristan Sutherland, Jamal Yorke, Chevron McLean, Kamol Bess (42.Zidane Sam), Diel Spring, Nigel Jahvon Jahvin Charles, Oalex Anderson, Akeem Williams, Cornelius Stewart, Kyle Lyndon Adonis Edwards (82.Kurtlon Williams). Trainer: Kendale Mercury.

30.03.2021, 22nd FIFA World Cup Qualifiers, CONCACAF First Round
Stadion „Ergilio Hato", Willemstad (Curaçao)
Referee: Henry Alberto Bejarano Matarrita (Costa Rica)
SAINT VINCENT AND THE GRENADINES - BRITISH VIRGIN ISLANDS   3-0(2-0)
VIN: Dwaine Peters Sandy, Jahvin Darren Tristan Sutherland, Jamal Yorke, Kamol Bess, Diel Spring (74.Renson Sayers), Oalex Anderson (89.Terrason Joseph), Akeem Williams, Kyle Lyndon Adonis Edwards (82.Azinho Amunike Andre Jr. Solomon), Kurtlon Williams (82.Erel Hector), Cornelius Stewart, Zidane Sam (89.Ted Roberts). Trainer: Kendale Mercury.
Goals: Oalex Anderson (10), Zidane Sam (20), Azinho Amunike Andre Jr. Solomon (86).

04.06.2021, 22nd FIFA World Cup Qualifiers, CONCACAF First Round
Estadio "Doroteo Guamuch Flores", Ciudad de Guatemala; Attendance: n/a
Referee: Erick Moisés Lezama Pavón (Nicaragua)
GUATEMALA - SAINT VINCENT AND THE GRENADINES   10-0(5-0)
VIN: Jadiel Chance, Jahvin Darren Tristan Sutherland, Jamal Yorke (80.Nazir Obain McBurnette), Tristan Marshall (90+1.Kenijah Joseph), Kamol Bess (33.Diel Spring), Ted Roberts, Gidson Francis, Brad Richards (46.Oryan Velox), Kyle Lyndon Adonis Edwards (71.Zidane Sam), Cornelius Stewart, Kurtlon Williams. Trainer: Kendale Mercury.

08.06.2021, 22nd FIFA World Cup Qualifiers, CONCACAF First Round
Kirani James Athletic Stadium, St. George's (Grenada); Attendance: 50
Referee: Fernando Guerrero Ramírez (Mexico)
SAINT VINCENT AND THE GRENADINES - CUBA   0-1(0-0)
VIN: Jadiel Chance, Jahvin Darren Tristan Sutherland, Jamal Yorke, Kamol Bess, Diel Spring (79.Brad Richards), Gidson Francis (84.Kurtlon Williams), Nigel Jahvon Jahvin Charles, Nazir Obain McBurnette, Kyle Lyndon Adonis Edwards, Cornelius Stewart, Oryan Velox (64.Dorren Hamlet). Trainer: Kendale Mercury.

02.07.2021, 16th CONCACAF Gold Cup Qualifiers, First Round
DRV PNK Stadium, Fort Lauderdale (United States); Attendance: 0
Referee: Oshane Nation (Jamaica)

HAITI - SAINT VINCENT AND THE GRENADINES   **6-1(3-1)**

VIN: Nigel Jahvon Jahvin Charles, Jahvin Darren Tristan Sutherland, Jamal Yorke, Kamol Bess, Tristan Marshall, Ted Roberts, Dorren Hamlet, Brad Richards, Nazir Obain McBurnette (79.Kenijah Joseph), Kyle Lyndon Adonis Edwards (71.Marlon Simmons), Kurtlon Williams. Trainer: Kendale Mercury.

Goal: Kyle Lyndon Adonis Edwards (42).

NATIONAL TEAM PLAYERS 2020/2021

Name	DOB	Club
Goalkeepers		
Jadiel CHANCE	08.08.1999	*North Leeward Predators FC Chateaubelair*
Dwaine Peters SANDY	19.02.1989	*Glenside Ball Blazers SC*
Defenders		
Tristan MARSHALL	19.12.2003	*Toronto Skillz (CAN)*
Chevron McLEAN	09.05.1996	*Billericay Town FC (ENG)*
Ted ROBERTS	31.10.2001	*System 3 FC Kingstown*
Jahvin Darren Tristan SUTHERLAND	10.11.1994	*System 3 FC Kingstown*
Jamal YORKE	09.10.1991	*Sion Hill FC*
Midfielders		
Kamol BESS	25.08.1996	*Bequia United FC Port Elizabeth*
Nigel Jahvon Jahvin CHARLES*	20.03.2003	*Camdonia Chelsea SC Lowmans*
Kyle Lyndon Adonis EDWARDS	15.01.1996	*Rio Grande Valley Vaqueros (USA)*
Gidson FRANCIS	01.04.1999	*BESCO Pastures United FC Layou*
Dorren HAMLET	16.07.1989	*BESCO Pastures United FC Layou*
Erel HECTOR	10.12.1999	*Avenues United FC Kingstown*
Kenijah JOSEPH		*Layou FC*
Terrason JOSEPH	26.06.2002	*Je Belle's FC*
Nazir Obain McBURNETTE	18.02.1993	*Hope International FC Kingstown*
Brad RICHARDS	07.11.1996	*Hope International FC Kingstown*
Renson SAYERS	17.11.2004	*System 3 FC Kingstown*
Diel SPRING	26.12.2000	*SKS Wisla Sandomierz (POL)*

*also fielded as goalkeeper

Forwards		
Oalex ANDERSON	11.11.1995	*Richmond Kickers (USA)*
Zidane SAM	24.07.1998	*Je Belle's FC*
Marlon SIMMONS	26.01.2003	*Bequia United FC Port Elizabeth*
Azinho Amunike Andre Jr. SOLOMON	12.10.1994	*System 3 FC Kingstown*
Cornelius STEWART	19.07.1989	*Maaziya S&RC Malé (MDV)*
Oryan VELOX	28.10.2004	*Layou FC*
Akeem WILLIAMS	29.04.1993	*Grenades FC Saint John's (ATG)*
Kurtlon WILLIAMS	21.06.1990	*North Leeward Predators FC Chateaubelair*
National coaches		
Kendale MERCURY [from 28.12.2018]		1970

SINT MAARTEN

The Country:	The FA:
Eilandgebied St. Maarten (Island Territory of Sint Maarten) Capital: Philipsburg Surface: 34 km² Population: 41,486 [2019] Time: UTC-4 Independent since: *overseas region of Holland*	Sint Maarten Soccer Association #28 Yohan Veer meer Street Madame Estate St. Maarten Year of Formation: 1986 Member of FIFA since: *not affiliated* Member of CONCACAF since: 2002

NATIONAL TEAM RECORDS

First international match:	03.04.1992: Sint Maarten - Cayman Islands 4-2
Most international caps:	Not known
Most international goals:	Not known

CONCACAF GOLD CUP		FIFA WORLD CUP	
1991	Did not enter	1930	-
1993	Qualifiers	1934	-
1996	Qualifiers	1938	-
1998	Qualifiers	1950	-
2000	*Withdrew*	1954	-
2002	Did not enter	1958	-
2003	Did not enter	1962	-
2005	*Withdrew*	1966	-
2007	Did not enter	1970	-
2009	Did not enter	1974	-
2011	Did not enter	1978	-
2013	Did not enter	1982	-
2015	Did not enter	1986	-
2017	Qualifiers	1990	-
2019	Qualifiers	1994	-
2021	Qualifiers	1998	-
		2002	-
		2006	-
		2010	-
		2014	-
		2018	-

F.I.F.A. CONFEDERATIONS CUP 1992-2017
None

OLYMPIC FOOTBALL TOURNAMENTS 1900-2016
None

CCCF (Confederación Centroamericana y del Caribe de Fútbol) CHAMPIONSHIPS 1941-1961
None

CONCACAF CHAMPIONSHIPS 1963-1989
None

CONCACAF NATIONS LEAGUE	
2019-2020	League C

CARIBBEAN CHAMPIONSHIPS 1989-2017				
1989	Qualifiers		1999	*Withdrew*
1991	Did not enter		2001	Did not enter
1992	Qualifiers		2005	Did not enter
1993	Final Tournament - Group Stage		2007	Did not enter
1994	Qualifiers		2008	Did not enter
1995	Qualifiers		2010	Did not enter
1996	Qualifiers		2012	Did not enter
1997	Qualifiers		2014	Did not enter
1998	Did not enter		2017	Qualifiers

SINT-MAARTEN CLUB HONOURS IN CONCACAF CLUB COMPETITIONS:

CONCACAF Champions Cup / CONCACAF Champions League 1962-2020
None

CONCACAF League 2017-2020
None

Caribbean Club Championship 1997-2021
None

CONCACAF Cup Winners Cup 1991-1995*
None

Copa Interamericana 1968-1998*
None

*defunct competitions

NATIONAL COMPETITIONS
TABLE OF HONOURS

2000/2001	Sporting Club
2001/2002	Victory Boys
2002/2003	*Not known*
2003/2004	*Not known*
2004/2005	*Not known*
2005/2006	C&D Connection
2006/2007	D&P Connection FC Philipsburg
2007/2008	*Not known*
2008/2009	*Not known*
2009/2010	*Not known*
2010/2011	*Not known*
2011/2012	*Not known*
2012/2013	*Not known*
2013/2014	NAGICO Insurance
2014/2015	Flames United SC Philipsburg
2015/2016	*Not held*
2016/2017	Reggae Lions Philipsburg
2017/2018	*Not held*
2018/2019	C&D Connection
2019/2020	*Not held*
2020/2021	Flames United SC Philipsburg

NATIONAL CHAMPIONSHIP
SMSA Senior League 2020/2021

1.	**Flames United SC Philipsburg**	18	15	3	0	75	-	15	48
2.	SCSA Eagles	18	14	1	3	93	-	19	43
3.	758 Boyz	18	11	2	5	66	-	24	35
4.	FC Soualiga	18	10	3	5	69	-	23	33
5.	C&D Connection FC	18	9	3	6	56	-	23	30
6.	SXM Crew	18	9	1	8	54	-	49	28
7.	Hot Spurs	18	6	5	7	42	-	51	23
8.	United Super Stars FC	18	3	1	14	26	-	120	10
9.	Belvedere FC	18	3	0	15	29	-	119	9
10.	Reggae Lions FC Philipsburg	18	0	1	17	8	-	75	1

NATIONAL TEAM
INTERNATIONAL MATCHES 2020/2021

No international activities for the Sint Maarten national team during the 2020/2021 season.

SURINAME

The Country:	The FA:
Republiek Suriname (Republic of Suriname) Capital: Paramaribo Surface: 163,821 km² Population: 579,990 [2018] Time: UTC-3 Independent since: 1975	Surinaamse Voetbal Bond Letitia Vriesdelaan #7; P.O. Box 1223, Paramaribo Year of Formation: 1920 Member of FIFA since: 1929 Member of CONCACAF since: 1965

NATIONAL TEAM RECORDS

First international match: 28.01.1921: Suriname - British Guiana 1-2
Most international caps: Marlon Felter – 48 caps (2004-2011)
Most international goals: Stefano Rodney Rijssel – 14 goals / 36 caps (since 2010)

CONCACAF GOLD CUP	
1991	Qualifiers
1993	*Withdrew*
1996	Qualifiers
1998	Did not enter
2000	Qualifiers
2002	Qualifiers
2003	*Withdrew*
2005	Qualifiers
2007	Qualifiers
2009	Qualifiers
2011	Qualifiers
2013	Qualifiers
2015	Qualifiers
2017	Qualifiers
2019	Qualifiers
2021	Final Tournament (*to be played*)

FIFA WORLD CUP	
1930	Did not enter
1934	Did not enter
1938	*Withdrew*
1950	Did not enter
1954	Did not enter
1958	Did not enter
1962	Qualifiers
1966	Qualifiers
1970	Qualifiers
1974	Qualifiers
1978	Qualifiers
1982	Qualifiers
1986	Qualifiers
1990	Did not enter
1994	Qualifiers
1998	Qualifiers
2002	Qualifiers
2006	Qualifiers
2010	Qualifiers
2014	Qualifiers
2018	Qualifiers

F.I.F.A. CONFEDERATIONS CUP 1992-2017

None

OLYMPIC FOOTBALL TOURNAMENTS 1908-2016

1908	-	1948	-	1972	Qualifiers	1996	Did not enter
1912	-	1952	-	1976	Qualifiers	2000	Qualifiers
1920	-	1956	-	1980	Qualifiers	2004	Qualifiers
1924	-	1960	Qualifiers	1984	Qualifiers	2008	Qualifiers
1928	-	1964	Qualifiers	1988	*Withdrew*	2012	Qualifiers
1936	-	1968	Qualifiers	1992	Qualifiers	2016	*Withdrew*

CCCF (Confederación Centroamericana y del Caribe de Fútbol) CHAMPIONSHIPS 1941-1961

1957 (Runners-up, as Curaçao), 1960

CONCACAF CHAMPIONSHIPS 1963-1989

1971, 1977, 1985

CONCACAF NATIONS LEAGUE

2019-2020	League B (*promoted to League A*)

CARIBBEAN CHAMPIONSHIPS 1989-2017

1989	Did not enter	1999	Qualifiers
1991	Qualifiers	2001	Final Tournament - Group Stage
1992	Final Tournament - Group Stage	2005	Qualifiers
1993	Did not enter	2007	Qualifiers
1994	Final Tournament - 4th Place	2008	Qualifiers
1995	Qualifiers	2010	Qualifiers
1996	Final Tournament - 4th Place	2012	Qualifiers
1997	Did not enter	2014	Qualifiers
1998	Qualifiers	2017	Qualifiers

SURINAMESE CLUB HONOURS IN CONCACAF CLUB COMPETITIONS:

CONCACAF Champions Cup / CONCACAF Champions League 1962-2020

Sport Vereniging Transvaal Paramaribo	2	1973, 1981

CONCACAF League 2017-2020

None

Caribbean Club Championship 1997-2021

None

CONCACAF Cup Winners Cup 1991-1995*

None

Copa Interamericana 1968-1998*

None

defunct competitions

NATIONAL COMPETITIONS
TABLE OF HONOURS

	CHAMPIONS
1923/1924	Olympia [city not known]
1924/1925	SV Transvaal Paramaribo
1925/1926	*No competition*
1926/1927	Ajax [city not known]
1927/1928	Ajax
1928/1929	*No competition*

1929/1930	*No competition*
1930/1931	Excelsior/Blauw Wit [city not known]
1931/1932	Cicerone [city not known]
1932/1933	Cicerone
1933/1934	Cicerone
1934/1935	Cicerone
1935/1936	SV Voorwaarts Paramaribo
1936/1937	SV Transvaal Paramaribo
1937/1938	SV Transvaal Paramaribo
1938/1939	Arsenal [city not known]
1939/1940	Arsenal
1940/1941	SV Voorwaarts Paramaribo
1942	*No competition*
1943	*No competition*
1944	*No competition*
1945	*No competition*
1946	*No competition*
1947	*No competition*
1948	MVV [city not known]
1949	MVV
1950	SV Transvaal Paramaribo
1951	SV Transvaal Paramaribo
1952	SV Voorwaarts Paramaribo
1953	SV Robinhood Paramaribo
1954	SV Robinhood Paramaribo
1955	SV Robinhood Paramaribo
1956	SV Robinhood Paramaribo
1957/1958	SV Voorwaarts Paramaribo
1958/1959	SV Robinhood Paramaribo
1960	*Championship abandoned*
1961	SV Leo Victor Paramaribo
1962	SV Transvaal Paramaribo
1963/1964	SV Leo Victor Paramaribo
1964	SV Robinhood Paramaribo
1965/1966	SV Transvaal Paramaribo
1966	SV Transvaal Paramaribo
1967	SV Transvaal Paramaribo
1968	SV Transvaal Paramaribo
1969	SV Transvaal Paramaribo
1970	SV Transvaal Paramaribo
1971	SV Robinhood Paramaribo
1972	*No competition*
1973	SV Transvaal Paramaribo
1974	SV Transvaal Paramaribo
1975/1976	SV Robinhood Paramaribo
1976	SV Robinhood Paramaribo
1977	SV Voorwaarts Paramaribo
1978	SV Leo Victor Paramaribo
1979	SV Robinhood Paramaribo
1980	SV Robinhood Paramaribo
1981	SV Robinhood Paramaribo
1982	SV Leo Victor Paramaribo

1983	SV Robinhood Paramaribo	
1984/1985	SV Robinhood Paramaribo	
1985/1986	SV Robinhood Paramaribo	
1986	SV Robinhood Paramaribo	
1987	SV Robinhood Paramaribo	
1988	SV Robinhood Paramaribo	
1989	SV Robinhood Paramaribo	
1990/1991	SV Transvaal Paramaribo	

	CHAMPIONS	CUP WINNERS
1991/1992	SV Transvaal Paramaribo	PVV Paramaribo
1992/1993	SV Leo Victor Paramaribo	*Not known*
1993/1994	SV Robinhood Paramaribo	*Not known*
1994/1995	SV Robinhood Paramaribo	*Not known*
1995/1996	SV Transvaal Paramaribo	SV Transvaal Paramaribo
1997	SV Transvaal Paramaribo	SV Robinhood Paramaribo
1998/1999	SNL Paramaribo	SV Robinhood Paramaribo
1999/2000	SV Transvaal Paramaribo	*No competition*
2000/2001	*No competition*	SV Robinhood Paramaribo
2001/2002	SV Voorwaarts Paramaribo	SV Transvaal Paramaribo
2002/2003	FCS Nacional Paramaribo	SV Leo Victor Paramaribo
2003/2004	Walking Bout Company Paramaribo	Super Red Eagles Paramaribo
2004/2005	SV Robinhood Paramaribo	FCS Nacional Paramaribo
2005/2006	Walking Bout Company Paramaribo	SV Robinhood Paramaribo
2006/2007	Inter Moengotapoe	SV Robinhood Paramaribo
2007/2008	Inter Moengotapoe	SV Transvaal Paramaribo
2008/2009	Walking Bout Company Paramaribo	Walking Bout Company Paramaribo
2009/2010	Inter Moengotapoe	SV Excelsior Meerzorg
2010/2011	Inter Moengotapoe	SV Notch Moengo
2011/2012	SV Robinhood Paramaribo	Inter Moengotapoe
2012/2013	Inter Moengotapoe	Walking Bout Company Paramaribo
2013/2014	Inter Moengotapoe	SV Leo Victor Paramaribo
2014/2015	Inter Moengotapoe	SV Nishan '42 Meerzorg
2015/2016	Inter Moengotapoe	SV Robinhood Paramaribo
2016/2017	Inter Moengotapoe	Inter Moengotapoe
2017/2018	SV Robinhood Paramaribo	SV Robinhood Paramaribo
2018/2019	Inter Moengotapoe	Inter Moengotapoe
2019/2020	*Competition abandoned*	*Competition abandoned*
2020/2021	*No competition*	*No competition*

NATIONAL CHAMPIONSHIP
Eerste Divisie 2020/2021

No championship was played due to COVID-19 pandemic.

NATIONAL CUP
Beker van Suriname Final 2020/2021

No competition was played due to COVID-19 pandemic.

NATIONAL TEAM
INTERNATIONAL MATCHES 2020/2021

24.03.2021	Paramaribo	Suriname - Cayman Islands	3-0(2-0)	(WCQ)
27.03.2021	Bradenton	Aruba - Suriname	0-6(0-3)	(WCQ)
04.06.2021	Paramaribo	Suriname - Bermuda	6-0(4-0)	(WCQ)
08.06.2021	Bridgeview	Canada - Suriname	4-0(1-0)	(WCQ)

24.03.2021, 22nd FIFA World Cup Qualifiers, CONCACAF First Round
Stadion "Dr. Ir. Franklin Essed", Paramaribo
Referee: Jorge Antonio Pérez Durán (Mexico)
SURINAME - CAYMAN ISLANDS **3-0(2-0)**
SUR: Warner Lloyd Hahn (73.Ishan Ernesto Arturo Kort), Ramon Stanley Remy Leeuwin (65.Ramon Stanley Remy Leeuwin), Kelvin Walther Gianini Leerdam, Damil Serena Dankerlui, Leo Myenty Janna Abena (88.Sersinho Rahi Eduard), Shaquille Pinas, Ryan Henk Donk, Roland Romario Alberg (87.Jerrel Wijks), Ivenzo Comvalius (87.Dimitrie Apai), Nigel Hasselbaink, Gleofilo Sabrino Rudewald Hasselbaink Vlijter. Trainer: Dean Gorré.
Goals: Shaquille Pinas (22), Ryan Henk Donk (38 penalty), Gleofilo Sabrino Rudewald Hasselbaink Vlijter (76).

27.03.2021, 22nd FIFA World Cup Qualifiers, CONCACAF First Round
IMG Academy, Bradenton (United States)
Referee: Ismail Elfath (United States)
ARUBA - SURINAME **0-6(0-3)**
SUR: Warner Lloyd Hahn, Kelvin Walther Gianini Leerdam, Damil Serena Dankerlui (46.Ramon Stanley Remy Leeuwin), Leo Myenty Janna Abena (71.Ramon Stanley Remy Leeuwin), Shaquille Pinas, Diego Marvin Biseswar (71.Dimitrie Apai), Ryan Henk Donk, Tjaronn Inteff Chefren Chery, Nigel Hasselbaink (80.Alvaro Xavier Verwey), Florian Marc Jozefzoon, Gleofilo Sabrino Rudewald Hasselbaink Vlijter (46.Roland Romario Alberg). Trainer: Dean Gorré.
Goals: Nigel Hasselbaink (20), Ryan Henk Donk (29), Nigel Hasselbaink (38, 55), Florian Marc Jozefzoon (70), Roland Romario Alberg (74).

02.06.2021, 22nd FIFA World Cup Qualifiers, CONCACAF First Round
Stadion "Dr. Ir. Franklin Essed", Paramaribo
Referee: Mario Alberto Escobar Toca (Guatemala)
SURINAME - BERMUDA **6-0(4-0)**
SUR: Warner Lloyd Hahn, Kelvin Walther Gianini Leerdam, Ridgeciano Delano Haps, Shaquille Pinas, Diego Marvin Biseswar (67.Mitchell Glenn Donald), Ryan Henk Donk (67.Ramon Stanley Remy Leeuwin), Ryan Koolwijk, Tjaronn Inteff Chefren Chery, Nigel Hasselbaink (67.Mitchell te Vrede), Florian Marc Jozefzoon (80.Ivenzo Comvalius), Sheraldo Becker (79.Dimitrie Apai). Trainer: Dean Gorré.
Goals: Sheraldo Becker (3), Nigel Hasselbaink (15), Sheraldo Becker (36), Nigel Hasselbaink (37), Nigel Hasselbaink (65), Shaquille Pinas (74).

08.06.2021, 22nd FIFA World Cup Qualifiers, CONCACAF First Round
SeatGeek Stadium, Bridgeview (United States)
Referee: Nima Saghafi (United States)
CANADA - SURINAME **4-0(1-0)**
SUR: Warner Lloyd Hahn, Kelvin Walther Gianini Leerdam (63.Damil Serena Dankerlui), Ridgeciano Delano Haps, Shaquille Pinas, Diego Marvin Biseswar (46.Florian Marc Jozefzoon), Ryan Henk Donk, Ryan Koolwijk, Tjaronn Inteff Chefren Chery, Ramon Stanley Remy Leeuwin (63.Ivenzo Comvalius), Nigel Hasselbaink (62.Mitchell te Vrede), Sheraldo Becker. Trainer: Dean Gorré.

NATIONAL TEAM PLAYERS 2020/2021

Name	DOB	Club
Goalkeepers		
Warner Lloyd HAHN	15.06.1992	RSC Anderlecht Bruxelles (BEL)
Ishan Ernesto Arturo KORT	01.06.2000	Jong Almere City (NED)
Defenders		
Leo Myenty Janna ABENA	12.12.1994	ŠK Slovan Bratislava (SVK)
Damil Serena DANKERLUI	24.08.1996	FC Groningen (NED)
Ryan Henk DONK	30.03.1986	Galatasaray SK İstanbul (TUR)
Ridgeciano Delano HAPS	12.06.1993	Feyenoord Rotterdam (NED)
Ramon Stanley Remy LEEUWIN	01.09.1987	AZ Alkmaar (NED)
Dion MALONE	13.02.1989	NAC Breda (NED)
Shaquille PINAS	19.03.1998	ADO Den Haag (NED)
Midfielders		
Roland Romario ALBERG	06.08.1990	Hyderabad FC (IND)
Diego Marvin BISESWAR	08.03.1988	Apollon Limassol FC (CYP)
Tjaronn Inteff Chefren CHERY	04.06.1988	Maccabi Haifa FC (ISR)
Ivenzo COMVALIUS	24.06.1997	NK Dugopolje (CRO)
Mitchell Glenn DONALD	10.12.1988	Büyükşehir Belediye Erzurumspor (TUR)
Sersinho Rahi EDUARD	04.09.1994	Inter Moengotapoe
Ryan KOOLWIJK	08.02.1985	Almere City (NED)
Kelvin Walther Gianini LEERDAM	24.06.1990	Inter Miami CF (USA)
Jerrel WIJKS	15.03.1998	Inter Moengotapoe
Forwards		
Dimitrie APAI	19.07.1994	Williams Connection FC (TRI)
Sheraldo BECKER	09.02.1995	1.FC Union Berlin (GER)
Nigel HASSELBAINK	21.11.1990	Hapoel Bnei Sakhnin FC (ISR)
Florian Marc JOZEFZOON	09.02.1991	Rotherham United FC (ENG)
Mitchell TE VREDE	07.08.1991	Al Fateh SC Al Hofuf (KSA)
Alvaro Xavier VERWEY	12.01.1999	SV Transvaal Paramaribo
Gleofilo Sabrino Rudewald Hasselbaink VLIJTER	17.09.1999	Beitar Jerusalem FC (ISR)
National coaches		
Dean GORRÉ [from 03.07.2018]		10.09.1970

TRINIDAD AND TOBAGO

The Country:	The FA:
Republic of Trinidad and Tobago	Trinidad and Tobago Football Association
Capital: Port of Spain	"Ato Boldon" Stadium
Surface: 5,128 km²	Balmain, Couva
Population: 1,366,725 [2020]	Year of Formation: 1908
Time: UTC-4	Member of FIFA since: 1944
Independent since: 1962	Member of CONCACAF since: 1964

NATIONAL TEAM RECORDS

First international match: 06.08.1934: Dutch Guiana - Trinidad and Tobago 3-3
Most international caps: Angus Anthony Eve – 117 caps (1994-2005)
Most international goals: Stern John – 70 goals / 115 caps (1995-2011)

CONCACAF GOLD CUP		FIFA WORLD CUP	
1991	Final Tournament (Group Stage)	1930	-
1993	Qualifiers	1934	-
1996	Final Tournament (Group Stage)	1938	-
1998	Final Tournament (Group Stage)	1950	Did not enter
2000	Final Tournament (Semi-Finals)	1954	Did not enter
2002	Final Tournament (Group Stage)	1958	Did not enter
2003	Qualifiers	1962	Did not enter
2005	Final Tournament (Group Stage)	1966	Qualifiers
2007	Final Tournament (Group Stage)	1970	Qualifiers
2009	Qualifiers	1974	Qualifiers
2011	Qualifiers	1978	Qualifiers
2013	Final Tournament (Quarter-Finals)	1982	Qualifiers
2015	Final Tournament (Quarter-Finals)	1986	Qualifiers
2017	Qualifiers	1990	Qualifiers
2019	Final Tournament (Group Stage)	1994	Qualifiers
2021	Final Tournament (*to be played*)	1998	Qualifiers
		2002	Qualifiers
		2006	Final Tournament (Group Stage)
		2010	Qualifiers
		2014	Qualifiers
		2018	Qualifiers

F.I.F.A. CONFEDERATIONS CUP 1992-2017

None

OLYMPIC FOOTBALL TOURNAMENTS 1908-2016							
1908	-	1948	-	1972	Did not enter	1996	Qualifiers
1912	-	1952	Qualifiers	1976	Qualifiers	2000	Qualifiers
1920	-	1956	-	1980	Qualifiers	2004	Qualifiers
1924	-	1960	-	1984	Qualifiers	2008	Qualifiers
1928	-	1964	-	1988	Qualifiers	2012	Qualifiers
1936	-	1968	Qualifiers	1992	Qualifiers	2016	Qualifiers

CCCF (Confederación Centroamericana y del Caribe de Fútbol) CHAMPIONSHIPS 1941-1961
None

CONCACAF CHAMPIONSHIPS 1963-1989
1967, 1969, 1971, 1973 (Runners-up), 1985, 1989 (3rd Place)

CONCACAF NATIONS LEAGUE	
2019-2020	League A

CARIBBEAN CHAMPIONSHIPS 1989-2017			
1989	Final Tournament - Winners	1999	Final Tournament - Winners
1991	Final Tournament - Runners-up	2001	Final Tournament - Winners
1992	Final Tournament - Winners	2005	Final Tournament - 3rd place
1993	Final Tournament - 3rd place	2007	Final Tournament - Runners-up
1994	Final Tournament - Winners	2008	Final Tournament - Group Stage
1995	Final Tournament - Winners	2010	Final Tournament - Group Stage
1996	Final Tournament - Winners	2012	Final Tournament - Runners-up
1997	Final Tournament - Winners	2014	Final Tournament - Runners-up
1998	Final Tournament - Runners-up	2017	Qualifiers

TRINIDAD AND TOBAGO CLUB HONOURS IN CONCACAF CLUB COMPETITIONS:

CONCACAF Champions Cup / CONCACAF Champions League 1962-2020		
Defence Force Football Club Chaguaramas	2	
CONCACAF League 2017-2020		
None		
Caribbean Club Championship 1997-2021		
Williams Connection FC	3	2002, 2006, 2009
Joe Public FC Tunapuna	2	1998, 2000
Central FC California	2	2015, 2016
United Petrotrin FC	1	1997
Defence Force Football Club Chaguaramas	1	2001
San Juan Jabloteh FC	1	2003
Caledonia AIA Malabar	1	2012
*CONCACAF Cup Winners Cup 1991-1995***		
None		
*Copa Interamericana 1968-1998***		
None		

*defunct competitions

NATIONAL COMPETITIONS
TABLE OF HONOURS

	CHAMPIONS	CUP WINNERS
1908	Clydesdale	-
1909	Casuals	-
1910	Shamrock	-
1911	Shamrock	-
1912	Casuals	-
1913	Casuals	-
1914	Clydesdale	-
1915	Clydesdale	-
1916	*No competition*	-
1917	*No competition*	-
1918	*No competition*	-
1919	Queen's Park	-
1920	Royal Sussex	-
1921	Casuals	-
1922	Shamrock	-
1923	Shamrock	-
1924	Shamrock	-
1925	Shamrock	-
1926	Sporting Club	-
1927	Maple Club	Shamrock
1928	Maple Club	Casuals
1929	Casuals	Everton
1930	Everton	Everton
1931	Everton	Everton
1932	Everton	Everton
1933	Queen's Royal College	*No competition*
1934	Casuals	Casuals
1935	Casuals	Sporting Club
1936	Sporting Club	Shamrock
1937	Sporting Club	United British Oilfields Trinidad
1938	Casuals	West Ham
1939	Notre Dame	Casuals
1940	Casuals	Maple Club
1941	Casuals	United British Oilfields Trinidad
1942	Colts	Spitfire
1943	Fleet Air Arm	United British Oilfields Trinidad
1944	Shamrock	Colts
1945	Colts	Colts
1946	Notre Dame	Maple Club
1947	Colts	Notre Dame
1948	Malvern	Colts
1949	Malvern	Maple Club & Carlton [shared]
1950	Maple Club	United British Oilfields Trinidad
1951	Maple Club	United British Oilfields Trinidad & Providence [shared]
1952	Maple Club	Malvern
1953	Maple Club	Maple Club

1954	Sporting Club	United British Oilfields Trinidad
1955	Sporting Club	Malvern
1956	Notre Dame	Trinidad Petroleum Development
1957	Colts	Shell & Shamrock [shared]
1958	Shamrock	Casuals
1959	Shamrock	Shamrock
1960	Maple Club	Malvern
1961	Maple Club	Malvern & Apex [shared]
1962	Maple Club	Dynamos
1963	Maple Club	Maple Club
1964	Paragon	Paragon
1965	Regiment	Malvern & BP Palo Seco [shared]
1966	Regiment	Regiment & Juniors [shared]
1967	Maple Club	Regiment
1968	Maple Club	Malvern
1969	Maple Club	Point Fortin
1970	Regiment	Maple Club
1971	*Championship not finished*	*No competition*
1972	Defence Force FC Chaguaramas	Maple Club
1973	Defence Force FC Chaguaramas	*No competition*
1974	Defence Force FC Chaguaramas	Defence Force FC Chaguaramas
1975	Defence Force FC Chaguaramas	Police FC Saint James
1976	Defence Force FC Chaguaramas	Falcons
1977	Defence Force FC Chaguaramas	Malvern
1978	Defence Force FC Chaguaramas	Falcons
1979	Police FC Saint James	*No competition*
1980	Defence Force FC Chaguaramas	*No competition*
1981	Defence Force FC Chaguaramas	Defence Force FC Chaguaramas
1982	ASL Sports Club	ASL Sports Club
1983	ASL Sports Club	ASL Sports Club
1984	Defence Force FC Chaguaramas	Motown United
1985	Defence Force FC Chaguaramas	Defence Force FC Chaguaramas
1986	Trintoc Palo Seco[1]	Trintoc Palo Seco
1987	Defence Force FC Chaguaramas	La Brea Angels
1988	Trintoc Palo Seco	Trintoc Palo Seco
1989	Defence Force FC Chaguaramas	Defence Force FC Chaguaramas
1990	Defence Force FC Chaguaramas	Police FC Saint James
1991	Police FC Saint James	Defence Force FC Chaguaramas
1992	Defence Force FC Chaguaramas	Motown United
1993	Defence Force FC Chaguaramas	Trintoc Palo Seco
1994	Police FC Saint James	Police FC Saint James
1995	Defence Force FC Chaguaramas	United Petrotrin Palo Seco
1996	Defence Force FC Chaguaramas	Defence Force FC Chaguaramas
1997	Defence Force FC Chaguaramas	United Petrotrin Palo Seco
1998	Joe Public FC Tunapuna	San Juan Jabloteh FC
1999	Defence Force FC Chaguaramas	Williams Connection FC
2000	Williams Connection FC	Williams Connection FC
2001	Williams Connection FC	Joe Public FC Tunapuna
2002	San Juan Jabloteh FC	Williams Connection FC
2003	San Juan Jabloteh FC	North East Stars Sangre Grande
2004	North East Stars Sangre Grande	*No competition*
2005	Williams Connection FC	San Juan Jabloteh FC

2006	Joe Public FC Tunapuna	WASA FC St. Joseph
2007	San Juan Jabloteh FC	Joe Public FC Tunapuna
2008	San Juan Jabloteh FC	Caledonia AIA Malabar
2009	Joe Public FC Tunapuna	Joe Public FC Tunapuna
2010/2011	Defence Force FC Chaguaramas	San Juan Jabloteh FC
2011/2012	Williams Connection FC	Caledonia AIA Malabar
2012/2013	Defence Force FC Chaguaramas	Caledonia AIA Malabar
2013/2014	Williams Connection FC	Williams Connection FC
2014/2015	Central FC California	North East Stars Sangre Grande
2015/2016	Central FC California	*No competition*
2016/2017	Central FC California	*No competition*
2017	North East Stars FC Arima	Williams Connection FC
2018	Williams Connection FC	*No competition*
2019/2020	Defence Force FC Chaguaramas	*No competition*
2020/2021	*No competition*	*No competition*

[1] became United Petrotrin Palo Seco in 1993.

Note: the National Championship had different names over the years: Port of Spain Football League (1908-1973), National League (1974-1995), Semi-Professional League (1996–1998), Professional Football League (1999–2001) and Pro League (since 2002).

NATIONAL CHAMPIONSHIP
TT Pro League 2020/2021

The championship was cancelled due to COVID-19 pandemic.

NATIONAL TEAM
INTERNATIONAL MATCHES 2020/2021

31.01.2021	Orlando	United States - Trinidad and Tobago	7-0(4-0)	(F)
25.03.2021	San Cristóbal	Trinidad and Tobago - Guyana	3-0(3-0)	(WCQ)
28.03.2021	Mayagüez	Puerto Rico - Trinidad and Tobago	1-1(0-0)	(WCQ)
05.06.2021	Nassau	Bahamas - Trinidad and Tobago	0-0	(WCQ)
08.06.2021	San Cristóbal	Trinidad and Tobago - Saint Kitts and Nevis	2-0(1-0)	(WCQ)
02.07.2021	F. Lauderdale	Trinidad and Tobago - Montserrat	6-1(3-0)	(GCQ)
06.07.2021	F. Lauderdale	Trinidad and Tobago - French Guiana	1-1; 8-7p	(GCQ)

31.01.2021, Friendly International
Exploria Stadium, Orlando; Attendance: 0
Referee: Héctor Said Martínez Sorto (Honduras)
UNITED STATES - TRINIDAD AND TOBAGO   7-0(4-0)
TRI: Adrian Jamal Foncette, Jamal Jack (82.Noah Powder), Josiah Trimmingham (64.Justin Julian Garcia), Leland Archer, Alvin John Jones, Jabari Mitchell, Andre Fortune II (58.Michel Yannick Poon-Angeron), Sean Bonval (56.Matthew Woo Ling), Ajani Fortune (56.Neveal Irwin Hackshaw), Ryan Telfer, Federico Peña (58.Karl Duane Muckette). Trainer: Terence William Fenwick (England).

25.03.2021, 22nd FIFA World Cup Qualifiers, CONCACAF First Round
Estadio Panamericano, San Cristóbal (Dominican Republic)
Referee: Randy Encarnacion Solano (Dominican Republic)
TRINIDAD AND TOBAGO - GUYANA   3-0(3-0)
TRI: Nicklas Bruus Jensen Frenderup, Robert Alfred Junior Primus, Sheldon Michael Louis Bateau (46.Judah García), Aubrey Rudolph Robert David, Neveal Irwin Hackshaw, Khaleem Shaquille Hyland, Joevin Martin Jones (77.Justin Julian Garcia), Daniel Shaquille Jabari Phillips, Michel Yannick Poon-Angeron, Levi Samuel García (58.Noah Powder), Ryan Telfer (77.Brent Sam). Trainer: Terence William Fenwick (England).
Goals: Levi Samuel García (7), Sheldon Michael Louis Bateau (15), Ryan Telfer (44).

28.03.2021, 22nd FIFA World Cup Qualifiers, CONCACAF First Round
Mayagüez Athletics Stadium, Mayagüez
Referee: Adonai Escobedo González (Mexico)
PUERTO RICO - TRINIDAD AND TOBAGO   1-1(0-0)
TRI: Nicklas Bruus Jensen Frenderup, Robert Alfred Junior Primus, Sheldon Michael Louis Bateau, Aubrey Rudolph Robert David, Neveal Irwin Hackshaw, Khaleem Shaquille Hyland (85.André Christopher Boucaud), Joevin Martin Jones (74.Jabari Mitchell), Daniel Shaquille Jabari Phillips (46.Karl Duane Muckette), Michel Yannick Poon-Angeron, Levi Samuel García, Ryan Telfer (70.Willis Deon Plaza). Trainer: Terence William Fenwick (England).
Goal: Joevin Martin Jones (54).

05.06.2021, 22nd FIFA World Cup Qualifiers, CONCACAF First Round
"Thomas Robinson" Stadium, Nassau; Attendance: n/a
Referee: Oliver Amet Vergara Rodríguez (Panama)
BAHAMAS - TRINIDAD AND TOBAGO   0-0
TRI: Adrian Jamal Foncette, Sheldon Michael Louis Bateau, Aubrey Rudolph Robert David, Shannon Gomez, Neveal Irwin Hackshaw, Keston Anthony Julien (62.Noah Powder), Joevin Martin Jones, Andre Fortune II (46.Daniel Shaquille Jabari Phillips), Karl Duane Muckette (70.Khaleem Shaquille Hyland), Levi Samuel García (70.Judah García), Ryan Telfer (62.Daniel Clive Carr). Trainer: Terence William Fenwick (England).

08.06.2021, 22nd FIFA World Cup Qualifiers, CONCACAF First Round
"Estadio Olímpico "Félix Sánchez", Santo Domingo (Dominican Republic)
Referee: Randy Encarnacion Solano (Dominican Republic)
TRINIDAD AND TOBAGO - SAINT KITTS AND NEVIS   2-0(1-0)
TRI: Adrian Jamal Foncette, Sheldon Michael Louis Bateau, Aubrey Rudolph Robert David, Justin Julian Garcia, Neveal Irwin Hackshaw, Khaleem Shaquille Hyland, Karl Duane Muckette (46.Michel Yannick Poon-Angeron), Jesse Williams, Judah García (46.Joevin Martin Jones), Levi Samuel García (90+3.Andre Fortune II), Ryan Telfer (71.Daniel Clive Carr). Trainer: Terence William Fenwick (England).
Goals: Karl Duane Muckette (36), Khaleem Shaquille Hyland (74).

02.07.2021, 16th CONCACAF Gold Cup Qualifiers, First Round
DRV PNK Stadium, Fort Lauderdale (United States); Attendance: 0
Referee: Bryan Hamed López Castellanos (Guatemala)
TRINIDAD AND TOBAGO - MONTSERRAT   6-1(3-0)
TRI: Nicklas Bruus Jensen Frenderup, Aubrey Rudolph Robert David, Alvin John Jones, Jelani Peters, Neveal Irwin Hackshaw, Triston Hodge (46.Ross Jeivon Russell Jr.), Khaleem Shaquille Hyland, Judah García (79.Andre Fortune II), Kevin Reginald Molino (67.Karl Duane Muckette), Marcus Leric Joseph Jr. (67.Reon Moore), Ryan Telfer (85.Isaiah Lee). Trainer: Angus Anthony Eve.
Goals: Kevin Reginald Molino (21 penalty), Marcus Leric Joseph Jr. (35), Ryan Telfer (45+2), Judah García (57), Reon Moore (68, 82).

06.07.2021, 16th CONCACAF Gold Cup Qualifiers, Second Round
DRV PNK Stadium, Fort Lauderdale (United States); Attendance: 0
Referee: Ismail Elfath (United States)
TRINIDAD AND TOBAGO   1-1(1-1,1-1); 8-7 on penalties
TRI: Nicklas Bruus Jensen Frenderup, Aubrey Rudolph Robert David, Ross Jeivon Russell Jr. (70.Justin Julian Garcia), Alvin John Jones, Jelani Peters, Neveal Irwin Hackshaw, Khaleem Shaquille Hyland (45+2.Karl Duane Muckette), Judah García (22.Andre Fortune II), Kevin Reginald Molino, Marcus Leric Joseph Jr. (46.Curtis Gonzales), Ryan Telfer (70.Reon Moore). Trainer: Angus Anthony Eve.
Goal: Kevin Reginald Molino (27).
Penalties: Karl Duane Muckette, Neveal Irwin Hackshaw, Jelani Peters, Andre Fortune II, Kevin Reginald Molino, Alvin John Jones, Judah García, Curtis Gonzales.

NATIONAL TEAM PLAYERS 2020/2021

Name	DOB	Club
Goalkeepers		
Adrian Jamal FONCETTE	10.10.1988	*Police FC Saint James*
Nicklas Bruus Jensen FRENDERUP	14.12.1992	*Ranheim IL (NOR)*
Defenders		
Leland ARCHER	08.01.1996	*Charleston Battery (USA)*
Sheldon Michael Louis BATEAU	29.01.1991	*KV Mechelen (BEL)*
Aubrey Rudolph Robert DAVID	13.04.1991	*Deportivo Saprissa San José (CRC)*
Justin Julian GARCIA	26.10.1995	*Defence Force FC Chaguaramas*
Shannon GOMEZ	05.10.1996	*Sacramento Republic (USA)*
Curtis GONZALES	26.01.1989	*Defence Force FC Chaguaramas*

Neveal Irwin HACKSHAW	21.09.1995	Indy Eleven Indianapolis (USA)
Triston HODGE	09.10.1994	Colorado Springs Switchbacks (USA)
Jamal JACK	17.12.1987	CSD Sacachispas Chiquimula (GUA)
Alvin John JONES	09.07.1994	Unattached
Joevin Martin JONES	03.08.1991	Inter Miami CF (USA)
Keston Anthony JULIEN	26.10.1998	FC Sheriff Tiraspol (MDA)
Jelani PETERS	17.12.1993	Pittsburgh Riverhounds (USA)
Noah POWDER	27.10.1998	Real Salt Lake (USA)
Robert Alfred Junior PRIMUS	10.11.1990	FC Bengaluru United (IND)
Ross Jeivon RUSSELL Jr.	09.09.1992	La Horquetta Rangers FC
Josiah TRIMMINGHAM	14.12.1996	Forward Madison (USA)
Jesse WILLIAMS	18.05.2001	Coleraine FC (NIR)

Midfielders

André Christopher BOUCAUD	10.10.1984	Unattached
Ajani FORTUNE	30.12.2002	Atlanta United II (USA)
Andre FORTUNE (II)	03.07.1996	Memphis 901 FC (USA)
Judah GARCIA	24.10.1999	NEROCA FC Manipur (IND)
Khaleem Shaquille HYLAND	05.06.1989	Al Batin FC (KSA)
Matthew Woo LING	15.09.1996	Iowa Western Reivers (USA)
Jabari MITCHELL	01.05.1997	Police FC Saint James
Kevin Reginald MOLINO	17.06.1990	Columbus Crew (USA)
Reon MOORE	22.09.1996	Defence Force FC Chaguaramas
Karl Duane MUCKETTE	01.07.1995	Unattached
Daniel Shaquille Jabari PHILLIPS	18.01.2001	Watford FC (ENG)
Michel Yannick POON-ANGERON	19.04.2001	CA Banfield (ARG)

Forwards

Sean BONVAL	07.03.1996	Central FC California
Daniel Clive CARR	30.11.1993	Rovaniemi Palloseura (FIN)
Levi Samuel GARCIA	20.11.1997	AEK Athína (GRE)
Marcus Leric JOSEPH Jr.	29.04.1991	Unattached
Isaiah LEE	21.09.1999	La Horquetta Rangers FC
Federico PEÑA	30.03.1999	Valour FC Winnipeg (CAN)
Willis Deon PLAZA	03.08.1987	Mohammedan SC Kolkata (IND)
Brent SAM	18.04.1996	Defence Force FC Chaguaramas
Ryan TELFER	04.03.1994	York 9 FC (CAN)

National coaches

Terence William FENWICK (England) [01.01.2020 – 11.06.2021]	17.11.1959
Angus Anthony EVE [from 12.06.2021]	23.02.1972

TURKS AND CAICOS ISLANDS

The Country:	The FA:
Turks and Caicos Islands	Turks and Caicos Islands Football Association
Capital: Cockburn Town	TCIFA National Academy
Surface: 430 km²	Venetian Road, P.O. Box 626, Providenciales
Population: 42,953 [2020]	Year of Formation: 1996
Time: UTC-5	Member of FIFA since: 1998
Independent since: *British overseas territory*	Member of CONCACAF since: 1996

NATIONAL TEAM RECORDS

First international match: 24.02.1999, Nassau: Bahamas - Turks and Caicos Islands 3-0
Most international caps: Lenford Singh – 19 caps (since 2006)
Most international goals: Billy Forbes – 8 goals / 15 caps (since 2008)

CONCACAF GOLD CUP	
1991	Did not enter
1993	Did not enter
1996	Did not enter
1998	Did not enter
2000	Qualifiers
2002	Did not enter
2003	Did not enter
2005	*Withdrew*
2007	Qualifiers
2009	Did not enter
2011	Did not enter
2013	Did not enter
2015	Qualifiers
2017	Did not enter
2019	Qualifiers
2021	Qualifiers

FIFA WORLD CUP	
1930	-
1934	-
1938	-
1950	-
1954	-
1958	-
1962	-
1966	-
1970	-
1974	-
1978	-
1982	-
1986	-
1990	-
1994	-
1998	-
2002	Qualifiers
2006	Qualifiers
2010	Qualifiers
2014	Qualifiers
2018	Qualifiers

F.I.F.A. CONFEDERATIONS CUP 1992-2017
None

OLYMPIC FOOTBALL TOURNAMENTS 1900-2016
None

CCCF (Confederación Centroamericana y del Caribe de Fútbol) CHAMPIONSHIPS 1941-1961	
None	

CONCACAF CHAMPIONSHIPS 1963-1989	
None	

CONCACAF NATIONS LEAGUE	
2019-2020	League C

CARIBBEAN CHAMPIONSHIPS 1989-2017			
1989	Did not enter	1999	Qualifiers
1991	Did not enter	2001	Did not enter
1992	Did not enter	2005	*Withdrew*
1993	Did not enter	2007	Qualifiers
1994	Did not enter	2008	Did not enter
1995	Did not enter	2010	Did not enter
1996	Did not enter	2012	Did not enter
1997	Did not enter	2014	Qualifiers
1998	Did not enter	2017	Did not enter

TURKS AND CAICOS ISLANDS CLUB HONOURS IN CONCACAF CLUB COMPETITIONS:

CONCACAF Champions Cup / CONCACAF Champions League 1962-2020
None

CONCACAF League 2017-2020
None

Caribbean Club Championship 1997-2021
None

*CONCACAF Cup Winners Cup 1991-1995**
None

*Copa Interamericana 1968-1998**
None

defunct competitions

NATIONAL COMPETITIONS
TABLE OF HONOURS

	CHAMPIONS
1999	Tropic All Stars
2000	Masters FC [city not known]
2001	SWA Sharks FC
2002	Beaches FC
2002/2003	Caribbean All Stars FC
2003/2004	KPMG United FC
2004/2005	KPMG United FC
2005/2006	Cost Right FC
2006/2007	Beaches FC
2007/2008	PWC Athletic
2008/2009	Digi FC
2009/2010	AFC Academy
2010/2011	Provopool FC
2011/2012	Cheshire Hall FC

2012/2013	Cheshire Hall FC
2013/2014	AFC Academy
2014/2015	AFC Academy
2015/2016	AFC Academy
2016/2017	Beaches FC
2018	Academy Jaguars
2019	Academy Jaguars
2019/2020	*Competition suspended*
2020/2021	*No competition*

NATIONAL CHAMPIONSHIP
WIV Provo Premier League 2020/2021

The championship was cancelled due to COVID-19 pandemic.

NATIONAL TEAM
INTERNATIONAL MATCHES 2020/2021

27.03.2021	San Cristóbal	*Turks and Caicos Islands - Nicaragua*	*0-7(0-3)*	*(WCQ)*
30.03.2021	San Cristóbal	*Belize - Turks and Caicos Islands*	*5-0(1-0)*	*(WCQ)*
05.06.2021	Providenciales	*Turks and Caicos Islands - Haiti*	*0-10(0-5)*	*(WCQ)*

27.03.2021, 22nd FIFA World Cup Qualifiers, CONCACAF First Round
Estadio Panamericano, San Cristóbal (Dominican Republic)
Referee: William Anderson (Puerto Rico)
TURKS AND CAICOS ISLANDS - NICARAGUA   0-7(0-3)
TCA: Pendieno Brooks, Jeff Beljour, Wildens Delva, Jerome Ledson, José Elcius, Mackenson Cadet, Rascari Cox (50.Alexander Bryan), Lenford Singh (65.Fred Dorvil), James McKnight, Billy Forbes, Wilkins Sylvain (21.Widlin Calixte). Trainer: Omar Edwards (Jamaica).

30.03.2021, 22nd FIFA World Cup Qualifiers, CONCACAF First Round
Estadio Panamericano, San Cristóbal (Dominican Republic)
Referee: Nima Saghafi (United States)
BELIZE - TURKS AND CAICOS ISLANDS   5-0(1-0)
TCA: Pendieno Brooks, Jeff Beljour (68.Lenford Singh), Wildens Delva, Jerome Ledson, Widlin Calixte, Alexander Bryan (77.Callum Park), Mackenson Cadet, José Elcius (57.Wilkins Sylvain), Rascari Cox, Billy Forbes, James McKnight. Trainer: Omar Edwards (Jamaica).

05.06.2021, 22nd FIFA World Cup Qualifiers, CONCACAF First Round
TCIFA National Academy, Providenciales
Referee: Diego Montaño Robles (Mexico)
TURKS AND CAICOS ISLANDS - HAITI   0-10(0-5)
TCA: Pendieno Brooks (46.Sebastian Guy Turbyfield), Jeff Beljour (73.Cory Williams), Jerome Ledson, Christopher Louisy, James Rene, José Elcius (58.Callum Park), Mackenson Cadet, Rascari Cox (46.Lenford Singh), Raymond Burey, Billy Forbes, Wilkins Sylvain (58.Wildens Delva). Trainer: Omar Edwards (Jamaica).

NATIONAL TEAM PLAYERS 2020/2021

Name	DOB	Club
Goalkeepers		
Pendieno BROOKS	04.01.2000	*SWA Sharks FC*
Sebastian Guy TURBYFIELD	19.12.2002	*Academy Eagles*
Defenders		
Jeff BELJOUR	04.04.1998	*Academy Jaguars*
Alexander BRYAN	05.12.1994	
Wildens DELVA	15.10.1991	*SWA Sharks FC*
Jerome LEDSON	28.12.1998	*Academy Jaguars*
Callum PARK	06.12.2004	*Academy Eagles*
James RENE	02.02.1986	
Lenford SINGH	08.08.1985	*SWA Sharks FC*
Cory WILLIAMS	22.03.2005	
Midfielders		
Mackenson CADET	20.01.2000	*Hardin-Simmons Cowboys (USA)*
Widlin CALIXTE	21.04.1990	*Beaches FC*
Rascari COX	13.07.1985	
José ELCIUS	06.11.2000	*Academy Jaguars*
Christopher LOUISY	06.04.2005	*Academy Falcons*
Forwards		
Raymond BUREY	03.09.1997	*Academy Jaguars*
Fred DORVIL	12.10.1995	*Beaches FC*
Billy FORBES	13.12.1990	*Miami FC (USA)*
James McKNIGHT	10.06.1994	*VEC Dublin (IRL)*
Wilkins SYLVAIN	20.10.1999	*Academy Eagles*
National coaches		
Omar EDWARDS (Jamaica) [from 18.02.2019]		30.05.1980

UNITED STATES

The Country:	The FA:
United States of America Capital: Washington D.C. Surface: 9,826,675 km² Population: 331,449,281 [2020] Time: UTC-5 to -10 Independent since: 1776	United States Soccer Federation 1801 South Prairie Avenue, Chicago, Illinois 60616 Year of Formation: 1913 Member of FIFA since: 1914 Member of CONCACAF since: 1961

NATIONAL TEAM RECORDS

First international match:	20.08.1916, Stockholm: Sweden - United States 2-3
Most international caps:	Cobi N'Gai Jones – 164 caps (1992-2004)
Most international goals:	Landon Timothy Donovan – 57 goals / 157 caps (2000-2014) Clinton Drew Dempsey – 57 goals / 141 caps (2004-2017)

CONCACAF GOLD CUP		FIFA WORLD CUP	
1991	**Final Tournament (Winners)**	1930	Final Tournament (3rd Place)
1993	Final Tournament (Runners-up)	1934	Final Tournament (Group Stage)
1996	Final Tournament (3rd Place)	1938	Qualifiers
1998	Final Tournament (Runners-up)	1950	Final Tournament (Group Stage)
2000	Final Tournament (Quarter-Finals)	1954	Qualifiers
2002	**Final Tournament (Winners)**	1958	Qualifiers
2003	Final Tournament (3rd Place)	1962	Qualifiers
2005	**Final Tournament (Winners)**	1966	Qualifiers
2007	**Final Tournament (Winners)**	1970	Qualifiers
2009	Final Tournament (Runners-up)	1974	Qualifiers
2011	Final Tournament (Runners-up)	1978	Qualifiers
2013	**Final Tournament (Winners)**	1982	Qualifiers
2015	Final Tournament (4th Place)	1986	Qualifiers
2017	**Final Tournament (Winners)**	1990	Final Tournament (Group Stage)
2019	Final Tournament (Runners-up)	1994	Final Tournament (2nd Round of 16)
2021	Final Tournament (*to be played*)	1998	Final Tournament (Group Stage)
		2002	Final Tournament (Quarter-Finals)
		2006	Final Tournament (Group Stage)
		2010	Final Tournament (2nd Round of 16)
		2014	Final Tournament (2nd Round of 16)
		2018	Qualifiers

F.I.F.A. CONFEDERATIONS CUP 1992-2017

1992 (3rd Place), 1999 (3rd Place), 2003, 2009 (Runners-up)

OLYMPIC FOOTBALL TOURNAMENTS 1908-2016							
1908	-	1948	FT-1/8 Finals	1972	FT/Group Stage	1996	FT/Group Stage
1912	-	1952	Preliminary Rd.	1976	Qualifiers	2000	FT/4th Place
1920	*Withdrew*	1956	Quarter-Finals	1980	Qualifiers	2004	Qualifiers
1924	FT-1/8 Finals	1960	Qualifiers	1984	FT/Group Stage	2008	FT/Group Stage
1928	FT-1/8 Finals	1964	Qualifiers	1988	FT/Group Stage	2012	Qualifiers
1936	FT-1/8 Finals	1968	Qualifiers	1992	FT/Group Stage	2016	Qualifiers

CCCF (Confederación Centroamericana y del Caribe de Fútbol) CHAMPIONSHIPS 1941-1961
None

CONCACAF CHAMPIONSHIPS 1963-1989
1985, 1989 (Runners-up)

NAFC (North American Football Confederation) CHAMPIONSHIPS 1947-1991
1947 (3rd Place), 1949 (Runners-up), 1990 (3rd Place, with „B"-Team), 1991 (Runners-up)

COPA AMÉRICA
2016

CONCACAF NATIONS LEAGUE	
2019-2020	League A

UNITED STATES CLUB HONOURS IN CONCACAF CLUB COMPETITIONS:

CONCACAF Champions Cup / CONCACAF Champions League 1962-2020		
Washington DC United	1	1998
Los Angeles Galaxy	1	2000
CONCACAF League 2017-2020		
None		
Caribbean Club Championship 1997-2021		
None		
CONCACAF Cup Winners Cup 1991-1995*		
None		
Copa Interamericana 1968-1998*		
Washington DC United	1	1998

defunct competitions

NATIONAL COMPETITIONS
TABLE OF HONOURS

CHAMPIONS

American League of Professional Soccer

1894	Baltimore Orioles

National Association Football League

1895	Bayonne Centerville
1897/1898	Paterson True Blues
1906/1907	West Hudson
1907/1908	Paterson Rangers
1908/1909	Clark AA
1909/1910	West Hudson
1910/1911	Jersey AC
1911/1912	West Hudson
1912/1913	West Hudson
1913/1914	Brooklyn FC
1914/1915	West Hudson
1915/1916	Alley Boys
1916/1917	Jersey AC
1917/1918	Paterson FC
1918/1919	Bethlehem Steel
1919/1920	Bethlehem Steel
1920/1921	Bethlehem Steel

American Soccer League I

1921/1922	Philadelphia Football Club
1922/1923	J & P Coats
1923/1924	Fall River Marksmen
1924/1925	Fall River Marksmen
1925/1926	Fall River Marksmen
1926/1927	Bethlehem Steel
1927/1928	Boston Wonder Workers
1928/1929	Fall River Marksmen
1929	Fall River Marksmen
1929/1930	Fall River Marksmen
1930	Fall River Marksmen
1930/1931	New York Giants
1932	New Bedford Whalers
1932/1933	Fall River Football Club

American Soccer League II

1933/1934	Kearney Irish
1934/1935	Philadelphia German-Americans
1935/1936	New York Americans
1936/1937	Kearny Scots
1937/1938	Kearny Scots
1938/1939	Kearny Scots
1939/1940	Kearny Scots
1940/1941	Kearny Scots
1941/1942	Philadelphia Americans
1942/1943	Brooklyn Hispano
1943/1944	Philadelphia Americans

1944/1945	Brookhattan	
1945/1946	Baltimore Americans	
1946/1947	Philadelphia Americans	
1947/1948	Philadelphia Americans	
1948/1949	Philadelphia Nationals	
1949/1950	Philadelphia Nationals	
1950/1951	Philadelphia Nationals	
1951/1952	Philadelphia Americans	
1952/1953	Philadelphia Nationals	
1953/1954	New York Americans	
1954/1955	Uhrik Truckers Philadelphia	
1955/1956	Uhrik Truckers Philadelphia	
1956/1957	New York Hakoah	
1957/1958	New York Hakoah	
1958/1959	New York Hakoah	
1959/1960	Colombo	
1960/1961	Ukrainian Nationals Philadelphia	
1961/1962	Ukrainian Nationals Philadelphia	
1962/1963	Ukrainian Nationals Philadelphia	
1963/1964	Ukrainian Nationals Philadelphia	
1964/1965	Hartford SC	
1965/1966	Roma SC	
1966/1967	Baltimore St. Gerards	
	North American Soccer League	**American Soccer League II**
1967/1968	Los Angeles Wolves (USA) Oakland Clippers (NPSL)	Ukrainian Nationals Philadelphia
1968	Atlanta Chiefs	Washington Darts
1969	Kansas City Spurs	Washington Darts
1970	Rochester Lancers	Philadelphia Ukrainians
1971	Dallas Tornado	New York Greeks
1972	New York Cosmos	Cincinnati Comets
1973	Philadelphia Atoms	New York Apollo
1974	Los Angeles Aztecs	Rhode Island Oceaneers
1975	Tampa Bay Rowdies	New York Apollo
1976	Toronto Metros-Croatia	Los Angeles Skyhawks
1977	New York Cosmos	New Jersey Americans
1978	New York Cosmos	New York Apollo
1979	Vancouver Whitecaps	Sacramento Gold
1980	New York Cosmos	Pennsylvania Stoners
1981	Chicago Sting	Carolina Lightnin'
1982	New York Cosmos	Detroit Express
1983	Tulsa Roughnecks	Jacksonville Tea Men
1984	Chicago Sting	-
	American Soccer League III	
1988	Washington Diplomats	
1989	Ft. Lauderdale Strikers	
1990	Maryland Bays	
	Major League Soccer	
1996	Washington DC United	
1997	Washington DC United	
1998	Chicago Fire	
1999	Washington DC United	

2000	Kansas City Wizards
2001	San Jose Earthquakes
2002	Los Angeles Galaxy
2003	San Jose Earthquakes
2004	Washington DC United
2005	Los Angeles Galaxy
2006	Houston Dynamo
2007	Houston Dynamo
2008	Columbus Crew SC
2009	Real Salt Lake
2010	Colorado Rapids
2011	Los Angeles Galaxy
2012	Los Angeles Galaxy
2013	Sporting Kansas City
2014	Los Angeles Galaxy
2015	Portland Timbers
2016	Seattle Sounders FC
2017	Toronto FC
2018	Atlanta United FC
2019	Seattle Sounders FC
2020	Columbus Crew SC

US Open Cup Winners:
1914: Brooklyn Field Club; 1915: Bethlehem Steel; 1916: Bethlehem Steel; 1917: Fall River Rovers; 1918: Bethlehem Steel; 1919: Bethlehem Steel; 1920: St. Louis Ben Millers; 1921: Brooklyn Robins Dry Dock; 1922: St. Louis Scullins Steel; 1923: Paterson FC; 1924: Fall River Marksmen; 1925: Shawsheen Indians; 1926: Bethlehem Steel; 1927: Fall River Marksmen; 1928: New York Nationals; 1929: New York Hakoah; 1930: Fall River Marksmen; 1931: Fall River FC; 1932: New Bedford Whalers; 1933: St. Louis Stix, Baer & Fuller; 1934: St. Louis Stix, Baer & Fuller; 1935: St. Louis Central Breweries; 1936: Philadelphia German-American; 1937: New York Americans; 1938: Chicago Sparta; 1939: Brooklyn St. Mary's Celtic; 1940: Baltimore SC & Chicago Sparta A & BA [shared]; 1941: Pawtucket FC; 1942: Pittsburgh Gallatin SC; 1943: Brooklyn Hispano; 1944: Brooklyn Hispano; 1945: New York Brookhattan; 1946: Chicago Vikings; 1947: Fall River Ponta Delgada; 1948: St. Louis Simpkins-Ford; 1949: Pittsburgh Morgan SC; 1950: St. Louis Simpkins-Ford; 1951: New York German-Hungarian; 1952: Pittsburgh Hamarville; 1953: Chicago Falcons; 1954: New York Americans; 1955: SC Eintracht; 1956: Pittsburgh Hamarville; 1957: St. Louis Kutis; 1958: Los Angeles Kickers; 1959: San Pedro McIlvane Canvasbacks; 1960: Philadelphia Ukrainian Nationals; 1961: Philadelphia Ukrainian Nationals; 1962: New York Hungaria; 1963: Philadelphia Ukrainian Nationals; 1964: Los Angeles Kickers; 1965: New York Ukrainians; 1966: Philadelphia Ukrainian Nationals; 1967: New York Greek-American; 1968: New York Greek American; 1969: New York Greek-American; 1970: SC Elizabeth; 1971: New York Hota; 1972: SC Elizabeth; 1973: Los Angeles Maccabee; 1974: New York Greek-American; 1975: Los Angeles Maccabee; 1976: San Francisco AC; 1977: Los Angeles Maccabee; 1978: Brooklyn Dodgers; 1979: Brooklyn Dodgers; 1980: New York Pancyprian Freedoms; 1981: Los Angeles Maccabee; 1982: New York Pancyprian Freedoms; 1983: New York Pancyprian Freedoms; 1984: New York AO Krete; 1985: San Francisco Greek-American AC; 1986: St. Louis Kutis; 1987: Washington Club Espana; 1988: St. Louis Busch Seniors; 1989: St. Petersburg Kickers; 1990: Chicago AAC Eagles; 1991: Brooklyn Italians; 1992: San Jose Oaks; 1993: San Francisco CD Mexico; 1994: San Francisco Greek-American; 1995: Richmond Kickers; 1996: Washington DC United; 1997: Dallas Burn; 1998: Chicago Fire; 1999: Rochester Rhinos; 2000: Chicago Fire; 2001: Los Angeles Galaxy; 2002: Columbus Crew SC; 2003: Chicago Fire; 2004: Kansas City Wizards; 2005: Los Angeles Galaxy; 2006: Chicago Fire; 2007: New England Revolution; 2008: Washington DC United; 2009: Seattle Sounders FC; 2010: Seattle Sounders FC; 2011: Seattle Sounders FC; 2012: Sporting

Kansas City; 2013: Washington DC United; 2014: Seattle Sounders FC; 2015: Sporting Kansas City; 2016: FC Dallas; 2017: Sporting Kansas City; 2018: Houston Dynamo; 2019: Atlanta United FC; 2020: *Competition cancelled.*

NATIONAL CHAMPIONSHIP
Major League Soccer 2020

Results

29.02.2020	DC United	-	Colorado Rapids	1-2(0-0)
	Montréal Impact	-	New England Revolution	2-1(1-1)
	Houston Dynamo	-	Los Angeles Galaxy	1-1(0-1)
	San Jose Earthquakes	-	Toronto FC	2-2(0-1)
01.03.2020	FC Dallas	-	Philadelphia Union	2-0(0-0)
	Orlando City	-	Real Salt Lake	0-0
	Nashville SC	-	Atlanta United	1-2(1-2)
	Vancouver Whitecaps	-	Sporting Kansas City	1-3(1-2)
	Columbus Crew	-	New York City FC	1-0(0-0)
	New York Red Bulls	-	FC Cincinnati	3-2(2-0)
	Seattle Sounders	-	Chicago Fire	2-1(0-0)
	Los Angeles FC	-	Inter Miami	1-0(1-0)
02.03.2020	Portland Timbers	-	Minnesota United FC	1-3(0-0)
07.03.2020	New England Revolution	-	Chicago Fire	1-1(1-0)
	Real Salt Lake	-	New York Red Bulls	1-1(0-1)
	FC Dallas	-	Montréal Impact	2-2(0-0)
	DC United	-	Inter Miami	2-1(0-1)
	Toronto FC	-	New York City FC	1-0(0-0)
08.03.2020	Atlanta United	-	FC Cincinnati	2-1(1-0)
	San Jose Earthquakes	-	Minnesota United FC	2-5(1-4)
	Sporting Kansas City	-	Houston Dynamo	4-0(2-0)
	Colorado Rapids	-	Orlando City	2-1(0-0)
	Los Angeles Galaxy	-	Vancouver Whitecaps	0-1(0-0)
	Seattle Sounders	-	Columbus Crew	1-1(0-1)
09.03.2020	Portland Timbers	-	Nashville SC	1-0(1-0)
	Los Angeles FC	-	Philadelphia Union	3-3(1-1)
13.08.2020	FC Dallas	-	Nashville SC	0-1(0-0)
17.08.2020	FC Dallas	-	Nashville SC	0-0
19.08.2020	Toronto FC	-	Vancouver Whitecaps	3-0(1-0)
21.08.2020	New York Red Bulls	-	New York City FC	1-0(0-0)
	Columbus Crew	-	Chicago Fire	3-0(1-0)
	New England Revolution	-	Philadelphia Union	0-0
22.08.2020	FC Cincinnati	-	DC United	0-0
	Minnesota United FC	-	Sporting Kansas City	1-2(1-1)
	Houston Dynamo	-	FC Dallas	0-0
	Toronto FC	-	Vancouver Whitecaps	1-0(1-0)
23.08.2020	Los Angeles FC	-	Los Angeles Galaxy	0-2(0-1)
	Atlanta United	-	Nashville SC	2-0(1-0)
	Inter Miami	-	Orlando City	3-2(2-1)
	Colorado Rapids	-	Real Salt Lake	1-4(1-0)
24.08.2020	Portland Timbers	-	Seattle Sounders	0-3(0-0)
25.08.2020	New York City FC	-	Columbus Crew	1-0(0-0)
26.08.2020	DC United	-	New England Revolution	1-2(0-2)
	Chicago Fire	-	FC Cincinnati	3-0(2-0)

	Philadelphia Union	-	New York Red Bulls	1-0(1-0)
	Montréal Impact	-	Vancouver Whitecaps	2-0(2-0)
	Sporting Kansas City	-	Houston Dynamo	2-5(1-2)
27.08.2020	Orlando City	-	Nashville SC	3-1(1-1)
29.08.2020	Montréal Impact	-	Toronto FC	0-1(0-0)
	Atlanta United	-	Orlando City	1-3(0-2)
30.08.2020	FC Cincinnati	-	Columbus Crew	0-0
	New York City FC	-	Chicago Fire	3-1(1-1)
	Philadelphia Union	-	DC United	4-1(3-0)
	New England Revolution	-	New York Red Bulls	1-1(1-1)
	FC Dallas	-	Minnesota United FC	3-1(2-0)
	Colorado Rapids	-	Sporting Kansas City	1-1(0-0)
	Los Angeles Galaxy	-	San Jose Earthquakes	3-2(1-1)
	Portland Timbers	-	Real Salt Lake	4-4(2-1)
31.08.2020	Nashville SC	-	Inter Miami	1-0(0-0)
	Seattle Sounders	-	Los Angeles FC	3-1(1-0)
02.09.2020	Toronto FC	-	Montréal Impact	0-1(0-1)
03.09.2020	Atlanta United	-	Inter Miami	0-0
	FC Cincinnati	-	Chicago Fire	0-0
	Columbus Crew	-	Philadelphia Union	1-0(0-0)
	New York Red Bulls	-	DC United	0-1(0-0)
	Houston Dynamo	-	Minnesota United FC	3-0(1-0)
	New England Revolution	-	New York City FC	0-2(0-0)
	Nashville SC	-	Orlando City	1-1(0-1)
	Sporting Kansas City	-	FC Dallas	1-1(1-1)
	Real Salt Lake	-	Seattle Sounders	2-2(0-1)
	Portland Timbers	-	Los Angeles Galaxy	2-3(0-1)
	Los Angeles FC	-	San Jose Earthquakes	5-1(1-0)
06.09.2020	Houston Dynamo	-	Sporting Kansas City	2-1(0-1)
	Orlando City	-	Atlanta United	1-1(1-0)
	Vancouver Whitecaps	-	Toronto FC	3-2(1-1)
	San Jose Earthquakes	-	Colorado Rapids	1-1(0-0)
07.09.2020	DC United	-	New York City FC	0-0
	New York Red Bulls	-	Philadelphia Union	0-3(0-1)
	Chicago Fire	-	New England Revolution	1-2(1-1)
	Columbus Crew	-	FC Cincinnati	3-0(0-0)
	Minnesota United FC	-	Real Salt Lake	4-0(0-0)
	Inter Miami	-	Nashville SC	0-0
	Seattle Sounders	-	Portland Timbers	1-2(1-1)
	Los Angeles Galaxy	-	Los Angeles FC	3-0(0-0)
10.09.2020	Inter Miami	-	Atlanta United	2-1(2-1)
	Minnesota United FC	-	FC Dallas	3-2(2-1)
	Montréal Impact	-	Toronto FC	1-2(0-1)
	Colorado Rapids	-	Houston Dynamo	1-1(0-0)
	Real Salt Lake	-	Los Angeles FC	3-0(1-0)
11.09.2020	Seattle Sounders	-	San Jose Earthquakes	7-1(5-0)
12.09.2020	Chicago Fire	-	Columbus Crew	2-2(2-0)
13.09.2020	DC United	-	New York Red Bulls	0-2(0-1)
	New York City FC	-	FC Cincinnati	2-1(1-0)
	Orlando City	-	Inter Miami	2-1(1-0)
	Philadelphia Union	-	New England Revolution	2-1(0-0)
	Nashville SC	-	Atlanta United	4-2(3-1)
	FC Dallas	-	Houston Dynamo	2-1(1-1)
	Real Salt Lake	-	Colorado Rapids	0-5(0-2)
14.09.2020	Sporting Kansas City	-	Minnesota United FC	1-0(0-0)

	Vancouver Whitecaps	-	Montréal Impact	2-4(1-2)
	Los Angeles FC	-	Portland Timbers	4-2(3-2)
	San Jose Earthquakes	-	Los Angeles Galaxy	0-0
17.09.2020	FC Dallas	-	Colorado Rapids	4-1(1-0)
	Vancouver Whitecaps	-	Montréal Impact	3-1(2-0)
19.09.2020	Seattle Sounders	-	Los Angeles FC	3-0(2-0)
	Sporting Kansas City	-	FC Dallas	2-3(0-1)
	New England Revolution	-	New York City FC	0-0
20.09.2020	Atlanta United	-	Inter Miami	1-2(1-2)
	New York Red Bulls	-	FC Cincinnati	0-1(0-0)
	Orlando City	-	Chicago Fire	4-1(2-0)
	Columbus Crew	-	Nashville SC	2-0(0-0)
	DC United	-	Toronto FC	2-2(1-1)
	Houston Dynamo	-	Minnesota United FC	2-2(0-2)
	Real Salt Lake	-	Vancouver Whitecaps	1-2(0-0)
	San Jose Earthquakes	-	Portland Timbers	1-6(1-2)
	Los Angeles Galaxy	-	Colorado Rapids	0-2(0-1)
21.09.2020	Montréal Impact	-	Philadelphia Union	1-4(1-2)
23.09.2020	New England Revolution	-	Montréal Impact	3-1(1-0)
24.09.2020	New York City FC	-	Toronto FC	0-1(0-0)
	Atlanta United	-	FC Dallas	1-0(0-0)
	Chicago Fire	-	Houston Dynamo	4-0(3-0)
	FC Cincinnati	-	Philadelphia Union	0-0
	Columbus Crew	-	Minnesota United FC	2-1(1-0)
	Sporting Kansas City	-	Orlando City	1-2(0-2)
	Inter Miami	-	New York Red Bulls	1-4(1-1)
	Nashville SC	-	DC United	1-0(0-0)
	Colorado Rapids	-	San Jose Earthquakes	5-0(1-0)
	Real Salt Lake	-	Los Angeles Galaxy	2-0(0-0)
	Portland Timbers	-	Seattle Sounders	1-0(1-0)
	Los Angeles FC	-	Vancouver Whitecaps	6-0(5-0)
26.09.2020	Nashville SC	-	Houston Dynamo	1-1(0-0)
27.09.2020	New York City FC	-	FC Cincinnati	4-0(3-0)
28.09.2020	DC United	-	New England Revolution	0-2(0-0)
	New York Red Bulls	-	Montréal Impact	4-1(2-1)
	Philadelphia Union	-	Inter Miami	3-0(1-0)
	Chicago Fire	-	Atlanta United	2-0(2-0)
	Toronto FC	-	Columbus Crew	3-1(0-1)
	Minnesota United FC	-	Real Salt Lake	0-0
	FC Dallas	-	Orlando City	0-0
	Vancouver Whitecaps	-	Portland Timbers	0-1(0-1)
	Los Angeles Galaxy	-	Seattle Sounders	1-3(0-2)
	Los Angeles FC	-	San Jose Earthquakes	1-2(1-0)
03.10.2020	Orlando City	-	New York Red Bulls	3-1(1-0)
04.10.2020	DC United	-	Atlanta United	0-4(0-2)
	Montréal Impact	-	Chicago Fire	2-2(1-1)
	New England Revolution	-	Nashville SC	0-0
	Toronto FC	-	Philadelphia Union	2-1(0-1)
	Houston Dynamo	-	Sporting Kansas City	1-2(0-1)
	Inter Miami	-	New York City FC	2-3(2-3)
	Minnesota United FC	-	FC Cincinnati	2-0(1-0)
	FC Dallas	-	Columbus Crew	2-2(1-0)
	Seattle Sounders	-	Vancouver Whitecaps	3-1(0-0)
	San Jose Earthquakes	-	Los Angeles Galaxy	2-1(1-1)
05.10.2020	Real Salt Lake	-	Los Angeles FC	1-3(0-2)

07.10.2020	Nashville SC	-	Minnesota United FC	0-0
08.10.2020	Colorado Rapids	-	Los Angeles FC	not played
	Atlanta United	-	Orlando City	0-0
	New York Red Bulls	-	Inter Miami	1-2(0-0)
	New England Revolution	-	Toronto FC	0-1(0-1)
	Philadelphia Union	-	FC Cincinnati	3-0(0-0)
	Columbus Crew	-	Montréal Impact	1-2(1-1)
	New York City FC	-	DC United	4-1(1-1)
	Houston Dynamo	-	FC Dallas	2-0(1-0)
	Sporting Kansas City	-	Chicago Fire	1-0(0-0)
	Seattle Sounders	-	Real Salt Lake	2-1(1-0)
	Los Angeles Galaxy	-	Portland Timbers	3-6(1-2)
	San Jose Earthquakes	-	Vancouver Whitecaps	3-0(0-0)
10.10.2020	Columbus Crew	-	Los Angeles FC	not played
	Inter Miami	-	Houston Dynamo	1-0(0-0)
11.10.2020	Colorado Rapids	-	Los Angeles Galaxy	not played
	Atlanta United	-	New York Red Bulls	0-1(0-0)
	Vancouver Whitecaps	-	Real Salt Lake	2-1(0-1)
	New York City FC	-	New England Revolution	1-2(0-1)
12.10.2020	FC Dallas	-	Minnesota United FC	not played
	Los Angeles FC	-	Seattle Sounders	3-1(1-0)
	Chicago Fire	-	DC United	2-1(2-0)
	FC Cincinnati	-	Toronto FC	0-1(0-1)
	Philadelphia Union	-	Montréal Impact	2-1(1-0)
	Sporting Kansas City	-	Nashville SC	2-1(0-1)
	Portland Timbers	-	San Jose Earthquakes	3-0(0-0)
15.10.2020	Seattle Sounders	-	Colorado Rapids	not played
	Montréal Impact	-	New England Revolution	2-3(1-2)
	FC Cincinnati	-	Columbus Crew	2-1(1-1)
	Orlando City	-	New York City FC	1-1(1-1)
	Toronto FC	-	New York Red Bulls	1-1(1-0)
	DC United	-	Philadelphia Union	2-2(0-0)
	Houston Dynamo	-	Nashville SC	1-3(0-3)
	Inter Miami	-	Atlanta United	1-1(0-0)
	FC Dallas	-	Sporting Kansas City	1-0(1-0)
	Real Salt Lake	-	Portland Timbers	2-1(2-0)
	Vancouver Whitecaps	-	Los Angeles FC	2-1(1-0)
	Los Angeles Galaxy	-	San Jose Earthquakes	0-4(0-1)
17.10.2020	Chicago Fire	-	Sporting Kansas City	2-2(1-1)
18.10.2020	Montréal Impact	-	Inter Miami	2-1(1-1)
19.10.2020	Colorado Rapids	-	Real Salt Lake	not played
	Columbus Crew	-	New York City FC	3-1(1-0)
	New York Red Bulls	-	Orlando City	1-1(0-0)
	FC Cincinnati	-	DC United	1-2(0-1)
	Toronto FC	-	Atlanta United	1-0(0-0)
	Minnesota United FC	-	Houston Dynamo	2-2(2-0)
	Portland Timbers	-	Los Angeles FC	1-1(0-0)
	Los Angeles Galaxy	-	Vancouver Whitecaps	1-0(0-0)
	San Jose Earthquakes	-	Seattle Sounders	0-0
20.10.2020	New England Revolution	-	Philadelphia Union	1-2(0-1)
21.10.2020	Nashville SC	-	FC Dallas	3-0(1-0)
22.10.2020	Colorado Rapids	-	Sporting Kansas City	not played
23.10.2020	Seattle Sounders	-	Portland Timbers	1-1(0-1)
24.10.2020	Nashville SC	-	New England Revolution	1-1(0-0)
	Inter Miami	-	Orlando City	2-1(1-1)

Date	Home		Away	Score
	Atlanta United	-	DC United	1-2(0-0)
25.10.2020	New York City FC	-	Montréal Impact	3-1(0-0)
	Chicago Fire	-	New York Red Bulls	2-2(0-1)
	FC Cincinnati	-	Minnesota United FC	0-1(0-0)
	Philadelphia Union	-	Toronto FC	5-0(2-0)
	Houston Dynamo	-	Columbus Crew	1-1(1-0)
	Sporting Kansas City	-	Colorado Rapids	4-0(0-0)
	Real Salt Lake	-	FC Dallas	0-0
	Vancouver Whitecaps	-	San Jose Earthquakes	2-1(0-1)
	Los Angeles FC	-	Los Angeles Galaxy	2-0(0-0)
28.10.2020	Montréal Impact	-	Nashville SC	0-1(0-1)
	Vancouver Whitecaps	-	Seattle Sounders	0-2(0-0)
29.10.2020	New York Red Bulls	-	New England Revolution	1-0(0-0)
	FC Cincinnati	-	Sporting Kansas City	0-1(0-0)
	Orlando City	-	Atlanta United	4-1(2-0)
	Philadelphia Union	-	Chicago Fire	2-1(1-1)
	Toronto FC	-	New York City FC	0-1(0-0)
	Minnesota United FC	-	Colorado Rapids	2-1(1-0)
	DC United	-	Columbus Crew	1-0(1-0)
	FC Dallas	-	Inter Miami	2-1(0-1)
	Portland Timbers	-	Los Angeles Galaxy	5-2(3-0)
	Los Angeles FC	-	Houston Dynamo	2-1(2-0)
	San Jose Earthquakes	-	Real Salt Lake	2-0(1-0)
31.10.2020	FC Dallas	-	Houston Dynamo	3-0(2-0)
01.11.2020	Nashville SC	-	Chicago Fire	1-1(1-1)
	Columbus Crew	-	Philadelphia Union	2-1(1-0)
02.11.2020	Sporting Kansas City	-	Minnesota United FC	not played
	Atlanta United	-	FC Cincinnati	2-0(2-0)
	New York City FC	-	New York Red Bulls	5-2(2-2)
	Montréal Impact	-	Orlando City	0-1(0-1)
	New England Revolution	-	DC United	4-3(1-2)
	Toronto FC	-	Inter Miami	2-1(0-1)
	Colorado Rapids	-	Seattle Sounders	3-1(2-1)
	Portland Timbers	-	Vancouver Whitecaps	1-0(0-0)
	Los Angeles Galaxy	-	Real Salt Lake	2-1(1-0)
05.11.2020	Orlando City	-	Columbus Crew	2-1(1-0)
	Minnesota United FC	-	Chicago Fire	2-2(0-1)
	Nashville SC	-	FC Dallas	0-1(0-1)
	Portland Timbers	-	Colorado Rapids	0-1(0-0)
	San Jose Earthquakes	-	Los Angeles FC	3-2(2-1)
	Los Angeles Galaxy	-	Seattle Sounders	1-1(0-0)
08.11.2020	Chicago Fire	-	New York City FC	3-4(3-3)
	Columbus Crew	-	Atlanta United	2-1(1-0)
	DC United	-	Montréal Impact	2-3(2-1)
	Inter Miami	-	FC Cincinnati	2-1(2-0)
	New York Red Bulls	-	Toronto FC	2-1(2-0)
	Orlando City	-	Nashville SC	2-3(1-1)
	Philadelphia Union	-	New England Revolution	2-0(1-0)
09.11.2020	Houston Dynamo	-	Colorado Rapids	1-2(0-0)
	Los Angeles FC	-	Portland Timbers	1-1(1-0)
	Minnesota United FC	-	FC Dallas	3-0(1-0)
	Real Salt Lake	-	Sporting Kansas City	0-2(0-1)
	Seattle Sounders	-	San Jose Earthquakes	4-1(0-0)
	Vancouver Whitecaps	-	Los Angeles Galaxy	3-0(2-0)

On 12.03.2020, the season entered a lengthy suspension due to the COVID-19 pandemic, several matches being cancelled.

On 10.06.2020, MLS announced that a bracket format dubbed the "MLS is Back Tournament" would begin on 08.07.2020 at ESPN Wide World of Sports Complex in Walt Disney World, and end with the final on 11.08.2020. The tournament was eventually won by the Portland Timbers, who as a result earned a berth in the 2021 CONCACAF Champions League. The MLS is Back Tournament introduced three regular season matches in the group stage.

The regular season later resumed a day after the tournament finished, and concluded on November 8. The playo-ffs began on November 20, 2020, with MLS Cup 2020 now being played on December 12. The 2020 season saw the addition of two new clubs, Club Internacional de Fútbol Inter Miami (Eastern Conference) and Nashville SC (Western Conference), which took Major League Soccer to 26 total teams. After the "MLS Is Back Tournament", due to COVID-19 difficulties led to MLS limiting teams to matches with teams in geographic proximity, Nashville SC was moved to the Eastern Conference due to geography.

On 29.10.2020, MLS announced that the final regular season standings and playoff qualification would be determined by points per game rather than by overall points. This was due to eight MLS clubs, all in the Western Conference, being unable to play all of their scheduled 23 regular season matches in time due to COVID-19 cases. Postponed matches were canceled.

	Eastern Conference								
1.	Philadelphia Union	23	14	4	5	44 - 20	47	(2.04)
2.	Toronto FC	23	13	5	5	33 - 26	44	(1.91)
3.	Columbus Crew SC	23	12	6	5	36 - 21	41	(1.78)
4.	Orlando City SC	23	11	4	8	40 - 25	41	(1.78)
5.	New York City FC	23	12	8	3	37 - 25	39	(1.70)
6.	New York Red Bulls	23	9	9	5	29 - 31	32	(1.39)
7.	Nashville SC	23	8	7	8	24 - 22	32	(1.39)
8.	New England Revolution Boston	23	8	7	8	26 - 25	32	(1.39)
9.	Montréal Impact*	23	8	13	2	33 - 43	26	(1.13)
10.	CIF Inter Miami	23	7	13	3	25 - 35	24	(1.04)
11.	Chicago Fire SC	23	5	10	8	33 - 39	23	(1.00)
12.	Atlanta United FC	23	6	13	4	23 - 30	22	(0.96)
13.	Washington DC United	23	5	12	6	25 - 41	21	(0.91)
14.	FC Cincinnati	23	4	15	4	12 - 36	16	(0.70)

*Montréal Impact changed its name to Club de Foot Montréal in 2021.
Please note: Teams ranked 1-6 were qualified for the MLS Cup Play-offs First Round, while teams ranked 7-10 were qualified for the Play-offs play-in Round.

Play-offs play-in Round [20.11.2020]	
New England Revolution Boston – Montréal Impact	2-1(1-0)
Nashville SC – CIF Inter Miami	3-0(2-0)

New England Revolution Boston and Nashville SC were qualified for the MLS Cup Play-offs First Round.

Western Conference

1.	Sporting Kansas City	21	12	6	3	38	-	25	39	(1.86)
2.	Seattle Sounders FC	22	11	5	6	44	-	23	39	(1.77)
3.	Portland Timbers	23	11	6	6	46	-	35	39	(1.70)
4.	Minnesota United FC	21	9	5	7	36	-	26	34	(1.62)
5.	Colorado Rapids	18	8	6	4	32	-	28	28	(1.56)
6.	FC Dallas	22	9	6	7	28	-	24	34	(1.55)
7.	Los Angeles FC	22	9	8	5	47	-	39	32	(1.45)
8.	San Jose Earthquakes	23	8	9	6	35	-	51	30	(1.30)
9.	Vancouver Whitecaps FC	23	9	14	0	27	-	44	27	(1.17)
10.	Los Angeles Galaxy	22	6	12	4	27	-	46	22	(1.00)
11.	Real Salt Lake	22	5	10	7	25	-	35	22	(1.00)
12.	Houston Dynamo	23	4	10	9	30	-	40	21	(0.91)

Please note: Teams ranked 1-8 were qualified for the MLS Cup Play-offs First Round.

Aggregate Table – Western & Eastern Conference

1.	Philadelphia Union	23	14	4	5	44	-	20	47	(2.04)
2.	Toronto FC	23	13	5	5	33	-	26	44	(1.91)
3.	Sporting Kansas City	21	12	6	3	38	-	25	39	(1.86)
4.	Columbus Crew SC	23	12	6	5	36	-	21	41	(1.78)
5.	Orlando City SC	23	11	4	8	40	-	25	41	(1.78)
6.	Seattle Sounders FC	22	11	5	6	44	-	23	39	(1.77)
7.	New York City FC	23	12	8	3	37	-	25	39	(1.70)
8.	Portland Timbers	23	11	6	6	46	-	35	39	(1.70)
9.	Minnesota United FC	21	9	5	7	36	-	26	34	(1.62)
10.	Colorado Rapids	18	8	6	4	32	-	28	28	(1.56)
11.	FC Dallas	22	9	6	7	28	-	24	34	(1.55)
12.	Los Angeles FC	22	9	8	5	47	-	39	32	(1.45)
13.	New York Red Bulls	23	9	9	5	29	-	31	32	(1.39)
14.	Nashville SC	23	8	7	8	24	-	22	32	(1.39)
15.	New England Revolution Boston	23	8	7	8	26	-	25	32	(1.39)
16.	San Jose Earthquakes	23	8	9	6	35	-	51	30	(1.30)
17.	Vancouver Whitecaps FC	23	9	14	0	27	-	44	27	(1.17)
18.	Montréal Impact	23	8	13	2	33	-	43	26	(1.13)
19.	CIF Inter Miami	23	7	13	3	25	-	35	24	(1.04)
20.	Los Angeles Galaxy	22	6	12	4	27	-	46	22	(1.00)
21.	Real Salt Lake	22	5	10	7	25	-	35	22	(1.00)
22.	Chicago Fire SC	23	5	10	8	33	-	39	23	(1.00)
23.	Atlanta United FC	23	6	13	4	23	-	30	22	(0.96)
24.	Washington DC United	23	5	12	6	25	-	41	21	(0.91)
25.	Houston Dynamo	23	4	10	9	30	-	40	21	(0.91)
26.	FC Cincinnati	23	4	15	4	12	-	36	16	(0.70)

Philadelphia Union, Columbus Crew SC, Atlanta United FC (as 2019 US Open Cup winners) and Portland Timbers were qualified for the 2021 CONCACAF Champions League.

2020 MLS Cup Play-offs

First Round [21-24.11.2020]

Orlando City SC – New York City FC	1-1(1-1,1-1,1-1); 6-5 pen
Columbus Crew SC – New York Red Bulls	3-2(1-1)
Toronto FC – Nashville SC	0-1(0-0,0-0)
Philadelphia Union – New England Revolution Boston	0-2(0-2)
Sporting Kansas City – San Jose Earthquakes	3-3(1-2,3-3,3-3); 3-0 pen
Minnesota United FC – Colorado Rapids	3-0(1-0)
Portland Timbers – FC Dallas	1-1(0-0,1-1,1-1); 7-8 pen
Seattle Sounders FC – Los Angeles FC	3-1(1-0)

Conference Semi-Finals [29.11.-03.12.2020]

Orlando City SC – New England Revolution Boston	1-3(1-2)
Columbus Crew SC – Nashville SC	2-0(0-0,0-0)
Seattle Sounders FC – FC Dallas	1-0(0-0)
Sporting Kansas City – Minnesota United FC	0-3(0-3)

2020 MLS Cup Conference Finals [06-07.12.2020]

Columbus Crew SC – New England Revolution Boston	1-0(0-0)
Seattle Sounders FC – Minnesota United FC	3-2(0-1)

2020 MLS Cup Final

12.12.2020, Mapfre Stadium, Columbus; Attendance: 1,500
Referee: Jair Marrufo
Columbus Crew SC – Seattle Sounders FC 3-0(2-0)
Columbus Crew: Eloy Victor Room, Harrison Afful, Jonathan Mensah (Cap), Josh Williams, Milton Nahuel Valenzuela, Aidan Morris, José Artur de Lima Junior "Artur" (88.Abdul-Fatai Alashe), Luis Mario Díaz Espinoza (90.Waylon Dwayne Francis Box), Lucas Manuel Zelarayán, Derrick Etienne Jr. (83.Hector Osvaldo Jiménez), Gyasi Zardes. Trainer: Caleb Porter.
Seattle Sounders: Stefan Frei, Alexander Roldan (60.Kelvin Leerdam), Yeimar Pastor Gómez Andrade, Shane Edward O'Neill (77.Jimmy Gerardo Medranda Obando), Nouhou Tolo (46.Bradley Shaun Smith), Cristian Roldan, João Paulo Mior (60.William Christopher Bruin), Joevin Martin Jones (46.Karl Gustav Johan Svensson), Marcelo Nicolás Lodeiro Benítez (Cap), Jordan Perry Morris, Raúl Mario Ruidíaz Misitich. Trainer: Brian Schmetzer.
Goals: 1-0 Lucas Manuel Zelarayán (25), 2-0 Derrick Etienne Jr. (31), 3-0 Lucas Manuel Zelarayán (82).

2020 Major League Soccer Winners: **Columbus Crew SC**

Top goalscorers (only regular season):

14 goals:	Diego Martín Rossi Marachlian (URU)	**(Los Angeles FC)**
12 goals:	Robert Berić (SVN)	(Chicago Fire SC)
	Raúl Mario Ruidíaz Misitich (PER)	(Seattle Sounders FC)
	Gyasi Zardes	(Columbus Crew SC)

NATIONAL CUP
„Lamar Hunt" US Open Cup 2020

Competition was cancelled due to COVID-19 pandemic.

"MLS IS BACK" TOURNAMENT
2020

The MLS is Back Tournament took place during the 2020 Major League Soccer season break after the league being suspended as a result of the COVID-19 pandemic. 24 teams of Major League Soccer participated in the tournament, FC Dallas and Nashville SC withdrew after several of their players tested positive for COVID-19 just before their first matches.

The tournament was held behind closed doors from July 8 to August 11, 2020, at the ESPN Wide World of Sports Complex in the Walt Disney World Resort in Bay Lake, Florida. The tournament champion, Portland Timbers, were qualified for the 2021 CONCACAF Champions League.

GROUP STAGE

Group winners, runners-up and four best third ranked teams were qualified for the Second Round of 16.

Group A

Date	Match	Score
08.07.2020	Orlando City SC - CIF Inter Miami	2-1(0-0)
09.07.2020	New York City FC - Philadelphia Union	0-1(0-0)
14.07.2020	New York City FC - Orlando City SC	1-3(1-2)
14.07.2020	Philadelphia Union - CIF Inter Miami	2-1(1-1)
20.07.2020	CIF Inter Miami - New York City FC	0-1(0-0)
20.07.2020	Philadelphia Union - Orlando City SC	1-1(0-0)

FINAL STANDINGS

#	Team	P	W	D	L	GF	-	GA	Pts
1.	**Orlando City SC**	3	2	1	0	6	-	3	7
2.	**Philadelphia Union**	3	2	1	0	4	-	2	7
3.	*New York City FC*	3	1	0	2	2	-	4	3
4.	CIF Inter Miami	3	0	0	3	2	-	5	0

Group B

Date	Match	Score
10.07.2020	Seattle Sounders FC - San Jose Earthquakes	0-0
14.07.2020	Chicago Fire SC - Seattle Sounders FC	2-1(0-0)
15.07.2020	Vancouver Whitecaps FC - San Jose Earthquakes	3-4(2-1)
19.07.2020	Chicago Fire SC - San Jose Earthquakes	0-2(0-0)
19.07.2020	Seattle Sounders FC - Vancouver Whitecaps FC	3-0(2-0)
23.07.2020	Chicago Fire SC - Vancouver Whitecaps FC	0-2(0-0)

FINAL STANDINGS

#	Team	P	W	D	L	GF	-	GA	Pts
1.	**San Jose Earthquakes**	3	2	1	0	6	-	3	7
2.	**Seattle Sounders FC**	3	1	1	1	4	-	2	4
3.	*Vancouver Whitecaps FC*	3	1	0	2	5	-	7	3
4.	Chicago Fire SC	3	1	0	2	2	-	5	3

Group C

Date	Match	Result
09.07.2020	Montréal Impact - New England Revolution Boston	0-1(0-0)
13.07.2020	Toronto FC - Washington DC United	2-2(2-0)
16.07.2020	Montréal Impact - Toronto FC	3-4(2-3)
17.07.2020	Washington DC United - New England Revolution Boston	1-1(0-0)
21.07.2020	Toronto FC - New England Revolution Boston	0-0
21.07.2020	Montréal Impact - Washington DC United	1-0(1-0)

FINAL STANDINGS

1.	**Toronto FC**	3	1	2	0	6 - 5	5
2.	**New England Revolution Boston**	3	1	2	0	2 - 1	5
3.	*Montréal Impact*	3	1	0	2	4 - 5	3
4.	Washington DC United	3	0	2	1	3 - 4	2

Group D

Date	Match	Result
12.07.2020	Sporting Kansas City - Minnesota United FC	1-2(1-0)
12.07.2020	Real Salt Lake - Colorado Rapids	2-0(1-0)
17.07.2020	Sporting Kansas City - Colorado Rapids	3-2(0-1)
17.07.2020	Real Salt Lake - Minnesota United FC	0-0
22.07.2020	Real Salt Lake - Sporting Kansas City	0-2(0-1)
22.07.2020	Colorado Rapids - Minnesota United FC	2-2(1-2)

FINAL STANDINGS

1.	**Sporting Kansas City**	3	2	0	1	6 - 4	6
2.	**Minnesota United FC**	3	1	2	0	4 - 3	5
3.	*Real Salt Lake*	3	1	1	1	2 - 2	4
4.	Colorado Rapids	3	0	1	2	4 - 7	1

Group E

Date	Match	Result
11.07.2020	Atlanta United FC - New York Red Bulls	0-1(0-1)
11.07.2020	FC Cincinnati - Columbus Crew SC	0-4(0-2)
16.07.2020	Atlanta United FC - FC Cincinnati	0-1(0-0)
16.07.2020	Columbus Crew SC - New York Red Bulls	2-0(1-0)
21.07.2020	Atlanta United FC - Columbus Crew SC	0-1(0-1)
22.07.2020	FC Cincinnati - New York Red Bulls	2-0(1-0)

FINAL STANDINGS

1.	**Columbus Crew SC**	3	3	0	0	7 - 0	9
2.	**FC Cincinnati**	3	2	0	1	3 - 4	6
3.	*New York Red Bulls*	3	1	0	2	1 - 4	3
4.	Atlanta United FC	3	0	0	3	0 - 3	0

Group F

13.07.2020	Los Angeles FC - Houston Dynamo	3-3(1-3)
13.07.2020	Los Angeles Galaxy - Portland Timbers	1-2(0-0)
18.07.2020	Portland Timbers - Houston Dynamo	2-1(1-0)
18.07.2020	Los Angeles FC - Los Angeles Galaxy	6-2(1-2)
23.07.2020	Los Angeles Galaxy - Houston Dynamo	1-1(0-1)
23.07.2020	Los Angeles FC - Portland Timbers	2-2(2-1)

FINAL STANDINGS

1.	**Portland Timbers**	3	2	1	0	6 - 4	7
2.	**Los Angeles FC**	3	1	2	0	11 - 7	5
3.	*Houston Dynamo*	3	0	2	1	5 - 6	2
4.	Los Angeles Galaxy	3	0	1	2	4 - 9	1

RANKING OF THIRD-PLACED TEAMS

1.	**Real Salt Lake**	3	1	1	1	2 - 2	4
2.	**Montréal Impact**	3	1	0	2	4 - 5	3
3.	**Vancouver Whitecaps FC**	3	1	0	2	5 - 7	3
4.	**New York City FC**	3	1	0	2	2 - 4	3
5.	New York Red Bulls	3	1	0	2	1 - 4	3
6.	Houston Dynamo	3	0	2	1	5 - 6	2

SECOND ROUND OF 16

25.07.2020	Orlando City SC - Montréal Impact	1-0(0-0)
25.07.2020	Philadelphia Union - New England Revolution Boston	1-0(0-0)
26.07.2020	Toronto FC - New York City FC	1-3(0-1)
26.07.2020	Sporting Kansas City - Vancouver Whitecaps FC	0-0; 3-1 pen
27.07.2020	San Jose Earthquakes - Real Salt Lake	5-2(1-1)
27.07.2020	Seattle Sounders FC - Los Angeles FC	1-4(0-2)
28.07.2020	Columbus Crew SC - Minnesota United FC	1-1(0-1,1-1,1-1); 3-5 pen
28.07.2020	Portland Timbers - FC Cincinnati	1-1(0-0,1-1,1-1); 4-2 pen

QUARTER-FINALS

30.07.2020	Philadelphia Union - Sporting Kansas City	3-1(3-1)
31.07.2020	Orlando City SC - Los Angeles FC	1-1(0-0,1-1,1-1); 5-4 pen
01.08.2020	San Jose Earthquakes - Minnesota United FC	1-4(0-2)
01.08.2020	New York City FC - Portland Timbers	1-3(1-1)

SEMI-FINALS

05.08.2020	Philadelphia Union - Portland Timbers	1-2(0-1)
06.08.2020	Orlando City SC - Minnesota United FC	3-1(2-0)

FINAL

11.08.2020	**Portland Timbers** - Orlando City SC	2-1(1-1)

THE CLUBS 2020

Please note: matches/(subs)/goals includes MLS Conference + "MLS is Back" tournament + Play-offs.

ATLANTA UNITED FOOTBALL CLUB

Foundation date: April 16, 2014
Address: 861 Franklin Gateway SE, 30067 Marietta, Georgia
Stadium: Mercedes-Benz Stadium, Atlanta (42,500)

THE SQUAD

	DOB	M	(s)	G
Goalkeepers:				
Bradley Edwin Guzan	09.09.1984	23		
Defenders:				
George Bello	22.01.2002	19	(1)	1
George Campbell	22.06.2001		(1)	
Edgar Eduardo Castillo Carrillo	08.10.1986	1	(3)	
Franco Nicolás Escobar (ARG)	21.02.1995	16		
Jon Gallagher (IRL)	23.02.1996	11	(5)	4
Brooks Howard Lennon	22.09.1997	19	(4)	2
Fernando Nicolás Meza (ARG)	21.03.1990	13		
Miles Gordon Robinson	14.03.1997	16	(1)	
Anton Charles Walkes (ENG)	08.02.1997	15	(2)	
Midfielders:				
Mohammed Adams (ENG)	23.09.1996	9	(4)	
Ezequiel Omar Barco (ARG)	29.03.1999	11	(4)	2
Luis Manuel Castro Cáceres (URU)	27.09.1995	3	(7)	
Jürgen Damm Rascón (MEX)	07.11.1992	7	(7)	
Emerson Schellas Hyndman	09.04.1996	16	(4)	2
Jeffrey Adam "Jeff" Larentowicz	05.08.1983	11	(8)	2
Gonzalo Nicolás Martínez (ARG)	13.06.1993	7		2
Matheus Rossetto (BRA)	03.06.1996	10	(5)	
Damián Marcelino Moreno (ARG)	25.06.1994	5	(1)	2
Jake David Mulraney (IRL)	05.04.1996	8	(10)	1
Eric Daian Remedi (ARG)	04.06.1995	12	(6)	1
Laurence Wyke (ENG)	20.09.1996	2	(5)	
Forwards:				
Adam Jahn	05.01.1991	13	(8)	3
Josef Alexander Martínez Mencia (VEN)	19.05.1993	1		
Erick Estéfano Torres Padilla (MEX)	19.01.1993	4	(9)	1
Jerome Williams Jr.	04.01.1998		(1)	
Tyler Wolff	13.02.2003	1	(4)	
Trainer:				
Franciscus "Frank" de Boer (NED) [23.11.2018-24.07.2020; Sacked]	15.05.1970	5		
Stephen Glass (SCO) [from 27.07.2020]	23.05.1976	18		

CHICAGO FIRE SOCCER CLUB

Foundation date: October 7, 1997
Address: 7773 South Harlem Avenue, 60455 Bridgeview, Illinois
Stadium: Soldier Field, Chicago (24,955)

THE SQUAD

	DOB	M	(s)	G
Goalkeepers:				
Kenneth Kronholm	14.10.1985	5		
Robert Shuttleworth	13.05.1987	17		
Connor Sparrow	10.05.1994	1		
Defenders:				
Jonathan Rey Bornstein	07.11.1984	13	(7)	1
Francisco Javier Calvo Quesada (CRC)	08.07.1992	22		1
Johan Kappelhof (NED)	05.08.1990	2	(2)	
Miguel Ángel Navarro Zárate (VEN)	26.02.1999	10	(9)	
Wyatt Omsberg	21.09.1995	2	(3)	
Mauricio Pineda	17.10.1997	23		3
Andre Reynolds II	02.05.2001		(2)	
Boris Sekulić (SRB)	21.10.1991	21		2
Carlos Terán Díaz (COL)	24.09.2000		(2)	
Midfielders:				
Micheal Azira (UGA)	22.08.1987	1	(5)	
Brandt James Bronico	20.06.1995	3	(7)	
Przemysław Frankowski (POL)	12.04.1995	16	(3)	3
Gastón Claudio Giménez (ARG)	27.07.1991	17	(1)	
Brian Gutiérrez	17.06.2003		(6)	
Álvaro Medrán Just (ESP)	15.03.1994	23		2
Djordje Aleksandar Mihailović	10.11.1998	14	(6)	2
Luka Stojanović (SRB)	04.01.1994	1	(1)	
Forwards:				
Ignacio Santiago Aliseda (ARG)	14.03.2000	16	(4)	1
Robert Berić (SVN)	17.06.1991	22	(1)	12
Elliot Collier (NZL)	22.02.1995	2	(19)	
Fabian Herbers (GER)	17.08.1993	18	(3)	4
Charles "CJ" Nana Kwabena Sapong	27.12.1988	4	(7)	2
Trainer:				
Raphaël Wicky (SUI) [from 27.12.2019]	26.04.1977	23		

FOOTBALL CLUB CINCINNATI

Foundation date: May 29, 2018
Address: 14 East 4th Street, Cincinnati, OH 45202
Stadium: Nippert Stadium, Cincinnati (32,250)

THE SQUAD

	DOB	M	(s)	G
Goalkeepers:				
Robert Edwards	11.08.1995	2		
Spencer McNair Richey	30.05.1992	9	(1)	
Przemysław Tytoń (POL)	04.01.1987	12		
Defenders:				
Saad Abdul-Salaam	08.09.1991	5	(3)	
Zico Bailey	27.08.2000	3	(2)	
Mathieu Deplagne (FRA)	01.10.1991	13	(2)	
Gregory Martin Garza	16.08.1991	7	(2)	
Andrew David Gutman	02.10.1996	15	(6)	
Nicholas Hagglund	14.09.1992	8	(3)	1
Tom Pettersson (SWE)	25.03.1990	13	(2)	
Maikel van der Werff (NED)	22.04.1989	11	(2)	
Kendall Jamaal Waston Manley (CRC)	01.01.1988	17		
Midfielders:				
Abdul-Fatai Alashe	21.10.1993		(3)	
Franuel "Frankie" Amaya	26.09.2000	21		1
Álvaro Martín Barreal (ARG)	17.08.2000	4	(1)	
Allan Enzo Cruz Leal (CRC)	24.02.1996	8	(6)	1
Siem de Jong (NED)	28.01.1989	8	(7)	
Joseph-Claude Gyau	16.09.1992	20	(1)	1
Yūya Kubo (JPN)	23.12.1993	15	(4)	3
Thomas McCabe	04.04.1998		(1)	
James Joseph McLaughlin	30.04.1993		(1)	
Haris Medunjanin (BIH)	08.03.1985	19	(2)	1
Kamohelo Mokotjo (RSA)	11.03.1991	6	(3)	
Adrien Regattin (MAR)	22.08.1991	7	(3)	
Caleb Stanko	26.07.1993	5	(8)	
Forwards:				
Rashawn Dally (JAM)	14.01.1997		(4)	
Franko Kovačević (CRO)	08.08.1999	1		
Jürgen Leonardo Locadia	07.11.1993	15	(2)	1
Kekuta Manneh (GAM)	30.12.1994	1	(1)	
Brandon Vázquez Toledo	14.10.1998	8	(11)	2
Trainer:				
Yoann Damet (FRA) [18.02.– 21.05.2020; Caretaker]	19.03.1990	2		
Jakob "Jaap" Stam (NED) [from 21.05.2020]	17.07.1972	21		

COLORADO RAPIDS				
Foundation date: June 6, 1995 **Address**: 1701 Bryant Street, Suite 700, 80204 Denver, Colorado **Stadium**: Dick's Sporting Goods Park, Commerce City (18,061)				

THE SQUAD	DOB	M	(s)	G
Goalkeepers:				
Clinton Robert Irwin	01.04.1989	4		
William Paul Yarbrough Story	20.03.1989	15		
Defenders:				
Alhassan "Lalas" Abubakar (GHA)	25.12.1994	18		1
Drew Moor	15.01.1984	5	(3)	1
Keegan Rosenberry	11.12.1993	17	(1)	1
Auston Levi-Jesaiah Trusty	12.08.1998	5	(3)	
Samuel Vines	31.05.1999	18	(1)	1
Daniel John Wilson (SCO)	27.12.1991	10		
Midfielders:				
Cole Bassett	28.07.2001	13	(2)	5
Nicolas Benezet (FRA)	24.02.1991	5	(8)	
Jeremy Kelly	21.10.1997	2	(6)	
Gabriel Nicolás Mezquida Sero (URU)	21.01.1992	2	(16)	1
Younes Namli (DEN)	20.06.1994	17	(1)	2
Sam Nicholson (SCO)	20.01.1995	2		
Kellyn Kai Perry-Acosta	24.07.1995	15	(1)	2
Jack Alexander Price (ENG)	19.12.1992	15	(2)	
Collen Warner	24.06.1988	4	(3)	
Forwards:				
Andre Bava Shinyashiki (BRA)	11.06.1997	14	(2)	4
Braian Alejandro Galván (ARG)	06.10.2000	2	(8)	1
Kei Ansu Kamara (SLE)	01.09.1984	5	(4)	3
Jonathan Jeremy Lewis	04.06.1997	8	(11)	5
Diego Iván Rubio Köstner (CHI)	15.05.1993	13	(4)	3
Trainer:				
Robin Lucius Fraser [from 25.08.2019]	17.12.1966	19		

COLUMBUS CREW SOCCER CLUB

Foundation date: May 10, 1994
Address: 1 Black and Gold Boulevard, 43211 Columbus, Ohio
Stadium: Mapfre Stadium, Columbus (19,968)

THE SQUAD

	DOB	M	(s)	G
Goalkeepers:				
Eloy Victor Room (CUW)	06.02.1989	19		
Andrew Tarbell	07.10.1993	8	(1)	
Defenders:				
Harrison Afful (GHA)	24.07.1986	24	(1)	1
Christopher Cadden	19.09.1996	3	(6)	
Waylon Dwayne Francis Box (CRC)	20.09.1990	2	(3)	
Aboubacar Kobele Keita	06.04.2000	10	(1)	
Jonathan Mensah (GHA)	13.07.1990	27		
Milton Nahuel Valenzuela (ARG)	13.08.1998	21	(2)	
Josh Williams	18.04.1988	15	(1)	
Vito Nova Wormgoor (NED)	16.11.1988	2		
Midfielders:				
Abdul-Fatai Alashe	21.10.1993	6	(3)	1
José Artur de Lima Junior "Artur" (BRA)	11.03.1991	24	(2)	3
Sebastian Berhalter	10.05.2001	4	(5)	
Emmanuel Agyenim Boateng (GHA)	17.01.1994	3	(9)	
Luis Mario Díaz Espinoza (CRC)	06.12.1998	17	(8)	
Derrick Etienne Jr. (HAI)	25.11.1996	10	(13)	2
Hector Osvaldo Jiménez	03.11.1988	4	(5)	
Youness Mokhtar (MAR)	29.08.1991	10	(9)	3
Aidan Morris	16.11.2001	3	(8)	
Darlington Joephillip Nagbe	19.07.1990	17	(1)	2
Pedro Miguel Martins Santos (POR)	22.04.1988	25		8
Forwards:				
Fanendo Adi (NGA)	10.10.1990	1	(10)	
Jordan Patrick Dear Hamilton (CAN)	17.03.1996		(2)	
Krisztián Németh (HUN)	05.01.1989	2	(3)	1
Gyasi Zardes	02.09.1991	24	(1)	14
Lucas Manuel Zelarayán (ARG)	20.06.1992	16	(4)	8
Trainer:				
Caleb Porter [from 04.01.2019]	18.02.1975	27		

WASHINGTON D.C. UNITED

Foundation date: 1995
Address: 2400 East Capitol Street Southeast, 20003 Washington, District of Columbia
Stadium: Audi Field, Buzzard Point, Washington D.C. (20,000)

THE SQUAD

	DOB	M	(s)	G
Goalkeepers:				
Abdul "Bill" Hamid	25.11.1990	17		
Christopher "Chris" Seitz	12.03.1987	6		
Defenders:				
Steven Mitchell Birnbaum	23.01.1991	10		
Frédéric Brillant (FRA)	26.06.1985	18	(1)	2
Oniel David Fisher (JAM)	22.11.1991	6	(9)	
Joseph Martín Mora Cortéz (CRC)	15.01.1993	19	(2)	
Chris Odoi-Atsem	27.05.1995	8	(7)	1
Donovan Pines	07.03.1998	15	(1)	3
Axel Sjöberg (SWE)	08.03.1991	2		
Midfielders:				
Mohammed Abu	04.11.1991	4	(2)	
Paul Joseph Arriola Hendricks	05.02.1995		(1)	
Yamil Rodrigo Asad (ARG)	24.07.1994	18	(5)	3
Russell Canouse	11.06.1995	15		2
Felipe Campanholi Martins (BRA)	30.09.1990	7		
Édison Michael Flores Peralta (PER)	14.05.1994	11	(2)	
Julian Gressel (GER)	16.12.1993	19	(3)	2
Federico Fernando Higuaín (ARG)	25.10.1984		(10)	2
Júnior Leonardo Moreno Borrero (VEN)	20.07.1993	20		
Moses Nyeman	05.11.2003	5	(6)	
Kevin Paredes	07.05.2003	9	(8)	
José Yordy Reyna Serna Sánchez (PER)	17.09.1993	3	(2)	
Ulises Segura Machado (CRC)	23.06.1993	7	(3)	
Forwards:				
Ola Williams Kamara (NOR)	15.10.1989	17	(5)	4
Gelmin Javier Rivas Boada (VEN)	23.03.1989	7	(6)	2
Erik Sorga (EST)	08.07.1999	6	(11)	1
Griffin McDorman Yow	25.09.2002	4	(8)	2
Trainer:				
Benjamin Robert "Ben" Olsen [01.2010-08.10.2020; Sacked]	03.05.1977	16		
Chad Ashton [from 08.10.2020]	26.10.1967	7		

FOOTBALL CLUB DALLAS

Foundation date: June 6, 1996 (*as Dallas Burn*)
Address: 9200 World Cup Way, Suite 202, 75034 Frisco, Texas
Stadium: Toyota Stadium, Frisco (20,500)

THE SQUAD

	DOB	M	(s)	G
Goalkeepers:				
José Luis González Gudina (MEX)	25.05.1995	2		
Jimmy Maurer	14.10.1988	18		
Phelipe Megiolaro Alves (BRA)	08.02.1999	1		
Kyle Zobeck	06.02.1990	3	(1)	
Defenders:				
Reginald Jacob Cannon	11.06.1998	5		
Matthew James Hedges	01.04.1990	20	(1)	
Matheus Simonete Bressaneli "Matheus Bressan" (BRA)	15.01.1993	13	(7)	
John Nelson	11.07.1998	10	(3)	
Fabrice-Jean "Fafà" Picault	23.02.1991	13	(7)	3
Bryan Reynolds	28.06.2001	16	(3)	
Reto Pirmin Ziegler (SUI)	16.01.1986	17	(3)	2
Midfielders:				
Bryan Josué Acosta Ramos (HON)	24.11.1993	10	(1)	
Michael David Barrios Puerta (COL)	21.04.1991	19	(4)	1
Edwin Cerrillo	03.10.2000		(2)	
Ryan Michael Hollingshead	16.04.1991	21	(1)	4
Paxton Pomykal	17.12.1999	1	(4)	1
Andrés Ricaurte Vélez (COL)	03.10.1991	15	(1)	1
Brandon Iván Servania	12.03.1999	4	(8)	
Francis Tanner Tessmann	24.09.2001	10	(11)	
Thiago dos Santos (BRA)	05.09.1989	21	(1)	
Forwards:				
Jesús David Ferreira Castro	24.12.2000	14	(7)	1
Franco Daniel Jara (ARG)	15.07.1988	18	(3)	7
Hárold Santiago Mosquera Caicedo (COL)	07.02.1995	5	(8)	4
Zdeněk Ondrášek (CZE)	22.12.1988	4	(1)	2
Ricardo Pepi	09.01.2003	4	(15)	3
Dante Isiah Sealy	17.04.2003		(5)	
Emmanuel "Ema" Twumasi (GHA)	18.05.1997		(5)	
Trainer:				
Luis "Luchi" Gonzalez [from 16.12.2018]	14.07.1980	24		

463

HOUSTON DYNAMO

Foundation date: December 15, 2005
Address: 1415 Louisiana Suite 3400, 77002 Houston, Texas
Stadium: BBVA Compass Stadium, Houston (22,039)

THE SQUAD

	DOB	M	(s)	G
Goalkeepers:				
Marko Marić (CRO)	03.01.1996	23		
Defenders:				
José Carlos Bizama Venegas (CHI)	25.06.1994	6	(2)	
Víctor Fernando Cabrera (ARG)	07.02.1993	8	(2)	
Maynor Alexis Figueroa Róchez (HON)	02.05.1983	19	(1)	2
Alejandro Enriquez Fuenmayor Castillo (VEN)	29.08.1996	3	(2)	
Sam Junqua	09.11.1996	2	(7)	1
Adam Stefan Lundqvist (SWE)	20.03.1994	21		
Aljaž Struna (SVN)	04.08.1990	16	(1)	
Zarek Chase Valentin	06.08.1991	18	(1)	
Midfielders:				
Darwin Adelso Cerén Delgado (SLV)	31.12.1989	18	(2)	1
Óscar Boniek García Ramírez (HON)	04.09.1984	7	(11)	
Nikolaj Hansen (DEN)	14.09.1994	8	(9)	2
Nico Lemoine	10.04.2000		(11)	
Tomás Martínez (ARG)	07.06.1995	3	(8)	
Thomas Liam McNamara	06.02.1991	2	(2)	
Marcelo Palomino	21.05.2001		(3)	
José Guillermo "Memo" Rodríguez	27.12.1995	20	(1)	5
Matías Gabriel Vera (ARG)	26.10.1995	20		
Wilfried Aimeric Jocelyn Ziri Zahibo (FRA)	21.08.1993	2	(2)	
Forwards:				
Alberth Josué Elis Martínez (HON)	12.02.1996	4	(2)	4
Ariel Daniel Lassiter Acuña (CRC)	27.09.1994	10	(6)	3
Mauro Andrés Manotas Páez (COL)	15.07.1995	15	(5)	3
Ronaldo Luis Peña Vargas (VEN)	10.03.1997		(1)	
Carlos Darwin Quintero Villalba (COL)	19.09.1987	20	(2)	7
Christian Ramirez	04.04.1991	8	(7)	2
Michael Salazar (BLZ)	15.11.1992		(1)	
Trainer:				
Tabaré "Tab" Ramos [from 25.10.2019]	21.09.1966	23		

CLUB INTERNACIONAL DE FÚTBOL MIAMI

Foundation date: January 28, 2018
Address: Miami, Florida
Stadium: Inter Miami CF Stadium, Fort Lauderdale (18,000)

THE SQUAD

	DOB	M	(s)	G
Goalkeepers:				
John McCarthy	04.07.1992	9		
Luis Ermita Robles	11.05.1984	15		
Defenders:				
Michael Ambrose	05.10.1993	4	(3)	1
Adolphe Joseph DeLaGarza	04.11.1987	6		
Jorge Nicolás Figal (ARG)	03.04.1994	22		
Leandro Martín González Pirez (ARG)	26.02.1992	16		2
Christian Frederick Bayoi Makoun Reyes (VEN)	05.03.2000	2	(2)	
Dylan Nealis	30.07.1998	11	(9)	
Alvas Elvis Powell (JAM)	14.07.1994	3	(2)	
Andrés Felipe Reyes Ambuila (COL)	08.09.1999	13		
Dane Brekken Shea	28.02.1990	6	(7)	4
Benjamin Sweat	04.09.1991	20	(3)	
Román Aureliano Torres Morcillo (PAN)	20.03.1986	4	(1)	
Midfielders:				
Luis Argudo	13.12.1995		(1)	
Jay Tyler Chapman (CAN)	01.01.1994	2	(6)	
Federico Fernando Higuaín (ARG)	25.10.1984		(4)	
Blaise Matuidi (FRA)	09.04.1987	15	(1)	1
Lewis Morgan (SCO)	30.09.1996	24		5
Matías Pellegrini (ARG)	11.03.2000	12	(8)	1
Rodolfo Gilbert Pizarro Thomas (MEX)	15.02.1994	18	(2)	4
William Alexander Trapp	15.01.1993	17	(5)	
Víctor Ulloa (MEX)	04.03.1992	17	(7)	
Forwards:				
Juan Sebastián Agudelo	23.11.1992	10	(5)	3
Julián Simón Carranza (ARG)	22.05.2000	5	(12)	2
Gonzalo Gerardo Higuaín (ARG)	10.12.1987	9		1
Jerome Julien Kiesewetter	09.02.1993		(2)	
Lee Nguyễn	07.10.1986		(5)	
Robbie Robinson	17.12.1998	4	(8)	
Trainer:				
Diego Martín Alonso López (URU) [from 30.12.2019]	06.04.1975	24		

LOS ANGELES FOOTBALL CLUB

Foundation date: October 30, 2014
Address: 818 W 7th Street, #1200, Los Angeles, CA 90017
Stadium: Banc of California Stadium, Los Angeles (22,000)

THE SQUAD

	DOB	M	(s)	G
Goalkeepers:				
Pablo Eduardo Sisniega Fink (MEX)	07.07.1995	15		
Kenneth Vermeer (NED)	10.01.1986	8		
Defenders:				
Tristan Michael Blackmon	12.08.1996	12	(3)	
Danilo Aparecido da Silva (BRA)	24.11.1986	1		
Erik Dueñas	18.10.2004		(2)	
Mohamed El-Mounir Abdussalam (LBY)	08.04.1992	4	(9)	1
Jordan Harvey	28.01.1984	9	(3)	
Dejan Jaković (CAN)	16.07.1985	12	(4)	1
Jesús David Murillo Largacha (COL)	18.02.1994	6		
Diego José Palacios Espinoza (ECU)	12.07.1999	15	(1)	
Eddie Livington Segura Martínez (COL)	02.02.1997	22	(1)	2
Mohamed Traoré (SEN)	15.08.2002	1		
Midfielders:				
Eduard Andrés Atuesta Velasco (COL)	18.06.1997	15	(3)	2
José Andoni Cifuentes Charcopa (ECU)	12.03.1999	13	(5)	1
Bryce Duke	28.02.2001	2	(9)	
Francisco Ginella Dabezies (URU)	21.01.1999	14	(9)	1
Mark-Anthony Kaye (CAN)	02.12.1994	16	(1)	3
Paul Brian Rodríguez Bravo (URU)	20.05.2000	18	(1)	2
Forwards:				
Latif Atta Blessing (GHA)	30.12.1996	19	(3)	1
Valentin Adama Diomandé (NOR)	14.02.1990		(1)	
Danny Musovski	30.11.1995	6	(9)	5
Andy Aryel Nájar Rodríguez (HON)	16.03.1993	1	(7)	
Kwadwo Opoku (GHA)	13.07.2001		(4)	
Adrien Alfredo Perez	13.10.1995	2	(8)	
Diego Martín Rossi Marachlian (URU)	05.03.1998	19		14
Christian Torres	15.04.2004	3	(6)	1
Carlos Alberto Vela Garrido (MEX)	01.03.1989	5	(3)	4
Bradley Edward Wright-Phillips (ENG)	12.03.1985	15	(4)	8
Trainer:				
Robert Frank Bradley [from 27.07.2017]	05.03.1958	23		

LOS ANGELES GALAXY

Foundation date: June 15, 1995
Address: 18400 Avalon Boulevard, Suite 100, Carson, 90746 Los Angeles, California
Stadium: Dignity Health Sports Park (ex-The StubHub Center), Carson (27,000)

THE SQUAD

	DOB	M	(s)	G
Goalkeepers:				
David Matthew Bingham	19.10.1989	18		
Jonathan Klinsmann	08.04.1997	4		
Defenders:				
Nicholas Brady DePuy	14.11.1994	15	(1)	
Rolf Günther Feltscher Martínez (VEN)	06.10.1990	13	(4)	
Giancarlo González Castro (CRC)	08.02.1988	9	(1)	1
Emiliano Adrián Insúa Zapata (ARG)	07.01.1989	22		
Daniel Steres	11.11.1990	20		1
Diedie Traoré (FRA)	15.01.1999		(6)	
Midfielders:				
Efraín Álvarez (MEX)	19.06.2002	6	(10)	1
Julian Vicente Araujo	13.08.2001	17		1
Joe Benny Corona Crespín	09.07.1990	12	(4)	1
Emil Cuello (ARG)	02.01.1997	2	(9)	
Jonathan dos Santos Ramírez (MEX)	26.04.1990	7	(6)	
Carlos Miguel Harvey Cesneros (PAN)	03.02.2000	1	(5)	
Aleksandar Katai (SRB)	06.02.1991	2		
Perry Allen Kitchen	29.02.1992	19	(2)	
Sacha Bryan Kljestan	09.09.1985	8	(7)	
Sebastian Lletget	03.09.1992	19	(2)	6
Forwards:				
Cameron Dunbar	22.10.2002	1	(3)	
Yony Alexander González Copete (COL)	11.07.1994	7	(2)	
Javier Hernández Balcazar (MEX)	01.06.1988	7	(5)	2
Kai Koreniuk (NED)	01.03.1998		(4)	1
Cristian David Pavón (ARG)	21.01.1996	22		10
Gordon Wild (GER)	16.10.1995		(3)	
Ethan Zubak	15.04.1998	11	(4)	2
Trainer:				
Guillermo Barros Schelotto (ARG) [02.01.2019-29.10.2020; Sacked]	04.05.1973	19		
Dominic Kinnear [from 29.10.2020]	26.07.1967	3		

MINNESOTA UNITED FOOTBALL CLUB

Foundation date: March 25, 2015
Address: Minneapolis-Saint Paul, Minnesota
Stadium: Allianz Field, Saint Paul (19,400)

THE SQUAD

	DOB	M	(s)	G
Goalkeepers:				
Tyler Austin Miller	12.03.1993	5		
Gregory Nicholas Ranjitsingh (TRI)	18.07.1993	3		
Dayne St. Clair (CAN)	09.05.1997	16		
Defenders:				
José Manuel Aja Livchich (URU)	10.05.1993	12	(1)	1
Michael Joseph Boxall (NZL)	18.08.1988	22		
Bakaye Dibassy (MLI)	11.08.1989	13	(1)	2
Chase Blair Gasper	25.01.1996	19	(2)	1
Brent Kallman	04.10.1990	3	(1)	
Romain Métanire (MAD)	28.03.1990	22		
James Mzamo Musa (NZL)	01.04.1992	2	(4)	
Ikenna Martin "Ike" Opara	21.02.1989	2		2
Midfielders:				
Osvaldo Alonso Moreno (CUB)	11.11.1985	11	(2)	
Thomás Chacón Yona (URU)	17.08.2000	1	(3)	
Hassani Dotson Stephenson	06.08.1997	13	(8)	1
Raheem Nathaniel Anfernee Edwards (CAN)	17.07.1995	2	(10)	
Ethan Christopher Finlay	06.08.1990	15	(2)	4
Ján Greguš (SVK)	29.01.1991	21		1
Marlon Hairston	23.03.1994	5	(6)	
Jacori Hayes	28.06.1995	6	(7)	1
Robin Lod (FIN)	06.08.1997	21	(2)	8
Emanuel Reynoso ARG)	16.11.1995	12	(4)	2
Forwards:				
Luis Antonio Amarilla Lencina (PAR)	25.08.1995	5	(2)	2
Noah James Billingsley (NZL)	06.08.1997		(1)	
Kei Ansu Kamara (SLE)	01.09.1984	6	(3)	1
Foster Langsdorf	14.12.1995		(1)	
Kevin Molino (TRI)	17.06.1990	18	(3)	13
Aaron Maxwell Schoenfeld (NED)	17.04.1990	3	(12)	1
Mason Vincent Toye	16.10.1998	6	(2)	1
Trainer:				
Adrian Paul Heath (ENG) [from 29.11.2016]	11.01.1961	24		

MONTRÉAL IMPACT

Foundation date: December 1, 1992
Address: 4750 Sherbrooke East Street, H1V 3S8 Montreal, Quebec, Canada
Stadium: Saputo Stadium, Montreal (19,619)

THE SQUAD

	DOB	M	(s)	G
Goalkeepers:				
Clément Diop Degoud (SEN)	13.10.1993	21		
James Pantemis (CAN)	21.02.1997	3		
Defenders:				
Luis Thomas Binks (ENG)	02.09.2001	21	(1)	
Zachary Bichotte Paul Brault-Guillard (CAN)	30.12.1998	20	(2)	
Rudy Camacho (FRA)	05.03.1991	15		1
Jorge Luis Corrales Cordero (CUB)	20.05.1991	13	(2)	
Rod Dodji Fanni (FRA)	06.12.1981	11	(2)	
Mustafa Kizza (UGA)	03.10.1999		(2)	
Jukka Raitala (FIN)	15.09.1988	15		
Joel Robert Waterman (CAN)	24.01.1996	6	(1)	
Karifa Yao (CAN)	20.09.2000	1	(1)	
Midfielders:				
Clément Bayiha (CAN)	08.03.1999	1	(3)	
Emanuel Fernando Maciel (ARG)	28.03.1997	11	(1)	
Samuel Piette (CAN)	12.11.1994	22		1
Amar Sejdič (BIH)	29.11.1996	8	(7)	2
Shamit Shome (CAN)	05.09.1997	4	(8)	
Saphir Sliti Taïder (ALG)	29.02.1992	11		4
Victor Mugubi Wanyama (KEN)	25.06.1991	21		2
Forwards:				
Bojan Krkić Pérez (ESP)	28.08.1990	15	(3)	4
Anthony Jackson-Hamel (CAN)	02.08.1993	3	(5)	
Lassi Lappalainen (FIN)	24.08.1998	7	(6)	4
Orji Okwonkwo (NGA)	19.01.1998	5	(9)	1
Romell Samir Quioto Robinson (HON)	09.08.1991	18	(2)	9
Ballou Jean-Yves Tabla (CAN)	31.03.1999		(5)	1
Mason Vincent Toye	16.10.1998	2	(5)	
Maximiliano Nicolás Urruti Mussa (ARG)	22.02.1991	10	(5)	5
Trainer:				
Thierry Daniel Henry (FRA) [from 14.11.2019]	17.08.1977	24		

NASHVILLE SOCCER CLUB

Foundation date: December 20, 2017
Address: *Not known*
Stadium: Nissan Stadium, Nashville (60,000)

THE SQUAD

	DOB	M	(s)	G
Goalkeepers:				
Joseph Willis	10.08.1988	26		
Defenders:				
Jalil Anibaba	19.10.1988	6	(7)	
Brayan Antonio Beckeles (HON)	28.11.1985	1	(1)	
Alistair Johnston (CAN)	08.10.1998	18	(3)	
Daniel Harry Lovitz	27.08.1991	24		1
Jack Maher	28.10.1999	2	(1)	
Jimmy Gerardo Medranda Obando (COL)	07.02.1994		(1)	
Eric Miller	15.01.1993	5	(2)	
David Romney	12.06.1993	26		1
Taylor Washington	16.08.1993	2	(15)	
Walker Dwain Zimmerman	19.05.1993	25		3
Midfielders:				
Tah Brian Anunga (CMR)	10.08.1996	10	(7)	
Handwalla Bwana (KEN)	25.06.1999		(4)	
Aníbal Casis Godoy Lemus (PAN)	10.02.1990	19	(2)	1
Derrick Jones Amaniampong	03.03.1997	9	(12)	
Matthew LaGrassa	27.01.1993	4	(5)	
Randall Enrique Leal Arley	14.01.1997	22	(2)	4
Michael Dax McCarty	30.04.1987	22	(2)	2
Hany Abubakr Mukhtar (GER)	21.03.1995	16	(2)	5
Alex Muyl	30.09.1995	18	(3)	
Forwards:				
David Accam (GHA)	28.09.1990	2	(5)	1
Dominique Badji (SEN)	16.10.1992	10	(2)	1
Jhonder Leonel Cádiz Fernández (VEN)	29.07.1995	3	(7)	2
Abu Danladi (GHA)	18.10.1995	7	(10)	2
Daniel Armando Rios Calderón (MEX)	22.02.1995	8	(13)	5
Alan Winn	18.02.1996	1	(6)	
Trainer:				
Gary Neil Smith (ENG) [from 01.01.2020]	03.12.1968	26		

NEW ENGLAND REVOLUTION BOSTON

Foundation date: 1994
Address: 1388 One Patriot Place, 2035 Foxborough, Massachusetts
Stadium: Gillette Stadium, Foxborough (20,000)

THE SQUAD

	DOB	M	(s)	G
Goalkeepers:				
Brad Burton Knighton	06.02.1985	1		
Matthew Turner	24.06.1994	26		
Defenders:				
Alexander Büttner (NED)	11.02.1989	15	(2)	
Antonio Delamea Mlinar (SVN)	10.06.1991	4	(1)	
Andrew Farrell	02.04.1992	23	(1)	
Henry Kessler	25.06.1998	23	(3)	1
Michael Ian Mancienne (ENG)	08.01.1988	4	(3)	
Matthew Ryan Polster	08.06.1993	12	(7)	
Seth Sinovic	28.01.1987		(1)	
Midfielders:				
Brandon Bye	29.11.1995	18	(6)	
Scott Caldwell	15.07.1991	18	(4)	
Carles Gil de Pareja Vicent (ESP)	22.11.1992	8	(2)	2
Diego Santiago Fagúndez Pepe (URU)	14.02.1995	9	(10)	1
DeJuan Lytelle Jones	24.06.1997	17	(5)	
Kekuta Manneh (GAM)	30.12.1994	2	(4)	1
Thomas Liam McNamara	06.02.1991	12	(6)	
Lee Nguyễn	07.10.1986	8	(6)	1
Kelyn Jaynes Rowe	02.12.1991	10	(9)	
Wilfried Aimeric Jocelyn Ziri Zahibo (FRA)	21.08.1993	1	(2)	
Forwards:				
Gustavo Leonardo Bou (ARG)	18.02.1990	18	(4)	8
Tajon Buchanan (CAN)	08.02.1999	15	(12)	3
Adam Buksa (POL)	12.07.1996	20	(7)	7
Teal Alexander Bunbury	27.02.1990	23	(3)	8
Cristian Anderson Penilla Caicedo (ECU)	02.05.1991	10	(7)	
Justin Gerard Rennicks	20.03.1999		(7)	
Trainer:				
Bruce Arena [from 14.05.2019]	21.09.1951	27		

NEW YORK CITY FOOTBALL CLUB

Foundation date: May 21, 2013
Address: 600 Third Avenue, 30th Floor, New York, NY 10016
Stadium: Yankee Stadium, New York (28,743)

THE SQUAD

	DOB	M	(s)	G
Goalkeepers:				
Sean Everet Johnson	31.05.1989	24		
Defenders:				
Alexander Martín Marquinho Callens Asín (PER)	04.05.1992	23		2
Maxime Chanot (LUX)	21.11.1989	21		1
Sebastien Uchechukwu Ibeagha	21.01.1992	2	(6)	
Rónald Alberto Matarrita Ulate (CRC)	09.07.1994	20	(2)	
James Hoban Sands	06.07.2000	16		
Joseph Scally	31.12.2002	1	(4)	
Midfielders:				
Nicolás Brian Acevedo Tabarez (URU)	14.04.1999	1	(12)	
Valentín Mariano José Castellanos Giménez (ARG)	18.03.1998	15	(8)	6
Jesús Manuel Medina Maldonado (PAR)	30.04.1997	19	(4)	5
Maximiliano Nicolás Moralez (ARG)	27.02.1987	11	(3)	1
Keaton Alexander Parks	06.08.1997	21	(3)	3
Alexander Michael Ring (FIN)	09.04.1991	24		4
Antonio Rocha	21.08.1983		(12)	1
Ismael Tajouri Shradi (LBY)	28.03.1991	6	(10)	3
Anton Lars Tinnerholm (SWE)	26.02.1991	23	(1)	4
Juan Pablo Torres	26.07.1999		(2)	
Gedion Zelalem	26.01.1997		(1)	
Guðmundur Þórarinsson (ISL)	15.04.1992	7	(13)	
Forwards:				
Héber Araujo dos Santos (BRA)	10.08.1991	11	(1)	1
Gary Sean Mackay-Steven (SCO)	31.08.1990	11	(12)	2
Alexandru Ionuț Mitriță (ROU)	08.02.1995	8	(4)	4
Trainer:				
Ronny Deila (NOR) [from 06.01.2020]	21.09.1975	24		

NEW YORK RED BULLS

Foundation date: 1994 (as *New York/New Jersey MetroStars*)
Address: One Harmon Plaza, Eighth Floor, 7094 Secaucus, New Jersey
Stadium: Red Bull Arena, Harrison, New Jersey (25,385)

THE SQUAD

	DOB	M	(s)	G
Goalkeepers:				
David Raagaard Jensen (DEN)	25.03.1992	10	(1)	
Ryan Meara	15.11.1990	14		
Defenders:				
Kyle Duncan	27.12.1997	22	(2)	3
Mandela Chinweizu Egbo (ENG)	17.08.1997	6	(3)	1
Aaron Ray Long	12.10.1992	16	(1)	2
Sean Nealis	13.01.1997	5	(1)	
Timothy Ryan Parker	23.02.1993	19	(1)	
Jason Quang-Vinh Pendant (FRA)	09.02.1997	18	(3)	
Patrick Seagrist	21.02.1998	3		
Amr Tarek Abdel-Aziz (EGY)	17.05.1992	10	(2)	
Midfielders:				
Cristian Sleiker Cásseres Yepes Jr. (VEN)	20.01.2000	14	(6)	2
Caden Clark	27.05.2003	4	(4)	3
Sean Akira Davis	08.02.1993	14	(1)	
Omir Guadalupe Fernandez Mosso	08.02.1999	5	(10)	2
Alex Muyl	30.09.1995		(2)	
Alejandro Sebastián Romero Gamarra "Kaku" (PAR)	11.01.1995	13	(4)	2
Daniel Royer (AUT)	22.05.1990	16	(5)	4
Marc Rzatkowski (GER)	02.05.1990	7	(10)	
Joshua Samuel Sims (ENG)	28.03.1997		(2)	
Jared Presson Stroud	10.07.1996	11	(10)	
Florian Valot (FRA)	13.02.1993	18	(6)	2
Dru Anthony Yearwood (ENG)	17.02.2000	9	(4)	
Forwards:				
Tom Barlow	08.07.1995	13	(9)	3
Mathias Jørgensen (DEN)	20.09.2000	2	(6)	
Benjamin Mines	13.05.2000	1	(4)	1
Samuel Tetteh (GHA)	28.07.1996	4	(6)	
Brian White	03.02.1996	10	(9)	6
Trainer:				
Chris Armas [06.07.2018 – 04.09.2020; Sacked]	27.08.1972	10		
Bradley Neil Carnell (RSA) [04.09.-06.10.2020; Caretaker]	21.01.1977	6		
Gerhard Struber (AUT) [from 06.10.2020]	24.01.1977	8		

ORLANDO CITY SOCCER CLUB

Foundation date: November 19, 2013
Address: 1540 International Parkway, 32746 Lake Mary, Florida
Stadium: Exploria Stadium, Orlando (25,500)

THE SQUAD

	DOB	M	(s)	G
Goalkeepers:				
Pedro David Gallese Quiróz (PER)	23.02.1990	20		
Brian Michael Rowe	16.11.1988	5		
Defenders:				
Antônio Carlos Cunha Capocasali Junior (BRA)	07.03.1993	20	(2)	1
Alexander Ray DeJohn	10.05.1991		(6)	
Robin Jansson (SWE)	15.11.1991	24		
João Gervásio Bragança Moutinho (POR)	12.01.1998	8		
Kamal Anthony Miller (CAN)	16.05.1997	10	(4)	
Ruan Gregório Teixeira (BRA)	29.05.1995	19	(3)	
Rodrigo Adrián Schlegel (ARG)	03.04.1997	7	(4)	
Kyle Smith	09.01.1992	13	(5)	
Midfielders:				
Jordan Bender	09.07.2001	1	(1)	
Joseph DeZart II (JAM)	09.06.1998	4	(7)	
Ocimar de Almeida Júnior "Júnior Urso" (BRA)	10.03.1989	22	(3)	4
Jhegson Sebastián Méndez Carabali (ECU)	26.04.1997	11	(8)	
Oriol Rosell Argerich (ESP)	07.07.1992	10		
Andrés Felipe Perea Castañeda (COL)	14.11.2000	11	(14)	
Mauricio Ernesto Pereyra Antonini (URU)	15.03.1990	16	(2)	2
Francisco Wellington Barbosa de Lisboa "Robinho" (BRA)	19.01.1995	2	(4)	
Forwards:				
Tesho Akindele (CAN)	31.03.1992	8	(11)	3
Alexander Antonio Alvarado Carriel (ECU)	21.04.1999		(2)	
Daryl Dike	03.06.2000	17	(2)	8
Dominic James Dwyer	30.07.1990	2		
David Loera	10.09.1998		(2)	
Matheus Aias Barrozo Rodrigues (BRA)	30.12.1996		(4)	1
Benjamin Stanley Michel	23.10.1997	8	(15)	5
Christopher Mueller	29.08.1996	19	(5)	10
Luís Carlos Almeida da Cunha "Nani" (POR)	17.11.1986	18	(3)	7
Santiago Patiño (COL)	10.03.1997		(2)	
Trainer:				
Óscar Alexander Pareja Gómez (COL)	10.08.1968	25		

PHILADELPHIA UNION

Foundation date: February 28, 2008
Address: 2501 Seaport Drive, Switch House Suite 500, 19103 Chester, Pennsylvania
Stadium: Subaru Park, Chester (18,500)

THE SQUAD

	DOB	M	(s)	G
Goalkeepers:				
Joseph T. Bendik	25.04.1989	1	(1)	
Andre Jason Blake (JAM)	21.11.1990	22		
Matthew Andrew Geary Freese	02.09.1998	1		
Defenders:				
Warren Creavalle	14.08.1990	4	(7)	
Jack Elliott (SCO)	25.08.1995	10	(8)	1
Raymon Gaddis	13.01.1990	16		
Jacob Glesnes (NOR)	25.03.1994	18	(2)	1
Olivier Mbaissidara Mbaizo (CMR)	15.08.1997	12	(2)	
Mark Alexander McKenzie	25.02.1999	23		2
Matthew Joseph Real	10.07.1999	5	(10)	1
Kai Wagner (GER)	15.02.1997	15		1
Midfielders:				
Brenden Russell Aaronson	22.10.2000	24		4
Alejandro Bedoya	29.04.1987	22		3
Jack de Vries	28.03.2002		(4)	
Anthony Fontana	14.10.1999	5	(13)	6
Ilson Pereira Dias Júnior "Ilsinho" (BRA)	12.10.1985	2	(21)	3
José Andrés Martínez Torres (VEN)	07.08.1994	15		
Jamiro Gregory Monteiro Alvarenga (CPV)	23.11.1993	23		3
Cole Turner	07.07.2001		(1)	
Andrew Wooten (GER)	30.09.1989	4	(12)	
Forwards:				
Cory Lamar Crossgill Burke (JAM)	28.12.1991		(6)	2
Kacper Przybyłko (POL)	25.03.1993	24		8
Sérgio Henrique Santos Gomes (BRA)	04.09.1994	18	(4)	8
Trainer:				
Jim Curtin [from 10.06.2014]	23.06.1979	24		

PORTLAND TIMBERS

Foundation date: 2009
Address: 1844 SW Morrison Street, 97205 Portland, Oregon
Stadium: Providence Park (formerly Jeld-Wen Field), Portland (25,218)

THE SQUAD

	DOB	M	(s)	G
Goalkeepers:				
Jeff Attinella	29.09.1988	1		
Steve Clark	14.04.1986	21		
Aljaž Ivačič (SVN)	29.12.1993	2		
Defenders:				
Pablo Alejandro Bonilla Serrada (VEN)	02.12.1999	11	(2)	
Julio César Cascante Solórzano (CRC)	03.10.1993	4	(1)	1
Chris Duvall	10.09.1991	9	(1)	
Marco Farfán	12.11.1998	9	(6)	
Larrys Mabiala Destin (COD)	08.10.1987	16	(2)	1
Jorge Luis Moreira Ferreira (PAR)	01.02.1990	1		
Bill Poni Tuiloma (NZL)	27.03.1995	9	(3)	1
Jorge Antonio Flores Villafaña	16.09.1989	18	(2)	2
Dario Župarić (CRO)	03.05.1992	19	(1)	
Midfielders:				
Dairon Estibens Asprilla Rivas (COL)	25.05.1992		(3)	
Sebastián Marcelo Blanco (ARG)	15.03.1988	8	(1)	2
Diego Ferney Chará Zamora (COL)	05.04.1986	18		1
Tomás José Conechny (ARG)	30.03.1998	3	(5)	
Andrés Alejandro Flores Mejía (SLV)	31.08.1990	3	(1)	1
Cristhian Fabián Paredes Maciel (PAR)	18.05.1998	9	(9)	
Diego Hernán Valeri (ARG)	01.05.1986	19	(4)	8
Eryk Tyrek Williamson	11.06.1997	18	(4)	3
Renzo José Zambrano (VEN)	26.08.1994	1	(4)	
Forwards:				
Blake Bodily	13.01.1998		(1)	
Yimmi Javier Chará Zamora (COL)	02.04.1991	16	(9)	4
Jeremy Edward Nirina Ebobisse Ebolo	14.02.1997	11	(8)	8
Marvin Antonio Loría Leitón (CRC)	24.04.1997	9	(9)	
Felipe Andrés Mora Aliaga (CHI)	02.08.1993	14	(6)	7
Jarosław Niezgoda (POL)	15.03.1995	7	(10)	7
Andy Jorman Polo Andrade (PER)	29.09.1994	8	(9)	1
Trainer:				
Giovanni Savarese Rubinaccio (VEN) [from 18.12.2017]	14.07.1971	24		

REAL SALT LAKE

Foundation date: 2004
Address: 9256 South State Street, 84070 Salt Lake City, Utah
Stadium: Rio Tinto Stadium, Sandy (20,213)

THE SQUAD

	DOB	M	(s)	G
Goalkeepers:				
Zachary Michael MacMath	07.08.1991	6		
David Ochoa	16.01.2001	1		
Andrew Putna	21.10.1994	15		
Defenders:				
Justen Glad	28.02.1997	14	(3)	1
Aaron Herrera	06.06.1997	20		
Erik Lee Holt	06.09.1996	4	(3)	
Chinedum Onuoha (ENG)	12.11.1986	15		
Marcelo Andrés Silva Fernández	21.03.1989	15		
Donald Austin "Donny" Toia	28.05.1992	19	(1)	
Midfielders:				
Kyle Robert Beckerman	23.04.1982	5	(5)	
Nick Besler	07.05.1993	6	(6)	
Maikel Chang Ramírez (CUB)	18.04.1991	12	(7)	1
Everton Luiz Guimarães Bilher (BRA)	24.05.1988	11	(3)	
Damir Kreilach (CRO)	16.04.1989	20	(1)	8
Justin Joseph Meram (Hikmat Azeez)	04.12.1988	13	(8)	3
Justin José Portillo	09.09.1992	3	(2)	
Jeizon Jesús Ramírez Chacón (VEN)	24.03.2001		(10)	
Pablo Enrique Ruiz (ARG)	20.12.1998	15	(3)	1
Albert Rusnák (SVK)	07.07.1994	15	(1)	3
Forwards:				
Corey Jacob Baird	30.01.1996	17	(4)	2
Christopher Garcia	13.01.2003		(1)	
Milan Iloski	29.07.1999		(1)	
Sam Garyahzon Johnson (LBR)	06.05.1993	3	(7)	1
Douglas Francisco Martínez Juárez (HON)	05.06.1997	9	(9)	2
Giuseppe Rossi (ITA)	01.02.1987	1	(6)	1
Tate Schmitt	28.05.1997	3	(1)	
Trainer:				
Freddy Juarez [from 11.08.2019]	01.04.1978	22		

SAN JOSE EARTHQUAKES

Foundation date: June 15, 1994 (*as San Jose Clash*)
Address: 451 El Camino Real, Suite 220, 95050 Santa Clara, California
Stadium: Earthquakes Stadium, San Jose (18,000)

THE SQUAD

	DOB	M	(s)	G
Goalkeepers:				
James Thomas Marcinkowski	09.05.1997	11		
Mario Daniel Vega (ARG)	03.06.1984	12		
Defenders:				
Oswaldo Alanís Pantoja (MEX)	18.03.1989	14		2
James Tanner Beason	23.03.1997	9		
Florian Jungwirth (GER)	27.01.1989	18	(1)	
Guram Kashia (GEO)	04.07.1987	6		
Nicholas Lima	17.11.1994	20	(1)	2
Marcos Johan López Lanfranco (PER)	20.11.1999	11	(2)	2
Paul Marie (FRA)	24.03.1995	3	(8)	1
Midfielders:				
Eric Santana Calvillo	02.01.1998	1	(6)	
Magnus Eriksson (SWE)	08.04.1990	5		1
Carlos Eduardo Fierro Guerrero (MEX)	24.07.1994	12	(4)	3
Gilbert Fuentes	21.02.2002		(1)	
Siad Haji	01.12.1999		(4)	
Judson Silva Tavares (BRA)	25.05.1993	20	(1)	
Luis Felipe Fernandes Rodrigues	29.01.1996	2	(3)	
Valeri Qazaishvili (GEO)	29.01.1993	8	(6)	2
Shea Salinas	24.06.1986	5	(18)	3
Jack Skahan	07.02.1998		(1)	
Thomas Palmer Thompson	15.08.1995	13	(7)	1
Jackson William Yueill	19.03.1997	21		1
Forwards:				
Cade Cowell	14.10.2003	4	(13)	1
Cristian Omar Espinoza (ARG)	03.04.1995	22	(1)	3
Daniel Hoesen (NED)	15.01.1991	3	(5)	1
Andrés Lorenzo Ríos (ARG)	01.08.1989	19	(3)	5
Christopher Elliott Wondolowski	28.01.1983	14	(8)	8
Trainer:				
Matías Jesús Almeyda (ARG) [from 08.10.2018]	21.12.1973	23		

SEATTLE SOUNDERS FOOTBALL CLUB

Foundation date: November 13, 2007
Address: 12 Seahawks Way, 98056 Renton, Washington
Stadium: Lumen Field, Seattle (39,419)

THE SQUAD

	DOB	M	(s)	G
Goalkeepers:				
Stefan Frei (SUI)	20.04.1986	26		
Defenders:				
Xavier Ricardo Arreaga Bermello (ECU)	28.09.1994	13	(1)	
Yeimar Pastor Gómez Andrade (COL)	30.06.1992	23		2
Joevin Martin Jones (TRI)	03.08.1991	14	(3)	2
Kelvin Leerdam (NED)	24.06.1990	19	(5)	3
Jimmy Gerardo Medranda Obando (COL)	07.02.1994		(3)	
Shane Edward O'Neill	02.09.1993	17	(5)	1
Bradley Shaun Smith	09.04.1994	1	(8)	
Nouhou Tolo (CMR)	23.06.1997	20	(6)	
Román Aureliano Torres Morcillo (PAN)	20.03.1986		(5)	
Midfielders:				
Joshua Atencio	31.01.2002		(5)	
Handwalla Bwana (KEN)	25.06.1997	2	(3)	1
Jordy José Delem (MTQ)	18.03.1993	9	(9)	
Ethan Dobbelaere	14.11.2002	1		
Miguel Ángel Ibarra Andrade	15.03.1990	3	(9)	
João Paulo Mior (BRA)	08.03.1991	21	(2)	2
Daniel Ulises "Danny" Leyva	05.05.2003	1	(1)	
Marcelo Nicolás Lodeiro Benítez (URU)	21.03.1989	24		8
Alexander Roldan	28.07.1996	7	(15)	
Cristian Roldan	03.06.1995	25	(1)	2
Harrison "Harry" Shipp	07.11.1991		(2)	
Karl Gustav Johan Svensson (SWE)	07.02.1987	11	(3)	1
Forwards:				
William Christopher "Will" Bruin	24.10.1989	5	(12)	2
Justin Shane Dhillon	06.06.1995		(1)	
Shandon Hopeau	01.12.1998	1	(4)	
Jordan Perry Morris	26.10.1994	22	(4)	11
Raúl Mario Ruidíaz Misitich (PER)	25.07.1990	21		14
Trainer:				
Brian Schmetzer [from 26.07.2016]	18.08.1962	26		

SPORTING KANSAS CITY

Foundation date: 1995 (*as Kansas City Wizzards*)
Address: 8900 State Line Road, Leawood, 66206 Kansas City, Kansas
Stadium: Children's Mercy Park [formerly Sporting Park], Kansas City (18,467)

THE SQUAD

	DOB	M	(s)	G
Goalkeepers:				
Tim Melia	15.05.1986	22		
Richard Sánchez Alcaraz (MEX)	05.04.1994	1	(1)	
Defenders:				
Matthew Scott Besler	11.02.1987	9	(1)	
Amadou Tidiane Dia	08.06.1993	11	(3)	
Cameron Duke	13.02.2001	2	(6)	
Andreu Fontàs Prat (ESP)	14.11.1989	3		1
Jaylin Chad Lindsey	27.03.2000	13	(1)	
Luís Carlos Ramos Martins (POR)	10.06.1992	9	(3)	
Roberto Punčec (CRO)	27.10.1991	20	(2)	
Winston Wiremu Reid (NZL)	03.07.1988	10	(2)	1
Graham Smith	25.11.1995	4		
Midfielders:				
Roger Aníbal Espinoza Ramírez (HON)	25.10.1986	14	(4)	3
Felipe Hernández (COL)	08.06.1998	8	(10)	
Ilie Sánchez Farrés (ESP)	21.11.1990	15	(2)	1
Gadi Kinda (ISR)	17.05.1994	16	(4)	6
Graham Jonathan Zusi	18.08.1986	14	(1)	1
Forwards:				
Gianluca Busio	28.05.2002	17	(4)	2
Gerso Fernandes (GNB)	23.02.1991	12	(9)	3
Erik Hurtado	15.11.1990	3	(14)	5
Alan Pulido Izaguirre (MEX)	08.03.1991	11	(1)	6
Johnathon Russell (SCO)	08.04.1990	19	(4)	6
Dániel Sallói (HUN)	19.07.1996	1	(6)	
Khiry Lamar Shelton	26.06.1993	19	(3)	5
Trainer:				
Peter Joseph Vermes [from 04.08.2009]	21.11.1966	23		

TORONTO FOOTBALL CLUB

Foundation date: 2005
Address: 170 Princes' Boulevard, ON M6K 3C3 Toronto, Canada
Stadium: BMO Field, Toronto (28,351)

THE SQUAD

	DOB	M	(s)	G
Goalkeepers:				
Alexander Nicholas "Alex" Bono	25.04.1994	3		
Quentin Westberg	25.04.1986	21		
Defenders:				
Auro Alvaro da Cruz Junior (BRA)	23.01.1996	18	(1)	
Laurent Franco Ciman (BEL)	05.08.1985	5	(7)	
Tony Gallacher (SCO)	23.07.1999	5	(5)	
Omar Alejandro Gonzalez	11.10.1988	22	(2)	
Richmond "Richie" Laryea (CAN)	07.01.1995	16	(5)	4
Chris Mavinga (COD)	26.05.1991	18	(2)	
Justin Morrow	04.10.1987	11	(4)	
Eriq Anthony Zavaleta	02.08.1992	3	(2)	
Midfielders:				
Michael Sheehan Bradley	31.07.1987	12	(1)	
Nicholas Lee DeLeon	17.07.1990	10	(12)	1
Marco Antonio "Marky" Delgado	16.05.1995	18	(1)	
Tsubasa Endoh (JPN)	20.08.1993	7	(10)	1
Liam Fraser (CAN)	13.02.1998	4	(10)	
Jahkeele Marshall-Rutty (CAN)	16.06.2004		(1)	
Noble Okello Ayo (CAN)	20.07.2000		(1)	
Jonathan Osorio (CAN)	12.06.1992	18		1
Alejandro Pozuelo Melero (ESP)	20.09.1991	24		9
Ralph-William Johnson Priso-Mbongue (CAN)	02.08.2002	1	(4)	
Forwards:				
Ifunanyachi Achara (NGA)	28.09.1997	1		1
Ayomide Akinola	20.01.2000	11	(5)	9
Josmer Volmy "Jozy" Altidore	06.11.1989	11	(3)	2
Griffin Dorsey	05.03.1999		(1)	
Erickson Yirson Gallardo Toro (VEN)	26.07.1996	2	(4)	
Patrick Michael Mullins	05.02.1992	4	(13)	1
Jayden Nelson (CAN)	26.09.2002	1	(6)	
Pablo Daniel Piatti (ARG)	31.03.1989	17	(1)	4
Jacob Shaffelburg (CAN)	26.11.1999	1	(3)	
Trainer:				
Greg Vanney [from 31.08.2014]	11.06.1974	24		

VANCOUVER WHITECAPS FOOTBALL CLUB

Foundation date: 2009
Address: Suite 550, 375 Water Street, V6B 5C6 Vancouver, British Columbia, Canada
Stadium: BC Place Stadium, Vancouver (22,120)

THE SQUAD

	DOB	M	(s)	G
Goalkeepers:				
Evan William Bush	06.03.1986	8		
Maxime Crépeau (CAN)	11.04.1994	4		
Thomas Hasal (CAN)	09.07.1999	8	(1)	
Bryan Meredith	02.08.1989	3		
Defenders:				
Ali Adnan Kadhim Al Tameemi (IRQ)	19.12.1993	20	(2)	2
Derek Austin Cornelius (CAN)	25.11.1997	11	(2)	
Érik Fernando Godoy (ARG)	16.08.1993	11	(1)	
Cristian Daniel Gutiérrez Zúñiga (CHI)	18.02.1997	7	(5)	
Jasser Khmiri (TUN)	27.07.1997	5		
Jakob Nerwinski	17.10.1994	18	(3)	2
Ranko Veselinović (SRB)	24.03.1999	16	(2)	
Midfielders:				
Michael Baldisimo (CAN)	13.04.2000	7	(6)	1
Hwang In-beom (KOR)	20.09.1996	5		
Janio Bikel Figueiredo da Silva (POR)	28.06.1995	12		
Patrick Metcalfe (CAN)	11.11.1998	2	(5)	
Leonard Owusu (GHA)	03.06.1997	14	(6)	
Damiano Daniele Pecile (CAN)	11.04.2002		(1)	
Ryan Raposo (CAN)	05.03.1999	2	(13)	
José Yordy Reyna Serna (PER)	17.09.1993	4	(4)	1
Andrew Patrick Rose (ENG)	13.02.1990	10	(3)	
Forwards:				
Thelonius "Theo" Bair (CAN)	27.08.1999	6	(10)	1
Lucas Daniel Cavallini (CAN)	28.12.1992	16	(2)	6
Cristián Andrés Dájome Arboleda (COL)	03.01.1994	18	(5)	3
Manuel David Milinković (FRA)	20.05.1994	11	(5)	1
Fredy Henkyer Montero Muñoz (COL)	26.07.1987	11	(5)	5
Tosaint Antony Ricketts (CAN)	06.08.1987	5	(11)	2
Russell Teibert (CAN)	22.12.1992	19	(1)	
Trainer:				
Marc Dos Santos (CAN) [from 07.11.2018]	26.05.1977	23		

SECOND LEVEL
United Soccer League 2020

Top-8 of each Conference were qualifeid for the Conference Play-offs.

Eastern Conference

1.	Louisville City FC	16	11	3	2	28	-	12	35	(2.19)
2.	Hartford Athletic	16	11	3	2	31	-	24	35	(2.19)
3.	Pittsburgh Riverhounds SC	16	11	4	1	39	-	10	34	(2.13)
4.	Tampa Bay Rowdies	16	10	3	3	25	-	11	33	(2.06)
5.	Charleston Battery	15	9	3	3	26	-	15	30	(2.00)
6.	Charlotte Independence	16	8	4	4	24	-	22	28	(1.75)
7.	Birmingham Legion FC	16	7	5	4	29	-	19	25	(1.56)
8.	Saint Louis FC	16	7	5	4	22	-	21	25	(1.56)
9.	Indy Eleven Indianapolis	16	7	7	2	21	-	19	23	(1.44)
10.	North Carolina FC	15	6	8	1	17	-	21	19	(1.27)
11.	Memphis 901 FC	15	4	7	4	24	-	31	16	(1.07)
12.	Sporting Kansas City II	16	5	10	1	21	-	30	16	(1.00)
13.	Miami FC	16	4	8	4	20	-	34	16	(1.00)
14.	New York Red Bulls II	16	5	11	0	30	-	37	15	(0.94)
15.	Atlanta United FC 2	16	3	10	3	23	-	33	12	(0.75)
16.	Philadelphia Union II	16	2	11	3	20	-	45	9	(0.56)
17.	Loudoun United FC Leesburg	13	1	9	3	10	-	28	6	(0.46)

Western Conference

1.	Reno 1868 FC	16	11	2	3	43	-	21	36	(2.25)
2.	Phoenix Rising FC	16	11	3	2	46	-	17	35	(2.19)
3.	San Antonio FC	16	10	3	3	30	-	14	33	(2.06)
4.	El Paso Locomotive FC	16	9	2	5	24	-	14	32	(2.00)
5.	Sacramento Republic FC	16	8	2	6	27	-	17	30	(1.88)
6.	New Mexico United	15	8	4	3	23	-	17	27	(1.80)
7.	FC Tulsa	15	6	2	7	21	-	16	25	(1.67)
8.	Los Angeles Galaxy II	16	8	6	2	29	-	32	26	(1.63)
9.	Orange County SC	16	7	6	3	18	-	18	24	(1.50)
10.	San Diego Loyal SC	16	6	5	5	17	-	18	23	(1.44)
11.	Austin Bold FC	16	5	4	7	30	-	26	22	(1.38)
12.	Tacoma Defience	16	4	10	2	25	-	32	14	(0.88)
13.	Colorado Springs Switchbacks	16	2	7	7	19	-	28	13	(0.81)
14.	Real Monarchs Real Salt Lake	16	3	11	2	14	-	25	11	(0.69)
15.	Las Vegas Lights FC	16	2	9	5	24	-	34	11	(0.69)
16.	Rio Grande Valley Toros	14	2	9	3	17	-	28	9	(0.64)
17.	Oklahoma City Energy FC	16	1	8	7	12	-	29	10	(0.63)
18.	Portland Timbers 2	16	3	13	0	20	-	50	9	(0.56)

Conference Play-offs

Quarter-Finals [10.10.2020]

Hartford Athletic - Saint Louis FC	0-1(0-0)
Tampa Bay Rowdies - Birmingham Legion FC	4-2(2-0)
Louisville City FC - Pittsburgh Riverhounds SC	2-0(1-0)
Charlotte Independence - Charleston Battery	1-2(0-1,1-1)
Reno 1868 FC - Los Angeles Galaxy II	4-1(2-1)
San Antonio FC - New Mexico United	0-1(0-0,0-0)
El Paso Locomotive FC - FC Tulsa	2-2 aet; 4-2 pen
Phoenix Rising FC - Sacramento Republic FC	1-0(0-0,0-0)

Conference Semi-Finals [17.10.2020]

Louisville City FC - Saint Louis FC	2-0(1-0)
Tampa Bay Rowdies - Charleston Battery	1-0(0-0)
Reno 1868 FC - Phoenix Rising FC	2-2 aet; 4-5 pen
El Paso Locomotive FC - New Mexico United	1-1 aet; 5-3 pen

Conference Finals [24.10.2020]

Louisville City FC - Tampa Bay Rowdies	1-2(1-2)
Phoenix Rising FC - El Paso Locomotive FC	1-1 aet; 4-2 pen

United Soccer League Final

01.11.2020, Al Lang Stadium, St. Petersburg
Tampa Bay Rowdies - Phoenix Rising FC   *cancelled*
The final was cancelled because several Tampa Bay Rowdies players were tested positive for COVID-19.

2020 United Soccer League Winner: **no title awarded**

NATIONAL TEAM
INTERNATIONAL MATCHES 2020/2021

12.11.2020	Swansea	Wales - United States	0-0	(F)
16.11.2020	Wiener Neustadt	United States - Panama	6-2(3-1)	(F)
09.12.2020	Fort Lauderdale	United States - El Salvador	6-0(5-0)	(F)
31.01.2021	Orlando	United States - Trinidad and Tobago	7-0(4-0)	(F)
25.03.2021	Wiener Neustadt	United States - Jamaica	4-1(1-0)	(F)
28.03.2021	Belfast	Northern Ireland - United States	1-2(0-1)	(F)
30.05.2021	St. Gallen	Switzerland - United States	2-1(1-1)	(F)
03.06.2021	Denver	Honduras - United States	0-1(0-0)	(CNL)
06.06.2021	Denver	United States - Mexico	3-2(1-1,2-2)	(CNL)
09.06.2021	Sandy	United States - Costa Rica	4-0(2-0)	(F)

12.11.2020, Friendly International
Liberty Stadium, Swansea; Attendance: 0
Referee: Nicholas Walsh (Scotland)
WALES - UNITED STATES   **0-0**
USA: Zackary Thomas Steffen, John Anthony Brooks, Matthew Miazga, Antonee Robinson, Sergiño Gianni Dest (87.Reginald Jacob Cannon), Sebastian Francisco Lletget (87.Ebeguowen Otasowie), Tyler Shaan Adams (71.João Lucas de Souza Cardoso), Weston James Earl McKennie, Giovanni Alejandro Reyna (79.Timothy Tarpeh Weah), Yunus Dimoara Musah (79.Nicholas Selson Gioacchini), Konrad de la Fuente (71.Ulysses Llanez Jr.). Trainer: Gregg Berhalter.

16.11.2020, Friendly International
Wiener Neustadt Stadion, Wiener Neustadt (Austria); Attendance: 0
Referee: Harald Lechner (Austria)
UNITED STATES - PANAMA   **6-2(3-1)**
USA: Zackary Thomas Steffen, Timothy Michael Ream, Matthew Miazga (80.Christopher Jeffrey Richards), Reginald Jacob Cannon, Sergiño Gianni Dest, Tyler Shaan Adams (62.João Lucas de Souza Cardoso), Weston James Earl McKennie, Giovanni Alejandro Reyna (68.Richard Ledezma), Yunus Dimoara Musah (76.Sebastian Francisco Lletget), Ulysses Llanez Jr. (62.Timothy Tarpeh Weah), Nicholas Selson Gioacchini (77.Sebastian Guerra Soto). Trainer: Gregg Berhalter.
Goals: Giovanni Alejandro Reyna (18), Nicholas Selson Gioacchini (22, 26), Sebastian Guerra Soto (83), Sebastian Francisco Lletget (87), Sebastian Guerra Soto (90+1).

09.12.2020, Friendly International
DRV PNK Stadium, Fort Lauderdale; Attendance: 0
Referee: Jose Raúl Torres Rivera (Puerto Rico)
UNITED STATES - EL SALVADOR   **6-0(5-0)**
USA: Abdul Bilal Hamid, Aaron Ray Long (83.Walker Dwain Zimmerman), Mark Alexander McKenzie, Samuel Marques Lloyd Vines (46.Marco Antonio Farfan), Julian Vicente Araujo (74.Kyle Barri Duncan), Paul Joseph Arriola Hendricks (58.Sebastian Guerra Soto), Sebastian Francisco Lletget (68.Kellyn Kai Perry-Acosta), Jackson William Yueill, Brenden Russell Aaronson, Christopher Matthew Mueller, Ayomide Bamidele Akinola (74.Đorđe Aleksandar Mihailović). Trainer: Gregg Berhalter.
Goals: Paul Joseph Arriola Hendricks (17), Christopher Matthew Mueller (20), Sebastian Francisco Lletget (23), Christopher Matthew Mueller (25), Ayomide Bamidele Akinola (27), Brenden Russell Aaronson (50).

31.01.2021, Friendly International
Exploria Stadium, Orlando; Attendance: 0
Referee: Héctor Said Martínez Sorto (Honduras)
UNITED STATES - TRINIDAD AND TOBAGO **7-0(4-0)**
USA: Matthew Charles Turner, Aaron Ray Long, Aaron Joseph Herrera (78.Francis Tanner Tessmann), Miles Gordon Robinson, Samuel Marques Lloyd Vines (64.George Oluwaseun Bello), Paul Joseph Arriola Hendricks (65.Daryl Dike), Kellyn Kai Perry-Acosta, Sebastian Francisco Lletget (46.Andrés Felipe Perea Castañeda), Jackson William Yueill (64.Cristian Nicolas Roldan), Jonathan Jeremy Lewis, Jesús David Ferreira Castro (64.Christopher Matthew Mueller). Trainer: Gregg Berhalter.
Goals: Jonathan Jeremy Lewis (2), Jesús David Ferreira Castro (9), Paul Joseph Arriola Hendricks (22), Paul Joseph Arriola Hendricks (41), Miles Gordon Robinson (52), Jonathan Jeremy Lewis (55), Jesús David Ferreira Castro (62).

25.03.2021, Friendly International
Wiener Neustadt Stadion, Wiener Neustadt (Austria); Attendance: 0
Referee: Christian-Petru Ciochirca (Austria)
UNITED STATES - JAMAICA **4-1(1-0)**
USA: Zackary Thomas Steffen, John Anthony Brooks, Aaron Ray Long (46.Christopher Jeffrey Richards), Reginald Jacob Cannon, Sergiño Gianni Dest (67.Antonee Robinson), Kellyn Kai Perry-Acosta, Sebastian Francisco Lletget, Christian Mate Pulisic (46.Brenden Russell Aaronson), Giovanni Alejandro Reyna (68.Nicholas Selson Gioacchini), Yunus Dimoara Musah (73.Lucas Daniel de la Torre), Joshua Thomas Sargent (82.Theoson-Jordan Siebatcheu Pefok). Trainer: Gregg Berhalter.
Goals: Sergiño Gianni Dest (34), Brenden Russell Aaronson (52), Sebastian Francisco Lletget (83, 90).

28.03.2021, Friendly International
Windsor Park, Belfast; Attendance: 0
Referee: Robert Jenkins (Wales)
NORTHERN IRELAND - UNITED STATES **1-2(0-1)**
USA: Zackary Thomas Steffen, Timothy Michael Ream, Matthew Miazga, Aaron Ray Long (63.Christopher Jeffrey Richards), Antonee Robinson, Sergiño Gianni Dest (46.Bryan Keith Reynolds Jr.), Kellyn Kai Perry-Acosta (74.Lucas Daniel de la Torre), Christian Mate Pulisic, Giovanni Alejandro Reyna (63.Brenden Russell Aaronson), Yunus Dimoara Musah (46.Sebastian Francisco Lletget), Theoson-Jordan Siebatcheu Pefok (63.Daryl Dike). Trainer: Gregg Berhalter.
Goals: Giovanni Alejandro Reyna (30), Christian Mate Pulisic (59 penalty).

30.05.2021, Friendly International
Kybunpark, St. Gallen; Attendance: 0
Referee: Harm Osmers (Germany)
SWITZERLAND - UNITED STATES **2-1(1-1)**
USA: Ethan Shea Horvath, John Anthony Brooks (61.Timothy Michael Ream), Mark Alexander McKenzie, Reginald Jacob Cannon (81.DeAndre Roselle Yedlin), Sergiño Gianni Dest, Sebastian Francisco Lletget (61.Yunus Dimoara Musah), Weston James Earl McKennie, Jackson William Yueill (61.Kellyn Kai Perry-Acosta), Brenden Russell Aaronson, Giovanni Alejandro Reyna (72.Timothy Tarpeh Weah), Joshua Thomas Sargent (72.Theoson-Jordan Siebatcheu Pefok). Trainer: Gregg Berhalter.
Goal: Sebastian Francisco Lletget (5).

03.06.2021, 1st CONCACAF Nations League, Semi-Finals
Empower File at Mile High Stadium, Denver; Attendance: 34,451
Referee: Oshane Nation (Jamaica)

HONDURAS - UNITED STATES   0-1(0-0)

USA: Zackary Thomas Steffen, John Anthony Brooks, Antonee Robinson (78.Reginald Jacob Cannon), Mark Alexander McKenzie, Sergiño Gianni Dest, Sebastian Francisco Lletget, Christian Mate Pulisic (90+4.Matthew Miazga), Weston James Earl McKennie, Jackson William Yueill (83.Kellyn Kai Perry-Acosta), Giovanni Alejandro Reyna (78.Brenden Russell Aaronson), Joshua Thomas Sargent (78.Theoson-Jordan Siebatcheu Pefok). Trainer: Gregg Berhalter.

Goal: Theoson-Jordan Siebatcheu Pefok (89).

06.06.2021, 1st CONCACAF Nations League, Final
Empower Field at Mile High Stadium, Denver; Attendance: 34,451
Referee: Bryan López Castellanos (Guatemala)

UNITED STATES - MEXICO   3-2(1-1,2-2)

USA: Zackary Thomas Steffen (69.Ethan Shea Horvath), Timothy Michael Ream (82.Tyler Shaan Adams), John Anthony Brooks, DeAndre Roselle Yedlin (105+1.Reginald Jacob Cannon), Mark Alexander McKenzie, Sergiño Gianni Dest (60.Timothy Tarpeh Weah), Kellyn Kai Perry-Acosta, Christian Mate Pulisic, Weston James Earl McKennie, Giovanni Alejandro Reyna (82.Sebastian Francisco Lletget), Joshua Thomas Sargent (68.Theoson-Jordan Siebatcheu Pefok). Trainer: Gregg Berhalter.

Goals: Giovanni Alejandro Reyna (27), Weston James Earl McKennie (82), Christian Mate Pulisic (114 penalty).

09.06.2021, Friendly International
Rio Tinto Stadium. Sandy; Attendance: 19,007
Referee: Tristley Bassue (Saint Kitts and Nevis)

UNITED STATES - COSTA RICA   4-0(2-0)

USA: Ethan Shea Horvath, Timothy Michael Ream, Antonee Robinson (82.Sergiño Gianni Dest), Mark Alexander McKenzie (46.Walker Dwain Zimmerman), Reginald Jacob Cannon, Sebastian Francisco Lletget, Tyler Shaan Adams (62.Jackson William Yueill), Brenden Russell Aaronson, Yunus Dimoara Musah (75.Kellyn Kai Perry-Acosta), Timothy Tarpeh Weah (46.Giovanni Alejandro Reyna), Daryl Dike (75.Theoson-Jordan Siebatcheu Pefok). Trainer: Gregg Berhalter.

Goals: Brenden Russell Aaronson (8), Daryl Dike (42), Reginald Jacob Cannon (52), Giovanni Alejandro Reyna (77 penalty).

NATIONAL TEAM PLAYERS 2020/2021

Name	DOB	Club
Goalkeepers		
Abdul Bilal "Bill" HAMID	25.11.1990	*Washington DC United*
Ethan Shea HORVATH	09.06.1995	*Club Brugge KV (BEL)*
Zackary Thomas STEFFEN	02.04.1995	*Manchester City FC (ENG)*
Matthew Charles TURNER	24.06.1994	*New England Revolution Boston*
Defenders		
Julian Vicente ARAUJO	13.08.2001	*Los Angeles Galaxy*
George Oluwaseun BELLO	22.01.2002	*Atlanta United*
John Anthony BROOKS	28.01.1993	*VfL Wolfsburg (GER)*
Reginald Jacob CANNON	11.06.1998	*Boavista FC Porto (POR)*
Sergiño Gianni DEST	03.11.2000	*FC Barcelona (ESP)*
Kyle Barri DUNCAN	08.08.1997	*New York Red Bulls*
Marco Antonio FARFAN	12.11.1998	*Portland Timbers*
Aaron Joseph HERRERA	06.06.1997	*Real Salt Lake*
Aaron Ray LONG	12.10.1992	*New York Red Bulls*
Mark Alexander McKENZIE	25.02.1999	*Philadelphia Union; 07.01.2021-> RKC Genk (BEL)*
Matthew MIAZGA	19.07.1995	*RSC Anderlecht Bruxelles (BEL)*
Đorđe Aleksandar MIHAILOVIĆ	10.11.1998	*Chicago Fire*
Timothy Michael "Tim" REAM	05.10.1987	*Fulham FC London (ENG)*
Bryan Keith REYNOLDS Jr.	28.06.2001	*AS Roma (ITA)*
Christopher Jeffrey RICHARDS	28.03.2000	*FC Bayern München (GER); 01.02.2021-> TSG 1899 Hoffenheim (GER)*
Antonee ROBINSON	08.08.1997	*Fulham FC London (ENG)*
Miles Gordon ROBINSON	14.03.1997	*Atlanta United FC*
Samuel Marques Lloyd VINES	31.05.1999	*Colorado Rapids*
DeAndre Roselle YEDLIN	09.07.1993	*Galatasaray SK İstanbul (TUR)*
Walker Dwain ZIMMERMAN	19.05.1993	*Nashville SC*
Midfielders		
Tyler Shaan ADAMS	14.02.1999	*RasenBallsport Leipzig (GER)*
João Lucas de Souza CARDOSO	20.09.2001	*SC Internacional Porto Alegre (BRA)*
Lucas Daniel DE LA TORRE	23.05.1998	*Heracles Almelo (NED)*
Richard LEDEZMA	06.09.2000	*PSV Eindhoven (NED)*
Sebastian Francisco LLETGET	03.09.1992	*Los Angeles Galaxy*
Weston James Earl McKENNIE	28.08.1998	*Juventus FC Torino (ITA)*
Yunus Dimoara MUSAH	29.11.2002	*Valencia CF (ESP)*
Ebeguowen OTASOWIE	06.01.2001	*Wolverhampton Wanderers FC (ENG)*
Andrés Felipe PEREA Castañeda	14.11.2000	*Orlando City SC*
Kellyn Kai PERRY-ACOSTA	24.07.1995	*Colorado Rapids*
Cristian Nicolas ROLDAN	03.06.1995	*Seattle Sounders FC*
Francis Tanner TESSMANN	24.09.2001	*FC Dallas*
Jackson William YUEILL	19.03.1997	*San Jose Earthquakes*

Forwards

Brenden Russell AARONSON	22.10.2000	*Philadelphia Union;*
		01.01.2021-> FC Red Bull Salzburg (AUT)
Ayomide Bamidele AKINOLA	20.01.2000	*Toronto FC (CAN)*
Paul Joseph ARRIOLA Hendricks	05.02.1995	*Washington DC United*
Konrad DE LA FUENTE	16.07.2001	*FC Barcelona (ESP)*
Daryl DIKE	03.06.2000	*Orlando City SC;*
		01.02.2021-> Barnsley FC (ENG)
Jesús David FERREIRA Castro	24.12.2000	*FC Dallas*
Nicholas Selson GIOACCHINI	25.07.2000	*Stade Malherbe Caen (FRA)*
Jonathan Jeremy LEWIS	04.06.1997	*Colorado Rapids*
Ulysses LLANEZ Jr.	02.04.2001	*SC Heerenveen (NED)*
Christopher Matthew MUELLER	29.08.1996	*Orlando City SC*
Christian Mate PULISIC	18.09.1998	*Chelsea FC London (ENG)*
Giovanni Alejandro REYNA	13.11.2002	*BV Borussia 09 Dortmund (GER)*
Joshua Thomas SARGENT	20.02.2000	*SV Werder Bremen (GER)*
Theoson-Jordan SIEBATCHEU Pefok	26.04.1996	*BSC Young Boys Bern (SUI)*
Sebastian Guerra SOTO	28.07.2000	*SC Telstar Ijmuiden (NED)*
Timothy Tarpeh WEAH	22.02.2000	*Lille OSC (FRA)*

National coaches

Gregg BERHALTER [from 02.12.2018]	01.08.1973

U.S. VIRGIN ISLANDS

The Country:	The FA:
United States Virgin Islands	USVI Soccer Federation
Capital: Charlotte Amalie	23-1 Bethlehem, PO Box 2346,
Surface: 346 km²	00581 Christiansted, Saint Croix
Population: 105,870 [2021]	Year of Formation: 1992
Time: UTC-4	Member of FIFA since: 1998
Independent since: *United States territory*	Member of CONCACAF since: 1987

NATIONAL TEAM RECORDS

First international match: 21.03.1998: Us Virgin Islands - British Virgin Islands 1-0
Most international caps: Not known
Most international goals: Not known

CONCACAF GOLD CUP	
1991	Did not enter
1993	Did not enter
1996	Did not enter
1998	Did not enter
2000	Qualifiers
2002	Qualifiers
2003	Qualifiers
2005	Qualifiers
2007	Qualifiers
2009	Did not enter
2011	Did not enter
2013	Did not enter
2015	Qualifiers
2017	Qualifiers
2019	Qualifiers
2021	Qualifiers

FIFA WORLD CUP	
1930	-
1934	-
1938	-
1950	-
1954	-
1958	-
1962	-
1966	-
1970	-
1974	-
1978	-
1982	-
1986	-
1990	-
1994	-
1998	-
2002	Qualifiers
2006	Qualifiers
2010	Qualifiers
2014	Qualifiers
2018	Qualifiers

F.I.F.A. CONFEDERATIONS CUP 1992-2017

None

OLYMPIC FOOTBALL TOURNAMENTS 1900-2016

2004 (Qualifiers), 2008 (Qualifiers)

CCCF (Confederación Centroamericana y del Caribe de Fútbol) CHAMPIONSHIPS 1941-1961

None

CONCACAF CHAMPIONSHIPS 1963-1989

None

CONCACAF NATIONS LEAGUE

2019-2020	League C

CARIBBEAN CHAMPIONSHIPS 1989-2017

1989	Did not enter	1999	Qualifiers
1991	Did not enter	2001	Qualifiers
1992	Did not enter	2005	Qualifiers
1993	Did not enter	2007	Qualifiers
1994	Did not enter	2008	Did not enter
1995	Did not enter	2010	Did not enter
1996	Did not enter	2012	Did not enter
1997	Did not enter	2014	Qualifiers
1998	Did not enter	2017	Qualifiers

U.S. VIRGIN ISLANDS CLUB HONOURS IN CONCACAF CLUB COMPETITIONS:

CONCACAF Champions Cup / CONCACAF Champions League 1962-2020

None

CONCACAF League 2017-2020

None

Caribbean Club Championship 1997-2021

None

CONCACAF Cup Winners Cup 1991-1995*

None

Copa Interamericana 1968-1998*

None

defunct competitions

NATIONAL COMPETITIONS
TABLE OF HONOURS

The champion of the US Virgin Islands is decided in a knockout tournament between the best of both St. Croix Soccer League and St. Thomas & St. John League.

	CHAMPIONS
1997/1998	MI Roc Masters
1998/1999	*No competition*
1999/2000	UWS Upsetters SC
2000/2001	*No competition*
2001/2002	Haitian Stars SC
2002/2003	*No competition*
2003/2004	*No competition*
2004/2005	Positive Vibes

2005/2006	New Vibes
2006/2007	Helenites FC Groveplace
2007/2008	Positive Vibes
2008/2009	New Vibes
2009/2010	*No competition*
2010/2011	*No competition*
2011/2012	Helenites FC Groveplace
2012/2013	New Vibes
2013/2014	Helenites FC Groveplace
2014/2015	Helenites FC Groveplace
2015/2016	Raymix SC
2016/2017	Raymix SC
2017/2018	*No competition*
2018/2019	Helenites FC Groveplace
2019/2020	*Not known*
2020/2021	*No competition*

St. Croix Soccer League Winners:
1968/69: Hess Oil Company; 1969-97: *Not known*; 1997/98: Helenites Groveplace; 1998/99: Unique FC Christiansted; 1999/00: Helenites Groveplace; 2000/01: Helenites Groveplace; 2001/02: Helenites Groveplace; 2002/03: Helenites Groveplace; 2003/04: Helenites Groveplace; 2004/05: Helenites Groveplace; 2005/06: Helenites Groveplace; 2006/07: Helenites Groveplace; 2007/08: Helenites Groveplace; 2008/09: Helenites Groveplace; 2009/10: Unique FC Christiansted; 2010/11: Helenites Groveplace; 2011/2012: Helenites Groveplace; 2012/2013: Rovers; 2013/2014: Helenites FC Groveplace; 2014/2015: Helenites FC Groveplace; 2015/2016: Helenites FC Groveplace; 2016/2017: Helenites FC Groveplace.

St. Thomas & St. John League Winners:
1995/1996: MI Roc Masters; 1996/1997: Saint John United SC Cruz Bay; 1997/1998: MI Roc Masters; 1998/1999: MI Roc Masters; 1999/2000: UWS Upsetters SC; 2000/2001: UWS Upsetters SC; 2001/2002: Waitikubuli United SC; 2002/2003: Waitikubuli United SC; 2003/2004: *Not known*; 2004/2005: Positive Vibes; 2005/2006: Positive Vibes; 2006/2007: Positive Vibes; 2007/2008: Positive Vibes; 2008/2009: New Vibes; 2009/2010: Positive Vibes; 2010/2011: *Not known*; 2011/2012: New Vibes; 2012/2013: Positive Vibes; 2013/2014: Positive Vibes; 2014/2015: Raymix SC; 2015/2016: Raymix SC; 2016/2017: Raymix SC.

NATIONAL CHAMPIONSHIP
US Virgin Islands Championship 2020/2021

The championship was cancelled due to COVID-19 pandemic.

NATIONAL TEAM
INTERNATIONAL MATCHES 2020/2021

21.03.2021	Fort Lauderdale	U.S. Virgin Islands - Anguilla	0-0	(F)
27.03.2021	Upper Bethlehem	U.S. Virgin Islands - Antigua and Barbuda	0-3(0-3)	(WCQ)
30.03.2021	St. George's	Grenada - U.S. Virgin Islands	1-0(1-0)	(WCQ)
02.06.2021	San Cristóbal	Montserrat - U.S. Virgin Islands	4-0(1-0)	(WCQ)
05.06.2021	Upper Bethlehem	U.S. Virgin Islands - El Salvador	0-7(0-2)	(WCQ)

21.03.2021, Friendly International
Training Ground at Inter Miami CF Stadium, Fort Lauderdale (USA); Attendance: 0
Referee: Juan Pablo Casas (United States)
U.S. VIRGIN ISLANDS - ANGUILLA   0-0
VIR: Lionel Brown (46.Erik Mozzo), Joshua Ramos, Grant Farrell, John Engerman (60.Quinn Farrell), Jett Blaschka, Dusty Good (52.Nakeeme Julian), Axel Bartsch, Jimson St. Louis, Konner Kendall (58.Humberto Delgado), Shomari Francis, Ramesses Moore-McGuinness (75.Seidon Thomas Nemeth). Trainer: Gilberto Damiano Maciel Jr. (Brazil).

27.03.2021, 22nd FIFA World Cup Qualifiers, CONCACAF First Round
Bethlehem Soccer Stadium, Upper Bethlehem
Referee: Trevester Richards (Saint Kitts and Nevis)
U.S. VIRGIN ISLANDS - ANTIGUA AND BARBUDA   0-3(0-3)
VIR: Lionel Brown, John Engerman, Grant Farrell, Quinn Farrell, Joshua Ramos, Dusty Good (71.Humberto Delgado), Jett Blaschka (85.Seidon Thomas Nemeth), Nakeeme Julian (58.Jacob Iller), Jimson St. Louis, Ramesses Moore-McGuinness (84.Timothy Herring), Axel Bartsch (84.Julius Brown). Trainer: Gilberto Damiano Maciel Jr. (Brazil).

30.03.2021, 22nd FIFA World Cup Qualifiers, CONCACAF First Round
Kirani James Athletic Stadium, St. George's
Referee: Sherwin Johnson (Guyana)
GRENADA - U.S. VIRGIN ISLANDS   1-0(1-0)
VIR: Lionel Brown, Grant Farrell, Quinn Farrell, John Engerman, Kassall Greene, Joshua Ramos, Jacob Iller (84.Axel Bartsch), Jett Blaschka (59.Julius Brown), Jimson St. Louis, Ramesses Moore-McGuinness (46.Humberto Delgado; 84. Konner Kendall), Timothy Herring (69.Mahari Cortijo). Trainer: Gilberto Damiano Maciel Jr. (Brazil).

02.06.2021, 22nd FIFA World Cup Qualifiers, CONCACAF First Round
Estadio Panamericano, San Cristóbal (Dominican Republic)
Referee: Selvin Brown Chavarria (Honduras)
MONTSERRAT - U.S. VIRGIN ISLANDS   4-0(1-0)
VIR: Lionel Brown, Karson Kendall, Jacob Iller, Joshua Ramos, Kassall Greene, MacDonald Taylor Jr., Zahmyre Harris (84.Dusty Good), Jimson St. Louis (84.Asante Herring), Julius Brown (64.Rakeem Michael Joseph), Ramesses Moore-McGuinness (46.John Engerman), Timothy Herring (64.William Schaffer). Trainer: Gilberto Damiano Maciel Jr. (Brazil).

05.06.2021, 22nd FIFA World Cup Qualifiers, CONCACAF First Round
Bethlehem Soccer Stadium, Upper Bethlehem; Attendance: 150
Referee: Ted Unkel (United States)
U.S. VIRGIN ISLANDS - EL SALVADOR   0-7(0-2)
VIR: Lionel Brown, Karson Kendall, Grant Farrell (46.Ramesses Moore-McGuinness), Jacob Iller, Joshua Ramos, Kassall Greene, MacDonald Taylor Jr. (75.Julius Brown), Dusty Good (59.William Schaffer), Jimson St. Louis (61.John Engerman), Asante Herring, Timothy Herring (59.Mahari Cortijo). Trainer: Gilberto Damiano Maciel Jr. (Brazil).

NATIONAL TEAM PLAYERS 2020/2021

Name	DOB	Club
Goalkeepers		
Lionel BROWN	01.09.1987	*Helenites FC Groveplace*
Erik MOZZO	25.12.1990	*FC Châlon-sur-Saône (FRA)*
Defenders		
John ENGERMAN	25.10.2000	*St. Bonaventure Bonnies (USA)*
Grant FARRELL	29.01.2000	*Truett McConell Bears (US)*
Kassall GREENE	08.09.1985	*Cayon Rockets FC (SKN)*
Nakeeme JULIAN	10.04.1999	*Helenites FC Groveplace*
Karson KENDALL	01.04.2000	*Kings Hammer FC (USA)*
Joshua RAMOS	25.04.2000	*AFA Olaine (LVA)*
Midfielders		
Axel BARTSCH	16.05.2002	*Occidental College Tigers (USA)*
Jett BLASCHKA	16.09.1999	*Marquette Golden Eagles (USA)*
Julius BROWN	06.01.2000	*Helenites FC Groveplace*
Mahari CORTIJO	31.01.2002	
Humberto DELGADO III	10.03.2000	
Quinn FARRELL	26.09.2002	*LSU Eunice Bengals (USA)*
Dusty GOOD	30.03.1987	*New Vibes*
Zahmyre HARRIS	14.10.1998	*GSW Hurricanes (USA)*
Jacob ILLER	03.10.2001	*Wright State Raiders (USA)*
Rakeem Michael JOSEPH	23.05.2000	*Empire FC Gray's Farm (ATG)*
Konner KENDALL	20.05.1997	*Moros FC (USA)*
Seidon Thomas NEMETH	19.08.1999	*Becker Hawks (USA)*
William SCHAFFER	05.07.2001	*Wright State Raiders (USA)*
Jimson ST. LOUIS	02.12.2002	*Southeastern CC Blackhawks (USA)*
MacDonald TAYLOR Jr.	22.03.1992	
Forwards		
Shomari FRANCIS	31.03.2001	*Prankton SC*
Asante HERRING	12.09.1997	*TSV Sonnefeld (GER)*
Timothy HERRING	07.05.2000	*Wabash Little Giants*
Ramesses MOORE-MCGUINESS	06.01.2000	

National coaches	
GILBERTO DAMIANO Maciel Jr. (Brazil) [from 07.10.2019]	1976